THE TURKISH COOKBOOK

THE TURKISH COOKBOOK

THE CULINARY TRADITIONS & RECIPES FROM TURKEY

MUSA DAĞDEVİREN

♦

INTRODUCTION

♦

This book is a culinary introduction to Turkish culture and its regional variations. Culinary culture is as old as humanity itself. The inquisitive spirit and creativity of humans is what sets us apart on this planet we share with myriad living organisms. We all need food to survive.

Regional foods can be ascribed to all communities past and present. Man spreads his culture as he wanders the earth. New ideas and methods continuously spread, be they wheat, corn, peppers, tomatoes, fire or even electricity, games and musical instruments.

Turkey's location and its historical heritage are key to shaping its culinary culture. Economy and religion also play their respective roles. Culinary culture reflects the wealth and fertility of an area. Landlocked and poor communities use basic ingredients and techniques out of necessity. Their range is limited and monotonous, often with little meat. Conversely, commercially vibrant, dynamic and fertile places, where the variety of ingredients and techniques is abundant, host a broad range of food with generous use of meat and spices.

Civilisations share common traits that build communities. We are in a way the culmination of all those before us. Wheat was domesticated in 10,000 BC in the Neolithic period in Çatalhöyük (near Konya) in Anatolia. Similar traditions were followed by the Urartu, Phrygians and Hittites. Ancient Greeks, Romans, Byzantines and Anatolian Seljuks have all made their unique mark followed by the reign of the Ottoman Empire for 620 years. Present-day Turkey and its culinary culture is a product of this rich heritage. A heritage shaped by the vast geography from the Mediterranean to Mesopotamia; from the Arab Peninsula to Africa, from Central Asia to Anatolia, to the Caucasus, Thrace and the Balkans throughout the span of history.

The world is an open table, we should enjoy it instead of focusing on how to separate flavours and faiths. Instead of praising the Armenians for their skill in olive oil dishes, the Kurds for meat, Turks for pastries, Ottoman Greeks for their seafood, we could coexist, with mutual respect to each other's values, faiths and way of life.

REGIONAL CUISINES

Turkey consists of seven geographical regions. These are the Mediterranean, Aegean, Marmara, Black Sea, Central Anatolia, Southeastern Anatolia and Eastern Anatolia. Each region has its own culinary identity shaped by its geography. The Marmara and the Aegean regions are neighbours with Greece, Bulgaria and the Balkan countries. The Black Sea region is next to Eastern Anatolia Russia, Georgia, Armenia, Azerbaijan and Iran. Southeastern Anatolia neighbours Syria, Iraq and Iran and the Mediterranean region with Syria and Cyprus. Central Anatolia is in the heart of the country, sharing borders with all other regions.

The Mediterranean, Aegean, Marmara and Black Sea regions have long sea borders. The locals consume a lot of fish and olive oil. The Black Sea region, however, seems to have moved on from its olive oil days towards butter, hazelnut oil and corn oil. Butter and animal fats are essential in Central, Southeastern and Eastern Anatolia. Southeastern Anatolia is a major olive and olive oil producer and consumer.

The backbone of our culinary consumption is vegetable and olive oil dishes, with fish dishes along the coasts. Also popular are wheat-based breads, bulgur and pastries followed by grain-based pilafs, meals and pulse-based dishes. Salads are important too. Sheep and goat are the most popular meats.

İstanbul is a cultural bridge between the continents of Europe and Asia. The Bosphorus is home to many local varieties of fish which are enjoyed during their respective seasons. August is the time for sardines. The season is in full swing until the end of winter. October and November is bluefish season. *Lakerda* (Cured Bonito, see p.286) preserved in salt, is prepared in season using large fish.

Tekirdağ in the Marmara region and its environs are famous for its olive oil and sunflower oil, *Şıra* (Grape Cordial, see p.456) and *Hardaliye* (Grapes Fermented with Mustard Seeds, see p.451) based on grape production, wine and *rakı* (see p.503) production, milk and milk products. Bursa is known for chestnut desserts, olives, İskender kebab, grilled meatballs and *şıra*. Bursa olives are enjoyed all around the world.

Hıdrellez (see p.500) is celebrated enthusiastically from May 6th in the rural Marmara region, with goat on a stick and stuffed goat. Homemade noodles, lamb confit, grape molasses, jams and marmalade are widely made. We should also mention İstanbul's love of *sahlep* and *boza*, both sold by street vendors. *Sahlep* (Orchid Tuber Milk, see p.450), made of orchid tubers, is a winter warmer. *Boza* (Fermented Grain Smoothie, see p.454), made of white millet, is a fermented drink consumed at room temperature. Both are even more delicious with a sprinkle of cinnamon. The pairing of *boza* with *leblebi* (see p.454) is a marriage made in heaven. Pilafs, stuffed mussels, roasted chestnuts, *simit*, corn, fish sandwiches, kebabs and *böreks* are all parts of the colourful urban street food scene in İstanbul. Tripe soup is popular all through the year but especially after nights at the *meyhane* as a local cure for a hangover.

The Marmara region and especially İstanbul and its environs have shaped our traditional dishes, reinterpreting them with local influences. Different regional cuisines and the multi-ethnic nature of this large metropolis have combined into a rich and diverse cuisine. Street vendors, bakeries, restaurants and kebab houses have always been the darlings of locals. Albanian, Bosnian, Bulgarian, Armenian, Rum (Ottoman Greek), Kurdish, Laz, Circassian,

Georgian, Arabic and Persian influences have made İstanbul cuisine what it is today. The multi-ethnic, multinational Ottoman Empire – made up of Christian, Jewish, Armenian and Muslim elements – live on in the cuisine of The City.

Peoples of different religions have used local produce and techniques to prepare their own ritualistic dishes. An example is the use of wheat dishes by the three Abrahamic religions. Muslim communities in our region prepare and share a wheat-based mourning dish called *aşure* (Noah's Pudding, see p.418) after the fast in the month of *Muharrem*. Another tradition related to this dessert makes reference to Noah. The ancient communities in our country respectfully preserve this tradition. Christian Armenians make a very similar dish for the New Year and name it *anuş abur*. Different faiths share a tradition of visiting graves of the dearly departed during religious festivals. Around Antakya, blueberry branches are collected and sold at cemetery gates. Christians, Jews and Muslims all buy them to place on the graves of their relatives. As the branches move in the wind, the sins of the dead move into the ether, cleansing the visitors in the process. Once the branches dry out, the poor collect them for their *tandır* ovens.

The culinary cultures we inherited from previous civilisations have influenced our current cuisine immensely. Different regions have their own local flavours and techniques. There are many food rituals for special occasions, the New Year, religious festivals, weddings and funerals. Many of our dishes are available in restaurants, even more made in home kitchens. The variety of our breads and pastries, the huge diversity of bulgur and rice dishes, the dominance of pulses, the variety of our meat cooking traditions and how we cook pulses and meat together makes Turkish cuisine unique. Milk products feature extensively in our dishes. Olive oil is so crucial in our culinary culture that we have a special category named 'olive oil dishes'. Butter, ghee, olive oil, tail fat, kidney fat and suet are all widely used. One-pot dishes are very popular too. There is a tradition of cooking food in its own juices. Cutlery is used extensively, but some dishes like sheep's head, fish and chicken are traditionally eaten by hand.

THE SIGNIFICANCE OF CULINARY CULTURE

Nomadic communities have more restricted means where agricultural societies provide better access to a variety of foods due to the increase in production. The discovery of new foods and cooking methods have vastly expanded culinary cultures. Urbanisation is a big influence leading to faster production and consumption of food. More affluent societies have better access to foods of other cultures whereas poor communities have to be creative with whatever is available. The rich have access to more meat, rice and bulgur whereas the poor in the same area make a version of the same dish with whatever is available to them.

The Abrahamic religions – Christianity, Judaism and Islam – have flourished beside one another throughout history. Religious rules and regulations differentiate food culture. Muslims and Jews cannot eat pork whereas Christians can. It is okay to eat rabbit for some believers, but not for others.

These religious rules have, however, been shaped within the common cultural contexts of our geography. For example, Muslims and Christians who live near each other generally make and eat the same foods, with minor differences attributable to religious dietary rules. The food eaten by a Christian living in Gaziantep is the same as that eaten by a Muslim in Gaziantep. Similarly a Muslim and Christian in Cappadocia eat the same food. So linking a dish strictly to a religious identity can also be troublesome. It is worth noting that *Topik* (see p.85), a typical Armenian dish skilfully prepared in İstanbul, might be unknown to Anatolian Armenians.

Turkey is a multi-religious, multicultural society. Different cultures have their own traditions. The Ramadan festival and the Festival of the Sacrifice in Muslims, peace rituals, prayers for rain, *Hıdrellez* and sacred months like Ramadan and *Muharrem* have enriched our culinary culture. *Çöreks*, *kandil simidi*, *helva* and *aşure* are good examples. Armenians, Rum (Ottoman Greeks), Assyrians and other Christians make special brioches and red eggs to celebrate Easter. They share these delicacies with all their friends and neighbours regardless of their religion.

The Black Sea region receives a lot of rain and people often pray for sunshine, whereas many other regions have rituals and prayers for rain. A plate of food offered to a neighbour always comes back with another dish. Returning an empty plate is considered disrespectful. Charity is a crucial component of our culture. All charitable work is to be done quietly. We have many proverbs reflecting the importance of food in our social interactions. 'A cup of coffee goes for forty years,' and 'That who goes to bed full while his neighbour is hungry, is not one of us' are some examples. The needy are quietly taken care of and protected by those better off. There is a tradition of solidarity, cooperation and peace. There is a strong bond between our culinary culture and traditions.

Food is the key to the soul of a society. Whenever I travel, I go off the beaten track and explore more authentic dishes to get a feel for the culture. This is also how I get to explore different regions in Turkey. Food is a constant link to our heritage. All culinary traditions are precious in their own way. Geographical possibilities and the ensuing diversity is key here. Getting to know different cuisines and enabling their interaction with one another is extremely valuable. Milestones in one's life like birth, death and marriage are all marked with food rituals. There is a dinner organised at a bride's family home just before she gets married, to symbolise that she has her destiny in her own hands. If a woman craves a specific food during pregnancy, she absolutely has to have it. otherwise a mark will appear on her baby's body. Young mothers are nurtured with *Kaynar* (Spiced Herbal Tea, see p.446), which is also applied to her belly, then washed off. Visitors are offered sherbet and sweet *kuymak* (cheese fondue), served warm or cold depending on the season. *Hedik* (Whole Wheat Stew, see p.329) is made of boiled wheat to celebrate the first baby tooth and comes with its own ritual. The first step of a baby is called *köstek*. The toes of the baby are tied together with thread, and sweets and snacks are placed around him. Local children form two teams and run a race. The winner of the race cuts the thread and lifts the baby onto his feet. He is also the winner of the presents! Of course he shares the goodies all around. The first haircut has its own ritual too. Depending on how well-off the family is, the hair is weighed and an equal amount of gold, sugar or nuts are distributed.

Keşkek (Pounded Lamb and Wheat, see p.317) is traditional wedding food. In Nizip, a new groom is taken to the Turkish bath early in the morning of the wedding. They all have kebabs later. The groom has some spleen and *küşneme* to take to the bride.

Family and neighbours provide the food when someone dies. *Helva* (Halva, see p.408) is made in the hope that the aroma brings peace to the soul of the dearly departed. Sweets are placed in miniature houses at the graves, people eat them and pray for the dead.

This book covers both our traditional dishes and regional ones. It is unique in providing an extensive collection of recipes within their geographical and cultural context. I hope it will attract the attention of Turkish food lovers as well as international ones.

HISTORY

Turkey is truly at the crossroads of the Mediterranean, the Black Sea, Europe and the Middle East. It is surrounded by seas on three sides and bridges Asia and Europe. Anatolia (meaning sunrise or East in Greek) has been home to many civilisations. The Hitites, Assyrians, Phrygians, Ancient Romans and the Roman, Seljuk, Byzantine and Ottoman Empires have all enriched with their culture and traditions. The empires had many religious and ethnic components resulting in diverse practices.

Turkey became a republic in 1923, and this started a period of intense interaction with the West. The economy gradually shifted its power base from agriculture to industry. Turkey has been preserving its traditions as it became an integral part of a global world.

The geography and climate of our country has shaped the living conditions of the different regions. Central Anatolia has low rainfall, hence is suitable for cultivation of grains and pulses.

The Aegean and the Mediterranean are popular tourist destinations with long coastal stretches and a milder climate. They grow our fruit and vegetables. The Black Sea region with its steady rainfall supplies us with fish, tea and other produce. The Marmara region, with İstanbul at its centre, is industrialised and densely populated. Eastern and Southeastern Anatolia are very hilly. Animal herding is done in the Eastern Mediterranean region. Southeastern Anatolia has provided many key parts of our culinary culture. Both agriculture and animal herding is widely done here. The diversity in the climate results in different produce and dishes.

Meat, grains, vegetables and pastries form the mainstay of Turkish cuisine. There are regional differences between the use of meat and the cooking techniques of grains and pastries. Meat is cooked with beans in the west of the country, but the eastern version incorporates aromatic herbs and grains. The connecting geographical threads through the country are the flatbreads made on a *sac* and the *böreks* made of *yufka*. The black *sac* is a folkloric vessel connecting the whole country. It is inverted and used as a wok to make *Kavurma* (Lamb Confit, see p.497). It is a very versatile cooking device used to cook fish and *külbastı* (cutlets).

The Turkish culinary identity is based on a diverse heritage nurtured by ingredients and techniques employed by many civilisations. *Çiğköfte* (steak tartar), *halka tatlısı, Hamsili Pilav* (Rice Pilaf with Anchovies, see p.302) and *Frik Pilavı* (Freekeh Pilaf, see p.326) have all moved from local delicacies to dishes enjoyed by the whole country. It is possible to trace culinary signs of all seven regions in metropolitan areas. Immigrants from small places tend to live together in big cities, and this makes it easier to keep their local culinary cultures alive.

Geography gives Turkish cuisine its unique character. *Kıyma Kebabı* was renamed *Adana Kebap* (Spicy Kofte Kebab, see p.206) after the influx of migrants to İstanbul from the region. The fried liver that was sold in the past by the Albanians was eventually named after them. *Çiğ Börek* is called *Tatar Böreği* (Fried Pasties, see p.342) these days. Urbanisation has caused an erosion in our culinary culture. We can talk about culinary culture but attributing nationalities to dishes is futile. Food has geography not nationality. I do not like referring to dishes as Armenian, Turkish, Arabic, Circassian, Rum or Kurdish. Geography and its cultural transformations determine culinary culture. Culture transforms with changes in location, interacts with the culture already there and enriches it.

MY EARLY DAYS IN THE KITCHEN

Relatives on my father's side were farmers and on my mother's side bakers. My father looked after pistachio, olive and fruit trees. I still remember the wild honey I tasted in a pistachio orchard. My father was my master of all things rural from pistachios to olives, olive oil and fresh cheeses.

INTRODUCTION

My elder brothers and I are restaurateurs with a baking background. In Nizip, Gaziantep, where I am from, food meant everything to us. The ridged bread, various *pides* and *böreks* were prepared at bakeries. The locals made trays of food at home and sent them off to local bakeries for a final taste test and baking. The filling for *Lahmacun* (Spiced Meat-Topped Flatbread, see p.380) was made at the butcher and then sent, along with other meat, to the local bakery for cooking, eaten with fresh flatbreads and *pide*. There used to be many street vendors who cooked chickpeas in bone broth and pulled their carts in front of bakeries for hungry aficionados in the early morning. The bakers knew who were the best cooks in Nizip. They got cross if they were not offered a piece of the food they baked for others.

The baker, butcher, greengrocer, kebab shop and pastry shop were all in the same area in Nizip. They somehow had a lot to do with one another. What is called ridged bread in urban areas was our staple. We always had it fresh. Sugar, sesame seeds, cartilage and lamb confit from the homes were added to this bread and turned into delicious *pide*. The fresh *pide* are dipped into olive oil and eaten with milk for breakfast. Fresh cheese is made of sheep's milk at the beginning of spring and eaten with the *pide*.

Working at a bakery was a great experience. The ingredients, the people and communicating with clients made me mature both as a baker and a person. I cannot over-emphasise the importance of baking in the Turkish culinary tradition.

During primary school we used to compare our mothers' food. Every mother had a special dish she made really well. I have always been interested in ingredients and cooking techniques. This curiosity eventually led me into my research and field work on the relationship between food and folklore. Discovering sources about our culinary history put things into a historical perspective, more of a continuum. My mother has been my inspiration and I still love to learn.

I came to İstanbul in 1979 to work at my uncle Ismet's restaurant. The meze, grilled dishes and fish fired my enthusiasm and broadened my horizons. I learnt about the restaurant trade at places run by my older brothers and uncles. In the 1980s we cooked with diverse ingredients, most locally produced. Street vendors and restaurants contributed to a vibrant and authentic food scene which is sadly no longer here because of wider access to mass-produced foods. The local food culture that was dominant in Nizip in my childhood has long been replaced by restaurant food. Restaurants do serve local specialties like ridged bread, *pide*, *lahmacun*, sheep's head and trotters soup, lentil soup, *karnıyarık* and *moussaka*. More efficient communication and urbanisation have unfortunately taken place at the expense of local cuisines.

Every August, we visited Özyurt, a village near my hometown Nizip to pick grapes. We used to stay there a few nights waiting for the grapes to dry. We would also make our sweet *Sucuk* (Spiced Salami, see p.496) and *Pestil* (Fruit Leather, see p.439). We made *Menemen* (Scrambled Eggs with Vegetables, see p.116), a dish with our own tomatoes and eggs. This is the first dish I remember making.

I worked at several restaurants and did a fair bit of field work before opening a tiny restaurant with four friends in 1986. This six-table diner eventually turned into Çiya and I eventually became the sole owner. This boutique hole-in-the-wall is still remembered with affection by aficionados. I would take orders for special dishes and cook them for the patrons who enjoyed them accompanied by classical music. A woman among our regulars made a comment about the name of the *İçli Köfte* (Kibbeh, see p.184) in the menu. She claimed it was called '*oruk*'. I immediately knew she was from Antakya since this is the local name for kibbeh. That is how I met my wife Zeynep!

My restaurant Çiya developed a reputation as a culinary wonderland of discovery. I experimented passionately with new foods, reading extensively and researching obscure local dishes in Anatolia. In 1998 we opened Çiya Sofrası, on the same street but with a new concept. Çiya Sofrası has always been known as a destination for the lesser known cuisines of Southeastern Anatolia and Eastern Mediterranean. It encompasses a larger area from Mesopotamia to Anatolia featuring Azeri, Georgian, Turkish, Arabic, Armenian, Kurdish, Rum, Assyrian, Laz, Circassian and Sephardic dishes. In 2001 we opened a bigger kebab restaurant on the same street. We now also have our own farm to supply our restaurants with the freshest produce. We make our own pickles, grow our own fruit and vegetables and make our own tomato and red bell pepper pastes with the ingredients we grow ourselves.

I have also been sharing my knowledge about Turkish culinary culture in high schools, universities and local councils both in Turkey and internationally. Since 2005 I have been publishing *Yemek ve Kültür* (*Food and Culture*) with an editorial board of academics covering the history, literature, etymology and folklore of food. Çiya Yayınları is a specialised publishing house focusing on documenting food history. The Çiya Foundation carries out research on our culinary culture and aims to compile a food dictionary of our country and document food culture.

ABOUT THIS BOOK

I have long been thinking about an extensive book about Turkish food. When Phaidon approached me about this project, I relished the opportunity to write for an international audience. Choosing the recipes was the hardest part. I included food rituals and folklore as well as the original names of some dishes. This is why some recipes have a second name in parentheses. This is only a glimpse of Turkish cuisine. Fieldwork was the most fun part. I visited people in their kitchens and made them food, while they cooked for me in return.

DAIRY-FREE

GLUTEN-FREE

ONE-POT

VEGAN

VEGETARIAN

X

LESS THAN 30 MINUTES

LESS THAN 5 INGREDIENTS

SOUPS

SOUP IN
TURKISH CULTURE

Soups have a vital place in Turkish culture and we have a vast range of festive and seasonal varieties. We have served thousands of different soups at Çiya. Some recipes are localised, traditionally made with ingredients determined by their immediate geography, but many soups are enjoyed countrywide.

When I was a child, soup was the quintessential breakfast dish. Breakfast culture in urban areas has changed over the years and soup has been replaced by tea with olives, cheese, *halva*, molasses, tahini, clotted cream, butter, eggs, honey, jams, sliced tomato and cucumber, chilli (chile), cress, parsley and mint. This trend has affected the countryside as well, to a slightly lesser extent, but soup is still present on the breakfast table. Soup is not only there when we start the day, but also when we end it. Night owls love their soup, especially the protein-rich tripe soup. *Paça Çorbasi* (Trotter Soup, see p.44) and *Beyran Çorbasi* (Lamb and Rice Soup, see p.42) are great favourites of early birds.

Turkish soups are usually cooked with bone broth, meat stock or plain water, but there are recipes made with vegetable, chicken or fish stock. Plain soups, or those using tomato paste, always use meat or chicken stock or bone broth. Homemade stock makes for a fabulous soup. If adding milk and yogurt to your soup, there is no need to use stock.

The stock quantity in the soup recipes should always have been be diluted at the ratio one part stock to two parts water. If using the stock recipes in the Pantry chapter (see pp.478–497), this information is provided therein. I strongly suggest you be mindful of this, though you can of course adjust this ratio according to personal preference.

TARHANA

The Turkish culinary canon encompasses a vast variety of *tarhana* (see p.503), which has a vital place in our culture. *Tarhana* is traditionally made during August and September, then consumed in the winter months of December, January, and February. Soup is the most popular *tarhana* dish, followed by pilaf, porridge, roast, fried, on bread, salad, as a snack and with freekeh.

Two types of *tarhana* are used in soups: *Diş Tarhanası* (Hulled Tarhana, p.495) and *Un Tarhanası* (Powdered Tarhana, p.494). Hulled tarhana is made of cracked wheat and yogurt. Ingredients can include *yarma*, barley, chickpeas, lentils, black-eyed peas, broad (fava) beans, green beans, peas, corn and crushed rice. Cooked with sour strained yogurt, it is fermented and dried into different shapes. Powdered tarhana is made of flour and yogurt and can include plain (all-purpose) flour, semolina flour, barley flour, chickpea flour, lentil flour, ground cornmeal (polenta), rice flour and stale bread, which is then cooked with sour strained yogurt.

Once you start delving into the rich and flavourful world of *tarhana*, you might find it hard to classify this versatile ingredient into just two types. It can be flavoured in any number of ways. As well as yogurt, sour cheese, *çökelek* whey and milk can be used to make it. Fruits also feature in its production: sour grapes, sour cherries, cranberries, rose hip, plum, blackthorn, wild pear, sour apple, overripe fruit, pomegranate, sumac and sour fruit straps. Meat and vegetables can also be used: lamb confit, dried meat, dried bone, dried belly, dried goose, preserved meats such as *Pastırma* (Cured Beef, see p.495) and *Sucuk* (Spiced Salami, see p.494); turnip, cabbage, spinach, chard, nettles, fresh black-eyed beans, fresh peas, fresh green beans, tomatoes, bell peppers, onions, garlic, mint, basil, dill, pennyroyal, wild thyme, chilli (red pepper) flakes, paprika and smoked paprika. And a variety of fats: olive oil, butter, tail fat and suet all have a place in Turkish *tarhana*.

◆

SOUP AS
SOCIAL MEMORY

Soups are the pride and joy of Turkey. The humble bowl of soup is much more even than that. It announces and facilitates our joy, grief, pain and lives. In Turkey, soup heals the sick and feeds the poor. *Tarhanas* (see p.28), *Paça Çorbasi* (Trotter Soup, see p.44) and *Beyran Çorbasi* (Lamb and Rice Soup, see p.42) are all curative soups for colds. Trotter Soup is believed to help with broken bones. Courgette (zucchini), potato, yogurt soup with mint, orzo and homemade noodle soup with milk are all good for the stomach.

Soups are laden with meaning in Turkey – they are distributed for charity at wakes, weddings and festivals. *Bayram Çorbası* (Festive Soup, see p.41) is made on festive occasions, and weddings have their own special soup. Following a death, a soup made of head and trotters is crucial to the ease of the departed, according to ancient tradition. The family of the deceased will distribute this soup, feeding at least seven neighbours and the poor, so the deceased can be made more comfortable.

The communities in our geography are all remarkably good at creating riches from nothing. A good example of this is offal soup. In Turkey, it is traditional to sacrifice animals for religious festivals. The head, tripe, trotters and intestines of the sacrificed animal are useless to many but invaluable to the poor. They take home the offal, clean it and make it into this delicious soup. The same resourcefulness applies to wild herbs, where *ışkın, gulik, cinçar, jağ, labada doc*, mushroom and watercress find a home in soups and other local dishes, especially in the spring. Some soup names, such as *Dulavrat Çorbası* (Widow's Soup, see p.23) are symbolic of this spirit, a celebration of the widow's creativity and resourcefulness.

Soup is the first dish I want to eat after a period away from home, no matter how short, which gives you an indication of how central it is to our culture – soup is what I miss the most.

ALACA SOUP
ALACA ÇORBASI

Region:	Gaziantep, Southeastern Anatolia	
Preparation time:	10 minutes, plus overnight soaking	
Cooking time:	1 hour 20 minutes	
Serves:		4

80 g	cracked wheat	⅔ cup/3 oz
80 g	whole red lentils	½ cup/3 oz
1 (120 g)	medium onion, sliced	1 (¾ cup/4 oz)
2 tbsp	chickpeas (garbanzo beans), soaked overnight and cooked	2 tbsp
¼ tsp	ground cumin	¼ tsp

For the sauce:		
60 ml	olive oil	¼ cup/2 fl oz
4	garlic cloves, finely chopped	4
1 tsp	dried chilli (red pepper) flakes	1 tsp
1 tbsp	tomato paste (see p.492)	1 tbsp
3½ tbsp	dried tarragon	¼ cup/3½ tbsp

 V   p.21

The name of this winter soup is derived from its colourful ingredients: *alaca* means multi-coloured in Turkish. If a man is serious about asking for a woman's hand in marriage, his family requests that she makes this soup. Her cooking skills may determine the groom's continued interest. Or so the legend goes.

♦

The day before, cook the cracked wheat in 500 ml (generous 2 cups/17 fl oz) simmering water for 5 minutes, then cover the pan and leave to soak overnight.

Bring a large saucepan with 2 litres (8½ cups/70 fl oz) of water to the boil, add the lentils and onions and simmer for 10 minutes, then reduce the heat, cover, and cook for a further 30 minutes. Add the cracked wheat together with the soaking water, the soaked and cooked chickpeas (garbanzo beans) and cumin, with ¼ teaspoon black pepper and ½ teaspoon salt. Cook, covered, for 20 minutes.

To make the sauce:
Heat the oil in a small saucepan over medium heat, add the garlic and cook for 30 seconds. Add the dried chilli (red pepper) flakes and cook for a further 3 minutes. Add the dried tarragon and cook for another minute. Pour the sauce into the soup and boil for 4 minutes. Transfer to bowls and serve.

♦

BULGUR WHEAT SOUP
BULGUR AŞI ÇORBASI

Region:	Konya, Central Anatolia	
Preparation time:	10 minutes	
Cooking time:	35 minutes	
Serves:		4

2 litres	meat stock (see p.489)	8½ cups/70 fl oz
90 g	coarse bulgur wheat	½ cup/3 oz
200 g	fresh spinach	⅞ cup/7 oz
1	lemon, quartered, to serve	1

For the sauce:		
70 g	butter	¾ cup/2¾ oz
60 g	onion, finely chopped	2¼ oz
4	garlic cloves, finely chopped	4
1 tbsp	tomato paste (see p.492)	1 tbsp
½ tsp	dried chilli (red pepper) flakes	½ tsp
¼ tsp	black pepper	¼ tsp
3½ tbsp	dried tarragon (or 10 g/¼ oz fresh tarragon)	¼ cup/3½ tbsp

This is a soup for the winter months.

♦

In a large saucepan, bring the meat stock to the boil with 1 teaspoon salt over medium heat. Reduce the heat, add the bulgur wheat and cook for 20 minutes. Finely slice the fresh spinach, add to the pan and cook for a further 10 minutes.

To make the sauce:
Heat the butter in a small saucepan over medium heat, add the onion and garlic and cook for 3 minutes. Add the tomato paste, dried chilli (red pepper) flakes, black pepper and dried tarragon and cook for 2 minutes.

Pour the sauce into the soup you have just prepared. Stir and remove from the heat. Serve with lemon wedges.

VERMICELLI SOUP
TEL ŞEHRİYE ÇORBASI

Region:		Kütahya, all regions
Preparation time:		15 minutes
Cooking time:		35 minutes
Serves:		4

60 ml	olive oil	¼ cup/2 fl oz
60 g	onion	⅜ cup/2 oz
2	garlic cloves	2
70 g	carrots	½ cup/2½ oz
1	celery stick (stalk)	1
1½ tsp	tomato paste (see p.492)	1½ tsp
2	bay leaves	2
1	hot chilli (chile), crushed	1
1.5 litres	chicken stock (see p.489), hot	6¼ cups/50 fl oz
70 g	vermicelli	¾ cup/2½ oz
10	flat-leaf parsley sprigs	10
6	dill sprigs	6
1	lemon, quartered	1

Some cooks add cooked, shredded chicken thighs along with their cooking juices to this soup. When made as a restorative, the chilli and tomato paste are substituted with 200 g/7 oz each of shelled peas and potatoes.

♦

Finely slice the onion, garlic, carrots and celery. Heat the oil in a large saucepan over medium heat, add the onion, garlic, carrot and celery and cook for 5 minutes, stirring occasionally. Add the tomato paste, bay leaves and chilli (chile) with ¼ teaspoon black pepper and ½ teaspoon salt. Stir for 1 minute, then add the hot chicken stock. Cook uncovered for 5 minutes, then reduce the heat, cover, and cook for a further 10 minutes. Add the vermicelli and cook for 10 minutes. Remove from the heat.

Remove the bay leaves with a slotted spoon. Transfer the soup to serving bowls. Finely slice the parsley and dill, then sprinkle over the top. Serve with lemon wedges.

NOODLE SOUP
KESME ÇORBASI

Region:		Bingöl, Eastern Anatolia
Preparation time:		5 minutes
Cooking time:		1 hour 15 minutes
Serves:		4

80 g	black lentils	½ cup/3 oz
60 g	butter	¼ cup/2¼ oz
1 (120 g)	medium onion, finely chopped	1 (¾ cup/4 oz)
½ tsp	dried chilli (red pepper) flakes	½ tsp
1½ tsp	tomato paste (see p.492)	1½ tsp
4 tsp	dried purple basil (or 6 sprigs fresh purple basil)	4 tsp
2 litres	vegetable stock (see p.488), hot	8½ cups/70 fl oz
80 g	homemade noodles (see p.493)	3 oz

This is a winter staple, usually served with dried beans, lamb confit and yogurt.

♦

In a large saucepan, boil the black lentils in 500 ml (generous 2 cups/17 fl oz) of water for 15 minutes, then drain and set aside.

Heat the butter in a large saucepan over medium heat, add the onions and cooked lentils and cook for 5 minutes. Add the dried chilli (red pepper) flakes, tomato paste and purple basil with 1½ teaspoon salt and cook for a further 2 minutes, stirring continuously. Add the hot vegetable stock, reduce the heat and simmer, covered, for 30 minutes. Add the homemade noodles and cook, uncovered, for a further 10 minutes. Serve warm.

SOUR SOUP
EKŞİLİ ÇORBA

Region:	Kastamonu, Black Sea Region	
Preparation time:	10 minutes	
Cooking time:	45 minutes	
Serves:	4	

80 g	butter	⅓ cup/3 oz
100 g	chanterelle mushrooms, finely chopped	1⅓ cups/ 3½ oz
80 g	dark coarse bulgur wheat	½ cup/3 oz
½ tsp	dried chilli (red pepper) flakes	½ tsp
1 tsp	dried oregano	1 tsp
2 litres	vegetable stock (see p.488), hot	8½ cups/ 70 fl oz
25 g	fruit leather (prune) (or 2 tbsp sour plum extract, see p.491)	1 oz 1 oz
1 tsp	dried marigold leaves, to serve	1 tsp

V

Mushrooms collected in the autumn are added to the warm, winter version of this soup. The cold summer version omits the butter and mushrooms. Some like it with onions and garlic.

◆

Heat the butter in a large saucepan over medium heat, add the mushrooms and cook for 5 minutes. Add the bulgur wheat, dried chilli (red pepper) flakes and oregano with ¼ teaspoon black pepper and 1½ teaspoon salt and cook for 10 minutes. Reduce the heat, add the hot stock and the prune leather or sour plum extract and simmer for 30 minutes. Serve with the marigold leaves sprinkled on top.

WIDOW'S SOUP
DULAVRAT ÇORBASI

Region:	Adana, Mediterranean Region	
Preparation time:	10 minutes, plus overnight soaking	
Cooking time:	20 minutes for lentils, 35 minutes for soup	
Serves:	4	

4 tbsp	green lentils, soaked overnight	4 tbsp
2 tbsp	olive oil	2 tbsp
60 g	onion, finely chopped	⅜ cup/2 oz
4	garlic cloves, finely chopped	4
1	chard leaf, finely chopped	1
1 tsp	hot dried chilli (red pepper) flakes	1 tsp
2 tsp	dried mint	2 tsp
¼ tsp	ground cumin	¼ tsp
1 tbsp	tomato paste (see p.492)	1 tbsp
2 tbsp	chickpeas (garbanzo beans), soaked overnight and cooked	2 tbsp
60 ml	Seville (bitter) orange juice	¼ cup/2 fl oz
70 g	homemade noodles (see p.493)	2¾ oz

V

Legend has it that the name of this winter soup came from a poor widow who was talented at making scraps from her pantry into a delicious soup for guests. This is an ode to her skill at making something tasty out of nothing.

◆

Drain the soaked green lentils. Cook in a saucepan of simmering water until soft – about 20 minutes for the lentils. Drain and set aside.

Heat the oil in a large saucepan over medium heat, add the onion and garlic and cook for 3 minutes. Add the chard, dried chilli (red pepper) flakes, dried mint, cumin and tomato paste with ¼ teaspoon black pepper and 1 teaspoon salt, then cook for 4 minutes. Add the soaked and cooked chickpeas (garbanzo beans) and cooked green lentils and 1.5 litres (6¼ cups/50 fl oz) hot water and simmer for 15 minutes. Add the Seville orange juice and noodles and cook for a further 10 minutes. Serve warm.

TOMATO SOUP
DOMATES ÇORBASI

Region:		Aydın, all regions
Preparation time:		15 minutes
Cooking time:		1 hour 5 minutes
Serves:		4

500 g	tomatoes, quartered	2½ cups/ 1 lb 2 oz
1 (80 g)	small onion, quartered	1 (½ cup/ 3 oz)
1 (20 g)	chilli (chile), quartered	1 (¾ oz)
60 ml	olive oil	¼ cup/2 fl oz
70 g	medium-grain rice	⅓ cup/2½ oz
2	garlic cloves, thinly sliced	2
½ tsp	dried chilli (red pepper) flakes	½ tsp
2 tbsp	honey	2 tbsp
6	flat-leaf parsley sprigs	6
4	slices of toast	4

● V   p.25

This dish is best prepared in the summer when tomatoes are at their prime. There are versions without rice, thickened with butter, flavoured with cheese or tomato juice.

♦

Preheat oven to 200°C/400 F/Gas Mark 6. Spread the tomatoes, onion and chilli over a baking tray (sheet). Drizzle with 2 tablespoons of the oil and sprinkle over ½ teaspoon salt. Bake in the hot oven for 30 minutes.

Transfer the roasted ingredients to a food processor and blitz to combine or slice them finely by hand.

Heat the remaining oil in a saucepan over medium heat. Add the rice, garlic and dried chilli (red pepper) flakes with ½ teaspoon black pepper and cook for 1 minute. Add the blended or sliced ingredients with ½ teaspoon salt. Keep stirring and cook for a further 10 minutes.

Reduce the heat, add 1.5 litres (6¼ cups/50 fl oz) hot water and cook for 20 minutes, until the consistency thickens. Remove from the heat, add the honey and mix well.

Dice the toast into croutons. Pour the soup into bowls and garnish with finely sliced parsley and croutons.

♦

ISOT PEPPER SOUP
İSOT ÇORBASI

Region:		Diyarbakır, Southeastern Anatolia
Preparation time:		10 minutes
Cooking time:		30 or 45 minutes
Serves:		4

100 g	small hot red bell peppers	½ cup/ 3½ oz
300 g	small red bell peppers	1¾ cups/ 11 oz
2 (240 g)	medium onions, quartered	2 (1⅝ cups/8 oz)
200 g	tomatoes	1 cup/7 oz
60 ml	olive oil	¼ cup/2 fl oz
6	garlic cloves, finely chopped	6
80 g	coarse bulgur wheat	⅜ cup/3 oz
2 tbsp	grape molasses	2 tbsp
2 tbsp	grape vinegar	2 tbsp
2 tsp	dried basil (or 5 sprigs fresh basil, finely chopped)	2 tsp

● ♦ V

The winter version of this soup is enjoyed warm, whereas the summer version (without the olive oil) is served cold. It is usually made using leftover tomatoes and bell peppers from the barbecue. If cooking on embers is not an option, oven-roasting is just fine.

♦

Thread the peppers, onion quarters and tomatoes on to skewers and char over barbecue embers for 3 minutes on each side. Alternatively, roast in the oven at 200°C/400 F/ Gas Mark 6 for 15 minutes. Transfer to a paper bag, seal and let rest for 5 minutes, then scrape away the charred bits and seeds, and finely slice.

Heat the oil in a large saucepan over medium heat, add the garlic and cook for 15–20 seconds. Add the bulgur wheat and cook for 4 minutes. Add the sliced peppers, onions and tomatoes and sauté for 3 minutes. Add ¼ teaspoon black pepper, 1 teaspoon salt and 2 litres (8½ cups/70 fl oz) hot water, reduce the heat and cook, covered, for 10 minutes. Add the grape molasses and grape vinegar and cook, covered, for a further 7 minutes. Serve in bowls, garnished with dried basil.

GRAPE MOLASSES SOUP
DIMS ÇORBASI (ÜZÜM PEKMEZİ ÇORBASI)

Region:	Adıyaman, Southeastern Anatolia	
Preparation time:	10 minutes, plus overnight soaking	
Cooking time:		40 minutes
Serves:		4

120 g	cracked wheat	1 cup/4 oz
60 g	butter	¼ cup/2¼ oz
40 g	sultanas	¼ cup/1½ oz
1 tsp	ground cloves	1 tsp
½ tsp	ground cinnamon	½ tsp
1 tsp	ground allspice	1 tsp
30 g	chickpeas (garbanzo beans),	¼ cup/
	soaked overnight and cooked	1 oz
60 ml	grape molasses	¼ cup/2 fl oz
2 tbsp	sesame seeds,	2 tbsp
	toasted and ground	

V

This simple, nutritious soup is a particular favourite for serving to children and new mothers during the winter months. Enjoyed warm or cold, this dish works really well as a side to fried bulgur balls.

♦

The day before, cook the cracked wheat in 500 ml (generous 2 cups/17 fl oz) simmering water for 5 minutes, then cover the pan and leave to soak overnight. At the same time, set the chickpeas (garbanzo beans) to soak in a separate bowl of water and leave overnight.

The next day, drain the soaked wheat.

Heat the butter in a large saucepan over medium heat, add the cooked cracked wheat and cook for 2 minutes. Add the sultanas, cloves, cinnamon and allspice with 1 teaspoon salt and cook for 1 minute. Reduce the heat, add 1.5 litres (6¼ cups/50 fl oz) hot water and the soaked and cooked chickpeas, cover and cook for 20 minutes. Add the grape molasses and cook for a further 10 minutes. Serve, sprinkled with the sesame seeds.

TURNIP SOUP
ÇELEM (ŞALGAM) ÇORBASI

Region:	Erzurum, Eastern Anatolia	
Preparation time:		15 minutes
Cooking time:		40 minutes
Serves:		4

60 g	butter	¼ cup/2¼ oz
60 g	onion, finely chopped	⅜ cup/2 oz
5	garlic cloves,	5
	finely chopped	
1 tsp	dried chilli	1 tsp
	(red pepper) flakes	
1 (70 g)	carrot, grated	1 (½ cup/2½ oz)
300 g	turnip, grated	2 cups/10½ oz
70 g	dried bean flour	½ cup/2¾ oz
	(or 70 g/⅓ cup/2¾ oz	
	dried cannellini beans,	
	crushed)	
250 ml	hot and sour	1 cup/8 fl oz
	pickling brine (see p.451)	

80 g	*kaymak* (clotted cream,	⅓ cup/3 oz
	see p.486)	
10	flat-leaf parsley sprigs	10
10	coriander (cilantro) sprigs	10

❁ V

This soup is popular in the winter months together with other dishes using the humble turnip. You are not considered a true local if you can't make this soup.

♦

Heat the butter in a large saucepan over medium heat, add the onion and garlic and cook for 2 minutes. Add the dried chilli (red pepper) flakes with ¼ teaspoon black pepper and 1 teaspoon salt. Squeeze any moisture out of the grated carrot and turnip. Add the grated carrot and turnip and cook for 5 minutes, mixing continuously. Add 2 litres (8½ cups/70 fl oz) hot water and cook for 5 minutes, then reduce the heat, cover, and cook for a further 10 minutes. At the end of this time, mash with a wooden spoon.

Mix the bean flour with the sour pickling brine and add to the soup. Cook uncovered for 10 minutes.

Serve in bowls, garnished with a dollop of clotted cream and sprinkle of finely chopped parsley and coriander.

COLLARD GREENS SOUP
KARALAHANA ÇORBASI

Region:		Rize, Black Sea Region
Preparation time:		15 minutes
Cooking time:		50 minutes
Serves:		4

50 g	suet (dried and smoked, if possible)	½ cup/2 oz
2	lamb bones with marrow, baked and halved	2
4	garlic cloves, finely chopped	4
60 g	onion, finely diced	⅜ cup/2 oz
70 g	cracked hominy corn	½ cup/2¾ oz
50 g	borlotti beans, cooked	¼ cup/2 oz
300 g	collard greens	2 cups/11 oz
2	marigold or basil sprigs	2

For the sauce:		
30 g	butter	⅛ cup/1 oz
2	garlic cloves, crushed	2
2 tsp	dried mint	2 tsp
½ tsp	dried chilli (red pepper) flakes	½ tsp

Another winter staple, this soup is traditionally made with smoked suet, which is dried on the rooftops of homes with weights on top. Some versions of the soup are mashed, and some add yogurt, ground cornmeal, flour and roux.

◆

Heat the suet in a large saucepan over medium heat, add the lamb bones and fry for 2 minutes. Add the garlic and onion and cook for 3 minutes. Add the cracked hominy corn and cooked borlotti beans and cook for 2 minutes. Add 2 litres (8½ cups/70 fl oz) boiling water, then reduce the heat and cook, covered, for 30 minutes.

Meanwhile, poach the collard greens in a separate saucepan for 5 minutes, then drain and discard the juice.

Wash and finely chop the collard greens and slice the marigold or basil leaves. Add to the pan with ¼ teaspoon black pepper and 1 teaspoon salt and cook for 10 minutes over low heat.

To make the sauce:
Heat the butter in a small saucepan over medium heat. Add the garlic, dried mint and dried chilli (red pepper) flakes and cook for 10 minutes.

Ladle the soup into serving bowls, stir through the sauce and serve.

CELERIAC SOUP
KEREVİZ ÇORBASI

Region:		İzmir, Aegean Region
Preparation time:		15 minutes
Cooking time:		35 minutes
Serves:		4

400 g	celeriac (celery root)	2½ cups/14 oz
60 g	onion	⅜ cup/2 oz
3	garlic cloves	3
70 g	carrots	½ cup/2½ oz
2 tbsp	olive oil	2 tbsp
1	long green dried pepper, crushed	1
100 g	strained yogurt	½ cup/3½ oz
10	dill sprigs, finely sliced	10

For the sauce:		
2 tbsp	olive oil	2 tbsp
2	garlic cloves, crushed	2
2 tsp	dried mint	2 tsp

This winter soup is believed to ease sore stomachs.

◆

Finely chop the celeriac (celery root), onion, garlic and carrots. Heat the oil in a large saucepan over medium heat. Add the chopped celeriac, onion, garlic, carrots and crushed dried pepper. Season with ¼ teaspoon black pepper and 1 teaspoon salt, then cook for 5 minutes. Add 1.5 litres (6¼ cups/50 fl oz) hot water, reduce the heat and cook, covered, for 20 minutes. At the end of this time, mash with a fork to a smooth purée.

Meanwhile, in a small saucepan, combine the yogurt with 500 ml (generous 2 cups/17 fl oz) cold water. Cook over medium heat for 10 minutes, always stirring in one direction. When it comes to the boil, add to the soup pan and cook for 2 minutes, then remove from the heat.

To make the sauce:
Heat the oil in a large saucepan over medium heat, add the garlic and cook for 5 minutes. Add the dried mint and cook for 5 seconds.

Stir the sauce through the soup, garnish with the dill and serve.

V

CRUSHED WHEAT TARHANA SOUP
DÖVME TARHANA ÇORBASI

Region:	Kahramanmaraş, all regions	
Preparation time:	10 minutes, plus overnight soaking	
Cooking time:	45 minutes for the soup	
Serves:		4

150 g	hulled tarhana (see p.495), soaked overnight	1 cup/5 oz
2 tbsp	chickpeas (garbanzo beans), soaked overnight and cooked	2 tbsp
1 (200 g)	turnip, peeled and finely diced	1 (1½ cups/ 7 oz)

For the sauce:		
70 g	(goat's milk) butter	⅓ cup/2¾ oz
5	garlic cloves, crushed	5
2 tsp	dried mint	2 tsp
2 tsp	dried chilli (red pepper) flakes	2 tsp

V

p.29

Several legends are associated with the origins of this popular cure for a cold. One recalls a local tent-dwelling couple who have a fight. While the husband goes to town, the wife starts a soup with yogurt and crushed wheat. On his return home, she pours the soup onto the reeds in anger. Later she realises that the soup has dried and is now more delicious. In another legend, a visiting Sultan asks for this soup when he journeys to Maraş. The locals pour the soup over reeds to dry as a memento from the Sultan. Since then, this soup has been known as *tarhana*.

◆

Drain the hulled tarhana, transfer to a bowl and knead for 5 minutes. Put it into a saucepan with 2 litres (8½ cups/ 70 fl oz) water, the soaked and cooked chickpeas (garbanzo beans), ¼ teaspoon black pepper and ½ teaspoon salt. Cook over medium heat for 10 minutes. Reduce the heat, add the turnip and cook for 30 minutes, until the soup thickens.

To make the sauce:
Heat the butter in a saucepan over medium heat, add the garlic and cook for 5 minutes. Add the dried mint and dried chilli (red pepper) flakes and cook for a further 5 seconds.

Ladle the soup into bowls. Drizzle with the sauce to serve.

◆

POWDERED TARHANA SOUP
TOZ TARHANA ÇORBASI

Region:	Çorum, Black Sea Region	
Preparation time:	10 minutes	
Cooking time:	30 minutes	
Serves:		4

30 g	butter	⅛ cup/1 oz
60 g	onion, finely chopped	⅜ cup/2 oz
1	fresh banana pepper (mild sweet pepper), finely chopped	1
2	garlic cloves, crushed	2
200 g	tomatoes, finely chopped	1 cup/7 oz
1½ tsp	tomato paste (see p.492)	1½ tsp
½ tsp	dried chilli (red pepper) flakes	½ tsp
1.5 litres	chicken stock (see p.489)	6¼ cups/50 fl oz
70 g	powdered tarhana (see p.494)	½ cup/2¾ oz
1 tsp	dried mint	1 tsp
2 tbsp	lemon juice	2 tbsp

This is a winter staple. You can buy powdered tarhana in Turkish groceries and Middle Eastern stores.

◆

Heat the butter in a large saucepan over medium heat, add the onion, pepper and garlic and cook for 2 minutes. Add the chopped tomatoes, tomato paste and dried chilli (red pepper) flakes and cook for a further 3 minutes. Stir in the chicken stock. Add the powdered tarhana in small increments and keep mixing to incorporate. Reduce the heat, add the dried mint and lemon juice with ½ teaspoon salt and simmer for 20 minutes, stirring continuously. Serve warm.

SPINACH SOUP
ISPANAK ÇORBASI

Region:		Sinop, Black Sea Region
Preparation time:		10 minutes, plus overnight soaking
Cooking time:		45 minutes–1½ hours for the beans,
		30 minutes for the soup
Serves:		4

100 g	borlotti beans, soaked overnight	½ cup/3½ oz
300 g	fresh spinach leaves, washed, patted dry and finely chopped	1⅓ cups/11 oz
2 tbsp	butter	2 tbsp
4	garlic cloves, crushed	4
1¼ tsp	salt	1¼ tsp

For the sauce:		
1	egg	1
150 g	strained yogurt	¾ cup/5 oz

For the dressing:		
2 tbsp	butter	2 tbsp
2 tsp	dried mint	2 tsp
½ tsp	dried chilli (red pepper) flakes	½ tsp

❦ V

This is an autumnal soup, which works equally well with dried spinach as it does with fresh. For a lighter, more summery version, omit the butter.
◆
Drain the soaked borlotti beans, then cook in a saucepan of simmering water until soft, about 45 minutes–1½ hours depending on age of beans. Drain, mash and set aside.

Warm a large saucepan over medium heat for 1 minute, add the spinach and steam, covered, for 10 minutes.

Heat the butter in another saucepan over medium heat, add the garlic and cook for 10 seconds. Add the mashed beans and spinach. Cook for 3 minutes. Add 1 litre (4¼ cups/ 34 fl oz) water and the salt. Cook for a further 10 minutes.

To make the sauce:
In a large saucepan, whisk 500 ml (generous 2 cups/17 fl oz) water with the egg and strained yogurt for 1 minute until well combined. Bring to the boil over medium heat, stirring continuously in the same direction. The stirring is vital to prevent the yogurt from curdling. When boiling, cook for a further 2 minutes then pour into the soup pan. Cook for a further 3 minutes, then remove from the heat.

To make the dressing:
Heat the butter in a small saucepan over medium heat, add the dried mint and dried chilli (red pepper) flakes and cook for 5 minutes.

Ladle the soup into bowls, drizzle with the dressing and serve warm.

NETTLE SOUP
ÇİNÇAR ÇORBASI

Region:		Artvin, Black Sea Region
Preparation time:		5 minutes
Cooking time:		20 minutes
Serves:		4

300 g	fresh nettles, washed, finely sliced	1⅓ cups/1 oz
40 g	plain (all-purpose) flour	⅓ cup/ 1½ oz
80 g	blue cheese	⅞ cup/3 oz
1	egg	1
2 tbsp	butter	2 tbsp

V Ⅹ

Çinçar is the local name for nettles. Those grown in the shade are believed to have stronger healing properties for clearing the lungs. This is a popular soup for the autumn and winter months.
◆
In a large saucepan over medium heat, bring 1 litre (4¼ cups/34 fl oz) water to the boil, then add the nettles and flour and cook for 10 minutes, stirring continuously. Add the blue cheese. If the cheese is already salty do not add any further salt. If not, add 1¼ teaspoon salt. Cook, stirring, for a further 5 minutes. Remove from the heat.

In a separate bowl, whisk the egg. Slowly mix 2 tablespoons of the soup into the egg until incorporated, then stir this mixture gradually back into the soup.

Finally, warm a saucepan and heat the butter for 1 minute.

Serve the soup hot in bowls, drizzled with the hot butter.

CURLY DOCK SOUP
TİRŞİK (YILAN PANCARI) ÇORBASI

Region:	Osmaniye, Mediterranean Region
Preparation time:	10 minutes, plus 2 days fermentation
Cooking time:	2 hours 15 minutes
Serves:	4

40 g	chickpeas (garbanzo beans)	¼ cup/1½ oz
120 g	cracked wheat	1 cup/4 oz
600 g	curly dock (wild sorrel, or spinach or Swiss chard), finely chopped	2⅔ cups/ 1 lb 5 oz
100 g	plain (all-purpose) flour	¾ cup/3½ oz
1¼ tsp	salt	1¼ tsp
120 ml	sumac extract (see p.491)	½ cup/4 fl oz
2 tbsp	olive oil	2 tbsp

♦ ♦ V

Curly dock, a wild herb, is also known as 'snake beet' as it is believed the snake transfers its venom to the herb. Locals have myriad names for this spring herb and as many ways to cook it. The Black Sea folk call it *livik, nivik* or *mivik*, Eastern Anatolians *gari*, Southeastern Anatolians *yılan pancarı*, Aegeans *yılan yastığı*. Follow all the preparatory steps for this soup to take the sting out of the herb.

♦

Pour 4 litres (16 cups/130 fl oz) water into a saucepan, add the chickpeas (garbanzo beans), cracked wheat and curly dock. Boil for 5 minutes, then remove from the heat.

Sprinkle the flour over the surface of the soup, put a lid on the pan, then wrap in a towel, making sure the whole pan is enclosed. Let ferment at room temperature for 2 days.

Uncover and skim off 90 percent of the flour, which will have formed a layer on the surface like clotted cream.

Add the salt and sumac extract and cook over medium heat, covered, for 10 minutes. Reduce the heat to low and simmer for 2 hours.

Warm the oil in a small saucepan over medium heat. Pour over the soup and serve.

♦

WATERCRESS SOUP
SU TERESİ ÇORBASI

Region:	Bilecik, Marmara Region
Preparation time:	10 minutes
Cooking time:	40 minutes
Serves:	4

100 g	broad (fava) beans (shelled and peeled)	½ cup/3½ oz
60 g	onion, finely chopped	⅜ cup/2 oz
3	garlic cloves, crushed	3
¼ tsp	ground cumin	¼ tsp
¼ tsp	*poy* (see p.502, optional)	¼ tsp
300 g	fresh watercress	9 cups/11 oz
2 tbsp	lemon juice	2 tbsp

For the sauce:		
2 tbsp	olive oil	2 tbsp
2	garlic cloves, crushed	2
½ tsp	dried chilli (red pepper) flakes	½ tsp

♦ ❀ ♦ V

Spring watercress grows in creeks and riverbeds. As well as being delicious raw, it is also used in soups, salads, wraps and sherbets.

♦

In a large saucepan over medium heat, bring 2 litres (8½ cups/70 fl oz) water to the boil, then add the broad (fava) beans, onion, garlic, cumin and *poy* (if using) with 1 teaspoon salt. Cook, covered, over low heat for 30 minutes, until the broad beans become the consistency of mash. Finely chop the watercress, then add it with the lemon juice and cook for a further 5 minutes, then remove from the heat.

To make the sauce:
Heat the oil in a small saucepan over medium heat, add the garlic and dried chilli (red pepper) flakes and cook for 5 seconds.

Serve in bowls, drizzled with a little sauce.

PUMPUM SOUP
PUMPUM ÇORBASI

Region:		Bartın, Black Sea Region
Preparation time:		5 minutes
Cooking time:		20 minutes
Serves:		4

30 g	butter	⅛ cup/1 oz
80 g	ground cornmeal (polenta)	generous ½ cup/ 3 oz
1.5 litres	meat stock, (veal or lamb, see p.489), hot	6¼ cups/ 50 fl oz

For the garnish:		
200 g	toasted bread	7 oz
30 g	butter	⅛ cup/1 oz
80 g	pastırma, (cured beef, see p.497), finely diced	3 oz
½ tsp	dried chilli (red pepper) flakes	½ tsp

✗   p.33

'*Pumpum*' is utterly onomatopoeic. The batter is very runny, slightly more so than pancake batter. Both hands are dipped into the batter and the pieces make a '*pum*' sound once they hit the hot oil. Some recipes use beignets instead of bread to make the croutons.

◆

Heat the butter in a saucepan over medium heat. Reduce the heat, add the ground cornmeal (polenta) and cook for 5 minutes. Add the hot stock. If the *pastırma* is salty do not add any salt, if it isn't salty then season with 1¼ teaspoon salt. Cook for 10 minutes, whisking continuously to prevent any lumps.

To make the garnish:
Dice the toasted bread into 5-mm (¼-inch) croutons. Heat the butter in a small saucepan over medium heat. Add the *pastırma*, dried chilli (red pepper) flakes and croutons and cook for 2 minutes.

Serve the soup in bowls, with the garnish drizzled on top.

◆

WEDDING SOUP
DÜĞÜN ÇORBASI

Region:		Afyon, all regions
Preparation time:		5 minutes
Cooking time:		2 hours 30 minutes
Serves:		4

500 g	lamb neck with bones	1 lb 2 oz
60 g	onion, quartered	⅜ cup/2 oz
2 tsp	salt	2 tsp
40 g	butter	3 tbsp/1½ oz
2 heaped tbsp	plain (all-purpose) flour	2 heaped tbsp
1 tsp	ground dried chilli (chile)	1 tsp
¼ tsp	black pepper	¼ tsp

For the sauce:		
1	egg	1
50 g	strained yogurt	¼ cup/2 oz

This soup is a menu staple of traditional restaurants. In some regions, it is distributed to the poor at the mosque after the Friday morning prayers. The stock takes time to make, but this can be reduced by using a pressure cooker (about 50 minutes with 2 litres/8½ cups/70 fl oz water).

◆

In a very large saucepan, bring 3.5 litres (14½ cups/ 118 fl oz) water, the lamb neck, onion and salt to the boil over medium heat. Boil for 5 minutes, skimming the surface with a slotted spoon. Reduce the heat to low and cook, uncovered, for 2 hours.

Remove the lamb neck from the pan and set aside to cool. Reserve the stock. Pull the meat off the bone in pieces.

Heat the butter in a saucepan over medium heat, stir in the flour and cook for 3 minutes. Add the ground chilli (chile) and cook for 10 seconds. Add the stock from the lamb and whisk to combine with the flour. Reduce the heat, add the pulled meat and black pepper. Cook for 10 minutes.

To make the sauce:
Whisk the egg and yogurt together, then add 2 tablespoons of the soup, stirring vigorously to prevent curdling.

Slowly pour the sauce into the pan and cook for a further 2 minutes, stirring continuously. Serve immediately.

YOGURT SOUP
ZOZAN (YAYLA) ÇORBASI

Region:		Kars, all regions
Preparation time:		5 minutes
Cooking time:		40 minutes
Serves:		4

1 litre	meat stock (see p.489)	4¼ cups/34 fl oz
100 g	medium-grain rice	½ cup/3½ oz
120 g	strained yogurt	½ cup/4 oz
1¼ tsp	salt	1¼ tsp
¼ tsp	black pepper	¼ tsp
50 g	butter	scant ¼ cup/2 oz
2 tsp	dried mint	2 tsp

This soup is popular all year round. For a lighter summer soup that can be eaten cold, omit the butter.

◆

In a saucepan, bring the stock and rice to the boil, then reduce the heat to low and cook, covered, for 25 minutes.

In a separate saucepan, mix the strained yogurt with 1 litre (4¼ cups/34 fl oz) water over medium heat. Bring to the boil, then slowly add to the first pan, mixing continuously until incorporated. Add the salt and black pepper. Cook for 5 minutes.

Heat the butter in a small saucepan over medium heat. Add the dried mint, cook for 10 seconds, then pour into the soup pan. Cook for a further 5 minutes. Serve warm.

❧

◆

YOGURT AND LENTIL SOUP
PESKÜTAN (PESKİTAN)

Region:		Sivas, Central Anatolia
Preparation time:		10 minutes, plus overnight soaking, plus 2 hours soaking
Cooking time:		50 minutes
Serves:		4

100 g	cracked wheat	⅞ cup/3½ oz
30 g	green lentils	¼ cup/1 oz
1 (80 g)	roasted lamb bone with a little meat on	1 (3 oz)
1¼ tsp	salt	1¼ tsp
100 g	peskütan (strained yogurt with çökelek), butter removed, thickened with strong flour	½ cup/3½ oz

For the sauce:		
60 g	butter	¼ cup/2¼ oz
60 g	onion, finely diced	⅜ cup/2 oz
2 tsp	dried mint	2 tsp

❧

This soup is traditionally sent to the immediate family of a deceased person at the time of the funeral. If you don't have a lamb bone to hand, you can use a bone stock instead: adding 200 ml (scant 1 cup/7 fl oz) bone broth (see p.490) and reducing the water to 1.5 litres (6¼ cups/50 fl oz). Peskütan is a type of çökelek (dry curd cottage cheese, see p.482) native to Sivas and its environs. It's made by boiling and draining Ayran (Salted Yogurt Drink, see p.452). If peskütan is unavailable, substitute 50 g (¼ cup/2 oz) sour strained yogurt and 100 g (½ cup/3½ oz) lor (fresh curd cheese, see p.485), mixed with 1 tablespoon plain (all-purpose) flour for 2 minutes.

The day before, cook the cracked wheat in 500 ml (generous 2 cups/17 fl oz) simmering water for 5 minutes. Cover the pan and leave to soak overnight.

The next day, soak the lentils in 250 ml (1 cup/8 fl oz) water for 2 hours. Drain the lentils and wheat. Set aside.

In a saucepan over medium heat, cook the green lentils, lamb bone and salt in 2.25 litres (10 cups/80 fl oz) water for 20 minutes. Skim the surface with a slotted spoon. Add the cracked wheat and cook for a further 10 minutes.

In another saucepan, whisk the peskütan and water for 5 minutes. Cook for 2 minutes over medium heat, stirring in the same direction. Add to the soup pan and cook for a further 8 minutes. Keep stirring in the same direction.

To make the sauce:
Heat the butter in a saucepan over medium heat, add the onion and cook for 1½ minutes. Add the dried mint and cook for 10 seconds. Pour the sauce on the soup and serve.

DRIED YOGURT AND LENTIL SOUP
ÇORTAN ÇORBASI

Region:	Şanlıurfa, Southeastern Anatolia	
Preparation time:	10 minutes, plus 1 hour soaking	
Cooking time:	50 minutes	
Serves:	4	

70 g	*kashk* (see p.485)	2¾ oz
150 g	hulled red lentils	1 cup/5 oz
40 g	dried black-eyed peas	¼ cup/1½oz
1 tsp	salt (do not use if *kashk* is already salty)	1 tsp

For the sauce:

50 g	ghee (see p.485)	¼ cup/2 oz
½ tsp	hemp seeds	½ tsp
1 (120 g)	medium onion, finely chopped	1 (¾ cup/4 oz)
2	garlic cloves, finely chopped	2
½ tsp	dried chilli (red pepper) flakes	½ tsp

4	fresh coriander (cilantro) sprigs, finely chopped	4
1	basil sprig, finely chopped	1

V

Also known as *kurut*, *keşk*, or *keş* soup, *kashk* (see p.485) is a dried yogurt product, which can be found in Middle Eastern stores or online. *Kashk* is a very popular snack with pregnant women as it leaves a tangy taste in the mouth. Added to soups, *Ayran* (Salted Yogurt Drink, see p.452) and many other dishes, it is believed to have healing and energy enhancing properties. It is consumed cold in the summer months and warm with added butter in the winter.

◆

Soak the *kashk* in 500 ml (generous 2 cups/17 fl oz) water until it dissolves, about 1 hour, then set aside.

In a saucepan, cook the red lentils and black-eyed peas in 1.5 litres (6¼ cups/50 fl oz) water over medium heat for 5 minutes. Skim the surface with a slotted spoon. Reduce the heat, cover, and cook for 25 minutes. Add the dissolved *kashk* and salt, if using, and cook for a further 10 minutes.

To make the sauce:
Heat the ghee in a small saucepan over medium heat, add the hemp seeds and cook for 10 seconds. Add the onion and garlic and cook for 3 minutes. Add the dried chilli (red pepper) flakes and cook for a further 10 seconds.

Pour the sauce into the soup and cook for 5 minutes.

Serve in bowls, garnished with fresh coriander (cilantro) and basil.

YOGURT AND CRACKED WHEAT SOUP
AYRAN AŞI ÇORBASI

Region:	Van, Eastern Anatolia	
Preparation time:	10 minutes, plus overnight soaking	
Cooking time:	40 minutes	
Serves:	4	

100 g	cracked wheat	⅞ cup/3½ oz
250 g	strained yogurt	1¼ cups/9 oz
1 (120 g)	courgette (zucchini), finely diced	1 (¾ cups/4 oz)
1 tbsp	plain (all-purpose) flour (optional)	1 tbsp
300 g	spinach, finely chopped	1⅓ cups/11 oz
½ bunch	fresh coriander (cilantro), finely chopped	½ bunch

V

This recipe can be made with either courgette (zucchini) or fresh chillies (chiles), depending on seasonal availability, and some local recipes substitute the fresh coriander (cilantro) with mint. It can be enjoyed warm or cold – if serving cold, leave out the flour.

◆

The day before, cook the cracked wheat in 500 ml (generous 2 cups/17 fl oz) simmering water for 5 minutes, then cover the pan and leave to soak overnight.

The next day, drain the cracked wheat and set aside.

In a large saucepan, whisk the yogurt into 1.5 litres (6¼ cups/50 fl oz) water until well combined. Add the cracked wheat and courgette (zucchini) and cook over medium heat for 20 minutes. Add the flour, if using, and mix until well combined. Add the spinach and 1¼ teaspoon salt and cook for 10 more minutes. Finally, mix in the fresh coriander (cilantro), and serve.

STRAINED LENTIL SOUP
SÜZME MERCİMEK ÇORBASI

Region:	Eskişehir, all regions
Preparation time:	10 minutes
Cooking time:	45 minutes
Serves:	4

150 g	split yellow lentils, washed	1 cup/5 oz
100 g	potato, quartered	3½ oz
1 (120 g)	medium onion, quartered	1 (¾ cup/4 oz)
½ tsp	ground cumin	½ tsp
½ tsp	ground turmeric	½ tsp
¼ tsp	white pepper	¼ tsp
1	lemon, quartered	1

For the sauce:

2 tbsp	olive oil	2 tbsp
¼ tsp	white pepper	¼ tsp
1 tsp	paprika	1 tsp

V

p.37

This is a popular soup all over the country. It is traditionally consumed in small quantities at the beginning of a meal, unlike other soups which are treated more like a main course. You can substitute beef, chicken or vegetable stock for the boiling water in this recipe.

♦

In a large saucepan over medium heat, add 1 litre (4¼ cups/34 fl oz) water, the yellow lentils, potato and onion with 1 teaspoon salt, bring to the boil, and cook for 10 minutes. Reduce the heat and cook for a further 25 minutes, until the soup thickens. Skim the surface using a slotted spoon.

Remove from the heat and mash the contents of the pan. Add 1 litre (4¼ cups/34 fl oz) boiling water, the cumin, turmeric and white pepper and whisk for 1 minute. Return to the heat and cook for a further 5 minutes.

To make the sauce:
Heat the oil in a large saucepan over medium heat. Add the white pepper and paprika and cook for 5 seconds.

Drizzle the sauce over the soup and serve immediately with wedges of lemon.

SOUR LENTIL SOUP
EKŞİLİ MALHUTA ÇORBA

Region:	Kilis, Southeastern Anatolia
Preparation time:	10 minutes
Cooking time:	1 hour 5 minutes
Serves:	4

100 g	red lentils, washed	¾ cup/3½ oz
1 (120 g)	medium onion	1 (¾ cup/4 oz)
6	garlic cloves	6
50 g	coarse bulgur wheat	¼ cup/2 oz
100 g	aubergine (eggplant)	⅜ cup/3½ oz
1½ tsp	dried mint	1½ tsp
¼ tsp	ground cumin	¼ tsp
150 g	fresh spinach	⅔ cup/5 oz
2 tbsp	lemon juice	2 tbsp

For the sauce:

2 tbsp	olive oil	2 tbsp
1 tsp	dried chilli (red pepper) flakes	1 tsp
1½ tsp	tomato paste (see p.492)	1½ tsp

V

This is a warming soup for the autumn and winter months. It is believed that when people make this soup and distribute it to the poor, snow will follow.

♦

In a large saucepan over medium heat, add 2.25 litres (10 cups/80 fl oz) water and the red lentils, bring to the boil, and cook for 5 minutes. Skim the surface with a slotted spoon. Reduce the heat and simmer for 30 minutes. Finely chop the onion and garlic, then add to the pan with the bulgur wheat.

Finely dice the aubergine (eggplant) and add it to the pan with the dried mint and cumin. Season with ¼ teaspoon black pepper and cook for 20 minutes. Finely chop the spinach then add it and the lemon juice. Season with 1 teaspoon salt and cook for a further 5 minutes.

To make the sauce:
Heat the oil in a small saucepan over medium heat, add the dried chilli (red pepper) flakes and tomato paste and cook for 2 minutes.

Add the sauce to the soup, mix for 1 minute, then serve.

EZO THE BRIDE'S SOUP
EZO GELİN ÇORBASI

Region:		Kilis, Southeastern Anatolia
Preparation time:		10 minutes
Cooking time:		1 hour
Serves:		4

200 g	red lentils	1½ cups/7 oz
1 litre	boiling water	4¼ cups/34 fl oz
1 tsp	salt	1 tsp
¼ tsp	black pepper	¼ tsp
1	lemon, quartered	1

For the sauce:

2 tbsp	olive oil	2 tbsp
1 (120 g)	medium onion, finely chopped	1 (¾ cup/4 oz)
6	garlic cloves, finely chopped	6
1 tsp	dried chilli (red pepper) flakes	1 tsp
2 tsp	dried mint	2 tsp
1 tbsp	tomato paste (see p.492)	1 tbsp

💧 🌿 ♦ V   p.39

Known as *Mahlûta Çorbası* in Southeastern Anatolia, this soup gained nationwide fame with the name *Ezo Gelin*. Legend has it that Ezo spent time in hospital. Towards the end of her stay, tired of bland food, Ezo made this soup. It has since been made famous by restaurants in İstanbul whose owners are from Southeastern Anatolia. This soup is made with bulgur wheat or rice and meat stock in the south.

♦

In a saucepan over medium heat, add 1.5 litres (6¼ cups/50 fl oz) water and the red lentils, bring to the boil, and cook for 10 minutes. Skim the surface with a slotted spoon. Reduce the heat and simmer, covered, for 30 minutes, until well combined. Add the boiling water, salt and black pepper. Cook for a further 10 minutes, whisking continuously.

To make the sauce:
Heat the oil in a saucepan over medium heat, add the onion and garlic. Cook for 3 minutes. Add the dried chilli (red pepper) flakes and dried mint. Cook for 10 seconds. Add the tomato paste and cook for 1 minute.

Pour the sauce into the boiling soup, cook for a further 2 minutes, then remove from the heat.

Serve in bowls with lemon wedges.

♦

WHITE CORN SOUP
AK MISIR ÇORBASI

Region:		Ordu, Black Sea Region
Preparation time:		5 minutes
Cooking time:		50 minutes
Serves:		4

120 g	cracked hominy corn	1 cup/4 oz
100 g	white cabbage, finely chopped	1 cup/3½ oz
⅛ tsp	black pepper	⅛ tsp
1½ tsp	salt	1½ tsp
375 ml	milk	generous 1½ cups/13 fl oz

For the sauce:

2	dried chillies (chiles), finely chopped	2
2	garlic cloves	2
30 g	walnuts	¼ cup/1 oz
6	fresh coriander (cilantro) sprigs, finely chopped	6
40 g	butter	3 tbsp/1½ oz

🌿 V

This soup is a cure-all in winter. People revert to it at times of stress, in hope of better times.

♦

In a large saucepan over low heat, cook the cracked hominy corn, cabbage, black pepper and salt in 2 litres (8½ cups/70 fl oz) water, covered, for 40 minutes.

In a separate small saucepan bring the milk to boiling point, then add to the soup pan and cook for 5 more minutes, mixing continuously.

To make the sauce:
With a pestle and mortar, pound the dried chilli (chile), garlic, walnuts and fresh coriander (cilantro) into a paste for 3 minutes.

Heat the butter in a small saucepan over medium heat. Add the pounded mixture to the hot butter and cook for 10 seconds.

Pour the sauce into the soup and serve.

SOUPS

CHICKPEA SOUP
NOHUT ÇORBASI

Region:	İstanbul, all regions
Preparation time:	5 minutes, plus overnight soaking
Cooking time:	1½ hours for chickpeas, 20 minutes for soup
Serves:	4

200 g	chickpeas (garbanzo beans), soaked overnight	1 cup/7 oz
1.5 litres	chicken stock (see p.489), boiling	6¼ cups/50 fl oz
¼ tsp	ground cumin	¼ tsp
½ tsp	ground turmeric	½ tsp
1 tbsp	ground sumac	1 tbsp

For the sauce:

50 g	butter	scant ¼ cup/2 oz
6	garlic cloves, crushed	6
½ tsp	dried chilli (red pepper) flakes	½ tsp

Locals hope for for rain during periods of drought. A portion of this chickpea soup is symbolically poured over dry fields in the hope that the soil will receive rain. Another version of this soup uses whole, unmashed chickpeas (garbanzo beans).

♦

Drain the chickpeas (garbanzo beans) and cook in a saucepan of simmering water until soft – about 1½ hours. Drain and set aside until cool enough to handle, then peel the chickpeas.

Put the chickpeas into a saucepan, add 500 ml (generous 2 cups/17 fl oz) of the boiling chicken stock, and mash. Add the remaining stock, cumin and turmeric with 1 teaspoon salt. Cook for 5 minutes over medium heat, whisking to combine. Reduce the heat to low and whisk for a further 5 minutes.

To make the sauce:
Heat the butter in a small saucepan over medium heat, add the garlic and cook for 1 minute, then add the dried chilli (red pepper) flakes and cook for a further 5 seconds.

Serve the soup in bowls with the sauce drizzled on top and sprinkled with sumac.

♦

EGYPTIAN SPINACH SOUP
MÜHLİYE ÇORBASI

Region:	Mersin, Mediterranean Region
Preparation time:	10 minutes
Cooking time:	45 minutes
Serves:	4

2 tbsp	olive oil	2 tbsp
1 (120 g)	medium onion, finely chopped	1 (¾ cup/4 oz)
5	garlic cloves, finely chopped	5
¾ tbsp	tomato paste (see p.492)	¾ tbsp
½ tsp	dried chilli (red pepper) flakes	½ tsp
2	sundried tomatoes	2
1	hot dried chilli (chile)	1
80 g	coarse bulgur wheat	⅜ cup/3 oz
30 g	dried *molokhia* (see p.502), crumbled (or 300 g/1⅓ cups/ 11 oz fresh *molokhia*)	⅛ cup/1 oz
¼ tsp	ground cumin	¼ tsp
2 tbsp	lemon juice	2 tbsp

A popular herb in the Middle East, *molokhia* or *mulukhiyah* (see p.502) is used in a variety of dishes. Legend goes that the slaves escaping the Pharaoh in Ancient Egypt had this herb with them, so it's also known as 'the Pharaoh herb' and is believed to give good health and a long life. Use fresh *molokhia* when in season; dry some in the spring for use in winter.

♦

Heat the oil in a large saucepan over medium heat, add the onion and garlic and cook for 3 minutes. Add the tomato paste and dried chilli (red pepper) flakes. Finely chop the sundried tomatoes and the hot dried chilli (chile), then add them to the pan and cook for 3 minutes. Add the bulgur wheat and cook, stirring continuously, for 2 minutes. If using fresh *molokhia*, wash and finely chop it. Add the *molokhia* and cook for 3 minutes, stirring continuously. Add 2 litres (8½ cups/70 fl oz) hot water, the cumin and lemon juice with ¼ teaspoon black pepper and 1 teaspoon salt, then cook for 10 minutes, stirring occasionally. Reduce the heat and cook for a further 20 minutes.

Serve in bowls.

WHEAT AND CHICKPEA SOUP
TOYGA ÇORBASI

Region:		Çankırı, Central Anatolia
Preparation time:		5 minutes, plus overnight soaking
Cooking time:		1½ hours for beans, 40 minutes for soup
Serves:		4

100 g	cracked wheat	⅞ cup/3½ oz
1 tbsp	dried cannellini (white) beans	1 tbsp
30 g	raisins	¼ cup/1 oz
100 g	strained yogurt	½ cup/3½ oz
2 tbsp	chickpeas (garbanzo beans), soaked overnight and cooked	2 tbsp
¼ tsp	black pepper	¼ tsp
1¼ tsp	salt	1¼ tsp
50 g	butter	¼ cup/2 oz
2 tsp	dried mint	2 tsp

V

Toyga Çorbası is a staple of the Central Anatolian diet. Wedding banquets in Çankırı will feature this soup, which they always make with raisins.

◆

The day before, cook the cracked wheat in 500 ml (generous 2 cups/17 fl oz) simmering water for 5 minutes, then cover the pan and leave to soak overnight. At the same time, set the beans and raisins to soak in separate bowls of water and leave overnight.

The next day, drain the soaked wheat, beans and raisins. Cook the beans in a saucepan of simmering water until soft – about 1½ hours. Drain and set aside.

In a large saucepan, mix the yogurt with 2 litres (8½ cups/ 70 fl oz) water until well combined. Add the cracked wheat, beans, raisins, cooked chickpeas, black pepper and salt. Cook over medium heat for 5 minutes, mixing vigorously to prevent the yogurt from curdling. Bring to the boil, then reduce the heat and simmer for 20 minutes.

Heat the butter in a small saucepan over medium heat. Add the dried mint, cook for 10 seconds, then pour into the soup pan. Cook for 5 more minutes and serve.

◆

FESTIVE SOUP (SWEET SOUP)
BAYRAM ÇORBASI (TATLI ÇORBA)

Region:		Sivas, Central Anatolia
Preparation time:		10 minutes, plus overnight soaking
Cooking time:		1½ hours for beans, 35 minutes for soup
Serves:		4

80 g	cracked wheat	⅔ cup/3 oz
2 tbsp	dried cannellini (white) beans	2 tbsp
2 tbsp	chickpeas (garbanzo beans), soaked overnight and cooked	2 tbsp
1	cinnamon stick	1
½ tsp	salt	½ tsp
50 g	walnut kernels, coarsely chopped	½ cup/2 oz
100 g	dried apricots, finely diced	½ cup/3½ oz
60 g	sultanas (golden raisins)	scant ½ cup/ 2¼ oz
4	dried figs, finely diced	4

💧 ◆ V

This soup is enjoyed hot or cold. Central Anatolians claim the naming rights to this dish, which is traditionally eaten cold just before the lamb confit at *Eid-al-Adha* (see p.501).

◆

The day before, cook the cracked wheat in 500 ml (generous 2 cups/17 fl oz) simmering water for 5 minutes, then cover the pan and leave to soak overnight. At the same time, set the dried beans to soak in a bowl of water and leave overnight.

The next day, drain the soaked beans. Cook the beans in a saucepan of simmering water until soft – about 1½ hours. Drain and set aside.

Warm a large saucepan over medium heat, add 1.5 litres (6¼ cups/50 fl oz) hot water, the cooked chickpeas and beans, cracked wheat, cinnamon and salt. When simmering, reduce the heat and cook, covered, for 20 minutes. Add the walnut kernels, dried apricots, sultanas (golden raisins) and dried figs and cook for a further 15 minutes. Remove the cinnamon before serving in bowls.

LAMB AND RICE SOUP
BEYRAN ÇORBASI

Region:	Gaziantep, Southeastern Anatolia	
Preparation time:	10 minutes	
Cooking time:	2 hours 10 minutes	
Serves:	4	

1 (600 g)	lamb shank on the bone, washed	1 (1 lb 5 oz)
80 g	medium-grain rice	½ cup/3 oz
40 g	suet	¼ cup/1½ oz
6	garlic cloves, crushed	6
1 tsp	dried chilli (red pepper) flakes	1 tsp
¼ tsp	black pepper	¼ tsp
1 tsp	salt	1 tsp
2 tbsp	lemon juice, to serve	2 tbsp

p.43

This is a local breakfast staple and can easily be made with leftovers, in which case simply heat butter, garlic, dried chilli (red pepper) flakes, rice and meat (in that order) for 5–10 seconds on very high heat, add some boiling meat stock, then cook for another minute and serve.

♦

Put the lamb shank into a saucepan with 4 litres (16 cups/130 fl oz) water and bring to the boil over medium heat, about 5 minutes. Skim off the foam with a slotted spoon. Reduce the heat and cook, covered, for 2 hours.

Meanwhile, cook the rice in a pan with 500 ml (generous 2 cups/17 fl oz) water for 30 minutes. Drain and set aside.

Remove the lamb and reserve the meat stock for later. Pull the lamb off the bone into large chunks.

Heat the suet in a saucepan over medium heat. Add the garlic and cook for 5 seconds, then add the dried chilli (red pepper) flakes and cook for 5 seconds. Add the reserved meat stock and lamb, cooked rice, black pepper and salt and cook, uncovered, for 5 minutes. Reduce the heat, cook for a further 5 minutes. Remove from the heat. Serve in bowls with a squeeze of lemon juice.

♦

LAMB'S BRAIN SOUP
TERBİYELİ BEYİN ÇORBASI

Region:	Manisa, Aegean Region	
Preparation time:	15 minutes, plus 1 hour soaking,	
Cooking time:	50 minutes	
Serves:	4	

4 (300 g)	lamb's brains	4 (11 oz)
4	bay leaves	4
6	black peppercorns	6
1	lemon, halved and seeded	1
2	garlic cloves	2
90 g	fresh peas, shelled	½ cup/3¼ oz
100 g	yogurt	½ cup/3½ oz
30 g	plain (all-purpose) flour	¼ cup/1 oz
1	egg yolk	1
2 tbsp	lemon juice	2 tbsp

For the sauce:		
10	flat-leaf parsley sprigs	10
4	dill sprigs	4
1	dried chilli (chile)	1
2	garlic cloves	2
2 tbsp	grape vinegar	2 tbsp
2 tbsp	olive oil	2 tbsp

Each and every Turkish kid grows up believing they will get smarter if they drink copious amounts of this soup, which is also seen as a cure for poor memory and anxiety.

♦

Soak the lamb's brains in 2 litres (8½ cups/70 fl oz) cold water for 1 hour, then drain and clean. In a saucepan, bring 2 litres (8½ cups/70 fl oz) water, the bay leaves, black peppercorns, lemon and ½ teaspoon salt to the boil over medium heat. Add the brains and boil for 20 minutes, skimming the surface with a slotted spoon. Remove the brains with a slotted spoon and set aside.

In a pestle and mortar, pound the garlic with ½ teaspoon salt. Add one brain and pound to a paste with the garlic. Stir the paste into the soup and boil for 5 minutes. Remove the bay leaf and lemon with a slotted spoon, then add the peas and cook for a further 5 minutes over medium heat.

Whisk the yogurt, flour, egg yolk and lemon juice together. Add a ladle of soup stock and combine thoroughly. Pour back into the soup slowly, stirring well, in one direction. Boil for 5 minutes, then reduce the heat. Dice the remaining brains and add to the soup. Cook for a further 5 minutes.

To make the sauce:
Finely slice the parsley and dill, then pound to a paste with the dried chilli and garlic. Stir in the vinegar and oil. Pour the sauce into the soup and serve immediately.

SOUPS

TRIPE SOUP
İŞKEMBE ÇORBASI

Region:		Ankara, all regions
Preparation time:		30 minutes
Cooking time:		1 hour 50 minutes
Serves:		4

700 g	tripe, washed	1 lb 8½ oz
500 g	bones, with marrow	1 lb 2 oz
1 (120 g)	medium onion, quartered	1 (¾ cup/4 oz)
5	black peppercorns	5
1	clove	1
2	garlic cloves	2
1 (70 g)	carrot, halved	1 (½ cup/½ oz)
2	bay leaves	2
1	slice of stale bread	1
½	lemon, halved and seeded	½

For the sauce:

3 tbsp	butter	3 tbsp
2 tbsp	grape vinegar	2 tbsp
6	garlic cloves, crushed	6
1 tsp	hot paprika	1 tsp

 p.45

Many a long night at the *meyhane* (see p.502) draws to a close with tripe soup. This soup is usually made with water buffalo tripe and bones, but sheep or lamb can be used instead.

♦

Put the tripe and bones into a saucepan with 1.5 litres (6¼ cups/50 fl oz) water, bring to the boil over medium heat and cook for 5 minutes. Drain, then wash the tripe and the bones in cold water. Return them to the pan, add 4 litres (16 cups/130 fl oz) water, the onion, black peppercorns, clove, garlic, carrot, bay leaves, stale bread and lemon halves and boil for 5 minutes. Skim the surface with a slotted spoon. Reduce the heat, then cook, covered, for 1½ hours.

Using a slotted spoon, remove the cooked tripe from the pot and finely dice. Remove the bone, scrape out the marrow and set aside. Strain the stock, return it to the pan and bring back to the boil over low heat.

Add the diced tripe back into the stock, cook for 5 minutes, then remove from the heat.

To make the sauce:
Warm a small saucepan over medium heat, melt the butter and reserved marrow together for 2 minutes.

Serve with the vinegar, crushed garlic and paprika. Season with 1 teaspoon black pepper. Everyone can add the sauce to their own taste.

♦

TROTTER SOUP
PAÇA ÇORBASI

Region:		Yalova, all regions
Preparation time:		10 minutes
Cooking time:		1 hour 45 minutes
Serves:		4

8 (1kg)	goat's or lamb's trotters, washed	8 (2 lb 3 oz)
1 tsp	salt	1 tsp
5	black peppercorns	5
2 tbsp	lemon juice	2 tbsp
1 (120 g)	medium onion, quartered	1 (¾ cup/4 oz)
2	slices of stale bread	2
2 tbsp	butter	2 tbsp
2 tbsp	grape vinegar	2 tbsp
8	garlic cloves, crushed	8
1	lemon, quartered	1

This soup is believed to heal broken bones. If you aren't comfortable with eating trotters on the bone, pick the meat off the bone before serving.

♦

Put the trotters into a saucepan with 2 litres (8½ cups/ 70 fl oz) water, bring to the boil over medium heat. Boil for 5 minutes, then drain. Return the trotters to the pan, add 4 litres (16 cups/130 fl oz) water with the salt, black peppercorns, lemon juice and onion. Boil, uncovered, for 5 minutes, skimming the surface with a slotted spoon. Reduce the heat, add the bread and cook, covered, for 1½ hours.

Drain, reserving the stock. Discard the bones, onion and bread. Bring the stock back to the boil, then add the trotters back to the soup. Heat the butter in a small saucepan over medium heat, then pour into the soup.

Ladle the soup into bowls, add a little vinegar and garlic to each bowl and serve with a wedge of lemon.

SCORPION FISH SOUP
ÇARPANA (İSKORPİT) ÇORBASI

Region:	Giresun, Black Sea Region	
Preparation time:	20 minutes	
Cooking time:	45 minutes	
Serves:	4	

1 (400 g)	scorpion fish (rascasse) or other firm, white-fleshed fish such as gurnard	1 (14 oz)
150 g	potato, peeled	5 oz
1 (120 g)	medium onion, quartered	1 (¾ cup/4 oz)
1 (70 g)	carrot, peeled	1 (½ cup/2½ oz)
4	bay leaves	4
6	black peppercorns	6
4	fennel seeds	4
4	garlic cloves, finely sliced	4
10	flat-leaf parsley sprigs	10
1	lemon, halved and seeded	1
2 tbsp	olive oil	2 tbsp
1	hot dried chilli (chile), crushed	1

p.47

Some prefer this soup smooth, while others want to feel the texture of each ingredient. The Turkish '*çarpana*' conveys how the sting of this fish feels: like an electric current!
♦
Fillet the fish, dice the flesh into 5-mm (¼-inch) pieces and set aside.

Put the head, bones and skin of the fish into a saucepan, cover with 1.5 litres (6¼ cups/50 fl oz) water and add the potato, onion, carrot, bay leaves, black peppercorns, fennel seeds, parsley, 1 of the lemon halves and half of the garlic with ½ teaspoon salt. Bring to the boil over medium heat for 5 minutes, skimming the surface with a slotted spoon. Reduce heat to low and simmer, covered, for 20 minutes. Strain, reserving the stock. Transfer the carcass to one bowl and the potato and carrot to another bowl. Pick the flesh from the carcass and set aside. Mash the vegetables.

Heat the oil in a saucepan over medium heat, add the remaining garlic and cook for 10 seconds. Add the mashed vegetables and cook for 1 minute. Add the reserved stock and whisk until incorporated. Reduce the heat, add the diced fish, dried chilli (chile) and ½ teaspoon salt. Cook for 10 minutes, stirring continuously. Add the picked flesh, then remove from the heat and let rest for 5 minutes.

Serve in bowls, garnished with a sprig of parsley and a final squeeze of lemon on top.

♦

CATFISH SOUP
YAYIN BALIĞI ÇORBASI

Region:	Erzincan, Eastern Anatolia	
Preparation time:	15 minutes	
Cooking time:	40 minutes, plus 5 minutes resting	
Serves:	4	

500 g	greengages or sour plums	3 cups/1 lb 2 oz
2 tbsp	walnut oil	2 tbsp
4	spring onions (scallions)	4
6	garlic cloves, crushed	6
400 g	catfish fillet, cleaned and diced	14 oz

For the sauce:

300 g	walnuts, crushed	2½ cups/11 oz
10	flat-leaf parsley sprigs	10
10	fresh basil sprigs	10

This freshwater fish is abundant in the River Euphrates as well as lakes and creeks in the area. Catfish is also enjoyed fried and in kebabs. It is preserved in a confit and in salt.
♦
In a saucepan, bring 1 litre (4¼ cups/34 fl oz) water and the plums to the boil over medium heat. Cook, covered, for 20 minutes. Let cool, then knead and remove the stones. Strain the plum juice through a sieve (strainer) and set aside.

Heat the oil in a saucepan over medium heat, add the finely chopped spring onions (scallions) and crushed garlic. Cook for 3 minutes. Add 1 litre (4¼ cups/34 fl oz) water. Season with 1 teaspoon salt and ¼ teaspoon black pepper, bring to the boil, then add the plum juice and cook, covered, for 2 minutes. Add the catfish and cook for 8 minutes, then remove from the heat.

To make the sauce:
In a pestle and mortar, pound the walnuts with the finely chopped parsley and basil to a paste.

Add the sauce into the soup and mix gently. Let rest for 5 minutes and serve.

SOUPS

◆

SALADS
&
APPETIZERS

◆

COLD DISHES IN TURKISH CULTURE

The recipes in this chapter are appetizers and side dishes and – in the case of the salads and dips – are all intended to be refreshing. Classifying them as 'meze' might have been an option, but falls short of the big picture. In Turkish society, meze dishes belong at the *meyhane* (wine and *raki* bars serving small traditional dishes), where the term is used as a generic name for cold dishes made with olive oil.

Lettuce-, cucumber- and tomato-based salads, *piyaz* (onion salads), bulgur- and legume-based salads, yogurt dishes and tzatziki, pastes and pickles are all popular side dishes at the Turkish table. And legume-based dishes such as *Humus* (Hummus, see p.72), *Fava* (Broad Bean Paste, see p.76) and *Topik* (see p.85) make ideal meals in their own right. There are also cooling one-dish meals for warmer days, which are popular on the menus of Turkish bath houses, such as *Kaşik Salatasi* (Spoon Salad, see p.59), *Bat* (Lentil and Walnut Salad, see p.88), *Batırık* (Bulgur and Pepper Dip, see p.87) and *Kisir* (Tabbouleh, see p.88). All of these cold dishes are always eaten with bread and accompanied by olive oil, olives and cheese.

The recipes only make sense when they are prepared in season. For instance, no-one in Turkey would eat pickles in the summer months. I am in favour of a bit of longing for dishes, for exercising some patience when ingredients are not in season. When it comes to food, absence really does make the heart grow fonder. Wait for the ingredients to reach their prime when the season comes.

PICKLES

Pickles are raw or cooked vegetables, fruit or mushrooms, combined with water, salt and vinegar, then fermented with stale bread, chickpeas (garbanzo beans) or wheat. The brine is savoured as much as the infinite varieties of pickles themselves. Pickles are not only a great side to pilafs and other dishes, but are also warm dishes in their own right in the winter months. An amazing example is the accompaniment of grape molasses and tahini halva with bread.

Pickles also have their own quirky rituals. Would you like to guarantee perfect pickles? All you need to do is cite the names of seven carefree souls during preparation. It is believed that the carefree make the best pickles!

SALADS AND LETTUCE

The term 'salads' refers to cold dishes made with raw vegetables, lettuce and greens, dressed with olive oil and lemon, vinegar, sumac or pomegranate molasses. Salads are our most popular side dish – we always serve a salad with pilafs, kebabs, meatballs and fish. As well as being sides for other meals of the day, many are also breakfast staples, such as *Zahter Salatasi* (Wild Thyme Salad, see p.56) and *Sürk Salatasi* (Sürk Cheese Salad, see p.70).

There are often many regional names for the same dish, reflecting differences in local ingredients. Tomato salad, for instance, ranges from 'tomato salad' to 'sour tomato extract', and in cities is called 'shepherd's salad'.

Often, greens are served unadorned, sometimes with only a squeeze of lemon. Lettuce is a good example of this. Lettuce can be eaten on-the-go as a snack with no accompaniment, or at home it might be simply given a sprinkle of sugar, a drizzle of molasses or a squeeze of lemon juice.

In my home town of Nizip, Gaziantep, from early April to early May, growers sell lettuces in big sacks carried by mules. People would shop in bulk for the home and eat lettuce as a snack all through the day. When lettuce was bought in bulk, the seller would not cut off the root. However, if it was to be eaten there and then, the customer would ask for the root to be trimmed. Once the root was cut off, that was it – that lettuce was yours, no returns accepted. Even if it was bitter, all you could do was buy another one. The outer leaves of the lettuce would be stripped off and given to the donkeys, sheep and goats, then the lettuce hearts washed in a common fountain and enjoyed on the spot.

Women long believed that a stroll in a lettuce orchard would purify their souls and give them eternal youth. And not so long ago there were even impromptu street festivals to celebrate the lettuce. Eating lettuce was the purpose of the day, and the unfortunate souls who ended up with bitter lettuce would be mercilessly teased. The furious victim would have to go and buy another lettuce hoping it would turn out sweet that time. If the second one was bitter as well, it could end in a duel – with the lettuce as the weapon!

All of these rituals affirm the vital role of raw vegetables and greens in Turkish culture.

TZATZIKI AND YOGURT DISHES

We mix yogurt with cucumber, purslane, thistle or lettuce root and call it *Cacik* (Tzatziki, see p.78). It has both runny and firm versions. A *raki* table calls for firm yogurt, whereas a side dish to accompany pilafs or other dishes needs to be runny. Cucumber, mint, yogurt and garlic are the ingredients of a classic tzatziki regardless of its consistency.

Confusingly, tzatziki is also another name for dishes made with fried green vegetables with chilli (chile) and poached spinach mixed with yogurt. These dishes are sometimes called *borani*, *yoğurtlusu* or *yoğurtlama* – they are cooling menu staples and served as breakfast dishes in some regions. No *raki* table would be complete without them.

PIYAZ

Piyaz, the word for 'onion' in Farsi and Kurdish, is the also name for a dried bean and onion salad in Turkey. This is a popular dish made with cooked dried beans, sliced onions, chopped parsley and boiled egg, dressed with vinegar and olive oil. There are of course regional differences in ingredients, although the addition of onions is a constant. The spectrum of *piyaz* dishes features black-eyed beans, green olives, boiled eggs, mung beans, chickpeas (garbanzo beans), lentils, potatoes, greens, spices, sour extracts and olive oil; the ingredients can be boiled or raw – they are all referred to as *piyaz*.

Over time, the humble *piyaz* has diverged from its original meaning of simply 'onion' and become a technique. It is not unusual to hear people saying that the onion should be sliced the right way for a *piyaz*, or a customer might order a *piyaz* 'without onion' at a restaurant.

Piyaz usually goes hand-in-hand with kebabs and meatballs, to cool the palate. It is also popular on its own. Some *piyaz* are seasonal: for instance, for *Maş Piyazı* (Mung Bean and Onion Salad, see p.68) fresh (green) garlic is an absolute must, which means that the dish needs to be made just before the fresh garlic shoots from its bulbs in the spring. This delicious dish is made exclusively in the spring in Turkey. *Hek-ê Piyazi* (Egg Salad, see p.64) is also a spring dish and made especially for *Nowruz* (New Year's) celebrations.

MASHES, HUMMUS AND OTHER DIPS

There is an abundance of cold dishes made from mashed, raw or cooked vegetables and legumes. The names and preparation techniques for dishes such as *Tarama* (Taramasalata, see p.71), *Tarator* (Almond and Garlic Sauce, see p.79), *Fava* (Broad Bean Paste, see p.76), *Humus* (Hummus, see p.72) and many of the dips, differ greatly among regions. Some dips are very fine; some are textured.

These dishes are not only served as sides or appetizers, but hold their own as independent dishes. *Fava*, for example, is a breakfast staple in some regions, whereas *Humus* is only eaten for lunch in others. These dishes are still made and consumed in traditional ways in rural areas, whereas they appear as sides at a *raki* table in urban areas. For instance, the Armenian community in İstanbul makes a chickpea (garbanzo bean) dish called *Topik* (see p.85) for Lent, and eventually renamed 'The Armenian Meze' by *meyhanes*.

COLD DISHES WITH BULGUR

Patties are the first dishes that come to mind for bulgur wheat – there are numerous versions, such as *Kürt Köftesi* (Kurdish Meatballs, see p.84) *and Fellah Köftesi* (Farmer's Meatballs, see p.84). If we are not making patties, then we are most likely adding raw greens, olive oil and a sour element to create dishes, such as *Kisir* (Tabbouleh, see p.88).

Çiğ Köfte (Spicy Lamb Tartare, see p.60) has a special place among the bulgur dishes in our culture, and has its own rituals. The ingredients are picked and chopped, then kneaded in a large tub placed in the middle of the floor where people dine. It is then squeezed into patties and eaten immediately. People with limited means who cannot afford meat often substitute potatoes for the meat and this version, also, needs to be eaten right after making, before the bulgur starts expanding. The best drink to accompany *Çiğ Köfte* is *Ayran* (Salted Yogurt Drink, see p.452). It should not be served with *raki*, since the tradition at a *meyhane* table is to eat over a long period, the flavour chemistry of the dish would be lost.

◆

SHEPHERD'S SALAD
ÇOBAN SALATASI

Region:		Bolu, all regions
Preparation time:		10 minutes
Serves:		4

400 g	tomatoes, diced into 5 mm (¼ inch) cubes	2 cups/14 oz
150 g	cucumber, diced into 5 mm (¼ inch) cubes	1 cup/5¼ oz
2	banana peppers (mild sweet peppers), sliced into crescents	2
1 (120 g)	medium onion, sliced	1 (¾ cup/4 oz)
¼ bunch	flat-leaf parsley, finely chopped	¼ bunch
¼ bunch	basil, finely chopped	¼ bunch

For the dressing:		
2 tbsp	olive oil	2 tbsp
2 tbsp	lemon juice	2 tbsp
1 tbsp	grape vinegar	1 tbsp
¼ tsp	salt	¼ tsp

♦ ❧ **V** ♦ Ⅹ   p.55 ◩

There is no mention of this popular salad anywhere until the 1950s. Shepherds probably took a few tomatoes and an onion in their sacks to eat for lunch. They smashed the onion, halved the tomatoes and ate them together in a rudimentary salad. City restaurants eventually refined the shepherd's salad, chopping the ingredients more finely: Some versions omit the olive oil; some add cottage cheese.
◆
Put all the salad ingredients into a large, deep bowl.

To make the dressing:
Mix the dressing ingredients in a separate bowl, then drizzle the dressing over the salad, mix gently and serve.

◆

LETTUCE SALAD
MARUL SALATASI

Region:		Malatya, Eastern Anatolia
Preparation time:		10 minutes
Serves:		4

500 g	lettuce hearts, washed, dried, and thinly sliced	7 cups/ 1 lb 2 oz
4	fresh purple basil sprigs, finely sliced	4
80 g	tulum cheese (a pungent, soft, crumbly goat's milk cheese)	⅞ cup/3 oz
50 g	walnuts, toasted and crushed	½ cup/2 oz
¼ tsp	salt	¼ tsp
80 g	sundried sour apricots, halved, then finely sliced	3 oz
2 tbsp	olive oil	2 tbsp

❧ **V** Ⅹ

During the month of April, women in Southeastern Anatolia, and especially in the towns of Adıyaman and Malatya, go to the local Turkish baths in large groups. This cleansing ritual continues in the lettuce fields, which are believed to spread calm and serenity. They pick the lettuce, eat some in the fields and take the rest home. Lettuce is eaten in salads, such as this one, or simply drizzled with grape molasses, sugar or honey. Lettuce is good to eat for seven to ten days after it is picked: after this time it acquires a bitter taste. Kids stealing lettuce from the fields is the worst nightmare of lettuce growers.
◆
Put the lettuce and purple basil into a large, deep bowl. Crumble the cheese with your hands and sprinkle it over the greens. Add the walnuts, salt, and dried apricots and drizzle with the olive oil. Give it a quick, gentle stir and serve.

WILD THYME (ZA'ATAR) SALAD
ZAHTER SALATASI

Region:	Hatay, Mediterranean Region	
Preparation time:	20 minutes	
Serves:	4	

150 g	fresh za'atar sprouts, washed and finely sliced	5¼ oz
¾ tsp	salt	¾ tsp
1 tsp	chilli (red pepper) flakes	1 tsp
1 tsp	tomato paste (see p.492)	1 tsp
1 bunch	spring onions (scallions), finely sliced	1 bunch
1 bunch	flat-leaf parsley, washed and finely chopped	1 bunch
1	pomegranate, seeds removed	1
80 g	walnuts, crushed	¾ cup/3 oz

For the dressing:

2 tbsp	pomegranate molasses	2 tbsp
60 ml	olive oil	¼ cup/2 fl oz

◖ ❦ V ◖ ✕   p.57

The wild varieties of thyme that grow in Turkey have a superior flavour to regular thyme. Za'atar grows abundantly in Southeastern Anatolia during April and May. The blossoms are picked and dried. This salad is made around Antakya and its environs. Za'atar is believed to cure infertility and diabetes and improve appetite. If you cannot source fresh za'atar, use the largest fresh thyme leaves you can find. Boil the thyme leaves for 1 minute, then run them under cold water. Rub the thyme leaves with a pinch of salt before use.

◆

In a large, deep bowl, combine the za'atar sprouts and ¼ teaspoon salt with your hands. Transfer to a fine sieve (strainer) and wash the za'atar, then dry with paper towels. Massage the leaves with your hands, then wash and dry the za'atar again.

In a large, deep bowl, combine the za'atar with the remaining ½ teaspoon salt, chilli (red pepper) flakes and tomato purée (paste) and mix by hand for 2 minutes. Add the spring onions (scallions), parsley, pomegranate seeds and walnuts and mix gently.

To make the dressing:
In a separate bowl, mix the dressing ingredients. Dress the salad, toss and serve.

◆

AUBERGINE WITH YOGURT
PATLICAN YOĞURTLAMASI

Region:	Burdur, all regions	
Preparation time:	15 minutes	
Cooking time:	1 hour	
Serves:	4	

1 (750 g)	aubergine (eggplant)	1 (1 lb 10 oz)
½ tsp	salt	½ tsp
2 tbsp	olive oil	2 tbsp
200 g	strained yogurt (goat's milk)	1 cup/7 oz
½ tsp	nigella seeds	½ tsp
1 tbsp	molasses	1 tbsp

❦ V

This dish is a life-saver on long, hot summer days. Very popular in the Mediterranean, Aegean and Southeastern Anatolia all through the summer months, this dish creates more aubergine (eggplant) lovers. It can be made with grilled or fried aubergine. Some send the aubergine to the local bakery. A variation on this dish can be made by replacing the nigella seeds and molasses with garlic.

◆

Preheat the oven to 200°C/400 F/Gas Mark 6.

Prick the aubergine (eggplant) a few times, then bake in the hot oven for 1 hour. Let cool, then peel.

Put the aubergine into a large bowl with the salt and olive oil and mash together. Add the yogurt, nigella seeds and molasses and mix for 3 minutes until well combined, then serve in individual bowls.

RED BEETROOT (BEET) SALAD
ÇÜKÜNDÜR (KIRMIZI PANCAR) SALATASI

Region:		Kastamonu, Black Sea Region
Preparation time:		20 minutes
Cooking time:		1 hour
Serves:		4

500 g	red beetroot (beets)	1 lb 2 oz
10	garlic cloves, quartered	10
2 tbsp	apple cider vinegar	2 tbsp
2 tbsp	lemon juice	2 tbsp
2 tbsp	filtered honey	2 tbsp
½ bunch	flat-leaf parsley	½ bunch
60 g	almonds, toasted	½ cup/2 oz
50 g	green olives, pitted	⅓ cup/1¾ oz
80 g	unsalted nigella-seed cheese	⅞ cup/3 oz

❧ V

This salad is a popular side to pilafs and *Keşkek* (Pounded Lamb and Wheat, see p.317). Some summer versions use raw beetroot, half cooked or grilled. If you cannot find nigella-seed cheese, use 80 g/3 oz unsalted cheese, such as cottage cheese or paneer, mixed with ½ teaspoon nigella seeds (black cumin seeds).

♦

Cook the beetroot (beets) in 2 litres (8½ cups/70 fl oz) water for 1 hour. Cool, peel and cut into 5-mm (¼-inch) cubes.

Put the garlic in a saucepan with 200 ml (scant 1 cup/7 fl oz) water. Boil for 5 minutes, then drain and set aside.

Put the beetroot and garlic into a large, deep bowl with ¾ teaspoon salt. In a separate bowl, whisk the vinegar, lemon juice and honey. Drizzle over the beetroot/garlic mixture. Stir well for 3 minutes to combine. Finely chop the parsley and coarsely chop the almonds. Add with the green olives and 2 tablespoons olive oil, and mix gently.

Cut the nigella-seed cheese into 5-mm (¼-inch) cubes, then sprinkle over the salad and serve.

♦

BRAIN SALAD
BEYİN SALATASI

Region:		Kırklareli, all regions
Preparation time:		10 minutes, plus 30 minutes soaking
Cooking time:		30 minutes, plus 15 minutes cooling
Serves:		4

¾ tsp	salt	¾ tsp
4 (325 g)	lamb's brains, washed	4 (11½ oz)
1 tbsp	apple cider vinegar	1 tbsp
4	bay leaves	4
5	black peppercorns	5
1	lemon, zest grated	1
For the dressing:		
2 tbsp	olive oil	2 tbsp
1 tbsp	apple cider vinegar	1 tbsp
2 tbsp	lemon juice	2 tbsp
2	garlic cloves, pounded	2
⅛ tsp	black pepper	⅛ tsp
3 bunches	flat-leaf parsley	3 bunches
1 bunch	spring onions (scallions)	1 bunch

💧 ❧

This is a very popular *meyhane* dish. It is believed to have healing properties for people with brain issues.

♦

In a bowl, dissolve ½ teaspoon salt in 1 litre (4¼ cups/34 fl oz) iced water. Soak the lamb's brains in the salt water for 30 minutes. Clean any blood off the nerve endings without damaging the brains, then remove from the water.

Pour 1 litre (4¼ cups/34 fl oz) water into a large saucepan and add the apple cider vinegar, bay leaves, peppercorns, the remaining ¼ teaspoon salt and the lemon zest. Lower the brains gently into the pan, one by one, making sure they don't sit on top of one another. Cook uncovered for 30 minutes over medium heat. Skim off the froth that forms on the surface of the water with a slotted spoon.

Once the brains are cooked, remove from the heat and let rest in the pan for 5 minutes. Remove the brains with a slotted spoon to a plate and let cool for 10 minutes.

To make the dressing:
Mix all the dressing ingredients in a separate bowl.

Combine the picked parsley leaves and finely sliced spring onions (scallions). Divide half of the mixture among four plates. Slice the brains into 1-cm (½-inch) wide strips and place on top. Sprinkle over the remainder of the parsley and onion mixture. Drizzle over the dressing and serve.

SPOON SALAD
KAŞIK SALATASI

Region:	Diyarbakır, Southeastern Anatolia
Preparation time:	15 minutes
Serves:	4

100 g	cucumber	⅔ cup/3½ oz
1 (120 g)	medium onion	1 (¾ cup/4 oz)
1	hot fresh green chilli	1
300 g	tomatoes	1½ cups/11 oz
2½ tsp	hot chilli (red pepper) flakes	2½ tsp
1½ tsp	tomato paste (see p.492)	1½ tsp
2 tbsp	ground sumac	2 tbsp
1½ tbsp	dried mint	1½ tbsp
½ bunch	purslane (or lamb's ear)	½ bunch
6	flat-leaf parsley sprigs	6
50 g	walnuts, toasted	½ cup/2 oz
2 tbsp	pomegranate molasses	2 tbsp
1	pomegranate, seeds removed	1

This is a cooling summer salad and is a popular side dish to bulgur pilafs, steak tartar and to serve with drinks. In Southeastern Anatolia it is known locally as *Bostana Salatası* (Orchard Salad) in Urfa and as *Pürpürüm Ekşisi* (Sour Purslane) in Gaziantep, but as *Kaşık Salatası* (Spoon Salad) in Diyarbakır. There is no olive oil in the dressing and this watery salad is eaten by the spoonful, hence the name.

♦

Finely slice the cucumber, onion, green chilli and tomatoes. Combine in a large, deep bowl with the chilli (red pepper) flakes, tomato paste, ground sumac, dried mint and ½ teaspoon salt, then mix for 2 minutes.

Finely chop the purslane and parsley. Coarsely chop the walnuts. Add along with the pomegranate molasses, pomegranate seeds and 500 ml (generous 2 cups/ 17 fl oz) ice-cold water and mix gently for 2 minutes until well combined.

Serve the salad in individual bowls, with spoons to eat it.

♦

PRAWN SALAD
TEKE SALATASI

Region:	Balıkesir, Marmara Region
Preparation time:	40 minutes
Cooking time:	15 minutes
Serves:	4

600 g	shell-on prawns (shrimp)	2 cups/1 lb 5 oz
1	lemon, zest grated	1
1 (100 g)	apple, quartered	1 (⅞ cup/3½ oz)
1 tbsp	pine nuts, toasted	1 tbsp
2 tbsp	currants	2 tbsp
1 (120 g)	medium red onion	1 (¾ cup/4 oz)
½ bunch	flat-leaf parsley	½ bunch

For the dressing:		
2 tbsp	lemon juice	2 tbsp
4 tbsp	orange juice	4 tbsp
⅛ tsp	ground ginger	⅛ tsp
pinch	saffron threads	pinch
½ tsp	ground cinnamon	½ tsp
2 tbsp	olive oil	2 tbsp
2 tbsp	grape vinegar	2 tbsp

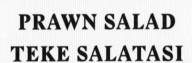

Teke is the name given to the local small prawns (shrimps). This salad is popular with home cooks and is served widely at *meyhanes* in İstanbul. There is also a version of this salad that omits the spices.

♦

Rinse and dry the prawns (shrimp). Pour 1.5 litres (6¼ cups/50 fl oz) water into a large saucepan, add the lemon zest and apple quarters and cook for 10 minutes. Add the prawns, cook for a further 5 minutes, then remove from the heat. Drain the prawns and let cool at room temperature for 20 minutes.

Peel the prawns, discarding the shells, and transfer to a large bowl. Add the pine nuts and currants and toss through. Slice the apple quarters into the salad.

To make the dressing:
In a separate bowl, combine all the dressing ingredients. Season with ½ teaspoon salt.

Slice the red onion into crescents. Finely chop the parsley. Pour the dressing over the prawn salad and mix. Arrange a layer of onion and parsley over each serving plate, top with the salad and serve.

SALTED MACKEREL SALAD
ÇİROZ SALATASI (KURU BALIK SALATASI)

Region:	İstanbul, Marmara Region	
Preparation time:	10 minutes (if using a stove-top smoker) or 40 minutes (if using a charcoal grill/barbecue)	
Cooking time:	15 minutes, plus 2 days soaking	
Serves:	4	

200 g	dried and salted mackerel	7 oz
60 ml	grape vinegar	¼ cup/2 fl oz

For the dressing:		
2 tbsp	olive oil	2 tbsp
1 tbsp	grape vinegar	1 tbsp

1 bunch	dill, leaves picked	1 bunch
½ bunch	flat-leaf parsley, leaves picked	½ bunch

💧 🌿 p.63

This is an appetizer to serve with drinks. Salted mackerel is available online or in Middle Eastern stores.

◆

Prepare a stove-top smoker with woodchips. Place over a high heat. When the wood is smoldering, turn the heat to low, place the fish on the rack, cover and smoke for 20 seconds. Alternatively, heat a charcoal grill/barbecue to medium. Meanwhile, soak your woodchips in water for 30 minutes. When ready, put the woodchips on the coals, place the mackerel on the grill rack and smoke for 20 seconds.

Pick the flesh from the bones and place in a muslin (cheesecloth). Massage the cloth with your hands for 3 minutes until the meat is in thin shreds. Place the shredded meat in a bowl, add 500 ml (generous 2 cups/17 fl oz) water and the grape vinegar. Cover and soak for 24 hours. The next day, drain the fish and place in a separate bowl.

To make the dressing:
Combine the olive oil and grape vinegar. Pour the dressing over the soaked fish. Cover and refrigerate for 24 hours.

Arrange the dill and parsley over four serving plates and top with the mackerel.

◆

SPICY LAMB TARTARE
ÇİĞ KÖFTE

Region:	Gaziantep, all regions	
Preparation time:	40 minutes	
Serves:	4	

100 g	dark bulgur wheat	½ cup/3½ oz
150 g	minced (ground) lamb	⅔ cup/5 oz
60 g	onion, finely sliced	⅜ cup/2 oz
6	garlic cloves, finely sliced	6
¼ tsp	allspice	¼ tsp
⅛ tsp	ground cumin	⅛ tsp
¼ tsp	ground cinnamon	¼ tsp
2 tbsp	tomato paste (see p.492)	2 tbsp
2 tsp	red bell pepper paste (see p.492)	2 tsp
1½ tbsp	dried chilli (red pepper) flakes	1½ tbsp
2	spring onions (scallions)	2
2	fresh (green) garlic	2
10	flat-leaf parsley sprigs	10
2	fresh mint sprigs	2
1 tbsp	lemon juice	1 tbsp
2 tbsp	olive oil	2 tbsp
16	lettuce leaves, to serve	16

💧

A local favourite, especially in Southeastern Anatolia, Eastern Anatolia and the Mediterranean Region, lamb tartare must be devoured as soon as it is ready. Use very fresh, lean minced (ground) lamb with any sinew trimmed. Lettuce, cress and fresh mint are popular sides to serve alongside this dish.

◆

Combine the bulgur wheat, lamb, onion, garlic, allspice, cumin and cinnamon with ¼ teaspoon black pepper and ½ teaspoon of salt in a large, deep bowl or tray and knead for 20 minutes.

Add the red bell pepper paste, tomato paste and dried chilli (red pepper) flakes and knead for a further 5 minutes.

Finely slice the spring onions (scallions) and fresh (green) garlic, then add and knead for 2 minutes. Finely slice the parsley and fresh mint, then add along with the lemon juice and olive oil and combine gently. Squeeze with your fingers and serve immediately on lettuce leaves.

WHITE BEAN SALAD
FASULYE PİYAZI

Region:		Antalya, all regions
Preparation time:		20 minutes, plus overnight soaking
Cooking time:		10 minutes
Serves:		4

200 g	small cannellini beans, soaked overnight, boiled until soft, drained	1 cup/7 oz

For the dressing:		
4	garlic cloves, crushed	4
1 tbsp	lemon juice	1 tbsp
60 ml	tahini (sesame seed paste)	¼ cup/ 2 fl oz
1 tbsp	grape vinegar	1 tbsp

1 (120 g)	medium onion,	1 (¾ cup/4 oz)
4	eggs, hard-boiled for 12 minutes	4
16	black olives, pitted	16
8	hot chillies (chiles)	8
8	flat-leaf parsley sprigs	8
2 tbsp	olive oil	2 tbsp

◦ ✿ V   p.63 ▢

This is a popular dish all over the country. Some versions omit the tahini and garlic. Tahini is more commonly used in Antalya. If the sauce is too thick, dilute with 60 ml (¼ cup/2 fl oz) water.
♦

Divide the cooked beans equally into four serving bowls.

To make the dressing:
Mix the garlic and lemon juice with ¼ teaspoon salt in a small bowl with a wooden spoon. Pour over the tahini a little at a time, making sure it is well combined after each addition. Add the vinegar and keep mixing for 1 minute.

Pour the sauce over the beans. Finely slice the onion and then scatter over the beans. Peel and quarter the hard-boiled eggs. Arrange the eggs and olives around the sides. Garnish each bowl with two chillies. Sprinkle with parsley, drizzle with olive oil and serve.

♦

MUSHROOM SALAD
EKŞİLİ MANTAR SALATASI

Region:		Kastamonu, Black Sea Region
Preparation time:		15 minutes
Cooking time:		1 hour
Serves:		4

500 g	beetroot (beets)	1 lb 2 oz
200 g	pickled mushrooms, finely diced	7 oz
2 tbsp	grape vinegar	2 tbsp
2 tbsp	lemon juice	2 tbsp
2	fresh (green) garlic, finely diced (or 3 garlic cloves, pounded)	2
¼ tsp	salt	¼ tsp
600 g	lettuce hearts	8 cups/1 lb 5 oz
1 bunch	cress, finely chopped	1 bunch
60 ml	olive oil	¼ cup/2 fl oz

◦ ✿ V ♦

October and November are mushroom season in the Black Sea region. Saffron milk cap mushrooms are enjoyed fresh in season – fried or roasted and used in pastry fillings – or pickled for later use in salads. If saffron milk cap mushrooms are not available to you, chanterelle mushrooms are a good substitute.
♦

Cook the beetroot (beets) in a pan of simmering water for 1 hour, then drain and cool. When cool enough to handle, dice into 5-mm (¼-inch) cubes.

In a large bowl, mix the beetroot, pickled mushrooms, grape vinegar, lemon juice, fresh (green) garlic and salt with your hands, until well combined. Add the lettuce hearts, cress and olive oil, toss gently and serve.

CHICKPEA SALAD
NOHUT PİYAZI

Region:	Adıyaman, Southeastern Anatolia	
Preparation time:	10 minutes, plus overnight soaking	
Cooking time:	1 hour 40 minutes	
Serves:	4	

200 g	chickpeas (garbanzo beans), soaked overnight	1 cup/7 oz
60 ml	olive oil	¼ cup/2¼ fl oz
1 (120 g)	medium onion, sliced into crescents	1 (¾ cup/4 oz)
2	garlic cloves, roughly chopped	2
1	small hot red bell pepper, sliced into crescents	1
2	sundried tomatoes, finely sliced	2
½ tsp	ground cumin	½ tsp
½ tsp	dried chilli (red pepper) flakes	½ tsp
1 tsp	ground sumac	1 tsp
2 tbsp	lemon juice	2 tbsp
½ bunch	flat-leaf parsley, finely sliced	½ bunch
6	fresh basil sprigs, finely sliced	6

This is popular street food in the region. Vendors cook the chickpeas (garbanzo beans) in a lamb stock and serve them in this fresh salad. Chickpea rolls are sold in front of bakeries and enjoyed in the early morning in homes and workplaces. This tradition is still strong in Gaziantep, Şanlıurfa and Adıyaman.

◆

Drain the soaked chickpeas (garbanzo beans), then cook in a saucepan of simmering water until soft, about 1½ hours. Drain and put the cooked chickpeas into a large bowl.

Heat the oil in a large saucepan over medium heat, add the onions and garlic and cook for 2 minutes. Add the bell pepper and sundried tomatoes and cook for a further minute. Add ½ teaspoon salt, then pour the mixture over the chickpeas and mix gently. Add the cumin, dried chilli (red pepper) flakes, sumac, lemon juice, parsley and basil, mix gently and serve.

p.65

EGG SALAD
HEK-Ê PİYAZ

Region:	Diyarbakır, Southeastern Anatolia	
Preparation time:	10 minutes	
Cooking time:	12 minutes	
Serves:	4	

8	eggs, hard-boiled for 12 minutes	8
4	fresh mint sprigs, finely sliced	4
4	dill sprigs, finely sliced	4
4	spring onions (scallions), finely sliced	4
4	cress sprigs, finely sliced	4
½ bunch	flat-leaf parsley, finely sliced	½ bunch
4	fresh coriander (cilantro) sprigs, finely sliced	4
½ tsp	ground cumin	½ tsp
2 tbsp	olive oil	2 tbsp

This is a popular spring dish in Southeastern Anatolia, especially served for the Festival of *Nowrouz* (New Year). Also known as *'nergisleme'* and 'eggs and onions', this can be served with lavash bread. If it is going to be served as a roll, the olive oil is omitted. You can use the discarded egg yolks as a filling for *kıbbeh* or to add to *kısır*. Alternatively, you could use the whole egg for this salad.

◆

Remove the yolks from the hardboiled eggs, if wished. Chop the egg whites into 5-mm (¼-inch) wide strips and put into a large bowl.

Add the fresh mint, dill, spring onions (scallions), cress, parsley, coriander (cilantro) and cumin with ½ teaspoon salt. Mix gently and serve drizzled with olive oil.

◆

SUNDRIED TOMATO SALAD WITH ONIONS
HIŞK (KURU TOMATOES) PİYAZI

Region:		Mardin, Southeastern Anatolia
Preparation time:		15 minutes, plus overnight soaking
Cooking time:		1 hour 45 minutes
Serves:		4

50 g	chickpeas (garbanzo beans), soaked overnight	¼ cup/2 oz
2 tbsp	olive oil	2 tbsp
4	garlic cloves, finely sliced	4
80 g	sundried tomatoes, soaked in water for 10 minutes, finely sliced	1½ cups/3 oz
8	spring onions (scallions), finely sliced	8
50 g	black olives, thinly sliced	½ cup/2 oz
1	dried red chilli (chile), finely sliced	1
4	fresh za'atars (or thyme) sprigs, finely sliced	4
2	fresh coriander (cilantro) sprigs, finely sliced	2
2 tbsp	pomegranate molasses	2 tbsp
60 g	walnuts, toasted, roughly chopped	½ cup/2¼ oz
5	flat-leaf parsley sprigs, finely sliced	5

⬤ ❧ V ◆

This dish is a winter staple and goes well in wraps. The dish is made with local twists in the Aegean, Mediterranean and Southeastern Anatolia regions. If your sundried tomatoes are unsalted, add an additional ½ teaspoon of salt.

◆

Drain the soaked chickpeas (garbanzo beans), then cook in a pan of simmering water until soft, about 1½ hours. Drain and set aside.

Heat the oil in a large saucepan over medium heat, add the garlic and cook for 5 seconds, then add the sundried tomatoes, spring onions (scallions) and cooked chickpeas and cook for 3 minutes. Add the black olives, dried chilli (chile) and fresh za'atar and cook for 10 minutes, mixing thoroughly. Add the fresh coriander (cilantro), cook for 1 minute, then remove from the heat. Sprinkle in the pomegranate molasses and walnuts, mix and let cool.

Once cooled, sprinkle with parsley and serve.

◆

SMASHED CUCUMBER
HIYAR DÖVMESİ

Region:		Bursa, all regions
Preparation time:		30 minutes
Serves:		4

300 g	cucumber, deseeded and crushed	2 cups/11 oz
1 (150 g)	large onion, finely sliced	1 (1 cup/5 oz)
½ tsp	salt	½ tsp
1½ tbsp	pine nuts, toasted	1½ tbsp
2	fresh basil sprigs	2
2 tbsp	olive oil	2 tbsp
60 ml	lemon juice	¼ cup/2 fl oz

⬤ ❧ V ◆ X

Smashed cucumber is enjoyed cold in the summer and is a popular side dish at a *rakı* table. Some prefer to use fresh mint instead of the basil.

◆

In a pestle and mortar, pound the cucumber, onion and salt for 10 minutes. Strain the cucumber and onions in a sieve, discarding the juice and transfer the pulp to a bowl.

Add 1½ tablespoons of the toasted pine nuts and fresh basil to the mortar and pound to a pulp for 2 minutes. Gradually add the olive oil and lemon juice into the mortar, then add the cucumber and onion mix. Pound everything together until the mixture turns white in colour.

Sprinkle with the remaining 1 tablespoon toasted pine nuts and serve.

SALADS & APPETIZERS

ONION SALAD (KEBAB SHOP VERSION)
PİYAZ SALATASI (KEBAPÇI SOĞAN SALATASI)

Region:		Adana, all regions
Preparation time:		10 minutes
Serves:		4

1 (120 g)	medium onion, finely sliced, then rubbed and washed in cold water	1 (¾ cup/4 oz)
1	red bell pepper, very finely sliced	1
1 tbsp	lemon juice	1 tbsp
2½ tbsp	ground sumac	2½ tbsp
1 bunch	flat-leaf parsley, finely sliced	1 bunch

Ⅰ ❁ V ♦ Ⅹ

This is a popular side salad served at kebab joints. Some versions omit the parsley or bell peppers. If you can't get good-quality sumac, use lemon juice to add sourness.

♦

In a large bowl, mix the onion, bell pepper, lemon juice and sumac with ¼ teaspoon salt together by hand for 1 minute, making sure all is well combined. Sprinkle the parsley over, gently mix and serve.

SPRING ONION SALAD (KEBAB SHOP VERSION)
TAZE SOĞAN SALATASI
(KEBAPÇI TAZE SOĞAN SALATASI)

Region:		Gaziantep, all regions
Preparation time:		10 minutes
Serves:		4

6	spring onions (scallions), finely sliced	6
1	red bell pepper, finely sliced	1
1 tbsp	lemon juice	1 tbsp
2½ tbsp	ground sumac	2½ tbsp
1 bunch	flat-leaf parsley, finely sliced	1 bunch
½ bunch	fresh basil, finely sliced	½ bunch

Ⅰ ❁ V ♦ Ⅹ

This humble salad is the perfect accompaniment to kebabs, especially in wraps.

♦

In a large bowl, mix the spring onions (scallions), bell pepper, lemon juice, sumac and parsley with ¼ teaspoon salt together by hand for 1 minute, making sure all is well combined. Sprinkle with the basil and serve.

MUNG BEAN AND ONION SALAD
MAŞ PİYAZI

Region:	Gaziantep, Southeastern Anatolia	
Preparation time:	20 minutes, plus overnight soaking	
Cooking time:		30 minutes
Serves:		4

120 g	mung beans, soaked overnight	⅔ cup/4 oz
½ tsp	dried chilli (red pepper) flakes	½ tsp
1 tsp	ground sumac	1 tsp
100 g	walnuts, roughly chopped	1 cup/3½ oz
2 tbsp	olive oil	2 tbsp
2 tbsp	pomegranate molasses	2 tbsp
2	spring onions (scallions)	2
2	fresh (green) garlic	2
2	fresh mint sprigs	2
10	flat-leaf parsley sprigs	10
4	fresh basil sprigs	4
2	fresh tarragon sprigs	2
100 g	pomegranate seeds	1¼ cups/3½ oz

For the dressing:

2	fresh (green) garlic	2
4	spring onions (scallions)	4
50 g	unsalted green olives, pitted, finely sliced	½ cup/2 oz
1	fresh red chilli (chile)	1
2 tbsp	olive oil	2 tbsp

◦ ✿ ◦ V

p.69 📷

This dish is known as *maşik* or *maşk-e* in and around Southeastern Anatolia. It is also made as a standalone meal.

◆

Drain the soaked mung beans, then cook in a pan of simmering water until soft, about 25 minutes. Drain.

Put the cooked mung beans into a large bowl, add ½ teaspoon of salt along with the dried chilli (red pepper) flakes, sumac, walnuts, olive oil and pomegranate molasses and gently combine.

To make the dressing:
Finely slice the fresh (green) garlic, spring onions (scallions), olives and the fresh chilli (chile). Heat the oil in a small saucepan over medium heat, add the sliced fresh (green) garlic, spring onions and chilli and cook for 3 minutes.

Meanwhile, finely slice the spring onions, fresh (green) garlic, mint, parsley, basil and tarragon. Pour the warm dressing over the mung bean mixture, then add the sliced spring onions, fresh (green) garlic, mint, parsley, basil, tarragon and pomegranate seeds. Toss gently and serve.

◆

OLIVE AND ONION SALAD
ZEYTİN PİYAZI

Region:	Gaziantep, Southeastern Anatolia	
Preparation time:		20 minutes
Serves:		4

150 g	unsalted green olives,	1½ cups/5 oz
50 g	walnuts	½ cup/2 oz
1 (120 g)	medium onion,	1 (¾ cup/4 oz)
1 tsp	tomato paste (see p.492)	1 tsp
1 tsp	dried chilli (red pepper) flakes	1 tsp
2 tbsp	olive oil	2 tbsp
3	spring onions (scallions)	3
8	flat-leaf parsley sprigs,	8
2 tbsp	pomegranate molasses	2 tbsp
100 g	pomegranate seeds	1¼ cups/3½ oz

◦ ✿ ◦ V X

This dish is made in the winter months. It is a popular lunch dish in Southeastern and Eastern Anatolia and the Eastern Mediterranean regions.

◆

Pit and quarter the green olives. Roughly chop the walnuts. Finely dice the onion. Put the green olives, walnuts, onion, tomato paste and dried chilli (red pepper) flakes into a large bowl. Season with ¾ teaspoon of salt. Add 1 tablespoon olive oil and gently mix with your hands.

Finely slice the spring onions (scallions) and parsley. Add the sliced spring onions to the bowl and gently mix, then sprinkle in the parsley and mix again.

Dress with the remaining 1 tablespoon olive oil and the pomegranate molasses and sprinkle the pomegranate seeds on top. Serve immediately.

SÜRK CHEESE SALAD
SÜRK (BAHARATLI KÜFLÜ PEYNİRLİ ÇÖKELEK) SALATASI

Region:		Adana, Mediterranean Region
Preparation time:		20 minutes
Serves:		4

1 (120 g)	medium onion, cut into thick crescents	1 (¾ cup/4 oz)
1	hot green chilli (chile), sliced into crescents	1
6	flat-leaf parsley sprigs, finely sliced	6
4	fresh basil sprigs, finely sliced	4
½ tsp	dried chilli (red pepper) flakes	½ tsp
40 g	*Sürk* (Spicy Hatay Cheese, see p.484)	1½ oz
60 ml	olive oil	2 fl oz/¼ cup
2 tbsp	pomegranate molasses	2 tbsp
400 g	tomatoes, sliced into crescents	2 cups/14 oz

◦ ❧ ✗

This salad is a regular breakfast dish during the summer months. It is also a staple of *meyhane* menus and is popular in Hatay or Antakya – the ancient city of Antioch – and Mersin, both neighbors of Adana.

♦

In a large bowl, combine the onion, chilli (chile), parsley, basil, chilli (red pepper) flakes and *sürk* with ¼ teaspoon salt. Add the olive oil and pomegranate molasses and mix for 3 minutes. Add the tomatoes and gently mix for 2 minutes. Cover and chill in the refrigerator for 5 minutes, then serve.

♦

SKY CHEESE (BLUE CHEESE)
GÖK PEYNİRİ (KÜFLÜ PEYNİR) OVMASI

Region:		Konya, Central Anatolia
Preparation time:		10 minutes
Cooking time:		40 minutes
Serves:		4

350 g	onions	2⅓ cups/12 oz
120 g	*küflü* blue cheese (sheep's milk)	4 oz
2 tbsp	filtered honey	2 tbsp
50 g	walnuts, pounded	½ cup/2 oz
4	toasted bread slices, cut into 1-cm (½-inch) squares (or 1 *yufka* pastry sheet, cut into 1-cm (½-inch) squares and deep-fried)	4

V

Fresh cheese prepared in an earthenware pot, or sheepskin or goatskin, is handed over to a pothole owner (or *obrukçu*) in the spring. The cheese is then buried in a natural pothole in the mountains for maturation. The *obrukçu* checks if the cheese is ready in January, but depending on the owner's taste, the cheese may spend up to three years in the pothole. Once it is returned to its owner, traditionally the first seven portions are distributed to neighbours with some flatbread to protect the produce from the evil eye. This dish is one of the first prepared with the new season's cheese.

♦

Preheat oven to 180°C/350°F/Gas Mark 4.

Put the onions in a baking tray and roast in the oven for 40 minutes, until the onions are soft.

In a large bowl, combine the *küflü* blue cheese, roasted onion and honey with a pinch of salt. Mix thoroughly for 3 minutes, rubbing everything together.

Divide among serving plates, sprinkle the walnuts over the top and serve with the toast or pastry croutons.

TARAMASALATA
TARAMA

Region:	İstanbul, Marmara Region
Preparation time:	25 minutes
Serves:	4

100 g	stale bread (crust removed)	3½ oz
60 g	onion, quartered	⅜ cup/2 oz
5	garlic cloves, crushed	5
200 g	fresh carp or pike roe, membrane discarded	7 oz
1 tbsp	lemon juice	1 tbsp
200 ml	olive oil	scant 1 cup/7 fl oz
3	flat-leaf parsley sprigs	3
3	dill sprigs	3

Served all through the year, taramasalata is a specialty of the Rum (Ottoman Greek) families in İstanbul. Over the years, this dish has worked its way onto all *meyhane* menus. As well as carp or pike, it can also be made from salmon, sea bass or mullet roe. Some versions omit the bread.

♦

Soak the bread in a small amount of water then squeeze out any excess moisture. Process the onion and the garlic in a food processor until well mashed. Add the soaked bread and ½ teaspoon salt and pulse the processor a few times to combine, then add the roe and lemon juice and then process for a further 5 minutes. As soon as the colour of the roe becomes paler, gradually add the olive oil while continuing to process. When all the olive oil is thoroughly combined, the final mixture should be a shade of white.

Finely slice the parsley and dill, then combine. Serve either underneath or sprinkled on top of the taramasalata.

♦

LENTIL DIP
MERCİMEK (DONDURMASI) EZMESİ

Region:	Muğla Ege, Aegean Region
Preparation time:	20 minutes
Cooking time:	45 minutes
Serves:	4

120 g	yellow lentils, washed	¾ cup/4 oz
1 (70 g)	carrot , peeled	1 (½ cup/2½ oz)
200 g	potato, peeled and quartered	1 cup/7 oz
½ tsp	ground cumin	½ tsp
1 tbsp	lemon juice	1 tbsp

For the dressing:		
1 (120 g)	medium onion	1 (¾ cup/4 oz)
1 tbsp	olive oil	1 tbsp
2 tsp	ground paprika	2 tsp

50 g	unsalted feta cheese	½ cup/2 oz
1½ tsp	pine nuts, toasted	1½ tsp
5	flat-leaf parsley sprigs	5
5	fresh mint sprigs	5

This lentil dip is made in the autumn and winter, traditionally during the olive harvest. It is usually followed by tahini halva.

♦

Fill a large saucepan with 1 litre (4¼ cups/34 fl oz) water and add the washed lentils, carrot, potato and ½ teaspoon salt. Bring to the boil, uncovered, and skim the surface with a slotted spoon. Then reduce the heat and cook, covered, for 30 minutes. Transfer to a food processor, add the cumin and lemon juice and blitz until smooth.

To make the dressing:
Slice the onion into thin crescents. Heat the oil in a small saucepan over medium heat, add the onion and ¼ teaspoon salt to the hot oil and cook for 10 minutes, stirring continuously. Add the paprika and cook for 10 seconds, then remove from the heat.

Put the lentil mash on to serving plates, drizzle with the dressing and garnish with feta cheese and pine nuts. Finish with a drizzle of olive oil and a sprinkle of finely sliced parsley and mint.

HUMMUS
HUMUS

Region:		Mersin, all regions
Preparation time:		30 minutes, plus overnight soaking
Cooking time:		about 1½ hours
Serves:		4

200 g	chickpeas (garbanzo beans), soaked overnight	1 cup/7 oz
4	garlic cloves, crushed	4
⅛ tsp	ground cumin	⅛ tsp
60 ml	tahini (sesame seed paste)	¼ cup/ 2 fl oz
2 tbsp	sesame oil	2 tbsp
60 ml	lemon juice	¼ cup/2 fl oz
1 tbsp	ground sumac	1 tbsp
½ tsp	dried chilli (red pepper) flakes	½ tsp
6	flat-leaf parsley sprigs, finely sliced	6
2 tbsp	olive oil	2 tbsp

♦ ⚘ ♦ V   p.73 ◻

Some local versions add butter, some *pastırma* (cured beef, see p.497).

♦

Drain the soaked chickpeas (garbanzo beans), then cook in a pan of simmering water until soft, about 1½ hours. Drain and let cool, then remove the skins.

Mash the chickpeas with the crushed garlic, cumin and ½ teaspoon salt either with a fork or in a food processor.

In a separate bowl, whisk the tahini, sesame oil and lemon juice, then add to the chickpea mash gradually, making sure all is smooth and well combined. If you prefer a more runny consistency, add a small amount of water to loosen the hummus.

Divide among serving plates, sprinkle with sumac, dried chilli (red pepper) flakes and parsley, then drizzle with olive oil and serve.

♦

CHEESE DIP
PEYNİR EZMESİ

Region:		Edirne, Marmara Region
Preparation time:		10 minutes
Serves:		4

150 g	*tulum* cheese (low salt), grated	5 oz
60 g	stale bread (crusts removed), soaked, drained and squeezed	2¼ oz
60 g	onion, finely sliced	⅜ cup/2 oz
2	garlic cloves	2
½ bunch	flat-leaf parsley, finely sliced	½ bunch
100 g	walnuts	1 cup/3½ oz
2½ tbsp	dried dill	2½ tbsp
1 tsp	hot paprika	1 tsp
2 tsp	dried oregano	2 tsp
2 tbsp	olive oil	2 tbsp

V ✕

On the day of *Hıdrellez* (see p.500) – a celebration of the arrival of spring in May – the whole village contributes to a communal table with bread, cheese, walnuts and other foods. A lamb confit is prepared and distributed to everyone with pilaf and this cheese dip. The purpose of the ritual is to guarantee the arrival of Hızır (deus-ex-machina) and Ilyas (Elijah), who hopefully grant everyone's wishes. Other local names include 'gypsy salad', *oğmaç* salad and *abdal aşı*. This cheese dip is most often enjoyed as an appetizer, but if it is going to be served as a main course, the amount of bread is increased, offcuts of goats cheese are added to the tulum cheese and the mixture is then made into patties before being rolled in egg wash and fried.

♦

In a pestle and mortar, pound the cheese and bread into a paste for 3 minutes. Add the onion, garlic, parsley and walnuts and pound for a further 3 minutes. Add the dill, paprika and oregano and stir to combine. Drizzle with olive oil and serve.

TOMATO DIP
DOMATES EZMESİ

Region:	Adana, Mediterranean Region	
Preparation time:	20 minutes	
Serves:	4	

400 g	tomatoes, very finely chopped	2 cups/14 oz
60 g	onion, very finely chopped	⅜ cup/2 oz
1	hot green chilli (chile), very finely chopped	1
5	flat-leaf parsley sprigs, very finely chopped	5
1½ tbsp	hot dried chilli (red pepper) flakes	1½ tbsp
2 tsp	dried mint	2 tsp
¼ tsp	ground cumin	¼ tsp
2 tbsp	ground sumac	2 tbsp
2 tbsp	pomegranate molasses	2 tbsp
100 g	tart pomegranate seeds	1¼ cup/3½ oz
100 g	walnuts, roughly crushed	1 cup/3½ oz
2 tbsp	olive oil	2 tbsp

This dish has a flame-roasted version as well as one made with tomato paste; some recipes include garlic; some cooks like to combine all the ingredients and chop them with a mezzaluna (a curved knife with a handle on each end), which yields a superior result. It is a popular side dish to kebabs.

♦

In a large bowl, combine the chopped tomatoes, onion, green chilli (chile) and parsley and mix well. Add the dried chilli (red pepper) flakes, dried mint, ground cumin, ground sumac and pomegranate molasses with ½ teaspoon salt and gently combine.

Transfer to serving plates and garnish with the pomegranate seeds and walnuts. Drizzle with olive oil and serve.

♦

AUBERGINE DIP
PATLICAN EZMESİ

Region:	İzmir, Aegean Region	
Preparation time:	10 minutes	
Cooking time:	1 hour 3 minutes	
Serves:	4	

600 g	aubergines (eggplants)	2½ cups/1 lb 5 oz
1 tbsp	lemon juice	1 tbsp
¾ tsp	salt	¾ tsp
¼ tsp	white pepper	¼ tsp
60 ml	olive oil	¼ cup/2 fl oz
6	garlic cloves, crushed	6

You could roast the aubergines (eggplants) in a wood-fired oven or on a barbecue for a superior taste. Some versions of this recipe even deep-fry the aubergines.

♦

Preheat oven to 200°C/400 F/Gas Mark 6. Prick the aubergines (eggplants) in a few places with a knife, put them on a baking tray (sheet) and roast for 1 hour. Remove from the oven and let cool for 5 minutes.

Peel the aubergines, put the flesh in a bowl, and add the lemon juice, salt and white pepper. Mix and crush with a wooden spoon.

Heat the oil in a large saucepan over medium heat, add the crushed garlic and cook for 5 seconds, then add the aubergine mixture to the pan and cook for 1 minute, mixing thoroughly with a wooden spoon.

Transfer to a platter to serve.

BELL PEPPER AND WALNUT DIP
MUHAMMARA

Region:		Kilis, Southeastern Anatolia
Preparation time:		15 minutes
Serves:		4

400 g	fresh, small, hot red bell peppers, finely sliced	2¼ cups/14 oz
8	garlic cloves	8
80 g	stale bread, crust removed	3 oz
60 g	walnuts	½ cup/2 oz
½ tsp	salt	½ tsp
½ tsp	ground coriander	½ tsp
½ tsp	ground cumin	½ tsp
1½ tbsp	tahini (sesame seed paste)	1½ tbsp
2 tbsp	pomegranate molasses	2 tbsp
2 tbsp	olive oil	2 tbsp

This dish is a specialty of Kilis, Halep and their environs. It is a breakfast staple as well as a great side to *rakı* (see p.503), and popular as part of a wedding banquet. The summer version of this dip uses fresh red bell peppers, whereas the winter one uses dried peppers. August is peak *muhammara* season since its key ingredient, the local red bell peppers, reach full flavour at this time. Some versions omit tahini and pomegranate molasses.

◆

In a pestle and mortar, pound the bell peppers, garlic, bread, walnuts, salt, ground coriander and cumin into a paste for 5 minutes. Add the tahini, half of the pomegranate molasses and half of the olive oil and mix.

Transfer to serving plates and drizzle with the remaining pomegranate molasses and then the remaining olive oil.

CHILLI AND WALNUT DIP
CEVİZLİ BİBER

Region:		Hatay, all regions
Preparation time:		25 minutes
Cooking time:		5 minutes
Serves:		4

100 g	dried red chillies (chiles), washed, deseeded	3½ oz
1 (120 g)	medium onion, finely sliced	1 (¾ cup/4 oz)
60 g	walnuts	½ cup/2 oz
80 g	breadcrumbs	⅞ cup/3 oz
½ tsp	ground cumin	½ tsp
2 tbsp	ground sumac	2 tbsp
½ tsp	salt	½ tsp
60 ml	olive oil	¼ cup/2 fl oz
4	flat-leaf parsley sprigs, finely sliced	4

The large red local chillies (*baş biber*), which are dried on strings, are eaten for breakfast, as snacks or with *öcce*. The chillies dried in the summer are eaten all year round. This dish is a popular side at *meyhanes*. Another recipe substitutes onion with 2 tablespoons tahini.

◆

Bring 500 ml (generous 2 cups/17 fl oz) water to the boil in a small saucepan, add the dried chillies (chiles) and boil for 5 minutes. Drain, then rinse in cold water.

In a pestle and mortar, pound the onion, walnuts and breadcrumbs for 5 minutes. Transfer the mixture to a large bowl.

Add the poached chilli to the mortar with the ground cumin, ground sumac and salt and pound into a paste for 5–10 minutes. Combine the chilli paste with the onion paste and mix in 2 tablespoons of the olive oil.

Serve, garnished with parsley and drizzled with the remaining olive oil.

BROAD BEAN PASTE
FAVA

Region:	İzmir, Aegean Region
Preparation time:	15 minutes
Cooking time:	35 minutes, plus 2¼ hours resting/chilling
Serves:	4

200 g	dried broad (fava) beans, washed and dried	1 cup/7 oz
1 (120 g)	medium onion, quartered	1 (¾ cup/4 oz)
4	garlic cloves	4
1 tbsp	lemon juice	1 tbsp
⅛ tsp	lemon zest	⅛ tsp
¼ tsp	white pepper	¼ tsp
½ tsp	salt	½ tsp
1½ tbsp	honey	1½ tbsp
6	dill sprigs, finely sliced	6
2 tbsp	olive oil	2 tbsp

   p.77

Popular with home cooks, fava is also a *meyhane* staple. Some cooks make fava with carrots as well as onions. In İstanbul, broad bean paste is set in moulds, while the version made in İzmir is more runny in consistency.

◆

Fill a large saucepan with 1 litre (4¼ cups/34 fl oz) water and add the broad (fava) beans, onion, garlic, lemon juice, lemon zest, white pepper and salt. Bring to the boil and skim the foam from the surface with a slotted spoon, then reduce the heat and cook, covered, for 30 minutes. Remove from the heat and let rest for 10 minutes.

Add the honey to the pan and mash the mixture, then add the dill and gently mix. Put the mixture into a bowl and let cool at room temperature. Once cooled, cover and chill in the refrigerator for 2 hours.

Serve in bowls, with a drizzle of oil on top.

◆

BROAD BEAN DIP
BAKLA EZMESİ

Region:	Hatay, Mediterranean Region
Preparation time:	10 minutes, plus 1 hour soaking
Cooking time:	2 hours 30 minutes
Serves:	4

200 g	dried broad (fava) beans, skin-on	1 cup/7 oz
½ tsp	salt	½ tsp
60 ml	tahini (sesame seed paste)	¼ cup/ 2 fl oz
8	garlic cloves, crushed	8
90 ml	lemon juice	6 tbsp/3 fl oz
½ tsp	ground cumin	½ tsp
2 tsp	dried chilli (red pepper) flakes	2 tsp
2 tbsp	ground sumac	2 tbsp
½ bunch	flat-leaf parsley, finely sliced	½ bunch
2 tbsp	olive oil	2 tbsp

This dish is eaten in the Mediterranean region, usually with pickles, fresh chillies (chiles) and radishes. Traditionally, broad (fava) bean dip is delivered to the Turkish baths the previous evening to be slow-cooked overnight in the fires of the baths. It is then eaten for breakfast. Local legend has it that a bowl of broad bean dip in the morning keeps you going throughout the day.

◆

Soak the dried broad (fava) beans in 500 ml (generous 2 cups/17 fl oz) water for 1 hour.

Drain the soaked beans and put into a large saucepan with 3 litres (12 cups/100 fl oz) water and the salt. Bring to the boil, then reduce the heat and simmer uncovered for 30 minutes. Skim the surface with a slotted spoon. Cover and cook for 2 hours.

Drain the cooked beans, reserving the cooking juices. Put the bean pulp into a food processor and blitz to a paste. In a large bowl, mix the tahini, garlic and lemon juice until thoroughly combined. Add the broad bean paste and 2 tablespoons of the reserved cooking juices and mix until combined.

Garnish with cumin, dried chilli (red pepper) flakes, sumac and parsley. Drizzle with olive oil and serve.

TZATZIKI
CACIK (JAJİ)

Region:		Van, all regions
Preparation time:		15 minutes
Serves:		4

200 g	cucumber, peeled, deseeded and finely sliced	1⅓ cups/7 oz
4	garlic cloves, crushed	4
3	spring onions (scallions), finely sliced	3
4	dill sprigs, finely sliced	4
300 g	yogurt (sheep's milk)	1½ cups/11 oz
½ tsp	salt	½ tsp
300 g	unsalted *lor* (fresh curd cheese, see p.485, or ricotta)	11 oz
2 tbsp	olive oil	2 tbsp

Many regions have their own way of making tzatziki. The most well-known version (strained yogurt, water, cucumber, garlic, dried mint and salt) is eaten as a side dish, but this version of the recipe is usually eaten in the mornings. Other versions use *jaji* cheese instead of yogurt, some use green bell peppers instead of cucumber.

♦

Put the cucumber in a large bowl and add the garlic, spring onions (scallions), dill, yogurt, salt and *lor*. Mix well and serve in smaller bowls with a drizzle of olive oil.

♦

FRESH ALMOND TZATZIKI
ÇAĞLA CACIĞI (TAZE BADEM CACIĞI)

Region:		Malatya, all regions
Preparation time:		15 minutes
Serves:		4

200 g	fresh almonds, finely sliced	2½ cups/7 oz
2	garlic cloves, finely sliced	2
2 tbsp	olive oil	2 tbsp
½ bunch	cress, finely sliced	½ bunch
2	fresh mint sprigs, finely sliced	2
2	flat-leaf parsley sprigs, finely sliced	2
½ tsp	salt	½ tsp
300 g	strained yogurt (sheep's milk)	1½ cups/11 oz

When almonds are in season, this tzatziki is used to accompany meat dishes, soups, lamb confit and wraps.

♦

In a large bowl, combine the almonds, garlic, 1 tablespoon of the olive oil, cress, mint and parsley with the salt and knead for 3 minutes. Stir in the strained yogurt.

Drizzle with the remaining 1 tablespoon olive oil and serve immediately.

ALMOND AND GARLIC SAUCE
TARATOR

Region:	İstanbul, Marmara Region
Preparation time:	10 minutes
Serves:	4

150 g	fresh almonds, skinned	2 cups/5 oz
6	garlic cloves	6
70 g	onion	½ cup/2¾ oz
¼ tsp	ground white pepper	¼ tsp
½ tsp	salt	½ tsp
2 tbsp	lemon juice	2 tbsp
100 g	stale bread (crusts removed), soaked, drained and squeezed	3½ oz

This is a very popular side dish to calamari and shrimps in all coastal areas, especially İstanbul, Thrace and their environs. Some add it to salads and fried vegetables for extra flavour; other recipes include yogurt or milk.

♦

In a pestle and mortar, pound the almonds, garlic, onion, white pepper and salt into a paste for 5 minutes. Add 1 tablespoon lemon juice and the bread and keep pounding for a further 2 minutes. Stir in the remaining lemon juice and serve.

ÇEMEN SPICED DIP
ÇEMEN

Region:	Tokat, Black Sea Region and Central Anatolia
Preparation time:	25 minutes
Serves:	4

250 ml	water, freshly boiled	1 cup/8 fl oz
15	garlic cloves, crushed	15
40 g	ground *çemen*	1½ oz
1 tsp	ground allspice	1 tsp
1 tsp	ground cloves	1 tsp
3 tbsp	hot dried chilli (red pepper) flakes	3 tbsp
50 g	paprika	½ cup/1¾ oz
1½ tsp	ground cumin	1½ tsp
½ tsp	ground cinnamon	½ tsp
½ tsp	black pepper	½ tsp
½ tsp	salt	½ tsp
200 g	ground hazelnuts	2 cups/7 oz

Çemen is a popular breakfast staple and a snack enjoyed at any time with a slice of bread. Every family in Central Anatolia has their own *çemen* recipe with a twist; the basic recipe of garlic, ground cumin, paprika, dried chilli (red pepper) flakes and black pepper is spiced differently according to taste. A nut-free version is used in making *Pastırma* (Cured Beef, see p.497) and for adding extra flavour to dishes.

♦

In a medium bowl, combine the boiling water, garlic and ground *çemen*, mix for 1 minute, then let rest for 10 minutes.

Add the allspice, cloves, dried chilli (red pepper) flakes, paprika, cumin, cinnamon, black pepper and salt, then knead for 5 minutes. Finally, add the ground hazelnuts and knead for a further 3 minutes.

Serve alongside bread and vegetables.

YOGURT DIP
HAYDARİ

Region:		İzmir, Aegean Region
Preparation time:		10 minutes
Serves:		4

400 g	strained yogurt (sheep's milk)	2 cups/14 oz
2 tsp	dried oregano	2 tsp
10	dill sprigs, finely sliced	10
1 tsp	dried mint	1 tsp
8	garlic cloves, crushed	8
½ tsp	salt	½ tsp
1 tbsp	apple cider vinegar	1 tbsp
2 tbsp	olive oil	2 tbsp

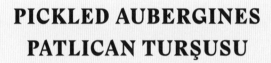

p.81

An great side dish with drinks.

♦

In a large bowl, mix the yogurt, oregano, dill and dried mint.

In a separate, smaller bowl, mix the garlic, salt and vinegar, then add to the yogurt mixture. Combine well.

Drizzle with olive oil and serve.

PICKLED AUBERGINES
PATLICAN TURŞUSU

Region:		Ankara, all regions
Preparation time:		30 minutes, plus 20 days fermentation
Cooking time:		45 minutes
Serves:		4

8	baby aubergines (eggplants)	8
1 bunch	flat-leaf parsley, stalks only	1 bunch
2	red bell peppers	2
2	lemons, finely sliced	2
½ bunch	dill	½ bunch

For the filling:

100 g	carrot	⅔ cup/3½ oz
100 g	white cabbage	1 cup/3½ oz
2	celery stalks	2
1	hot red chilli (chile)	1
2	fresh mint sprigs	2
15	garlic cloves, peeled, quartered	15
5	black peppercorns	5
2 tbsp	lemon juice	2 tbsp

For the brine:

500 ml	grape vinegar	2 cups/17 fl oz
2 tbsp	grape molasses	2 tbsp
½ tsp	rock salt or sea salt	½ tsp
10	garlic cloves, quartered	10

Legend goes that seven people of good character and humour are namechecked during the pickling of the aubergines (eggplants) in an earthenware pot. If the pickles work, the right names were spoken. If not, well, too bad... perhaps those people are not good after all. Some variations omit the water in the brine and use only oil.

♦

Prick a few holes in the aubergines (eggplants) and put into a large saucepan with 2 litres (8½ cups/70 fl oz) water. Bring to the boil, then turn down the heat and simmer for 40 minutes. Drain and set aside.

In a separate small pan, poach the flat-leaf parsely stalks in boiling water for 5 minutes, then drain and set aside.

To make the filling:
Finely slice the carrot, cabbage, celery stalks, hot red chilli (chile) and fresh mint. In a bowl, thoroughly combine all the filling ingredients. Season with ½ teaspoon salt.

Make a 4-cm (1½-inch) cut lengthwise down the aubergines and fill the cavities with the stuffing. Quarter the red bell peppers lengthwise and use a piece to cover each stuffed cavity. Tie each into a parcel with a parsley stalk.

To make the brine:
Mix the brine ingredients together with 1 litre (4¼ cups/ 34 fl oz) water. Put the stuffed aubergines into a 2-litre (70-fl oz) sterilized jar. Push the lemon slices around the sides of the jar. Add the dill and pour in the brine. Seal the jar and leave to ferment in a cool, dark place for 20 days. The pickles will keep for up to a year when kept in a sealed jar and refrigerated.

PICKLED GHERKINS
HIYAR TURŞUSU

Region:		Bursa, all regions
Preparation time:	20 minutes, plus 20 days fermentation	
Serves:		4

16 (5 cm)	gherkins	16 (2 inch)
1	fresh chilli (chile), halved	1
16	garlic cloves	16
2 tbsp	raw chickpeas (garbanzo beans)	2 tbsp
½ bunch	dill	½ bunch

For the brine:		
3	garlic cloves, crushed	3
2½ tsp	rock salt or sea salt	2½ tsp

Small gherkins are picked in the autumn. Gherkins are enjoyed raw in all regions and as a popular side to pilafs. Believe it or not, some like it with halva! Gherkins are commercially grown around Ankara and Bursa.

♦

Put the gherkins, chilli (chile) and garlic into a 1.5-litre (50-fl oz) sterilized jar. Put the raw chickpeas (garbanzo beans) in a square of muslin (cheesecloth), tie into a sack and put into the jar. Press everything down with your hand. Add the dill and press down again.

To make the brine:
Mix the garlic and salt in a large bowl with 1 litre (4¼ cups/34 fl oz) water.

Pour the brine into the jar. Seal the jar and leave to ferment in a cool, dark place for 20 days.

After 20 days, remove the muslin sack before serving. The pickles will keep for up to a year when kept in a sealed jar and refrigerated.

♦

PICKLED CABBAGE
LAHANA TURŞUSU

Region:		Niğde, all regions
Preparation time:		20 minutes, plus 21 days fermentation
Serves:		4

800 g	white cabbage, cut into 5-cm (2-inch) pieces	8 cups/1 lb 12 oz
15	garlic cloves	15
1	fresh fennel sprig, chopped	1
2	fresh chillies (chiles), quartered	2
150 g	carrot, peeled, chopped into 2.5-cm (1-inch) slices	1 cup/5 oz
1 (200 g)	turnip, quartered	1 (7 oz)
2 tsp	rock salt or sea salt	2 tsp
2 tbsp	raw chickpeas (garbanzo beans)	2 tbsp
1	slice of bread, crumbled	1

For the brine:		
2 tsp	rock salt or sea salt	2 tsp

If you are short on time, you can poach the cabbage first. If you take this shortcut, omit the bread and chickpeas (garbanzo beans) and add 200 ml (scant 1 cup/7 fl oz) grape vinegar to the poaching water.

♦

In a large bowl, combine the white cabbage, garlic, fennel, chillies (chiles), carrot, turnip and salt and knead for 5 minutes. Cover the bowl with a muslin (cheesecloth) and let rest for 1 day.

The next day, pack the mixture into a 2-litre (70-fl oz) sterilized jar.

To make the brine:
Mix the salt in a large bowl with 2.25 litres (10 cups/ 80 fl oz) water.

Put the chickpeas (garbanzo beans) and the bread in a square of muslin (cheesecloth), tie into a sack and put into the jar. Pour in the brine. Seal the jar and leave to ferment in a cool, dark place for 20 days.

After 20 days, remove the muslin sack before serving. The pickles will keep for up to a year when kept in a sealed jar and refrigerated.

PICKLED GREEN BEANS
FASULYE TURŞUSU

Region:		Giresun, all regions
Preparation time:		10 minutes, plus 15 days fermentation
Cooking time:		20 minutes
Serves:		4

600 g	fresh green beans (de-stringed), cooked in boiling water for 20 minutes, drained	1 lb 5 oz
1	fresh hot chilli (chile), finely sliced	1
10	garlic cloves, finely sliced	10
4	fresh basil sprigs	4

For the brine:

| 90 ml | lemon juice | 6 tbsp/3 fl oz |
| 2 tsp | rock salt or sea salt | 2 tsp |

The autumn green beans are best for pickling. These pickles are ready between 15–20 days after preparation and are eaten all though the winter. They are a popular side and a versatile ingredient for other dishes. Most commonly, they are roasted with onions or eggs.

◆

Pack the cooked beans, chilli (chile) and garlic into a 1-litre (30-fl oz) sterilized jar. Press down with your hand and add the basil. Fill the jar with water, then add the lemon juice and salt. Seal the jar and leave to ferment in a cool, dark place for 15 days.

The pickles will keep for up to a year when kept in a sealed jar and refrigerated.

◆

PICKLED BELL PEPPERS
BİBER TURŞUSU

Region:		Uşak, all regions
Preparation time:		10 minutes, plus 20 days fermentation
Serves:		4

600 g	green chillies	1 lb 5 oz
15	garlic cloves	15
200 g	tomatoes, halved	1 cup/7 oz

For the brine:

200 ml	grape vinegar	scant 1 cup/7 fl oz
2 tbsp	lemon juice	2 tbsp
60 ml	grape molasses	¼ cup/2 fl oz
2½ tsp	rock salt or sea salt	2½ tsp
50 g	barley	⅓ cup/2 oz

Another regional method for making these pickles cooks the same ingredients over medium heat for 10 minutes. They are then cooled and enjoyed the same day, without waiting for fermentation to occur.

◆

Prick the chillies (chiles) all over with a fork then put into a 1.5-litre (50-fl oz) sterilized jar along with the garlic. Press down and add the tomatoes.

To make the brine:
Mix the vinegar, lemon juice, grape molasses and salt in a large bowl with 1 litre (4¼ cups/34 fl oz) water.

Put the barley in a square of muslin (cheesecloth), tie into a sack and put into the jar. Pour in the brine. Seal the jar and leave to ferment in a cool, dark place for 20 days.

After 20 days, remove the muslin sack before serving. The pickles will keep for up to a year when kept in a sealed jar and refrigerated.

FARMER'S MEATBALLS
FELLAH KÖFTESİ (ÇİFTÇİ KÖFTESİ)

Region:		Adana, Mediterranean Region
Preparation time:		30 minutes
Cooking time:		15 minutes
Serves:		4

150 g	dark bulgur wheat	⅔ cup/5 oz
1 tsp	sweet bell pepper paste (see p.492) 1 tsp	
1½ tsp	tomato paste (see p.492)	1½ tsp
100 g	tomato, grated	½ cup/3½ oz
⅛ tsp	ground cumin	⅛ tsp
1½ tbsp	dried mint	1½ tbsp
2 tbsp	olive oil	2 tbsp
6	garlic cloves, finely sliced	6
1 tsp	dried chilli (red pepper) flakes	1 tsp
300 g	spinach leaves	1⅓ cup/11 oz
50 g	walnuts, roughly crushed	½ cup/2 oz
2 tbsp	pomegranate molasses	2 tbsp

◊ ◊ V

Fellah is a name given to the Nusayris (Arab Alawites) who live around Adana, Mersin and Antakya by the Sunnis in the region. Arab Alawites call this dish *sarımsaklı köfte* (garlic meatballs), which is eaten cold on summer days.
♦
Combine the bulgur wheat, pepper paste, tomato paste, tomato, ground cumin, dried mint and ¼ teaspoon salt in a large, deep bowl or tray and knead for 20 minutes. When the mixture starts resembling a dough, take small pieces and roll into 1-cm (½-inch) balls. Make small dents in the balls with a fingertip.

In a large saucepan, bring 1 litre (4¼ cups/34 fl oz) water and ⅛ teaspoon salt to the boil. Add the bulgur balls to the pan and simmer for 5 minutes.

Heat the oil in a saucepan over medium heat, add the garlic and dried chilli (red pepper) flakes and cook for 10 seconds. Add the spinach and remaining ⅛ teaspoon of salt and cook for 5 minutes, mixing continuously. Remove from the heat, then add the cooked bulgur balls, walnuts and pomegranate molasses to the pan. Mix well before serving.

♦

KURDISH MEATBALLS
KÜRT KÖFTESİ

Region:		Van, Eastern Anatolia
Preparation time:		30 minutes
Cooking time:		25 minutes
Serves:		4

150 g	fine dark bulgur wheat	⅔ cup (5 oz)
1	egg	1
½ tsp	salt	½ tsp
40 g	butter	3 tbsp/1½ oz
2 (240 g)	medium onions, finely sliced	2 (1⅝ cups/8 oz)
50 g	green lentils, cooked	⅓ cup/2 oz
2 tsp	dried basil (or 5 sprigs fresh basil)	2 tsp

For the dressing:		
2 tbsp	butter	2 tbsp
½ tsp	dried chilli (red pepper) flakes	½ tsp

200 g	plain yogurt	1 cup/7 oz

V

This dish is known as squeezed meatballs among Kurds and 'Kurdish meatballs' among the rest of the population. Also known as *çimdik köfte* and *sıkma köfte* in the region, these vegetarian meatballs are popular with children.
♦
Combine the bulgur wheat, egg and ¼ teaspoon of salt in a large, deep bowl or tray and knead for 20 minutes. Divide the mixture into 24 equal pieces and squeeze into patties.

In a large saucepan, bring 1 litre (4¼ cups/34 fl oz) of water to the boil. Add the bulgur patties and simmer for 5 minutes, until the patties rise to the surface. Remove with a slotted spoon to paper towels. Reserve the cooking water.

Heat the butter in a saucepan over medium heat, add the onion and cook for 10 minutes, mixing continuously. Add the cooked lentils and basil, then add the patties with 200 ml (1 cup/7 fl oz) of their cooking water. Cook for 2 minutes.

Transfer to serving bowls while you make the dressing.

To make the dressing:
Heat the butter in a small saucepan over low-medium heat, add the dried chilli (red pepper) flakes and gently cook for 5 minutes.

Pour a little yogurt over each serving, drizzle with the dressing and serve.

TOPIK
TOPİK

Region:	İstanbul, Marmara Region	
Preparation time:	30 minutes, plus overnight soaking, plus 2½ hours resting and chilling	
Cooking time:		2½ hours
Serves:		4

For the filling:

8 (1 kg)	medium onions, sliced	8 (2 lb 3 oz)
1 tsp	salt	1 tsp
40 g	raisins	¼ cup/1½ oz
3 tbsp	pine nuts, toasted	3 tbsp
½ tsp	ground allspice	½ tsp
¼ tsp	ground cloves	¼ tsp
¼ tsp	black pepper	¼ tsp
60 ml	tahini (sesame seed paste)	¼ cup/ 2 fl oz

For the shells:

250 g	chickpeas (garbanzo beans), soaked overnight	2 cups/9 oz

2 tbsp	olive oil	2 tbsp
1 tsp	ground cinnamon	1 tsp

▲ ❧ ◆ **V**

This Armenian dish, eaten during Lent, has become a staple on *meyhane* menus. A popular shortcut involves making a paste out of boiled chickpeas (garbanzo beans) or mixing chickpea paste with potato paste and skipping the boiling stage. The recipe below is the original. You will need four 30 × 30-cm (12 × 12-inch) squares of muslin (cheesecloth). The *topik* can also be served with a squeeze of lemon on top.

◆

To make the filling:
Put the onions and ½ teaspoon salt into a large, deep saucepan and cook over medium heat for 20 minutes, stirring continuously. Turn the heat to low, put the lid on the pan and cook for 1 hour, stirring every 15 minutes, until the onions are caramelized. Remove from the heat, add the raisins, pine nuts, allspice, cloves and black pepper and mix thoroughly. Mix in the tahini, then transfer the mixture to a bowl and let cool for 30 minutes.

To make the shells:
Drain and shell the soaked chickpeas (garbanzo beans), then run them through a mincer (grinder) and place in a bowl. Add the remaining ½ teaspoon salt and knead for 2 minutes until a dough forms. Lightly moisten the muslin (cheesecloth) squares and place a quarter of the chickpea dough in the middle of one square. Place a second muslin square on top and press gently to form a 20-cm (8-inch) diameter circle. Remove the top muslin square and repeat until you have four paste circles.

Spoon a quarter of the filling mixture into the middle of each shell. Shape into balls, enclosing the filling inside the shells. Wrap each muslin square around a ball and tie with a piece of string to secure.

Bring a large saucepan of water to the boil. Lower the muslin parcels into the water, cover and bring back to the boil. Boil for 1 hour. Using a slotted spoon, remove the parcels to a tray and let cool for 30 minutes. Transfer the parcels to the refrigerator to chill for 1½ hours.

Unwrap the parcels and arrange the balls on a serving platter. Garnish with a drizzle of olive oil and use the cinnamon to sprinkle a cross shape on the top of each ball.

♦

LENTIL PATTIES
MERCİMEKLİ KÖFTE

Region:	Osmaniye, all regions
Preparation time:	15 minutes
Cooking time:	45 minutes, plus 10 minutes resting
Serves:	4

100 g	red lentils, washed	½ cup/3½ oz
50 g	fine bulgur wheat	¼ cup/2 oz
4 tbsp	olive oil	4 tbsp
1 (120 g)	medium onion	1 (¾ cup/4 oz)
5	garlic cloves	5
2½ tsp	dried chilli (red pepper) flakes	2½ tsp
1½ tbsp	tomato paste (see p.492)	1½ tbsp
1½ tsp	red bell pepper paste (see p.492)	1½ tsp
⅛ tsp	ground cumin	⅛ tsp
2	spring onions (scallions)	2
½ bunch	flat-leaf parsley	½ bunch
2	fresh basil sprigs	2
2	fresh coriander (cilantro)	2

2 bunches	cress	2 bunches
150 g	radishes, sliced	5 oz

◦ ♦ V

Lentil patties are a favourite in Southeastern Anatolia and the Eastern Mediterranean, but have spread to the rest of the country. Local versions range from mild to spicy. This is a satisfying meal in itself together with *Ayran* (Salted Yogurt Drink, see p.452) and salad.

♦

In a saucepan over medium heat, add the lentils to 1 litre (4¼ cups/34 fl oz) water and simmer for 30 minutes. When cooked, whisk the lentils and water until combined. Add the bulgur wheat, ½ teaspoon salt, cover and rest for 10 minutes.

Transfer the mixture to a large, deep bowl or tray.

Meanwhile, finely slice the onion and garlic. Heat a frying pan (skillet) until hot. Add 2 tablespoons of the oil and heat for 1 minute. Add the onion and garlic and cook for 3 minutes. Add the dried chilli (red pepper) flakes and half of the tomato and pepper pastes and cook for 2 minutes.

Add the remaining 2 tablespoons of the oil, tomato and pepper pastes to the lentils along with the cumin and ⅛ teaspoon black pepper. Knead for 1 minute. Finely slice the spring onions (scallions), parsley, basil and coriander (cilantro) and add to the cooked onion and garlic mixture, then knead gently for a further 5 minutes.

Squeeze large walnut-sized pieces of the mixture into patties. Serve garnished with the cress and radish slices.

♦

BUTTERY PATTIES
YAĞLI KÖFTE

Region:	Şanlıurfa, Southeastern Anatolia
Preparation time:	40 minutes
Serves:	4

100 g	tomatoes, grated	½ cup/3½ oz
1 (120 g)	medium onion	1 (¾ cup/4 oz)
8	garlic cloves	8
150 g	dark bulgur wheat, cooked	⅔ cup/5 oz
50 g	walnuts, crushed	½ cup/2 oz
4 tsp	red bell pepper paste (see p.492)	4 tsp
1 tbsp	tomato paste (see p.492)	1 tbsp
2 tsp	dried chilli (red pepper) flakes	2 tsp
⅛ tsp	ground cumin	⅛ tsp
70 g	ghee (see p.485)	⅓ cup/2¾ oz
½ bunch	flat-leaf parsley	½ bunch
4	fresh basil sprigs	4

½ bunch	cress, leaves only, washed	½ bunch
½ bunch	fresh mint leaves, washed	½ bunch
1	*Kaşik Salatası* (Spoon Salad, see p.59)	1

This dish is perfect for cooling off during those sizzling summer days.

♦

Grate the tomatoes into a large bowl or deep tray. Finely slice the onion and garlic and add to the tomatoes, then combine with the bulgur wheat, walnuts, pepper paste, tomato paste, dried chilli (red pepper) flakes, ground cumin, and ghee. Season with ½ teaspoon salt and ¼ teaspoon black pepper. Knead the mixture well with your hands for 20 minutes.

Finely slice the parsley and basil, then add to the mixture and knead gently for a further 5 minutes.

Divide into 16 equal pieces. Squeeze each piece into a patty, place on a plate and garnish with cress and fresh mint. Serve with *Kaşik Salatası* (Spoon Salad, see p.59) on the side.

BULGUR AND PEPPER DIP
BATIRIK

Region:	Mersin, Mediterranean Region	
Preparation time:	30 minutes	
Cooking time:	5 minutes	
Serves:	4	

80 g	dark bulgur wheat	⅜ cup/3 oz
1½ tsp	red bell pepper paste (see p.492)	1½ tsp
1½ tsp	tomato paste (see p.492)	1½ tsp
200 g	tomatoes, finely chopped	1 cup/7 oz
1¾ tsp	dried chilli (red pepper) flakes	1¾ tsp
60 g	onion, finely chopped	⅜ cup/2 oz
3½ tsp	sundried tomatoes	3½ tsp
1	fresh green chilli, finely sliced	1
⅛ tsp	ground cumin	⅛ tsp
1 tbsp	dried mint	1 tbsp
100 g	peanuts, toasted	1 cup/3½ oz
2 tbsp	sesame seeds, toasted	2 tbsp
2 tbsp	tahini (sesame seed paste)	2 tbsp
2 tbsp	lemon juice	2 tbsp
2 tbsp	pomegranate molasses	2 tbsp
4	spring onions (scallions),	4
70 g	cucumber	½ cup/2¾ oz
¼ bunch	flat-leaf parsley	¼ bunch
2	fresh basil sprigs	2
2	romaine or cos lettuce leaves	2
6	romaine or cos lettuce leaves	6
2 tbsp	olive oil	2 tbsp

♦ ♦ V

This dish is a popular on hot summer days. Some prefer it without the addition of water, which gives the dish a loose texture and so it is eaten with a spoon.

♦

In a large bowl, combine the bulgur wheat, pastes, tomatoes, dried chilli (red pepper) flakes and onion. Pound the sun-dried tomatoes in a pestle and mortar then add to the bowl with the green chilli, cumin and dried mint. Season with ½ teaspoon salt. Mix thoroughly, kneading by hand for 10 minutes.

Crush the toasted peanuts and sesame seeds. Add to the bowl and continue to knead the mixture for 2 minutes. Add the tahini (sesame seed paste), lemon juice and pomegranate molasses and knead for a further 2 minutes.

Finely slice the spring onions (scallions), cucumber, parsley, basil and lettuce leaves. Add to the bowl and mix for a further 2 minutes. Add 400 ml (1⅔ cups/14 fl oz) ice-cold water and knead into the mixture, then divide equally between 4 plates and let chill for 10 minutes.

Poach the 6 lettuce leaves briefly in boiling water, then drain and immediately refresh under cold running water. Slice the lettuce into 4-cm (1½-inch) slices and divide among serving plates. Add the *batırık*, drizzle with olive oil and serve.

♦

CRACKED WHEAT WITH YOGURT
MASTEDEN (YOĞURTLU DÖVME)

Region:	Hakkâri, Eastern Anatolia	
Preparation time:	5 minutes, plus overnight soaking	
Cooking time:	10 minutes	
Serves:	4	

150 g	cracked wheat	1¼ cups/5 oz
200 g	strained yogurt (sheep's milk)	1 cup/7 oz
50 g	scented pink rose petals, finely sliced	2 oz
2 tbsp	grape molasses	2 tbsp

V

This dish can also be made with 1 litre (4¼ cups/34 fl oz) of iced water and served cold in the summer months. Some versions omit the grape molasses.

♦

Bring a saucepan of water to a simmer, add the cracked wheat and gently simmer for 10 minutes. Remove from the heat, cover, and let soak overnight.

The next day, drain the wheat and put into a large bowl. Add the yogurt and rose petals, season with ½ teaspoon salt and mix well. Drizzle with the molasses and serve.

TABBOULEH

KISIR

Region:	Hatay, Mediterranean Region	
Preparation time:	40 minutes	
Serves:	4	

120 g	fine dark bulgur wheat, cooked	generous ½ cup/ 4 oz
1 tbsp	red bell pepper paste (see p.492)	1 tbsp
1 tbsp	tomato paste (see p.492)	1 tbsp
2½ tsp	dried chilli (red pepper) flakes	2½ tsp
¼ tsp	ground cumin	¼ tsp
200 g	tomatoes, grated	1 cup/7 oz
1 (120 g)	medium onion, finely sliced	1 (¾ cup/4 oz)
4	spring onions (scallions),	4
½ bunch	fresh mint	½ bunch
1 bunch	flat-leaf parsley	1 bunch
2 tbsp	pomegranate molasses	2 tbsp
60 ml	olive oil	¼ cup/2 fl oz
16	romaine lettuce leaves	16

◖ ◆ V

p.89

This is Turkey's favourite bulgur salad and there are plenty of regional variations. It is served with boiled fresh vine leaves when they are in season.

◆

In a large, deep bowl or tray, combine the bulgur wheat, red bell pepper paste, tomato paste, dried chilli (red pepper) flakes, ground cumin, grated tomatoes and onions. Season with ½ teaspoon salt. Knead the mixture well with your hands for 20 minutes.

Finely slice the spring onions (scallions), fresh mint and parsley. Add to the mixture and knead for a further 5 minutes.

In a separate bowl, combine the pomegranate molasses and olive oil. Add to the other ingredients and mix gently. Serve on romaine lettuce leaves.

◆

LENTIL AND WALNUT SALAD

BAT

Region:	Tokat, Black Sea Region	
Preparation time:	20 minutes	
Cooking time:	10 minutes	
Serves:	4	

100 g	green lentils, cooked and cooled	1 cup/3½ oz
300 g	tomatoes, finely sliced	1½ cups/10½ oz
60 g	onion, finely sliced	⅜ cup/2 oz
4	spring onions (scallions), finely sliced	4
1½ tsp	tomato paste (see p.492)	1½ tsp
2½ tsp	dried chilli (red pepper) flakes	2½ tsp
60 g	walnuts, crushed	¾ cup/2¼ oz
6	dill sprigs, finely sliced	6
2	basil sprigs, finely sliced	2
4	flat-leaf parsley sprigs, finely sliced	4
2 tbsp	cranberry extract (see p.491)	2 tbsp
40	crisp, fresh vine leaves	40

◖ ✿ ◆ V Ⅹ

A popular dish year-round, *Bat* is served with vine leaves in brine when the fresh ones are no longer in season.

◆

In a large bowl, mix together the cooked lentils, tomatoes, onion, spring onions (scallions), tomato paste, dried chilli (red pepper) flakes and walnuts. Season with ½ teaspoon salt. Add the dill, basil and parsley and gently mix. Finally, mix in 400 ml (1⅔ cups/14 fl oz) iced water and the cranberry extract.

Serve in bowls with the fresh vine leaves on the side.

◆

VEGETABLES
EGGS
&
PULSES

◆

VEGETABLE AND OLIVE OIL DISHES

OLIVE OIL

'Olive oil dishes' traditionally means meat-free dishes in our culture, however the use of the term is not limited to vegetable recipes – olive oil is widely used with meat, poultry and fish and even in some desserts. Legend has it that Christian meat and dairy restrictions during Lent is the reason behind our dishes of vegetables, greens, herbs and legumes cooked in olive oil, which are in fact sometimes called 'Lent dishes'.

Vegetables such as green beans, okra, leeks and celeriac (celery root), cooked in olive oil with some onions and very little water, are popular all over the country. This type of dish, and ones prepared with poached greens, are served cold at restaurants, and are eaten as soon as they are ready or on the same day.

Herbs and fresh seasonal greens might be poached and the olive oil added afterwards, or they are cooked directly in olive oil. Sea samphire, euphorbia (sütleğen) and nettles are poached and dressed with olive oil and a souring agent and eaten immediately. Herbs such as mallow, and sarsaparilla (diken ucu) are roasted in olive oil with eggs.

Examples of warm olive oil dishes are the ones made with eggs: Menemen (Scrambled Eggs with Vegetables, see p.116), Çılbır (Poached Eggs and Yogurt, p.96) and Ayvanet (Diced Omelette with Yogurt Sauce, p.105). All must eaten immediately after preparation – they do not store well.

Vegetables fried in olive oil are great warm or cold. Even though the vegetables lose their freshness once cold, they are still tasty. However, as always, fresh is best. We have a saying about reheating dishes: 'A meal cannot be cooked twice.' Local culture insists that olive oil dishes are eaten on the same day that they are cooked.

There are many local variations in the preparation of olive oil dishes, some dependant on the climate and personal tastes. For instance, in the Aegean Region, black-eyed peas are poached and dressed with a garlic and olive oil dressing, whereas elsewhere the same dish is made by frying the black-eyed peas with onions, garlic, pepper and tomato.

Olive oil is vital to Turkish culture. Let us consider the olive groves – the main olive and olive oil production centres of Turkey. We hold the olive tree dear, and even believe it to be sacred. The healing properties of olive oil and olives are widely accepted, and olive oil was also once used for lighting.

Olive production still has its home in the Marmara, Aegean, Mediterranean and Southeastern Anatolia regions. The Black Sea region used to have an olive culture, although it has become scarce. Olive oil production was a vital part of the region before 1923, but cultural and urban transformation has contributed to the decline in olive oil culture in the region.

MY CHILDHOOD

In Nizip, Gaziantep, where I was born and bred, bakeries started the day bright and early – as they tend to do! As a young apprentice, I began work at 2 a.m. My baking career began in primary school. In fact, I have distant memories of my daily commute to the bakery even before I started school. I remember being afraid of the dark on my way to work. The master bakers helped me get over my fear and this is where olive oil comes in.

In Nizip, November was when olives were picked and turned into fresh olive oil. There were olive oil presses at the nearby *masmana* (soap makers). Locals would bring their freshly picked olives and the pressing would start in the very early hours of the morning. The smell of the fresh oil would travel all the way to the bakery, around the same time as the ridged breads were coming out of the oven, usually 4 a.m. The still-warm bread would be wrapped in newspapers. 'Run to the *masmana*,' my masters would say, 'before the bread gets cold, or else...' Warm bread and olive oil are a match made in heaven.

I would run as fast as I could to make sure the bread was still hot when I arrived at the *masmana*. The caretaker was always eager for his 'cut'. He would dunk all of the warm breads in the fresh olive oil, keep a couple of breads for himself and return the rest. Tea and milk would be ready by then. Everyone would dig into the bread with olive oil and I always got a piece. It was the best taste – etched in my memory forever. This is why olives and olive oil will always have a special place in my heart.

That was also the season my mum would make *Bazlama* (Bazlama Flatbread, see p.394) or *Pişi* (Fried Bread, see p.395), frying them in the olive oil made from our own olives. We would eat them plain or sprinkled with salt, pepper, sugar and ground cloves. Sometimes we would add salt and crushed garlic to the fresh olive oil, mix it in and dunk in the freshly made *bazlama*. They were small, thin and crusty, and just when you thought that they could not get any better, there was the dunk.

BROAD BEANS AND EGGS IN OLIVE OIL

When my mother died, my nephew's wife made roasted broad (fava) beans and eggs in olive oil, saying 'Auntie Feride [my mother] loved this dish and made it so well. Here is my version in her memory.'

My mum did in fact often make *Yumurtali Bakla Kavurmasi* (Fresh Broad Beans with Eggs, see p.104), but only from February to March when fresh broad beans were in season. So, we all gathered around the table prepared by my nephew's wife. The moment I broke a piece of the *Yufka Ekmeği* (Thin Flatbread, see p.378) and scooped up a morsel of the broad bean dish, I realized that it was nothing like my mother's food. It was as if my mother was saying 'Long gone are the days of my broad beans – no more, ever!'

Eating my mum's broad beans with eggs had been pure joy. We would make sure not a single drop went to waste, but we were never able to replicate it – we could only make our own versions in tribute. This is why I believe that there is no such thing as learning from a master in the kitchen. The best we can do is to imitate our mothers.

POACHED EGGS AND YOGURT
ÇILBIR

Region:		Bilecik, all regions
Preparation time:		5 minutes
Cooking time:		10 minutes
Serves:		4

1 tbsp	apple cider vinegar	1 tbsp
½ tsp	salt	½ tsp
8	eggs	8

For the yogurt sauce:

400 g	Greek yogurt	2 cups/14 oz
4	garlic cloves, crushed	4
¼ tsp	salt	¼ tsp

For the dressing:

2 tbsp	olive oil	2 tbsp
½ tsp	dried chilli (red pepper) flakes	½ tsp

❀ V X   p.97 📷

A poached egg per person is placed on a tray and an evil-eye bead is then placed under one. The wishes of the person who finds the evil eye bead are granted for the day. The dish has many local variations. It can be served with yogurt, milk, tomato paste, minced meat or spinach.

♦

Pour 3 litres (12 cups/100 fl oz) water into a saucepan, add the vinegar and salt, bring to the boil over high heat, then reduce to a gentle simmer. One at a time, crack the eggs into a bowl and gently add to the water, keeping the yolks intact. Poach for 3 minutes, making sure the eggs do not touch one another – you should be able to poach 4 at a time. Remove this batch from the pan with a slotted spoon and place directly into serving bowls. Poach the second batch.

To make the yogurt sauce:
Mix the yogurt, garlic and salt in a separate bowl.

To make the dressing:
Heat the oil in a small saucepan over medium heat, add the dried chilli (red pepper) flakes and cook for 5 seconds.

Pour the yogurt sauce over the poached eggs, then drizzle with the dressing and serve.

♦

POACHED FRESH BLACK-EYED PEAS
TAZE BÖRÜLCE HAŞLAMASI

Region:		Muğla, Aegean Region
Preparation time:		10 minutes
Cooking time:		20 minutes
Serves:		4

600 g	fresh black-eyed peas	1 lb 5 oz
¼ tsp	salt	¼ tsp
6	garlic cloves, crushed	6
60 ml	verjuice (see p.494)	¼ cup/2 fl oz
60 g	stale white breadcrumbs	1 cup/2¼ oz
100 g	walnuts, crushed	1 cup/3½ oz
60 ml	olive oil	¼ cup/2 fl oz
¼ tsp	salt	¼ tsp

💧 ♦ V X

A summer dish that, in the Mediterranean and Southeastern Anatolian regions, is made by frying fresh black-eyed peas, onion, garlic, bell peppers and tomatoes. This method is known as *loğlaz* in Southeastern Anatolia and *löbye* in the Mediterranean. Some recipes omit the stale bread and walnuts.

♦

Pour 1 litre (4¼ cups/34 fl oz) water into a large saucepan, add the black-eyed peas and salt and cook over medium heat, covered, for 20 minutes. Drain and set aside.

In a large bowl, mix the garlic, verjuice, breadcrumbs, walnuts, olive oil and salt for 2 minutes, until well combined. Add the black-eyed peas, mix well and serve.

STEAMED NETTLES
ISIRGAN BUĞULAMASI

Region:	Denizli, all regions
Preparation time:	5 minutes
Cooking time:	20 minutes
Serves:	4

600 g	fresh nettles, washed	2⅔ cups/ 1 lb 5 oz
60 ml	olive oil	¼ cup/2 fl oz
4	garlic cloves, crushed	4
½ tsp	salt	½ tsp
¼ tsp	black pepper	¼ tsp
200 g	*lor* (fresh curd cheese, see p.485, or ricotta)	1 cup/7oz

❀ V X

This spring and summer dish is believed to have healing properties. In place of the *lor*, you can add either yogurt or eggs.

♦

Pour 1 litre (4¼ cups/34 fl oz) water into a steamer or large saucepan with a steamer basket or heatproof colander on top (making sure it does not touch the water). Bring to the boil, add the nettles and steam, covered, for 15 minutes.

Heat the oil in a saucepan over medium heat, add the garlic and cook for 10 seconds. Transfer the steamed nettles to the pan, add the salt and black pepper and cook for 2 minutes, stirring continuously. Add the *lor*, and cook for a further 1 minute, stirring. Remove from the heat and serve.

♦

BORAGE WITH WALNUTS
CEVİZLİ HODAN

Region:	Bolu, Marmara and Black Sea Regions
Preparation time:	10 minutes
Cooking time:	20 minutes
Serves:	4

400 g	borage leaves, chopped	14 oz
6	garlic cloves	6
100 g	walnuts	1 cup/3½ oz
1 tbsp	dried rose petals, crushed	1 tbsp
½ tsp	salt	½ tsp
2 tbsp	olive oil	2 tbsp
2 tbsp	lemon juice	2 tbsp

💧 ❀ ♦ V X

In Turkey, wild borage heralds the spring as the snow starts to melt. It tastes like mushrooms and is loved in the Marmara and western Black Sea regions. Locally, it's known as *zılbıt, zıbıdık, ıspıt, tomara* and *galdirik.* The branches are often pickled, and the flowers used in *kaygana* and *maya* and mash. In fact, this recipe also works well with borage flowers. Other local variations include a fried version, as well as recipes using lamb confit, eggs and *pastırma* (cured beef, see p.497).

♦

In a large saucepan, bring 1.5 litres (6¼ cups/5 fl oz) water to the boil, add the chopped borage and cook for 20 minutes. Drain well.

Meanwhile, with a pestle and mortar, pound the garlic, walnuts, dried rose petals and salt for 5 minutes. Stir through the olive oil and lemon juice.

Combine the warm borage with the walnut sauce in a large bowl and mix well. Serve immediately.

SAUTÉED BROAD BEANS
İÇ BAKLA HAŞLAMASI

Region:		Manisa, all regions
Preparation time:		5 minutes
Cooking time:		30 minutes
Serves:		4

2 tbsp	olive oil	2 tbsp
1 (120 g)	medium onion, finely chopped	1 (¾ cup/4 oz)
2	fennel fronds, finely chopped	2
400 g	fresh broad (fava) beans, outer skins removed	2 cups/ 14 oz
1 tbsp	lemon juice	1 tbsp
½ tsp	salt	½ tsp

Also known as 'donkey's broad beans', this is a popular street food when in season. Cooking broad (fava) beans the right way requires skill: vendors poach the beans (in their shells) in lemon water and salt. Local broad bean eating contests are famous in the Aegean, Mediterranean and Southeastern Turkey – a rite of passage for local youth, who more often than not take the competition too far. Broad beans are also a popular medium for fortune tellers. Placing a broad bean under your pillow is the key to your wishes coming true!

◆

Heat the oil in a large saucepan over medium heat. Add the onion and fennel and cook for 10 minutes, stirring continuously. Add the broad (fava) beans, lemon juice and ½ teaspoon salt and sauté for 5 minutes. Cover and cook for a further 10 minutes. Serve immediately.

◆

SAUTÉED AUBERGINES
BAŞ KAVURMASI

Region:		Adana, Mediterranean Region
Preparation time:		10 minutes, plus 15 minutes soaking
Cooking time:		50 minutes
Serves:		4

4	small aubergines (eggplants), peeled, quartered lengthwise, but not cut through at the stem	4
60 ml	olive oil	¼ cup/2 fl oz
1 (120 g)	medium onion, sliced into crescents	1 (¾ cup/4 oz)
10	garlic cloves, quartered	10
2	green bell peppers, chopped	2
2	green chilli (chile) peppers, chopped	2
2 tsp	red bell pepper paste (see p.492)	2 tsp
1 tsp	dried chilli (red pepper) flakes	1 tsp
1 tsp	dried mint	1 tsp
1 tsp	salt	1 tsp
750 g	tomatoes, chopped	3¾ cups/ 1 lb 10 oz
2 tbsp	pomegranate molasses (see p.490)	2 tbsp

This dish is made with the small, long aubergines (eggplants) that are available in the region in August. Japanese or Italian aubergines, about 5 × 10 cm (2 × 5 inches), will therefore work best, if you can find them.

◆

Put the aubergines (eggplants) in a bowl, cover with 1 litre (4¼ cups/34 fl oz) salted water and let soak for 15 minutes. Drain and rinse, then pat dry with paper towels.

In a large saucepan, heat the olive oil over medium heat to 155°C/310°F. Add the aubergines and fry each side for 2 minutes, turning regularly, for a total of 8 minutes. Transfer to a plate.

In the same pan, fry the onion, garlic and peppers for 10 minutes, stirring continuously. Add the red bell pepper paste, dried chilli (red pepper) flakes, dried mint and salt and cook for 1 minute. Add the tomatoes and cook for 5 minutes, stirring continuously. Add the aubergines back to the mixture and mix gently until well combined. Drizzle in the pomegranate molasses. Reduce the heat and cook, covered, for 20 minutes.

Serve warm or cold.

SEA SAMPHIRE
DENİZ BÖRÜLCESİ

Region:		İzmir, Aegean Region
Preparation time:		10 minutes
Cooking time:		10 minutes
Serves:		4

600 g	marsh samphire	1 lb 5 oz
4	garlic cloves, crushed	4
60 ml	olive oil	¼ cup/2 fl oz
2 tbsp	lemon juice	2 tbsp

♦ ❧ ♦ V ⁘ Χ   p.101

This dish is made in the spring and summer. Also known as sea bean, sea pickle and glasswort, samphire is naturally salty, so this doesn't require any additional salt.

♦

Pour 1.5 litres (6¼ cups/50 fl oz) water into a saucepan and bring to the boil over medium heat. Add the samphire to the pan and boil for 10 minutes.

Drain and refresh the samphire under cold running water. Holding each piece of samphire by the stem, pull out and discard the hard centre of each stem and put the soft flesh into a bowl.

Combine the garlic, olive oil and lemon juice in a separate bowl and mix well. Dress the samphire and serve.

♦

VEGETARIAN STUFFED AUBERGINE
İMAMBAYILDI

Region:		İstanbul, all regions
Preparation time:		25 minutes, plus 15 minutes soaking
Cooking time:		1 hour or 1 hour 15 minutes, plus cooling time
Serves:		4

4 (each 6 × 20 cm)	aubergines (eggplants), stems attached, partially peeled in alternating strips lengthwise	4 (each 2¼ × 8 inch)
560 ml	olive oil, for frying	2½ cups/ 19 fl oz
500 g	onions, sliced	3⅓ cups/ 1 lb 2 oz
16	garlic cloves, finely sliced	16
4	banana peppers (mild sweet peppers), de-seeded and finely sliced	4
¼ tsp	black pepper	¼ tsp
2 tsp	sugar	2 tsp
¾ tsp	salt	¾ tsp
200 ml	fresh tomato juice, warmed	¾ cup/ 7 fl oz

♦ ❧ ♦ V

Another version of this dish substitutes courgettes (zucchini) for the aubergines (eggplants). You can finish the cooking here either in the oven or on the stove.

♦

Put the aubergines (eggplants) in a bowl, cover with 1 litre (4¼ cups/34 fl oz) salted water and let soak for 15 minutes. Drain and rinse, then pat dry with paper towels.

In a large saucepan, heat 500 ml (generous 2 cups/17 fl oz) of the olive oil over medium heat to 155°C/310°F. Poke 3 slots in each aubergine (eggplant) with a knife, then place the aubergines in the hot oil and fry for 5 minutes, turning every minute. Remove with a slotted spoon and drain in a colander. Let cool.

Heat the remaining 60 ml (¼ cup/2 fl oz) olive oil in a separate pan (ovenproof, if you intend to finish cooking in the oven). Add the onion, garlic, banana pepper, black pepper, sugar, and salt and cook for 30 minutes, stirring continuously. Remove from the heat, transfer the mixture to a large bowl, add the parsley and mix well.

If you intend to cook the stuffed aubergines in the oven, preheat to 160°C/325°F/Gas Mark 3.

Add the cooled aubergines back to the pan used for cooking the onions. Make a long lengthwise cut in each aubergine, without cutting all the way through. Stuff each aubergine equally with the onion stuffing mixture. Add the warm tomato juice and cook in the hot oven for 30 minutes. Alternatively, cook over low heat for 15 minutes.

Place on a serving platter and enjoy hot or cold.

FRIED AUBERGINE WITH GARLIC SAUCE
PATLICAN PAÇASI

Region:		İstanbul, Marmara
Preparation time:	15 minutes, plus 15 minutes soaking
Cooking time:		10 minutes
Serves:		4

4 (600 g)	small Japanese or Italian aubergines (eggplants), peeled	4 (1 lb 5 oz)
100 g	plain (all-purpose) flour	¾ cup/ 3½ oz
500 ml	olive oil, for frying	generous 2 cups/ 17 fl oz

For the sauce:		
60 ml	grape vinegar	¼ cup/2 fl oz
10	garlic cloves, crushed	10
8	flat-leaf parsley sprigs, finely sliced	8

🌢 V 🌢

Summer is not really summer without this dish.
◆
Put the aubergines (eggplants) in a bowl, cover with 1 litre (4¼ cups/34 fl oz) salted water and let soak for 15 minutes. Drain and rinse, then pat dry with paper towels. Cut widthwise into 1-cm (½-inch) slices, then coat the slices on both sides in the flour.

In a large saucepan, heat the olive oil over medium heat to 155°C/310°F. Fry the aubergine slices for 2 minutes on each side. Remove with a slotted spoon to a colander to drain.

To make the sauce:
Mix the grape vinegar, garlic and parsley in a bowl with ¼ teaspoon black pepper and ¾ teaspoon salt. Arrange the fried aubergine slices in a circle in a wide sauté pan. Drizzle the sauce over the top, then cook over low heat for 5 minutes.

Serve warm or cold.

◆

FRIED 'PİRÇİKLİ' CARROTS
PİRÇİKLİ KIZARTMASI

Region:		Kilis, Southeastern Anatolia
Preparation time:		10 minutes
Cooking time:	35 minutes, plus 5 minutes resting
Serves:		4

60 ml	olive oil	¼ cup/2 fl oz
8 (500 g)	small yellow carrots with stems, peeled, cut into quarters lengthwise	8 (1 lb 2 oz)
1 (120 g)	medium onion, finely diced	1 (¾ cup/4 oz)
6	garlic cloves, finely sliced	6
1 tsp	tomato paste (see p.492)	1 tsp
1 tsp	dried chilli (red pepper) flakes	1 tsp
½ tsp	ground coriander	½ tsp
2 tbsp	pomegranate molasses (see p.490)	2 tbsp
4	fresh coriander (cilantro) sprigs, finely sliced	4

🌢 🌿 V 🌢

The yellow carrots which are available in Southeastern Anatolia in winter are the main ingredient for this dish. *Pirçikli* is the local name for these carrots.
◆
Heat the oil in a large saucepan over medium heat, add the carrots and cook for 6 minutes, turning halfway through. Add the onion and garlic and cook for 5 minutes, mixing continuously. Add the tomato paste, dried chilli (red pepper) flakes and ground coriander with ¼ teaspoon black pepper and ½ teaspoon salt and cook for a further 2 minutes. Reduce the heat, add 200 ml (scant 1 cup/ 7 fl oz) water and cook, covered, for 15 minutes. Add the pomegranate molasses, turn off the heat and let rest for 5 minutes.

Sprinkle with coriander (cilantro) and serve.

FRIED LEEKS IN TARATOR SAUCE
TARATORLU PIRASA KIZARTMASI

Region:		Çanakkale, Marmara
Preparation time:		10 minutes
Cooking time:		25 minutes
Serves:		4

800 g	leeks, chopped into	8 cups/
	2.5-cm (1-inch) pieces	1 lb 12 oz
6	eggs	6
100 g	plain (all-purpose) flour	¾ cup/3½ oz
250 ml	olive oil	1 cup/8 fl oz

For the tarator sauce:

50 g	stale bread	2 oz
50 g	almonds	generous ⅓ cup/2 oz
5	garlic cloves	5
2 tbsp	lemon juice	2 tbsp
4	flat-leaf parsley sprigs	4
1	fresh basil sprig	1
⅛ tsp	white pepper	⅛ tsp

V

Roasted and fried vegetables are commonly served with a tarator sauce in the Marmara, Aegean and Mediterranean regions. In winter, tarator is served with leeks and fish, but it is also drizzled on pastries and meat dishes. Pine nuts, walnuts or hazelnuts may be used instead of almonds. Some recipes include yogurt, others tahini.

♦

In a large saucepan, bring 1 litre (4¼ cups/34 fl oz) water and ¼ teaspoon salt to the boil over a high heat. Add the leeks to the pan and boil for 15 minutes, then drain.

Whisk the eggs in a bowl and put the flour in a separate bowl next to it. Coat the leeks with egg, then with flour.

In a large saucepan, heat the olive oil over medium heat to 155°C/310°F. Fry the leeks for 2 minutes on each side. Remove with a slotted spoon to paper towels to drain.

To make the tarator sauce:
Soak the bread in water then squeeze out any excess moisture. Blitz all the sauce ingredients in a food processor. Season with ¼ teaspoon salt.

Pour the tarator sauce over the leeks and mix gently. Transfer to plates and serve warm or cold.

GRILLED VEGETABLES
SACA BASMA

Region:		Şanlıurfa, Southeastern Anatolia
Preparation time:		10 minutes
Cooking time:		25 minutes
Serves:		4

12	dried bell peppers	12
12	sundried tomatoes	12
12	dried aubergines (eggplants),	12
	sliced into 1-cm (½-inch) pieces	
1 (120 g)	medium onion,	1 (¾ cup/4 oz)
	cut into thin rings	
60 ml	olive oil	¼ cup/2 fl oz
6	garlic cloves, crushed	6
½ tsp	dried chilli (red pepper) flakes	½ tsp
1 tsp	dried oregano	1 tsp
	(or ground dried za'atar)	

2	Açık Ekmek (Lavash Bread,	2
	see p.394), halved	2
4	flat-leaf parsley sprigs, leaves only	4
2	fresh mint sprigs, leaves only	2

◊ V ◊

A *sac*, which gives its name to this dish, is a shallow, iron plate or sheet pan, traditionally used in Turkey for grilling. If a *sac* is not available, this dish can be made in a regular iron skillet or a wok. If you wish, this dish can be cooked without oil, just add a drizzle of olive oil before serving. You can buy dried aubergines (eggplants) and dried bell peppers at some Turkish and Middle Eastern stores.

♦

Bring a large saucepan with 1 litre (4¼ cups/34 fl oz) water to the boil, add the dried peppers and boil for 5 minutes. Use a slotted spoon to transfer the peppers to paper towels and pat dry. Meanwhile, to the same boiling water, add the sundried tomatoes and dried aubergines (eggplants) and boil for 10 minutes. Drain and pat dry with paper towels.

In a bowl, combine the cooked bell peppers, sundried tomatoes, aubergines and onion, olive oil, garlic, dried chilli (red pepper) flakes, oregano and ½ teaspoon salt.

Heat a wide sac (iron skillet or wok) until smoking. Arrange the vegetables on the cooking surface and grill for 1 minute, turn with a spatula and cook for 1 minute on the other side. Repeat 3 times, cooking for 8 minutes in total.

Fill the *açık ekmek* with the grilled vegetables and serve as wraps, sprinkled with fresh parsley and mint.

VEGETABLES, EGGS & PULSES

BEANS AND BULGUR WHEAT
FASULYE DİBLE

Region:		Giresun, Black Sea Region
Preparation time:		10 minutes
Cooking time:		50 minutes, plus 10 minutes resting
Serves:		4

60 ml	olive oil	¼ cup/2 fl oz
1 (120 g)	medium onion, finely sliced	1 (¾ cup/4 oz)
1½ tbsp	tomato paste (see p.492)	1½ tbsp
500 g	fresh green beans, strings removed, halved lengthwise, then finely sliced	3⅓ cups/ 1 lb 2 oz
¾ tsp	salt	¾ tsp
50 g	coarse bulgur wheat	¼ cup/2 oz

 V ◆

Dible is the local name given to the technique used to make this dish, which is native to Ordu and Giresun. The crucial factors here are the addition of the grain into the well in middle of the beans and the minimal amount of water used. No stirring is necessary. Many fruit and vegetables are prepared this way. The bulgur wheat can be substituted with medium-grain rice (such as Baldo) or corn.

◆

Heat the oil in a large saucepan over medium heat, add the onion and sauté for 3 minutes. Add the tomato paste and cook for 2 minutes. Add the beans and sauté for 10 minutes, stirring continuously. Add the salt and sauté for 5 minutes.

Reduce the heat and make a 4-cm (1½-inch) well in the middle of the beans then add the bulgur. Pour in 200 ml (scant 1 cup/7 fl oz) water and cook, covered, for 30 minutes. Remove from the heat and let rest for 10 minutes.

Mix until combined and serve immediately.

◆

FRESH BROAD BEANS WITH EGGS
YUMURTALI BAKLA KAVURMASI

Region:	Nizip, Gaziantep, Southeastern Anatolia
Preparation time:	20 minutes
Cooking time:	40 minutes
Serves:	4

200 ml	olive oil	¾ cup/7 fl oz
200 g	onions, peeled, sliced into ¼-cm (⅛-inch) pieces	1⅓ cup/7 oz
750 g	fresh broad (fava) beans, in their pods, ends trimmed, sliced into ¼-cm (⅛-inch) pieces	4 cups/ 1 lb 10 oz
5	spring onions (scallions), finely chopped	5
5	fresh garlic, finely chopped	5
¾ tsp	chilli (chile) flakes	¾ tsp
1 tsp	salt	1 tsp
¼ tsp	black pepper	¼ tsp
5	eggs	5
5	mint sprigs, finely chopped	5

◆ ✿ V ◆

This was my mother's signature dish. I really felt the loss after she was gone when I realized no one else (including me) was able to make this dish quite as well as she did.

◆

Heat the oil in a saucepan over medium heat, add the onions and sauté for 2 minutes, mixing with a wooden spoon. Add the broad (fava) beans and fry for a further 3 minutes. Reduce the heat, cover with paper and cook for 20 minutes over low heat. Remove the paper, add the spring onions (scallions) and garlic. Add the chilli (chile) flakes, salt and black pepper and cook for 5 minutes, stirring gently. Cover and cook for a further 5 minutes over low heat.

Crack the eggs into a glass bowl and mix with a fork. Add the fresh mint and cook, stirring for 10 seconds. Pour the eggs over the other ingredients. Cover and cook for 1 minute. Cook uncovered for a further 3 minutes, stirring gently.

Serve with *Yufka Ekmeği* (Thin Flatbread, see p.378), more spring onions and a glass of *Ayran* (Salted Yogurt Drink, see p.452). This dish is not eaten with a fork but wrapped into small pieces of the bread.

DICED OMELETTE WITH YOGURT SAUCE
AYVANET

Region:		Bitlis, Eastern Anatolia
Preparation time:		5 minutes
Cooking time:		10 minutes
Serves:		4

8	eggs	8
2 tbsp	plain (all-purpose) flour	2 tbsp
¼ tsp	salt	¼ tsp
2 tbsp	olive oil	2 tbsp

For the yogurt sauce:

200 g	Greek yogurt	1 cup/7 oz
4	garlic cloves, crushed	4
2	basil sprigs, finely sliced	2
¼ tsp	salt	¼ tsp

For the dressing:

2 tbsp	olive oil	2 tbsp
1	garlic clove, crushed	1
½ tsp	dried chilli (red pepper) flakes	½ tsp

V X

This dish is traditionally made at the beginning of winter to express gratitude in prayer. The ritual is completed when a portion of the dish is placed at the graves of the ancestors. People believe that the soul of the deceased visits the family home on the days this dish is prepared, and that their wishes will be granted and happy times will follow. This ritual is repeated several times throughout the year.

♦

In a large bowl, whisk the eggs, flour and salt for 2 minutes, until well combined.

Heat a frying pan (skillet) over medium heat and add 1 tablespoon of the olive oil. Pour the egg mixture into the pan, spreading to coat the bottom. Cook for 2 minutes on one side, then transfer the omelette to a plate. Heat the remaining olive oil in the pan and add the omelette back to the pan to cook for 2 minutes on the other side.

Transfer the cooked omelette to a chopping board and cut into 1-cm (½-inch) squares.

To make the sauce:
In a separate bowl, mix the yogurt, garlic, basil and salt.

To make the dressing:
Heat the oil in a saucepan over medium heat. Add the garlic and dried chilli (red pepper) flakes. Cook for 10 seconds.

Pour the yogurt sauce over the omelette squares, then pour the dressing over the top and serve immediately.

SALTED YOGURT WITH ONIONS
BEZİRGAN KEBABI (TUZLU YOĞURT KAVURMASI)

Region:		Hatay, Mediterranean Region
Preparation time:		10 minutes
Cooking time:		20 minutes
Serves:		4

60 ml	olive oil	¼ cup/2 fl oz
3 (360 g)	medium onions, sliced into crescents	3 (2⅜ cups/ 12 oz)
1 tsp	dried chilli (red pepper) flakes	1 tsp
300 g	salted Greek yogurt (goat's milk or strained goat's milk yogurt)	1½ cups/ 11 oz
2	fresh basil sprigs, chopped	2

❀ V X

Making yogurt and cheese from goat's milk is highly popular in the Mediterranean spring. The yogurt is boiled in huge copper cauldrons with salt and stored in glass jars for the winter. It goes well with bread in the morning and as a snack at any time of day. The name *Bezirgân Kebabı* is a local name implying riches.

♦

Heat the oil in a large saucepan over medium heat, add the onions and cook for 15 minutes, mixing occasionally. Add the dried chilli (red pepper) flakes and cook for 2 minutes. Add the salted yogurt and cook for a further 2 minutes, mixing well. Serve immediately, sprinkled with basil.

VEGETABLES, EGGS & PULSES

STUFFED ARTICHOKES IN OLIVE OIL
ZEYTİNYAĞLI ENGİNAR

Region:		Yalova, all regions
Preparation time:		10 minutes
Cooking time:		45 minutes, plus 10 minutes resting
Serves:		4

60 ml	olive oil	¼ cup/2 fl oz
2 (240 g)	medium onions, diced	2 (1⅝ cups/ 8½ oz)
6	garlic cloves, quartered	6
100 g	carrots, finely diced	⅔ cup/3½ oz
150 g	fresh broad (fava) beans, shelled	¾ cup/5 oz
¾ tsp	salt	¾ tsp
4	fresh artichoke hearts, trimmed 10-cm (4-inches) wide	4
2 tbsp	lemon juice	2 tbsp
60 g	fresh peas, shelled	⅓ cup/2¼ oz
2 tsp	sugar	2 tsp
4	dill sprigs	4

♦ ❀ **V** ♦   p.107 📷

This is a spring dish. Artichokes are preserved in the summer for winter consumption. Keep the fresh artichoke hearts in acidulated water until you are ready to cook them.
♦
Heat the oil in a large saucepan over medium heat, add the onion and sauté for 5 minutes. Add the garlic, carrot, broad (fava) beans, and ½ teaspoon of the salt and fry for 5 minutes. Add the artichoke hearts to the pan and cook for a further 5 minutes, stirring continuously. Remove from the heat. Add the lemon juice and mix.

Remove the artichoke hearts from the pan and place them in a separate large saucepan.

Stir the peas into the mixture left in the pan, then use the mixture to fill the artichoke hearts. Add 500 ml (generous 2 cups/17 fl oz) of water, ¼ teaspoon of salt and the sugar to the pan with the artichokes, then cover with a layer of parchment paper and put the lid on the pan. Cook over low heat for 30 minutes. Remove from the heat and let rest, covered, for 10 minutes.

Garnish with dill and serve.

♦

CELERIAC AND CARROT IN ORANGE
ZEYTİNYAĞLI KEREVİZ

Region:		İzmir, all regions
Preparation time:		15 minutes
Cooking time:		30 minutes, plus 10 minutes resting
Serves:		4

60 ml	olive oil	¼ cup/2 fl oz
1 (120 g)	medium onion, cut into 1-cm (½-inch) crescents	1 (¾ cup/ 4 oz)
150 g	carrot, chopped into 2-cm (¾-inch) crescents	1 cup/ 5 oz
600 g	celeriac (celery root) peeled, chopped into 2-cm (¾-inch) wedges	4 cups/ 1 lb 5 oz
2 tbsp	lemon juice	2 tbsp
100 ml	orange juice	scant ½ cup/ 3½ fl oz
⅛ tsp	grated orange zest	⅛ tsp
1 tsp	sugar	1 tsp
½ tsp	salt	½ tsp

♦ ❀ **V** ♦

This aromatic celeriac (celery root) dish is enjoyed in the Aegean and Marmara regions in the autumn and winter. Home cooks love preparing it for their guests, and it is served more as a side than a main course. Some recipes do not add any liquids but prefer to cook the celeriac in its own juices.
♦
Heat the oil in a large saucepan over medium heat, add the onion and carrot and sauté for 5 minutes. Add the celeriac (celery root) and cook for 5 minutes.

Reduce the heat and add the lemon juice, orange juice, orange zest, sugar and salt to the pan along with 200 ml (scant 1 cup/7 fl oz) water. Cook, covered, for 20 minutes. Remove from the heat and let rest for 10 minutes. Serve immediately.

SPICY SQUASH
KABAK ÇİNTMESİ

Region:	Diyarbakır, Southeastern Anatolia
Preparation time:	15 minutes
Cooking time:	40 minutes, plus 10 minutes resting
Serves:	4

60 ml	olive oil	¼ cup/2 fl oz
1 (120 g)	medium onion, thinly sliced	1 (¾ cup/4 oz)
4	garlic cloves, thinly sliced	4
2	fresh chillies (chiles), finely sliced	2
3 (500 g)	summer squash, thinly sliced	3 (1 lb 2 oz)
¾ tsp	salt	¾ tsp
½ tsp	dried chilli (red pepper) flakes	½ tsp
1 tsp	dried mint	1 tsp
300 g	tomatoes, diced	1½ cups/11 oz
6	fresh coriander (cilantro) sprigs, finely sliced	6
6	flat-leaf parsley sprigs, finely sliced	6

This is a summer dish enjoyed with flatbreads as a delicious vegetarian meal.

◆

Heat the oil in a large saucepan over medium heat, add the onion, garlic and chillies (chiles) and cook for 5 minutes, mixing continuously. Add the squash, salt, dried chilli (red pepper) flakes and dried mint, and cook for 10 minutes, mixing continuously. Add the tomatoes and cook for 5 minutes, mixing occasionally. Reduce the heat and cook, covered, for 20 minutes. Remove from the heat and let rest for 10 minutes.

Add the coriander (cilantro) and parsley to the pan, stir the herbs in gently and serve.

SOUR OKRA
BAMYA

Region:	Konya, all regions
Preparation time:	10 minutes
Cooking time:	45 minutes, plus 10 minutes resting
Serves:	4

2 tbsp	olive oil	2 tbsp
1 (120 g)	medium onion, finely sliced	1 (¾ cup/4 oz)
10	garlic cloves, quartered	10
500 g	fresh okra, stems trimmed	5 cups/1 lb 2 oz
1 tsp	dried chilli (red pepper) flakes	1 tsp
1 tsp	salt	1 tsp
¼ tsp	black pepper	¼ tsp
2 tbsp	lemon juice	2 tbsp
1 kg	tomatoes	5 cups/2 lb 4 oz
1	basil sprig, leaves only	1

Okra is a popular ingredient for casseroles and soups, and is also fried and roasted. This recipe shows slight variations among regions. The gelatinous secretions of okra is believed to have healing properties, the dish should never be too slimy. A popular summer vegetable, okra is dried during the warmer months for winter use.

◆

Heat the oil in a large saucepan over medium heat, add the onion and garlic and cook for 5 minutes. Add the okra, dried chilli (red pepper) flakes, salt and black pepper and cook for 3 minutes, mixing continuously. Add the lemon juice and tomatoes and cook for 5 minutes, mixing continuously. Reduce the heat and cook, covered, for 30 minutes. Remove from the heat and let rest for 10 minutes.

Transfer to plates, sprinkle with fresh basil and serve.

FRIED TOMATOES
DOMATES TAVASI

Region:	Gaziantep, Southeastern Anatolia
Preparation time:	15 minutes, plus 10 minutes soaking
Cooking time:	50 minutes
Serves:	4

150 g	aubergine (eggplant), peeled and finely diced	⅝ cups/ 5 oz
60 ml	olive oil	¼ cup/2 fl oz
1 (120 g)	medium onion, finely diced	1 (¾ cup/4 oz)
10	garlic cloves, finely sliced	10
3	green chillies (chiles), finely diced	3
1 tsp	tomato paste (see p.492)	1 tsp
1 tsp	red bell pepper paste (see p.492)	1 tsp
1 tsp	dried chilli (red pepper) flakes	1 tsp
1.5 kg	tomatoes, finely diced	7½ cups/ 3 lb 5 oz
40 g	coarse bulgur wheat	¼ cup/1½ oz
⅛ tsp	black pepper	⅛ tsp
¾ tsp	salt	¾ tsp
6	flat-leaf parsley sprigs, finely sliced	6
5	fresh purple basil sprigs, finely sliced	5

This dish is made out of ripe tomatoes in the summer months. Some recipes omit the grains, some others add meat.

◆

Soak the aubergine (eggplant) in 1 litre (4¼ cups/34 fl oz) of salted water for 10 minutes, then drain, rinse and set aside.

Heat the oil in a large saucepan over medium heat, add the onion, garlic and green chillies (chiles) and cook for 5 minutes. Add the tomato paste, red bell pepper paste and dried chilli (red pepper) flakes and cook for 5 minutes. Add the aubergine and cook for 5 minutes, mixing continuously. Reduce the heat, add the tomatoes, bulgur wheat, black pepper and salt and cook for 35 minutes. Remove from the heat, add the parsley and basil, mix gently and serve.

◦ V ◦

◆

SOUR LEEKS
EKŞİLİ PIRASA

Region:	Afyon, all regions
Preparation time:	10 minutes
Cooking time:	35 minutes
Serves:	4

60 ml	olive oil	¼ cup/2 fl oz
600 g	leeks, sliced	6 cups/1 lb 5 oz
150 g	carrot, finely diced	1 cup/5 oz
1½ tbsp	tomato paste (see p.492)	1½ tbsp
1 tsp	red bell pepper paste (see p.492)	1 tsp
1 tsp	sugar	1 tsp
½ tsp	salt	½ tsp
40 g	medium-grain rice	¼ cup/1½ oz
2 tbsp	lemon juice	2 tbsp
500 ml	hot water	generous 2 cups/17 fl oz

This winter dish is made all around the country, but is especially popular in the Aegean and Marmara regions. This is a specialty of home cooks. Some recipes use grape vinegar instead of lemon juice as a souring agent.

◆

Heat the oil in a large saucepan over medium heat, add the leeks, carrots, tomato paste, red bell pepper paste, sugar and salt and cook for 5 minutes, mixing gently. Reduce the heat, add the rice, lemon juice and hot water and cook, covered, for 30 minutes. Serve immediately.

◦ ✿ V ◦

GREEN BEANS IN OLIVE OIL
ZEYTİNYAĞLI TAZE FASULYE

Region:	Ankara, all regions
Preparation time:	15 minutes
Cooking time:	45 minutes, plus 10 minutes resting
Serves:	4

This dish is made and eaten in the summer months. Beans are dried in summer for winter use.

◆

Heat the oil in a large saucepan over medium heat, add the onion, garlic, and bell pepper and cook for 5 minutes. Add the beans and cook for 5 minutes. Add the tomatoes and salt and cook, stirring, for 5 minutes. Cover and cook for a further 30 minutes. Remove from the heat and let rest for 10 minutes before serving.

60 ml	olive oil	¼ cup/2 fl oz
2 (240 g)	medium onions, finely sliced	2 (1⅝ cups/ 8½ oz)
4	garlic cloves, finely sliced	4
1	green bell pepper, de-seeded and finely sliced	1
600 g	green beans, strings removed, cut lengthwise, then cut into 3 pieces	4 cups/ 1 lb 5 oz
1 kg	tomatoes, finely diced	5 cups/ 2 lb 4 oz
½ tsp	salt	½ tsp

💧 🌿 **V** ◆   p.111 📷

◆

BANANA PEPPERS IN MILK
SÜTLÜ BİBER YEMEĞİ

Region:	Tekirdağ, Marmara Region
Preparation time:	5 minutes
Cooking time:	40 minutes, plus 10 minutes resting
Serves:	4

This is a summer dish.

◆

Heat the oil in a large saucepan over medium heat, add the onion and cook for 5 minutes. Add the banana peppers and cook for 15 minutes, stirring continuously. Add the salt and black pepper and cook for 1 minute, then add the boiling milk. Cook, uncovered, for 15 minutes, stirring occasionally. Remove from the heat and let rest for 10 minutes before serving.

2 tbsp	olive oil	2 tbsp
1 (120 g)	medium onion, finely sliced	1 (¾ cup/4 oz)
8	banana peppers (mild sweet peppers), finely diced	8
¾ tsp	salt	¾ tsp
¼ tsp	black pepper	¼ tsp
1 litre	boiling milk	4¼ cups/34 fl oz

🌿 **V**

MAYA (GREEN TOMATOES)
MAYA (YEŞİL DOMATES YEMEĞİ)

Region:		Bartın, all regions
Preparation time:		15 minutes
Cooking time:		45 minutes
Serves:		4

60 ml	olive oil	¼ cup/2 fl oz
1 (120 g)	medium onion, finely sliced	1 (¾ cup/4 oz)
4	garlic cloves, finely sliced	4
1	hot fresh chilli (chile), finely sliced	1
40 g	coarse bulgur wheat	¼ cup/1½ oz
600 g	green tomatoes, finely diced	3 cups/1 lb 5 oz
100 g	red tomato, grated	½ cup/3½ oz
1 tsp	dried mint	1 tsp
¾ tsp	salt	¾ tsp

💧 V ◆

This dish is made in the autumn. The winter version uses pickled tomatoes when fresh are not available.

◆

Heat the oil in a large saucepan over medium heat, add the onion, garlic and chilli (chile) and cook for 5 minutes. Add the coarse bulgur wheat, green and red tomatoes, dried mint and salt and cook for 10 minutes, mixing continuously. Reduce the heat and cook, covered, for 30 minutes. Serve immediately.

◆

SOUR PURSLANE
PÜRPÜRÜM EKŞİSİ

Region:		Elazığ, all regions
Preparation time:		15 minutes
Cooking time:		1 hour
Serves:		4

80 g	dried black-eyed peas	½ cup/3 oz
2 tbsp	olive oil	2 tbsp
1 (120 g)	medium onion, finely sliced	1 (¾ cup/4 oz)
6	garlic cloves, finely sliced	6
1	red chilli (chile), finely sliced	1
1½ tbsp	tomato paste (see p.492)	1½ tbsp
1 tsp	dried chilli (red pepper) flakes	1 tsp
300 g	tomatoes, finely sliced	11 oz
¼ tsp	black pepper	¼ tsp
½ tsp	salt	½ tsp
2 tbsp	lemon juice	2 tbsp
600 g	fresh wild purslane, chopped	1 lb 5 oz
2 tsp	dried mint	2 tsp

💧 🌿 V ◆

The wild variety of purslane, which grows everywhere in the summer, is most flavoursome. Purslane salad with yogurt is loved all over the country as well purslane soups and wraps. People believe purslane strengthens the bones. When the wild version is in abundance, storks are expected to deliver babies for those yearning couples. The Turkish idiom 'seeing the stork in the air' means you will be travelling a lot. This dish is a local favourite in Southeastern Anatolia and the Mediterranean. It is enjoyed hot or cold at home. The icy and oil-free version is very popular in the heat.

◆

In a large saucepan, bring 1 litre (4¼ cups/34 fl oz) water to the boil, add the black-eyed peas and boil for 20 minutes, then drain and set aside.

Heat the oil in a large saucepan over medium heat, add the onion, garlic and red chilli (chile) and cook for 5 minutes. Add the tomato paste and dried chilli (red pepper) flakes and cook for 2 minutes. Add the tomatoes, black-eyed peas, black pepper and salt and cook for 10 minutes, mixing occasionally. Reduce the heat, stir in the lemon juice, purslane and dried mint, then add 500 ml (generous 2 cups/17 fl oz) water and cook, covered, for 10 minutes. Serve immediately.

FRIED SPRING ONIONS
SOĞAN TAVASI

Region:	Karaman, Central Anatolia
Preparation time:	10 minutes
Cooking time:	25 minutes, plus 10 minutes resting
Serves:	4

2 tbsp	olive oil	2 tbsp
600 g	spring onions (scallions), trimmed	1 lb 5 oz
60 g	almonds, blanched	½ cup/2¼ oz
50 g	dried apricots, quartered	½ cup/2 oz
2 tbsp	grape vinegar	2 tbsp
¼ tsp	black pepper	¼ tsp
½ tsp	salt	½ tsp
200 ml	hot water	scant 1 cup/7 fl oz

This winter dish is believed to have healing properties. Locals like burying the outer skin of the spring onions hoping that their wishes will come true.

◆

Heat the oil in a large saucepan over medium heat, add the spring onions (scallions) and the almonds and cook for 10 minutes. Reduce the heat, add the apricots, grape vinegar, black pepper, salt and hot water, and cook, covered, for 15 minutes. Let rest for 10 minutes, then serve.

AUBERGINE PATTIES
PATLICANLI KÖFTE

Region:	Malatya, Eastern Anatolia
Preparation time:	35 minutes, plus 10 minutes resting
Cooking time:	40 minutes
Serves:	4

2 tbsp	olive oil	2 tbsp
1 (120 g)	medium onion, finely sliced	1 (¾ cup/4 oz)
1 tbsp	tomato paste (see p.492)	1 tbsp
1 tsp	dried chilli (red pepper) flakes	1 tsp
200 g	aubergine (eggplant), peeled, finely diced	¾ cup/ 7 oz
1 tbsp	dried basil	1 tbsp
60 ml	verjuice (see p.494)	¼ cup/2 fl oz
½ tsp	salt	½ tsp

For the patties:		
150 g	fine bulgur wheat	⅔ cup/5 oz
¼ tsp	salt	¼ tsp
1 tbsp	plain (all-purpose) flour	1 tbsp
2 tsp	dried basil	2 tsp

This is a popular dish, served warm or cold to take the edge off the summer heat.

◆

To make the patties:
Mix the bulgur wheat, salt and 2 tablespoons of water in a large bowl or tray and let rest for 10 minutes. Add the flour and dried basil and knead for 20 minutes, wetting your hands regularly. Roll the mixture into 1-cm (½-inch) balls. Transfer the balls to a tray and set aside.

Heat the oil in a large saucepan over medium heat, addthe onions and cook for 3 minutes. Add the tomato paste and dried chilli (red pepper) flakes and cook for 2 minutes. Add the aubergine (eggplant) and cook, stirring, for 5 minutes. Add the dried basil, verjuice, salt and 1.5 litres (6¼ cups/50 fl oz) water and cook, covered, for 20 minutes. Add the patties and cook, uncovered, for 10 minutes.

Serve immediately.

VEGETABLES, EGGS & PULSES

COURGETTE FRITTERS
MÜCVER

Region:	Sinop, all regions
Preparation time:	15 minutes
Cooking time:	25 minutes
Serves:	4

500 g	courgettes (zucchini)	3⅓ cup/1 lb 2 oz
1 (120 g)	medium onion,	1 (¾ cup/4 oz)
4	spring onions (scallions)	4
1	fresh garlic	1
½ bunch	flat-leaf parsley	½ bunch
½ bunch	dill	½ bunch
1 tsp	dried mint	1 tsp
5	eggs	5
50 g	plain (all-purpose) flour	⅓ cup/2 oz
250 ml	olive oil, for frying	1 cup/8 fl oz

For the sauce:

400 g	yogurt	2 cups/14 oz
4	garlic cloves, crushed	4
1	dill sprig, leaves picked	1

V   p.115

A summer dish, traditionally made after making stuffed courgettes (zucchini), so that the leftover courgette flesh does not go to waste. Some versions add 50 g/2 oz feta cheese to the recipe below.

◆

Peel the courgettes (zucchini) and grate into a bowl. Finely slice the onion, spring onions (scallions), garlic, parsley and dill. Add to the courgette flesh. Add the dried mint, then season with ¼ teaspoon black pepper and ½ teaspoon salt. Knead for 3 minutes, until well incorporated.

In a separate bowl, whisk the eggs and flour. Add the whisked egg mixture to the other ingredients and knead for a further 2 minutes to combine.

In a large saucepan, heat the olive oil over medium heat to 155°C/310°F. Place a ¼ cup of the fritter mixture into the hot oil and fry for 2 minutes on each side. Use a slotted spoon to remove to paper towels while you prepare the rest, until all the mixture is used up.

To make the sauce:
Mix the yogurt and garlic in a separate bowl, then season with ¼ teaspoon salt and garnish with dill. Arrange the fritters on a platter and serve with the yogurt sauce.

◆

HERB AND CHEESE FRITTERS
SÖCCE

Region:	Kilis, Southeastern Anatolia
Preparation time:	15 minutes
Cooking time:	25 minutes
Serves:	4

4	spring onions (scallions)	4
4	fresh garlic	4
½ bunch	flat-leaf parsley	½ bunch
½ bunch	fresh mint	½ bunch
2	fresh basil sprigs	2
1 tsp	dried chilli (red pepper) flakes	1 tsp
¼ tsp	ground cumin	¼ tsp
½ tsp	ground coriander	½ tsp
¼ tsp	black pepper	¼ tsp
80 g	cheese (preferably sheep's milk, unsalted)	scant 1 cup/ 3 oz
5	eggs	5
50 g	plain (all-purpose) flour	⅓ cup/2 oz
250 ml	olive oil, for frying	1 cup/8 fl oz

V

This dish is traditionally made at the very beginning of spring when the fresh garlic first appears. Vegetables are added to the herbs depending on the season. There is a version with meat, usually lamb but also occasionally chicken or fish.

◆

Finely slice the spring onions (scallions), fresh garlic, parsley, mint and basil, then combine in a large bowl with the dried chilli (red pepper) flakes, ground cumin, ground coriander and black pepper. Grate the cheese into the bowl and then season with ½ teaspoon salt. Knead for 5 minutes, until well combined. In a separate bowl, whisk the eggs and the flour. Add to the cheese mixture, and knead to combine.

In a large saucepan, heat the olive oil over medium heat to 155°C/310°F. Place a ¼ cup of the fritter mixture into the hot oil and fry for 2 minutes on each side. Use a slotted spoon to remove to paper towels while you prepare the rest, until all the mixture is used up.

Serve immediately.

VEGETABLES, EGGS & PULSES

SCRAMBLED EGGS WITH VEGETABLES
MENEMEN

Region:		İzmir, all regions
Preparation time:		15 minutes
Cooking time:		30 minutes
Serves:		4

60 ml	olive oil	¼ cup/2 fl oz
1 (120 g)	medium onion, finely sliced	1 (¾ cup/4 oz)
4	garlic cloves, finely sliced	4
4	banana peppers (mild sweet peppers), finely sliced	4
2 tsp	red bell pepper paste (see p.492)	2 tsp
1 tsp	dried chilli (red pepper) flakes	1 tsp
½ tsp	black pepper	½ tsp
½ tsp	salt	½ tsp
600 g	tomatoes, finely sliced	3 cups/1 lb 5 oz
4	eggs	4
10	flat-leaf parsley sprigs, finely sliced	10

◐ ❧ V   p.117 📷

In some regions, this dish is made only with tomatoes and peppers, omitting the onions and garlic. Some versions use butter. Famous as a bachelor or student favourite, it is eaten at all meals as a main or a side dish.

◆

Heat the oil in a large saucepan over medium heat, add the onions and garlic and cook for 5 minutes. Add the banana peppers and cook for 2 minutes. Add the red bell pepper paste, dried chilli (red pepper) flakes, ¼ teaspoon of the black pepper and all the salt and cook for 2 minutes. Add the tomatoes and cook for a further 15 minutes. Crack the eggs on top of the mixture and let cook for 1 minute without mixing. Start mixing the eggs in, cooking for a further 2 minutes, then remove from the heat.

Sprinkle the parsley on top and mix through only once, gently. Sprinkle with the remaining ¼ teaspoon of black pepper and serve.

ABBOT'S BEANS
VARTABED

Region:		Adana, Mediterranean Region
Preparation time:		10 minutes, plus overnight soaking
Cooking time:		1½ hours for beans, plus 5 minutes
Serves:		4

120 g	dried cannellini beans, soaked overnight	⅔ cup/4 oz
½ tsp	salt	½ tsp
60 ml	tahini (sesame seed paste)	¼ cup/2 fl oz
90 ml	lemon juice	6 tbsp/3 fl oz
6	garlic cloves, crushed	6
2 tbsp	olive oil	2 tbsp
1 tsp	dried chilli (red pepper) flakes	1 tsp
6	flat-leaf parsley sprigs, leaves only	6
¼ tsp	ground cumin	¼ tsp

◐ ❧ V ◆

Also known as 'the priest's dish', *vartabed* means 'priest' in Armenian. Another version of this dish serves the beans drizzled with tahini on toast.

◆

Drain the soaked beans, then cook in a large saucepan of simmering water until soft, about 1½ hours. Drain and put the cooked beans on a serving plate and season with salt.

In a small bowl, mix the tahini, lemon juice and garlic with 60 ml (¼ cup/2 fl oz) water. Drizzle over the beans.

Heat the oil in a small saucepan over medium heat, add the dried chilli (red pepper) flakes and cook for 10 seconds. Drizzle over the beans, then sprinkle with the parsley and cumin and serve.

BORLOTTI BEAN PILAKI
KIRMIZI LOBYE (BARBUNYA PİLAKİ)

Region:		Artvin, all regions
Preparation time:		20 minutes, plus overnight soaking
Cooking time:	1 hour 40 minutes, plus 10 minutes resting
Serves:		4

160 g	borlotti (cranberry) beans, soaked overnight	1 cup/5½ oz
60 ml	olive oil	¼ cup/2 fl oz
2 (240 g)	medium onion, finely sliced	2 (1⅝ cups/ 8½ oz)
8	garlic cloves, quartered	8
200 g	carrot, diced into 1-cm (½-inch) cubes	1⅓ cups/7 oz
1½ tsp	tomato paste (see p.492)	1½ tsp
4	dried chillies (chiles), crushed	4
½ tsp	dried chilli (red pepper) flakes	½ tsp
150 g	potatoes, diced into 1-cm (½-inch) cubes	⅔ cup/5 oz
1 tbsp	dried basil	1 tbsp
½ tsp	salt	½ tsp
2 tbsp	lemon juice	2 tbsp
¼ tsp	black pepper	¼ tsp
2 tbsp	honey	2 tbsp
½ bunch	flat-leaf parsley,	½ bunch

💧 🌿 **V**

p.119 📷

This dish is eaten warm in the winter months and cold in the summer and is an integral part of *meyhane* menus. You could substitute the borlotti (cranberry) beans with other pulses for this dish.

♦

Drain the soaked beans, then cook in a large saucepan of simmering water until soft, about 1 hour. Drain.

Heat the oil in a large saucepan over medium heat, add the onion, garlic and carrot and cook for 10 minutes. Add the tomato paste, dried chilli (chile) and dried chilli (red pepper) flakes and cook for 1 minute. Add the borlotti (cranberry) beans, potato, dried basil and salt and cook for 3 minutes.

Reduce the heat, add 500 ml (generous 2 cups/17 fl oz) hot water and lemon juice and cook, covered, for 20 minutes.

Remove from the heat, add black pepper and honey. Finely slice the parsley and mix gently into the beans. Let rest for 10 minutes, then serve.

♦

BAKED CELERIAC
FIRINDA KEREVİZ

Region:		Edirne, Marmara
Preparation time:		15 minutes
Cooking time:		40 minutes
Serves:		4

400 g	celeriac (celery root)	2½ cups/14 oz
100 g	carrot	⅔ cup/3½ oz
1 (120 g)	medium onion	1 (¾ cup/4 oz)
10	garlic cloves	10
100 ml	orange juice	scant ½ cup/ 3½ fl oz
2 tbsp	orange zest	2 tbsp
2 tbsp	lemon juice	2 tbsp
¼ tsp	black pepper	¼ tsp
½ tsp	salt	½ tsp
60 ml	olive oil	¼ cup/2 fl oz
½ bunch	dill, finely sliced	½ bunch

💧 🌿 **V** ♦

This dish is a local favourite in Edirne, Marmara and the Aegean regions during the winter months. Celeriac (celery root) is believed to be one of those cure-all root vegetables, enjoyed stuffed and roasted and served with yogurt when in season.

♦

Preheat oven to 180°C/350°F/Gas Mark 4.

Peel and chop the celeriac (celery root) and carrot into 2-cm (¾-inch) wedges, then chop the onion into thin wedges. Combine all the ingredients apart from the dill in a large roasting pan and toss well. Bake in the hot oven for 40 minutes, stirring every 10 minutes. Remove from the oven and mix in the dill before serving.

FIG AND PISTACHIO CASSEROLE
ÇATLAK (HAM ERKEK İNCİR) KAVURMASI

Region:	Gaziantep, Southeastern Anatolia	
Preparation time:	15 minutes	
Cooking time:	35 minutes	
Serves:	4	

60 ml	olive oil	¼ cup/2 fl oz
1 (120 g)	medium onion	1 (¾ cup/4 oz)
1 tbsp	tomato paste (see p.492)	1 tbsp
1 tsp	dried chilli (red pepper) flakes	1 tsp
300 g	small unripe figs	2 cups/1 oz
80 g	pistachio kernels	¼ cup/3 oz
6	spring onions (scallions)	6
4	fresh garlic	4
2 tbsp	pomegranate molasses (see p.490)	2 tbsp
6	flat-leaf parsley sprigs, finely sliced	6

The male fig (the caprifig) has many local onomatopoeic names, such as *çatlak*, *patlak* and *tum*, referring to how it crunches when eaten. This dish is made from figs picked in the spring and is believed to increase fertility.

◆

Heat the oil in a large saucepan over medium heat. Finely slice the onion, add to the pan and cook for 5 minutes. Add the tomato paste and dried chilli (red pepper) flakes and cook for 2 minutes. Slice the figs in half and add to the pan with the pistachios and cook for 5 minutes.

Finely chop the spring onions (scallions) and fresh garlic. Add them to the pan with ¼ teaspoon black pepper and ½ teaspoon salt and cook for 15 minutes, stirring occasionally. Add the pomegranate molasses and cook for 5 minutes, stirring occasionally. Add the finely sliced parsley and serve.

p.121

MUALLE
MUALLE

MUALLE

Region:	Hatay, Mediterranean Region	
Preparation time:	30 minutes, plus 20 minutes soaking	
Cooking time:	1 hour 15 minutes, plus 1 hour 10 minutes resting	
Serves:	4	

600 g	aubergines (eggplant), chopped into 4-cm (1½-inch) pieces	2¼ cups/ 1 lb 5 oz
80 g	green lentils	½ cup/3 oz
1 kg	tomatoes	5 cups/2 lb 4 oz
2	green bell peppers	2
1 (120 g)	medium onion	1 (¾ cup/4 oz)
6	garlic cloves, quartered	6
2 tsp	red bell pepper paste (see p.492)	2 tsp
1 tsp	tomato paste (see p.492)	1 tsp
1 tsp	dried mint	1 tsp
2 tbsp	pomegranate molasses (see p.490)	2 tbsp
½ bunch	purple basil	½ bunch
60 ml	olive oil	¼ cup/2 fl oz

This is a summer dish made with seasonal vegetables. Another version uses the method for *imambayıldı* (stuffed aubergines/eggplants).

◆

Put the aubergines (eggplant) in a bowl, cover with 1.5 litres (6¼ cups/50 fl oz) water and 2 teaspoons salt and let soak for 20 minutes. Drain and rinse.

Meanwhile, bring a saucepan with 1 litre (4¼ cups/34 fl oz) water to the boil, add the lentils and cook for 15 minutes. Turn off the heat and let rest for 10 minutes, then drain.

Finely dice the tomatoes, bell peppers and onion. Combine in a bowl with the garlic, red pepper paste, tomato paste, dried mint, pomegranate molasses and ½ teaspoon salt and knead for 5 minutes until well combined.

Coat the bottom of a small casserole dish with about half of the aubergines, layer half of the green lentils on top of this, then layer half of the vegetable mix on top. Repeat the layers one more time. Finally, add a layer of purple basil and press down the contents of the casserole until the juices float to the top. Pour over the olive oil. Cover and cook over low heat, for 1 hour.

Let rest for 1 hour before serving.

VEGETABLES, EGGS & PULSES

◆

STUFFED
&
WRAPPED DISHES

◆

DOLMAS

SARMAS

Stuffed and wrapped dishes (*dolmas*) are culinary showstoppers in our culture. They are the jewels in the crown, an ode to the unification of many cultures that make up our country. The varieties are endless, embracing the hot, the sweet, the sour, the salty and the spicy, and they are cherished and devoured all over the country. No festival or celebration would be complete without them. No *dolma* simply means no celebration!

A *dolma* is anything that is stuffed with a mixture of meat, rice, bulgur or a similar grain. Stuffed bell peppers, aubergines (eggplant) and tripe are classic examples of *dolmas*. Vegetables that have been stuffed and sewn up are also called *dolmas* and there are of course local variations.

The copious array of *dolmas* is further enlarged by endless variations in local techniques and seasonal ingredients. Fillings of meat, butter, olive oil, milk, yogurt, tomato paste, tahini, leaves, fruit and vegetables all make them uniquely delicious in their own way. In my hometown of Nizip, stuffing dried vegetables is traditional. Dried courgettes (zucchini), aubergines and bell peppers all work well. And when it comes to size, the rule is 'the smaller the better' as it is an indication of skill. The masters of stuffing and rolling are the women of our country. I would not like to exclude all men from the rank of masters, however our mothers are the real angels of *dolma*-making.

Sarmas are where a filling is rolled or wrapped inside leaves or vegetables, for example vine leaves, cherry leaves or slices of aubergine. Anything and everything can be stuffed: flowers, fruits, vegetables, an endless selection of leaves, fish, poultry, sheep, goats and offal (variety meats), even calico sacks.

All wrapped and rolled dishes with meat and rice or bulgur are now known as either *dolmas* or *sarmas* in cities, but these dishes were all called simply *dolma* in Ottoman İstanbul. The same applies to Eastern Anatolia where, regardless of technique, both *dolmas* and *sarmas* are known only as *dolmas*. A *dolma* can be with or without meat. Meatless *dolmas* and *sarmas* made with olive oil are called 'fake *dolmas*'.

◆

DOLMA DECADENCE IN THE TURKISH BATH

Apart from being popular everyday dishes, *dolmas* add another element of decadence to the *hamam* (Turkish bath) tradition. The day before a *hamam* day is busy, with all the wrapping and rolling. The *dolmas* will be taken to the *hamam* the next day and stored in the refrigerators there. After the ritual in the hot rooms, the fun continues in the cooler section, where the *dolmas*, along with other dishes such as *piyaz*, are enjoyed with cool drinks.

Anytime is a good time to visit a *hamam*, there is no need to wait for a special occasion. The fortieth day after a baby's birth or a wedding is traditionally celebrated at a *hamam*. I started going to the *hamam* regularly at a very young age. I still love it. The joy and spirit of the preparations are etched in my memory. The trick was to edge up to the best *dolmas* and go for it! Although the refrigerators would always be supervised, we would go and say that our sisters, mothers or aunties had been asking for the *dolmas* and we would secretly gulp them down. My mother's *dolmas* were among the very best.

The olive oil *dolmas* with bulgur were exceptionally delicious, especially at the *hamam*. It was as if they tasted even better there, cooling off the *hamam*, reviving us all and adding joy to the experience.

◆

STUFFED CALICO SACKS

Stuffed calico sacks (*çuval dolması*) is a dish quite specific to our culinary culture. In the district of Çorum İskilip, the word *dolma* specifically refers to this unique dish. Another name for it is *ca dolması*. It is made on special occasions, for charity and at weddings. There are *dolma* masters in the region who take their orders in advance. The process is tedious. Par-boiled rice is tied into calico sacks, which are then placed on trays set on trivets in large copper cauldrons. Meat, onions, salt and a little water are added to the cauldron, and it is covered with parchment paper and a lid, which is then sealed tight with dough. A stone is placed on top and a tiny, pin-sized hole is made in the dough. Then the cauldron is left to cook over a wood fire for 18 hours.

It is definitely a dish for large gatherings. Depending on the number of guests, there could be five, ten or even twenty cauldrons going. Each sack contains 4–5 kilos of rice and each cauldron takes 2–3 sacks in addition to 10–15 kilos of sheep or veal meat. The *dolmas* are prepared a day ahead and someone always makes sure that there is a steady supply of wood for the fire. If this important job is not carried out properly, the person gets a bad name and the *dolma* goes to waste, so their task is crucial.

The next day, the owner of the *dolma* arrives with local dignitaries and the lid is removed with prayers and blessings. The *dolma* maker traditionally complains that the stone on the lid is too heavy to lift. The *dolma* owner gets the message and tips the chef who generously kept the vigil. Et voilà! The stone which weighed a ton now is as light as a feather. The trivet and the tray are removed, the rice is poured into the copper cauldrons and the juices of the melt-in-the-mouth meat are poured over the rice. A popular side dish is a vinegar *cacık* known as *salata* in the region.

STUFFED APPLES
ELMA DOLMASI

Region:		Niğde, all regions
Preparation time:		20 minutes, plus 15 minutes soaking
Cooking time:		50 minutes
Serves:		4

4 (6 × 6 cm)	hard red apples	4 (2½ × 2½ inch)
2 tbsp	lemon juice	2 tbsp

For the filling:

70 g	butter	⅓ cup/2½ oz
300 g	medium-fat minced (ground) veal	1⅓ cup/11 oz
60 g	medium-grain rice, cooked	⅜ cup/2 oz
100 g	crushed walnuts	1 cup/3½ oz
1 tsp	ground cinnamon	1 tsp
2 tbsp	lemon juice	2 tbsp
1 tbsp	apple molasses	1 tbsp
2 tbsp	apple cider vinegar	2 tbsp

❧   p.129 ▢

A dervish who visited Teney (Yeşilyurt) in Niğde noticed that no one set foot in the mosque. The villagers explained this was once a Christian village and that the old souls became restless if they did. The dervish suggested they make *halva* for the deceased to gain their blessing. Stuffed apples became a symbolic dish for this blessing.

♦

Slice the tops off the apples. Set aside. Hollow out the apples, finely slice the flesh, put in a bowl and discard the cores. Soak the cases in water with the lemon juice for 15 minutes.

Preheat oven to 160°C/325°F/Gas Mark 3.

To make the filling:
Heat the butter in a saucepan over medium heat, add the veal and season with ½ teaspoon salt and cook for 15 minutes. Add the cooked rice, walnuts, cinnamon, lemon juice, apple molasses, apple cider vinegar and chopped apple and cook for another minute, until well combined.

Remove the apples from the lemon water. Poke holes in them. Fill equally with the mixture, press firmly, replace the lids, then place in a roasting pan and pour over 200 ml (scant 1 cup/7 fl oz) lemon water. Bake for 30 minutes.

♦

STUFFED COLLARD GREENS
KARALAHANA SARMASI

Region:		Rize, Karadeni
Preparation time:		35 minutes, plus pre-roasting the bones
Cooking time:		1 hour 20 minutes
Serves:		4

40 (8 × 10 cm)	collard greens leaves (reserve any leftover leaves)	40 (3 × 4 inches)
50 g	butter	¼ cup/2 oz

For the stuffing:

200 g	cracked hominy corn	½ cup/7 oz
300 g	minced (ground) veal brisket	1⅓ cups/11 oz
3 (360 g)	medium onions, finely sliced	3 (2⅜ cups/12 oz)
½ tsp	dried chilli (red pepper) flakes	½ tsp
1 tsp	dried mint	1 tsp
2	dill sprigs, finely sliced	2
4 (10-cm)	pre-roasted bones from veal brisket, flesh on	4 (4-inch)

❧

Collard greens are commonly eaten in the winter months. The cracked hominy corn (known in the region as *korkota*) can be substituted with rice or bulgur wheat.

♦

Cook the collard greens leaves in 2 litres (8½ cups/ 70 fl oz) water for 5 minutes, then drain and set aside.

To make the stuffing:
Rinse the hominy corn. Mix the corn, veal, onions, dried chilli, dried mint and dill in a bowl or tray. Season with ½ teaspoon black pepper and ¼ teaspoon salt. Divide the mixture into 40 equal parts.

Spread a collard greens leaf out on a work surface, veins facing up. Spread a line of stuffing along the longer side. Roll the leaf around the stuffing for one full turn, then fold in the sides and continue rolling. Arrange the roasted veal bones at the bottom of a saucepan, cover with the leftover collard greens leaves, then arrange the stuffed rolls on top.

Heat 1 litre (4¼ cups/34 fl oz) water along with the butter and ¼ teaspoon salt in a saucepan for 5 minutes. Pour over the rolls. Cover most of the surface area with an inverted plate. Cook, uncovered, over medium heat for 10 minutes. Reduce the heat and cook, covered, for 1 hour. Serve.

STUFFED PUMPKIN
BALKABAĞI DOLMASI

Region:		Sakarya, all regions
Preparation time:		20 minutes, plus 20 minutes soaking
Cooking time:	1 hour 40 minutes, plus 15 minutes resting	
Serves:		4

1 (12 × 8 cm)	pumpkin, top cut off and reserved for a lid, hollowed out, de-seeded	1 (4¾ × 3 inches)
2 tbsp	grape molasses	2 tbsp
¼ tsp	ground cinnamon	¼ tsp
200 ml	orange juice	scant 1 cup/7 fl oz

For the stuffing:		
150 g	medium-grain rice	1 cup/5 oz
2 tbsp	olive oil	2 tbsp
1 (120 g)	medium onion	1 (¾ cup/4 oz)
60 g	almonds, roasted	½ cup/2¼ oz
1 tsp	ground cinnamon	1 tsp
6	flat-leaf parsley sprigs	6
4	dill sprigs	4

Depending on the size of the cook's family, 8–10 kg (17 lb 10 oz–22 lb 1 oz) pumpkins are used for this dish. Some recipes use peeled pumpkin.

♦

Preheat oven to 160°C/325°F/Gas Mark 3. Put the grape molasses, ground cinnamon and ¼ teaspoon salt into the pumpkin, seal with the reserved lid and bake in the hot oven for 30 minutes. Remove and set aside.

To make the stuffing:
Soak the rice in 600 ml (2½ cups/20 fl oz) water with ½ teaspoon salt for 20 minutes. Drain and rinse. Heat the oil in a large saucepan over medium heat. Finely slice the onion, add to the pan and cook for 3 minutes. Add the almonds and rice and cook for 3 minutes. Stir in the ground cinnamon, ¼ teaspoon black pepper and ½ teaspoon salt and remove from the heat. Finely slice the parsley and dill, then add to the pan and mix gently.

Fill the pumpkin with the stuffing. Pour in the orange juice and seal tight with the pumpkin lid. Bake in the hot oven for 1 hour.

Remove from the oven and let rest for 10 minutes, then remove the lid and aerate for a few minutes more. Cut the pumpkin into 4 pieces and serve with the stuffing.

♦

STUFFED COUSA SQUASH
SAKIZ KABAĞI DOLMASI

Region:		Muğla, all regions
Preparation time:		25 minutes, plus 20 minutes soaking
Cooking time:		1 hour, plus 10 minutes resting
Serves:		4

8 (5 × 10 cm)	cousa (summer) squash	8 (2 × 5 inch)
150 g	tomato, finely sliced	¾ cup/5 oz
1½ tsp	tomato paste (see p.492)	1½ tsp
2	garlic cloves, crushed	2
2 tbsp	olive oil	2 tbsp

For the stuffing:		
120 g	medium-grain rice	¾ cup/4 oz
100 ml	olive oil	scant ½ cup/3½ fl oz
4 (600 g)	large onions, finely sliced	4 (4 cups/1 lb 5 oz)
50 g	walnuts, crushed	½ cup/2 oz
1 tsp	dried mint	1 tsp
½ bunch	flat-leaf parsley	½ bunch
½ bunch	dill	½ bunch

Cousa squash are enjoyed in many ways – fried, cooked in olive oil and stuffed – all over the country. Vegetables stuffed with meat are considered the real deal, whereas ones without are considered to have been made in a hurry! Turkish Sephardic Jews have a signature recipe: the stuffing is made with caramelised sugar, stale bread and minced (ground) meat.

♦

To make the stuffing:
Soak the rice in 500 ml (generous 2 cups/17 fl oz) boiling water with ½ teaspoon salt for 20 minutes, then rinse. Heat the oil in a saucepan over medium heat, add the onions and cook for 20 minutes. Add the rice and walnuts and cook for 10 minutes. Add the dried mint and season with ¼ teaspoon black pepper and ½ teaspoon salt. Cook for 1 minute. Remove from the heat. Finely slice the parsley and dill, then add to the pan and mix gently.

Slice the tops off the squash and set aside. Hollow out the squash and make shallow cuts in the peel. Fill with the stuffing. Replace the tops. Pack the squash vertically, as close together as possible, in a saucepan. Add the sliced tomatoes, tomato paste, garlic, olive oil, ¼ teaspoon salt and 200 ml (scant 1 cup/7 fl oz) water. Cook, covered, over low heat for 30 minutes. Rest for 10 minutes and serve.

STUFFED ARTICHOKES
ENGİNAR DOLMASI

Region:		İzmir, Aegean Region
Preparation time:		25 minutes, plus 20 minutes soaking
Cooking time:		40 minutes, plus 10 minutes resting
Serves:		4

4 (6 × 8 cm)	tender artichokes	4 (2½ × 3 inches)
2 tbsp	lemon juice	2 tbsp
4	vine leaves	4
5	garlic cloves, peeled	5
20	green plums	20
½ tsp	sugar	½ tsp

For the stuffing:		
120 g	medium-grain rice	¾ cup/4 oz
1 (120 g)	medium onion	1 (¾ cup/4 oz)
2	spring onions (scallions)	2
6	flat-leaf parsley sprigs	6
4	fresh mint sprigs	4
1½ tbsp	pine nuts, toasted	1½ tbsp
2½ tbsp	raisins	2½ tbsp
100 ml	olive oil	scant ½ cup/3½ fl oz
½ tsp	sugar	½ tsp

There is no need to remove the choke if the artichokes are the tender egg-sized ones of early spring. Instead of trimming the leaves and stuffing the centres, leave the leaves and stuff in between them.

♦

Trim the artichokes, remove the choke and soak in 1.5 litres (6¼ cups/50 fl oz) water with 2 tbsp lemon juice.

To make the stuffing:
Soak the rice in 1 litre (4¼ cups/34 fl oz) water with ½ teaspoon of salt for 20 minutes. Drain and rinse under running water until translucent.

Finely slice the onion, spring onions (scallions), parsley and mint. Mix the rice with the rest of the filling ingredients and ¼ teaspoon salt in a large bowl or deep tray with your hands. Divide the mixture into 4 equal parts.

Remove the artichokes from the lemon water and stuff the filling into the cavities. Place the vine leaves on top.

Put the artichokes into a saucepan and sprinkle the garlic and plums on top. Pour 800 ml (3¼ cups/27 fl oz) lemon water into the pan, along with the sugar and ¼ teaspoon of salt. Drizzle in the olive oil. Cover with parchment paper and the lid, then cook for 40 minutes over a low heat.

Remove from heat and rest for 10 minutes before serving.

STUFFED COURGETTE FLOWERS
KABAK ÇİÇEĞİ DOLMASI

Region:		Balıkesir, all regions
Preparation time:		25 minutes, plus 1 hour soaking
Cooking time:		40 minutes, plus 10 minutes resting
Serves:		4

20	courgette (zucchini) flowers	20
2 tbsp	lemon juice	2 tbsp
2 tbsp	olive oil	2 tbsp

For the stuffing:		
160 g	medium-grain rice	1 cup/5½ oz
2 (240 g)	medium onions	2 (1⅝ cups/8½ oz)
4	spring onions (scallions),	4
2	fresh mint sprigs	2
200 g	tomato	1 cup/7 oz
10	flat-leaf parsley sprigs,	10
½ tsp	dried chilli (red pepper) flakes	½ tsp
2 tbsp	olive oil	2 tbsp

Courgette (zucchini) flowers open at sunrise in summer and close if not picked immediately. The stuffing is prepared earlier and placed in the blossoms as soon as they open.

♦

Soak the rice in 500 ml (generous 2 cups/17 fl oz) boiling water with ¼ teaspoon salt for 1 hour. Drain and rinse under running water until translucent.

To make the stuffing:
Finely slice the onion, spring onions (scallions), fresh mint, tomato and parsley, then combine with the rice, dried chilli (red pepper) flakes, olive oil, ¼ teaspoon black pepper and ½ teaspoon salt in a large bowl or deep tray. Mix until well combined.

Fill the courgette flowers evenly with the stuffing. Twist to close the flowers and pack them close together, arranged vertically, in a large pan with the twisted ends on top.

Mix the lemon juice and oil with ¼ teaspoon salt and 500 ml (generous 2 cups/17 fl oz) water. Drizzle over the flowers. Cover with parchment paper and the lid, then cook over low heat for 40 minutes. Rest for 10 minutes before serving.

STUFFED & WRAPPED DISHES

COURGETTES STUFFED WITH MEAT
ETLİ KABAK DOLMASI

Region:		Bursa, all regions
Preparation time:		25 minutes, plus 30 minutes soaking
Cooking time:		45 minutes, plus 10 minutes resting
Serves:		4

8 (10 × 5 cm)	small courgettes (zucchini), tops cut off and reserved, hollowed out	8 (4 × 2 inch)
¼ tsp	black pepper	¼ tsp
¼ tsp	salt	¼ tsp
1 (2 kg)	rack of lamb ribs	1 (4 lb 8 oz)

For the stuffing:		
80 g	medium-grain rice	½ cup/3 oz
¾ tsp	salt	¾ tsp
50 g	coarse bulgur wheat	¼ cup/2 oz
250 g	minced (ground) veal brisket	1⅛ cups/9 oz
1 (120 g)	medium onion, finely sliced	1 (¾ cup/4 oz
10	flat-leaf parsley sprigs, finely sliced	10
5	dill sprigs, finely sliced	10
2 tbsp	olive oil	2 tbsp
1½ tsp	tomato paste (see p.492)	1½ tsp
½ tsp	dried chilli (red pepper) flakes	½ tsp
¼ tsp	black pepper	¼ tsp
¼ tsp	ground cumin	¼ tsp

For the sauce:		
150 g	tomatoes, finely sliced	¾ cup/5 oz
1½ tsp	tomato paste (see p.492)	1½ tsp
2	garlic cloves, crushed	2
¼ tsp	salt	¼ tsp

400 g	Greek yogurt	2 cups/14 oz
5	dill sprigs, finely sliced	5
1	garlic clove, crushed	1
¼ tsp	salt	¼ tsp

This is a summer dish. Some recipes use rice or bulgur wheat only.

♦

Soak the rice for the stuffing in 200 ml (scant 1 cup/7 fl oz) water with ¼ teaspoon of the salt for 30 minutes. Drain and rinse, then set aside.

Meanwhile, soak the courgettes (zucchini) in 1.5 litres (6¼ cups/50 fl oz) water with the salt and pepper for 15 minutes. Drain and set aside.

To make the stuffing:
Combine the rice, bulgur wheat, veal, onion, parsley, dill, olive oil, tomato paste, dried chilli (red pepper) flakes, black pepper, cumin and the remaining ½ teaspoon of salt in a large bowl or deep tray. Mix until well combined.

Fill the courgettes with the stuffing, dividing it equally.

Put the rack of lamb ribs in a large saucepan. Arrange the stuffed courgettes on top of the ribs, stuffing side up. Turn the courgette tops upside down and place on top of the stuffing.

To make the sauce:
In a bowl, mix 400 ml (1⅔ cups/14 fl oz) water with the sliced tomatoes, tomato paste, garlic and salt.

Pour the sauce around the courgettes in the pan. Cook, covered, over low heat for 45 minutes. Remove from the heat and rest for 10 minutes.

In a separate small bowl, mix the yogurt, dill, garlic and salt. Transfer the *dolmas* to serving plates and serve with the lamb ribs and yogurt sauce.

STUFFED AUBERGINE WITH OLIVE OIL
ZEYTİNYAĞLI PATLICAN DOLMASI

Region:	İstanbul, all regions
Preparation time:	30 minutes, plus 30 minutes soaking
Cooking time:	1 hour 30 minutes
Serves:	4

8	hollow dried aubergines (eggplants)	8
1 (150 g)	tomato, cut into 8 slices	1 (5 oz)
2 tbsp	olive oil	2 tbsp

For the stuffing:		
60 ml	olive oil	¼ cup/2 fl oz
1½ tbsp	pine nuts	1½ tbsp
4 (450 g)	onions, finely sliced	4 (1 lb)
160 g	medium-grain rice	5½ oz
30 g	currants	¼ cup/1 oz
1½ tsp	ground cinnamon	1½ tsp
1½ tsp	allspice	1½ tsp
2 tsp	ground paprika	2 tsp
1 tsp	dried mint	1 tsp
½ bunch	dill, finely chopped	½ bunch

This is the quintessential recipe for *dolmas* made with olive oil. Small bell peppers work well too. Hollow dried aubergines (eggplants) are available in some Turkish or Middle Eastern food stores. Alternatively, use 4 Japanese or Italian aubergines, measuring 5 × 8 cm (2 × 3 inches).

◆

If using fresh aubergines (eggplants), remove the stems, partially peel them in stripes, halve and then hollow them out. Soak in 1.5 litres (6¼ cups/50 fl oz) water with 2 teaspoons salt for 15 minutes. Drain, rinse and set aside.

To make the stuffing:
Soak the rice in 500 ml (generous 2 cups/17 fl oz) boiling water with ¼ teaspoon salt for 30 minutes, then rinse.

Heat the oil in a sauté pan over medium heat, add the pine nuts and cook for 1 minute. Add the onions and cook for 10 minutes, mixing continuously. Add the rice and cook for 13 minutes. Stir in the currants, cinnamon, allspice, paprika, dried mint and ¾ teaspoon salt, cook for 2 minutes until combined. Remove from the heat. Gently stir in the dill.

Fill the aubergines with the stuffing mixture. Arrange the stuffed aubergines in a saucepan, making sure the stuffing is on top and seal each with a slice of tomato. Add 500 ml (generous 2 cups/17 fl oz) water and the olive oil to the pan. Cover and cook over low heat for 1 hour, then serve.

◆

AUBERGINE WITH MIXED MEAT STUFFING
MÜLEBBES DOLMASI

Region:	Mardin, Southeastern Anatolia
Preparation time:	20 minutes, plus 15 minutes soaking
Cooking time:	45 minutes
Serves:	4

8 (5 × 10 cm)	Japanese or Italian aubergines (eggplants)	8 (2 × 4 inches)
6	eggs	6
500 ml	olive oil	2 cups/17 fl oz
5 (25 cm)	gumwood or pine sticks	5 (10 inch)
300 g	unripe, sour grapes	1¾ cups/11 oz
400 ml	meat stock (see p.489)	1⅔ cups/14 fl oz

For the stuffing:		
80 g	medium-grain rice	½ cup/3 oz
2 (240 g)	medium onions	2 (1⅝ cups/8 oz)
150 g	minced (ground) veal	⅔ cup/5 oz
150 g	minced (ground) lamb	⅔ cup/5 oz

This *dolma* is made with the small aubergines (eggplants) local to Southeastern Anatolia. The oldest sources on Turkish cooking make references to this dish. It is traditionally made in the summer months.

◆

Soak the aubergines (eggplants) in 1.5 litres (6¼ cups/50 fl oz) water with 2 teaspoons salt for 15 minutes. Drain, rinse and set aside.

To make the stuffing:
In a bowl, combine the rice, finely sliced onions, veal and lamb with ¼ teaspoon black pepper and ½ teaspoon salt.

Fill the aubergines with the stuffing and seal with the reserved tops. Make a few holes on top of the aubergines with a knife. Whisk the eggs in a separate bowl.

In a saucepan, heat the oil over medium heat to 155°C/310°F. Coat the aubergines with the eggs and fry in the hot oil for 2 minutes on each side, cooking both sides evenly.

Arrange the sticks at the bottom of a saucepan and layer the aubergines on top. Cover with the grapes. Add the stock and ¼ teaspoon salt. Cook, covered, over low heat for 30 minutes. Drizzle with the cooking juices and serve.

STUFFED DRIED PEPPERS, COURGETTES AND AUBERGINES
KOFİK DOLMASI
(KURU BİBER VE KURU PATLICAN DOLMASI)

Region: Elazığ, all regions
Preparation time: 30 minutes
Cooking time: 1 hour 10 minutes, plus 10 minutes resting
Serves: 4

4	dried bell peppers	4
4	dried courgettes (zucchini)	4
4	dried aubergines (eggplants)	4
1	lamb rib bone	1
1	lamb brisket bone	1
2 tbsp	butter	2 tbsp
2 tbsp	olive oil	2 tbsp
2	garlic cloves, finely sliced	2
60 g	onion, finely sliced	⅜ cup/2¼ oz
1½ tsp	tomato paste (see p.492)	1½ tsp
½ tsp	dried chilli (red pepper) flakes	½ tsp
¼ tsp	salt	¼ tsp
200 ml	sumac water (see p.491)	scant 1 cup/ 7 fl oz
4	spring onions (scallions)	4
250 g	Greek yogurt	1¼ cup/9 oz

For the filling:

80 g	medium-grain rice	½ cup/3 oz
60 g	fine bulgur wheat	generous ¼ cup/ 2¼ oz
400 g	minced (ground) lamb, finely sliced with a cleaver	2 cups/14 oz
2 (240 g)	medium onions, finely sliced	2 (1½ cups/ 8 oz)
6	flat-leaf parsley sprigs, finely sliced	6
1½ tsp	tomato paste (see p.492)	1½ tsp
2 tsp	red bell pepper paste (see p.492)	2 tsp
½ tsp	dried chilli (red pepper) flakes	½ tsp
¼ tsp	black pepper	¼ tsp
30 g	butter	⅛ cup/1 oz
2 tbsp	olive oil	2 tbsp
100 ml	sumac water (see p.491)	scant ½ cup/ 3½ fl oz
½ tsp	salt	½ tsp

p.135 📷

Some versions of this dish are vegetarian, made with olive oil and just rice or bulgur wheat.

♦

Bring a large saucepan with 1 litre (4¼ cups/34 fl oz) water to the boil, add the dried peppers and boil for 5 minutes. Use a slotted spoon to transfer the peppers to paper towels. Meanwhile, to the same boiling water, add the dried courgettes (zucchini) and dried aubergines (eggplants) and boil for 10 minutes. Drain and set aside on paper towels.

To make the filling:
Mix the rice, bulgur wheat, lamb, onions, parsley, tomato paste, red bell pepper paste, dried chilli (red pepper) flakes, black pepper, butter, olive oil, sumac water and salt in a large bowl or deep tray for 1 minute, until well combined.

Divide the filling equally among the dried courgettes, eggplants and bell peppers, making sure it fills each vegetable three-quarters full. Put the rib bones and brisket into a large saucepan and arrange the stuffed vegetables on top.

Heat the butter and olive oil in a large saucepan over medium heat, add the garlic and onions and cook for 1 minute. Add the tomato paste, dried chilli (red pepper) flakes and the salt and cook for a further 1 minute. Remove from the heat, add the sumac water and mix for a further 1 minute.

Pour the mixture over the stuffed vegetables, partially cover with a plate and cook for 10 minutes over medium heat, until it comes to the boil. Reduce the heat and cook, covered, for a further 40 minutes.

Remove from the heat and let rest for 10 minutes. Serve with spring onions (scallions) and yogurt.

SORREL AND LOR ROLLS
LOR DOLMASI

Region:		Bayburt, Black Sea Region
Preparation time:		25 minutes
Cooking time:		35 minutes
Serves:		4

For the filling:

150 g	fine bulgur wheat	⅔ cup/5 oz
400 g	*lor* (fresh curd cheese, see p.485, or ricotta)	1¾ cups/ 14 oz
50 g	clotted cream (see p.486)	¼ cup/2 oz
60 g	onion, finely sliced	⅜ cup/2 oz
1 tbsp	dried basil	1 tbsp
2 tbsp	butter, melted	2 tbsp

40 (6 × 15 cm)	fresh sorrel leaves,	40 (2½ × 6 inches)
500 ml	milk	generous 2 cups/17 fl oz
50 g	clotted cream (see p.486)	¼ cup/2 oz

For the sauce:

50 g	butter	¼ cup/2 oz
2 (240 g)	medium onions	2 (1⅝ cups/8½ oz)

V

p.137

This dish is a spring specialty as it relies on fresh seasonal sorrel leaves and *lor* (a fresh sheep's milk curd cheese similar to ricotta). A local favourite around Erzurum and Kars.

♦

Preheat oven to 160°C/325°F/Gas Mark 3.

To make the filling:
Wash the bulgur wheat in hot water and then rinse. Put the bulgur wheat, fresh cheese, clotted cream, onion, dried basil and butter with ¼ teaspoon black pepper and ½ teaspoon salt in a large bowl or deep tray and knead to combine. Divide the mixture into 40 equal parts.

Soak the sorrel leaves in boiling water then drain. Place some filling in a leaf, making sure that the side with the veins is on the inside. Roll once, starting from one corner, then fold in the two neighbouring corners to enclose the filling and keep rolling. Place the rolls in a large oven dish.

To make the sauce:
Slice the onion into 5-mm (¼-inch) strips. Heat the butter in a large sauté pan over medium heat, add the onions and ¼ teaspoon salt and cook, stirring, for 5 minutes.

Pour the sauce over the rolls. Mix together the milk and clotted cream with ¼ teaspoon black pepper, and pour over the rolls, then bake in the hot oven for 30 minutes. Transfer to a serving platter.

♦

STUFFED CABBAGE
BEYAZ LAHANA SARMASI

Region:		Gaziantep, all regions
Preparation time:		30 minutes
Cooking time:	50 minutes, plus 10 minutes resting	
Serves:		4

40 (6 × 10 cm)	thin, white cabbage leaves (reserve any leftover)	40 (2½ × 4 inches)
1	whole rack of lamb ribs	1
60 ml	olive oil	¼ cup/2 fl oz

For the stuffing:

150 g	coarse bulgur wheat,	⅔ cup/5 oz
2 (240 g)	medium onions, finely sliced	2 (8½ oz)
6	garlic cloves, finely sliced	6
450 g	lamb, finely diced	2 cups/1 lb
1 tbsp	red bell pepper paste (see p.492)	1 tbsp
1 tbsp	tomato paste (see p.492)	1 tbsp
½ tsp	dried chilli (red pepper) flakes	½ tsp

This dish is made in the winter months. Another version replaces the meat with walnuts and adds olive oil.

♦

Boil the cabbage leaves in 2 litres (8½ cups/70 fl oz) water for 5 minutes, then drain and set aside.

To make the stuffing:
Rinse the bulgur wheat and then combine with the onion, garlic, lamb, red bell pepper paste, tomato paste, dried chilli (red pepper) flakes, ¼ teaspoon black pepper and ¾ teaspoon salt in a large bowl or deep tray and mix gently with your hands. Divide the stuffing into 40 equal parts.

Spread a cabbage leaf out on a work surface, veins facing up. Spread a piece of stuffing in a line along the longer side. Roll the leaf around the stuffing for one full turn, then fold in the sides and continue rolling. Arrange the lamb ribs in the bottom of a saucepan, cover with the leftover leaves and arrange the stuffed cabbage rolls on top.

Heat 500 ml (2 cups/17 fl oz) water in a saucepan with the oil and ¼ teaspoon salt for 5 minutes. Pour over the rolls. Cover most of the surface area with a plate. Cook, covered, over low heat for 40 minutes. Rest for 10 minutes and serve.

STUFFED & WRAPPED DISHES

STUFFED FISH DOLMAS
BALIK DOLMASI

Region:	İstanbul, Marmara Region
Preparation time:	45 minutes, plus 20 minutes soaking
Cooking time:	30 minutes
Serves:	4

4 (5 × 20 cm)	mackerel	4 (2 × 8 inches)
3	eggs	3
50 g	plain (all-purpose) flour	⅓ cup/2 oz
400 ml	olive oil	1⅔ cups/14 fl oz

For the stuffing:

60 g	medium-grain rice	scant ½ cup/ 2¼ oz
¾ tsp	salt	¾ tsp
100 ml	olive oil	scant ½ cup/3½ fl oz
3 (360 g)	medium onions, finely sliced	3 (2⅜ cups/ 12 oz)
1½ tbsp	pine nuts	1½ tbsp
40 g	currants	scant ½ cup/1½ oz
1 tsp	ground cinnamon	1 tsp
¼ tsp	cloves	¼ tsp
¼ tsp	ground cardamom	¼ tsp
¼ tsp	black pepper	¼ tsp
½ tsp	ground allspice	½ tsp
3	dill sprigs, finely sliced	3
5	flat-leaf parsley sprigs, finely sliced	5

In İstanbul, legend has it that Rum (Ottoman Greek) tavern owners prepared this dish and delivered it to their Muslim customers, who took a break from the *meyhanes*, or taverns, during the month of *Ramadan*, hoping that it would serve as a reminder. Hence the alternative name for this dish, 'forget-me-not'. Some replace the rice with bulgur wheat in this recipe, which also works well with freshwater fish.

♦

To prepare the mackerel, break the tail bone, but do not remove the tail. Remove the guts through the cavity behind the ear. Rinse and dry the fish, then massage the flesh for 5 minutes. Remove the spine through the cavity behind the ear by applying pressure with one hand and pulling out the bones with the other. Any flesh removed in the process can be picked from the bones and set aside in a bowl together with half the flesh removed with the help of a hooked knife. Alternatively, ask your fishmonger to prepare the fish for stuffing.

To make the stuffing:
Soak the rice in 1 litre (4¼ cups/34 fl oz) water with ¼ teaspoon of the salt for 20 minutes. Drain and rinse.

Heat the olive oil in a sauté pan over medium heat, add the onions and cook for 15 minutes, mixing continuously. Add the pine nuts and cook for 5 minutes. Add the reserved fish flesh, rice, currants, ground cinnamon, cloves, ground cardamom, black pepper, ground allspice and remaining ½ teaspoon of salt and cook for 3 minutes. Remove from the heat, add the dill and parsley and mix well.

Stuff the cavities of each fish equally with the stuffing mixture, being careful not to split the bellies.

Whisk the eggs in a shallow bowl or tray. Put the flour in a separate shallow bowl or tray.

In a large saucepan, heat the olive oil over medium heat to 155°C/310°F. Coat the fish with the eggs and then the flour, then place them in the hot oil. Fry for 2 minutes on each side. Serve immediately.

STUFFED LAMB RIBS
KABURGA DOLMASI

Region:		Mardin, all regions
Preparation time:	30 minutes, plus 1 hour soaking	
Cooking time:		4 hours 30 minutes
Serves:		4

1 × 2 kg	whole rack of lamb ribs, untrimmed	1 × 4 lb 4 oz
2 tbsp	olive oil	2 tbsp
½ tsp	salt	½ tsp
1 (120 g)	medium onion, quartered	(¾ cup/4 oz)
1½ tsp	tomato paste (see p.492)	1½ tsp
2	bay leaves	2
10	black peppercorns	10
1 tbsp	ground paprika	1 tbsp

For the sealing dough:

100 g	plain (all-purpose) flour	¾ cup/ 3½ oz

For the stuffing:

200 g	medium-grain rice	1¼ cups/7 oz
¾ tsp	salt	¾ tsp
70 g	butter	⅓ cup/2¾ oz
200 g	carrot, finely sliced	1½ cups/7 oz
1	parsley sprig, finely sliced	1
1 tsp	dried oregano	1 tsp
100 g	almonds	¾ cup/3½ oz
½ tsp	black pepper	½ tsp
½ tsp	ground coriander	½ tsp
1½ tsp	tomato paste (see p.492)	1½ tsp
1 tsp	ground paprika	1 tsp
2 tbsp	olive oil	2 tbsp

The lamb ribs are usually brought to the table whole for theatrical effect before the addition of the sauce. The sauce is also popular as a soup. Another serving suggestion is to get the rice ready, de-bone the meat and serve on top of the rice.

This recipe can also be made without using a trivet or rack, in a large deep roasting pan, in which case add only 2 litres (8½ cups/70 fl oz) water. It can also be cooked, covered, in a 180°C/350°F/Gas Mark 4 oven for 2 hours.

◆

To make the stuffing:
Soak the rice in 1 litre (4¼ cups/34 fl oz) water with ¼ teaspoon of the salt for 1 hour. Drain and rinse under running water until translucent.

Heat the butter in a large saucepan over medium heat, add the rice and fry for 15 minutes. Add the carrot, parsley, dried oregano, almonds, black pepper, ground coriander, tomato paste, ground paprika, olive oil and remaining ½ teaspoon of the salt and cook for 5 minutes.

Using a sharp knife, make a cavity between the rib and the meat of the lamb rack, making sure you do not cut all the way through. Fill the cavity with the stuffing mixture and use a trussing needle and cooking string to sew the opening closed.

Heat the olive oil in a very large saucepan or casserole (Dutch oven) over medium heat, add the stuffed lamb , season with ¼ teaspoon of the salt and fry on each side for 4 minutes to seal. Put a 20 × 20 cm (8 × 8 inch) trivet or rack in the pan. Pour in 4 litres (16 cups/130 fl oz) water, add the onion, tomato paste, bay leaves, remaining ¼ teaspoon salt, black peppercorns and paprika. Place a 30 cm (12 inch) metal plate on top of the trivet.

To make the sealing dough:
In a separate bowl, work the flour and 60 ml (¼ cup/ 2 fl oz) water to a soft dough and roll out to a long sausage shape. Cover the pan/casserole and stick the dough around the lid to seal it thoroughly and make it airtight. Cook for 4 hours over very low heat.

Divide into four and serve on the bone or pull the meat and serve on top of pilaf.

STUFFED MUSSELS
MİDYE DOLMASI

Region: İstanbul, all regions
Preparation time: 20 minutes, plus 20 minutes soaking
Cooking time: 1 hour, plus 10 minutes resting
Serves: 4

24	fresh large mussels	24
2 tbsp	olive oil	2 tbsp
1 tbsp	lemon juice	1 tbsp

For the stuffing:

100 g	medium-grain rice	generous ½ cup/3½ oz
60 ml	olive oil	¼ cup/2 fl oz
2 (240 g)	medium onions, finely sliced	2 (1⅝ cups/8½ oz)
1½ tbsp	pine nuts	1½ tbsp
30 g	currants	¼ cup/1 oz
½ tsp	ground allspice	½ tsp
1 tsp	ground cinnamon	1 tsp
¼ tsp	ground cloves	¼ tsp

p.141

This popular street food is also made at home. The home-made version uses currants and pine nuts, whereas the street version does not. The stuffed mussels made in İzmir have dried mint and black pepper; the ones made in İstanbul omit these and add allspice and cinnamon.

♦

To make the stuffing:
Soak the rice in 600 ml (2½ cups/20 fl oz) warm water with ½ teaspoon salt for 20 minutes. Drain and rinse. Heat the oil in a sauté pan over medium heat, add the onion and cook for 10 minutes. Add the rice, pine nuts and currants and cook for 5 minutes. Add the allspice, cinnamon, cloves, ¼ teaspoon each of black pepper and salt and cook for a further 2 minutes. Reduce the heat, add 100 ml (scant ½ cup/3½ fl oz) water and cook, covered, for 10 minutes.

Clean the mussel shells and then open at the wide ends, keeping the pointed ends connected. Fill each shell with stuffing. Close with the other shell. Place in a pan over low heat. Weigh down with a plate. Cook, covered, for 5 minutes.

Meanwhile, in a separate pan, bring 400 ml (1⅔ cups/14 fl oz) water, the olive oil, lemon juice and ¼ teaspoon salt to the boil. Pour over the stuffed mussels and cook, covered, for a further 30 minutes. Let rest for 10 minutes and transfer to serving platters.

♦

VEGETARIAN STUFFED VINE LEAVES
ZEYTİNYAĞLI YAPRAK SARMASI

Region: Muğla, all regions
Preparation time: 30 minutes, plus 20 minutes soaking
Cooking time: 1 hour 15 minutes, plus 10 minutes resting
Serves: 4

40	fresh vine leaves	40
2 tbsp	olive oil	2 tbsp
2 tbsp	lemon juice	2 tbsp

For the stuffing :

2 tbsp	olive oil	2 tbsp
4 (600 g)	large onions, finely sliced	4 (4 cups/1 lb 5 oz)
100 g	medium-grain rice	generous ½ cup/3½ oz
½ bunch	flat-leaf parsley	½ bunch
½ bunch	dill	½ bunch
1 tsp	dried mint	1 tsp
1 tsp	sugar	1 tsp
¼ tsp	black peppercorns	¼ tsp

Bulgur wheat, tomato paste and walnuts are used in the stuffing in the eastern Mediterranean Region and Southeastern Anatolia. This is a summer dish.

♦

Soak the vine leaves in 1 litre (4¼ cups/34 fl oz) hot water for 10 minutes, then drain and set aside. Soak the rice for the stuffing in 500 ml (generous 2 cups/17 fl oz) warm water with ½ teaspoon salt for 20 minutes, then rinse.

To make the stuffing:
Heat the oil in a saucepan over medium heat, add the onions. Cook for 20 minutes, stirring continuously. Add the rice and cook for 5 minutes. Finely slice the parsley and dill and then add to the pan with the dried mint, sugar, black peppercorns and ½ teaspoon salt. Cook for 1 minute. Remove from the heat. Divide the stuffing among the vine leaves. Spread each vine leaf out on a work surface, veins facing up. Spread a piece of stuffing in a line along the longer side. Roll the leaf around the stuffing for one full turn, then fold in the sides and continue rolling.

Arrange the *dolmas* in a wide saucepan. Add the oil, lemon juice and 500 ml (generous 2 cups/17 fl oz) water. Cover most of the surface area with a plate. Cook, uncovered, for 5 minutes over medium heat. Reduce the heat, cover, and cook for 40 minutes. Rest for 10 minutes before serving.

STUFFED SPLEENS
DALAK DOLMASI

Region:		Diyarbakır, all regions
Preparation time:		20 minutes, plus 20 minutes soaking
Cooking time:		1 hour 20 minutes, plus 3 hours chilling
Serves:		4

8	fresh lamb's spleens	8
50 g	plain (all-purpose) flour	⅓ cup/2 oz
4	eggs, whisked	4
60 ml	olive oil	¼ cup/2 fl oz
4	flat-leaf parsley sprigs, finely chopped	4

For the stuffing:		
120 g	medium-grain rice	¾ cup/4 oz
50 g	butter	¼ cup/2 oz
3 (360 g)	medium onions	3 (2⅜ cups/12 oz)
30 g	currants	¼ cup/1 oz
2 tbsp	pine nuts, toasted	2 tbsp
½ bunch	dill, finely chopped	½ bunch
1 tsp	ground cinnamon	1 tsp
½ tsp	ground allspice	½ tsp

This specialty of the Armenians of İstanbul and Diyarbakır has a short season, made between the end of winter and early spring from the spleens of suckling lambs.

♦

Make a 1-cm (½-inch) hole in the wider plane of each spleen. Remove three-quarters of the flesh with a spoon, without damaging the outer membrane. Set both aside.

To make the stuffing:
Soak the rice in 500 ml (2 cups/17 fl oz) warm water with ½ teaspoon salt for 20 minutes, then rinse. Heat the butter in a sauté pan over medium heat. Add the onions and cook for 15 minutes. Add the rice and cook for 5 minutes. Add the currants, pine nuts, dill, cinnamon, allspice, ¼ teaspoon black pepper and ½ teaspoon salt. Remove from the heat.

Stuff the spleens. Bring 3 litres (12 cups/100 fl oz) water and ¼ teaspoon salt to the boil in a pan. Add the spleens, reduce the heat and cook, covered, for 45 minutes. Remove and set aside to cool. Chill in the refrigerator for 3 hours.

Slice the spleens into 1-cm (½-inch) rounds. Put the flour and eggs into bowls. In a pan, heat the oil over medium heat to 155°C/310°F. Coat the spleen with flour, egg and flour again. Fry for 1 minute on each side. Sprinkle with parsley.

TRIPE STUFFED WITH RICE AND MEAT
KİBE (İŞKEMBE) DOLMASI

Region:		Diyarbakır, all regions
Preparation time:		25 minutes
Cooking time:		2 hours 45 minutes
Serves:		4

4 × 800 g	lamb's stomachs (tripe)	4 × 1 lb 12 oz
2	lamb bones with marrow	2
1	lamb brisket bone	1
1 (70 g)	carrot	1 (½ cup/2¼ oz)
1 tbsp	lemon juice	1 tbsp
6	black peppercorns	6

For the stuffing:		
2 (240 g)	medium onions	2 (1⅝ cups/8 oz)
½ bunch	flat-leaf parsley	½ bunch
160 g	medium-grain rice	1 cup/5½ oz
200 g	lamb, fatty, finely sliced	1 cup/7 oz
½ tsp	ground coriander	½ tsp
1½ tsp	tomato paste (see p.492)	1½ tsp
½ tsp	dried chilli (red pepper) flakes	½ tsp
¼ tsp	ground cumin	¼ tsp

A dish for special occasions and the winter months, this is also known as 'stuffed belly'. Some recipes use cracked wheat or coarse bulgur wheat. It can also be made in 1 hour in a pressure cooker, with 1.75 litres (7½ cups/60 fl oz) water.

♦

To make the stuffing:
Finely slice the onions and parsley. Mix all the stuffing ingredients in a bowl or deep tray until well combined. Season with ¼ teaspoon black pepper and ¾ teaspoon salt.

Clean the tripe well. Divide the mixture into four and stuff the tripe, leaving a 2-cm (¾-inch) space at the top. Use a trussing needle and cooking string to sew up the top of the tripe in crosses, making sure it is nice and tight.

Put the stuffed tripe, bones, carrot, lemon juice and black peppercorns and ¼ teaspoon salt into a large saucepan with 3.5 litres (14½ cups/118 fl oz) water and bring to the boil over medium heat, about 15 minutes. Skim the surface with a slotted spoon. Reduce the heat and cook, covered, for 2½ hours. Transfer the stuffed tripe to plates and serve.

STUFFED & WRAPPED DISHES

GOŞTEBERG (STUFFED TRIPE)
GOŞTEBERG (KOYUN ETİ DOLMASI)

Region:		Ağrı, Eastern Anatolia
Preparation time:		25 minutes, plus overnight soaking
Cooking time:		2 hours 50 minutes
Serves:		4

1	unbroken sheep's stomach (tripe), well cleaned	1

For the stuffing:

1 kg	leg of lamb, diced into 2-cm (1-inch) pieces	2 lb 4 oz
300 g	shallots, peeled	3 cups/11 oz
300 g	wild *goşteberg*, cleaned, cut into 1-cm (½-inch) slices *or*	3 cups/11 oz
2	medium leeks, cut into 1-cm (½-inch) slices	
2 tsp	dried oregano	2 tsp
½ tsp	ground cumin	½ tsp
½ tsp	black pepper	½ tsp
½ tsp	ground coriander, finely sliced	½ tsp
60 g	chickpeas (garbanzo beans), soaked overnight	½ cup/ 2¼ oz
50 g	butter	3½ tbsp/2 oz
¾ tsp	salt	¾ tsp

For the basting sauce:

2 tbsp	olive oil	2 tbsp
½ tsp	ground cumin	½ tsp
¼ tsp	black pepper	¼ tsp
½ tsp	ground paprika	½ tsp
¼ tsp	salt	¼ tsp

½ bunch	flat-leaf parsley	½ bunch
1	red radish, sliced into thin crescents	1
1	lemon, quartered	1
1	*Açık Ekmek* (Lavash Bread, see p.394) quartered	1

Goşteberg means lamb meat in Kurdish. It is also the name of a local herb. The lamb meat is chopped into pieces, mixed with wild *goşteberg* and placed in tripe, which is then placed in sheepskin. The sheepskin is sealed. To cook this dish, traditionally the locals dig a hole in the ground, and a fire is lit within the hole. Once the hole is hot enough, the fire is removed, stones are placed in the hole on top of which the sheepskin is placed. Another fire is lit on top of the sheepskin and the dish is then cooked for 4–5 hours. Jumping over fire is a *Newrouz* (New Year) tradition. People dance around the fire, play music and celebrate the arrival of spring.

◆

Put the tripe into a large saucepan with 3 litres (12 cups/ 100 fl oz) water and bring to the boil over medium heat. Reduce the heat and simmer for 1 hour, then drain and rinse in plenty of cold water.

Preheat oven to 160°C/325°F/Gas Mark 3.

To make the stuffing:
Mix the lamb, shallots, *goşteberg* or leeks, dried oregano, cumin, black pepper, ground coriander, drained chickpeas (garbanzo beans), butter and salt in a large bowl or deep tray, until well combined.

Stuff the tripe loosely with the stuffing mixture and roll. Tie into a parcel with cooking string to seal.

To make the basting sauce:
Mix the olive oil, cumin, black pepper, ground paprika and salt in a bowl.

Put the stuffed tripe into a large roasting pan and cover in the basting sauce. Cover with parchment paper and bake in the hot oven for 1½ hours.

Remove the parchment paper, baste the tripe with the cooking juices and return to the oven for a further 10 minutes. Remove the string and bake for a final 10 minutes to brown the top.

Cut the tripe into 8 pieces and serve with parsley, red radish, lemon wedges and *açık ekmek*.

STUFFED INTESTINES
MUMBAR (BUMBAR) DOLMASI

Region:		Siirt, all regions
Preparation time:		30 minutes
Cooking time:		1 hour 45 minutes
Serves:		4

2 metres	sheep's intestines,	80 inches
2	lamb bones with marrow	2
1	lamb brisket bone	1
2 tbsp	lemon juice	2 tbsp
1 (70 g)	carrot	1 (½ cup/2¼ oz)
5	black peppercorns	5

For the filling :		
400 g	minced (ground) lamb	1¾ cups/14 oz
	brisket and back strap	
200 g	medium-grain rice	1 cup/7 oz
2 (240 g)	medium onions, finely sliced	2 (1⅝ cups/ 8½ oz)
1 bunch	flat-leaf parsley	1 bunch
½ tsp	black pepper	½ tsp
2 tsp	dried basil	2 tsp

♦ ❧   p.145 📷

Mumbar is made with rice or bulgur wheat and chickpeas (garbanzo beans); liver, lungs, and so on, may be added to the filling. The dish is traditionally made on the first day of spring and during *Eid-al Adha* (see p.503). Once cooked, *mumbar* can be served in its own cooking juices or fried in olive oil.

♦

To make the filling:
Mix the lamb, rice, onion, parsley (including stems), black pepper, dried basil and ¾ teaspoon salt in a large bowl or deep tray, until well combined.

Clean the lamb's intestine well, then fill with the filling mixture using a funnel and your thumb and index finger. Squeeze the intestine with your palm to move the filling along. Repeat the squeezing process four times. Make sure that the filling is distributed evenly and that the intestine isn't over-stuffed. Poke three evenly spaced holes along the length with the tip of a knife.

Put the bones, lemon juice, carrot, black peppercorns and ¼ teaspoon salt into a saucepan with 3 litres (12 cups/100 fl oz) water and bring to the boil over medium heat. Reduce the heat, skim the surface with a slotted spoon and add the stuffed intestine. Cook, covered, for 1½ hours. Transfer to a serving platter.

♦

OFFAL MEATBALLS
CİĞER DOLMASI (SARMASI)

Region:		Edirne, all regions
Preparation time:	30 minutes, plus 30 minutes soaking	
Cooking time:		50 minutes
Serves:		4

1	lamb's pluck (lungs, liver and heart)	1
120 g	medium-grain rice	¾ cup/4 oz
6	spring onions (scallions)	6
10	flat-leaf parsley sprigs	10
4	dill sprigs	4
2	fresh mint sprigs	2
½ tsp	ground cinnamon	½ tsp
¼ tsp	ground cumin	¼ tsp
1 tsp	dried oregano	1 tsp
2 tbsp	olive oil	2 tbsp
1	piece of caul fat, cut into 8 × 10-cm (4-inch) pieces	1
1	egg, whisked	1
	Yufka Ekmeği (Thin Flatbread), to serve (see p.378)	

♦

This dish is only made in the spring with lamb or kid goat.

♦

Boil the lungs in 1.5 litres (6¼ cups/50 fl oz) water with ¼ teaspoon salt for 10 minutes, then drain. Discard the liver membrane. Dice the offal very finely and set aside.

Soak the rice in 1 litre (4¼ cups/34 fl oz) boiling water with ¼ teaspoon salt for 30 minutes. Drain and rinse.

Preheat oven to 160°C/325°F/Gas Mark 3. Line a large baking tray (pan) with parchment paper. Finely sliced the spring onions (scallions), parsley, dill and mint. Mix with the diced offal, rice, cinnamon, cumin, dried oregano and olive oil in a bowl or deep tray. Season with ¼ teaspoon black pepper and ¾ teaspoon salt.

Soak the caul fat pieces in warm water. Remove the fat from the soaking water and put into a bowl, making sure the lacy fat covers the base. Add an eighth of the meatball mixture, then cover all the mixture with the caul fat to make a ball. Brush thoroughly with egg wash. Put into the lined baking tray. Repeat for all 8 balls.

Pour 200 ml (scant 1 cup/7 fl oz) water into the tray around the meatballs. Bake in the oven for 40 minutes, until browned. Serve with *Yufka Ekmeği* (Thin Flatbreads).

STUFFED & WRAPPED DISHES

STUFFED CHICKEN
TAVUK DOLMASI

Region:		Bursa, all regions
Preparation time:	20 minutes, plus 10 minutes soaking	
Cooking time:	1 hour 20 minutes, plus 10 minutes resting	
Serves:		4

1 (2.5kg)	chicken	1 (5 lb 8oz)
½ tsp	olive oil, for oiling	½ tsp
480 g	potatoes	2 cups/1 lb 1 oz
(480 g)	medium onions	8 (3⅛ cups/1 lb 1 oz)

For the stuffing:

200 g	medium-grain rice	1 cup/7 oz
70 g	butter	⅔ stick/2¾ oz
60 g	onion, finely sliced	2¼ oz
60 g	almonds, skinned	½ cup/2¼ oz
¼ tsp	ground cinnamon	¼ tsp
¼ tsp	ground cardamom	¼ tsp
120 g	chestnuts, peeled and crushed	4 oz
100 g	dried apricots, quartered	1 cup/3½ oz

For the seasoning oil:

4	garlic cloves, crushed	4
1½ tsp	dried oregano	1½ tsp
⅛ tsp	black pepper	⅛ tsp
2 tbsp	olive oil	2 tbsp

p.147 📷

In Bursa, the chicken is served whole and shared around the table. Lamb, rabbit, turkey and other fowl are stuffed whole, the only difference being whether rice or bulgur wheat is used in the stuffing. The liver is usually added, together with currants and pine nuts.

♦

Preheat oven to 160°C/325°F/Gas Mark 3.

To make the stuffing:
Soak the rice in 1 litre (4¼ cups/34 fl oz) hot water with ¼ teaspoon salt for 10 minutes. Drain and rinse.

Heat the butter in a sauté pan over medium heat, add the onion and cook for 3 minutes. Reduce the heat, add the rice and almonds and cook for 7 minutes, stirring continuously. Add 500 ml (generous 2 cups/17 fl oz) hot water, cinnamon, cardamom, ⅛ teaspoon black pepper and ¼ teaspoon salt. Cook, covered, for 10 minutes. Remove from the heat and rest for 10 minutes. Add the crushed chestnuts and dried apricots, then toss gently.

To make the seasoning oil:
Mix the garlic, dried oregano, black pepper, olive oil and ¼ teaspoon salt for 1 minute in a bowl. Massage the chicken with this mixture, inside and out.

Oil a roasting pan. Fill the chicken with the stuffing. Put the chicken into the oiled pan. Add the potatoes and onions, 500 ml (generous 2 cups/17 fl oz) water and ½ teaspoon salt. Roast in the hot oven for 1 hour, checking regularly. Divide into pieces and serve.

♦

AUBERGINES STUFFED WITH QUAIL
PATLICANLI BILDIRCIN DOLMASI

Region:		Yalova, all regions
Preparation time:		10 minutes
Cooking time:		55 minutes
Serves:		4

60 ml	olive oil	¼ cup/2 fl oz
4 × 250 g	plump quails	4 × 9 oz
4 (480 g)	medium onions, sliced into thin crescents	4 (3⅛ cups/ 1 lb 1 oz)
20	garlic cloves	20
4 (1 kg)	large aubergines (eggplants), hollowed out 5 cm (2 inch) in the middle	4 (2 lb 4 oz)
2 tbsp	grape molasses	2 tbsp

This dish is made with plump quails in the hunting season. If your quails are skinny you will need to add 2 tablespoons of butter when cooking.

♦

Preheat oven to 160°C/325°F/Gas Mark 3.

Heat the oil in a large sauté pan over medium heat. Season the quails with ¼ teaspoon black pepper and ½ teaspoon salt, then cook for 2 minutes on each side. Remove the quails from the pan and set aside. Add the onion, garlic and ¼ teaspoon salt and cook for 10 minutes, stirring occasionally. Remove the onion and garlic and set aside. Add the aubergine (eggplant) to the pan and cook for 2 minutes on each side. Remove from the pan and set aside. Finally, add the grape molasses and 200 ml (scant 1 cup/7 fl oz) water to the same pan and boil for 2 minutes.

Put the aubergines on a baking tray (pan). Stuff them first with the quails, then the onion and garlic mixture. Pour over the hot grape molasses. Bake for 30 minutes.

STUFFED & WRAPPED DISHES

STUFFED QUINCES
AYVA DOLMASI

Region:		İstanbul, all regions
Preparation time:		20 minutes, plus 20 minutes soaking
Cooking time:	1 hour 35 minutes, plus 10 minutes resting	
Serves:		4

4 (6 × 10 cm)	quinces, peeled, tops removed and reserved, hollowed out and flesh reserved	4 (2½ x 5 inches)
40 g	butter	3 tbsp/1½ oz
60 ml	grape molasses	¼ cup/2 fl oz
400 ml	meat stock (see p.489), boiling	1⅔ cups/14 fl oz

For the stuffing:

120 g	medium-grain rice	¾ cup/4 oz
60 g	butter	¼ cup/2¼ oz
2 (240 g)	medium onions, finely sliced	2 (1⅝ cups/8½ oz)
200 g	minced (ground) lamb	1 cup/7 oz
30 g	currants	¼ cup/1 oz
1 tbsp	toasted pine nuts	1 tbsp
½ tsp	ground cinnamon	½ tsp
⅛ tsp	black pepper	⅛ tsp
¼ tsp	ground allspice	¼ tsp
400 ml	meat stock (see p.489), boiling	1⅔ cups/14 fl oz
½ bunch	dill, finely sliced	½ bunch

This is a winter dish. Some recipes add tomato paste.

◆

Soak the rice for the stuffing in 600 ml (2½ cups/20 fl oz) warm water with ½ teaspoon salt for 20 minutes. Drain and rinse.

Preheat oven to 160°C/325°F/Gas Mark 3.

To make the stuffing:
Heat the butter in a large sauté pan over medium heat, add the onions and cook for 5 minutes. Add the lamb and cook for 10 minutes. Add the rice, currants, pine nuts, ground cinnamon, black pepper, ground allspice and ½ teaspoon salt and cook for 5 minutes, mixing continuously. Reduce the heat, add the boiling meat stock and simmer, covered, for 10 minutes. Remove from the heat.

Finely chop the reserved quince flesh and add to the stuffing mixture with the dill and mix until well combined. Fill the hollowed out quinces equally with the stuffing mixture and cover with the quince tops. Sit the stuffed quinces upright in a small roasting pan.

Add the butter, grape molasses and meat stock to the pan you used for the stuffing and mix for 3 minutes over low heat. Pour over the stuffed quinces.

Bake for 1 hour in the hot oven. Let rest for 10 minutes and serve.

STUFFED SQUASH ROLLS WITH YOGURT
KATIKLI DOLMA (KATIKLI SARMA)

Region:	Bitlis, Eastern Anatolia
Preparation time:	20 minutes
Cooking time:	50 minutes
Serves:	4

1	winter squash, peeled, sliced into 3-mm (⅛-inch) discs, then into 40 strips, each 4 × 10-cm (1½ × 4-inches)	1
¼ tsp	salt	¼ tsp
400 ml	meat stock (see p.489)	1⅔ cups/14 fl oz

For the stuffing:

100 g	fine bulgur wheat, washed in hot water	½ cup/3½ oz
250 g	minced (ground) goat	1 cup/9 oz
1 (120 g)	medium onion, finely sliced	1 (¾ cup/4 oz)
½ bunch	flat-leaf parsley, finely sliced	½ bunch
4	fresh basil spr gs, finely sliced	4
¼ tsp	black pepper	¼ tsp
½ tsp	dried chilli (red pepper) flakes	½ tsp
½ tsp	salt	½ tsp

For the dressing:

50 g	butter	¼ cup/2 oz
4	garlic cloves, crushed	4
½ tsp	dried chilli (red pepper) flakes	½ tsp

For the yogurt sauce:

250 g	Greek yogurt (goat's milk)	1¼ cups/9 oz
¼ tsp	salt	¼ tsp

This is a winter staple. '*Katık*' refers to yogurt here. Both fresh or dried squash yields a delicious *dolma*. Squash is sliced and dried specifically for this dish. This is an everyday dish which nonetheless always finds itself a place on the table on special occasions.

◆

Massage the squash strips with the salt and set aside.

To make the stuffing:
Mix the bulgur wheat, goat, onion, parsley, basil, black pepper, dried chilli (red pepper) flakes and salt in a large bowl or deep tray for 1 minute. Divide into 40 equal parts.

Spread the squash strips out on a work surface, add a piece of the stuffing to each and roll to enclose.

Arrange the rolls at the bottom of a large, wide saucepan and pour over the meat stock. Cook, covered, over low heat for 30 minutes.

To make the dressing:
Heat the butter in a large sauté pan over medium heat, add the garlic and cook for 10 seconds. Add the dried chilli (red pepper) flakes and fry for a further 10 seconds. Transfer to a small serving bowl.

To make the yogurt sauce:
Whisk the yogurt with the salt in a separate bowl.

Serve the squash rolls, drizzled with the yogurt sauce and the fried garlic and chilli dressing.

STUFFED BREAD
EKMEK DOLMASI

Region:	Aydın and Manisa, Aegean Region	
Preparation time:		25 minutes
Cooking time:		1 hour 20 minutes
Serves:		4

4 (8-cm)	round loaves of whole wheat bread, tops cut off and reserved, hollowed out, the removed bread crumbed and dried	4 (3-inch)
60 ml	olive oil	¼ cup/2 fl oz
4	garlic cloves, crushed	4
4 (25-cm)	olive tree twigs	4 (10-inch)
500 ml	lamb/veal stock (see p.489)	generous 2 cups/ 17 fl oz

For the stuffing:		
2 tbsp	olive oil	2 tbsp
2 (240 g)	medium onions, finely sliced	2 (2½ cups/ 8½ oz)
500 g	lamb, finely chopped	1⅝ cups/1 lb 2 oz
4	spring onions (scallions), finely sliced	4
1 tsp	tomato paste (see p.492)	1 tsp
100 g	unsalted green olives, seeded, quartered	1 cup/3½ oz
100 g	walnuts, crushed	1 cup/3½ oz
½ tsp	dried chilli (red pepper) flakes	½ tsp
½ tsp	black pepper	½ tsp
¾ tsp	salt	¾ tsp
1 bunch	flat-leaf parsley, finely sliced	1 bunch
4	fresh mint sprigs, finely sliced	4
2	fresh basil sprigs, finely sliced	2
2	dill sprigs, finely sliced	2

For the sauce:		
250 g	Greek yogurt	1¼ cups/9 oz
4	garlic cloves, crushed	4
2	flat-leaf parsley sprigs, finely sliced	2
¼ tsp	salt	¼ tsp

p.151 📷

This is a popular Ramadan dish. A special round loaf is baked during Ramadan and used for this dish.

♦

Preheat oven to 150°C/300°F/Gas Mark 2.

To make the stuffing:
Heat the olive oil in a sauté pan over medium heat, add the onions and cook for 5 minutes. Add the lamb and cook for 15 minutes. Add the spring onions (scallions), tomato paste, green olives, walnuts, dried chilli (red pepper) flakes, black pepper and salt and cook, stirring, for 5 minutes. Add the reserved breadcrumbs and cook for 2 minutes. Remove from the heat, add the parsley, fresh mint, fresh basil and dill and mix.

Mix olive oil and garlic in a bowl, then liberally massage the insides and crust of the loaf shells with the mixture. Put the loaves on a baking sheet and bake in the hot oven for 20 minutes, until crisp. Remove from the oven, then tightly pack with the stuffing mixture and put the loaf lids on top.

Put the olive twigs into the bottom of a large saucepan and put the stuffed loaves on top. Pour in the stock and cook over low heat, covered, for 30 minutes. Remove the pan lid every 10 minutes and ladle some of the stock over the loaves.

To make the sauce:
Mix the yogurt, garlic, parsley and salt in a bowl.

Place the stuffed loaves on a large serving platter, pour over the remaining stock and then the yogurt sauce.

STUFFED VINE LEAVES WITH SOUR CHERRIES
VİŞNE DOLMASI (SARMASI)

Region: Kütahya, all regions
Preparation time: 30 minutes, plus 20 minutes soaking
Cooking time: 1 hour 10 minutes
Serves: 4

60	fresh vine leaves	60
250 g	sour cherries, pitted	1⅛ cups/9 oz
2 tbsp	olive oil	2 tbsp

For the stuffing:

120 g	medium-grain rice	¾ cup/4 oz
1 tsp	salt	1 tsp
2 tbsp	olive oil	2 tbsp
3 (360 g)	medium onions, finely sliced	3 (2⅜ cups/ 12 oz)
½ tsp	ground cinnamon	½ tsp
1½ tsp	dried mint	1½ tsp
⅛ tsp	black pepper	⅛ tsp
100 g	sour cherries, pitted, finely chopped	½ cup/3½ oz

p.153 📷

Older culinary resources refer to this dish as 'fake' stuffed vine leaves – the 'genuine' ones containing meat. The cherries can be substituted with other sour summer fruit.

♦

Soak the vine leaves in 1 litre (4¼ cups/34 fl oz) hot water for 10 minutes. Drain, reserving the soaking water. Set aside.

Soak the rice for the stuffing in 600 ml (2½ cups/20 fl oz) warm water with ½ teaspoon salt for 20 minutes, then rinse.

To make the stuffing:
Heat the oil in a sauté pan over medium heat, add the onions and cook for 10 minutes. Add the rice and cook for 5 minutes. Add the ground cinnamon, dried mint, black pepper and ½ teaspoon salt. Cook, stirring, for 5 minutes. Add the sour cherries and 60 ml (¼ cup/2 fl oz) of the reserved soaking water. Reduce the heat and cook, covered, for 10 minutes. Remove the lid and stir gently.

Spread each leaf on a work surface, veins facing up. Spread a line of stuffing along the longer side. Roll the leaf around the stuffing for one full turn, fold in the sides and continue rolling. Arrange the rolls in a saucepan. Crush the cherries, then scatter over the rolls. Mix the oil and ⅛ teaspoon salt with 200 ml (scant 1 cup/7 fl oz) soaking water. Pour over the rolls. Cover most of the surface area with an inverted plate. Cook, covered, over low heat for 40 minutes. Serve.

♦

STUFFED VINE LEAVES
YAPRAK SARMASI

Region: Amasya, all regions
Preparation time: 30 minutes, plus 10 minutes soaking
Cooking time: 1 hour 5 minutes, plus 10 minutes resting
Serves: 4

60	fresh vine leaves	60
50 g	butter	¼ cup/2 oz
500 g	lamb backstrap (medium fat), diced into 2-cm (1-inch) chunks	1 lb 2 oz
750 ml	meat stock (see p.489)	3 cups/25 fl oz

For the stuffing:

100 g	coarse bulgur wheat	½ cup/3½ oz
200 g	minced (ground) mutton	1 cup/7 oz
2 (240 g)	medium onions, finely sliced	2 (1⅝ cups/ 8½ oz)
150 g	tomato, finely sliced	¾ cup/5 oz
1½ tsp	tomato paste (see p.492)	1½ tsp
¼ tsp	ground cumin	¼ tsp

The summer version uses fresh vine leaves, while leaves preserved in brine are substituted in winter.

♦

Soak the vine leaves in 1 litre (4¼ cups/34 fl oz) hot water for 10 minutes, then drain and set aside.

To make the stuffing:
Mix the bulgur wheat, mutton, onion, sliced tomatoes, tomato paste and ground cumin in a bowl or deep tray. Season with ¼ teaspoon black pepper and ½ teaspoon salt. Divide the mixture into 48 equal parts.

Spread the vine leaves out on a work surface, veins facing up. Fill 48 leaves with a piece of stuffing, folding the leaf around it to make 2-cm (1-inch) square parcels.

Heat the butter in a saucepan over medium heat, add the lamb and cook for 10 minutes, stirring continuously.

Layer the remaining leaves in a copper or cast-iron pan. Spread half of the lamb on top. Add the stuffed leaves, then cover with the remaining lamb. Pour the stock over and season with ¼ teaspoon salt. Cover with a plate. Cook for 10 minutes, bringing to the boil. Reduce the heat. Cook, covered, for 45 minutes. Rest for 10 minutes before serving.

STUFFED & WRAPPED DISHES

STUFFED ONIONS
PİYAZ (SOĞAN) DOLMASI

Region:	Van, all regions
Preparation time:	25 minutes
Cooking time:	1 hour 35 minutes, plus 10 minutes resting
Serves:	4

8	large onions, peeled	8
60 ml	grape vinegar	¼ cup/2 fl oz
1 litre	lamb or veal stock	4¼ cups/34 fl oz

For the filling:

70 g	butter	⅓ cup/2½ oz
250 g	minced (ground) veal	1⅛ cup/9 oz
150 g	tomato, finely sliced	¾ cup/5 oz
1½ tsp	tomato paste (see p.492)	1½ tsp
100 g	medium-grain rice	½ cup/3½ oz
50 g	fine bulgur wheat	¼ cup/2 oz
½ tsp	dried chilli (red pepper) flakes	½ tsp
½ bunch	flat-leaf parsley	½ bunch
½ bunch	fresh basil	½ bunch

p.155

This winter dish is a litmus test for a newlywed woman to see if she is a good cook. The bride and groom taste four versions of this dish: spicy, sweet, salty and sour. The different tastes symbolise the balancing act of marriage.

◆

Make a cut in the top of each onion, to about halfway through. In a saucepan, bring 3 litres (12 cups/100 fl oz) water and 1 teaspoon of salt to the boil over medium heat. Add the onions and cook, covered, for 30 minutes. Drain and rinse under cold running water. Separate three outside layers of the onion and chop the removed middle sections.

To make the filling:
Heat the butter in a pan over medium heat, add the chopped onions and cook for 10 minutes. Add the veal and cook for 15 minutes. Add the tomatoes, tomato paste, rice, bulgur wheat and dried chilli (red pepper) flakes. Season with ½ teaspoon salt and ¼ teaspoon black pepper. Cook for 5 minutes. Remove from heat and mix in the finely sliced herbs.

Divide the filling equally between the onion shells. Put the stuffed onions into a saucepan. Add the vinegar and stock. Cook, covered, over low heat for 30 minutes. Remove the from the heat and rest for 10 minutes before serving.

◆

STUFFED GHERKINS
ŞIHILMAHŞİ

Region:	Kilis, Southeastern Anatolia
Preparation time:	20 minutes
Cooking time:	50 minutes
Serves:	4

8	fresh gherkins	8
500 ml	meat stock (see p.489), hot	2 cups/17 fl oz

For the marinade:

4	garlic cloves, crushed	4
1 tbsp	olive oil	1 tbsp

For the stuffing:

200 ml	olive oil	scant 1 cup/7 fl oz
500 g	lean mutton, trimmed	1 lb 2 oz
150 g	roasted chickpeas (garbanzo beans)	5 oz
1 bunch	flat-leaf parsley	1 bunch

For the sauce:

500 g	Greek yogurt	2½ cups/1 lb 2 oz
3	garlic cloves, crushed	3
1 bunch	flat-leaf parsley	1 bunch

Courgettes (zucchini) or Japanese or Italian eggplants can be used for this dish if gherkins are unavailable.

◆

To make the marinade:
Mix the garlic and olive oil with ¼ teaspoon black pepper, and ¼ teaspoon salt in a large bowl. Coat the gherkins, inside and out in the marinade.

To make the stuffing:
In a large saucepan, heat the olive oil over medium heat until hot. Add the gherkins and fry evenly for 3 minutes. Remove with a slotted spoon to drain on paper towels.

Season the mutton with ½ teaspoon black pepper and ½ teaspoon salt and add to the hot oil. Fry for 15 minutes, mixing continuously. Add the roasted chickpeas (garbanzo beans) and cook for 5 minutes. Remove from the heat, add the parsley and mix well. Stuff the gherkins with the meat mixture. Arrange them vertically in a saucepan. Add the meat stock and cook, covered, over low heat for 20 minutes. Remove from the heat and let rest for 5 minutes.

To make the sauce:
In a bowl, mix the yogurt, garlic, parsley and ⅛ teaspoon salt for 1 minute. Transfer the stuffed gherkins to serving plates, drizzle with the sauce and serve.

RED MEAT

MEAT IN TURKISH CULTURE

Meat is loved in Turkey and we have it as often as our means allow. In our cusine, red meat translates to five main dishes: kebabs, grilled *külbastı* (cutlets), meatballs, *kavurma* (confit, or sautéed chunks) and stews. Lamb and mutton are the favourite red meats by far and tradition holds that, when cooking meat, it should contain no blood whatsoever. The animal cooked with its own blood is believed to be still alive.

We do not pour any sauce over our meat dishes. Meat dishes cooked with added water are called 'stews' and dry-roasted dishes are 'kebabs'. Stews are made with very little water and no extra sauce, to keep all their flavours intact. Likewise, meat dishes with yogurt get all their flavour from their ingredients – common flavourings include fresh and dried fruit, vegetables, molasses, honey, hot chilli, pomegranate, sumac, plums, unripe grapes, milk and clotted cream. Kebabs with *tirit* (see p.503) are served with sizzling butter with chilli (chile) and tomato sauce with meat stock.

A popular technique for meat dishes is to make a stew cooked with bulgur wheat. Many of the meatball stews are good examples. All of these dishes are cooked in liquid; some are cooked in diluted tomato paste, some in yogurt and some in plain water, meat or chicken stock.

There are also dried and preserved meat dishes: *Pastırma* (Cured Beef, p.497), *Sucuk* (Spiced Salami, p.496) and *Kavurma* (Lamb Confit, p.497).

Turkish food is a communal affair; we love eating with family and friends, especially outdoors. On outings, meatballs and kebabs are preferred over stews – stews are considered home food. There are plenty of popular fast-food outlets producing meatballs, grilled *külbastı*, *şiş kebab*, *döner kebab* and *cağ kebab*. Kebab shawarmas, *kuyu kebabı* and oven kebabs are also much loved.

MEAT WITH FRUIT

Many red meat dishes are paired with fruit: stews, hot pots, sautés, kebabs, pilafs and confits, among others. Quinces, apples, pears, apricots, sour cherries, cherries, grapes, figs, rosehips, cranberries, pomegranates, lemons, oranges, loquats and unripe almonds are all widely used. The dominant flavour oscillates between sweet, sour and hot, depending on the region. Some like sweet and sour, others hot and sour. A good example is *Ekşili Kebap* (Sour Kebab, p.189) made with pomegranate molasses, which is hot-sour-sweet. Another is *Ayvali Yahni or Ayva Yahnisi* (Lamb and Quince Stew, see p.474), made with lamb and grape molasses, which is sweet and sour. Sultana *borani*, with main ingredients of meat and grapes, is sweet. The meat and fruit transform themselves and each other.

KEBABS

Kebabs come in all shapes and sizes. There is *şiş kebab*, *kuyu kebabı*, *oven kebab*, *külbastı*, *büryan*, meatball kebab and *döner kebab*, among others. In a nutshell, any meat on a skewer grilled over embers is called a kebab. Barbecued kebabs are either spicy or mild, marinated or plain. Meat is finely chopped with a *zırh* (a curved cleaver) or a knife, salt and pepper is added, along with vegetables, and it is squeezed on to a skewer. There are kebabs with no added ingredients where the cooking technique names the dish, such as *tandır kebabı* or *fırın kebabı*. Another example is *külbastı* (cutlets), which is large, flat pieces of meat cooked on a heated grill or over embers. When finely sliced or minced (ground) meat is mixed with the right ingredients and rolled into little balls, the dish is called *köfte* (meatballs). Meatballs are grilled or pan-fried. Some have breadcrumbs, some don't. The liquid the meatballs are cooked in gives the name to the dish, such as meatballs in water, milk, tomato paste or clotted cream.

KAVURMA

Most households make their *Kavurma* (Lamb Confit, see p.497) in the winter months and bury it in earthenware pots. When the *kavurma* is ready, it is distributed to seven poor families first, as families who make their own *kavurma* are usually quite well off. This tradition is similar to the families distributing the meat of the sacrificed sheep to the poor first. *Kavurma* is the traditional way of preserving the rest of the sacrificed animal. It is consumed cold or added to soups, pilafs and egg dishes. It is also eaten at funerals and has a traditional role in ceremonies with prayer for rain.

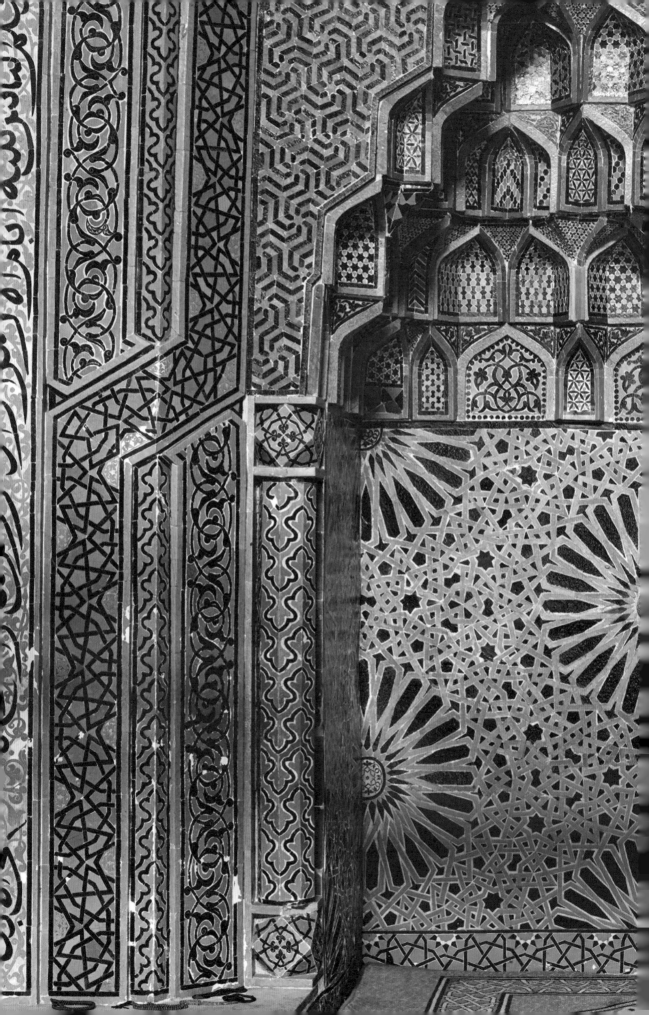

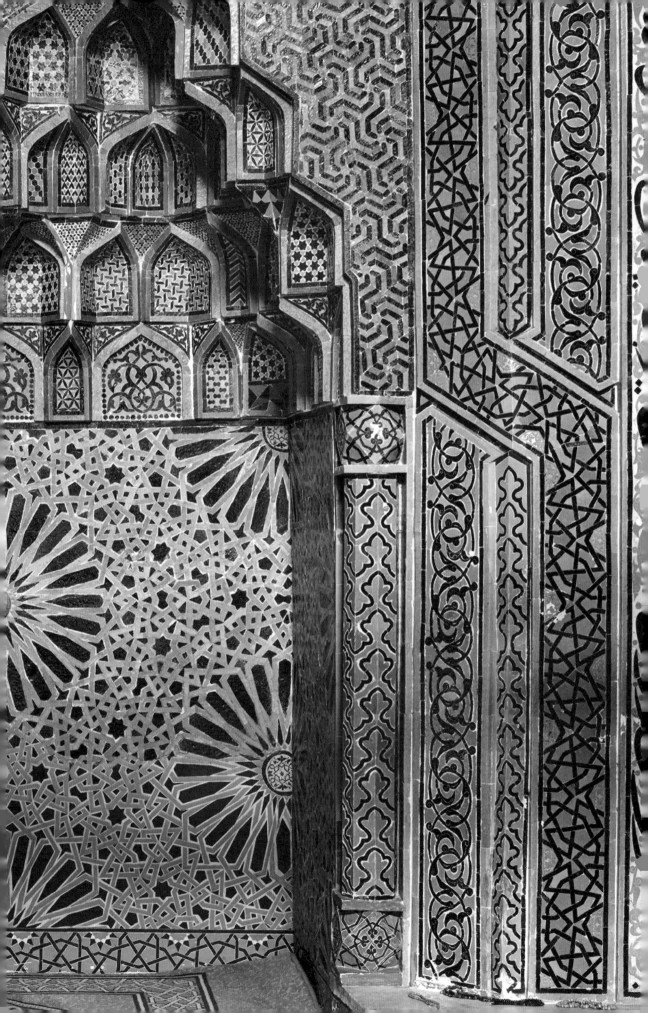

LAMB AND GARLIC STEW
ŞİVEYDİZ

Region:	Gaziantep, Southeastern Anatolia	
Preparation time:	10 minutes, plus overnight soaking	
Cooking time:	1 hour 50 minutes	
Serves:	4	

800 g	lamb shoulder, on the bone, cut into 4 pieces	1 lb 12 oz
60 g	chickpeas (garbanzo beans), soaked overnight, drained	⅓ cup/2¼ oz
8	fresh garlic, without the green leaves	8
8	spring onions (scallions), without the green leaves	8
300 g	strained Greek yogurt	1½ cups/11 oz
3 tbsp	ghee (see p.485)	3 tbsp
1 tbsp	dried mint	1 tbsp

p.163

This dish is best made in the spring, just before the fresh garlic bulbs develop.

◆

In a saucepan, cook the lamb and chickpeas (garbanzo beans) with 1.5 litres (6¼ cups/50 fl oz) water over a low heat, covered, for 1 hour. Chop the fresh garlic and spring onions (scallions) into 2-cm (¾-inch) strips and then add to the pan with ⅛ teaspoon black pepper and ¾ teaspoon salt and cook for 30 minutes.

In a small saucepan over medium heat, mix the strained yogurt with 500 ml (generous 2 cups/17 fl oz) water and bring to the boil, stirring in one direction only. Pour the yogurt mixture into the saucepan with the lamb and cook, uncovered, for 10 minutes. Remove from the heat.

Heat the ghee in a small saucepan over medium heat, add the dried mint and cook for 5 minutes. Pour the mixture into the saucepan with the lamb and stir to combine, then serve.

◆

LAMB AND CHICKPEAS
ETLİ NOHUT

Region:	Yozgat, all regions	
Preparation time:	15 minutes, plus overnight soaking	
Cooking time:	1 hour 20 minutes	
Serves:	4	

280 g	chickpeas (garbanzo beans), soaked overnight, drained	1½ cups/10 oz
60 g	butter	¼ cup/2¼ oz
1 (120 g)	medium onion,	1 (¾ cup/4 oz)
6	garlic cloves	6
400 g	lamb shoulder, finely diced	14 oz
2	lamb bones with marrow, cracked	2
200 g	carrots, finely diced	1½ cups/7 oz
1 tbsp	tomato paste (see p.492)	1 tbsp
1 tsp	red bell pepper paste (see p.492)	1 tsp
½ tsp	dried chilli (red pepper) flakes	½ tsp
¼ tsp	ground cumin	¼ tsp
1.5 litres	meat stock (see p.489), boiling	6¼ cups/50 fl oz
1 tbsp	lemon juice	1 tbsp

A favourite dish for weddings, it is ususally eaten in the winter with pilaf. This dish is also made without the tomato paste and with fresh vegetables.

◆

Simmer the chickpeas (garbanzo beans) in a large saucepan with 1.5 litres (6¼ cups/50 fl oz) water for 1 hour, then drain.

Meanwhile, heat the butter in a large cast-iron pan over medium heat. Finely slice the onion and garlic, add to the pan and cook for 5 minutes. Add the lamb shoulder and lamb bones and cook for 10 minutes. Add the carrot, tomato paste, red bell pepper paste, dried chilli (red pepper) flakes and cumin. Season with ⅛ teaspoon black pepper and 1 teaspoon salt, then cook for 5 minutes. Reduce the heat, pour in the meat stock and lemon juice and cook, covered, for 30 minutes. Add the cooked chickpeas and cook for 20 minutes. Remove the bones before serving.

LAMB, CURD AND SORREL SOUP
KELEDOŞ

Region:		Van, Eastern Anatolia
Preparation time:		20 minutes, plus overnight soaking
Cooking time:		2 hours
Serves:		4

800 g	lamb shoulder on the bone	1 lb 12 oz
40 g	cracked wheat, soaked overnight	⅓ cup/1½ oz
50 g	dried cannellini beans, soaked overnight	¼ cup/2 oz
30 g	chickpeas (garbanzo beans), soaked overnight	¼ cup/1 oz
2 tbsp	green lentils, soaked overnight	2 tbsp
100 g	dried keledoş (a kind of sorrel), rinsed in hot water (or 1 kg/ 2 lb 4 oz dried spinach)	3½ oz
80 g	kashk (see p.485), pulverized	3 oz
1	Açık Ekmek (Ridged Bread, see p.394)	1

For the garnish:

50 g	butter	¼ cup/2 oz
1 (120 g)	medium onion, finely sliced	1 (¾ cup/4 oz)
2 tbsp	hemp seeds	2 tbsp
1 tbsp	basil	1 tbsp
1 tsp	dried chilli (red pepper) flakes	1 tsp

This dish is made in the winter months, on special occasions and days that celebrate peace. There are many extended clans in Southeastern Turkey who have their differences: this dish is made to celebrate once they maintain peace. It can also be made without meat.

♦

Cut the lamb shoulder into 4 pieces. Bring a saucepan of 3 litres (12 cups/100 fl oz) water to the boil. Drain the cracked wheat, beans and chickpeas (garbanzo beans). Add to the boiling water with the lamb shoulder. Reduce the heat and simmer, uncovered, for 5 minutes. Skim the foam off the surface with a slotted spoon. Cover, then cook for 1 hour. Drain the green lentils and add, then cook, covered, for 10 minutes. Finely slice the keledoş or spinach, add and cook for a further 30 minutes.

Ladle 200 ml (scant 1 cup/7 fl oz) of the cooking juices from the pan into another bowl and mix in the kashk. Add back into the pan and cook for a further 10 minutes.

To make the garnish:
Heat the butter in a large saucepan over medium heat, add the onion and cook for 5 minutes. Add the hemp seeds and cook for 1 minute. Finally, add the dried basil and dried chilli (red pepper) flakes and cook for a further 1 minute.

Toast the Açık Ekmek, break it apart and divide equally among serving plates. Top with the cooked soup and pour over the hot garnish.

♦

LAMB AND TİRİT BREAD STEW
TİRİT

Region:		Gaziantep, all regions
Preparation time:		10 minutes
Cooking time:		1 hour 10 minutes
Serves:		4

60 ml	olive oil	¼ cup/2 fl oz
400 g	lamb shoulder, finely diced	14 oz
10	garlic cloves, crushed	10
2 tsp	tomato paste (see p.492)	2 tsp
1 tsp	red bell pepper paste (see p.492)	1 tsp
1 tsp	dried chilli (red pepper) flakes	1 tsp
2 litres	meat stock (see p.489), hot	8½ cups/70 fl oz
60 ml	lemon juice	¼ cup/2 fl oz
400 g	stale Açık Ekmek (Ridged Bread, see p.394)	14 oz
4	flat-leaf parsley sprigs	4

This popular winter staple, with many regional variations, is made regularly to use up stale bread. Poultry, eggs, meat stock, fish and yogurt are all local favourite ingredients. There is a vegetarian version too. The traditional way to serve it is in the middle of a communal table.

♦

Heat the olive oil in a large saucepan over medium heat, add the lamb shoulder and cook for 10 minutes. Add the garlic and cook for 10 minutes. Add the tomato paste, bell pepper paste and dried chilli (red pepper) flakes. Season with ¼ teaspoon black pepper and ¾ teaspoon salt, then cook for a further 5 minutes. Reduce the heat, add the meat stock and cook, covered, for 40 minutes. Stir in the lemon juice.

Dice the bread into 1-cm (½-inch) pieces and divide equally among 4 heat-resistant serving bowls. Top with the stew and cooking juices. Set the bowls over low-medium heat and boil for 2 minutes. Sprinkle with finely sliced parsley and serve (warning guests that the bowls are hot).

RED MEAT

LAMB AND CROÛTON STEW
PAPARA

Region:	Eskişehir, all regions
Preparation time:	10 minutes
Cooking time:	30 minutes
Serves:	4

400 g	minced (ground) lamb	14 oz
50 g	butter	¼ cup/2 oz
2 (240 g)	medium onions	2 (1⅝ cups/8½ oz)
4	banana peppers (mild sweet peppers)	4
1 tsp	dried oregano	1 tsp
¼ tsp	ground cinnamon	¼ tsp

For the sauce:		
500 g	Greek yogurt	2½ cups/1 lb 2 oz
4	garlic cloves, crushed	4
4	dill sprigs	4
4	flat-leaf parsley sprigs	4

400 g	dried stale bread	14 oz
500 ml	meat stock (see p.489)	generous 2 cups/ 17 fl oz
2	flat-leaf parsley sprigs	2

Yet another dish to use up stale bread, *papara* and *tirit* are the two names of the same dish prepared by cooking stale bread in meat stock. The toppings depend on what the family can afford. Meat stock, chicken stock, minced meat, lamb confit are all popular. This dish is presented in a tray and is shared by the whole family. Most families make *tirit* or *papara* at least 15 to 20 times a year. Many a story is shared around this humble dish. Some like it with *topaç kavurması* and with lemon, garlic and chilli. These dishes are mentioned in ancient culinary records.

◆

Heat a saucepan over medium heat. Add the lamb and cook until the fat has rendered out, stirring occasionally. Finely slice the onions and banana peppers, then add to the pan with the butter and cook for 5 minutes. Add the oregano, cinnamon, ¼ teaspoon black pepper and ½ teaspoon salt and cook for a further 10 minutes.

To make the sauce:
Mix the yogurt, garlic, finely sliced dill and parsley in a bowl. Season with ¼ teaspoon salt.

Dice the bread into 5-mm (¼-inch) pieces and divide equally among 4 heat-resistant (stainless steel, copper or heavy ceramic) serving bowls. Boil the meat stock with ½ teaspoon black pepper and ¼ teaspoon salt then pour over the bread. Pour the yogurt sauce over, then top with the stew. Set the bowls over low-medium heat and boil for 2 minutes. Sprinkle with finely sliced parsley and serve (warning guests that the bowls are hot).

LAMB AND BEAN CASSEROLE
KURU FASULYE

Region:	Erzurum, all regions
Preparation time:	10 minutes, plus overnight soaking
Cooking time:	1 hour 15 minutes
Serves:	4

280 g	dried cannellini beans, soaked overnight	1½ cups/ 10 oz
60 g	butter	¼ cup/2¼ oz
1 (120 g)	medium onion	1 (¾ cup/4 oz)
6	garlic cloves	6
400 g	lamb shoulder (medium fat),	14 oz
1 tbsp	tomato paste (see p.492)	1 tbsp
1 tsp	red bell pepper paste (see p.492)	1 tsp
½ tsp	dried chilli (red pepper) flakes	½ tsp
8	dried red chillies (chiles)	8
1.5 litres	meat stock (see p.489), boiling	6¼ cups/50 fl oz

Local variations substitute the lamb with bones or *sucuk* (spicy sausage, see p.496). Some recipes use both lamb and *pastırma* (cured beef, see p.497).

◆

Drain the beans and then place in a large covered saucepan with 2 litres (8½ cups/70 fl oz) water and simmer for 1 hour, skimming off the foam with a slotted spoon from time to time. Drain when cooked.

Meanwhile, heat the butter in a large cast-iron pan over medium heat. Finely slice the onion and garlic, add to the pan and cook for 5 minutes. Finely dice the lamb shoulder and add to the pan, then cook for 10 minutes. Add the tomato paste, red bell pepper paste and dried chilli (red pepper) flakes. Season with ⅛ teaspoon black pepper and 1 teaspoon salt, then cook for 5 minutes. Pour in the hot meat stock and cook, covered, for 30 minutes. Gently stir in the cooked white beans and cook, covered, for a final 15 minutes.

LAMB CASSEROLE
ALUCİYE

Region: Mardin, Southeastern Anatolia
Preparation time: 15 minutes
Cooking time: 1 hour 20 minutes, plus 5 minutes resting
Serves: 4

600 g	lamb, diced into 2-cm (1¾-inch) pieces	1 lb 5 oz
60 ml	olive oil	¼ cup/2 fl oz
60 g	onion, finely sliced	⅜ cup/2¼ oz
4	garlic cloves, finely sliced	4
1	summer squash, finely sliced	1
8	spring onions (scallions), finely sliced, white and green parts separated	8
200 ml	sour plum extract (see p.491)	scant 1 cup/ 7 fl oz
1 bunch	flat-leaf parsley	1 bunch
½ bunch	fresh coriander (cilantro)	½ bunch

p.167

This dish is made in the spring when plums are in season. Devotees like preserving greengages or sour plums during the spring months for use in the winter. This dish is delicious hot or cold.

♦

Add the lamb and 1.5 litres (6¼ cups/50 fl oz) water to a large saucepan over medium heat and cook for 5 minutes. Skim off the foam on the surface with a slotted spoon. Reduce the heat and simmer, covered, for 1 hour.

Meanwhile, 20 minutes before the lamb is ready, heat the olive oil in a large saucepan over medium heat, add the onion and garlic and cook for 1 minute. Add the summer squash and the whites of the spring onions (scallions) and cook for 2 minutes. Add the spring onion greens with ⅛ teaspoon black pepper and ¾ teaspoon salt and cook for a further 1 minute. Stir in the sour plum extract, cook for 1 minute, then pour this mixture into the saucepan with the lamb and cook for 20 minutes.

Remove from the heat and let rest for 5 minutes. Finely slice the parsley and coriander (cilantro), sprinkle over the casserole and serve.

♦

BAKED LAMB WITH PLUMS
ERİK TAVASI

Region: Gaziantep, Southeastern Anatolia
Preparation time: 10 minutes
Cooking time: 1 hour 30 minutes, plus 10 minutes resting
Serves: 4

60 ml	olive oil	¼ cup/2 fl oz
600 g	lamb shoulder, diced into 2-cm (¾-inch) pieces	1 lb 5 oz
4	garlic cloves, peeled	4
1 tbsp	tomato paste (see p.492)	1 tbsp
1 tsp	hot red bell pepper paste	1 tsp
½ tsp	dried chilli (red pepper) flakes	½ tsp
1 litre	meat stock (see p.489), hot	4¼ cups/ 34 fl oz
40	greengages or sour plums	40

Greengage plums are used in many dishes in our country. The locals around Nizip love preparing this dish in the spring, just before the plums start getting some colour. It is even more delicious when cooked in a wood-fired oven. Once ready, the earthenware pots are sent to the local bakery to be cooked in the communal oven. The traditional side dish is rice pilaf with vermicelli.
♦
Preheat oven to 200°C/400°F/Gas Mark 6.

Heat the olive oil in a large casserole dish (Dutch oven) over medium heat until very hot, add the lamb shoulder and cook for 10 minutes. Add the garlic and cook for 2 minutes. Add the tomato paste, red bell pepper paste and dried chilli (red pepper) flakes. Season with ⅛ teaspoon black pepper and ¾ teaspoon salt and cook for 3 minutes.

Add the meat stock, then bake in the hot oven for 40 minutes. Add the plums and cook, covered, for a final 30 minutes.

Rest for 10 minutes before serving the lamb in its own cooking juices.

RED MEAT

LAMB AND OKRA
BAMYA EKŞİSİ

Region:		Konya, all regions
Preparation time:		20 minutes
Cooking time:		1 hour 10 minutes
Serves:		4

300 g	lamb	11 oz
50 g	ghee (see p.485)	3½ tbsp/2 oz
1 (120 g)	medium onion	1 (¾ cup/4 oz)
6	garlic cloves	6
1	small bell pepper	1
300 g	tomatoes	1½ cups/11 oz
1½ tsp	tomato paste (see p.492)	1½ tsp
1 tsp	red bell pepper paste (see p.492)	1 tsp
1 tsp	dried chilli (red pepper) flakes	1 tsp
1.5 litres	meat stock (see p.489)	6¼ cups/50 fl oz
200 ml	verjuice (see p.494) (or 3 tbsp lemon juice)	scant 1 cup/ 7 fl oz
500 g	fresh okra	1 lb 2 oz

This dish is made in the summer months. The winter version uses dried okra.

♦

Dice the lamb into 2-cm (¾-inch) pieces. Heat the ghee in a large saucepan over medium heat, add the lamb and cook for 10 minutes.

Finely slice the the onion, garlic and bell pepper, add to the pan and cook for 10 minutes.

Finely slice the tomatoes and add to the pan with the tomato paste, red bell pepper paste and dried chilli (red pepper) flakes. Season with ⅛ teaspoon black pepper and ¾ teaspoon salt, then cook for 5 minutes.

Reduce the heat, pour in the meat stock and verjuice and cook, covered, for 20 minutes. Top and tail the okra, then add to the pan and cook for a further 20 minutes before serving.

♦

MEATBALLS IN YOGURT SAUCE
TAPPUŞ ORUĞU

Region:		Hatay, Mediterranean Region
Preparation time:		20 minutes
Cooking time:		1 hour 5 minutes
Serves:		4

60 g	onion	⅜ cup/2¼ oz
200 g	potato	1 cup/7 oz
200 g	fine bulgur wheat	⅞ cup/7 oz
200 g	finely minced (ground) lean lamb	1 cup/7 oz
½ tsp	ground cumin	½ tsp
6	garlic cloves, crushed	6
1 tsp	dried mint	1 tsp
1 tsp	dried chilli (red pepper) flakes	1 tsp
1 tbsp	dried basil	1 tbsp
1 tbsp	tomato paste (see p.492)	1 tbsp
500 ml	olive oil	generous 2 cups/17 fl oz

For the sauce:		
2	fresh basil sprigs	2
4	flat-leaf parsley sprigs	4
1	spring onion (scallion)	1
1	fresh garlic	1
500 g	Greek yogurt	2½ cups/1 lb 2 oz

This dish is made in the autumn and winter months, as well as during religious festivals. The bride-to-be makes this for the groom and his family when they visit to ask for her hand in marriage.

♦

Place the potato in a large saucepan of water, bring to the boil and boil for 40 minutes. When cooked, remove from the pan and mash.

Grate the onion, then strain and collect the juice. With wet hands, mix the fine bulgur wheat, lamb, mashed potato, onion juice, cumin, garlic, dried mint, dried chilli (red pepper) flakes, dried basil, ½ teaspoon salt, ¼ teaspoon black pepper, tomato paste and olive oil in a large bowl or deep tray and knead for 15 minutes, until well combined. Divide the mixture into 12 equal parts and roll into 6-cm (2¼-inch) flat discs.

Heat the olive oil in a sauté pan over medium heat, until hot. Fry the meatballs in batches, for 3 minutes on each side.

To make the sauce:
Finely slice the basil, parsley, spring onions (scallions) and garlic. Mix together with the yogurt and ¼ teaspoon salt.

Serve the meatballs with a small bowl of yogurt sauce on the side of each serving.

RED MEAT

LAMB AND APRICOT STEW
KAYISI YAHNİSİ

Region:	Malatya, all regions
Preparation time:	15 minutes
Cooking time:	1 hour 10 minutes, plus 10 minutes resting
Serves:	4

70 g	ghee (see p.485)	⅓ cup/2¾ oz
500 g	lamb backstrap, diced	1 lb 2 oz
1	cinnamon stick	1
40	shallots, peeled	40
100 g	apricot kernels, soaked in boiling water for 5 minutes, peeled	3½ oz
500 ml	meat stock (see p.489), hot	generous 2 cups/ 17 fl oz
300 g	dried apricots, each quartered	1½ cups/11 oz

This dish is made in the winter months. Some versions include chickpeas (garbanzo beans), while some prefer sour apricots. Other dried fruits also work well in this dish.

◆

Dice the lamb into 2-cm (1-inch) pieces. Heat the ghee in a large saucepan over medium heat, add the lamb and sauté on each side for 2 minutes. Add the cinnamon stick, shallots and apricot kernels and cook for 10 minutes. Season with ¼ teaspoon black pepper and ½ teaspoon salt, then cook for 2 minutes. Reduce the heat, add the meat stock, cover tightly and simmer for 30 minutes. Add the dried apricots and cook for a further 20 minutes.

Let rest for 10 minutes before serving.

LAMB KEBAB
KUŞBAŞI KEBABI

Region:	Gaziantep, all regions
Preparation time:	15 minutes, plus overnight marinating
Cooking time:	20–40 minutes
Serves:	4

800 g	lean lamb loin, trimmed of sinew, diced into 3-cm (1-¼ inch) chunks	1 lb 12 oz
200 g	lamb tail fat, diced into small chunks	7 oz
400 g	tomatoes, quartered	2 cups/14 oz
8	banana peppers	8

For the marinade :		
200 ml	olive oil	scant 1 cup/7 fl oz
15	garlic cloves, crushed	15
50 g	Greek yogurt	¼ cup/2 oz
1 tbsp	tomato paste (see p.492)	1 tbsp
2 tsp	red bell pepper paste (see p.492)	2 tsp
2 tbsp	dried chilli (red pepper) flakes	2 tbsp
1 tsp	dried oregano	1 tsp
4	*Tirnakli Ekmek* (Pide Flatbread, see p.376)	4
1	*Piyaz Salatası* (Onion Salad, see p.67)	1

There is also a plain version of this dish where there is no marinade. The meat is seasoned with salt and spices as it is being grilled. If you don't have a barbecue, you can use a regular grill (broiler). You will need 8 long cast-iron skewers or 10 flat wooden skewers (soaked).

◆

To make the marinade:
Mix the olive oil, garlic, yogurt, tomato paste, red bell pepper paste, dried chilli (red pepper) flakes, dried oregano, ½ teaspoon black pepper and 1 teaspoon salt in a bowl for 5 minutes. Add the lamb loin and tail fat, mix through, cover and marinate overnight in the refrigerator.

The next day, prepare a barbecue for cooking or preheat a grill (broiler) to high. Thread the marinated meat and tail fat onto each of the skewers, alternating 1 piece of tail fat between 2 pieces of meat. Pack snugly. Place 2 pieces of tomato and 1 banana pepper on each skewer.

Set the skewers 8 cm (3 inches) above the hot embers and cook for 3 minutes on each side, 12 minutes in total, turning every 30 seconds. Alternatively, grill (broil) the skewers for 5–6 minutes on each side, turning frequently.

Warm the *Tirnakli Ekmek* (flatbreads) on the barbecue or grill for 30 seconds on each side.

Cut the flatbreads into quarters lengthwise. Use them to draw off the meat from the skewers onto serving platters, on top of the cut breads. Serve with the *Piyaz Salatası*.

RED MEAT

RACK OF LAMB WITH QUINCE
AYVALI TARAKLI

Region:	Gaziantep, Southeastern Anatolia	
Preparation time:		15 minutes
Cooking time:		50 minutes
Serves:		4

1.5 kg	rack of lamb	3 lb 5 oz
2 tbsp	olive oil	2 tbsp
1 tsp	dried chilli (red pepper) flakes	1 tsp

For the sauce:

100 g	ghee (see p.485)	scant ½ cup/3½ oz
1	hot chilli (chile)	1
2 (600 g)	quinces	2 (1 lb 5 oz)
1 (120 g)	medium onion	1 (¾ cup/4 oz)
8	garlic cloves	8
1 tbsp	red bell pepper paste (see p.492)	1 tbsp
1 tbsp	tomato paste (see p.492)	1 tbsp
1	cinnamon stick	1
500 ml	lamb/veal stock, hot (see p.489)	generous 2 cups/ 17 fl oz
2 tbsp	pomegranate molasses	2 tbsp

Taraklı refers to ribs in the Southeastern Anatolian vernacular. Made in the autumn and winter months when quinces are available, it is cooked in earthenware pots.

◆

Preheat oven to 180°C/350°F/Gas Mark 4. Cut the rack of lamb into 8 equal pieces. Stir together the lamb, oil and dried chilli (red pepper) flakes in a large bowl with ¼ teaspoon black pepper and ½ teaspoon salt for 1 minute until the meat is well seasoned.

Heat a large saucepan over medium heat until hot, then add the lamb and sear for 2 minutes on each side. Remove the lamb to a plate and set aside.

To make the sauce:
Heat the ghee in the same pan until hot. De-seed and quarter the quinces. Quarter the onion. Cut the chilli (chile) lengthwise and then crosswise into quarters. Add the quince, onion, chilli and garlic, then cook for 5 minutes. Add the red bell pepper paste, tomato paste, cinnamon stick and lamb and cook for 3 minutes, stirring continuously. Add the stock, pomegranate molasses and ½ teaspoon salt. Cook for a further 2 minutes, stirring continuously.

Transfer the mixture a large earthenware pot or casserole (Dutch oven), cover tightly and cook in the hot oven for 30 minutes. Serve immediately.

◆

LAMB AND AUBERGINE STEW WITH SUMAC
MEFTUNE

Region:	Diyarbakır, Southeastern Anatolia	
Preparation time:		30 minutes
Cooking time:		1 hour 15 minutes
Serves:		4

600 g	aubergine (eggplant), peeled	1 lb 5 oz
60 g	tail fat or ghee, melted	¼ cup/2¼ oz
600 g	lamb rib meat, diced into 2-cm (¾-inch) pieces	1 lb 5 oz
60 g	onion, finely sliced	⅜ cup/2¼ oz
10	garlic cloves, finely sliced	10
2	fresh chillies (chiles)	2
1½ tsp	tomato paste (see p.492)	1½ tsp
1 tsp	red bell pepper paste (see p.492)	1 tsp
1 tsp	smoked dried chilli (red pepper) flakes	1 tsp
1.5 kg	tomatoes, finely diced	7½ cups/3 lb 5 oz
200 ml	sumac extract (see p.491)	scant 1 cup/ 7 fl oz

This summer dish is also made with other seasonal vegetables, such as globe artichokes, courgettes (zucchini), beans or okra. The recipe is recorded in old recipe books without the tomato paste, tomatoes and peppers.

◆

Soak the aubergine (eggplant) in 1.5 litres (6¼ cups/ 50 fl oz) water with 1 teaspoon salt for 15 minutes. Drain, rinse, squeeze out any excess water and pat dry with paper towels. Finely dice and set aside.

Heat the fat or ghee in a saucepan over medium heat, add the lamb and cook for 5 minutes on both sides. Remove the lamb and set aside. Add the onion and garlic to the same pan and cook for 10 minutes. Finely slice the chillies (chiles). Add to the pan with the tomato paste, red bell pepper paste and smoked dried chilli (red pepper) flakes. Season with ⅛ teaspoon black pepper and ¾ teaspoon salt, then cook for 5 minutes. Add the aubergine and cook for 5 minutes, mixing continuously.

Return the lamb to the pan and push down into the mixture so it sits at the bottom. Reduce the heat, add the tomatoes and the sumac extract and cook over low heat, covered, for 40 minutes. Remove from the heat, mix thoroughly and serve.

RED MEAT

STEWED GOAT WITH PICKLES
ÇORTİ AŞI

Region:		Muş, Eastern Anatolia
Preparation time:		15 minutes, plus overnight soaking
Cooking time:		1 hour 35 minutes
Serves:		4

300 g	*Lahana Turşusu* (Pickled Cabbage see p.82)	11 oz
100 g	*Biber Turşusu* (Pickled Bell Peppers, see p.83)	3½ oz
80 g	chickpeas (garbanzo beans), soaked overnight	⅜ cup/3 oz
80 g	cracked wheat, soaked overnight	⅔ cup/3 oz
1 (120 g)	medium onion	1 (¾ cup/4 oz)
2	chard leaf ribs	2
4 (1 kg)	goat shoulders on the bone	4 (2 lb 3 oz)
500 ml	pickling brine	generous 2 cups/ 17 fl oz
1 litre	meat stock (see p.489)	4¼ cups/ 34 fl oz

For the sauce:

3 tbsp	ghee (see p.485)	3 tbsp
60 g	onion, finely sliced	⅜ cup/2¼ oz
½ tsp	dried chilli (red pepper) flakes	½ tsp
1 tbsp	dried basil	1 tbsp

This is a very popular dish around Muş, Bitlis and their surrounding areas in the winter months. The pickles and brine provide enough salt for the dish. There is also a vegetarian version consisting of patties made up of bulgar, garlic and salt that replace the meatballs, which are added to the dish in the last 10 minutes of cooking.

◆

Preheat oven to 160°C/325°F/Gas Mark 3.

Rinse and finely slice the pickled cabbage and pickled bell peppers. Rinse and drain the chickpeas (garbanzo beans) and cracked wheat. Finely slice the onion and chard leaf ribs. Mix the pickles, chickpeas, cracked wheat, onion and chard leaf ribs in a large bowl or deep tray. Spread half of the mixture over the bottom of a casserole dish (Dutch oven). Arrange the goat shoulder meat on top, then cover with the rest of the mixture. Add the pickling brine and meat stock, cover tightly and cook in the hot oven for 1½ hours.

To make the sauce:
Heat the ghee in a small saucepan over medium heat, add the onions and cook for 2 minutes. Add the dried chilli (red pepper) flakes and dried basil and cook for 10 seconds.

Serve the stew on individual plates with the sauce.

◆

SAUTÉED SPICED LAMB
SAC KAVURMA

Region:		Ankara, all regions
Preparation time:		10 minutes
Cooking time:		40 minutes
Serves:		4

100 g	tail fat or ghee, melted	scant ½ cup/ 3½ oz
600 g	lamb backstrap, finely diced	1 lb 5 oz
1 (120 g)	medium onion	1 (¾ cup/4 oz)
2	red chillies (chiles)	2
2	green chillies (chiles)	2
1 tsp	dried chilli (red pepper) flakes	1 tsp
¼ tsp	ground cumin	¼ tsp
1 tsp	dried oregano	1 tsp
300 g	tomatoes	1½ cups/11 oz

This dish is the ultimate *Eid-al-Adha* feast. It is roasted in its own fat.
◆
Heat a large *sac* (see p.503), iron skillet or wok until very hot. Add the tail fat or ghee and heat for 1 minute. Add the lamb backstrap and sauté for 10 minutes, mixing continuously.

Finely dice the onion, add to the pan and sauté for 10 minutes. Finely dice the red and green chillies (chiles), add to the pan and sauté for 5 minutes. Add the dried chilli (red pepper) flakes, cumin and dried oregano. Season with ¼ teaspoon black pepper and ¾ teaspoon salt, then sauté for 3 minutes.

Finely dice the tomatoes. Reduce the heat, add the diced tomatoes and cook for 5 minutes, mixing gently, and then cook without mixing for a final 5 minutes.

RED MEAT

FESTIVE MEATBALL AND CHICKPEA STEW
TIKLİYE

Region:	Şanlıurfa, Southeastern Anatolia	
Preparation time:	10 minutes, plus overnight soaking	
Cooking time:		1 hour 50 minutes
Serves:		4

60 g	chickpeas (garbanzo beans), soaked overnight, drained	⅓ cup/2¼ oz
4 × 200-g	cuts of lamb shoulder on the bone	4 × 7-oz
2 tbsp	medium-grain rice	2 tbsp
200 g	strained Greek yogurt	1 cup/7 oz

For the meatballs:		
100 g	fine bulgur wheat	1¼ cups/3½ oz
150 g	minced (ground) lamb (lean, sinew trimmed)	5 oz
60 g	onion, finely sliced	⅜ cup/2¼ oz

For the sauce:		
2 tbsp	butter	2 tbsp
1 tbsp	dried mint	1 tbsp

p.173

This is a dish for religious festivals. Other local recipes use cracked rice, lentils, chickpea flour (besan) and legumes instead of bulgur wheat. Cooking the chickpeas (garbanzo beans) and meat in a pressure cooker with 1.5 litres (6¼ cups/50 fl oz) water reduces the cooking time significantly.

♦

In a saucepan, simmer the chickpeas (garbanzo beans), lamb and ¾ teaspoon salt in 3 litres (12 cups/100 fl oz) water, covered, for 1 hour. Add the rice and cook for 30 minutes.

To make the meatballs:
Combine the bulgur wheat, lamb and onion with ⅛ teaspoon black pepper and ⅛ teaspoon salt in a bowl or deep tray. Knead for 15 minutes, until well combined. Roll the mixture into very small, round meatballs, approximately 1 cm (½ inch) in size. Add the meatballs to the stew, bring it back to the boil, then reduce the heat.

Whisk the yogurt together with 250 ml (1 cup/8 fl oz) cold water in a small saucepan. Bring to the boil and cook for 1 minute, then remove from the heat. Reduce the heat and simmer for 10 minutes, stirring in the same direction. Add the mixture with a pinch of black pepper to the stew, cook for 5 minutes, then remove from the heat.

To make the sauce:
Briefly heat the butter in a saucepan over medium heat, add the dried mint and fry for 5 seconds. Pour the sauce into the stew and serve, along with the cooking juices.

♦

MEATBALLS IN MILK
SÜTLÜ KÖFTE

Region:	Bartın, Black Sea Region	
Preparation time:		20 minutes
Cooking time:	30 minutes, plus 5 minutes resting	
Serves:		4

800 g	veal shoulder, chopped	1 lb 12 oz
1 (120 g)	medium onion, finely sliced	1 (¾ cup/4 oz)
½ bunch	flat-leaf parsley	½ bunch
¼ tsp	ground cumin	¼ tsp
50 g	butter	¼ cup/2 oz

For the saffron sauce:		
2 litres	milk	8½ cups/70 fl oz
pinch	saffron threads, soaked in in 60 ml (¼ cup/2 fl oz) boiling water for 20 minutes	pinch

This winter dish works as a litmus test to see how skilful a potential bride is. It is presented at wedding banquets with pilaf and fruit compote. Peas are sometimes substituted with dried black-eyed peas or chickpeas.

♦

Combine the veal, onion, finely sliced flat-leaf parsley and ground cumin in a bowl or deep tray. Season with ¼ teaspoon black pepper and ½ teaspoon salt, then knead for 2 minutes. Roll the mixture into 24 meatballs. Heat the butter in a saucepan over medium heat, add the meatballs and fry for 2 minutes on each side, 8–10 minutes in total.

To make the sauce:
Meanwhile, in a separate saucepan, boil the milk with a generous pinch of salt, stirring in one direction only.

Reduce the heat under the meatballs and add the hot milk and ¼ teaspoon black pepper and simmer for 10 minutes. Add the saffron in its soaking water and cook for 2 minutes. Remove from the heat and let rest for 5 minutes. Serve the meatballs with the saffron sauce.

MEATBALLS IN WHITE LEMON SAUCE
TERBİYELİ EKŞİ KÖFTE

Region:	Tekirdağ, all regions
Preparation time:	25 minutes
Cooking time:	55 minutes
Serves:	4

For the meatballs:

600 g	minced (ground) veal shoulder (medium fat)	1 lb 5 oz
60 g	broken rice	⅓ cup/2 oz
60 g	onion, grated, strained and juice collected	⅜ cup/ 2¼ oz
1	egg	1
2 tbsp	dried basil	2 tbsp
¼ tsp	ground cumin	¼ tsp
¼ tsp	black pepper	¼ tsp
½ tsp	salt	½ tsp

2 tbsp	olive oil	2 tbsp
60 g	onion, finely sliced	⅜ cup/2¼ oz
4	garlic cloves, finely sliced	4
200 g	carrots, finely diced	1⅓ cups/7 oz
300 g	potatoes, finely diced	1⅓ cups/11 oz
1	celery stick (stalk), finely diced	1
250 g	shelled peas	1⅔ cups/9 oz
¼ tsp	black pepper	¼ tsp
½ tsp	salt	½ tsp
1.5 litres	meat stock (see p.489)	6¼ cups/ 50 fl oz

For the white lemon sauce:

2 tbsp	lemon juice	2 tbsp
2 tbsp	grape vinegar	2 tbsp
2	egg yolks	2
6	flat-leaf parsley sprigs, very finely sliced	6

This winter dish is very popular at wedding banquets and is served with pilaf and fruit compote.

♦

In a large saucepan, simmer the chickpeas (garbanzo beans), lamb shoulder and salt in 3 litres (12 cups/100 fl oz) water, covered, for 1 hour. Add the rice and cook for a further 30 minutes.

To make the meatballs:
Knead the veal, rice, onion juice, egg, dried basil, cumin, black pepper and salt in a large bowl or deep tray for 5 minutes. Roll the mixture into 2-cm (¾-inch) meatballs.

Heat the olive oil in a large saucepan over medium heat, add the onion and garlic and cook for 2 minutes. Add the carrots, potatoes, celery and peas and cook for 5 minutes. Add the black pepper and salt and cook for 2 minutes.

Reduce the heat, add the meat stock and cook, covered, for 10 minutes. Add the meatballs and continue to cook, covered, for 30 minutes. Remove from the heat.

To make the white lemon sauce:
Mix the lemon juice, grape vinegar, eggs yolks and parsley in a small bowl.

Drizzle the sauce into the meatball pan, gently stir through, then let rest for 2 minutes before serving.

MOTHERS AND DAUGHTERS
ANALI KIZLI

Region:	Adana, Mediterranean Region	
Preparation time:	30 minutes, plus overnight soaking	
Cooking time:	1 hour 45 minutes	
Serves:		4

60 g	chickpeas (garbanzo beans), soaked overnight and drained	⅓ cup/2¼ oz
500 g	shoulder of lamb, diced into 2-cm (¾-inch) pieces	1 lb 2 oz
60 ml	olive oil	¼ cup/2 fl oz
6	garlic cloves, crushed	6
60 g	onion, finely sliced	⅜ cup/2¼ oz
1½ tsp	tomato paste (see p.492)	1½ tsp
1½ tsp	red bell pepper paste (see p.492)	1½ tsp
1 tbsp	dried mint	1 tbsp
2	tomatoes, grated	2
60 ml	pomegranate molasses	¼ cup/2 fl oz
¼ tsp	salt	¼ tsp
⅛ tsp	black pepper	⅛ tsp

For the meatballs:

200 g	fine bulgur wheat	⅞ cup/7 oz
300 g	lean minced (ground) lamb	11 oz
2	garlic cloves, crushed	2
¼ tsp	salt	¼ tsp
1 tsp	tomato paste (see p.492)	1 tsp
1	egg	1
60 g	onion, grated, strained and juice collected	⅜ cup/ 2¼ oz
⅛ tsp	ground cumin	⅛ tsp
¼ tsp	black pepper	¼ tsp

For the stuffing:

1	lamb's caul fat, chopped	1
70 g	walnuts, crushed	scant ½ cup/2½ oz
2	garlic cloves, crushed	2
1½ tsp	dried mint	1½ tsp
1 tsp	dried chilli (red pepper) flakes	1 tsp
2	flat-leaf parsley sprigs, finely sliced	2
¼ tsp	salt	¼ tsp

This winter dish has many different local names and fillings. In the Eastern Mediterranean it is called both Mothers and Daughters and Sour Meal (due to the pomegranate molasses), Southeastern Anatolia calls it *Şırşırı-Lıklıkı*, and Bland Meatballs (because they contain so little meat) in Eastern Anatolia. This dish is a wedding banquet staple together with pilaf and fruit compote.

♦

In a large saucepan, bring the chickpeas (garbanzo beans), lamb shoulder and 1.5 litres (6¼ cups/50 fl oz) water to the boil over medium heat. Reduce the heat and cook, covered, for 1 hour.

To make the stuffing:
Mix the caul fat, walnuts, garlic, mint, dried chilli (red pepper) flakes, parsley and salt in a bowl for 3 minutes, until well combined. Divide the mixture into 8 equal parts and roll into balls. Refrigerate until needed.

To make the meatballs:
With wet hands, knead the bulgur wheat, lamb, garlic, salt, tomato paste, egg, onion juice, cumin and black pepper in a large bowl or deep tray for 15 minutes, until well combined. Roll half the mixture into 1-cm (½-inch) balls. Divide the other half of the mixture into 8 equal parts, roll each piece in your palm and create a cavity in the middle with your index finger. Fill each cavity with the chilled stuffing balls. Make sure the stuffing is fully enclosed inside the meatball.

Heat the olive oil in a large saucepan over medium heat, add the garlic and the onions and cook for 1 minute. Add the tomato paste, red bell pepper paste and dried mint and cook for 2 minutes. Add the tomatoes, pomegranate molasses, salt and black pepper and cook for 5 minutes. Add this mixture to the pan with the chickpeas and lamb and cook, covered, for another 30 minutes.

Turn the heat to medium, add all the meatballs to the pan and cook, uncovered, for 15 minutes, until all the meatballs have floated to the surface.

Transfer to bowls to serve.

MEATBALLS WITH SOUR CHERRIES
VİŞNELİ KÖFTE

Region:	Gaziantep, Southeastern Anatolia	
Preparation time:	20 minutes	
Cooking time:	40 minutes	
Serves:	4	

100 g	ghee (see p.485)	scant ½ cup/3½ oz
1 (120 g)	medium onion	1 (¾ cup/4 oz)
6	garlic cloves, finely sliced	6
1½ tsp	tomato paste (see p.492)	1½ tsp
1 tsp	red bell pepper paste (see p.492)	1 tsp
1	cinnamon stick	1
¼ tsp	ground cloves	¼ tsp
1 tsp	dried chilli (red pepper) flakes	1 tsp
250 g	sour cherries	9 oz
1 litre	meat stock (see p.489), hot	4¼ cups/ 34 fl oz

For the meatballs:

60 g	onion	⅜ cup/2¼ oz
500 g	lean minced (ground) lamb	1 lb 2 oz
1 tsp	dried chilli (red pepper) flakes	1 tsp
5	flat-leaf parsley sprigs	5
2½ tbsp	pine nuts, toasted	2½ tbsp

Served on squares of crisp flatbread or bread, this is a summer dish, made in sour cherry season.

♦

To make the meatballs:
Grate the onion, strain and collect the juice. Mix the lamb, onion juice, dried chilli (red pepper) flakes, ⅛ teaspoon black pepper and ¼ teaspoon salt in a large bowl or deep tray and knead for 5 minutes. Roll the mixture into 1-cm (½-inch) meatballs.

Heat the ghee in a large saucepan over medium heat, add the meatballs and fry for 5 minutes, shaking the pan every now and then. Remove the meatballs with a slotted spoon. Add the onion and garlic to the pan and cook for 5 minutes. Add the tomato paste, red bell pepper paste, cinnamon, cloves, dried chilli (red pepper) flakes and ½ teaspoon salt and cook for 2 minutes.

Strain the sour cherries, collecting the juice, and then pit them. Add the sour cherries to the pan and cook, stirring gently, for 10 minutes. Add the meatballs and cook for a further 5 minutes, stirring gently. Reduce the heat, add the sour cherry juice and meat stock and cook, covered, for 10 minutes.

Sprinkle with finely sliced flat-leaf parsley and pine nuts and serve.

♦

LAMB ON CRACKED WHEAT
SERBİDEV

Region:	Şırnak, Southeastern Anatolia	
Preparation time:	10 minutes, plus overnight soaking	
Cooking time:	1 hour 5 minutes	
Serves:	4	

150 g	cracked wheat, soaked overnight	1¼ cups/5 oz
800 g	lamb	1 lb 12 oz
100 g	butter	scant ½ cup/3½ oz
10	garlic cloves, crushed	10
½ tsp	dried chilli (red pepper) flakes	½ tsp
80 g	kashk (dried fresh cheese or yogurt, see p.485), ground	3 oz
6	flat-leaf parsley sprigs	6
2	fresh basil sprigs	2

This dish is cooked on special occasions.

♦

Drain the cracked wheat and then simmer in 2 litres (8½ cups/70 fl oz) water and ¼ teaspoon salt, covered, for 1 hour. Reduce the heat and keep warm until ready to serve.

Meanwhile, dice the lamb into 2-cm (¾-inch) pieces. Heat the butter in a saucepan over medium heat. Turn the heat up to high, add the lamb and garlic and sauté for 10 minutes, stirring occasionally. Reduce the heat to medium and cook for 20 minutes. Add the dried chilli (red pepper) flakes and ½ teaspoon salt. Sauté for a further 1 minute.

Simmer the ground kashk with 500 ml (generous 2 cups/ 17 fl oz) water for 5 minutes. Arrange the cooked cracked wheat on plates, pour the simmering kashk into the middle of the wheat. Top with the meat, drizzle with the cooking oils, then sprinkle with finely sliced fresh parsley and basil before serving.

RED MEAT

GOAT MEATBALLS WITH YOGURT SAUCE
ŞEKALOK

Region:		Bitlis, Eastern Anatolia
Preparation time:		25 minutes, plus overnight soaking
Cooking time:		1 hour 35 minutes
Serves:		4

70 g	chickpeas (garbanzo beans), soaked overnight	⅜ cup/2½ oz
70 g	green lentils, soaked overnight	½ cup/ 2½ oz
1	spring onion (scallion)	1
1	fresh garlic clove	1
100 g	dried cucumber peel, soaked overnight	3½ oz
1 litre	meat stock (see p.489), boiling	4¼ cups/ 34 fl oz

For the meatballs:

400 g	lean minced (ground) goat	14 oz
80 g	fine bulgur wheat	⅜ cup/3 oz
1 tbsp	dried basil	1 tbsp

For the yogurt sauce:

300 g	Greek yogurt	1½ cups/11 oz
2	fresh basil sprigs	2
4	garlic cloves	4

For the onion sauce:

50 g	butter	¼ cup/2 oz
60 g	onion, chopped	⅜ cup/2¼ oz
1 tsp	dried chilli (red pepper) flakes	1 tsp

Cucumber skins are dried in summer and preserved for the winter months, which is when this dish is made. If you can't find dried cucumber peel, make your own with 200 g/ 7 oz of fresh cucumber peel, sprinkled with ¼ teaspoon of salt and dried out in a very low oven for 1 day.

♦

Drain the chickpeas (garbanzo beans) and lentils. Simmer the chickpeas in 2 litres (8½ cups/70 fl oz) water for 1 hour, then drain. Meanwhile, simmer the green lentils in 1.5 litres (6¼ cups/50 fl oz) water for 30 minutes, then drain.

To make the meatballs:
Mix the goat, bulgur wheat, dried basil and ¼ teaspoon black pepper and ½ teaspoon salt in a large bowl or deep tray and knead for 5 minutes. Roll the mixture into 1-cm (½-inch) meatballs.

Put the spring onion (scallion) and fresh garlic into the bottom of a large saucepan and put the meatballs on top. Drain and slice the cucumber peel into 1-cm (½-inch) slices. Add the cooked chickpeas, cooked lentils and cucumber peel, then pour in the boiling meat stock and ½ teaspoon salt. Cover and cook for 10 minutes over medium heat, then reduce the heat and simmer for 20 minutes. Let rest for 5 minutes.

To make the yogurt sauce:
Mix the yogurt, fresh basil, garlic and ¼ teaspoon salt in a bowl for 1 minute.

To make the onion sauce:
Heat the butter in a large saucepan over medium heat, add the onions and fry for 1 minute. Add the dried chilli (red pepper) flakes and fry for 10 seconds. Serve the meatball stew drizzled with the yogurt sauce and the onion sauce.

♦

BRAISED LAMB
ZÜLBİYE

Region:		Konya, Central Anatolia
Preparation time:		10 minutes
Cooking time:		1 hour
Serves:		4

100 g	ghee (see p.485)	scant ½ cup/3½ oz
400 g	lamb shoulder	14 oz
40	shallots, peeled	40
1½ tbsp	tomato paste (see p.492)	1½ tbsp
1 litre	meat stock (see p.489), hot	4¼ cups/34 fl oz
2 tbsp	grape vinegar	2 tbsp
2	bay leaves	2

One for the winter months, rice pilaf goes really well with this dish.

♦

Dice the lamb shoulder into 2-cm (¾-inch) pieces. Heat the ghee in a large saucepan over medium heat, add the lamb shoulder and cook for 15 minutes. Add the shallots and cook for 10 minutes. Add the tomato paste, season with ⅛ teaspoon black pepper and ¾ teaspoon salt, then cook for 1 minute. Reduce the heat, add the hot meat stock, grape vinegar and bay leaves and cook, covered, for a further 30 minutes.

Serve in its own cooking juices.

RED MEAT

STEAMED MEATBALLS
SUSUZ MEATBALLS (BUĞULAMA KÖFTE)

Region:		İstanbul, all regions
Preparation time:		30 minutes
Cooking time:		1 hour
Serves:		4

For the meatballs:

1 tsp	mustard seeds	1 tsp
1 tbsp	sultanas (golden raisins)	1 tbsp
1 (120 g)	medium onion, finely sliced	¾ cup/ 4 oz
800 g	finely minced (ground) lamb	1 lb 12 oz
1½ tsp	ground cinnamon	1½ tsp
½ tsp	black pepper	½ tsp
¾ tsp	salt	¾ tsp

For the sauce:

¼ tsp	salt	¼ tsp
2	bay leaves	2
1	cinnamon stick	1
50 g	butter	¼ cup/2 oz
1 tbsp	lemon juice	1 tbsp
1 tbsp	grape vinegar	1 tbsp
2 tsp	tomato paste (see p.492)	2 tsp
1½ tbsp	oregano honey	1½ tbsp
½ tsp	mustard powder	½ tsp
½ tsp	dried chilli (red pepper) flakes	½ tsp
2	garlic cloves, crushed	2
¼ tsp	*poy* (see p.502)	¼ tsp

For the sealing dough:

100 g	plain (all-purpose) flour	¾ cup/ 3½ oz

This dish is also known as 'waterless meatballs', since they are steamed, not boiled. Some versions omit the sauce.
♦

To make the meatballs:
In a mortar and pestle, pound together the mustard seeds, sultanas and onion for 5 minutes. Transfer to a large bowl or deep tray and knead with the lamb, ground cinnamon, black pepper and salt, until well combined. Divide into 24 pieces and roll each one into a meatball.

To make the sauce:
Combine 250 ml (1 cup/8 fl oz) of water, the salt, bay leaves, cinnamon stick, butter, lemon juice, grape vinegar, tomato paste, honey, mustard powder, dried chilli (red pepper) flakes, garlic and *poy* in a medium metal bowl and mix for 1 minute. Put the bowl inside a large saucepan. Arrange the meatballs in the space around the bowl, then cover the saucepan with a tight lid.

To make the sealing dough:
In a separate bowl, work the flour and 60 ml (¼ cup/ 2 fl oz) water to a soft dough and roll out to a long sausage shape. Stick the dough around the pan lid to seal it thoroughly and make it airtight.

Cook over low heat for 1 hour.

Serve with the sauce on the side.

MEATBALLS IN SPICY TOMATO SAUCE
TOPALAK

Region:	İsparta, Mediterranean Region
Preparation time:	30 minutes
Cooking time:	30 minutes
Serves:	4

200 g	fine bulgur wheat	⅞ cup/7 oz
200 g	lean minced (ground) lamb	7 oz
60 g	onion, grated, strained and juice collected	⅜ cup/2¼ oz
¼ tsp	ground cumin	¼ tsp
½ tsp	dried chilli (red pepper) flakes	½ tsp
4	garlic cloves, crushed	4
1	egg	1
½ tsp	salt	½ tsp

For the sauce:

50 g	butter	¼ cup/2 oz
6	garlic cloves, crushed	6
60 g	onion, finely sliced	⅜ cup/2¼ oz
2	banana peppers, finely sliced	2
1 tsp	dried chilli (red pepper) flakes	1 tsp
1 tbsp	tomato paste (see p.492)	1 tbsp
2	fresh basil sprigs, finely sliced	2
¼ tsp	black pepper	¼ tsp
¼ tsp	salt	¼ tsp
300 g	tomatoes, finely sliced	1½ cups/11 oz
2 tbsp	grape vinegar	2 tbsp
2 tbsp	grape molasses	2 tbsp
4	flat-leaf parsley sprigs, finely sliced	4

2	flat-leaf parsley sprigs, finely sliced	2
60 g	sesame seeds, toasted	scant ½ cup/ 2¼ oz

Central Anatolian recipes have many local variations. *Topalak* means 'round' in Turkish. Children absolutely love this winter dish!

♦

Mix the bulgur wheat, lamb mince, onion juice, ground cumin, dried chilli (red pepper) flakes, garlic, eggs and ¼ teaspoon of the salt in a large bowl or deep tray and knead for 20 minutes until all is well combined, wetting your hands every now and then. Roll the mixture into 1-cm (½-inch) meatballs.

To make the sauce:
Heat the butter in a large saucepan over medium heat, add the garlic and onion and cook for 2 minutes. Add the banana peppers and cook for 2 minutes. Add the dried chilli (red pepper) flakes, tomato paste, 1 of the fresh basil sprigs, black pepper and salt and cook for 1 minute. Reduce the heat, add the tomatoes, grape vinegar and grape molasses, simmer for 10 minutes. Let rest on the lowest heat while you cook the meatballs.

Bring 2 litres (8½ cups/70 fl oz) water with the remaining ¼ teaspoon of salt to the boil in a large saucepan over medium heat. Add the meatballs and cook for 10 minutes.

Ladle out 200 ml (scant 1 cup/7 fl oz) of the meatball cooking water and add it to the simmering sauce. Add the remaining fresh basil and the parsley and cook for 3 minutes.

Transfer the cooked meatballs to serving bowls with a slotted spoon. Drizzle with the sauce, and sprinkle with the parsley and sesame seeds.

LAMB AND WALNUT RICE WITH MEATBALLS
KRİS

Region:	Hakkâri, Eastern Anatolia
Preparation time:	20 minutes, plus overnight soaking
Cooking time:	1 hour 35 minutes
Serves:	4

500 g	lamb ribs, cut into 2 × 3-cm (¾ × 1¼-inch) pieces	1 lb 2 oz
1 (120 g)	medium onion, finely sliced	1 (¾ cup/4 oz)
½ tsp	salt	½ tsp
70 g	chickpeas (garbanzo beans), soaked overnight, drained	⅜ cup/2½ oz
50 g	medium-grain rice	¼ cup/2 oz
100 g	walnuts, halved, soaked overnight and drained	1 cup/3½ oz
100 g	raisins	¾ cup/3½ oz

For the meatballs:

300 g	lean minced (ground) lamb	11 oz
50 g	broken rice	⅓ cup/2 oz
¼ tsp	black pepper	¼ tsp
¼ tsp	ground coriander	¼ tsp
¼ tsp	salt	¼ tsp

For the sauce:

3 tbsp	butter	3 tbsp
1 tbsp	tomato paste (see p.492)	1 tbsp
200 ml	sumac extract (see p.491)	scant 1 cup/ 7 fl oz

This is a dish for weddings, celebrations of peace and other festive occasions.

◆

In a large saucepan, bring the lamb ribs, onion, salt, chickpeas (garbanzo beans) and 3 litres (12 cups/100 fl oz) of water to the boil over medium heat, about 5 minutes. Skim off the foam on the surface with a slotted spoon. Reduce the heat, cover and cook for 40 minutes. Add the rice and cook for 20 minutes. Add the walnuts and raisins and cook for a further 5 minutes. Remove from the heat.

To make the meatballs:
Mix the lamb, broken rice, black pepper, ground coriander and salt in a large bowl or deep tray and knead for 5 minutes, until well combined. Roll the mixture into 2-cm (¾-inch) meatballs.

Add the meatballs to the saucepan, return to a low heat and cook, covered, for 15 minutes.

To make the sauce:
Heat the butter in a small saucepan over medium heat, add the tomato paste and cook for 2 minutes. Add the sumac extract and cook for a further 3 minutes.

Add the sauce to the meatball pan, cook over a medium heat for 5 minutes, then serve.

SPICED LAMB WITH AUBERGINE AND YOGURT
ALİ NAZİK

Region:	Gaziantep, Southeastern Anatolia
Preparation time:	10 minutes
Cooking time:	1 hour 10 minutes, plus cooling
Serves:	4

50 g	ghee (see p.485)	3½ tbsp/2 oz
100 g	lamb brisket, finely chopped	3½ oz
500 g	lamb backstrap, finely chopped	1 lb 2 oz
1	red chilli (chile), finely sliced	1
1	green chilli (chile), finely sliced	1
6	garlic cloves, finely sliced	6
½ tsp	salt	½ tsp
1 tsp	dried chilli (red pepper) flakes	1 tsp
¼ tsp	black pepper	¼ tsp

For the aubergine (eggplant) with yogurt:

1 kg	aubergines (eggplants)	4 cups/2 lb 3 oz)
50 g	ghee (see p.485)	3½ tbsp/2 oz
6	garlic cloves, crushed	6
½ tsp	salt	½ tsp
¼ tsp	black pepper	¼ tsp
500 g	strained Greek yogurt	2½ cups/1 lb 2 oz

A summer dish, *alinazik* is even more delicious when made in a wood-fired oven. There is a plain version, known as *söğürme,* made without yogurt, using bell peppers, tomatoes and garlic along with the aubergines (eggplants).
◆
Preheat oven to 200°C/400°F/Gas Mark 6.

Arrange the aubergines (eggplants) on a baking tray (sheet), prick them with the tip of a knife a few times and bake in the hot oven for 1 hour. Remove the aubergines from the oven, set aside until cool enough to handle, then peel.

Meanwhile, heat the ghee in a large saucepan over medium heat, add the lamb meat and cook for 15 minutes. Add the red and green chillies (chiles) and cook for 3 minutes. Add the garlic, salt, dried chilli (red pepper) flakes and black pepper and cook for a further 2 minutes. Keep warm while you make the aubergine with yogurt.

To make the aubergine with yogurt:
Heat the ghee in a small saucepan over medium heat, add the garlic and fry for 10 seconds. Add the peeled aubergine, salt and black pepper and cook for 5 minutes, mixing and pressing with a wooden spoon to combine. Remove from the heat, add the yogurt and mix until well combined.

Transfer the aubergine with yogurt mixture to serving bowls and make a well in the middle of each serving. Put a portion of the spiced lamb into each indentation and serve.

LAMB WITH AUBERGINE MASH
HÜNKÂR BEĞENDİ

Region:		İstanbul, all regions
Preparation time:		15 minutes
Cooking time:		1 hour 15 minutes, plus cooling
Serves:		4

800 g	lamb loin	1 lb 12 oz
100 g	ghee (see p.485)	scant ½ cup/3½ oz
¼ tsp	white pepper	¼ tsp
1 litre	lamb/veal stock (see p.489), boiling	4¼ cups/34 fl oz

For the aubergine (eggplant) mash:

1 kg	round, seedless aubergines (eggplants)	4 cups/2 lb 3 oz
50 g	butter	¼ cup/2 oz
1 tbsp	plain (all-purpose) flour	1 tbsp
¼ tsp	grated nutmeg	¼ tsp
¼ tsp	white pepper	¼ tsp
1 litre	milk, hot	4¼ cups/34 fl oz
70 g	unsalted *kasar* or *kashkaval* cheese (mature hard cheeses), grated	2¾ oz

p.183

The aubergines (eggplants) can be charred on barbecue embers. Some recipes omit the stock and sauté the peppers and tomatoes with the meat; some omit the cheese and milk.

♦

Preheat oven to 200°C/400°F/Gas Mark 6. Arrange the aubergines (eggplants) on a baking tray (sheet), prick a few times with the tip of a knife and bake in the hot oven for 1 hour. Remove the aubergines from the oven, set aside until cool enough to handle, then peel.

Dice the lamb into 3-cm (1¼-inch) pieces. Heat the ghee in a saucepan over medium heat. Add the lamb, white pepper and ½ teaspoon salt. Cook for 2 minutes on each side. Add the stock, reduce the heat and cook, covered, for 1 hour.

To make the mash:
Heat the butter in a sauté pan over medium heat, add the peeled aubergines and cook for 5 minutes, pressing and mixing continuously with a wooden spoon. Add the flour, nutmeg and white pepper with ½ teaspoon salt and mix for 1 minute. Reduce the heat, add the milk and cook, mixing continuously, for 5 minutes. Add the cheese and cook, stirring, for 3 minutes, then remove from the heat.

Transfer the aubergine mash to a shallow serving platter and top with the lamb.

♦

BRAISED LAMB SHANKS WITH LETTUCE
KUZU KAPAMA

Region:		İstanbul, all regions
Preparation time:		20 minutes
Cooking time:		1 hour 40 minutes
Serves:		4

90 ml	olive oil	6 tbsp/3 fl oz
4	lamb shanks on the bone	4
½ bunch	chard	½ bunch
1	lettuce (Romaine or Cos)	1
6	spring onions (scallions)	6
6	fresh garlic	6
6	dill sprigs, finely chopped	6
2	fennel fronds, finely chopped	2
10	black peppercorns	10
2 tbsp	lemon juice	2 tbsp
1 tbsp	plain (all-purpose) flour	1 tbsp

For the sealing dough:

100 g	plain (all-purpose) flour	¾ cup/3½ oz

The trick with this dish is not to stir at all during cooking and to make sure that the pot is completely airtight. The name '*kapama*' (sealed) refers to this technique.

♦

In a frying pan (skillet), heat 2 tablespoons of the olive oil. Add the lamb shanks and ¼ teaspoon of salt. Sear for 3 minutes on each side. Remove from the pan and set aside.

Slice the chard, lettuce, spring onions (scallions) and fresh garlic into 2-cm (¾-inch) pieces. Mix with the dill, fennel fronds, black peppercorns, lemon juice, flour, ½ teaspoon salt and 2 tablespoons of the oil until well combined.

In a cast-iron pan or casserole (Dutch oven), combine the remaining 2 tablespoons of oil, ¼ teaspoon salt and half of the lettuce. Arrange the lamb shanks on top and pour over their cooking oil. Top with the remaining lettuce. Pour in 1.5 litres (6¼ cups/50 fl oz) water. Cover with a tight lid.

To make the sealing dough:
In a separate bowl, work the flour with 60 ml (¼ cup/ 2 fl oz) water to a soft dough and roll out to a sausage shape. Stick the dough around the lid to seal and make it airtight. Cook for 1½ hours over 135°C/275°F heat.

RED MEAT

KIBBEH
İÇLİ KÖFTE

Region:		Adana, all regions
Preparation time:		45 minutes
Cooking time:		45 minutes
Serves:		4

¼ tsp	salt	¼ tsp

For the filling:

250 g	coarsely minced (ground) lamb loin	9 oz
1 (120 g)	medium onion, finely sliced	1 (¾ cup/4 oz)
100 g	walnuts, crushed	1 cup/3½ oz
¼ tsp	black pepper	¼ tsp
¼ tsp	salt	¼ tsp
½ bunch	flat-leaf parsley, finely sliced	½ bunch
2	fresh basil sprigs, finely sliced	2
80 g	tart pomegranate seeds	1 cup/3 oz

For the meatballs:

200 g	fine bulgur wheat	⅞ cup/7 oz
300 g	lean very finely minced (ground) lamb mince	11 oz
60 g	onion, grated, strained and juice collected	⅜ cup/2¼ oz
½ tsp	salt	½ tsp
¼ tsp	ground cumin	¼ tsp
½ tsp	dried chilli (red pepper) flakes	½ tsp
½ tsp	white pepper	½ tsp

For the sauce:

60 g	butter	¼ cup/2¼ oz
4	garlic cloves, crushed	4

p.185 📷

One for special occasions, this dish can be made in many different ways. There are fried, baked and steamed versions, as well as vegetarian and sweet variations.
♦
To make the filling:
Heat a large saucepan over medium heat until hot, then add the lamb and cook for 15 minutes, stirring occasionally. Once the meat releases its fat, add the onion, walnuts, black pepper and salt and cook for a further 15 minutes, stirring occasionally. Remove from the heat and let cool while you make the meatball mixture.

When cool, add the parsley, fresh basil and pomegranate seeds and mix well. Divide the filling mixture into 12 equal parts.

To make the meatballs:
Combine the bulgur wheat, lamb, onion juice, salt, cumin, dried chilli (red pepper) flakes and white pepper in a large bowl or deep tray and mix well with wet hands for 20 minutes. Divide the meatball mixture into 12 equal parts. Put each piece into your palm and, with wet fingers, make a cavity. Fill the cavity with the filling mixture and seal the meatball mixture meticulously around it, so it will stay intact when boiled. Press gently between your palms to flatten. Repeat to make 12 meatballs.

Meanwhile, bring 2 litres (8½ cups/70 fl oz) of water and ¼ teaspoon of salt to the boil in a large saucepan. Poach the meatballs in the boiling water for 10 minutes.

To make the sauce:
Heat the butter in a small saucepan over medium heat, add the garlic and fry for 1 minute.

Transfer the cooked meatballs to a serving plate and pour the sauce over to serve.

TANTUNI LAMB WRAPS
TANTUNİ DÜRÜMÜ

Region:		Mersin, Mediterranean Region
Preparation time:		20 minutes
Cooking time:		1 hour 10 minutes
Serves:		4

800 g	lean lamb backstrap	1 lb 12 oz
80 g	tail fat or ghee	⅓ cup/3 oz
2	green chillies (chiles)	2
1 tbsp	dried chilli (red pepper) flakes	1 tbsp
¼ tsp	ground cumin	¼ tsp

For the salad:		
60 g	onion	⅜ cup/2¼ oz
200 g	tomatoes	1 cup/7 oz
1	green chilli (chile)	1
½ bunch	flat-leaf parsley and basil	½ bunch
2	fresh mint sprigs	2
2 tsp	ground sumac	2 tsp
2 tbsp	Seville orange juice	2 tbsp
1 tsp	dried chilli (red pepper) flakes	1 tsp

4	*Açık Ekmek* (Lavash Bread, see p.394)	4

p.187

This dish evolved into a local delicacy from a humble early-morning snack of brisket or offal sold by street vendors to workers in the vegetable markets.

◆

Trim the lamb of any sinew and simmer in 2 litres (8½ cups/ 70 fl oz) water with ¾ teaspoon of salt, covered, for 1 hour. Drain and cool, cut into strips before dicing very finely.

To make the salad:
Slice the onion into thin crescents. Finely slice the tomato, green chilli (chile), fresh basil, flat-leaf parsley and mint. Gently mix the tomatoes, onion, chilli, basil, parsley, mint, sumac, orange juice (or lemon juice), dried chilli (red pepper) flakes and ¼ teaspoon salt in a large bowl, until well combined.

Heat the tail fat or ghee in a large saucepan over medium heat, add the lamb and cook for 2 minutes, stirring continuously. Finely slice the green chillies (chiles) and add to the pan with the dried chilli (red pepper) flakes, cumin, ¼ teaspoon black pepper, and ¼ teaspoon salt and cook for 5 minutes, stirring continuously. Transfer the mixture to a bowl.

Briefly press the flatbreads to the pan to warm up and soak up some of the oil. Arrange the lamb mixture on top of the flatbreads and add the salad. Fold the flatbreads in at the sides and roll into wraps, making sure the filling is completely enclosed. Cut in half and serve on a plate or as a snack wrapped in paper.

◆

STEWED RIBS WITH DRIED APPLES
GÂH YAHNİSİ

Region:		Erzincan, Eastern Anatolia
Preparation time:		10 minutes, plus overnight soaking
Cooking time:		2 hours
Serves:		4

30 g	butter	⅛ cup/1 oz
24 (each)	lamb rib pieces,	24 (each)
3 × 5 cm)	on the bone	1 × 2 inches)
2 (240 g)	medium onions, finely diced	2 (1⅝ cups/ 8½ oz)
100 g	dried cannellini beans, soaked overnight	½ cup/3½ oz
50 g	cracked wheat, soaked overnight	⅜ cup/2 oz
100 g	*gâh* (dried sour apples), soaked overnight	⅞ cup/3½ oz
1	cinnamon stick	1

Gâh is the Turkish name given to dried meat or fruit, especially dried apples and quinces. This is one of the oldest and most popular recipes of the region. *Gâh* is a popular snack in the winter, which also works well served alongside salted sundried ribs.

◆

Heat the butter in a large saucepan over medium heat. Add the ribs and fry for 3 minutes on each side, then remove from the pan. Add the onions to the pan and cook for 10 minutes.

Drain the beans and cracked wheat. Reduce the heat, add the beans and cracked wheat to the pan with the lamb ribs. Season with ¼ teaspoon black pepper and ¾ teaspoon salt, then pour in 3 litres (12 cups/100 fl oz) hot water and cook, covered, for 1 hour. Drain the *gâh* (dried sour apples) and add to the pan with the cinnamon stick and cook, covered, for a further 40 minutes.

RED MEAT

CONFIT GOAT WITH GARLIC MEATBALLS
KİTELFUM (SARIMSAKLI KÖFTE)

Region:		Siirt, Southeastern Anatolia
Preparation time:		30 minutes
Cooking time:		15 minutes
Serves:		4

600 g	goat confit (see *kavurma*, lamb confit, p.497)	1 lb 5 oz
½ tsp	dried chilli (red pepper) flakes	½ tsp
1	fresh green basil sprig	1

For the meatballs:		
200 g	fine bulgur wheat	⅞ cup/7 oz
15	garlic cloves, crushed	15
1	egg	1
¼ tsp	ground coriander	¼ tsp
¼ tsp	ground turmeric	¼ tsp
¼ tsp	ground cumin	¼ tsp

p.189

This dish is a breakfast staple.

◆

To make the meatballs:
Knead the fine bulgur wheat, garlic, egg, ground coriander, turmeric, cumin and ¼ teaspoon salt in a large bowl or deep tray for 15 minutes, until well combined. Divide the mixture into 20 balls and flatten them into discs between your palms.

Bring 1.5 litres (6¼ cups/50 fl oz) of water and ¼ teaspoon salt to the boil in a large saucepan over medium heat. Add the meatballs and boil for 10 minutes. Remove with a slotted spoon, reserving the cooking water.

Meanwhile, in a separate saucepan, warm through the confit goat and dried chilli (red pepper) flakes for 10 minutes.

Arrange the boiled meatballs on a serving platter and layer with the goat confit. Drizzle over 200 ml (scant 1 cup/ 7 fl oz) of the meatball cooking water, then sprinkle with finely sliced fresh basil and serve.

◆

TURNIP AND MUTTON STACKS
ŞALGAM ÇULLAMASI

Region:		Erzurum, Eastern Anatolia
Preparation time:		20 minutes
Cooking time:		1 hour, plus 10 minutes cooling
Serves:		4

80 g	medium-grain rice	½ cup/3 oz
2 (6 × 8 cm)	turnips	2 (2½ × 3 inch)
400 g	minced (ground) mutton	14 oz
1 (120 g)	medium onion, finely sliced	1 (¾ cup/4 oz)
1 tsp	dried chilli (red pepper) flakes	1 tsp
4	flat-leaf parsley sprigs	4
2	fresh tarragon sprigs	2
4	eggs	4
50 g	ground cornmeal (polenta)	⅓ cup/2 oz
50 g	plain (all-purpose) flour	⅓ cup/2 oz
500 ml	olive oil	generous 2 cups/17 fl oz

For the sauce:		
400 g	Greek yogurt	2 cups/14 oz
½ bunch	fresh coriander (cilantro)	½ bunch
1	garlic clove, crushed	1
1	hot red chilli (chile), sliced	1
2 tbsp	grape vinegar	2 tbsp

The humble turnip is believed to have many healing properties. Locals use it extensively in the winter in many dishes and soups. There is a vegetarian version as well.

◆

Cook the rice in 500 ml (generous 2 cups/17 fl oz) water for 30 minutes. Drain and set aside. Meanwhile, cut each turnip into 4 slices and cook in 2 litres (8½ cups/70 fl oz) water for 5 minutes. Drain and set aside. Heat a large sauté pan over medium heat, until very hot. Add half of the mutton and cook for 10 minutes, mixing occasionally. Add the onion, dried chilli (red pepper) flakes and ½ teaspoon salt and cook for a further 10 minutes. Transfer the cooked meat to a large bowl or deep tray and let cool for 10 minutes. Add the remaining uncooked mutton, cooked rice, finely sliced parsley and tarragon and knead gently for 5 minutes, until well combined. Divide the mixture into 4 equal parts. Arrange the meat mixture on top of a piece of turnip and top with another piece of turnip. Repeat to create 4 turnip and meat stacks. Whisk the eggs in a bowl for 1 minute. Mix the ground cornmeal (polenta) and flour in a separate bowl. Heat the olive oil in a large sauté pan over medium heat, until very hot. Coat each turnip and meat stack with egg wash and then flour. Add to the pan and fry for 4 minutes on each side, turning carefully.

To make the sauce:
Mix the yogurt, finely sliced fresh coriander (cilantro), garlic, chilli (chile), grape vinegar and ¼ teaspoon salt in a bowl. Transfer the fried turnip stacks to a serving platter and drizzle with the yogurt sauce.

RED MEAT

SOUR KEBABS
EKŞİLİ KEBAP

Region:	Kilis, Southeastern Anatolia	
Preparation time:	20 minutes, plus 10 minutes soaking	
Cooking time:	1 hour 10 minutes	
Serves:	4	

1 (300 g)	Japanese or Italian aubergine (eggplant), peeled, quartered lengthwise then cut into thirds, yielding 12 pieces	1 (11 oz)
50 g	tail fat or ghee, melted, strained	2 oz
28	shallots, peeled	28
¾ tsp	dried chilli (red pepper) flakes	¾ tsp
1.5 kg	tomatoes, grated, strained and juice reserved	3 lb 5 oz
60 ml	pomegranate molasses	¼ cup/2 fl oz

For the kebabs:

400 g	lamb shoulder finely and gently chopped with a *zırh* (a curved cleaver)	14 oz

4	*Açik Ekmek* (Ridged Bread, see p.394), diced into 2-cm (¾-inch) pieces	4
6	flat-leaf parsley sprigs, finely sliced	6

💧 🌿 🍚

If you don't have a *zırh* (a curved cleaver) or even a regular meat cleaver, combine the lamb shoulder, lamb brisket, salt and black pepper and put through a meat mincer (grinder). You will also need 8 long cast-iron skewers or 16 regular wooden skewers (soaked).

♦

Prepare barbecue coals for cooking.

Soak the aubergine (eggplant) in 2 litres (8½ cups/70 fl oz) water with 2 teaspoons of salt for 10 minutes. Drain and rinse, and squeeze excess water out. Set aside.

To make the kebabs:
Knead the lamb with ½ teaspoon black pepper in a bowl for 3 minutes. Divide the mixture into 16 equal parts. Mould each on to a skewer and squeeze the ends tightly with your palms, working each to a 10-cm (4-inch) flat roll.

Set the skewers 8 cm (3 inches) above the hot embers and sear for 5 seconds on each side, then cook for 2 minutes on each side, turning regularly. Once cooked, slide off the skewers, cut into 3 pieces and transfer to a bowl.

Heat the tail fat or ghee in a large saucepan over medium heat, add the shallots to and cook for 15 minutes, stirring regularly. Add the aubergine and cook for a further 10 minutes. Reduce the heat and add the dried chilli (red pepper) flakes, ¼ teaspoon black pepper, ¼ teaspoon of salt and the tomato juice. Cook, covered, for 20 minutes.

Add the kebabs to the pan and cook for 10 minutes. Add the pomegranate molasses and cook for a final 2 minutes.

Spread a layer of bread over each plate and top with the hot mixture, making sure each plate has an equal amount of meat and vegetables. Sprinkle with parsley and enjoy.

İZMİR-STYLE MEATBALLS
İZMİR KÖFTESİ

Region:		İzmir, all regions
Preparation time:		30 minutes
Cooking time:		40 minutes
Serves:		4

600 g	minced (ground) veal shoulder (medium fat)	1 lb 5 oz
1 (120 g)	medium onion, grated	1 (¾ cup/4 oz)
80 g	stale breadcrumbs, soaked in water and squeezed dry	3 oz
1	egg	1
3	flat-leaf parsley sprigs, finely sliced	3
½ tsp	dried chilli (red pepper) flakes	½ tsp
½ tsp	ground cloves	½ tsp
¼ tsp	black pepper	¼ tsp
½ tsp	salt	½ tsp
600 g	potatoes, peeled and quartered lengthwise	2⅔ cups/1 lb 5 oz
8	long chillies (chiles)	8

For the sauce:

800 g	tomatoes, grated, drained and juice reserved	4 cups/1 lb 12 oz
1½ tsp	tomato paste (see p.492)	1½ tsp
1 tsp	red bell pepper paste (see p.492)	1 tsp
⅛ tsp	black pepper	⅛ tsp
⅛ tsp	salt	⅛ tsp
2 tbsp	olive oil	2 tbsp
2	garlic cloves, crushed	2
⅛ tsp	ground cumin	⅛ tsp

Some recipes make this dish with lamb.

◆

Preheat oven to 160°C/325°F/Gas Mark 3.

Knead the veal, onion, breadcrumbs, egg, parsley, dried chilli (red pepper) flakes, cloves, black pepper and salt in a large bowl or deep tray for 5 minutes. Divide the mixture into 20 equal parts and roll into 7-cm (2¾-inch) meatballs.

Arrange the meatballs, alternating with the potatoes and chillies (chiles) in a roasting pan.

To make the sauce:
In a separate bowl, mix the tomato juice, tomato paste, red bell pepper paste, black pepper, salt, olive oil, garlic and cumin.

Pour the mixture over the meatballs and bake in the hot oven for 40 minutes.

Serve immediately.

STACKED MEATBALLS AND VEGETABLES
DİZME

Region:	Diyarbakır, Southeastern Anatolia	
Preparation time:		20 minutes
Cooking time:		1 hour 5 minutes
Serves:		4

24 (4-cm)	potatoes, halved	24 (1½-inch)

For the meatballs:

800 g	lamb shoulder and brisket, finely chopped	1 lb 12 oz
1 (120 g)	medium onion, finely sliced	1 (¾ cup/4 oz)
70 g	carrot, finely sliced	½ cup/2¾ oz
1	sweet green chilli (chile), finely sliced	1
1	hot red chilli (chile), finely sliced	1
6	garlic cloves, finely sliced	6
4	sprigs dill, finely sliced	4
6	flat-leaf parsley sprigs, finely sliced	6
2 tsp	dried basil	2 tsp
¼ tsp	black pepper	¼ tsp
½ tsp	cumin	½ tsp
⅛ tsp	dried tarragon	⅛ tsp
1 tsp	salt	1 tsp

For the sauce:

500 ml	fresh tomato juice	generous 2 cups/ 17 fl oz
2 tbsp	olive oil	2 tbsp
2 tbsp	verjuice (see p.494) (or lemon juice)	2 tbsp
2	garlic cloves, crushed	2
¼ tsp	salt	¼ tsp
¼ tsp	black pepper	¼ tsp
½ tsp	dried chilli (red pepper) flakes	½ tsp

A dish for the winter months; apples, quinces, turnips, celery, loquats, courgettes (zucchini), tomatoes and aubergines (eggplants) can all be used in this dish. Some like to roast the meatballs in the oven and grill or fry the vegetables in oil. Ideally, the meat would be chopped with a *zırh* (a curved cleaver), but a regular cleaver, sharp knife or meat grinder will work just fine too.

♦

Preheat oven to 200°C/400°F/Gas Mark 6.

To make the meatballs:
Gently knead the lamb, onion, carrot, chillies (chiles), garlic, dill, flat-leaf parsley, dried basil, black pepper, cumin, tarragon and salt in a large bowl or deep tray for 5 minutes, until well combined. Divide the mixture into 24 equal parts and roll into balls.

Arrange the potatoes and meatballs in a deep, round, 20-cm (8-inch) diameter baking pan (if not available, a 20 × 20-cm/8 × 8-inch roasting pan will do). Working from the outside in, alternate between a potato half, then a meatball, then another potato half, and so on.

To make the sauce:
Mix the tomato juice, olive oil, verjuice, garlic, salt, black pepper and dried chilli (red pepper) flakes in a bowl for 1 minute.

Pour the sauce over the potatoes and meatballs. Cover with foil and bake in the hot oven for 55 minutes. Remove the foil and return to the oven for 10 minutes to brown the top.

Serve immediately.

AUBERGINE MOUSSAKA
PATLICAN OTURTMA

Region:		Edirne, all regions
Preparation time:		15 minutes
Cooking time:		50 minutes
Serves:		4

200 ml	olive oil	scant 1 cup/7 fl oz
2 (600 g)	bell aubergines	2 (1 lb 5 oz)
	(eggplants), peeled in stripes,	
	topped and halved crosswise	
4	long green chillies (chiles)	4
1 (150 g)	tomato, quartered crosswise	1 (5 oz)

For the filling:

400 g	minced (ground) veal shoulder	14 oz
2 (240 g)	medium onions	2 (1⅝ cups/8½ oz)
2	long green chillies (chiles),	2
4	garlic cloves	4
50 g	butter	¼ cup/2 oz
1 tsp	dried chilli (red pepper) flakes	1 tsp
300 g	tomatoes, finely sliced	1½ cups/11 oz

❧

This popular dish is on the menus of traditional restaurants all summer long. Home cooks love this ancient cooking technique with fried vegetables and minced meat which is sometimes substituted with finely chopped meat.

◆

Preheat oven to 160°C/325°F/Gas Mark 3.

Heat the oil in a sauté pan over medium heat, until hot. Add the aubergines (eggplants) and fry for 5 minutes on each side. Remove to drain in a colander.

To make the filling:
Heat a sauté pan over medium heat, until hot. Add the veal and cook until it has absorbed its own juices. Finely slice the onions, long green chillies (chiles) and garlic. Add with the butter, dried chilli (red pepper) flakes, ¼ teaspoon black pepper and ½ teaspoon salt and cook for 5 minutes. Add the tomatoes and cook for 10 minutes, stirring occasionally.

Press the filling through a sieve (strainer) and reserve the juices. Pour the juices into a 20 × 20-cm (8 × 8-inch) baking pan. Arrange the aubergines vertically in the pan. Press their middles with a spoon to make an indentation, then load with the filling, making sure it is distributed equally. Place the long green chillies and tomato quarters on top. Bake in the hot oven for 20 minutes, then serve.

◆

COURGETTE MOUSSAKA
KABAK MUSAKKA

Region:		Kocaeli, all regions
Preparation time:		10 minutes
Cooking time:		1 hour 5 minutes
Serves:		4

1 kg	courgettes (zucchini)	7 cups/2 lb 4 oz
500 ml	olive oil	2 cups/17 fl oz
(200 g)	tomato, quartered crosswise	1 (7 oz)
4	long green chillies (chiles)	4

For the meat sauce:

500 g	minced (ground) lamb	1 lb 2 oz
2 (240 g)	medium onions	2 (1⅝ cups/8½ oz)
4	long green chillies (chiles),	4
5	garlic cloves	5
2 tbsp	olive oil	2 tbsp
400 g	tomatoes, finely sliced	2 cups/14 oz
2 tsp	tomato paste (see p.492)	2 tsp
½ tsp	dried chilli (red pepper) flakes	½ tsp
¼ tsp	ground cinnamon	¼ tsp

💧 ❧

Although courgette (zucchini) and aubergine (eggplant) are the most popular vegetables used for this summer dish, other vegetables can be used. Some skip the frying stage.

◆

Preheat oven to 160°C/325°F/Gas Mark 3.

Cut the courgettes (zucchini) into 1-cm (½-inch) slices. Heat the oil in a sauté pan over medium heat, until very hot. Add the courgette slices and fry for 2 minutes on each side. Remove with a slotted spoon to drain in a colander.

To make the meat sauce:
Heat a sauté pan over medium heat, until very hot. Add the lamb and cook for 15 minutes, stirring occasionally. Finely slice the onions, long green chillies (chiles) and garlic. Add to the pan with the oil and cook for 10 minutes. Add the tomatoes, tomato paste, dried chilli (red pepper) flakes, cinnamon, ¼ teaspoon black pepper and ½ teaspoon salt. Cook for 15 minutes, stirring occasionally.

Layer the courgette slices in a 20 × 20-cm (8 × 8-inch) baking pan. Spread the meat sauce on top in an even layer. Top with the tomatoe slices and chillies. Bake in the hot oven for 20 minutes, then serve.

AUBERGINE CASSEROLE
PATLICAN SİLKME

Region:		Kütahya, all regions
Preparation time:		20 minutes
Cooking time: 1 hour 30 minutes, plus 10 minutes resting		
Serves:		4

3 (600 g)	Japanese or Italian aubergines (eggplants), peeled, cut into 2-cm (¾-inch) slices	3 (1 lb 5 oz)
100 g	ghee (see p.485)	scant ½ cup/3½ oz
800 g	lamb backstrap, diced into 2-cm (¾-inch) pieces	1 lb 12 oz
1 (120 g)	medium onion	1 (¾ cup/4 oz)
1	small bell pepper	1
1.5kg	tomatoes	7½ cups/3 lb 5 oz
2 tbsp	grape vinegar	2 tbsp
1½ tsp	tomato paste (see p.492)	1½ tsp
1 tsp	dried chilli (red pepper) flakes	1 tsp

This dish is made all over the country in the summer months. This is a very traditional cooking method mentioned widely in old culinary records. Those earlier versions do not include tomatoes and chilli (chile) from the New World. There are meatless versions of this recipe as well, using chickpeas (garbanzo beans).

♦

Soak the aubergine (eggplant) slices in 2 litres (8½ cups/ 70 fl oz) water with 1½ teaspoons of salt for 10 minutes, then drain, rinse and pat dry with paper towels.

Heat the ghee in a saucepan over medium heat, add the lamb and sauté for 3 minutes on each side. Remove with a slotted spoon. Add the aubergine to the same pan and sauté for 3 minutes on each side, then cook for a further 5 minutes, shaking every now and then. Finely slice the onion, bell pepper and tomatoes and add with ⅛ teaspoon black pepper and ¾ teaspoon of salt and cook for 5 minutes, shaking occasionally.

In a separate bowl, whisk the vinegar, tomato paste and dried chilli (red pepper) flakes. Reduce the heat and return the lamb to the pan, layering it over the vegetables. Add the vinaigrette and cook, covered, for 1 hour. Rest for 10 minutes, then invert the pan on to a serving platter.

♦

BRAISED LAMB
TAS KEBABI

Region:		Ankara, all regions
Preparation time:		10 minutes
Cooking time:		2 hours, plus 10 minutes resting
Serves:		4

1 kg	lamb backstrap and shoulder (medium fat), diced into 2-cm (¾-inch) pieces	2 lb 3 oz
250 g	shallots	2½ cups/9 oz
2	fresh chillies (chiles), finely diced	2
¼ tsp	black pepper	¼ tsp
¼ tsp	ground cardamom	¼ tsp
2 tbsp	olive oil	2 tbsp
1½ tsp	salt	1½ tsp
50 g	butter	¼ cup/2 oz
200 g	coarse bulgur wheat	⅞ cup/7 oz

This traditional dish is made all year round at any excuse, but people tend to cook braised lamb to celebrate an achievement or because things went their way. Nowadays it is popular 'elite' restaurant fare, made from poached veal and presented with peas in tomato paste and mashed potatoes. This version has nothing to do with the authentic recipe below, made using a bowl. *Tas* in Turkish means bowl. Both rice and bulgur can be used in the recipe.

♦

Mix the lamb, shallots, chillies (chiles), black pepper, cardamom, olive oil and 1¼ teaspoons salt in a large bowl or deep tray for 1 minute, until well combined.

Put the mixture into a heavy-based pan or casserole (Dutch oven). Invert a 15 × 20-cm (6 × 8-inch) copper, metal or ceramic bowl over the mixture. Place a weight on top to make an airtight seal. Pour 2 litres (8½ cups/70 fl oz) water around and cook, covered, over low heat for 1½ hours.

Add the butter, bulgur wheat and remaining ¼ teaspoon of salt to the pot, around the bowl, without removing the bowl. Cover and cook for a further 30 minutes.

Remove from the heat and let rest for 10 minutes. Take the pan/casserole to the table, remove the lid and the weighted bowl and serve the meat and the pilaf together.

LADIES' THIGHS MEATBALLS
KADINBUDU KÖFTE

Region:		İstanbul, all regions
Preparation time:		20 minutes, plus 20 minutes soaking
Cooking time:		45 minutes
Serves:		4

¼ tsp	salt	¼ tsp
4	eggs	4
100 g	plain (all-purpose) flour	¾ cup/ 3½ oz
200 ml	olive oil	scant 1 cup/ 7 fl oz

For the meatballs:

70 g	medium-grain rice	⅓ cup/2¾ oz
¾ tsp	salt	¾ tsp
600 g	minced (ground) lamb	1 lb 5 oz
1 (120 g)	medium onion, finely sliced	1 (¾ cup/4 oz)
4	dill sprigs, finely sliced	4
6	flat-leaf parsley sprigs, finely sliced	6
¼ tsp	black pepper	¼ tsp
¼ tsp	ground cumin	¼ tsp

For the sauce:

500 g	Greek yogurt	2½ cups/ 1 lb 2 oz
4	garlic cloves, crushed	4
2	dill sprigs, finely sliced	2
4	flat-leaf parsley sprigs, finely sliced	4
¼ tsp	salt	¼ tsp

p.195 📷

These big meatballs must have taken their name from their voluptuous shape, accentuated by the cooked rice. This ancient recipe has always been known by the same name, an insight into societal characteristics. It is especially popular in Van where it is known as 'eggy meatballs'. It is known as a 'peace dish' in the region and is made mostly in the summer. This dish can be prepared with all types of meat. A shortcut is to mix pre-cooked minced (ground) meat with pre-cooked rice.

♦

Soak the rice for the meatballs in 500 ml (generous 2 cups/17 fl oz) hot water with ¼ teaspoon of salt for 20 minutes. Drain, rinse and set aside.

To make the meatballs:
Knead the rice, lamb, onion, dill, parsley, the remaining ½ teaspoon of the salt, black pepper and cumin in a large bowl or deep tray for 5 minutes.

Divide the mixture into 8 equal pieces. Roll each piece in your palm, then taper slightly to get an oval shape.

Bring 2 litres (8½ cups/70 fl oz) water and the salt to the boil in a large saucepan. Reduce the heat, place the meatballs carefully in the water and simmer, covered, for 30 minutes. Remove the meatballs with a slotted spoon.

Whisk the eggs in a bowl. Put the flour in a separate bowl.

Heat the olive oil in a large sauté pan over medium heat, until very hot. Roll the meatballs in the flour and then in the egg, then fry for 1 minute on each side, about 2 minutes in total.

To make the sauce:
Mix together the yogurt, garlic, dill, parsley and salt.

Serve the meatballs with the yogurt sauce on the side.

MEATBALLS WITH PARSLEY
MAYDANOZLU KÖFTE

Region:	İstanbul, all regions
Preparation time:	20 minutes
Cooking time:	35 minutes
Serves:	4

For the meatballs:		
800 g	minced (ground) lamb	1 lb 12 oz
1 (120 g)	medium onion, finely chopped	1 (¾ cup/4 oz)
2 bunches	flat-leaf parsley	2 bunches
60 g	ghee (see p.485)	¼ cup/2¼ oz
1 (120 g)	medium onion	1 (¾ cup/4 oz)
1	small bell pepper	1
60 ml	grape vinegar	¼ cup/2 fl oz

p.197

These meatballs are even more delicious when cooked over charcoal.

♦

To make the meatballs:
Knead the lamb and onion with ¼ teaspoon black pepper and ½ teaspoon salt in a bowl or deep tray for 5 minutes. Divide the mixture into 20 equal parts and roll into balls.

Arrange half of the parsley leaves in the bottom of a sauté pan with a lid and set aside. Heat the ghee in another sauté pan over medium heat, until hot. Fry the meatballs for 3 minutes on each side, about 6 minutes in total. Remove with a slotted spoon and layer over the parsley leaves.

Slice the onion and bell pepper into thin crescents. Add the onion, ¼ teaspoon each of black pepper salt. Cook for 5 minutes. Add the bell pepper and cook for 5 minutes. Add the vinegar and 200 ml (1 cup/7 fl oz) water. Boil for 2 minutes.

Sprinkle the remaining parsley leaves over the meatballs and pour over the sauce. Cover and simmer for 10 minutes.

♦

RABBIT MEATBALLS WITH SUMAC EXTRACT
EKŞİLİ TAVŞAN KÖFTESİ

Region:	Malatya, all regions
Preparation time:	20 minutes
Cooking time:	25 minutes, plus 5 minutes resting
Serves:	4

For the meatballs:		
60 g	onion	⅜ cup/2¼ oz
600 g	minced (ground) rabbit	1 lb 5 oz
100 g	fine bulgur wheat	½ cup/3½ oz
1 tsp	ground sumac	1 tsp
1 tsp	dried chilli (red pepper) flakes	1 tsp
60 g	onion	⅜ cup/2¼ oz
4	garlic cloves	4
70 g	carrot	½ cup/2¾ oz
2	dried chillies (chiles)	2
2	sun-dried tomatoes	2
60 g	ghee (see p.485)	¼ cup/2¼ oz
1 tbsp	tomato paste (see p.492)	1 tbsp
1 tsp	dried chilli (red pepper) flakes	1 tsp
200 ml	sumac extract (see p.491)	scant 1 cup/ 7 fl oz
4	flat-leaf parsley sprigs	4
2	fresh basil sprigs	2

The making and eating of this dish is a communal affair. It is endemic to the eastern parts of Southeastern Anatolia. The hunters come home with the rabbits, the neighbors gather and prepare this dish and the joy is shared around.

♦

To make the meatballs:
Grate the onion, then strain and collect the juice. Knead the rabbit, bulgur wheat, ¼ teaspoon black pepper, ground sumac, ½ teaspoon salt, dried chilli (red pepper) flakes and onion juice in a large bowl or deep tray for 5 minutes. Roll the mixture into 2-cm (¾-inch) meatballs.

Finely slice the onion, garlic, carrot, dried chillies (chiles) and sun-dried tomatoes. Heat the ghee in a large sauté pan over medium heat, add the onion, garlic, carrot and dried chilli (chiles) and cook for 5 minutes. Add the tomato paste, dried chilli (red pepper) flakes, ¼ teaspoon black pepper and ½ teaspoon salt and cook for 1 minute. Add the sun-dried tomatoes and cook for 2 minutes. Pour in 1 litre (4¼ cups/34 fl oz) of hot water and cook for 5 minutes. Reduce the heat, add the meatballs and cook, covered, for 5 minutes. Add the sumac extract and cook, covered, for a further 5 minutes.

Let rest for 5 minutes, then sprinkle with finely sliced parsley and basil and serve.

DRY MEATBALLS
KURU KÖFTE

Region:		Tekirdağ, all regions
Preparation time:		20 minutes
Cooking time:		25 minutes
Serves:		4

750 ml	olive oil, for frying	3 cups/25 fl oz
300 g	potatoes, finely diced	1⅓ cups/11 oz
2	banana peppers, finely sliced	2

For the meatballs:		
800 g	finely minced (ground) veal shoulder	1 lb 12 oz
100 g	stale bread, soaked, drained and excess water squeezed out	3½ oz
60 g	onion, grated, strained and juice collected	⅜ cup/2¼ oz
½ tsp	ground cumin	½ tsp
1	egg	1
50 g	plain (all-purpose) flour	⅓ cup/2 oz

½ bunch	flat-leaf parsley	½ bunch
½ tsp	ground sumac	½ tsp

p.199

Both sausage and disc shapes are popular for these meatballs. Delicious hot or cold, they are a picnic favourite and no Turkish mother would send a child on a long trip without a sizeable supply of these meatballs.

♦

To make the meatballs:
Knead the veal shoulder, stale bread, onion juice, cumin and egg with ¼ teaspoon black pepper and 1 teaspoon salt in a large bowl or deep tray for 5 minutes, until well combined. Roll the mixture into 2-cm (¾-inch) meatballs. Sprinkle a separate tray with flour, transfer the meatballs to it and shake the meatballs around in the tray to ensure they are evenly coated with flour.

In a large saucepan, heat the olive oil over medium heat to 155°C/310°F. Place the potatoes in the hot oil and fry evenly for 5 minutes. Remove with a slotted spoon to drain on paper towels. Place the banana peppers in the oil and fry for 4 minutes. Remove with a slotted spoon to drain on paper towels. Place the meatballs in the oil, making sure they do not touch one another, and fry for 3 minutes. Remove with a slotted spoon to drain on paper towels.

In a small bowl, gently mix the finely sliced parsley and sumac. Arrange the fried meatballs and vegetables on serving plates and sprinkle with the parsley and sumac mixture.

♦

VEAL MEATBALLS ON PICKLES
ABDİGOR KÖFTESİ

Region:		Ağrı, Eastern Anatolia
Preparation time:		15 minutes
Cooking time:		30 minutes
Serves:		4

800 g	lean veal shoulder, trimmed and pounded or minced (ground)	1 lb 12 oz
1 (120 g)	medium onion, grated	1 (¾ cup/4 oz)
1	egg	1

100 g	Lahana Turşusu (Pickled Cabbage see p.82)	3½ oz
100 g	pickled chillies	3½ oz

The cooking juices of these meatballs makes a fine stock for plain pilaf. Some versions of this recipe omit the eggs. This dish can also be served cold. Slice the meatballs 5-mm (¼-inch) thick, mix together 60 ml (¼ cup/2 fl oz) grape vinegar, 4 crushed garlic cloves, ¼ teaspoon salt and 2 sprigs of finely sliced flat-leaf parsley, then drizzle over the cold meatballs.

♦

In a large saucepan, bring 3 litres (12 cups/100 fl oz) water and ½ teaspoon salt to the boil. Keep it simmering while you prepare the meatballs.

Knead the veal shoulder, onion and egg together with ¼ teaspoon black pepper, ½ teaspoon salt and 200 ml (scant 1 cup/7 fl oz) water in a bowl or deep tray for 5 minutes. Divide the mixture into 4 equal parts. Collect the mixture with your hands and carefully drop into the simmering water. Simmer the meatballs over medium heat, covered, for 25 minutes. Serve with the pickles.

SLOW-COOKED GOAT AND LAMB
TESTİ KEBABI

Region:		Burdur, all regions
Preparation time:		15 minutes
Cooking time:		2 hours
Serves:		4

1 kg	lamb or goat shoulder and loin, diced into 2.5-cm (1-inch) pieces	2 lb 3 oz
400 g	shallots, peeled	4 cups/14 oz
4	banana peppers	4
1 kg	tomatoes, finely diced	5 cups/2 lb 3 oz
1 tsp	salt	1 tsp
½ tsp	ground cumin	½ tsp
¼ tsp	black pepper	¼ tsp
½ tsp	dried chilli (red pepper) flakes	½ tsp
100 g	butter	½ cup/3½ oz

For the sealing dough:

100 g	plain (all-purpose) flour	¾ cup/3½ oz

p.201

The traditional way to cook this dish is in the open air, on the embers of a fire, in an earthenware pot, wider at the top than at the bottom. This is a picnic favourite. Different regions make their own versions – the lamb version with more vegetables is widely cooked around Yozgat and the surrounding area.

♦

Mix the meat, shallots, banana peppers, tomatoes, salt, cumin, black pepper and dried chilli (red pepper) flakes in a large bowl or deep tray for 2 minutes, until well combined.

Put half of the butter into an earthenware pot or casserole dish (Dutch oven). Add the meat mixture, then top with the remaining butter. Cover with a tight lid.

To make the sealing dough:
In a separate bowl, work the flour and 60 ml (¼ cup/ 2 fl oz) water to a soft dough and roll out to a long sausage shape. Stick the dough around the lid to seal it thoroughly and make it airtight.

Cook over low heat for 2 hours.

Transfer to serving platters and serve immediately.

♦

THE IRONMONGER'S KEBAB
DEMİRCİ KEBABI

Region:		Manisa, Aegean Region
Preparation time:		15 minutes
Cooking time:		2 hours 30 minutes, plus 15 minutes cooling
Serves:		4

2 (2 kg)	goat legs, on the bone, quartered	2 (4 lb 6 oz)
1 tsp	salt	1 tsp
5	black peppercorns	5
1 tsp	dried chilli (red pepper) flakes	1 tsp
¼ tsp	black pepper	¼ tsp
pinch	dried marjoram	pinch
60 ml	lemon juice	¼ cup/2 fl oz
400 g	celeriac (celery root), thinly sliced	1½ cups/14 oz

Legend has it that the origins of this kebab lie in the *Demirci* near Manisa. *Demirci* means ironmonger in Turkish. The dish was prepared by cooking chunks of meat on the bone in cauldrons. The meat was then deboned, spiced and baked in the ironmonger's oven. It is offered to droppers-by. This dish is believed to have healing properties and make the ironmongers even stronger. Some recipes omit the celeriac (celery root) and some versions bake the goat meat overnight in a hot oven.

♦

In a saucepan, simmer the goat in 3 litres (12 cups/100 fl oz) water with the salt and peppercorns, covered, for 2 hours. Remove from the pan, reserve the stock and let cool. Once the goat is cool enough to handle, pull the meat off the bones and put into a muslin (cheecloth) or a clean dish towel tied loosely. Pound with a pestle or rolling pin for 10 minutes until tenderized. Transfer to a bowl, add the dried chilli (red pepper) flakes, black pepper, dried marjoram and half of the lemon juice. Mix until well combined.

Preheat oven to 160°C/325°F/Gas Mark 3. Arrange a layer of celeriac (celery root) in a roasting pan and drizzle with the remaining lemon juice. Layer the meat on top and press firmly. Pour over the reserved stock. Bake in the oven for 30 minutes, until brown. Divide among serving plates, giving everyone an equal amount of goat and celeriac.

RED MEAT

RABBIT KEBABS
GÖMLEKLİ TAVŞAN KEBABI

Region:		Edirne, Marmara Region
Preparation time:		15 minutes, plus 10 minutes soaking
Cooking time:		1 hour
Serves:		4

600 g	potatoes	2⅔ cups/1 lb 5 oz
4 (480 g)	medium onions	4 (3⅛ cups/1 lb 1 oz)
8 (1.6 kg)	rabbit legs, deboned, halved	8 (3 lb 8 oz)
60 ml	grape vinegar	¼ cup/2 fl oz
3½ tbsp	honey	3½ tbsp
1 tsp	ground turmeric	1 tsp
½ tsp	ground cumin	½ tsp
½ tsp	*poy* (see p.502)	½ tsp
½ tsp	ground cardamom	½ tsp
½ tsp	ground cinnamon	½ tsp
10	garlic cloves, crushed	10
1 tsp	salt	1 tsp
¼ tsp	black pepper	¼ tsp
1 tbsp	dried oregano	1 tbsp
1 tsp	mustard powder	1 tsp
4 (each 25 × 25 cm)	lamb caul fat pieces, intact, soaked in 2 litres (8½ cups/70 fl oz) warm water for 10 minutes	4 (each 10 × 10 inches)
8	flat-leaf parsley sprigs, finely sliced	8

If you don't have a barbecue, you can use a regular grill (broiler). You will need 4 long cast-iron skewers or 8 regular wooden skewers (soaked).

♦

Preheat oven to 180°C/350°F/Gas Mark 4. Bake the potatoes and onions in a roasting tray in the oven, covered, for 55 minutes. Uncover and cook for a further 5 minutes.

Prepare a barbecue for cooking or preheat a grill (broiler) to high.

Meanwhile, in a bowl, massage the vinegar and honey into the rabbit, then let rest for 1 minute. In a separate bowl, mix together the turmeric, cumin, *poy*, cardamom, cinnamon, garlic, salt, black pepper, dried oregano and mustard powder. Add the mixture to the meat and massage in for 5 minutes.

If using long cast-iron skewers and a barbecue:
Thread 4 pieces of rabbit lengthwise onto the skewers, leaving 10 cm (4 inches) space at either end. Wrap the meat entirely in the caul fat. Set the skewers 8 cm (3 inches) above the hot embers and cook, turning every 2 minutes, for a total of 16 minutes, until the caul fat is browned.

If using wooden skewers and a regular grill:
Use 2 pieces of rabbit and half a piece of caul fat per skewer. Grill (broil) for 20 minutes, turning every 5 minutes.

Draw the cooked meat from the skewers and transfer to plates. Peel the baked potatoes and onions and add to the serving plates. Sprinkle with parsley and serve.

KEBAB WITH YOGURT
YOĞURTLU KEBAP

Region:		Bursa, all regions
Preparation time:		15 minutes
Cooking time:		30 minutes
Serves:		4

For the yogurt sauce:

400 g	Greek yogurt (sheep's milk)	2 cups/14 oz
4	garlic cloves, crushed	4
¼ tsp	salt	¼ tsp

For the kebabs:

400 g	lamb shoulder, finely chopped with a *zırh* (a curved cleaver)	14 oz
400 g	lamb brisket, finely chopped with a *zırh* (a curved cleaver)	14 oz
1 tsp	salt	1 tsp
½ tsp	black pepper	½ tsp

For the hot sauce:

2 tbsp	butter	2 tbsp
1	red bell pepper, grilled, peeled and finely sliced	1
2	garlic cloves, crushed	2
1 tsp	tomato paste (see p.492)	1 tsp
½ tsp	dried chilli (red pepper) flakes	½ tsp
¼ tsp	black pepper	¼ tsp
¼ tsp	salt	¼ tsp
200 ml	meat stock (see p.489), hot	scant 1 cup/ 7 fl oz

4	*Açik Ekmek* (Ridged Bread, see p.394)	4
4	banana peppers (mild sweet peppers)	4
3 tbsp	butter	3 tbsp

The ideal cooking method for this dish is barbecuing the meat outdoors on embers. You will need 4 long cast- iron skewers or 8 regular wooden skewers (soaked). The long iron skewers, if using, should be turned every 30 seconds. If you don't have a *zırh* (a curved cleaver) for chopping the meat, use regular minced (ground) lamb shoulder and brisket.

♦

Preheat a grill (broiler) to high or prepare a barbecue for cooking.

To make the yogurt sauce:
Mix the yogurt, garlic and salt in a bowl and set aside.

To make the hot sauce:
Heat the butter in a large saucepan over medium heat, add the grilled bell pepper and garlic and cook for 2 minutes. Add the tomato paste, dried chilli (red pepper) flakes, black pepper and salt and cook for 2 minutes. Add the meat stock and cook for a further 5 minutes. Set aside.

To make the kebabs:
Knead the lamb, salt and black pepper in a large bowl or deep tray for 3 minutes until well combined. Divide the mixture into 8 equal parts. Mould around skewers, squeezing each with your palms into a flattened 12-cm (4¾-inch) roll.

Cook the kebabs for 3 minutes on each side under the hot grill or over the barbecue embers, turning regularly.

Crisp the breads and banana peppers on the grill or barbecue. Dice the bread into 1-cm (½-inch) pieces and place on serving platters. Pour over half of the sauce and then drizzle with the yogurt mixture. Once the kebabs are cooked, arrange the skewers on top in a crossed shape and drizzle with the remaining sauce.

Heat the butter in a small saucepan until hot, drizzle over the platters and serve with the banana peppers placed on top.

MEATBALLS WITH CUMIN
KİMYONLU KÖFTE

Region:		İstanbul, all regions
Preparation time:		15 minutes
Cooking time:		20 minutes
Serves:		4

For the meatballs:

1 (120 g)	medium onion,	1 (¾ cup/4 oz)
½ bunch	flat-leaf parsley	½ bunch
400 g	minced (ground) veal shoulder	14 oz
400 g	minced (ground) veal brisket	14 oz
½ tsp	ground cumin	½ tsp

1 (120 g)	medium onion	1 (¾ cup/4 oz)
1 (200 g)	tomato	1 (7 oz)
8	banana peppers (mild sweet peppers)	8

♦ ❧ ◗   p.205

Grilled meatballs have many local variations. Some like them spicy, some plain, some with onions or garlic, some with or without bread. Sizes vary too.
♦
Preheat a grill (broiler) to high or prepare a barbecue for cooking.

To make the meatballs:
Finely slice the onion and parsley. Knead the veal, onion, parsley and cumin with ¼ teaspoon black pepper and ¾ teaspoon salt in a large bowl or deep tray for 5 minutes, until well combined. Divide the mixture into 20 equal parts and form into flattened discs, about 4 × 6 cm (1½ × 2½ inches).

Quarter the onion and tomato. Cook the meatballs, onion and tomato quarters, and banana peppers under the hot grill or over barbecue embers for 3 minutes on each side.

Serve immediately, making sure each plate has an equal amount of the meat and vegetables.

♦

STUFFED AUBERGINE
KARNIYARIK

Region:		Afyon, all regions
Preparation time:		15 minutes
Cooking time:		1 hour
Serves:		4

500 ml	olive oil	2 cups/17 fl oz
4 (1 kg)	Japanese (thin) aubergines (eggplants), pricked with a knife	4(2 lb 3 oz)
4	banana peppers	4
1 (100 g)	tomato, quartered crosswise	1 (3½ oz)

For the filling:

500 g	lean minced (ground) lamb	1 lb 2 oz
2 (240 g)	medium onions, finely sliced	2 (1⅝ cups/ 8½ oz)
1 tbsp	olive oil	1 tbsp
5	garlic cloves, finely sliced	5
4	fresh chillies (chiles), finely sliced	4
600 g	tomatoes, finely sliced	3 cups/ 1 lb 5 oz
2 tsp	tomato paste (see p.492)	2 tsp
½ tsp	dried chilli (red pepper) flakes	½ tsp

♦ ❧

This summer dish could also be made with currants and pine nuts.
♦
Preheat oven to 160°C/325°F/Gas Mark 3.

Heat the olive oil in a large sauté pan over medium heat, until very hot. Add the aubergines (eggplants) and fry for 3 minutes on each side. Remove with a slotted spoon to drain in a colander.

To make the filling:
Heat a sauté pan over medium heat, until very hot. Add the lamb to the pan and cook for 15 minutes, stirring occasionally. Stir through the onions, olive oil and garlic, put the fresh chillies (chiles) on top of the lamb and cook for a further 10 minutes. Stir through the sliced tomatoes, tomato paste and dried chilli (red pepper) flakes with ¼ teaspoon black pepper and ½ teaspoon salt. Cook for a further 5 minutes.

Press the filling mixture through a sieve (strainer) and reserve the juices.

Pour the juices into a 30 × 30-cm (12 × 12-inch) baking pan. Put the aubergines into the pan and split them lengthways, making sure you don't cut all the way through. Stuff the cavities with the filling and garnish with banana peppers and tomatoes. Bake in the hot oven for 20 minutes, then serve.

RED MEAT

SPICY KOFTE KEBAB
ACILI KIYMA KEBABI

Region:		Adana, all regions
Preparation time:	25 minutes, plus 10 minutes chilling	
Cooking time:		25 minutes
Serves:		4

For the kebab mixture:

60 g	onion, finely sliced	⅜ cup/2¼ oz
1	fresh chilli (chile), finely sliced	1
1½ tbsp	dried chilli (red pepper) flakes	1½ tbsp
⅛ tsp	black pepper	⅛ tsp
⅛ tsp	ground cumin	⅛ tsp
¾ tsp	salt	¾ tsp
400 g	lamb shoulder, trimmed of sinew, finely chopped with a *zırh* (a curved cleaver)	14 oz
100 g	lamb brisket, trimmed of sinew, finely chopped with a *zırh* (a curved cleaver)	3½ oz
100 g	tail fat or ghee	scant ½ cup/ 3½ oz

For the salsa :

60 g	onion, sliced	⅜ cup/2¼ oz
1	red bell pepper, sliced	1
½ bunch	flat-leaf parsley, finely chopped	½ bunch
2 tsp	ground sumac	2 tsp
300 g	tomatoes, sliced	1½ cups/11 oz
2	fresh mint sprigs, finely chopped	2
2 tbsp	olive oil	2 tbsp
¼ tsp	salt	¼ tsp

4	*Tirnakli Ekmek* (Pide Flatbread, see p.376)	4
8	banana peppers (mild sweet peppers)	8

p.207 ◻

This dish is known as 'Adana kebab' in the big cities. The same technique applies to the version without chilli (chile), which is known as 'mild kofte kebab'. If you don't have a *zırh* (a curved cleaver), combine the lamb shoulder, lamb brisket, salt and fat and put through a meat mincer (grinder). If you don't have a barbecue, you can use a regular grill (broiler). You will need 5 long cast-iron skewers or 10 regular wooden skewers (soaked).

♦

Prepare a barbecue for cooking or preheat a grill (broiler) to high.

To make the kebab mixture:
Mix the onion, chilli (chile), dried chilli (red pepper) flakes, black pepper, cumin and salt in a large bowl for 1 minute, until well combined. Add the lamb shoulder, brisket and tail fat or ghee and gently mix for 5 minutes. Cover and chill in the refrigerator for 10 minutes.

To make the salsa:
Mix the onion, red bell pepper, parsley, sumac, mint, tomatoes, olive oil and salt in a large bowl for 2 minutes. Chill in the refrigerator until ready to serve.

Take the kebab mixture out of the fridge.

If using long cast-iron skewers and a barbecue:
Divide the kebab mixture into 4 pieces. Mould each piece on to a cast-iron skewer to make a 15-cm (6-inch) flattened roll and squeeze the two ends firmly. Thread the banana peppers on to another skewer. Set the skewers 8 cm (3 inches) above the hot barbecue embers and cook for 3 minutes on each side, turning them every 30 seconds.

If using wooden skewers and a regular grill:
Divide the mixture into 8 pieces and make the kebabs slightly shorter, about 10 cm (4 inches), and thread the banana peppers on to 2 skewers. Grill (broil) for 5–6 minutes on each side, turning as required.

Add the flatbreads to the barbecue or grill and cook for 2 minutes, turning them every 30 seconds.

Quarter the flatbreads lengthwise and divide among serving plates. Use the bread to draw off the meat and the peppers from the skewers and transfer to the plates. Serve with the salsa.

PEAR KEBABS
ARMUT KEBABI

Region:	Kilis, all regions
Preparation time:	20 minutes
Cooking time:	40 minutes, plus 30 minutes cooling
Serves:	4

100 ml	olive oil	scant ½ cup/3½ fl oz
4 (4 × 6 cm)	Japanese or Italian aubergines (eggplants), stem trimmed but left on, peeled in stripes	4 (1½ × 2½ inches)
2	eggs	2
60 g	plain (all-purpose) flour	½ cup/2 oz

For the kebab mixture:

1 kg	lean minced (ground) lamb	2 lb 3 oz
60 g	onion, grated, strained and juice collected	⅜ cup/2¼ oz
¼ tsp	black pepper	¼ tsp
1 tsp	salt	1 tsp
1	egg	1
4	cloves	4

For the sauce :

60 ml	ghee (see p.485)	¼ cup/2 fl oz
10	garlic cloves, finely sliced	10
1 tsp	dried chilli (red pepper) flakes	1 tsp
1 tsp	red bell pepper paste (see p.492)	1 tsp
2 tsp	tomato paste (see p.492)	2 tsp
400 ml	tomato juice	1⅔ cups/ 14 fl oz
400 ml	meat stock (see p.489)	1 ⅔ cups/ 14 fl oz
1 tsp	black mustard seeds	1 tsp
½ tsp	salt	½ tsp
¼ tsp	black pepper	¼ tsp
1	cinnamon stick	1
2 tbsp	grape vinegar	2 tbsp
2 tbsp	grape molasses	2 tbsp
1 (600 g)	pear, peeled, quartered	1 (1 lb 5 oz)

This dish is made in the summer months when small aubergines (eggplants) are in season.

◆

Heat the olive oil in a large sauté pan over medium heat, until very hot. Add the aubergines (eggplants) and fry for 3 minutes on each side. Remove with a slotted spoon to drain in a colander and reserve the cooking oil. Let cool for 30 minutes.

To make the kebab mixture:
Knead the lamb, onion juice, black pepper, salt and egg in a large bowl or deep tray for 5 minutes, until well combined. Divide the mixture into 4 equal parts and make a hole in the middle of each with your thumb. Place the cooled aubergines in the holes and enclose them with the kebab mixture, making sure the stems stick out. Push 1 clove into the bottom of each stuffed meat patty.

Whisk 2 eggs in a shallow bowl. Put the flour into a separate shallow bowl nearby.

Heat the reserved oil over medium heat to 155°C/310°F. Coat the pear kebabs in eggs and then flour, then fry them in the hot oil for 2 minutes on each side. Remove with a slotted spoon and set aside.

To make the sauce:
Heat the ghee in a large saucepan over medium heat, add the garlic and fry for 1 minute. Add the dried chilli (red pepper) flakes, red bell pepper paste and tomato paste and fry for 2 minutes. Add the tomato juice, meat stock, mustard seeds, salt, black pepper, cinnamon stick, grape vinegar and grape molasses and boil for 5 minutes.

Reduce the heat, add the pear quarters and the fried kebabs and cook for 20 minutes.

Serve immediately.

ORUK KEBAB
ORUK KEBABI

Region:		Kilis, Southeastern Anatolia
Preparation time:		20 minutes, plus 20 minutes soaking
Cooking time:		25 minutes
Serves:		4

8	banana peppers (mild sweet peppers)	8
2 (200 g)	tomatoes, quartered	2 (7 oz)

For the kebab mixture:

400 g	lamb shoulder, trimmed of sinew, finely chopped with a *zırh* (a curved cleaver)	14 oz
200 g	lamb brisket, trimmed of sinew, finely chopped with a *zırh* (a curved cleaver)	7 oz
60 g	onion, finely sliced	⅜ cup/2¼ oz
6	garlic cloves, finely sliced	6
¼ tsp	black pepper	¼ tsp
2 tsp	dried mint	2 tsp
1 tsp	dried chilli (red pepper) flakes	1 tsp
¾ tsp	salt	¾ tsp
¼ tsp	allspice	¼ tsp
¼ tsp	ground cinnamon	¼ tsp
50 g	fine bulgur wheat, soaked in 60 ml (¼ cup/2 fl oz) apple juice for 20 minutes	¼ cup/2 oz
60 g	walnuts, finely sliced	½ cup/2 oz

4	*Açik Ekmek* (Ridged Bread, see p.394)	4
1	*Piyaz Salatası* (Onion Salad, see p.67)	1
1	lemon, quartered	1

This kebab can also be baked in the oven or deep-fried. If you don't have a barbecue, you can use a regular grill (broiler). If you don't have a *zırh* (a curved cleaver) for chopping the meat, use regular minced (ground) lamb shoulder and brisket. You will need 5 long cast-iron skewers or 10 flat wooden skewers (soaked).

♦

Prepare a barbecue for cooking or preheat a grill (broiler) to high.

To make the kebab mixture:
Knead the lamb, onion, garlic, black pepper, dried mint, dried chilli (red pepper) flakes, salt, allspice, cinnamon, soaked bulgur wheat and walnuts in a large bowl or deep tray for 5 minutes, until well combined. Divide the kebab mixture into 4 equal parts, form each one into a 20-cm (8-inch) roll and skewer through the middle (if using wooden skewers, split into 8 parts and make the rolls 10 cm (4 inches) long). Squeeze with your palms, especially on the ends, to ensure the meat is snug on the skewers. Thread the banana peppers and tomatoes on to another skewer/s.Set the skewers 8 cm (3 inches) above the hot barbecue embers and cook for 4 minutes on each side, turning every 30 seconds.

Alternatively, grill (broil) the skewers for 3 minutes per side.

Add the *Açik Ekmek* (bread) to the barbecue or grill and warm for 2 minutes, turning every 30 seconds. Slice the bread into quarters lengthwise and arrange on plates. Use the bread to draw the meat off the skewers and top the bread on the plates. Serve with a side of *Piyaz Salatası* and lemon wedges.

CHERRY KEBAB
KİRAZLI KEBAP

Region:	Mersin, Mediterranean Region	
Preparation time:		20 minutes
Cooking time:		45 minutes
Serves:		4

24	shallots, peeled	24
40	sour black cherries, pitted	40
50 g	butter	¼ cup/2 oz
¼ tsp	black pepper	¼ tsp
¼ tsp	ground ginger	¼ tsp
1 tsp	dried chilli (red pepper) flakes	1 tsp
¼ tsp	salt	¼ tsp
1	cinnamon stick	1
400 ml	cherry juice	1 ⅔ cups/14 fl oz
2 tbsp	lemon juice	2 tbsp
60 g	pine nuts	⅜ cup/2 oz

For the kebab mixture:

400 g	lamb shoulder, trimmed of sinew, finely chopped with a *zırh* (a curved cleaver)	14 oz
200 g	lamb brisket, trimmed of sinew, finely chopped with a *zırh* (a curved cleaver)	7 oz
60 g	onion, finely sliced	⅜ cup/2¼ oz
¾ tsp	salt	¾ tsp
½ tsp	black pepper	½ tsp
1 tsp	ground cinnamon	1 tsp

4	*Açik Ekmek* (Ridged Bread, see p.394) 2 slices toasted and diced; 2 slices cut into 8 triangles	4

p.211

Instead of the cherries, you can use sour cherries and *mahlepi* (mahleb) – an aromatic spice made by grinding the seeds of a certain type of wild cherry. If you don't have a barbecue, you can use a regular grill (broiler). If you don't have a *zırh* (a curved cleaver) for chopping the meat, use regular minced (ground) lamb shoulder and brisket. You will need 4 long cast-iron skewers or 8 flat wooden skewers (soaked).

◆

Prepare a barbecue for cooking or preheat a grill (broiler) to high.

To make the kebab mixture:
Knead the lamb, onion, salt, black pepper and ground cinnamon in a large bowl or deep tray for 5 minutes, until well combined. Divide the mixture into 40 equal parts and roll into balls.

Thread the skewers alternately with 3 shallots, 5 meatballs and 5 cherries (shallot / cherry / meat / cherry / meat / shallot / meat / cherry / meat / cherry / meat / cherry / shallot). Make sure they are really snug.

Set the skewers 8 cm (3 inches) above the hot barbecue embers and cook for 5 minutes on each side, turning every 30 seconds. Draw off the meat, shallots and cherries into a bowl.

Alternatively, grill (broil) the skewers for 3 minutes per side.

Heat the butter in a large sauté pan over medium heat, add the cooked shallots, black pepper, ground ginger, dried chilli (red pepper) flakes, salt and cinnamon stick and fry for 3 minutes. Add the meat and cook for a further 2 minutes. Reduce the heat, add the cherry juice and lemon juice and cook, covered, for 10 minutes. Add the cherries and cook for a further 10 minutes. Remove from the heat, add the pine nuts and stir through.

Arrange the diced bread in pasta plates and spoon the hot dish over the top. Serve with the bread triangles on the side.

KEBAB WITH AUBERGINE
PATLICANLI KEBAP

Region:	Şanlıurfa, Southeastern Anatolia	
Preparation time:		20 minutes
Cooking time:		30–50 minutes
Serves:		4

For the kebab mixture:

400 g	lamb shoulder, trimmed of sinew, finely chopped with a *zırh* (a curved cleaver)	14 oz
200 g	lamb brisket, trimmed of sinew, finely chopped with a *zırh* (a curved cleaver)	7 oz
100 g	tail fat, finely chopped with a *zırh* (a curved cleaver)	3½ oz
¾ tsp	salt	¾ tsp
¼ tsp	black pepper	¼ tsp
4 (1 kg)	Japanese or Italian aubergines (eggplants), sliced	4 (2 lb 3 oz)
4 (600 g)	tomatoes, quartered	4 (1 lb 5 oz)
8	banana peppers (mild sweet peppers)	8
1 (120 g)	medium onion, quartered	1 (¾ cup/ 4 oz)
4	*Açık Ekmek* (Ridged Bread, see p.394)	4

p.213

Locals would start making this dish only after summer well and truly arrives – it is made with the mid- to late-summer aubergines (eggplants). Brought to the table in the tray after resting, the dish is placed in the middle of a communal table, and the onions are served in a separate plate. People help themselves with a piece of *Açık Ekmek* (Lavash Bread, see p.394) in hand. The burnt bits are pushed aside and the aubergine, tomatoes and chilli are wrapped together with the meat and onions according to taste. *Ayran* (Salted Yogurt Drink, see p.452) is a great beverage to accompany this dish.

You will need 6 long cast-iron skewers, or 10 flat wooden skewers (soaked). If you don't have a *zırh* (a curved cleaver), combine the lamb shoulder, lamb brisket and tail fat and put through a meat mincer (grinder). Alternatively, you can make this dish in the oven. Alternate the meat and aubergine in a roasting pan and fill in the gaps with the tomatoes and chillies (chiles). Bake covered in a 200°C/400°F/Gas Mark 6 oven for 50 minutes and uncovered for a further 10 minutes.

◆

Prepare a barbecue for cooking or preheat a grill (broiler) to high.

To make the kebab mixture:
Knead the lamb, tail fat, salt and black pepper in a large bowl or deep tray for 3 minutes, until well combined. Divide the mixture into 24 equal parts and roll into balls.

Alternate the meatballs with the aubergine slices on each skewer, making sure each skewer has 6 meatballs and 4 slices of aubergine (3 meatballs and 2 aubergine slices if using the shorter wooden skewers). Skewer the tomatoes and chillies separately.

Set the skewers 8 cm (3 inches) above the hot barbecue embers and cook for 10 minutes, turning every 30 seconds.

Alternatively, grill (broil) the skewers for 10 minutes, turning frequently.

Draw everything off the skewers into a roasting pan. Seal tightly with aluminum foil, set 8 cm (3 inches) above the ashes of the barbecue and let rest for 5 minutes, or place in a 180°C/350°F/Gas Mark 4 oven for 20 minutes.

Alternatively, all the cooking can be done in the oven. The roasting pan should be covered and cooked for 45 minutes at 180°C/350°F/Gas Mark 4, then uncovered for 5 more minutes.

Serve with *Açik Ekmek* and onion.

ONION KEBABS
SOĞAN KEBABI

Region:	Gaziantep, Southeastern Anatolia	
Preparation time:		10 minutes
Cooking time:		40 minutes
Serves:		4

400 g	lamb shoulder, trimmed of sinew, finely chopped with a *zırh* (a curved cleaver)	14 oz
200 g	lamb brisket, trimmed of sinew, finely chopped with a *zırh* (a curved cleaver)	7 oz
100 g	tail fat, finely chopped with a *zırh* (a curved cleaver)	3½ oz
¾ tsp	salt	¾ tsp
¼ tsp	black pepper	¼ tsp
48	sweet shallots, roots trimmed, peeled	48

For the sauce:		
200 ml	lamb/veal stock (see p.489), hot	scant 1 cup/ 7 fl oz
60 ml	pomegranate molasses (see p.490)	4 tbsp/ 2 fl oz
¼ tsp	black pepper	¼ tsp
¼ tsp	salt	¼ tsp

p.215

In the winter, this dish is prepared at home and taken to the local bakery for cooking in the communal oven. In the spring, fresh garlic is used with the same technique.

You will need 8 long cast-iron skewers or 12 flat wooden skewers (soaked). If you don't have a *zırh* (a curved cleaver), combine the lamb shoulder, lamb brisket and tail fat and put through a meat mincer (grinder). You can also alternate the meatballs and onions in a roasting pan and cook in a 180°C/350°F/Gas Mark 4 oven for 50 minutes with the oven door closed, and then another 10 minutes basted with the sauce and the oven door open.

♦

Prepare a barbecue for cooking or preheat a grill (broiler) to high.

Knead the lamb, tail fat, salt and black pepper in a large bowl or deep tray for 3 minutes, until well combined. Divide the mixture into 48 equal pieces and roll into balls.

Alternate the meat and onions on each skewer until you have 6 meatballs and 6 onions on each (4 meatballs and 4 onions if using the shorter wooden skewers), snugly stacked.

Set the skewers 8 cm (3 inches) above the barbecue embers and cook for 10 minutes, turning every 30 seconds.

Alternatively, grill (broil) the skewers for 10 minutes, turning frequently.

Draw everything off the skewers into a roasting pan.

To make the sauce:
Mix the stock, pomegranate molasses, black pepper and salt with 200 ml (scant 1 cup/7 fl oz) of hot water in a bowl for 1 minute, until well combined.

Pour the sauce over the meat and onions. Seal tightly with aluminum foil, set 8 cm (3 inches) above the ashes of the barbecue and let rest for 20 minutes before serving.

LOQUAT KEBABS
YENİDÜNYA KEBABI

Region:	Gaziantep, Southeastern Anatolia
Preparation time:	25 minutes
Cooking time:	25 minutes
Serves:	4

24	loquats (preferably thin-skinned), halved, deseeded, seed-beds cleaned	24

For the kebab mixture:

400 g	lamb shoulder, trimmed of sinew, finely chopped with a *zırh* (a curved cleaver)	14 oz
200 g	lamb brisket, trimmed of sinew, finely chopped with a *zırh* (a curved cleaver)	7 oz
60 g	onion, finely sliced	⅜ cup/2¼ oz
¾ tsp	salt	¾ tsp
½ tsp	black pepper	½ tsp

For the sauce:

50 g	butter	¼ cup/2 oz
4	garlic cloves, finely sliced	4
1 (200 g)	tomato, grilled, peeled and crushed	1 (1 cup/7 oz)
4	banana peppers (mild sweet peppers), grilled, peeled and crushed	4
¼ tsp	black pepper	¼ tsp
½ tsp	dried chilli (red pepper) flakes	½ tsp
½ tsp	salt	½ tsp
200 ml	meat stock (see p.489), hot	scant 1 cup/ 7 fl oz
2 tbsp	grape molasses	2 tbsp
2	fresh tarragon sprigs, finely sliced	2

🌿 ⬤   p.217 📷

The loquat is also known as the Maltese plum in Turkey. The thin skinned version is better for cooking, however if not available the thick skinned one can be used as well. The best results will be achieved with fruit that is just ripe. This dish is made in the spring and some versions omit the sauce. You will need 4 long cast-iron skewers or 6 flat wooden skewers (soaked). It can easily be made in the oven, if you prefer, by baking it, covered, for 30 minutes at 200°C/400°F/Gas Mark 6. If you don't have a *zırh* (a curved cleaver), combine the lamb shoulder and lamb brisket and put through a meat mincer (grinder).

♦

Prepare a barbecue for cooking or preheat a grill (broiler) to high.

To make the kebab mixture:
Knead the lamb, onion, salt and black pepper in a large bowl or deep tray for 5 minutes, until well combined. Divide the mixture into 24 equal parts and roll into balls.

Thread half a loquat on to a skewer, seed-bed facing up, thread on a meatball then thread another loquat, seed-bed facing down. Repeat until you have 4–6 sets on each skewer.

Set the skewers 8 cm (3 inches) above the hot barbecue embers and cook for 8 minutes, turning every 30 seconds.

Alternatively, grill (broil) the skewers for 8 minutes, turning frequently.

Draw the cooked kebabs on to a serving plate.

To make the sauce:
Heat the butter in a large sauté pan over medium heat, add the garlic, tomatoes, banana peppers, black pepper, dried chilli (red pepper) flakes and salt and cook for 5 minutes. Reduce the heat and add the meat stock, grape molasses and fresh tarragon, bring to the boil and boil for a further minute. Add the cooked kebab meat to the pan and cook for a final 3 minutes.

Serve the grilled loquats with the meat sauce.

POULTRY
&
GAME

POULTRY IN
TURKISH CULTURE

The cooking methods for poultry and game birds are endless: kebabs, cutlets, pilaf, soup, fried, poached, baked, steamed, roasted, stuffed or stewed. Stews can be plain or with tomato paste, milk, clotted cream, sweet, sour or hot. Game birds are poached or baked with a little oil, pan-fried, barbecued, cooked in a tandoor, on the spit or as a kebab. Goose, duck, chicken and turkey dishes such as *Keşkek* (Pounded Lamb and Wheat, see p.317), *Helise* (Pounded Rooster, see p.231) and *Perde Pilavı* (Veiled Rice Pilaf, p.314) add a decadent touch to weddings and other special occasions. And poorer families create wonders out of chicken livers, necks, giblets and wings.

THE SEASON
FOR GAME BIRDS

Partridge meat is eaten in the autumn and winter months. Duck, grouse, starling, woodcock and quail are among our traditional game fare. Sustainability is key here. Greedy hunters are shunned in our society and seen as wasteful. There are strict limits in hunting season. Unfortunately, our game birds are no longer in abundance. Chicken, duck or turkey make great alternatives to game birds in all of the recipes in this chapter. The traditional bird will be the one featured in the recipe, but feel free to substitute.

◆

FAT IS FLAVOUR, FRESH IS BEST

Our rich cultural heritage suggests how and when certain foods and dishes are to be eaten. We eat poultry and game birds both on and off the bone. The cooking times for farmed poultry is always shorter – free range birds take much longer to cook. The vital issue here is to choose the bird with the most fat. Don't be afraid of fat when it comes to poultry and game. Fat is flavour. I also suggest choosing sustainable and reliable farmers. Buy only what you need, and cook and eat it on the same day. The taste of the dish depends on how fresh your bird is – 'fresh is best'. Let this be your mantra for a lifetime of delicious cooking.

◆

THE BRIDE AND GROOM CHICKEN

Here is a sweet but surviving tradition:
The Chicken and the Bride and Groom.

Shortly before the wedding, the bride's family and friends pay a visit to the groom's family. The day is known but the time is not. In the middle of the night, they gather in front of the groom's family home. One of the friends dresses up as an imam and a few dress up as women. They ring the doorbell and dance in front of the house. The mayhem continues until the groom comes to the door. The neighbours, despite being woken up, tolerate or even participate in the fun and frolics. But the whole charade is not as innocent as it seems – there is a group with their eyes on the groom's chicken coup. While the family is distracted, they steal all the chickens. This tradition is called 'chicken theft' and is not limited to the groom's house. The chickens kept by his extended family and friends are all fair game! All the plunder is taken to the bride's family and the chickens prepared as part of the wedding banquet, on top of the pilaf, fried, roasted, stuffed, grilled or as kebabs.

Chicken theft is still very popular in rural areas. In the more practical urban version, the groom's family presents the bride's family with a live or cooked chicken.

Another tradition is the sacrifice of a rooster to bless the home of the newlyweds. This is done in front of the house just before the inhabitants step across the threshold. A drop of the rooster's blood is smeared on the foreheads of the bride and groom and the rooster is given away to the poor. This is an ongoing tradition in the Marmara region and its surrounding countryside.

SPICY DUMPLING SOUP
ARABAŞI

Region:		Yozgat, all regions
Preparation time:		10 minutes
Cooking time:		2 hours 20 minutes, plus 1 hour resting
Serves:		4

For the dough:

100 g	plain (all-purpose) flour	¾ cup/ 3½ oz
¼ tsp	salt	¼ tsp
1.5 kg	full-fat woodcock meat	3 lb 5 oz
1 tsp	salt	1 tsp
10	garlic cloves, crushed	10
2 tsp	dried chilli (red pepper) flakes	2 tsp
2 tsp	red bell pepper paste (see p.492)	2 tsp
2 tsp	tomato paste (see p.492)	2 tsp
60 ml	lemon juice	¼ cup/2 fl oz
½ tsp	black pepper	½ tsp

This is a specialty of the Central Anatolia, Aegean and Mediterranean regions. A staple of winter get-togethers and celebrations, the dish comes with a cheeky ritual: the person who drops the 'dough' from their spoon into the soup is the designated host of the next gathering. In some communities, the forfeit for dropping the dough is to buy gifts for everyone at the table. This dish is also made with turkey, chicken and rabbit.

♦

To make the dough:
Bring 1 litre (4¼ cups/34 fl oz) water to the boil in a saucepan. As soon as it comes to the boil, add the flour and salt. Cook over low heat for 20 minutes, whisking continuously. Pour the mixture into a moistened 25-cm (10-inch) diameter, deep-sided tray and rest, uncovered, at room temperature for 1 hour. Transfer the tray to the refrigerator.

Meanwhile, put the woodcock meat and salt into a very large saucepan with 4 litres (16 cups/130 fl oz) water and cook, covered, over low heat for 2 hours. Remove the woodcock from the pan with a slotted spoon and pick the meat off the bones. Keep the stock simmering.

Skim the fat from the simmering stock with a ladle until you have 200 ml (scant 1 cup/7 fl oz). Transfer the fat to a large sauté pan over medium heat and cook for about 1 minute. Add the garlic and dried chilli (red pepper) flakes to the hot fat and fry for 1 minute. Add the red bell pepper paste and tomato paste and cook for 3 minutes. Add the woodcock meat and cook for 5 minutes.

Add the woodcock mixture back into the simmering stock, turn the heat up and boil for 5 minutes. Add the lemon juice and black pepper and mix in for 1 minute. Transfer the soup to a serving bowl, about 15 cm (6 inches) wide by 10 cm (4 inches) deep.

Take the dough tray out of the refrigerator. Cut the centre out of the dough, to roughly the diameter of your serving bowl (15 cm/6 inches), and cut the removed section into 2.5 cm (1 inch) squares. Arrange the dough squares around the sides of the tray. Place the soup bowl in the middle of the empty section on the tray and serve.

To eat, scoop up a square of the wobbly dough and an equal amount of the hot and sour woodcock soup in your spoon and enjoy.

CHICKEN AND LENTIL STEW
GOGOLLU AŞ

Region:		Kars, Eastern Anatolia
Preparation time:		15 minutes
Cooking time:		1 hour 5 minutes
Serves:		4

250 ml	olive oil	1 cup/8 fl oz
100 g	leavened bread dough, cut into 1-cm (½-inch) wide discs	3½ oz
80 g	ghee (see p.485)	⅓ cup/3 oz
1 (70 g)	carrot, finely diced	1 (½ cup/2¾ oz)
1 (60 g)	onion, finely sliced	1 (⅜ cup/2¼ oz)
4	garlic cloves, finely sliced	4
300 g	chicken thighs, skinless, finely diced	11 oz
1 tsp	salt	1 tsp
¼ tsp	white pepper	¼ tsp
80 g	green lentils	½ cup/3 oz
1 litre	chicken stock (see p.489), hot	4¼ cups/34 fl oz
200 g	potatoes, finely diced	1 cup/7 oz
70 g	homemade noodles (see p.493)	2¾ oz
½ tsp	ground turmeric	½ tsp
½ bunch	fresh coriander (cilantro), finely sliced	½ bunch

This dish is made in the winter months. *Gogol* is the name given to the little balls of dough. Children love devouring these marble-like delicacies.

♦

In a large saucepan, heat the olive oil over medium heat to 155°C/310°F. Fry the bread discs for 5 minutes until crisp. Remove with a slotted spoon to drain on paper towels. Set aside.

Heat the ghee in a large saucepan over medium heat, add the carrot, onion and garlic and cook for 3 minutes. Add the chicken, salt, white pepper and green lentils, in that order, and cook for 5 minutes. Pour in 1 litre (4¼ cups/34 fl oz) water and cook, covered, for 20 minutes. Pour in the chicken stock and continue to cook, covered, for 10 minutes. Add the potatoes and cook, still covered, for 10 minutes. Remove the lid, add the homemade noodles and cook for 7 minutes. Finally, add the fried dough and cook for 3 minutes.

Remove from the heat, gently stir through the ground turmeric and fresh coriander (cilantro) and serve.

♦

BRAISED CHICKEN
KÜL

Region:		Edirne, Marmara Region
Preparation time:		5 minutes
Cooking time:		1 hour 20 minutes
Serves:		4

100 g	butter	½ cup/3½ oz
8 (800 g)	chicken drumsticks	8 (1 lb 12 oz)
4	garlic cloves, crushed	4
½ tsp	black pepper	½ tsp
¾ tsp	salt	¾ tsp
70 g	plain (all-purpose) flour	½ cup/ 2¾ oz

Also known in the Aegean Region, this winter dish is a trademark of the migrants from the Balkans.

♦

Heat the butter in a saucepan over medium heat, add the chicken and sauté for 2 minutes on each side, about 10 minutes in total. Strain off the fat and set aside in a bowl.

Add the garlic, black pepper and salt to the pan and sauté for 1 minute, stirring gently. Reduce the heat, add 1.5 litres (6¼ cups/50 fl oz) water and cook, covered, for 1 hour.

Heat the reserved fat in a separate saucepan over medium heat. Add the flour and stir vigorously with a wooden spoon for 1 minute, making sure it doesn't burn. Strain in the chicken cooking juices and cook for 2 minutes, mixing continuously, to thicken. Add the cooked chicken drumsticks to the pan and cook, uncovered, for a further 5 minutes before serving.

CHICKEN IN MILK
SÜTLÜ TAVUK

Region:		Erzurum, Eastern Anatolia
Preparation time:		10 minutes
Cooking time:		50 minutes, plus 10 minutes resting
Serves:		4

50 g	butter	¼ cup/2 oz
4	garlic cloves, finely sliced	4
600 g	chicken thighs, diced into 2.5-cm (1-inch) pieces	1 lb 5 oz
1 tsp	salt	1 tsp
¼ tsp	black pepper	¼ tsp
70 g	medium-grain rice	⅓ cup/2¾ oz
1 litre	hot milk	4¼ cups/34 fl oz
100 g	dried clotted cream (see p.486)	2¼ cups/3½ oz
500 g	fresh nettles, finely sliced	1 lb 2 oz
2	fresh tarragon sprigs, finely sliced	2
60 g	blue cheese	⅝ cup/2¼ oz

This traditional fare is a winter cure-all in Eastern Anatolia, especially for sore stomachs and breathing difficulties. It is especially popular with newlyweds and is referred to as 'bride and groom's chicken'.

♦

Heat the butter in a large saucepan over medium heat, add the garlic and cook for 30 seconds. Add the chicken, salt and pepper and cook for 3 minutes. Add the rice and cook for 2 minutes. Reduce the heat, add 1 litre (4¼ cups/ 34 fl oz) hot water and cook, covered, for 20 minutes. Add the milk and the clotted cream and cook, uncovered, for 10 minutes. Add the nettles, tarragon and blue cheese and cook for a final 10 minutes.

Let rest for 10 minutes and serve.

♦

OKRA WITH CHICKEN
TAVUKLU BAMYA

Region:		Amasya, all regions
Preparation time:		15 minutes
Cooking time:		50 minutes, plus 5 minutes resting
Serves:		4

100 ml	olive oil	scant ½ cup/3½ fl oz
500 g	chicken thighs, finely chopped	1 lb 2 oz
1 (120 g)	medium onion, finely sliced	1 (¾ cup/4 oz)
10	garlic cloves, finely sliced	10
1	small red bell pepper, finely sliced	1
½ tsp	dried chilli (red pepper) flakes	½ tsp
2 tbsp	lemon juice	2 tbsp
300 g	young, fresh okra, outer skin of the stem area gently peeled	11 oz
200 ml	fresh tomato juice, hot	scant 1 cup/ 7 fl oz
200 ml	chicken stock (see p.489), hot	scant 1 cup/ 7 fl oz

Okra soup, okra with lamb, as well as okra with chicken are widely made dishes, which are popular at wedding banquets. Okra is strung out to dry in the summer sun for later use in the winter, while the summer version of this dish uses fresh okra. The soup made from dried okra is a specialty of Konya and its environs. It is believed to aid digestion, and is served after dessert at the end of a feast.

♦

In a large saucepan, heat the olive oil over medium heat to 155°C/310°F. Add the chicken and sauté for 5 minutes. Remove the chicken with a slotted spoon to a bowl. Add the onion, garlic and bell peppers to the hot oil and sauté for 10 minutes, turning regularly. Add the dried chilli (red pepper) flakes, lemon juice and okra with ¼ teaspoon black pepper and 1 teaspoon salt, and cook gently for 10 minutes, stirring with a wooden spoon. Add the chicken back to the pan and cook for a further 10 minutes. Reduce the heat, add the tomato juice and chicken stock and cook, covered, for a final 10 minutes.

Remove from the heat and let rest for 5 minutes before serving.

MEATBALLS STUFFED WITH APRICOTS
MAKİYAN

Region:	Mardin, Southeastern Anatolia	
Preparation time:	20 minutes, plus 1 hour soaking	
Cooking time:	45 minutes	
Serves:	4	

100 g	almond meal	⅔ cup/3½ oz
100 g	butter	scant ½ cup/3½ oz
16	shallots	16
500 g	chicken thighs, diced into 2.5-cm (1-inch) pieces	1 lb 2 oz
¼ tsp	ground cinnamon	¼ tsp

For the stuffed apricots:

150 g	walnuts	1½ cups/5 oz
¼ tsp	ground cinnamon	¼ tsp
4	dried apricots, soaked in water for 1 hour, drained	4

For the meatballs:

500 g	minced (ground) mutton	1 lb 2 oz
50 g	rice flour	⅓ cup/2 oz
60 g	onion, grated, strained and juice collected	⅜ cup/2¼ oz

A winter specialty endemic to Mardin, Siirt and Diyarbakır, mentioned in old sources, this dish is traditionally made to celebrate peace after tense periods between clans. It is also made on the last day a new bride spends with her parents in the hope that her new home will enjoy good health, happiness and fortune.

♦

Mix the almond meal with 1.5 litres (6¼ cups/50 fl oz) water, strain the liquid into a bowl. Set the pulp aside.

To make the stuffed apricots:
Mix the walnuts and cinnamon in a bowl, then stuff the mixture into the soaked dried apricots. Set aside.

To make the meatballs:
Knead the mutton, rice flour, onion juice and almond pulp with ¼ teaspoon black pepper and ½ teaspoon salt in a bowl or deep tray for 5 minutes, until well combined. Divide into 4 equal parts and roll into balls. Make a hole in each ball, stuff an apricot inside and enclose.

Heat the butter in a saucepan over medium heat, add the shallots and cook for 10 minutes. Add the chicken and cook for 10 minutes. Reduce the heat, add the almond milk, ¼ teaspoon black pepper and ½ teaspoon salt and cook, covered, for 10 minutes. Add the meatballs and cook for 10 minutes, stirring frequently, until cooked through.

Sprinkle with ground cinnamon and serve.

♦

CHICKEN WITH FRUIT LEATHER
PESTİLLİ TAVUK ÇULLAMASI

Region:	Tunceli, all regions	
Preparation time:	10 minutes	
Cooking time:	30 minutes	
Serves:	4	

2 (800 g)	whole chicken breasts, halved and pounded thin with a meat tenderizer	2 (1 lb 12 oz)
½ tsp	salt	½ tsp
¼ tsp	black pepper	¼ tsp
½ tsp	ground cinnamon	½ tsp
4 (15 × 15 cm)	mulberry fruit leather (straps)	4 (6 × 6 inches)
6	eggs	6
100 g	plain (all purpose) flour	¾ cup/3½ oz
100 g	walnuts, finely crushed	1 cup/3½ oz
150 g	butter	⅔ cup/5 oz
400 g	Greek yogurt, to serve	2 cups/14 oz

Another name for this dish is 'sweet chicken'. A potential bride makes this dish with chicken and eggs taken from the groom's house. The prospective mother-in-law decides if her cooking skills are good enough to please her son.

♦

Put the chicken breasts into a steamer pan filled with 1 litre (4¼ cups/34 fl oz) water, bring to the boil and steam for 20 minutes. Remove from the steamer and season both sides of the chicken with salt, black pepper and ground cinnamon. Wrap the chicken in the mulberry fruit leather (straps) and seal tight.

Whisk the eggs in a shallow bowl. Put the flour and walnuts each in separate shallow bowls nearby.

Heat the butter in a large sauté pan over medium heat until very hot. Coat the chicken parcels in egg, then in flour, then egg, then walnuts, then flour again. Place in the hot butter and cook for 2 minutes on each side.

Serve immediately, with Greek yogurt on the side.

FORGET ME
UNUT BENİ

Region:	Şanlıurfa, Southeastern Anatolia	
Preparation time:	1 hour 40 minutes, plus overnight soaking	
Cooking time:		1 hour 25 minutes
Serves:		4

For the meatballs:

70 g	cracked rice (or 70 g/½ cup/ 2¾ oz rice flour)	⅓ cup/2¾ oz
200 g	finely minced (ground) lean lamb	7 oz
60 g	onion, grated, strained, juice collected and pulp reserved	⅜ cup/2¼ oz
1	egg	1
100 g	chickpeas (garbanzo beans), boiled in 1 litre (4¼ cups/ 34 fl oz) water and soaked overnight, then drained	½ cup/ 3½ oz
400 g	turkey leg, boned and finely diced	14 oz

For the yogurt sauce:

300 g	Greek yogurt	1½ cups/11 oz

For the dressing:

60 g	ghee (see p.485)	¼ cup/2¼ oz
3	garlic cloves, crushed	3
2 tsp	dried mint	2 tsp

❧

This dish is traditionally made on the day house guests leave. The facetious name, known around Şanlıurfa and also Birecik, means 'don't forget how I looked after you'. A variation includes poultry meatballs in a lamb broth. The lamb version is known as '*yuvalama*' (dumplings) in Gaziantep and is a popular festive dish. The meatballs can also be fried before they are added to the dish.
♦
Soak the rice for the meatballs in 500 ml (generous 2 cups/ 17 fl oz) warm water for 1 hour. Drain, then pound in a pestle and mortar to the size of semolina grains. Set aside.

In a saucepan, cook the chickpeas (garbanzo beans) in 2.25 litres (10 cups/80 fl oz) water for 40 minutes over medium heat. Add the turkey and cook for a further 20 minutes.

To make the meatballs:
Meanwhile, combine the lamb, cracked rice or rice flour, onion pulp, onion juice and egg with ¼ teaspoon each of black pepper and salt in a bowl. Knead for 15 minutes, until combined. Roll into 1-cm (½-inch) meatballs.

To make the yogurt sauce:
In a small saucepan, mix the yoghurt with 500 ml (generous 2 cups/17 fl oz) water for 2 minutes, until well combined. Set the pan over medium heat and stir in a single direction until it starts to boil. Keep boiling and stirring for 2 minutes, then remove from the heat.

Add the meatballs to the pan with the chickpeas and turkey. Reduce the heat, add ½ teaspoon salt and cook for 5 minutes. Mix in the yogurt sauce and ½ teaspoon black pepper, cook for a further 10 minutes. Remove from the heat.

To make the dressing:
Heat the ghee in a small saucepan over medium heat, add the garlic and dried mint and cook for 10 seconds. Gently stir the dressing into the dish and serve immediately.

TURKEY AND AUBERGINE CASSEROLE
HİNDİLİ PATLICAN SİLKME

Region:		Kocaeli, all regions
Preparation time:		15 minutes, plus 10 minutes soaking
Cooking time:		40 minutes
Serves:		4

2 (600 g)	Italian or Japanese aubergines (eggplants), peeled lengthwise in stripes, sliced into 2-cm (¾-inch) discs	2 (1 lb 5 oz)
150 g	butter	⅔ cup/5 oz
60 ml	olive oil	¼ cup/2 fl oz
800 g	turkey meat, chopped into 2-cm (¾-inch) pieces	1 lb 12 oz
2 (240 g)	medium onions, thinly sliced	2 (1⅝ cups/8½ oz)
1 litre	fresh tomato juice, hot	4¼ cups/34 fl oz
2 tbsp	apple cider vinegar	2 tbsp
1 tbsp	dried oregano	1 tbsp
½ tsp	dried chilli (red pepper) flakes	½ tsp

Garlic yogurt is a popular side to this dish.

◆

Soak the aubergine (eggplant) slices in 2 litres (8½ cups/70 fl oz) water with ¾ teaspoon salt for 10 minutes. Drain and squeeze dry.

Heat the butter and olive oil in a large saucepan over medium heat, add the turkey and cook for 5 minutes. Remove with a slotted spoon and set aside.

Add the aubergine slices to the same pan and cook for 3 minutes on each side. Remove with a slotted spoon and set aside.

Add the onions to the same pan and cook for 5 minutes, mixing continuously. Return the turkey to the pan and layer the fried aubergine slices on top. Reduce the heat, add the tomato juice, apple cider vinegar, dried oregano, dried chilli (red pepper) flakes, ¼ teaspoon black pepper, and 1 teaspoon salt and cook, covered, for 20 minutes.

Serve immediately.

◆

FRIED POACHED CHICKEN
TAVUK ÇULLAMA

Region:		Konya, all regions
Preparation time:		20 minutes
Cooking time:	1 hour 25 minutes, plus 20 minutes cooling	
Serves:		4

4 (1.4 kg)	chicken legs on the bone	4 (3 lb)
1 (70 g)	carrot	1 (½ cup/2¾ oz)
1	celery stick	1
60 g	onion, quartered	⅜ cup/2¼ oz
6	garlic cloves	6
5	black peppercorns	5
1 tsp	salt	1 tsp
4	eggs	4
100 g	plain (all purpose) flour	¾ cup/3½ oz
100 g	butter	½ cup/3½ oz
2 tbsp	grape vinegar	2 tbsp
2 tbsp	lemon juice	2 tbsp
¼ tsp	black pepper	¼ tsp
½ tsp	mustard powder	½ tsp
2	fresh tarragon sprigs	2
4	flat-leaf parsley sprigs	4

Another winter dish, the poached chicken can also be coated with eggs and flour and deep-fried whole or baked.

◆

In a large covered saucepan, simmer the chicken legs in 2 litres (8½ cups/70 fl oz) water with the carrot, celery, onion, garlic, black peppercorns and ¾ teaspoon salt for 1 hour. Strain, reserving the stock. Set the chicken legs aside to cool for 20 minutes. Transfer the carrot, celery stick, onion and garlic to a mortar and pestle and pound to a paste. Whisk the eggs in a shallow bowl. Put the flour in a separate shallow bowl nearby.

Heat the butter in a large sauté pan over medium heat until very hot. Coat the chicken legs in eggs and then flour, place in the hot butter and cook for 2 minutes on each side, about 10 minutes in total. Arrange the chicken legs snugly in the bottom of a separate large saucepan.

In a large bowl, mix the pounded carrot and onion paste with the grape vinegar, lemon juice, black pepper, mustard powder and the remaining ¼ teaspoon salt, until well combined. Stir in 250 ml (1 cup/8 fl oz) of the reserved chicken stock. Pour this mixture over the chicken legs in the pan. Cover and cook over low heat for 5 minutes. Add the finely sliced tarragon and parsley and cook, covered, for another 2 minutes and serve.

POULTRY & GAME

POUNDED ROOSTER
HELİSE

Region:		Ağrı, all regions
Preparation time:		10 minutes, plus overnight soaking
Cooking time:		2 hours 10 minutes
Serves:		4

200 g	cracked wheat,	1⅔ cups/
	soaked overnight, drained	7 oz
¾ tsp	salt	¾ tsp
1 kg	rooster meat, off the bone	2 lb 4 oz
2 (240 g)	medium onions,	2 (1⅝ cups/
	sliced into thin crescents	8½ oz)
½ tsp	black pepper	½ tsp

For the sauce:		
100 g	butter	¼ cup/3½ oz
50 g	honey (oregano flower)	2 oz

This winter dish exists in many local guises, also known as *harisa, herise, herse, aşir, aşür, dövme, keşkek* and *keşka*. Although usually made with lamb, variations include game, poultry, mutton and goat. The dish symbolizes peace and is popular at weddings and other special occasions. Some recipes omit the honey, while others use molasses.

♦

Put the cracked wheat in a bowl, cover with hot water (just off the boil) and rest for 5 minutes. Drain and set aside.

Sprinkle the bottom of a heavy saucepan or casserole (Dutch oven) with salt, then cover with half of the rooster meat, fatty skin facing down. Add a layer of half the cracked wheat and then a layer of half the onions. Repeat with the remaining half of the ingredients. Add the black pepper and 2 litres (8½ cups/70 fl oz) water. Simmer, covered, over low heat for 2 hours.

Keeping the pan/casserole over low heat, pound the stew into a pulp with a wooden pestle or the end of a rolling pin, until sticky. Remove from the heat.

To make the sauce:
Heat the butter in a saucepan over medium heat, add the honey and cook for 1 minute, mixing continuously. Transfer to plates, drizzle with the sauce and serve.

♦

THICK AND RICH CHICKEN STEW
ŞIPSİ

Region:		Sakarya, Marmara Region
Preparation time:		15 minutes
Cooking time:		1 hour 15 minutes
Serves:		4

1 (1.5 kg)	whole chicken, quartered	1 (3 lb 5 oz)
1 (120 g)	onion, quartered	1 (¾ cup/4 oz)
4	garlic cloves	4
½ tsp	ground coriander	½ tsp

For the garlic and walnut oil:		
2	garlic cloves	2
10	coriander seeds	10
1	dried chilli (chile)	1
60 g	walnuts, crushed	½ cup/2¼ oz

For the roux:		
50 g	butter	¼ cup/2 oz
2	garlic cloves, crushed	2
70 g	plain (all-purpose) flour	½ cup/2¾ oz
1 litre	milk	4¼ cups/34 fl oz
½ tsp	ground coriander	½ tsp

At a family meal, *şipsi* is served in a single dish. The chicken neck is offered to the son, the wings to the daughter, the breast to the mother and thighs to the father.

♦

In a saucepan, simmer the chicken, onion, garlic, ground coriander, ¼ teaspoon black pepper and ¾ teaspoon salt in 1 litre (4¼ cups/34 fl oz) water over low heat, covered, for 1 hour. Strain through a colander, reserving the stock in one bowl and the chicken in another. Set both aside.

To make the garlic and walnut oil:
Heat a sauté pan over medium heat until hot, add the garlic, coriander seeds, dried chilli (chile) and walnuts and dry-roast for 2 minutes, mixing continuously. Pound with a pestle and mortar for 5 minutes. Steam a piece of muslin (cheesecloth), place the pulp inside, squeeze to strain the oil into a bowl. Set aside the remaining pulp in another bowl.

To make the roux:
Heat the butter in a saucepan over low heat, add the garlic and cook for 10 seconds. Add the flour and cook for 3 minutes, stirring continuously. Stir in the chicken stock, milk, ground coriander, ¼ teaspoon black pepper and ¼ teaspoon salt and cook for 2 minutes, bringing to the boil. Add the cooked chicken pieces and cook, covered, for 5 minutes. Stir through the garlic and walnut oil and serve.

POULTRY & GAME

DUCK STEW OVER BREAD
ÖRDEK TİRİDİ

Region:		Manisa, all regions
Preparation time:		15 minutes
Cooking time:		2 hours 20 minutes
Serves:		4

1 (1.2 kg)	duck, meat only (full-fat)	1 (2 lb 10 oz)
5	black peppercorns	5
60 g	onion, quartered	⅜ cup/2¼ oz

For the yogurt sauce:

300 g	Greek yogurt	1½ cups/11 oz
4	garlic cloves, crushed	4

For the sauce:

50 g	butter	¼ cup/2 oz
6	garlic cloves, crushed	6
2 tsp	dried chilli (red pepper) flakes	2 tsp
1½ tsp	tomato paste (see p.492)	1½ tsp
400 ml	fresh tomato juice	1 ⅔ cups/14 fl oz

400 g	stale *Tirnakli Ekmek* (Pide Flatbread, see p.376), diced into 1-cm (½-inch) cubes	14 oz
4	parsley sprigs, finely sliced	4

Made using the ducks hunted in the winter, *tirit* is traditionally made with stale flatbreads and meat stock. There are other versions with mushroom, milk and *ayran*.

♦

In a saucepan, boil the duck meat, peppercorns, onions and ¾ teaspoon salt in 3 litres (12 cups/100 fl oz) water over medium heat for 5 minutes. Skim the surface with a slotted spoon. Cook, covered, over low heat for a further 2 hours.

Remove the duck from the pan and shred the meat. Reserve 600 ml (2½ cups/20 fl oz) of the cooking stock.

To make the yogurt sauce:
Mix the yogurt, garlic and ¼ teaspoon salt in a bowl for 1 minute, until well combined.

To make the sauce:
Heat the butter in a saucepan over medium heat, add the garlic and cook for 1 minute. Add the dried chilli (red pepper) flakes and cook for 30 seconds. Add the tomato paste and cook for 1 minute. Reduce the heat, add the duck, stock, tomato juice, ¼ teaspoon each of black pepper and salt. Cook for 5 minutes, until the juices have been absorbed.

Set 4 heat-resistant serving bowls over low heat. Add the bread cubes and ladle 100 ml (scant ½ cup/3½ fl oz) of the sauce into each bowl. Add the yogurt sauce and finally the duck in its sauce. Serve each with a sprinkle of parsley.

ROOSTER STEW WITH YOGURT
YOĞURTLU HOROZ YAHNİSİ

Region:		Kilis, Southeastern Anatolia
Preparation time:		10 minutes
Cooking time:	1 hour 10 minutes, plus 5 minutes resting	
Serves:		4

100 g	butter	½ cup/3½ oz
4	rooster thighs, off the bone	4
4 (600 g)	potatoes, peeled, soaked in water to prevent browning	2⅔ cups/ 1 lb 5 oz
8	shallots, peeled	8
8	garlic cloves, quartered	8
pinch	safflower (false saffron) or saffron	pinch

For the sauce:

300g	strained yogurt	1½ cups/11 oz
1	egg	1

Locals serve this dish with *Adi Pilav* (Plain Rice Pilaf, see p.306) or *Bulgar Pilavi* (Bulgur Pilaf, see p.318).

♦

Heat the butter in a large saucepan over medium heat. Halve the rooster thighs and add to the pan and cook on each side for 3 minutes. Add the potatoes and shallots and cook for 5 minutes. Add the garlic with ½ teaspoon black pepper and 1 teaspoon salt, then cook for 1 minute. Reduce the heat, add 1.5 litres (6¼ cups/50 fl oz) hot water and cook, covered, for 40 minutes.

To make the sauce:
In a small saucepan over medium heat, combine the strained yogurt and egg with 500 ml (generous 2 cups/ 17 fl oz) water for 3 minutes, stirring in one direction only.

Reduce the heat under the main pan, stir in the sauce and cook, uncovered, for 10 minutes. Remove from the heat, sprinkle with the safflower or saffron, and rest for 5 minutes before serving.

BRIDEGROOM'S SHANKS
DAMAT PAÇASI

Region:		Tekirdağ, Marmara Region
Preparation time:		25 minutes
Cooking time:		1 hour 15 minutes
Serves:		4

4 (1 kg)	chicken thighs	4 (2 lb 3 oz)
4	black peppercorns	4
100 g	butter, melted	½ cup/3½ oz
3	*Yufka Ekmeği*	3
	(Thin Flatbreads, see p.378)	

For the white sauce:

3	eggs	3
150 g	strained yogurt	¾ cup/5 oz
50 g	plain (all-purpose) flour	⅓ cup/2 oz
2 tbsp	apple cider vinegar	2 tbsp
6	garlic cloves, crushed	6
60 g	almonds	½ cup/2¼ oz

For the butter sauce:

50 g	butter	¼ cup/2 oz
1 tsp	dried chilli	1 tsp
	(red pepper) flakes	

This is a traditional winter dish of the migrants from the Balkan Wars who live in the Aegean and Marmara regions. It is a dish prepared for bridegrooms, hence the name.

♦

Preheat oven to 180°C/350°F/Gas Mark 4. In a saucepan, simmer the chicken, peppercorns and ½ teaspoon salt with 2 litres (8½ cups/70 fl oz) water, covered, for 1 hour.

Meanwhile, grease a 25-cm (10-inch) round baking pan with 2 tablespoons butter. Line the pan with 1 flatbread and drizzle with 2 tablespoons butter. Repeat for each flatbread. Trim the overflowing edges of the bread and put in the bottom of the pan. Bake in the hot oven for 20 minutes. Shred the chicken and scatter over the flatbreads. Drizzle over 200 ml (1 cup/ 7 fl oz) of the stock. Set the rest aside.

To make the white sauce:
In a bowl, whisk together the eggs, yogurt, flour, vinegar, garlic and ¼ teaspoon salt for 2 minutes. Add the remaining stock and whisk for another minute. Drizzle over the chicken and flatbreads. Sprinkle with the almonds and bake in the oven for a further 10 minutes.

To make the butter sauce:
Heat the butter in a saucepan over medium heat, add the dried chilli (red pepper) flakes and sauté for 30 seconds. Drizzle over the baked dish and serve immediately.

♦

PARTRIDGE PÂTÉ
KEKLİK DÖVMESİ

Region:		Bitlis, Southeastern Anatolia
Preparation time:		15 minutes
Cooking time:		1 hour 30 minutes
Serves:		4

2 (1 kg)	partridges, quartered	2 (2 lb 3 oz)
600 g	potatoes, peeled	2⅔ cups/1 lb 5 oz
1 (120 g)	onion, quartered	1 (¾ cup/4 oz)
3	black peppercorns	3
200 ml	milk	scant 1 cup/ 7 fl oz
½ tsp	ground cumin	½ tsp
½ tsp	ground turmeric	½ tsp
1 tsp	ground coriander	1 tsp

For the sauce:

60 g	butter	¼ cup/2¼ oz
50 g	walnuts, crushed	½ cup/2 oz
2	garlic cloves, crushed	2
1 tsp	dried chilli (red pepper) flakes	1 tsp

This autumn dish can also be made with a selection of herbs, and dried and fresh vegetables. The partridge can be substituted with other poultry, wild or domesticated.

♦

In a large saucepan, simmer the partridge, potatoes, onion, peppercorns and ¾ teaspoon salt with 1.5 litres (6¼ cups/50 fl oz) water over low heat, covered, for 1 hour 10 minutes.

Remove the partridge pieces with a slotted spoon, but keep the pan simmering. Take the meat off the bone and shred, then return it to the pan. Add the milk, cumin, ground turmeric, ground coriander and ¼ teaspoon black pepper. Cook for 10 minutes while pounding the mixture with a wooden pestle (or the end of a rolling pin). Remove from the heat when the consistency of the paste is quite sticky.

To make the sauce:
Heat the butter in a large saucepan over low heat, add the walnuts and cook for 1 minute. Add the garlic and dried chilli (red pepper) flakes and cook for 10 seconds. Remove from the heat.

Drizzle the partridge pâté with the sauce and serve.

PIGEON HOT POT
GÜVEÇTE GÜVERCİN

Region:		Kayseri, all regions
Preparation time:		20 minutes
Cooking time:		1 hour 10 minutes
Serves:		4

150 g	butter	⅔ cup/5 oz
4	fledgling pigeons	4
1 (120 g)	medium onion, sliced into thin rounds	1 (¾ cup/4 oz)
1	garlic clove, peeled	1
2	small bell peppers, sliced into thin rounds	2
½ tsp	black pepper	½ tsp
400 g	potatoes, halved	2 cups/14 oz
1 kg	tomatoes, cut into 1-cm (½-inch) slices	5 cups/2 lb 3 oz)
1 tsp	dried oregano	1 tsp
1 tsp	dried chilli (red pepper) flakes	1 tsp

Pigeons were bred in special houses across the regions specifically for this dish. This tradition still persists in many places in Southeastern Anatolia, as well as Gesi near Kayseri. The latter was the main pigeon breeding area for the Ottoman court. This dish has always been a delicacy enjoyed by the crème de la crème of society.

◆

Preheat oven to 180°C/350°F/Gas Mark 4.

Heat 100 g (scant ½ cup/3½ oz) of the butter in a sauté pan over medium heat, add the pigeons and sauté for 4 minutes on each side. Transfer the pigeons to an earthenware cooking pot or casserole (Dutch oven), making sure the more boney parts are at the bottom.

Add the onion, garlic, bell peppers, black pepper and ½ teaspoon salt to the sauté pan and cook for 10 minutes.

Coat the pigeons with the onion and peppers, then cover with a layer of potatoes, then a layer of tomatoes. Sprinkle in the dried oregano and chilli (red pepper) flakes with ½ teaspoon salt. Add the remaining butter to the pot/casserole and bake, covered, in the oven for 30 minutes. Remove the lid and cook, uncovered, for a final 10 minutes.

WHEAT AND WOODCOCK PASTE
ÇULLUK ETLİ KEŞKEK

Region:		Sakarya, all regions
Preparation time:		15 minutes, plus overnight soaking
Cooking time:		3 hours 5 minutes
Serves:		4

2 (1.5 kg)	plump woodcocks	2 (3 lb 5 oz)
1 (120 g)	onion, quartered	1 (¾ cup/4 oz)
200 g	cracked wheat, soaked overnight and drained	1⅔ cups/7 oz
¾ tsp	salt	¾ tsp
¼ tsp	ground cumin	¼ tsp
¼ tsp	black pepper	¼ tsp
1 tsp	dried oregano	1 tsp

For the sauce:		
50 g	butter	¼ cup/2 oz
60 g	crushed walnuts	½ cup/2¼ oz
½ tsp	dried chilli (red pepper) flakes	½ tsp

Keşkek – made by beating meat with wheat using a traditional technique – is also known as *keşka*, *herse*, *herise*, *aşir* and *aşur* in other parts of the country. Rooster, goose, duck, chicken and lamb are widely used as well as woodcock. It is an impressive part of wedding banquets, usually made in the winter when most game is hunted.

◆

Preheat oven to 160°C/325°F/Gas Mark 3.

Put the woodcocks, onion, cracked wheat, salt, cumin, black pepper, dried oregano and 3 litres (12 cups/100 fl oz) water into an earthenware cooking pot or casserole (Dutch oven). Seal tightly and bake in the hot oven for 3 hours.

Transfer the woodcocks to a bowl and pull the meat off the bone. Put the pulled meat back into the pot/casserole and mash or pound the meat and the cooked wheat into a paste with the back of a wooden spoon for 10 minutes.

To make the sauce:
Heat the butter in a large saucepan over medium heat, add the walnuts and sauté for 1 minute. Add the dried chilli (red pepper) flakes and sauté for 30 seconds.

Transfer the paste to serving plates, drizzle with the sauce and serve.

ROOSTER HOT POT
HOROZ ETLİ GÜVEÇ

Region:	Adana, Mediterranean Region	
Preparation time:	20 minutes	
Cooking time:	1 hour 10 minutes	
Serves:	4	

2 (2 kg)	small roosters, meat only, chopped into 2-cm (¾-inch) pieces	2 (4 lb 6 oz)
400 g	potatoes, chopped into 2-cm (¾-inch) pieces	2 cups/14 oz
1.5 kg	tomatoes, chopped into 2-cm (¾-inch) pieces	3 lb 5 oz
4	green bell peppers, chopped into 2-cm (¾-inch) pieces	4
3	garlic cloves, peeled	3
2 tsp	red bell pepper paste (see p.492)	2 tsp
1 tsp	dried chilli (red pepper) flakes	1 tsp
1 tbsp	dried oregano	1 tbsp
200 ml	olive oil	scant 1 cup/7 fl oz

This dish can also be made with pre-fried rooster meat. Chicken is fine, too.

◆

Preheat oven to 180°C/350°F/Gas Mark 4.

Mix the rooster meat, potatoes, tomatoes, bell peppers, garlic, red bell pepper paste, dried chilli (red pepper) flakes, dried oregano and olive oil with ½ teaspoon black pepper and 1 teaspoon salt in a large bowl for 3 minutes.

Transfer the mixture to an earthenware cooking pot or casserole (Dutch oven). Bake in the hot oven for 1 hour 10 minutes.

Transfer to serving platters and serve.

◆

PULLED PARTRIDGE
KEKLİK UFALAMASI

Region:	Elazığ, Doğu Anadolu, Eastern Anatolia	
Preparation time:	15 minutes	
Cooking time:	2 hours 20 minutes	
Serves:	4	

4 (2 kg)	partridges	4 (4 lb 6 oz)
1½ (180 g)	medium onions: 1 onion sliced; ½ onion left in one piece	1½ (1⅛ cups/ 6 oz)
100 g	butter	½ cup/3½ oz
100 g	crushed walnuts	1 cup/3½ oz
2 tsp	dried oregano	2 tsp
¼ tsp	black pepper	¼ tsp
½ tsp	salt	½ tsp
½ tsp	dried chilli (red pepper) flakes	½ tsp
1	Yufka Ekmeği (Thin Flatbreads, see p.378), dried, torn into pieces	1
½ bunch	flat-leaf parsley, finely sliced	½ bunch
½ bunch	fresh basil, finely sliced	½ bunch
160 g	pomegranate seeds	2 cups/5½ oz

Partridges are at their most plump and juicy in autumn, which is when this dish is made. You could substitute partridge with rabbit or chicken.

◆

Boil the partridges in 3 litres (12 cups/100 fl oz) water with the ½ onion for 2 hours, then remove the meat with a slotted spoon and shred. Set aside.

Heat the butter in a large saucepan over medium heat, add the sliced onions and walnuts and cook for 10 minutes. Add the shredded partridge meat, dried oregano, black pepper, salt and dried chilli (red pepper) flakes and cook for another 10 minutes.

Put the flatbread in the middle of a deep 40-cm (16-inch) diameter tray. Heap the sautéed meat on top, followed by the parsley, fresh basil and pomegranate seeds. Toss for 2 minutes, until well combined.

Serve immediately.

CHARGRILLED CHICKEN
TAVUK KÜLBASTI

Region:		İstanbul, all regions
Preparation time:		15 minutes, plus 2 hours chilling
Cooking time:		20 minutes
Serves:		4

4 (800 g)	chicken legs, skin removed, de-boned, pounded to 1-cm (½-inch) thick	4 (1 lb 12 oz)
1 tsp	ground cinnamon	1 tsp
60 g	onion, grated, strained and juice collected	⅜ cup/2¼ oz
½ tsp	black pepper	½ tsp
¾ tsp	salt	¾ tsp
100 g	butter, melted	½ cup/3½ oz
2 (240 g)	medium onions, thinly sliced	2 (1⅝ cups/ 8½ oz)
1 (300 g)	tomato, sliced	1½ cups/11 oz
4	banana peppers (mild sweet peppers)	4

A grill (broiler) will do for this dish, if you don't have access to a barbecue.

◆

Mix the chicken meat, ground cinnamon, onion juice, black pepper and salt in a large bowl, until well combined. Cover and chill in the refrigerator for 2 hours.

Meanwhile, prepare a barbecue for cooking or preheat a grill (broiler) to high.

Remove the chicken from the refrigerator. Generously brush the chicken, onion slices, tomatoes and banana peppers with melted butter. Cook the chicken and vegetables 8 cm (3 inches) above the hot barbecue embers for 3 minutes on each side. Alternatively, grill (broil), turning as required. Apply more butter as required.

Setting the banana peppers aside, arrange the tomatoes and onions snugly in the bottom of an ovenproof pan and top with the chicken. Cover and cook over the ashes of the barbecue for a further 10 minutes. Alternatively, grill (broil), turning as required.

Transfer to serving plates and serve with the banana peppers.

◆

BARBECUED DUCK PARCEL KEBABS
GÖMLEK KEBABI

Region:		Çanakkale, all regions
Preparation time:		15 minutes, plus 10 minutes soaking
Cooking time:		15 minutes
Serves:		4

1 (1 kg)	whole duck, meat taken off the bone, divided into 20 pieces	1 (2 lb 3 oz)
60 ml	olive oil	¼ cup/2 fl oz
1 (120 g)	medium onion, grated	1 (¾ cup/4 oz)
1 tsp	ground cinnamon	1 tsp
½ tsp	black pepper	½ tsp
½ tsp	salt	½ tsp
20 (5 × 5 cm)	lamb caul fat pieces, soaked in water for 10 minutes, rinsed	20 (2 × 2 inches)
1	*Piyaz Salatası* (Onion Salad, see p.67), to serve	1

This dish is made in the winter months, during the hunting season. Variations on this recipe use other poultry, mutton, goat or veal instead of the duck. If you don't have a barbecue, you can use a grill (broiler). You will need 4 long cast-iron skewers or 10 flat wooden skewers (soaked).

◆

Prepare a barbecue for cooking or preheat a grill (broiler) to high.

Mix the duck meat, olive oil, onion, ground cinnamon, black pepper and salt in a large bowl or deep tray, until well combined. Divide into 20 equal pieces.

Spread each piece of caul fat out on a work surface, put a piece of the duck mixture in the middle and fold the caul fat inwards from all corners to make a parcel. Thread the parcels on to skewers, making sure that they remain intact.

Set the skewers 8 cm (3 inches) above the hot barbecue embers and cook for 10 minutes, turning them every minute. Alternatively, grill (broil) for 10 minutes, turning as required.

Serve with fresh *Piyaz Salatası*.

FRIED GOOSE LIVER
KAZ CİĞERİ KIZARTMASI

Region:		Ardahan, Eastern Anatolia
Preparation time:		15 minutes
Cooking time:		15 minutes
Serves:		4

100 g	plain (all purpose) flour	¾ cup/ 3½ oz
400 g	fresh goose liver, diced into 1-cm (½-inch) pieces	14 oz
500 ml	goose fat	generous 2 cups/ 17 fl oz
300 g	potatoes, diced into 1-cm (½-inch) pieces	1⅓ cups/11 oz
1 tsp	ground paprika	1 tsp
½ tsp	ground cumin	½ tsp
2 tsp	ground sumac	2 tsp
½ bunch	parsley, finely sliced	½ bunch
2	spring onions (scallions), finely sliced	2

This dish can be eaten hot or cold depending on preference. The recipe also works with other poultry and game birds.

◆

Put the flour in a shallow bowl and toss the goose livers in the flour until well coated. Transfer to a colander and toss again to remove excess flour. Set aside.

In a large saucepan, heat the goose fat over medium heat to 155°C/310°F. Place half of the potatoes into the hot fat and cook for 5 minutes. Remove from the pan with a slotted spoon to drain on paper towels. Cook the remaining half of the potatoes in the same way. Finally, place the goose livers into the hot fat and cook for 30 seconds. Remove with a slotted spoon.

Arrange the cooked potatoes on a serving platter and layer the fried livers on top. Sprinkle with the paprika, cumin and sumac with ¼ teaspoon black pepper and 1 teaspoon salt and gently stir through. Garnish with parsley and spring onions (scallions) and then serve.

◆ ⏳

FRIED GIBLETS
TAŞLIK KAVURMASI

Region:		Tekirdağ, all regions
Preparation time:		15 minutes
Cooking time:		40 minutes
Serves:		4

200 ml	olive oil	scant 1 cup/7 fl oz
4 (480 g)	medium onions, finely diced	4 (3⅛ cups/ 1 lb 1 oz)
200 g	rooster giblets, cleaned and finely diced	7 oz
200 g	chicken giblets, cleaned and finely diced	7 oz
1	small green bell pepper, finely diced	1
1	small red bell pepper, finely diced	1
6	garlic cloves, quartered	6
1 tsp	dried oregano	1 tsp
¼ tsp	ground cumin	¼ tsp
¼ tsp	dried chilli (red pepper) flakes	¼ tsp
300 g	tomatoes, finely diced	½ cups/11 oz
½ bunch	flat-leaf parsley, finely sliced	½ bunch

The giblets of other poultry and wild game can be used for this dish, as well as the innards of chickens and roosters. There is also a plain version without onions, tomatoes or bell pepper, and also a version with only onions.

◆

Heat a large *sac* (see p.503), iron skillet or wok until very hot. Add the olive oil and heat through, then add the onion and sauté for 10 minutes, stirring continuously. Add the rooster giblets and sauté for 5 minutes. Add the chicken giblets and sauté for 10 minutes. Add the green and red bell peppers and garlic and sauté for 5 minutes. Add the dried oregano, cumin and dried chilli (red pepper) flakes with ¼ teaspoon black pepper and ¾ teaspoon salt and sauté for 1 minute. Add the tomatoes and sauté for 3 minutes. Reduce the heat and cook, uncovered, for a final 5 minutes.

Sprinkle with parsley and serve.

◆ 🌿

♦

OFFAL

♦

OFFAL IN TURKISH CULTURE

♦

Offal (variety meats) is the name we give to the innards, heads and trotters (feet) of goats, sheep and cattle. Offal is sold at special stores in Turkey and the dishes made with it are showstoppers in our culture. The variety is endless and encompasses all parts of the head, trotters, lungs, liver, spleen, heart, kidney, sweetbreads, visceral fat, oxtail, stomach and intestines.

Cooking techniques for offal range from stuffed tripe to kebabs, grills to confits, patties, pâtés, stews and soups. Poaching and baking in traditional and tandoori ovens are also popular techniques.

OFFAL SEASON

♦

We eat offal all the time but more so during the winter. We love goat, cow, veal and sheep trotters. Trotter soup comes to the rescue every time we have a broken bone (even doctors are in consensus that this folk remedy really works). Liver is an all-round folk remedy too. In a nutshell, we believe that offal is good for us.

FRESH OFFAL

Fresh is of course best, even more so with offal than with meat or poultry. Fresh meats or poultry are traditionally consumed the same day or the day after. With offal, cooking on the day of purchase is critical.

The best offal is from lamb or veal. Female or male, the animal has to be neutered or its meat will be tasteless and have a distinctive smell. The offal of castrated animals is the most delicious. The living conditions of livestock also matter – the closer to natural conditions, the better. Less stress means more delicious milk, meat, liver.

THE OFFAL KEBAB SHOP

In my hometown of Nizip, Gaziantep, the bakery I worked at was next door to a butcher. There was heavy traffic between the shops. Kebab shop owners would rush to the butchers immediately after the offal was delivered. They would buy the lungs, suet and sweetbreads at 4 a.m. and take it back to their shops. The spleen, heart, kidneys, liver and lungs would be meticulously threaded on skewers. The pieces of lung that would not go on skewers would be roasted with the suet. Vegetables would be prepared and the embers would reach the perfect heat. In the small hours of the morning, farmers, coffee shop owners, night watchmen, the pious on their way to the mosque for prayers, fruit growers, early risers, employers and employees, those on their way to the Turkish bath after a wedding... all frequented the kebab shop.

The quirkiness of kebab shop owners and their customers is worth mentioning. The fresh delicacies on skewers are served to the more prestigious patrons, along with other delicacies like liver which still has its blood. A groom fresh out of the Turkish bath and his friends receive preferential treatment too.

There is usually no offal left by 9 a.m. Most owners close shop by 10 or 11 a.m.

Traditionally, offal kebab shops avoid other cuts of meat. However, the early morning offal kebab is not a countrywide delicacy. Tripe soup is usually eaten late at night and so are sweetbreads. Fried liver is eaten for lunch and dinner. There is a time of the day for every type of offal.

FRIED TRIPE
KIRKKAT KAVURMASI

Region:		Adana, all regions
Preparation time:		15 minutes
Cooking time:	1 hour 25 minutes, plus cooling time	
Serves:		4

4	lamb tripe (omasum), thoroughly cleaned	4
150 g	suet	1¼ cups/5 oz
2 (240 g)	medium onions, sliced	2 (1⅝ cups/ 8½ oz)
2	chillies (chiles), thinly sliced	2
½ tsp	ground cumin	½ tsp
1 tsp	dried oregano	1 tsp
1 tsp	dried chilli (red pepper) flakes	1 tsp
¼ tsp	black pepper	¼ tsp
¾ tsp	salt	¾ tsp
2 tbsp	ground sumac	2 tbsp
1 bunch	flat-leaf parsley, finely sliced	1 bunch

p.247

All types of tripe (from the four chambers of ruminant animals) are commonly used in Turkish cooking; omasum, reed tripe and rumen tripe are often roasted, stewed or used in *dolmas* (stuffed dishes). Fried tripe is made in the winter months. Tripe and especially tripe soup is believed to be the best hangover cure after a long night at a *meyhane* (see p.502). *Rakı* (see p.503), the traditional drink served at a *meyhane*, is over 40% alcohol. Tripe dishes do the trick when you want a slow transition back to reality.

♦

Put the lamb tripe into a pressure cooker with 1 litre (4¼ cups/34 fl oz) water and cook for 50 minutes. Drain and let cool. When cool, roll the tripe up and slice crosswise into 2-mm (⅛-inch) strips.

Heat a large *sac* (see p.503), iron skillet or wok until very hot. Add the suet and heat through, then add onions and chillies (chiles) and sauté for 15 minutes. Add the lamb tripe and sauté for 10 minutes. Add the cumin, dried oregano, dried chilli (red pepper) flakes, black pepper and salt and sauté for another 5 minutes.

In a separate bowl, toss the sumac and parsley together.

Transfer the fried tripe to a serving platter and sprinkle the parsley and sumac mixture on top.

♦

TRIPE IN SOUR SAUCE
EKŞİLİ KARIN (İŞKEMBE)

Region:		Bursa, Marmara
Preparation time:		15 minutes
Cooking time:	1 hour, plus cooling time	
Serves:		4

600 g	water buffalo tripe, thoroughly cleaned	1 lb 5 oz
2	fresh garlic, finely chopped	2
2 tbsp	lemon juice	2 tbsp
1 tbsp	grape vinegar	1 tbsp
1 tsp	paprika	1 tsp
¼ tsp	ground cumin	¼ tsp
½ bunch	flat-leaf parsley, finely chopped	½ bunch
4	spring onions (scallions), finely chopped	4
60 ml	olive oil	¼ cup/2 fl oz

If you can't source water buffalo tripe, then substitute either veal or sheep tripe instead. Some recipes for this dish recommend frying the tripe first.

♦

Put the tripe into a pressure cooker with 1 litre (4¼ cups/ 34 fl oz) water and cook for 1 hour. Drain and let cool, then finely chop.

Gently mix the chopped tripe, fresh garlic, lemon juice, grape vinegar, paprika and cumin with ¼ teaspoon black pepper and ¾ teaspoon salt in a large bowl for 1 minute. Add the parsley, spring onions (scallions) and olive oil and mix for a further 1 minute.

Serve immediately.

SAUTÉED LIVER AND LUNGS
CİĞER KAVURMASI

Region:	Gaziantep, Southeastern Anatolia	
Preparation time:	15 minutes	
Cooking time:	50 minutes, plus 10 minutes cooling	
Serves:	4	

300 g	lamb liver	11 oz
300 g	lamb lungs	11 oz
150 g	tail fat or ghee, finely chopped	⅔ cup/ 5 oz
4 (480 g)	medium onions, finely diced	4 (3⅛ cups/ 1 lb 1 oz)
1½ tsp	tomato paste (see p.492)	1½ tsp
2 tsp	paprika	2 tsp
1 tsp	hot dried chilli (red pepper) flakes	1 tsp
½ tsp	ground cumin	½ tsp
¼ tsp	ground cloves	¼ tsp
1 bunch	flat-leaf parsley	1 bunch
1	Piyaz Salatsı (Onion Salad, see p.67)	1
4	Açik Ekmek (Ridged Bread, see p.394)	4

This dish, which is also popular in Şanlıurfa, is traditionally eaten as a wrap in *Açik Ekmek* (Ridged Bread, see p.394). Some recipes use both liver and lung, whereas others use only lung.

♦

Remove the membrane from the lamb liver and lamb lungs, then trim away any sinew. In a large saucepan, bring 2 litres (8½ cups/70 fl oz) water and 1 teaspoon salt to a boil. Add the liver and lungs and simmer, covered, for 20 minutes. Drain and rinse with cold water. Let cool, then chop finely.

Heat the tail fat or ghee in a large saucepan over medium heat, add the onions and sauté for 10 minutes, stirring continuously. Add the chopped lungs and liver and sauté for 10 minutes, stirring occasionally. Add the tomato paste, paprika, hot dried chilli (red pepper) flakes, ground cumin, ground cloves with ¼ teaspoon black pepper and 1 teaspoon salt and sauté for 10 minutes, stirring occasionally. Remove from the heat, gently mix in the finely sliced parsley and serve with fresh *Piyaz Salatsı* and *Açik Ekmek*.

♦

SAUTÉED LIVER WITH VEGETABLES
SEBZELİ CİĞER KAVURMASI

Region:	Malatya, all regions	
Preparation time:	15 minutes	
Cooking time:	35 minutes	
Serves:	4	

2 (240 g)	medium onions	2 (1⅝ cups/8½ oz)
1	green bell pepper	1
100 g	butter	½ cup/3½ oz
4	garlic cloves, quartered	4
600 g	lamb liver, membrane removed, sinew trimmed	1 lb 5 oz
500 g	tomatoes, diced into 2-cm (¾-inch) pieces	2½ cups/ 1 lb 2 oz
2 tsp	dried chilli (red pepper) flakes	2 tsp
2 tsp	dried oregano	2 tsp
½ bunch	fresh basil	½ bunch
½ bunch	flat-leaf parsley	½ bunch

This dish is made in the winter and early spring. It is believed to give an immediate injection of vitality and energy to those feeling a bit under the weather. It is popular with home cooks and restaurants alike, especially in Southeastern Anatolia. Specialised eateries usually sell out their liver dishes by mid morning. The kebab version, on skewers, includes fresh chillies in the summer and dried ones in the winter. The same dish is made using lungs as well. The name remains the same.

♦

Dice the onion and green bell pepper into 2-cm (¾-inch) pieces. Heat the butter in a large saucepan over medium heat, add the onion and sauté for 5 minutes. Add the bell pepper and garlic and sauté for 5 minutes. Add the liver, sauté for 5 minutes, then add the tomatoes and sauté for another 5 minutes. Reduce the heat, add the dried chilli (red pepper) flakes, oregano, ¼ teaspoon black pepper and ¾ teaspoon salt and cook, covered, for 10 minutes.

Finely slice the fresh basil and parsley. Sprinkle over the liver and serve.

🌿 ◆

SWEET AND SOUR LIVER
SİRKELİ CİĞER

Region:		Çorum, all regions
Preparation time:		15 minutes
Cooking time:		25 minutes, plus 5 minutes resting
Serves:		4

60 ml	olive oil	¼ cup/2 fl oz
60 g	onion, finely chopped	⅜ cup/2¼ oz
4	garlic cloves, finely chopped	4
600 g	veal liver, membrane removed, sinew trimmed	1 lb 5 oz
2	spring onions (scallions)	2
2 tbsp	plain (all-purpose) flour	2 tbsp
¼ tsp	ground cumin	¼ tsp
500 ml	tomato juice, hot	2 cups/17 fl oz
60 ml	grape vinegar	¼ cup/2 fl oz
2 tbsp	apple molasses	2 tbsp

6	parsley sprigs, finely sliced	6
4	dill sprigs, finely sliced	4

Liver is believed to cure anemia and improve eyesight. It is also claimed to boost immunity and energy. It is fried, stewed, roasted and added to pilafs. This dish is very popular in the spring and summer.

◆

Heat the olive oil in a large saucepan over medium heat, add the onions and garlic and sauté for 1 minute. Dice the veal liver into 1-cm (½-inch) pieces. Add to the pan and sauté for 5 minutes. Finely chop the spring onions (scallions), add to the pan and sauté for 2 minutes. Add the flour, ¼ teaspoon black pepper, cumin and ¾ teaspoon salt and sauté for 2 minutes. Reduce the heat, add the tomato juice, grape vinegar and apple molasses and cook, covered, for 15 minutes. Remove from the heat and rest for 5 minutes.

Sprinkle with the finely sliced parsley and dill and serve immediately.

POACHED BRAINS
BEYİN HAŞLAMA

Region:		İzmir, Aegean Region
Preparation time:		20 minutes, plus 1 hour soaking
Cooking time:		55 minutes
Serves:		4

1	veal brain, membrane removed	1
2 tbsp	lemon juice	2 tbsp
60 ml	apple cider vinegar	¼ cup/2 fl oz
150 g	carrot	1 cup/5 oz
200 g	celeriac (celery root), peeled	1⅓ cups/ 7 oz
60 ml	olive oil	¼ cup/2 fl oz
4	garlic cloves, crushed	4
150 g	shelled peas	1 cup/5 oz

For the sauce:		
60 ml	lemon juice	¼ cup/2 fl oz
4	dill sprigs, finely sliced	4
4	parsley sprigs, finely sliced	4
2	egg yolks	2

Offal is believed to improve cognitive function and brain-related issues. Sheep's and goat's brain is preferred to cow's brain. However, the latter is used in cooking as well.

◆

Thoroughly clean the veal brain in cold water. Dice the brain into 2-cm (¾-inch) pieces. In a saucepan, soak the brain pieces in 2 litres (8½ cups/70 fl oz) water, the lemon juice, vinegar and ¾ teaspoon salt for 1 hour.

Slice the carrot and celeriac (celery root) into 1-cm (½-inch) pieces. Heat the oil in a saucepan over medium heat, add the garlic, carrot and celeriac and sauté for 5 minutes. Strain off 1.5 litres (6¼ cups/50 fl oz) brain soaking water, add to the pan and cook, covered, for 15 minutes. Add the peas and continue to cook, covered, for 15 minutes. Reduce the heat and add the brain gently to the pan, together with the remaining soaking water. Cook, covered, for 15 minutes.

To make the sauce:
Ladle out 60 ml (¼ cup/2 fl oz) of the cooking juices into a bowl and mix in the lemon juice, dill, parsley and egg yolks for 1 minute, until well combined. Pour the sauce gradually back into the pan and gently mix once to combine. Serve immediately.

OFFAL

VEAL TONGUE
DİL SÖĞÜŞ

Region:		Malatya, all regions
Preparation time:		10 minutes
Cooking time:		1 hour, plus cooling time
Serves:		4

1 (1 kg)	veal tongue	1 (2 lb 3 oz)
2	cloves	2
2	black peppercorns	2
3	fennel seeds	3
1 tbsp	lemon juice	1 tbsp
2 tsp	dried oregano	2 tsp
½ tsp	dried chilli (red pepper) flakes	½ tsp
¼ tsp	ground cumin	¼ tsp
1 bunch	flat-leaf parsley, leaves picked	1 bunch
2 tbsp	olive oil	2 tbsp

p.251 📷

A favourite of the pre-dawn (*sahur*) meal observed during Ramadan. Some versions omit the olive oil, spices and parsley.

◆

Put the veal tongue into a pressure cooker with 1.5 litres (6¼ cups/50 fl oz) water, the cloves, peppercorns, fennel seeds and lemon juice. Cook for 1 hour. Let cool, then skin, de-bone and slice into 3-mm (⅛-inch) pieces

In a separate bowl, mix the dried oregano, dried chilli (red pepper) flakes and cumin with ¼ teaspoon each of black pepper and salt.

Arrange the parsley leaves on a serving platter and place the veal tongue slices on top. Drizzle the veal tongue with some olive oil and sprinkle with the spice mixture before serving.

VEAL JOWL
KELLE ETİ KAVURMASI

Region:		Ankara, all regions
Preparation time:		10 minutes
Cooking time:		1 hour 35 minutes
Serves:		4

800 g	veal cheek, cleaned	1¼ cups/ 1 lb 12 oz
150 g	suet	5 oz
3 (360 g)	medium onions, sliced into crescents	3 (2⅜ cups/12 oz)
3	small bell peppers, sliced into crescents	3
½ tsp	ground cumin	½ tsp
2 tsp	dried oregano	2 tsp
1 tsp	dried chilli (red pepper) flakes	1 tsp
¼ tsp	black pepper	¼ tsp
¾ tsp	salt	¾ tsp

During *Eid al Ahda* (Festival of Sacrifice) those who slaughter the animals are given the head, intestines and tripe. Veal jowl is considered the meat of the poor. It is an important dish that signifies making something delicious out of almost nothing. If bell peppers are unavailable, substitute more onions.

◆

Put the veal into a pressure cooker with 1 litre (4¼ cups/ 34 fl oz) water and cook for 1 hour. Drain and let cool, then shred the meat.

Heat a large *sac* (see p.503), iron skillet or wok until very hot. Add the suet and heat through, then add the onions and sauté for 5 minutes. Add the bell peppers and sauté for 10 minutes, then add the shredded veal cheeks and sauté for 2 minutes, stirring occasionally. Add the cumin, oregano, dried chilli (red pepper) flakes, black pepper and salt and sauté for 10 minutes. Reduce the heat and cook for a further 2 minutes, without stirring, to make sure that all the water is absorbed.

Serve immediately.

PATÉ
CİĞER DÖVMESİ

Region:		Kars, Eastern Anatolia
Preparation time:		10 minutes
Cooking time:		20 minutes
Serves:		4

600 g	lamb liver, membrane removed, sinew trimmed, cut into 6 pieces	1 lb 5 oz
¾ tsp	salt	¾ tsp
20	garlic cloves	20
6	black peppercorns	6
4	fresh coriander (cilantro) sprigs, finely chopped	4

For the sauce:

50 g	butter	¼ cup/2 oz
1 tsp	dried chilli (red pepper) flakes	1 tsp

❧ ✶

This dish is also made with other offal and preserved for a long time in tallow.

◆

In a large saucepan, bring 2 litres (8½ cups/70 fl oz) water to a boil over medium heat, add the liver, salt, garlic and black peppercorns and cook, covered, for 15 minutes. Drain well, then transfer to a food processor and process to a paste.

To make the sauce:
Heat the butter in a large saucepan over medium heat, add the dried chilli (red pepper) flakes and sauté for 30 seconds.

Transfer the pâté to serving plates, drizzle with the butter sauce, sprinkle with fresh coriander (cilantro) and serve.

◆

HEAD CHEESE
KELLE SÖĞÜŞ

Region:		İzmir, Aegean Region
Preparation time:		40 minutes
Cooking time:		1 hour, plus cooling time
Serves:		4

2	lamb heads with brains, skinned and cleaned in cold water	2
2 tbsp	lemon juice	2 tbsp
60 ml	apple cider vinegar	¼ cup/2 fl oz
¾ tsp	salt	¾ tsp
4	spring onions (scallions), finely chopped	4
½ bunch	flat-leaf parsley, finely chopped	½ bunch
½ tsp	ground cumin	½ tsp
2 tsp	dried oregano	2 tsp
1 tsp	paprika	1 tsp

● ❧ ◗

This is a popular street food, traditionally consumed in wraps. If your pressure cooker is not big enough to fit a whole head, use a very large saucepan and simmer, covered, for 2 hours in 4 litres (16 cups/130 fl oz) water.

◆

Put the head in a pressure cooker with 2 litres (8½ cups/70 fl oz) water, the lemon juice, apple cider vinegar and salt and cook for 1 hour. Let cool.

When cool enough to handle, remove the eyes, cheeks and tongue from the head. Remove and discard the hard tissue in the eye and the bone and hard pieces of the tongue. Use a small cleaver to break the skull and remove the brain. Pull out all the meat and arrange on serving plates, making sure the various parts are divided equally.

Serve, sprinkled with spring onions (scallions), parsley, cumin, dried oregano and paprika.

♦

VEAL HEAD CHEESE PATTIES
BAŞ ETİ KÖFTESİ

Region:	İstanbul, all regions
Preparation time:	25 minutes
Cooking time:	10 minutes
Serves:	4

4	banana peppers (mild sweet peppers)	4
1 (120 g)	medium onion, sliced into thin rings	1 (¾ cup/ 4 oz)
200 g	tomato, cut into 4 round slices	1 cup/7 oz
¼ tsp	salt	¼ tsp

For the meatballs:		
600 g	veal head meat (medium fat)	1 lb 5 oz
70 g	veal fat (from the thigh)	2½ oz
80 g	suet	⅝ cup/3 oz
2 (240 g)	medium onions, quartered	2 (1⅝ cup/ 8½ oz)
150 g	stale bread	5 oz
½ tsp	ground cumin	½ tsp
½ tsp	paprika	½ tsp
¼ tsp	black pepper	¼ tsp
1 tsp	salt	1 tsp

If you don't have a barbecue, you can use a grill (broiler) for this recipe.

♦

Prepare a barbecue for cooking or preheat a grill (broiler) to high.

To make the meatballs:
Combine the veal head meat with the suet, onion and stale bread and run twice through a meat mincer (grinder). Alternatively, chop together very finely until completely combined.

Knead the veal mixture, cumin, paprika, black pepper and salt in a large bowl or deep tray for 5 minutes, until well combined. Divide the mixture into 32 equal parts and form into flat patties.

Cook the patties 8 cm (3 inches) above the hot barbecue embers for 2 minutes on each side, then for a further 1 minute on each side. Cook the banana peppers and onions likewise. Sprinkle the tomatoes with the salt and cook in the same manner. Alternatively, grill (broil) everything for 3 minutes, turning as required.

Serve, making sure that each plate has an equal amount of the patties and vegetables.

♦

LAMB'S LIVER MEATBALLS
CİĞER TAPLAMA

Region:	Bitlis, Eastern Anatolia
Preparation time:	20 minutes, plus 10 minutes resting
Cooking time:	15 minutes
Serves:	4

400 g	lamb liver, membrane removed, sinew trimmed	14 oz
60g	onion, quartered	⅜ cup/2¼ oz
150 g	fine bulgur wheat	⅔ cup/5 oz
½ bunch	flat-leaf parsley, finely chopped	½ bunch
3–5 tbsp	dried basil	3–5 tbsp
¼ tsp	ground cumin	½ tsp

For the sauce:		
100 g	butter	scant ½ cup/ 3½ oz
2 tsp	dried chilli (red pepper) flakes	2 tsp

This winter dish is very popular on special occasions.

♦

Combine the liver with the onion and run through a meat mincer (grinder). Alternatively, chop together very finely.

Mix the liver and onion mixture with the bulgur wheat, parsley, dried basil, cumin, ¼ teaspoon black pepper and ½ teaspoon salt in a bowl, until well combined. Rest for 10 minutes, then knead for a further 4 minutes. Divide into 20 equal parts, roll into balls and flatten into discs.

In a saucepan, bring 3 litres (12 cups/100 fl oz) water and ½ teaspoon salt to a boil over medium heat. Add the meatballs and cook for 10 minutes. When the meatballs rise, remove with a slotted spoon and transfer to plates.

To make the sauce:
Heat the butter in a saucepan over medium heat, add the dried chilli (red pepper) flakes and sauté for 10 seconds.

Drizzle the meatballs with the sauce and serve.

OFFAL

SWEETBREAD KEBABS
UYKULUK KEBABI

Region:	Gaziantep, all regions
Preparation time:	15 minutes
Cooking time:	15 minutes
Serves:	4

600 g	lamb (or mutton) sweetbreads, washed, diced into 2-cm (¾-inch) pieces	1 lb 5 oz
60 g	onion, diced into 2-cm (¾-inch) pieces	⅜ cup/2¼ oz
60 ml	olive oil	¼ cup/2 fl oz
6	garlic cloves, crushed	6
½ tsp	salt	½ tsp
½ tsp	black pepper	½ tsp
¼ tsp	ground cumin	¼ tsp
1 tsp	dried chilli (red pepper) flakes	1 tsp
1 bunch	flat-leaf parsley, leaves only	1 bunch

p.255

This dish is made particularly at the beginning of spring when sweetbread is at its prime. It used to be associated with the old slaughterhouse in Sütlüce, but still survives as a street food. If you don't have a barbecue, you can use a grill (broiler). You will need 4 long cast-iron skewers or 8 flat wooden skewers (soaked).

♦

Prepare a barbecue for cooking or preheat a grill (broiler) to high.

Mix the sweetbreads, onions, olive oil, garlic, salt, black pepper, cumin and dried chilli (red pepper) flakes in a large bowl or deep tray for 3 minutes, until well combined. Divide into 4 or 8 parts and mould around the skewers.

Set the skewers 8 cm (3 inches) above the hot embers and cook for 3 minutes on each side, turning them every minute. Alternatively, grill (broil), turning as required.

Serve immediately on a bed of parsley leaves.

♦

LIVER KEBABS
PERDELİ CİĞER KEBABI

Region:	Diyarbakır, all regions
Preparation time:	20 minutes
Cooking time:	15 minutes
Serves:	4

600 g	lamb liver, membrane removed, sinew trimmed, diced into 2-cm (¾-inch) pieces	1 lb 5 oz
¼ tsp	black pepper	¼ tsp
¼ tsp	ground cinnamon	¼ tsp
1 tsp	dried chilli (red pepper) flakes	1 tsp
¼ tsp	cumin seeds	¼ tsp
½ tsp	ground coriander	½ tsp
½ tsp	salt	½ tsp
60 g	onion, finely chopped	⅜ cup/2¼ oz
4 (10 × 20 cm)	pieces of caul fat, soaked in water for 10 minutes, rinsed	4 (4 × 8 inches)

1	*Piyaz Salatsı* (Onion Salad, see p.67)	1
4	*Açik Ekmek* (Ridged Bread, see p.394)	4

Traditionally served in the morning with *Açik Ekmek* (Ridged Bread, see p.394), the kebab is first drawn onto a plate, drizzled with vinegar and garlic, then rested, covered, on barbecue ashes for 10 minutes. It can also be made without the caul fat, or another technique replaces the caul fat with tail fat, alternating pieces of liver with tail fat on the skewers. If you don't have a barbecue, you can use a grill (broiler). You will need 4 long cast iron skewers or 8 flat wooden skewers (soaked).

♦

Prepare a barbecue for cooking or preheat a grill (broiler) to high.

Mix the liver, black pepper, ground cinnamon, dried chilli (red pepper) flakes, cumin seeds, coriander, salt and onion in a large bowl or deep tray, until well combined. Divide the mixture equally among the skewers, then cover with the caul fat, making sure all the liver mixture is entirely enclosed.

Set the skewers 8 cm (3 inches) above the hot embers and cook for 10 minutes, turning them every minute. Alternatively, grill (broil) in the same manner.

Transfer to plates and serve with the *Piyaz Salatsı* and *Açik Ekmek*.

CHITTERLINGS
KOKOREÇ

Region:	İstanbul, Marmara Region and İzmir, Aegean Region	
Preparation time:	10 minutes	
Cooking time:	20–30 minutes	
Serves:	4	

1	lamb fore-stomach (rumen tripe), thoroughly cleaned	1
1	large lamb intestine, thoroughly cleaned	1
1	small lamb intestine, thoroughly cleaned	1
1	lamb caul fat	1
1 tsp	paprika	1 tsp
2 tsp	dried oregano	2 tsp
½ tsp	ground cumin	½ tsp
½ tsp	salt	½ tsp

p.257

Also known as *Lamb Sarma* and *Lamb Büryan*, chitterlings are eaten throughout the year, although this popular street food is at its prime in the spring, when suckling lamb is in season. İstanbul locals buy the prepared chitterlings from the offal vendors and boil for an hour over low heat, poking the intestines with a knife every now and then. They then bake it in the oven, together with the tomatoes, rice, spring onions (scallions), dill and spices. In İzmir, it is enjoyed in a bread roll with cumin and paprika, whereas cumin, dried chilli (red pepper) flakes, oregano, tomatoes and banana peppers are preferred by the citizens of İstanbul. Some like it sliced and fried in egg wash, served with rice and orzo pasta. If you don't have a barbecue, you can use a grill (broiler). You will need a long cast-iron skewer.

♦

Prepare a barbecue for cooking or preheat a grill (broiler) to high.

Wrap the lamb fore-stomach (rumen tripe) around the skewer starting from the pointy end. Unravel the large intestine and wrap around it. When you reach the end of the skewer, start wrapping the intestine in the opposite direction. Continue until you have wrapped the whole large intestine around the skewer. Take the small intestine, tie off at one end of the skewer and work your way to the end, wrapping in diagonal crosses. Finish off with a tight knot. Wrap the caul fat around the skewers.

Set the skewer 8 cm (3 inches) above the hot embers and grill for 20 minutes, turning frequently. After 10 minutes, poke a few holes in it with the tip of a sharp knife or with a packing needle. Alternatively, grill (broil) for 30 minutes, turning as required.

Remove from the skewer and slice into 1-cm (½-inch) wide discs, then coarsely chop into small pieces. Sprinkle with paprika, dried oregano, cumin and salt and serve as is or in a bread roll.

OFFAL

RAM'S TESTICLES
TAŞAK KEBABI (BİLLUR KEBABI)

Region:		Muğla, all regions
Preparation time:		15 minutes
Cooking time:		15 minutes
Serves:		4

4	ram testicles, halved, skinned, each half quartered, then rinsed in cold water	4
1 (120 g)	medium onion, finely sliced	1 (¾ cup/4 oz)
10	garlic cloves	10
60 ml	olive oil	¼ cup/2 fl oz
100 g	tail fat (lamb) or suet, diced	¾ cup/ 3½ oz
2	sprigs flat-leaf parsley, finely sliced	2

p.259

The lovers of this dish anticipate the spring when the ram's testicles are at their biggest. If you don't have a barbecue, you can use a grill (broiler). You will need 8 long cast-iron skewers or 16 wooden skewers (soaked).

♦

Prepare a barbecue for cooking or preheat a grill (broiler) to high.

Toss the testicles, onions, garlic, olive oil, tail fat and parsley in a large bowl or deep tray with ½ teaspoon each of black pepper and salt, until well combined. Thread onto the skewers making sure that a piece of the tail fat or suet is at the beginning, in the middle and at the end.

Set the skewers 8 cm (3 inches) above the hot embers and cook for 3 minutes on each side, turning them every minute. Alternatively, grill (broil), turning as required.

Serve immediately.

♦

BAKED SHEEP'S HEAD
FIRIN KELLE

Region:		Sivas, all regions
Preparation time:	15 minutes, plus 10 minutes soaking	
Cooking time:		3 hours
Serves:		4

4	lamb heads with brain, skinned, thoroughly cleaned in cold water	4
4 (480 g)	medium onions, quartered	4 (3⅛ cups/ 1 lb 1 oz)
5	black peppercorns	5
1 tsp	salt	1 tsp
1	piece of caul fat (intact), soaked in warm water for 10 minutes, rinsed	1
5	cloves	5
2 tsp	dried oregano	2 tsp

This dish is extremely popular early in the morning or is served at the communal Turkish bath houses. Right after the bathing finishes, the group moves to a cooler part of the bath house to eat and socialise. Some offal shops in İstanbul make this dish every day in a traditional or tandoori oven. Sheep's head aficionados keep an eye on the window of the offal shop, ready to make a move when they see a sheep's head. The tradition in Sivas is to go straight to a sheep's head shop right after morning prayers. The shop owner would chop the head with a cleaver and serve it with a raw onion. It is devoured by hand. A Turkish saying recommends that chicken, fish and head are always eaten by hand: *Tavuk balık kelle, bunlar yenir elle.*

♦

Preheat oven to 180°C/350°F/Gas Mark 4.

Put the lamb heads into a large casserole (Dutch oven) or copper pan, cover with 2 litres (8½ cups/70 fl oz) water and add half of the onion quarters, black peppercorns and salt. Cover with the caul fat and add the cloves. Cover tightly and bake in the hot oven for 2 hours 40 minutes.

Remove from the oven and turn oven up to 220°C/425°F/ Gas Mark 7.

Transfer the heads to a large, deep roasting pan. Pour 600 ml (2½ cups/20 fl oz) of the cooking juices over the heads, return to the oven and bake for 5–10 minutes. Use a cleaver to cut each head in half through the forehead. Transfer to serving plates, sprinkle with dried oregano and serve with the remaining raw onion quarters.

OFFAL

FRIED BRAINS
BEYİN ÇULLAMA (KIZARTMA)

Region:		Antalya, all regions
Preparation time:		15 minutes, plus 1 hour soaking
Cooking time:		30 minutes, plus 1 hour chilling
Serves:		4

1	veal brain, membrane removed	1
2 tbsp	lemon juice	2 tbsp
60 ml	apple cider vinegar	¼ cup/2 fl oz
100 g	plain (all purpose) flour	¾ cup/3½ oz
60 ml	olive oil	¼ cup/2 fl oz

For the egg wash:

4	eggs	4
3	spring onions (scallions)	3
6	flat-leaf parsley sprigs	6
3	dill sprigs	3
½ tsp	ground cumin	½ tsp

p.261

This spring dish is a specialty of the Sephardic Jews in Turkey. It is made of brain coated in egg wash and fried, then served with parsley and slices of lemon.

◆

Thoroughly clean the veal brain in cold water then put it to soak in a saucepan with 2 litres (8½ cups/70 fl oz) water, the lemon juice, vinegar and ¾ teaspoon salt for 1 hour.

Set the pan over low heat, cover and slowly bring to a boil, about 15 minutes. Remove from the heat and let rest for 5 minutes. Use a slotted spoon to remove the brain from the pan and rinse with cold water. Refrigerate for 1 hour.

To make the egg wash:
In a bowl, whisk the eggs together for 1 minute. Finely slice the spring onions (scallions), parsley and dill, then add to the eggs with the cumin and ¼ teaspoon black pepper and ¼ teaspoon salt. Whisk everything together. Put the flour into a separate shallow bowl.

Divide the chilled veal brain into 4 equal pieces. In a saucepan, heat the oil over medium heat to 155°C/310°F. Coat the brain pieces in egg wash, then in flour and place in the hot oil. Fry for 2 minutes on each side. Transfer to serving platters and serve immediately.

◆

FRIED OXTAIL, AUBERGINE AND WALNUT PATTIES
PÖÇ KÖFTESİ KIZARTMASI

Region:		Çankırı, Central Anatolia
Preparation time:		20 minutes, plus 10 minutes soaking
Cooking time:		1 hour 35 minutes, plus cooling time
Serves:		4

600 g	oxtail, quartered	1 lb 5 oz
1 (800 g)	bell aubergine (eggplant), peeled in vertical stripes, quartered	1 (1 lb 12 oz)
2 tsp	salt	2 tsp
200 ml	olive oil	scant 1 cup/7 fl oz
1 (120 g)	medium onion, sliced into crescents	1 (¾ cup/4 oz)
100g	walnuts	1 cup/3½ oz
¼ tsp	black pepper	¼ tsp
½ tsp	ground cinnamon	½ tsp
50 g	*khask* (dried yogurt, see p.485), grated	2 oz
4	dill sprigs, finely chopped	4
4	parsley sprigs, finely chopped	4
2	eggs	2
2 tbsp	grape vinegar	2 tbsp

Seasonal vegetables are used in this popular special occasion and *meyhane* dish.

◆

Put the oxtail into a pressure cooker with 1.5 litres (6¼ cups/ 50 fl oz) water and cook for 1 hour 10 minutes. Let cool, then take the meat off the bone and shred. Reserve the stock.

Meanwhile, soak the aubergine (eggplant) in 2 litres (8½ cups/70 fl oz) water with 1½ teaspoons salt for 10 minutes. Drain, rinse and pat dry the aubergine quarters.

Heat 60 ml (¼ cup/2 fl oz) of the olive oil in a sauté pan over medium heat. Add the onions and sauté for 5 minutes. Add the walnuts and sauté for 1 minute. Add the shredded oxtail, black pepper, ground cinnamon and remaining ½ teaspoon of salt and sauté for 5 minutes. Remove from the heat and let cool. When cool, add the *kashk* or *kurut* (dried yogurt), dill, parsley and eggs and mix for 1 minute.

In a saucepan, heat the remaining oil over medium heat to 155°C/310°F. Place the aubergine quarters in the hot oil and fry for 4 minutes on one side. Turning the aubergines, coat each fried side with a quarter of the oxtail/egg mixture and fry for a further 4 minutes. Reduce the heat, add 250 ml (1 cup/8 fl oz) of the oxtail stock and the grape vinegar and cook, covered, for 10 minutes. Serve immediately.

OFFAL

ALBANIAN-STYLE FRIED LIVER
CİĞER TAVASI (ARNAVUT CİĞERİ)

Region:	İstanbul, Marmara Region	
Preparation time:	15 minutes	
Cooking time:	15 minutes	
Serves:	4	

600 g	lamb liver, membrane and sinew trimmed	1 lb 5 oz
100 g	plain (all-purpose) flour	¾ cup/3½ oz
750 ml	olive oil	3 cups/25 fl oz
200 g	potato, diced into small cubes and patted dry	1 cup/7 oz
1 tsp	paprika	1 tsp
¼ tsp	ground cumin	¼ tsp
½ bunch	flat-leaf parsley, finely sliced	½ bunch
1	*Piyaz Salatsı* (Onion Salad, see p.67)	1

♦ ✕   p.263 📷

Most street vendors selling fried liver in the streets of old İstanbul were Albanian, hence the name. To remove any blood from the liver, wash and then soak it in 1 litre (4¼ cups/34 fl oz) milk with an onion for at least 2 hours but ideally 24 hours.

♦

Dice the lamb liver into small cubes. Put the flour in a shallow bowl. Toss the liver pieces in the flour until coated, then shake off the excess flour.

In a large saucepan, heat the olive oil over medium heat to 155°C/310°F. Gently place the potato in the hot oil and fry for 5 minutes. Remove with a slotted spoon to a deep tray. Gently place the liver pieces in the hot oil and fry for 30 seconds, until they float to the top. Use a slotted spoon to remove the liver from the pan to the tray.

Sprinkle the fried liver and potato with the paprika and cumin. Season with ⅛ teaspoon black pepper and ½ teaspoon salt and mix gently. Transfer to serving bowls and serve with a side of *Piyaz Salatsı*.

♦

DEEP-FRIED THINLY SLICED LIVER
YAPRAK CİĞER TAVASI

Region:	Edirne, Marmara Region	
Preparation time:	10 minutes	
Cooking time:	10 minutes	
Serves:	4	

150 g	plain (all-purpose) flour	1 cup/5 oz
¼ tsp	white pepper	¼ tsp
600 g	young buffalo calf liver (or veal liver), membrane removed, sinew trimmed, shaved into 1-mm (¹⁄₁₆-inch) thick slices, washed, drained	1 lb 5 oz
750 ml	sunflower oil (or olive oil)	3 cups/ 25 fl oz
12	dried chillies (chiles)	12
1 tsp	dried oregano	1 tsp
1 tsp	dried chilli (red pepper) flakes	1 tsp
¼ tsp	ground cumin	¼ tsp
1	*Fasulye Piyazı* (White Bean Salad, see p.62), to serve	1

♦ ✕

This is the signature dish of Edirne, believed to give one an immediate burst of energy. It is popular with home cooks as well as special shops in the region. This is the only dish these eateries serve. It is preferred mostly in the winter. Those who are sensitive to the strong smell of liver soak it in half a litre of milk mixed with an egg. It is then fried in the local sunflower oil.

♦

Put the flour, white pepper and ½ teaspoon salt in a shallow bowl. Toss the liver slices in the flour until coated, then shake off the excess flour.

In a large saucepan, heat the sunflower oil over medium heat to 155°C/310°F. Gently place the dried chillies (chiles) in the hot oil and fry for 1 minute, then transfer with a slotted spoon to a serving plate. Gently place the liver slices in the hot oil and fry for 30 seconds–1 minute, until they float to the top. Use a slotted spoon to remove the liver and place on top of the dried chillies.

In a separate bowl, mix the oregano, dried chilli (red pepper) flakes, cumin and ½ teaspoon salt. Sprinkle over the fried liver and chillies. Serve with *Fasulye Piyazı*.

◆

FISH
&
SEAFOOD

◆

FRESHWATER FISH

◆

SALTWATER FISH

◆

Turkish culinary culture embraces both saltwater and freshwater fish. People who live in coastal areas enjoy saltwater fish, whereas those who live near mountains, by lakes, creeks and by rivers such as the Euphrates naturally eat a variety of freshwater fish.

The mantra 'fresh is best' applies particularly to fish. There are countless ways to cook fish: deep-frying, grilling, on skewers, steaming and baking, to name a few. Stews, soups and patties are popular too. And fish and olive oil are a marriage made in heaven. Other seafoods, like mussels, calamari, shrimp and octopus, are fried, cooked in hot pots or added to salads. These dishes are popular in the Marmara and Aegean regions.

Fish is also commonly dried, pickled and preserved in brine. Sun-dried mackerel is a perennial favourite, and bonito and tuna are delicious preserved in salt. Another prevalent method is drying fish roe and preserving it in wax.

Freshwater fish are prepared in many different ways. They are used in omelettes, pâté, dried, baked in hot pots, roasted and salted. Freshwater fish can be cooked with fruit, garlic, or onions, and they can be spiced or marinated. They are used in kebabs, deep-fried, cooked in pastry, tandoors, baked and steamed.

Fish are seasonal. The fishing season starts mid-September and saltwater fish are always preferred over freshwater fish. Bonito opens the fish season in mid-September. The early, small and skinny variety is called 'the gypsy bonito' in İstanbul. By October and November the fish start to get oily and more rotund. This is the favourite season for fish aficionados. Sustainable, seasonal, moderate consumption is ideal. There is nothing like a seasonal, saltwater fish.

Whatever the cooking technique, deep-frying, shallow-frying or baking, the key is to preserve moisture. All that the fish asks of us is to be cooked to retain its moisture without burning or overcooking.

MEMORIES
OF THE SEA

HOLY
MACKEREL

I used to have a group of friends who would get together for the sole purpose of eating fish. They were local fishmongers from Beylerbeyi in İstanbul. We used to catch up once a month, drink *rakı* and eat fish, either fried or grilled. These fishermen liked using rods. Those freshly caught fish were so delicious. None of them were chefs, but when it came to fish they knew everything there was to know and more. Only a handful of these friends still fish and sell their catch to restaurants or special customers.

At one time, fishmongers, especially those who sold anchovies, had stalls with barbecues. Any customer questioning the freshness of the fish would immediately be given a sample to figure it out for themselves. This tradition was called 'crappy fish' or 'crappy kebab' in Çanakkale. Some clients would have their fish with a glass of *rakı* right there and then. It had to be quick, as everyone would want a piece of the fish. You still see the term 'crappy fish' appear on menus and at festivals.

Some believe that fish is holy. The particular sacred fish is carp, found in *Balıklıgöl*, a lake in Şanlıurfa in Southeastern Turkey. This particular fish is never consumed. Legend has it that when Abraham started a fire in Nemrut, the fire turned into water and the embers of the fire turned into fish. Locals believe that whoever eats the sacred fish will be cursed.

MILK-POACHED FISH IN PLUM SAUCE
SÜTLÜ BALIK

Region:		İstanbul, Marmara Region
Preparation time:		20 minutes, plus 1 hour soaking
Cooking time:		1 hour, plus resting
Serves:		4

16	rockling fish, cleaned	16
1 tbsp	salt	1 tbsp
60 ml	apple cider vinegar	¼ cup/2 fl oz

For the plum sauce:		
500 g	greengages or sour plums	1 lb 2 oz
¾ tsp	salt	¾ tsp
1 tsp	sugar	1 tsp
60 ml	olive oil	¼ cup/2 fl oz

p.271

A trademark dish of Sephardic Jews, this is made in early spring and summer, just before the plums ripen.

♦

Soak the rockling in 3 litres (12 cups/100 fl oz) cold water, with the salt and the apple cider vinegar, for 1 hour. Drain and pat dry.

To make the plum sauce:
Put the plums and 1.5 litres (6¼ cups/50 fl oz) water in a saucepan over medium heat, cover and bring to the boil. Cook for 40 minutes, then remove from the heat. Let rest, uncovered, until cooled, then mash the plums. Strain the plums, discarding the pulp and reserving the juice.

Pour the plum juice into a large saucepan, add the salt, sugar and olive oil and bring to a boil over medium heat for 5 minutes. Reduce the heat, add the fish and cook, covered, for 7 minutes. Remove from the heat, keep the lid on and let rest for 5 minutes before serving.

♦

ROCKLING FISH IN SOUR PLUM SAUCE
ERİKLİ GELİNCİK BALIĞI

Region:		İzmir, Aegean Region
Preparation time:		15 minutes
Cooking time:		25 minutes, plus 5 minutes resting
Serves:		4

60 ml	olive oil	¼ cup/2 fl oz
1 (120 g)	medium onion, sliced into thin rings	1 (¾ cup/4 oz)
2	banana peppers, (mild sweet peppers) sliced into thin rings	2
200 g	saffron milk cap mushrooms, sliced into thin strips	2⅔ cups/7 oz
1 tsp	salt	1 tsp
4 (2 kg)	bream (or other white fish), cleaned, filleted, skin removed	4 (4 lb 6 oz)
10	black peppercorns	10
6	garlic cloves, crushed	6
2 litres	milk, hot	8½ cups/70 fl oz
1	fennel frond, finely sliced	1
6	flat-leaf parsley sprigs, finely sliced	6

This a staple dish of the *meyhanes* (see p.502) of İzmir. Sometimes a whole fish is used and it can also be made with tomatoes and lemon. Other white fish could be used in place of the bream, if you can't find any. Likewise, you can use aromatic chanterelles if saffron milk cap mushrooms are unavailable.

♦

Heat the olive oil in a large saucepan over medium heat, add the onions, banana peppers, mushrooms and salt and sauté for 7 minutes. Add the fish fillets, black peppercorns, garlic, milk and fennel and cook, partially covered, for 15 minutes. Remove from the heat, stir in the parsley and let rest for 5 minutes.

Transfer to serving bowls and serve.

FISHCAKES WITH POACHED EGGS
BALIK KÖFTELİ ÇILBIR

Region:		Van, Eastern Anatolia
Preparation time:		30 minutes
Cooking time:		30 minutes
Serves:		4

For the fishcakes:

600g	freshwater fish, minced (ground)	1 lb 5 oz
60 g	onion, finely sliced	⅜ cup/2¼ oz
100 g	stale bread, crustless, soaked and excess water squeezed	3½ oz
½ bunch	parsley, finely sliced	½ bunch
¼ cup	dried tarragon (optional)	¼ cup
2 tbsp	dried basil	2 tbsp
½ tsp	dried chilli (red pepper) flakes	½ tsp
¼ tsp	black pepper	¼ tsp
½ tsp	salt	½ tsp
60g	plain (all-purpose) flour	½ cup/2¼ oz
60 ml	olive oil	¼ cup/2 fl oz
4	spring onions (scallions)	4
½ bunch	dill	½ bunch
500g	hazelwort (European wild ginger) or spinach, washed, finely sliced	2¼ cups/1 lb 5 oz
½ bunch	flat-leaf parsley	½ bunch
200 ml	sumac extract (see p.491)	scant 1 cup/7 fl oz
1 tbsp	tomato paste (see p.492)	1 tbsp
½ tsp	dried chilli (red pepper) flakes	½ tsp
2 tbsp	dried tarragon	2 tbsp
¼ tsp	black pepper	¼ tsp
½ tsp	salt	½ tsp
4	eggs	4

For the yogurt sauce:

500g	Greek yogurt	2½ cups/1 lb 2 oz
2	garlic cloves, crushed	2
¼ tsp	salt	¼ tsp

For the butter sauce:

50g	butter	¼ cup/2 oz
½ tsp	dried chilli (red pepper) flakes	½ tsp

This dish is made in the autumn and winter. It is especially delicious with the freshwater fish of Lake Van, although any fleshy freshwater fish will work here – just make sure it doesn't have too many bones. Hazelwort is a widely used local ingredient. It is a wild herb, which is never grown but always picked in the wild. Hazelwort is also known as wild spinach, but its nutritional benefits are far superior to that of spinach. If you don't have any stale bread for the fishcakes, you can substitute the same quantity of soaked fine bulgur wheat.

◆

To make the fishcakes:
Combine the minced (ground) fish, onion, bread, parsley, dried tarragon (if using) and basil, dried chilli (red pepper) flakes, black pepper and salt in a large bowl or deep tray and knead for 5 minutes, until well combined. Divide the mixture into 20 equal parts and roll into patties.

Sprinkle the flour over a shallow tray. Add the patties to the tray and give them a shake to make sure they are all well coated in flour.

Heat the olive oil in a large sauté pan over medium heat, add the patties and fry on each side for 1 minute. Remove from the pan with a slotted spoon to drain on paper towels. Add the spring onions (scallions) to the pan and sauté for 3 minutes. Add the dill, hazelwort or spinach and parsley and sauté for 3 minutes. Add the sumac extract, tomato paste, dried chilli (red pepper) flakes, dried tarragon, black pepper and salt and sauté for 30 seconds. Pour in 1 litre (4¼ cups/34 fl oz) hot water, bring to a boil and cook for 5 minutes. Reduce the heat, return the fishcakes to the pan and cook, covered, for 5 minutes.

Crack the eggs into the pan, making sure the yolks remain intact. Cover and cook for a final 3 minutes, without stirring.

Divide the mixture among serving plates, making sure that the eggs are on top.

To make the yogurt sauce:
Mix the yogurt, garlic and salt in a bowl for 1 minute.

To make the butter sauce:
Heat the butter in a large saucepan over medium heat, add the dried chilli (red pepper) flakes and sauté for 10 seconds.

Pour the yogurt sauce over the poached eggs, then drizzle the butter sauce over everything and serve.

CUTTLEFISH IN TOMATO SAUCE
DOMATESLİ SÜBYE

Region:		Balıkesir, Marmara Region
Preparation time:		20 minutes,
		plus 20 minutes marinating
Cooking time:		35 minutes, plus 5 minutes resting
Serves:		4

600 g	cuttlefish (or calamari), cleaned, quartered	1 lb 5 oz
30g	honey (pine)	1½ tbsp/1 oz
200 ml	soda water	scant 1 cup/7 fl oz
100 ml	olive oil	scant ½ cup/3½ fl oz
1 (120 g)	medium onion, quartered	1 (¾cup/ 4 oz)
2	small bell peppers, quartered	2
2	bay leaves	2
6	garlic cloves, quartered	6
600 g	tomatoes, quartered	3 cups/1 lb 5 oz
2 tsp	apple cider vinegar	2 tsp
1	fresh oregano sprig, finely sliced	1
½ tsp	dried chilli (red pepper) flakes	½ tsp
6	black peppercorns	6
6	flat-leaf parsley sprigs,	6

This *meyhane* (see p.502) favourite, served either as a side or main course, is made extensively by home cooks.

◆

In a large bowl, combine the cuttlefish with the honey and soda water, knead for 10 minutes, then set aside to marinate for 20 minutes.

Heat the olive oil in a large saucepan over medium heat, add the onions and sauté for 5 minutes. Add the bell peppers, bay leaves and garlic and sauté for 5 minutes. Add the tomatoes, apple cider vinegar, oregano, dried chilli (red pepper) flakes and black peppercorns with ¾ teaspoon salt and cook, uncovered, for 5 minutes. Reduce the heat, add the cuttlefish and its marinade to the pan and cook, covered, for 15 minutes. Remove from the heat and let rest for 5 minutes.

Sprinkle with finely sliced parsley and serve.

FRESHWATER FISH WITH GOOSE LIVER
CİĞERLİ BALIK

Region:		Kars, Eastern Anatolia
Preparation time:		15 minutes, plus 1 hour soaking
Cooking time:		45 minutes
Serves:		4

600 g	freshwater fish fillet, such as sea bass, diced	1 lb 5 oz
60 ml	apple cider vinegar	¼ cup/2 fl oz
300 g	potatoes, diced	11 oz
2 (240 g)	medium onions, diced	2 (1⅝ cups/ 8½ oz)
4	dried apricots, soaked and drained	4
4	sour prunes	4
10	black peppercorns	10
½ tsp	ground cinnamon	½ tsp
2 tsp	dried oregano	2 tsp
150 g	goose fat	5 oz
300 g	goose liver, diced	11 oz

This dish is made in the winter months, traditionally in a tandoor oven. Some recipes use turmeric instead of cinnamon.

◆

Soak the diced fish fillet in 3 litres (12 cups/100 fl oz) cold water, with the apple cider vinegar and 1 teaspoon salt, for 1 hour. Drain, rinse and pat dry.

Preheat oven to 190°C/375°F/Gas Mark 5.

In a large roasting pan, mix the diced fish, potatoes, onions, dried apricots, sour prunes, black peppercorns, cinnamon, dried oregano, goose fat and 1 teaspoon salt for 1 minute, until well combined.

Bake in the hot oven for 30 minutes. Mix the goose liver into the pan and return to the oven for a further 15 minutes.

Serve immediately.

STONE-BAKED FISH
PİLEKİDE BALIK

Region:	Rize, Black Sea Region
Preparation time:	10 minutes, plus 1 hour soaking
Cooking time:	1 hour pre-heating, plus 20 minutes
Serves:	4

1 kg	sea bass fillet, with skin, cleaned, quartered	2 lb 3 oz
60 ml	apple cider vinegar	¼ cup/2 fl oz
1 bunch	kale	1 bunch
1 (120 g)	medium onion, thinly sliced	1 (¾ cup/ 4 oz)
10	black peppercorns	10
1	fresh corn on the cob	1
100 g	butter	½ cup/3½ oz

p.275

Pileki are plate-shaped stones used for making pickles and bread and sometimes for baking fish. If a *pileki* stone is not available, any heat-resistant oval stone (about 20 × 30cm/8 × 12 inches) or a heavy pan that retains heat well can be used. Some recipes heat the stone and place it in the pan with the ingredients. Alternatively, the ingredients can be put into a baking dish and baked in a 200°C/400°F/Gas Mark 6 oven for 20 minutes.

◆

Soak the sea bass fillet in 3 litres (12 cups/100 fl oz) cold water, with the apple cider vinegar and 1 teaspoon salt, for 1 hour. Drain and pat dry.

To heat the stone or pan, prepare a barbecue or wood fire outdoors. Put one or two *pileki* stones or a cast-iron pan with a lid on to heat, piling a layer of coals or firewood on top. Let it heat up for 1 hour. Carefully remove the *pileki* stones or pan and clean by lighting a fire inside the pan and then brushing it with a bundle of dry herb sprigs.

Working quickly, put the ingredients in the following order on the stone or into the pan: half of the kale, half of the onions, 5 black peppercorns, ¼ teaspoon salt, the sea bass, the remaining onions, the remaining black peppercorns and ¼ teaspoon salt. Grate the fresh corn on top. Dot with the butter, then top with the remaining kale. Cover with another pre-warmed *pileki* stone, *sac* or lid. Let rest for 15 minutes. Serve, making sure each portion has an equal amount of everything.

◆

BAKED BLUEFISH
FIRINDA LÜFER

Region:	İstanbul, Marmara Region
Preparation time:	10 minutes
Cooking time:	25 minutes
Serves:	4

4 (25-cm)	bluefish	4 (10-inch)
60 ml	olive oil	¼ cup/2 fl oz
2 tbsp	lemon juice	2 tbsp
60 g	onion, grated, strained and juice collected	⅜ cup/2¼ oz
1 tsp	ground cinnamon	1 tsp

1 bunch	rocket (arugula)	1 bunch
1 (120 g)	medium red onion, quartered	1 (¾ cup/4 oz)
1	lemon, quartered	1

Bluefish is the signature fish of İstanbul. It is so integral to the city's culinary culture that the locals have a different name for each size of this fish. *Yaprak, çinekop, sarıkanat, lüfer* and *kofana* all refer to bluefish at different stages of growth. Mostly *lüfer* (28–35 cm/11–14 inches long) are caught these days in order to protect the species, and always with a handline. The varying sizes of bluefish do taste slightly different: *lüfer* is by far the most delicious. Bluefish is traditionally eaten by hand. If you cannot source bluefish, sea bass, turbot, mackerel or bonito can be used instead. Grilling (broiling) works well for this recipe too.

◆

Preheat oven to 200°C/400°F/Gas Mark 6.

Clean and pat dry the bluefish. Mix the oil, lemon juice, onion juice and ground cinnamon with ½ teaspoon black pepper and 1 teaspoon salt in a bowl for 1 minute. Put the bluefish into a large roasting pan, pour over the mixture and bake in the oven for 20 minutes.

Serve with rocket (arugula), red onion and lemon wedges.

BAKED ANCHOVIES WITH VEGETABLES
FIRINDA SEBZELİ HAMSİ

Region:		Ordu, Black Sea Region
Preparation time:		30 minutes, plus 1 hour soaking
Cooking time:		30 minutes
Serves:		4

800 g	anchovies, heads and spines removed, cleaned	1 lb 12 oz
60 ml	apple cider vinegar	¼ cup/2 fl oz
200 g	potato, diced	1 cup/7 oz
1 (120 g)	medium onion, finely diced	1 (¾ cup/ 4 oz)
4	garlic cloves, quartered	4
300 g	tomatoes, finely diced	1½ cups/11 oz
3	banana peppers (mild sweet peppers), each sliced into 3 lengthwise	3
1	lemon, halved, seeded and sliced	1
½ bunch	flat-leaf parsley, finely chopped	½ bunch
100 ml	olive oil	scant ½ cup/3½ fl oz
1 tsp	dried chilli (red pepper) flakes	1 tsp
50 g	butter, diced	¼ cup/2 oz

This dish is prepared at home between October and January and then taken to be baked in the wood-fired ovens of the local bakery. This traybake is then shared by the whole family. Anchovies in brine work well here too.
◆

Soak the anchovies in 3 litres (12 cups/100 fl oz) cold water, with the apple cider vinegar and 1 teaspoon salt, for 1 hour. Drain, rinse and pat dry.

Preheat oven to 200°C/400°F/Gas Mark 6.

Put the potato, onion, garlic, tomatoes, banana peppers, lemon, parsley, olive oil, dried chilli (red pepper) flakes and ½ teaspoon black pepper into a roasting pan and gently toss to combine. Bake in the oven for 20 minutes.

Remove from the oven and stir through. Turn the oven up to 220°C/425°F/Gas Mark 7. Lay the anchovies on top of the vegetables and dot with the butter. Return to the oven for a further 10 minutes.

Serve, making sure the anchovies and vegetables are divided equally.

BAKED FISH WITH TAHINI
FIRINDA TAHİNLİ BALIK

Region:		Mersin, Mediterranean Region
Preparation time:		10 minutes
Cooking time:		30 minutes
Serves:		4

60 ml	olive oil	¼ cup/2 fl oz
1 (1.2 kg)	rockfish fillet, quartered	1 (2 lb 10 oz)
1 tsp	salt	1 tsp
6	flat-leaf parsley sprigs, finely sliced	6

For the sauce:

60 ml	tahini (sesame seed paste)	¼ cup/2 fl oz
4	garlic cloves, crushed	4
60 ml	lemon juice	¼ cup/2 fl oz
1 tsp	dried chilli (red pepper) flakes	1 tsp
½ tsp	ground coriander	½ tsp
¼ tsp	ground cumin	¼ tsp
¼ tsp	black pepper	¼ tsp

You could also grill (broil) the fish for this recipe and drizzle the sauce over; a whole fish would also work.
◆

Preheat oven to 200°C/400°F/Gas Mark 6.

Grease a roasting pan with 2 tablespoons of the olive oil and put the rockfish into the pan, flesh side up. Sprinkle with the remaining olive oil and salt. Bake in the hot oven for 15 minutes.

To make the sauce:
Mix the tahini, garlic, lemon juice, dried chilli (red pepper) flakes, ground coriander, ground cumin and black pepper with 200 ml (scant 1 cup/7 fl oz) water in a bowl, until well combined.

When the fish has had 15 minutes in the oven, pour the sauce over the fish. Spoon any oils in the bottom of the pan over the fish as well and return to the oven for a further 15 minutes.

Serve the baked fish in its own cooking juices and sprinkled with parsley.

FRIED SARDINES
İSTAVRİT KIZARTMASI

Region:		İstanbul, Marmara Region
Preparation time:		10 minutes, plus 1 hour soaking
Cooking time:		10 minutes
Serves:		4

40	sardines, cleaned	40
60 ml	apple cider vinegar	¼ cup/2 fl oz
1¼ tsp	salt	1¼ tsp
100g	plain (all-purpose) flour	¾ cup/ 3½ oz
1 litre	olive oil	4¼ cups/34 fl oz
1 (120 g)	red onion, quartered	1 (¾ cup/4 oz)
1 bunch	rocket (arugula)	1 bunch
1	lemon, quartered	1

Sardines are the archetypal İstanbul fish. They are very much loved and cooked extensively at home especially in the autumn and winter.

◆

Soak the sardines in 3 litres (12 cups/100 fl oz) cold water, with the apple cider vinegar and 1 teaspoon of the salt, for 1 hour. Drain, rinse and pat dry.

Mix the flour and the remaining ¼ teaspoon of salt in a shallow bowl. Coat the sardines in the flour and shake off the excess.

In a large saucepan, heat the olive oil over medium heat to 155°C/310°F. Place the sardines in the hot oil and let fry for 2 minutes. Remove the fish with a slotted spoon as soon as they rise up to the surface.

Serve immediately with red onions, rocket (arugula) and lemon wedges.

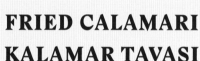

FRIED CALAMARI
KALAMAR TAVASI

Region:		Balıkesir, Marmara Region and Aegean Region
Preparation time:		10 minutes
Cooking time:		25 minutes
Serves:		4

4 (5 x 8 cm)	fresh calamari, cartilage removed, thinly sliced lengthwise	4 (2 × 3 inch)
100 g	caster (superfine) sugar	½ cup/ 3½ oz
200 ml	soda water	scant 1 cup/ 7 fl oz
150 g	plain (all-purpose) flour	1 cup/5 oz
1.5 litres	olive oil	6¼ cups/ 50 fl oz
1	*Tarator* (Almond and Garlic Sauce, see p.79)	1
1	lemon, quartered	1

This dish has become synonymous with *meyhanes* (see p.502). It is prepared and eaten all through the year, especially in the autumn and winter.

◆

In a large bowl, knead the calamari with the sugar for 5 minutes, until the sugar foams. Add the soda water and knead for another 5 minutes. Rinse the calamari in cold water and pat dry.

Put the flour in a shallow bowl, add the calamari and toss to coat in the flour. Shake off excess flour.

In a large saucepan, heat the olive oil over medium heat to 155°C/310°F. Place the calamari in the hot oil and let fry for 1 minute. Remove from the pan with a slotted spoon 10 seconds after they rise to the surface.

Serve immediately with *Tarator* and lemon wedges.

PRAWN HOT POT
GÜVEÇTE KARİDES

Region:		İstanbul, Marmara Region
Preparation time:		15 minutes
Cooking time:		40 minutes
Serves:		4

150 g	butter	⅔ cup/5 oz
1 (120 g)	medium onion, finely diced	1 (¾ cup/4 oz)
1	small green bell pepper, finely diced	1
1	small red bell pepper, finely diced	1
200 g	porcini mushrooms, finely diced	2⅔ cups/7 oz
20	garlic cloves, quartered	20
2 tsp	dried oregano	2 tsp
1 tbsp	sweet paprika	1 tbsp
1 tsp	dried chilli (red pepper) flakes	1 tsp
600 g	prawns (shrimps), shelled, de-veined	1 lb 5 oz

❧   p.279 📷

Some cooks like adding grated *kaşar* cheese to the prawns (shrimps) in the final baking of this dish.

♦

Preheat oven to 220°C/425°F/Gas Mark 7.

Heat the butter in a large saucepan over medium heat, add the onions and red and green bell peppers and sauté for 10 minutes. Add the mushrooms and sauté for 10 minutes. Add the garlic and sauté for 5 minutes. Add the dried oregano, sweet paprika and dried chilli (red pepper) flakes with ½ teaspoon black pepper and 1 teaspoon salt and sauté for a further 1 minute.

Warm a baking dish over medium heat for 3 minutes, then pour the contents of the saucepan into the warmed dish. Bake in the hot oven for 5 minutes. Remove from the oven, add the prawns (shrimps), mix through and return to the oven for a final 5 minutes.

Serve immediately in the baking dish.

♦

TROUT HOT POTS
GÜVEÇTE ALABALIK

Region:		Sakarya, all regions
Preparation time:		15 minutes
Cooking time:		20 minutes
Serves:		4

600 g	tomatoes, quartered	3 cups/1 lb 5 oz
4	banana peppers (mild sweet peppers)	4
8	black morel mushrooms, cleaned	8
1 (120 g)	onion, cut into 8 wedges	1 (¾ cups/4 oz)
12	garlic cloves	12
20	black peppercorns	20
4 (25-cm)	trout, cleaned	4 (10-inch)
½ tsp	salt	½ tsp
200 g	butter	1 cup/7 oz

❧

Here the trout is baked, but it could also be grilled (broiled) or battered and fried.

♦

Preheat oven to 200°C/400°F/Gas Mark 6.

Divide the tomatoes, banana peppers, mushrooms, onion, garlic, black peppercorns and trout among 4 individual baking dishes, layering in that order. Sprinkle with salt and dot with the butter. Bake in the oven for 10 minutes.

Remove from the oven and turn the vegetables, basting the fish and vegetables with the cooking juices. Return to the oven for a further 10 minutes.

Serve to the table in the individual dishes.

OCTOPUS HOT POT
GÜVEÇTE AHTAPOT

Region:	Muğla, Aegean Region
Preparation time:	20 minutes
Cooking time:	1 hour 10 minutes, plus 5 minutes resting
Serves:	4

For the octopus:

1 (3 kg)	octopus	1 (6 lb 10 oz)
4 tsp	apple cider vinegar	4 tsp
½	lemon, seeded	½
1	cinnamon stick	1
4	cloves	4

300 g	potato	1⅓ cups/11 oz
200 g	carrot	1½ cups/7 oz
1	fresh fennel bulb	1
1	celery stalk	1
2 (240 g)	medium onions	2 (1⅝ cups/8½ oz)
10	garlic cloves	10
60 ml	olive oil	¼ cup/2 fl oz
4	bay leaves	4
6	black peppercorns	6
2 tbsp	lemon juice	2 tbsp

This recipe is popular in Bodrum, where local octopuses are dried in the sun for a few hours and then grilled. Another method adds pre-chopped octopus to the other ingredients and is then simply baked in a 200°C/400°F/Gas Mark 6 oven for 1 hour. Some prefer the grill (broiler) to the oven and some poach the octopus instead of cooking it in the pressure cooker.

◆

To cook the octopus:
Put the octopus, apple cider vinegar, lemon, cinnamon stick and cloves into a pressure cooker with 1 litre (4¼ cups/34 fl oz) water and ¼ teaspoon salt. Cook on medium heat for 30 minutes. Let rest for 5 minutes. Remove the octopus and slice into 3-cm (1¼-inch) pieces.

Preheat oven to 200°C/400°F/Gas Mark 6.

Slice the potato, carrot, celery and fennel into 3-cm (1¼-inch) pieces. Slice the onion into 2-cm (¾ inch) pieces. Mix the diced potato, carrot, celery, fennel and onion with the garlic, olive oil, bay leaves, black peppercorns and lemon juice in a large bowl, until well combined. Season with ¾ teaspoon salt. Put the mixture into a casserole dish (Dutch oven) and bake in the hot oven for 30 minutes.

Remove the casserole and turn the oven up to 220°C/425°F/Gas Mark 7. Add the octopus to the dish and gently mix for 1 minute, then return to the oven for a final 10 minutes. Serve immediately.

FRIED FRESHWATER SCRAPER
SIRAZ KIZARTMASI

Region:	Konya, Central Anatolia
Preparation time:	10 minutes, plus 10 minutes resting
Cooking time:	10 minutes
Serves:	4

4 (25-cm)	longsnout scraper (or other freshwater fish), cleaned, scaled, gills removed	4 (10-inch)
1 litre	olive oil	4¼ cups/34 fl oz

1	*Çoban Salatası* (Shepherd's Salad, see p.54)	1

This dish is a specialty of Beyşehir and the surrounding areas. Longsnout scraper is a freshwater fish found only in Turkey, so substitute any medium-sized freshwater fish, such as trout.

◆

Using a sharp knife, make small indentations in the fish from top to tail, sprinkle with ¼ teaspoon salt and rub into the fish, then let rest for 10 minutes.

In a large saucepan, heat the olive oil over medium heat to 155°C/310°F. Place the fish in the hot oil and fry on both sides for 5 minutes.

Serve immediately, with *Çoban Salatası*.

BISHOP'S STEW
PAPAZ YAHNİSİ

Region:	Trabzon, Black Sea Region	
Preparation time:	20 minutes	
Cooking time:	35 minutes	
Serves:	4	

300 g	potatoes	1⅓ cups/11 oz
2	celery stalks	2
2	leeks	2
2	spring onions (scallions)	2
1 bunch	chard	1 bunch
1	fresh garlic	1
½ bunch	parsley	½ bunch
½ bunch	dill	½ bunch
200 ml	olive oil	scant 1 cup/7 fl oz
1	lemon, halved lengthwise, seeded, thinly sliced	1
1 tsp	ground cinnamon	1 tsp
½ tsp	sweet paprika	½ tsp
2 (30-cm)	bonitos, head and tail removed, cleaned, sliced into 6 pieces	2 (12-inch)

Legend goes that this dish was made by bishops in the past. It is a traditional taste with quite a few regional variations. Some recipes add wine, while others make it with poached veal. Muslims prefer to use vinegar. Depending on the main ingredient, the vinegar version is known as lamb or veal stew. The greens in this dish can be changed depending on the season. Traditionally the dish is sent to the local bakery for cooking in the communal ovens. Mackerel, anchovy and garfish are all suitable alternatives to bonito.

◆

Preheat oven to 200°C/400°F/Gas Mark 6.

Dice the potatoes. Finely slice the celery, leeks, spring onions (scallions), chard, garlic, parsley and dill. Mix with half of the oil, the lemon slices, cinnamon, paprika and ½ teaspoon each of black pepper and salt in a large bowl or deep tray for 3 minutes, kneading until well combined.

Arrange half of this mixture on the bottom of a roasting pan and layer the bonito pieces on top. Sprinkle with ½ teaspoon salt. Layer the rest of the mixture on top, drizzle over the remaining olive oil and add 250 ml (1 cup/ 8 fl oz) water. Bake, covered, in the oven for 30 minutes.

Increase the heat to 240°C/475°F/Gas Mark 9, uncover, and bake for a final 5 minutes. Serve immediately.

◆

FRIED FISH BRAINS
BEYİN KIZARTMASI

Region:	Şanlıurfa, Southeastern Anatolia	
Preparation time:	10 minutes	
Cooking time:	10 minutes	
Serves:	4	

4	eggs	4
4	garlic cloves, quartered	4
1 tsp	dried chilli (red pepper) flakes	1 tsp
½ tsp	ground cardamom	½ tsp
4	flat-leaf parsley sprigs	4
100g	plain (all-purpose) flour	¾ cup/ 3½ oz
100 ml	olive oil	scant ½ cup/3½ fl oz
600g	fish brains (large fish)	1 lb 5 oz

1 bunch	mustard greens	1 bunch
½ bunch	parsley	½ bunch
1	lemon, quartered	1

This is a specialty of Birecik and the surrounding areas. As well as being fried, fish brains are also commonly poached and grilled on skewers.

◆

Mix the eggs, garlic, dried chilli (red pepper) flakes and ground cardamom in a shallow bowl. Finely slice the parsley and add to the bowl with ½ teaspoon black pepper and ½ teaspoon salt, mix until well combined. Put the flour into a separate shallow bowl nearby.

Heat the olive oil in a large saucepan over medium heat. Chop the fish brains into 3-cm (1¼-inch) pieces. Coat the fish brains in the egg mixture and then in the flour, then place in the hot oil and fry for 2 minutes on each side.

Serve immediately, with mustard greens, parsley and lemon wedges.

FISH & SEAFOOD

FRIED ANCHOVIES
HAMSİ TAVA

Region:	Trabzon, Black Sea Region	
Preparation time:	10 minutes, plus 1 hour soaking	
Cooking time:	5 minutes	
Serves:	4	

60	anchovies, heads removed, cleaned	60
1¼ tsp	salt	1¼ tsp
60 ml	apple cider vinegar	¼ cup/2 fl oz
100 g	fine cornmeal (polenta)	¾ cup/3½ oz
50 g	plain (all-purpose) flour	⅓ cup/2 oz
60 g	onion, thinly sliced	⅜ cup/2¼ oz
100 ml	corn oil	scant ½ cup/3½ fl oz

p.283

This recipe is traditionally prepared in the local fish pans, which come with a special lid. Haddock and mullet are popular substitutes for the anchovies, especially in the Black Sea Region. Some versions omit the onions.

◆

Soak the anchovies in 3 litres (12 cups/100 fl oz) cold water, with 1 teaspoon of the salt and the apple cider vinegar, for 1 hour. Drain, rinse and pat dry.

Mix the cornmeal (polenta) and flour in a bowl. Toss the anchovies in the bowl to cover in the flour mixture.

In a separate bowl, squeeze the onions with the remaining ¼ teaspoon of salt and set aside.

In a large sauté pan or frying pan (skillet), heat half of the corn oil over medium heat to 155°C/310°F. Shake off the excess flour from the anchovies and place in the pan in a circular formation, closely packed and fanning out from the middle. Make sure that the anchovies are not actually on top of one another. Fry for 2 minutes on the first side. Turn the fish out in one movement on to a large flat plate or pan lid. You will need to turn the pan upside down and keep a bowl underneath to collect the excess oil. Take care to protect your hands and arms from the hot oil.

Add the remaining corn oil to the pan and heat to 155°C/310°F. Add the onions to the pan, then slide the anchovies off the plate or pan lid on top of the onions, fried side up. Pour the collected excess frying oil back over the fish and fry for a further 3 minutes.

Use the plate or lid once more to turn out the dish, draining the oil into a bowl. Serve with the onions on top.

◆

DRIED MACKEREL
ÇİROZ (KURU BALIK)

Region:	İstanbul, Marmara Region	
Preparation time:	10 minutes	
Cooking time:	11 days	
Serves:	4	

16	thin mackerel, gills removed, cleaned	16
2 kg	coarse sea salt	7 cups/ 4 lb 6 oz

Mackerel migrate to the Black Sea to give birth and are caught on their return, exhausted and skinny, by fishermen of the Marmara Sea. These mackerel are dried for 10–15 days, hung on strings. This takes place in April and May and is a technique used by İstanbul's fishermen. When dried, the mackerel is lightly grilled, then pounded in a pestle and mortar to remove the skin and bones. Discard the skin and bones and enjoy the rest. Use dried mackerel in *Çiroz Salatası* (Salted Mackerel Salad, see p.60).

◆

Put the mackerel into a deep tray and massage with the coarse sea salt. Let rest for 1 day in the refrigerator, covered with clingfilm (plastic wrap). Rinse with plenty of cold water and pat dry. Tie strings to the mackerel tails and hang outdoors in a sunny spot, using a net to protect the fish from flies. The mackerel will be ready in 10 days. Alternatively, use a dehydrator set a 70°C for 15 minutes.

FISH & SEAFOOD

FRIED MUSSELS
MİDYE TAVA

Region:	İstanbul, Marmara Region and	
	İzmir, Aegean Region	
Preparation time:	5 minutes	
Cooking time:	5 minutes	
Serves:	4	

150 g	plain (all-purpose) flour	1 cup/5 oz
80	medium-sized mussels	80
	(meat removed from shells)	
1 litre	olive oil	4¼ cups/
		34 fl oz
1 tsp	salt	1 tsp
1	*Tarator* (Almond and	1
	Garlic Sauce, see p.79)	

💧 ⬥ 𝙓 ⁘   p.285 📷

A very popular street food and all-time favourite snack in İstanbul, this dish is made most often in the autumn and winter.

♦

Put the flour in a shallow bowl, add the mussels and toss to coat in the flour. Shake off any excess flour.

In a large saucepan, heat the olive oil over medium heat to 155°C/310°F. Place the mussels in the hot oil and fry for 1 minute. Remove the mussels with a slotted spoon as soon as they rise up to the surface. Drain on paper towels.

Serve with a sprinkle of salt and a side of *Tarator*.

♦

BAKED CATFISH PATTIES
KARABALIKLI TAPPUŞ ORUĞU

Region:	Hatay, Mediterranean Region	
Preparation time:	20 minutes, plus 20 minutes soaking	
Cooking time:	20 minutes	
Serves:	4	

200 ml	olive oil	scant 1 cup/7 fl oz
1 kg	catfish, minced (ground)	2 lb 3 oz
100g	fine bulgur wheat,	½ cup/3½ oz
	soaked in 100 ml	
	(scant ½ cup/3½ fl oz)	
	water for 20 minutes	
1 (120 g)	medium onion,	1 (¾ cup/
	finely sliced	4 oz)
10	garlic cloves, finely sliced	10
1 tbsp	tomato paste (see p.492)	1 tbsp
2 tsp	paprika	2 tsp
½ tsp	ground cumin	½ tsp
2 tsp	dried mint	2 tsp
1 tsp	dried chilli	1 tsp
	(red pepper) flakes	
2 tbsp	pomegranate molasses	2 tbsp
	(see p.490)	
1 tsp	ground cloves	1 tsp
½ tsp	black pepper	½ tsp
1 tsp	salt	1 tsp
1 bunch	rocket (arugula), to serve	1 bunch

💧 ⬥

Karabalık is a freshwater fish, also known as 'meat fish'. Any freshwater fish with red flesh is ideal, such as catfish. *Tappuş* describes how the patties are made into balls and flattened, a local word to Antakya and its environs. In a variation on this recipe, the fish is not boned, but skinned and baked in the oven with vegetables.

♦

Preheat oven to 200°C/400°F/Gas Mark 6 and oil a baking tray (sheet) with half of the olive oil.

Knead the fish, bulgur wheat, onion, garlic, tomato purée (paste), paprika, cumin, dried mint, dried chilli (red pepper) flakes, pomegranate molasses, ground cloves, black pepper and salt in a large bowl or deep tray for 10 minutes, until well combined. Divide the mixture into 12 equal parts, then roll into balls and flatten into discs.

Arrange the patties on the oiled baking tray. Drizzle with the remaining olive oil and bake in the hot oven for 20 minutes.

Serve with a crisp rocket (arugula) salad.

CURED BONITO
LAKERDA

Region:		İstanbul, Marmara Region
Preparation time:		30 minutes, plus 5 hours soaking, plus 20 days curing, plus 8 hours resting, plus 1 hour chilling
Serves:		4

1 (1 kg)	bonito (or large mackerel)	1 (2 lb 3 oz)
2.25 kg	coarse sea salt (or rock salt)	8 cups/ 4 lb 16 oz
10	bay leaves	10
20	black peppercorns	20
1 (120 g)	medium red onion, cut into thin rings, thoroughly rinsed	1 (¾ cup/4 oz)
½ bunch	flat-leaf parsley, thinly sliced	½ bunch
2 tbsp	olive oil	2 tbsp
½ tsp	black pepper	½ tsp

♦ ❧   p.287 📷

This is prepared in the bonito season, towards the end of September, ready to be consumed when fresh fish is not available. Traditionally made at home, these days it is available ready-made in fishmongers and is popular in the Black Sea Region as well as İstanbul. Some cooks prefer to preserve the fish whole, applying weight on top to remove the oils.

♦

Cut the fins off the back of the bonito. Slit the belly, clean the insides and cut in half. Cut out the brown triangular piece in each half and brush off any remaining brown bits. Clean around the spine with a pin. Rinse the pieces well under high-pressure running water.

Put the bonito into a large bowl with 3 litres (12 cups/ 100 fl oz) water and 3½ tablespoons of the salt, cover and let soak in the refrigerator for 1 hour. Drain and discard the brine. Repeat 4 more times, replacing the brine each time. Take the bonito out of the bowl, and rinse and dry both the fish and bowl thoroughly. Place the bonito back in the bowl, cover with the remaining 2 kg (7 cups/ 4 lb 6 oz) of salt and rest to let all the juices seep out, about 3 hours.

Take 500 g (2 cups/1 lb 2 oz) of the salt covering the bonito and add to a large, deep airtight container. Arrange the bonito pieces vertically in the salt, making sure that the pieces do not touch one another or the sides of the container. Add the bay leaves and the black peppercorns. Top with the remaining salt, seal the container and keep in the refrigerator for 20 days. Turn the container upside down every other day.

After 20 days, wash all the salt off the bonito. Put the bonito into a large bowl with 3 litres (12 cups/100 fl oz) water, cover and let rest in the refrigerator for 1 hour. Drain and discard the water. Repeat this 4 more times, changing the water each time. After the final water change, rinse and dry the bonito thoroughly and place in another bowl. Cover and chill in the refrigerator for a further 1 hour.

Cut the bonito in half and debone, making sure that the flesh remains intact. Remove the skin. Cut the prepared bonito flesh into thin slices. Serve on a bed of red onions and parsley with a drizzle with olive oil and a sprinkling of black pepper.

SARDINES GRILLED IN VINE LEAVES
ASMA YAPRAKLI SARDALYA

Region:	Çanakkale, Marmara Region	
Preparation time:	20 minutes	
Cooking time:	10 minutes	
Serves:	4	

20	fresh vine leaves	20
40	sardines, cleaned and rinsed	40
½ tsp	salt	½ tsp

p.289

This dish is prepared in the month of August when the sardines are in their prime, and nice and oily. Another version wraps the sardines individually in the vine leaves. If you don't have a barbecue, you can use a grill (broiler) for this recipe.

♦

Prepare a barbecue for cooking or preheat a grill (broiler) to high.

Arrange 10 fresh vine leaves on one side of a fish grill. Place the sardines on top of the vine leaves and sprinkle with salt. Arrange the remaining vine leaves over the top and close the fish grill.

Set the fish grill 8 cm (3 inches) above the hot embers and grill for 3 minutes on each side, making sure that the leaves don't burn.

Alternatively, grill (broil) in the same manner.

Serve immediately, with the sardines in the vine leaves.

♦

SWORDFISH KEBABS
KILIÇ ŞİŞ

Region:	İstanbul, Marmara Region	
Preparation time:	15 minutes, plus 2 hours marinating	
Cooking time:	15 minutes	
Serves:	4	

1	lemon, diced into 12 pieces, juice reserved	1
1	large tomato, diced into 12 (2-cm/¾ inch) pieces	1
1	small bell pepper, diced into 12 (2-cm/¾ inch) pieces	1
1 (120 g)	medium onion, diced into 12 (2-cm/¾ inch) pieces, juice reserved	1 (¾ cup/ 4 oz)
12	bay leaves	12
4	garlic cloves, crushed	4
100 ml	olive oil	scant ½ cup/ 3½ fl oz
1 tsp	ground cinnamon	1 tsp
½ tsp	paprika	½ tsp
½ tsp	black pepper	½ tsp
1 tsp	salt	1 tsp
800 g	swordfish fillet, de-boned, skinned, diced into 24 (3-cm/1¼-inch) pieces	1 lb 12 oz

Some like to serve this dish plain, without the vegetables. You will need 4 long cast-iron skewers or 8 flat wooden skewers (soaked).

♦

Mix the lemon, lemon juice, tomato, bell pepper, onion, onion juice, bay leaves, garlic, olive oil, ground cinnamon, paprika, black pepper and salt in a large bowl, until well combined. Add the swordfish, cover and marinate in the refrigerator for 2 hours.

Prepare a barbecue for cooking or preheat a grill (broiler) to high.

Thread the vegetables and fish on to the skewers in the following order: bay leaf / onion / bell pepper / tomato / lemon / swordfish / lemon / tomato / bell pepper / bay leaf.

Set the skewers 8 cm (3 inches) above the hot embers and grill for 3 minutes on each side. Alternatively, grill (broil) in the same manner.

Serve immediately.

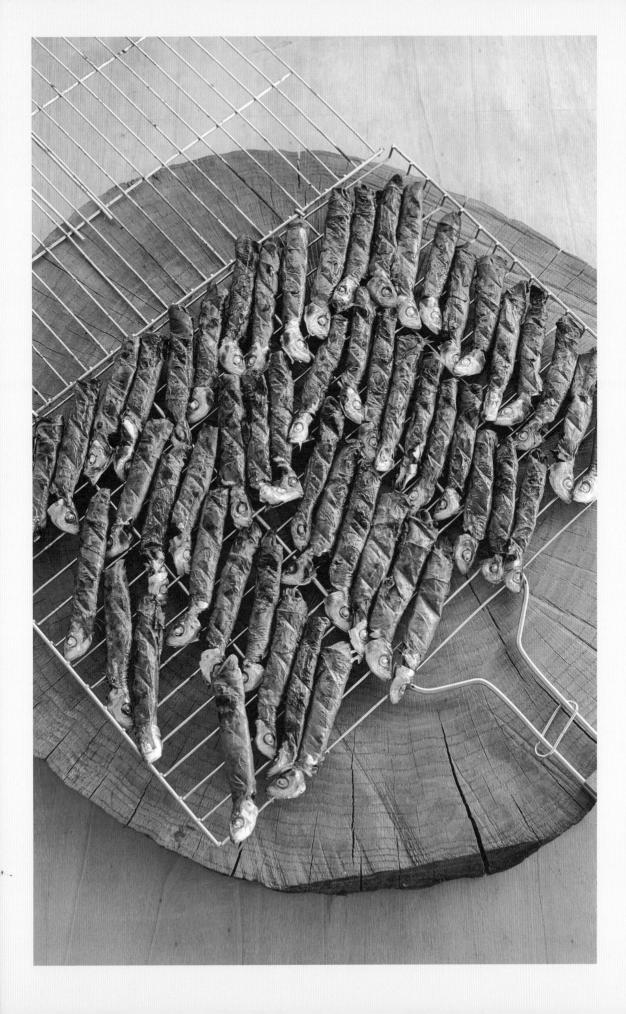

CATFISH KEBABS
BALIK KEBABI

Region:	Şanlıurfa, Southeastern Anatolia	
Preparation time:	15 minutes, plus 1 hour soaking, plus overnight chilling	
Cooking time:	10 minutes	
Serves:	4	

800 g	catfish, cleaned	1 lb 12 oz
60 ml	apple cider vinegar	¼ cup/2 fl oz

For the marinade:

1 tbsp	tomato paste (see p.492)	1 tbsp
2 tsp	red bell pepper paste (see p.492)	2 tsp
2 tsp	dried chilli (red pepper) flakes	2 tsp
10	garlic cloves, crushed	10
150 ml	olive oil	⅔ cup/5 fl oz
2 tsp	dried oregano	2 tsp
1	lemon, thinly sliced	1

1 bunch	cress	1 bunch
4	spring onions (scallions)	4
1 bunch	flat-leaf parsley	1 bunch

 p.291

If you don't have a barbecue, you can use a grill (broiler) for this recipe. You will need 4 long cast-iron skewers or 8 flat wooden skewers (soaked).

◆

Dice the catfish into 3-cm (1¼-inch) pieces. Soak the catfish in 3 litres (12 cups/100 fl oz) cold water, with the apple cider vinegar and 1 teaspoon salt, for 1 hour. Drain, rinse and pat dry.

To make the marinade:
Combine all the marinade ingredients in a large bowl with ½ teaspoon black pepper, ¼ teaspoon salt and mix for 2 minutes. Add the fish and let marinate for 3 minutes. Cover with clingfilm (plastic wrap) and chill in the refrigerator overnight.

Prepare a barbecue for cooking or preheat a grill (broiler) to high. Take the fish out of the marinade and reserve the marinade. Divide the marinated fish into 4 or 8 equal parts and arrange on the skewers.

Set the skewers 8 cm (3 inches) above the hot embers and grill for 2 minutes on each side. Brush the fish with the reserved marinade and cook for another 1 minute on each side. Repeat once more. Alternatively, grill (broil) in the same manner.

Transfer to plates and serve with cress, spring onions (scallions) and parsley.

◆

FISH WITH SOUR CHERRIES
VİŞNELİ BALIK

Region:	Adıyaman, Southeastern Anatolia	
Preparation time:	15 minutes	
Cooking time:	30 minutes, plus 5 minutes resting	
Serves:	4	

800 g	catfish fillet (or other freshwater fish)	1 lb 12 oz
200 ml	olive oil	scant 1 cup/7 fl oz
2 (240 g)	medium onions, finely diced	2 (1⅝ cups/ 8½ oz)
200g	almonds	1½ cups/7 oz
2	garlic cloves, quartered	2
1	cinnamon stick	1
1 tsp	ground fennel seeds	1 tsp
500g	sour cherries, pitted	2¼ cups/ 1 lb 2 oz
30g	honey (oregano flower)	1½ tbsp/1 oz
½ bunch	flat-leaf parsley	½ bunch

This dish is a summer delight. Made by Christians during periods of mourning and Lent, it has become more widely cooked by the rest of the population over the years.

◆

Dice the catfish into 3-cm (1¼-inch) pieces. Heat the olive oil in a large saucepan over medium heat, add the catfish and fry for 2 minutes on each side. Remove from the pan with a slotted spoon and set aside.

Sprinkle ½ teaspoon salt over the diced onions. Add the onion and almonds to the pan and cook for 7 minutes.

Add the garlic, cinnamon stick, fennel seeds, sour cherries to the pan and mix through. Season with ½ teaspoon black pepper and ½ teaspoon salt and cook for 1 minute. Reduce the heat and simmer for 10 minutes. Return the catfish to the pan and cook for a further 5 minutes. Remove from the heat, stir in the honey and finely sliced parsley, cover and let rest for 5 minutes before serving.

FISH & SEAFOOD

SOLE KEBAB
DİL ŞİŞ

Region: İzmir, Aegean Region
Preparation time: 15 minutes, plus 2 hours chilling
Cooking time: 10 minutes
Serves: 4

4 (30-cm)	sole, filleted, each fillet cut into 5 equal pieces (40 pieces in total)	4 (12-inch)
150 ml	olive oil	⅔ cup/5 fl oz
4	garlic cloves, crushed	4
¼ tsp	lemon zest	¼ tsp
¾ tsp	salt	¾ tsp
	Çoban Salatası (Shepherd's Salad, see p.54)	

 p.293

This dish is made in all the coastal areas in Turkey, but the best sole kebabs are always made in İzmir. Some vendors are known to sell one thousand portions in a single day! If you don't have a barbecue, you can use a grill (broiler) for this recipe. You will need 4 long cast-iron skewers or 8 flat wooden skewers (soaked).

♦

Mix the sole, olive oil, garlic, lemon zest and salt in a large bowl, cover with clingfilm (plastic wrap) and chill in the refrigerator for 2 hours.

Prepare a barbecue or preheat a grill (broiler) to high. Take the fish out of the marinade and reserve the marinade. Roll each piece of fish before threading on to the skewers.

Set the skewers 8 cm (3 inches) above the hot embers and grill for 2 minutes on each side, turning frequently. Keep the reserved marinade (in a heat-resistant bowl or pan) warm. Baste the fish with the marinade and grill for a further 1 minute on each side. Alternatively, grill (broil) the fish, keeping the marinade warm in a pan over low heat.

Draw the grilled fish on to serving platters and drizzle the warm marinade on top. Serve with the Çoban Salatası.

♦

EEL KEBABS
YILAN BALIĞI KEBABI

Region: Hatay, Mediterranean Region
Preparation time: 10 minutes, plus 1 hour soaking, plus 5 hours marinating
Cooking time: 10 minutes
Serves: 4

1.2 kg	freshwater eel, skinned, cleaned, chopped into 4-cm (1½-inch) pieces	2 lb 10 oz
60 ml	apple cider vinegar	¼ cup/2 fl oz
12	Seville orange leaves or bay leaves	12

For the marinade:

2 tbsp	olive oil	2 tbsp
2 tbsp	lemon juice	2 tbsp
½ tsp	ground cumin	½ tsp
1 tbsp	dried basil	1 tbsp
2 tsp	dried chilli (red pepper) flakes	2 tbsp
½ tsp	salt	½ tsp

Eel is caught in the murky water, directly after the rainfall in April. The local varieties of eel are very oily, so the fish is plunged into water during cooking to get rid of any excess oil. You will need 4 long cast-iron skewers or 8 flat wooden skewers (soaked).

♦

Soak the eel in 3 litres (12 cups/100 fl oz) cold water, with the apple cider vinegar and 1 teaspoon salt, for 1 hour. Drain, rinse and pat dry.

To make the marinade:
Combine all the marinade ingredients in a large bowl with ½ teaspoon salt. Add the eel, cover with clingfilm (plastic wrap) and chill in the refrigerator for 5 hours.

Prepare a barbecue for cooking or preheat a grill (broiler) to high. Fill a large bucket with cold water and set nearby.

Remove from the refrigerator and divide into 4 or 8 equal parts, reserving the marinade. Thread tightly onto skewers, alternating the eel with the orange or bay leaves.

Set the skewers 8 cm (3 inches) above the hot embers and grill for 2 minutes on each side. Plunge the skewers into the bucket of water for 3 seconds. Remove from the bucket, brush the eel with the reserved marinade and grill for a further 2 minutes on each side. Alternatively, grill (broil) in the same manner. Draw the eel on to plates and serve.

◆

PILAFS

◆

PILAF
CULTURE

Pilaf has many important characteristics. Rice is usually cooked using the absorption method and is the traditional ingredient for pilaf, but it can also be made with bulgur wheat. In urban areas, the bulgur version is also called *pilaf*, whereas in the countryside these dishes are called *aş* and named after the defining added ingredients, such as tomatoes or orzo pasta. A pilaf accompanies every dish at the Turkish table. Vegetable dishes, with or without meat, and chicken dishes are almost always served with a pilaf. Some pilafs are dishes in their own right, enriched with meat, liver, chicken and beans. Pilaf and *Cacık* (Tzatziki, see p.78), as well as pilaf and sweet fruit compotes, are marriages made in heaven.

Pilafs also have the ritualistic role of carrying us through seasons and rites of passage. The *Perde Pilavı* (Veiled Rice Pilaf, p.314) of Southeastern Anatolia is a wedding banquet staple. The pine nuts, almonds, currants and pastry in this pilaf have symbolic meanings. The pine nuts represent the groom, the almonds the bride, the currants the children and the pastry the home. The rice is believed to bring prosperity. *Keşkek* (Pounded Lamb and Wheat, p.317) is yet another wedding banquet and special occasion staple.

PILAF
TRADITIONS

Another popular dish for seasonal rituals is *Dortulu* bulgur (*aş*) pilaf, made for the *Hıdırellez* spring festivities on May 6th. In the village of Bayraktar in Kocaeli, in the Marmara region, charity collectors visit each house with a horse and carriage or tractor in tow. Everyone has to donate something, be it bulgur wheat, oil, salt, meat or flour. Some contribute in big sacks, some give away only meagre amounts of pantry staples, others donate roosters, chickens or ducks. Those who do not give bring bad luck upon themselves.

The collected goods are cooked in a communal kitchen by volunteer veteran chefs. On the day of *Hıdırellez*, *dortulu* pilaf is made over large wood fires and given out to the multitude. This is an ongoing annual tradition. The ritual of making certain foods at the change of seasons or on special occasions is related to local beliefs and customs.

PILAF TECHNIQUES
AND INGREDIENTS

When making pilaf, the rice must be soaked in salted water and then rinsed with a lot of water in order to get rid of the starch. This is the key to a delicious pilaf. Then there are different cooking techniques, including roasting, absorption, poaching and steaming. Roasting and absorption are the most popular.

When roasting, heat the olive oil or butter to sizzling hot, add the washed rice to the hot fat and cook over low heat for 10–20 minutes, stirring gently. Add hot meat or chicken stock, bring to the boil and then simmer until all the juices are absorbed.

In the absorption method, the washed rice is added to plain water or stock and simmered until all the juices are absorbed. The pan is then removed from the heat and the pilaf topped with sizzling hot butter, which is stirred in gently. The pilaf is served after resting for 15 minutes.

If you choose the boiling method, bring the water to the boil, add the washed rice, drain when cooked and stir in the butter.

Yet another technique has the washed rice added to a steamer or placed directly on top of meat cooking in a pot. This is called 'dry pilaf', 'waterless pilaf' or 'steamed pilaf'. Bulgur wheat, on the other hand, is usually used without soaking, although some prefer to rinse it. Bulgur wheat is added straight into the butter or boiling water and is usually cooked with meat, chicken or vegetable stock using the absorption method. Since the bulgur is parboiled and dried, its resting time is only 5 minutes, compared to the 15–20 minutes required for rice. Bulgur is sometimes roasted with meat or other ingredients and these pilafs are finished with the addition and absorption of boiling water.

Mashes constitute another category of pilaf, where the ingredients are pounded together. The most popular ingredients are fine and coarse bulgur wheat, rice, cracked wheat and ground cornmeal (polenta) with added vegetables, meat, pulses, yogurt, milk, cheese and grape molasses. Mashes are runnier than pilafs – the consistency changes according to local preferences. Some like it more grainy, some like it pounded to a thick paste. Grains and legumes ooze into one another, ending up in a runny pilaf. Mashes are eaten immediately without resting. Local names for mashes are *haşıl*, *papa*, *gulul* and *şile*. Also in this book are dishes made with cracked wheat: *dövme*, *herse* (or *herise*), *hedik* and *keşkek*. *Keşkek* is prepared with cracked wheat and can be plain or with meat, chicken, rooster, duck or woodcock. Once the grains and the meat are cooked, they are pounded into a paste with a thick wooden stick or a wooden spoon. The juices are absorbed and we end up with a thick glutinous mash which is served with melted butter.

Pilafs made with various forms of noodles are also covered in this section. First and foremost is couscous, which has many techniques and recipes. Couscous is usually prepared with bulgur wheat, flour and eggs. Semolina is another popular ingredient. Homemade pasta noodles are prepared fresh, cut and then cooked immediately. Cut-up pasta noodles are also called 'couscous'. The two most popular techniques for cooking both couscous and homemade noodles are roasting and absorption.

TOMATO RICE
DOMATESLİ PİLAV

Region:		İstanbul, all regions
Preparation time:		10 minutes, plus 1 hour soaking
Cooking time:		35 minutes, plus 10 minutes resting
Serves:		4

300 g	medium-grain rice	1½ cups/11 oz
2½ tsp	salt	2½ tsp
70 g	butter	⅓ cup/2¾ oz
60 g	onion, finely chopped	⅜ cup/2¼ oz
200 ml	meat stock (see p.489), boiling	scant 1 cup/7 fl oz
250 ml	fresh tomato juice, boiling	1 cup/8 fl oz
½ tsp	black pepper	½ tsp

🌱 ◖   p.301

This is a popular side to main dishes, eaten especially at the end of summer.

◆

Put the rice into a large bowl, add 2 teaspoons of the salt and pour over 1 litre (4¼ cups/34 fl oz) boiling water. Soak for 1 hour at room temperature. Drain and rinse the rice under cold running water, until the water runs clear. Drain the rice in a colander for 5 minutes.

Heat the butter in a saucepan over medium-low heat, add the rice and the remaining ½ teaspoon of salt and sauté for 7 minutes, stirring gently. Add the onions and sauté for 3 minutes. Add the meat stock, tomato juice and black pepper and cook, covered, for 20 minutes.

Remove from the heat, tightly cover the pan with a dish towel, then seal tight with the pan lid. Wrap the entire pan in another dish towel and rest for 10 minutes.

Unwrap the pilaf, stir gently and serve.

◆

BASIL RICE
REYHANLI PİLAV

Region:		Erzincan, Eastern Anatolia
Preparation time:		30 minutes, plus 1 hour soaking
Cooking time:		45 minutes, plus 10 minutes resting
Serves:		4

200 g	medium-grain rice	1 cup/7 oz
2½ tsp	salt	2½ tsp
100 g	butter	½ cup/3½ oz
150 g	carrot, finely sliced	1 cup/5 oz
4	spring onions (scallions), finely chopped	4
1	fresh garlic, finely sliced	1
2 tsp	dried mint	2 tsp
¼ tsp	black pepper	¼ tsp
100 g	coarse bulgur wheat, washed	½ cup/3½ oz
½ bunch	fresh basil, finely sliced	½ bunch
¼ bunch	dill, finely sliced	¼ bunch
½ bunch	flat-leaf parsley, finely sliced	½ bunch
100 g	*tulum* cheese, to serve	3½ oz

◖ V

This is a summer dish made when the community come together to sun-dry the harvested mulberries. There is a winter version using sun-dried vegetables instead of the fresh herbs.

◆

Put the rice into a large bowl, add 2 teaspoons of the salt and pour over 1 litre (4¼ cups/34 fl oz) boiling water. Soak for 1 hour at room temperature. Drain and rinse the rice under cold running water, until the water runs clear. Drain the rice in a colander for 5 minutes.

Heat the butter in a large saucepan over medium heat, add the carrots and sauté for 2 minutes. Add the spring onions (scallions), fresh garlic and dried mint and sauté for 3 minutes. Add the black pepper and remaining ½ teaspoon of salt and pour over 600 ml (2½ cups/ 20 fl oz) boiling water. Cook, covered, for 15 minutes. Turn the heat up to high, add the rice and cook, uncovered, for 5 minutes. Reduce the heat back down to low, then add the bulgur wheat. Cook, covered, for a further 15 minutes.

Remove the pan from the heat and add the fresh basil, dill and parsley on top of the pilaf. Do not stir. Tightly cover the pan with a dish towel, making sure it does not touch the herbs, then seal tight with the pan lid. Wrap the entire pan in another dish towel and rest for 10 minutes.

Unwrap the pilaf, gently stir through the cheese and serve.

RICE PILAF WITH ANCHOVIES
HAMSİLİ PİLAV

Region:		Rize, Black Sea Region
Preparation time:		20 minutes, plus 1 hour soaking
Cooking time:		1 hour 5 minutes
Serves:		4

For soaking:		
100 g	currants	¾ cup/3½ oz
1 kg	anchovies, heads removed, cleaned	2 lb 3 oz
60 ml	apple cider vinegar	¼ cup/2 fl oz
300 g	medium-grain rice	1½ cups/11 oz
2 tsp	salt	2 tsp

For the pilaf:		
120g	butter	½ cup/4 oz
½ tsp	salt	½ tsp
100 g	pine nuts, toasted	¾ cup/3½ oz
1 (120 g)	medium onion, finely sliced	1 (¾ cup/4 oz)
½ tsp	ground allspice	½ tsp
1 tsp	ground cinnamon	1 tsp
10	black peppercorns	10
½ bunch	dill	½ bunch

❋　　　　　　　　　　　　　　　p.303 📷

This rice dish is made throughout the autumn and winter, as well as for special occasions.

◆

Put the currants to soak in a bowl with 200 ml (scant 1 cup/7 fl oz) water for 1 hour.

Meanwhile, put the anchovies into a separate bowl with 3 litres (12 cups/100 fl oz) water and the apple cider vinegar to soak for 1 hour. Drain, rinse and set aside.

Put the rice into a large bowl, add the salt and pour over 1 litre (4¼ cups/34 fl oz) boiling water. Soak for 1 hour at room temperature. Drain and rinse the rice under cold running water, until the water runs clear. Drain the rice in a colander for 5 minutes.

To make the pilaf:
Heat 80 g (generous ⅓ cup/3 oz) of the butter in a large saucepan over medium heat, add the rice, salt and pine nuts and sauté for 7 minutes. Add the onions and sauté for 3 minutes. Turn the heat up, add the allspice, cinnamon and black peppercorns, along with 600 ml (2½ cups/ 20 fl oz) boiling water and boil for 1 minute. Reduce the heat and simmer, covered, for 15 minutes. Remove from the heat and sprinkle the currants into the pan. Tightly cover the pan with a dish towel, making sure that it doesn't touch the pilaf, then seal tight with the pan lid. Wrap the entire pan in another dish towel and rest for 20 minutes. Unwrap the pilaf, stir gently and gently stir in the dill.

While the pilaf is resting, preheat oven to 200°C/400°F/ Gas Mark 6 and use 2 tablespoons of the remaining butter to grease a 20-cm (8-inch) round sandwich cake pan.

Arrange some of the anchovies upright around the sides of the cake pan, making sure that their tails poke outside the pan. Arrange the remaining anchovies to cover the bottom of the pan, each overlapping the next, working from outside in. Spoon the pilaf over the anchovies and fold the fish tails back over the top of the rice. Cover the pilaf with the remaining anchovies in the same pattern as before. Brush the top with the remaining 2 tablespoons of butter and cover with aluminium foil. Bake in the hot oven for 10 minutes, then remove the foil and bake for a further 5 minutes.

To serve, turn the anchovy pilaf out of the pan on to a serving platter.

RICE PILAF WITH ORZO
ŞEHRİYELİ PİRİNÇ PİLAVI

Region:		İzmir, all regions
Preparation time:		10 minutes, plus 1 hour soaking
Cooking time:		30 minutes, plus 20 minutes resting
Serves:		4

300 g	medium-grain rice	1½ cups/11 oz
2½ tsp	salt	2½ tsp
100 g	butter	½ cup/3½ oz
70 g	orzo pasta	½ cup/2¾ oz
900 ml	chicken stock (see p.489), boiling	3¾ cups/30 fl oz
½ tsp	black pepper	½ tsp

p.305 📷

A great side with stews, this dish is popular all over the country. It is served at wedding banquets in some regions.

◆

Put the rice into a large bowl, add 2 teaspoons salt and pour over 1 litre (4¼ cups/34 fl oz) boiling water. Soak for 1 hour at room temperature. Drain and rinse the rice under cold running water, until the water runs clear. Drain the rice in a colander for 5 minutes.

Heat the butter in a large saucepan over medium heat, add the orzo pasta and sauté for 4 minutes, stirring continuously, until the orzo starts to brown. Reduce the heat, add the rice and cook for 10 minutes, stirring occasionally. Add the chicken stock, black pepper and remaining ½ teaspoon salt and cook, covered, for 15 minutes. Remove from the heat, tightly cover the pan with a dish towel, then seal tight with the pan lid. Wrap the entire pan in another dish towel and let rest for 20 minutes. Unwrap the pilaf, stir gently and serve.

◆

CHICKEN RICE
TAVUKLU PİLAV

Region:		Edirne, all regions
Preparation time:		20 minutes, plus overnight soaking, plus 1 hour soaking
Cooking time:		1½ hours pre-cooking, plus 30 minutes, plus 10 minutes resting
Serves:		4

80 g	chickpeas (garbanzo beans), soaked overnight	⅜ cup/3 oz
1 (2.5 kg)	chicken	1 (5 lb 8 oz)
300 g	medium-grain rice	1½ cups/11 oz
2½ tsp	salt	2½ tsp
100 g	butter	½ cup/3½ oz
½ tsp	black pepper	½ tsp

Hunters like to substitute game birds for the chicken in this favourite of home cooks. It is a popular street snack.

◆

Drain the soaked chickpeas (garbanzo beans), then cook in a saucepan of simmering water until soft, about 1½ hours. Drain, shell and set aside.

Meanwhile, bring a saucepan with 2 litres (8½ cups/70 fl oz) water to a boil, add the chicken and simmer for 1 hour 15 minutes. Drain, reserving 700 ml (2¾ cups/23 fl oz) of the chicken stock. Pick all the chicken meat from the bones and set aside.

Meanwhile, put the rice into a large bowl, add 2 teaspoons salt and pour over 1 litre (4¼ cups/34 fl oz) hot water. Soak for 1 hour at room temperature. Drain and rinse the rice under cold running water, until the water runs clear. Drain the rice in a colander for 5 minutes.

Heat the butter in a large saucepan over medium-low heat, add the rice and sauté for 10 minutes, mixing occasionally. Pour the reserved chicken stock into the pan and add the cooked chickpeas, chicken meat and remaining ½ teaspoon salt. Reduce the heat and simmer, covered, for 15 minutes.

Remove from the heat, tightly cover the pan with a dish towel, then seal tight with the pan lid. Wrap the entire pan in another dish towel and let rest for 10 minutes. Unwrap the pilaf, stir gently, sprinkle with black pepper and serve.

LAMB AND APRICOT RICE
HAŞLAMA PİLAVI

Region:		Van, Eastern Anatolia
Preparation time:		15 minutes
Cooking time:		25 minutes
Serves:		4

¾ tsp	salt	¾ tsp
300 g	medium-grain rice	1½ cups/11 oz
pinch	saffron	pinch
100 g	butter	scant ½ cup/3½ oz
200 g	lamb, finely diced	7 oz
60 g	onions, finely diced	⅜ cup/2¼ oz
80 g	apricot kernels (like bitter almonds), soaked in hot water for 10 minutes, drained and peeled	3 oz
6	dried apricots, finely diced	6
¼ tsp	black pepper	¼ tsp

This is a special dish for celebrations all over the country. It is called the 'wedding pilaf' in some regions.

◆

In a large saucepan, bring 3 litres (12 cups/100 fl oz) water and ½ teaspoon of the salt to a boil over medium heat. Add the rice, bring back to a boil and cook, covered, for 15 minutes.

Put the saffron into a bowl and add 1 tablespoon of the rice cooking water. Set aside.

Meanwhile, heat the butter in a large sauté pan over medium heat, add the lamb and sauté for 5 minutes, mixing continuously. Add the onions and sauté for 10 minutes, then add the apricot kernels, dried apricots, black pepper and the remaining ¼ teaspoon of salt and sauté for 5 minutes.

Drain the cooked rice, stir through the saffron water, then cover and let rest for 1 minute. Transfer the rice to plates, top with the lamb mixture and serve.

MILK RICE
SÜTLÜ PİLAV

Region:		Isparta, Mediterranean Region
Preparation time:		10 minutes, plus 1 hour soaking
Cooking time:		30 minutes, plus 10 minutes resting
Serves:		4

300 g	medium-grain rice	1½ cups/11 oz
2½ tsp	salt	2½ tsp
300 ml	milk	1¼ cups/10 fl oz
60 ml	rose water	¼ cup/2 fl oz
¼ tsp	black pepper	¼ tsp
80 g	toasted almonds, slivered	½ cup/3 oz
2 tbsp	rose petals	2 tbsp
50 g	dried clotted cream (see p.486, optional)	2 oz
200 g	*lor* (fresh curd cheese, see p.485)	7 oz

For the sauce:		
100 g	butter	scant ½ cup/3½ oz
1 tbsp	grape molasses	1 tbsp
½ tsp	ground cinnamon	½ tsp

An everyday dish popular with home cooks, milk rice is traditionally made to celebrate the first steps of a toddler with ingredients collected from the neighborhood.

◆

Put the rice into a large bowl, add 2 teaspoons salt and pour over 1 litre (4¼ cups/34 fl oz) hot water. Soak for 1 hour at room temperature. Drain and rinse the rice under cold running water, until the water runs clear. Drain the rice in a colander for 5 minutes.

In a large saucepan, combine 200 ml (scant 1 cup/7 fl oz) water with the milk, rose water, black pepper, the remaining ½ teaspoon salt, almonds, rose petals and dried clotted cream. Bring to a boil over medium heat, then add the rice, turn the heat up and bring back to a boil. Boil for 5 minutes, then reduce the heat and simmer for 15 minutes. Remove from the heat and rest for 10 minutes.

To make the sauce:
Heat the butter in a small saucepan over medium heat, add the grape molasses and ground cinnamon and cook for 1 minute, mixing continuously.

Stir the *lor* into the pilaf, then transfer to serving plates. Pour over the sauce and serve.

V

STEAMED LAMB AND RICE PILAF
SUSUZ PİLAV

Region:		İstanbul, all regions
Preparation time:		25 minutes, plus 1 hour soaking
Cooking time:		30 minutes, plus 10 minutes resting
Serves:		4

300 g	medium-grain rice	1½ cups/11 oz
2½ tsp	salt	2½ tsp
2 tbsp	mastic (plant resin)	2 tbsp
1 tsp	sugar	1 tsp
1 tsp	ground cinnamon	1 tsp
½ tsp	black pepper	½ tsp
3 (360 g)	medium onions, finely chopped	3 (2⅜ cups/ 12 oz)
60 ml	olive oil	¼ cup/2 fl oz
600 g	fatty lamb, diced	1 lb 5 oz

For the sealing dough:

6 tbsp	plain (all-purpose) flour	6 tbsp

The making of this pilaf requires a lot of care, cooked over very low heat with just meat juices and no additional water. You will need two cast-iron saucepans or casseroles (Dutch ovens) with lids: one about 25-cm (10-inches) in diameter; the other about 15-cm (6-inches) in diameter.

♦

Put the rice into a large bowl, add 2 teaspoons salt and pour over 1 litre (4¼ cups/34 fl oz) boiling water. Soak for 1 hour at room temperature. Drain and rinse the rice under cold running water, until the water runs clear. Drain the rice in a colander for 5 minutes.

Pound the mastic with the sugar in a mortar and pestle.

To make the sealing dough:
In a separate bowl, work the flour and 2 tablespoons water to a soft dough and roll out to a long sausage shape.

Mix the mastic, ground cinnamon, black pepper, the remaining ½ teaspoon salt, onions, olive oil and lamb for 5 minutes in a bowl.

Put the smaller of the two cast-iron pans or casseroles (Dutch ovens) inside the larger one and pour 1 litre (4¼ cups/34 fl oz) water into the smaller vessel. Arrange the lamb mixture in the larger pan, around the outside of the smaller pan, and then arrange the rice likewise. Put the lid on the larger pan and seal with the dough, making sure it is completely airtight. Simmer over low heat for 1½ hours.

Remove the lid and the smaller pan. Stir, then cover again and let rest for 10 minutes. Transfer to plates and serve.

♦

RICE WITH MEAT STOCK
SÜZME PİLAV

Region:		Van, all regions
Preparation time:		5 minutes
Cooking time:		25 minutes, plus 15 minutes resting
Serves:		4

1 tsp	salt	1 tsp
400 g	medium-grain rice, washed	2 cups/ 14 oz
200 ml	meat stock (see p.489)	scant 1 cup/ 7 fl oz
100 g	ghee (see p.485)	scant ½ cup/3½ oz

This is a basic pilaf made all over the country.

♦

In a large saucepan, bring 3 litres (12 cups/100 fl oz) water and the salt to a boil over medium heat. Add the rice, bring back to a boil and cook, uncovered, for 12 minutes. Drain the rice and add back to the empty pan. Pour over the meat stock, bring to a simmer and cook over very low heat for 5 minutes.

Meanwhile, heat the ghee in a small saucepan over medium heat.

Pour the hot ghee into the cooked rice and stir gently. Remove from the heat, tightly cover the pan with a dish towel, then seal tight with the pan lid. Wrap the entire pan in another dish towel and let rest for 15 minutes. Unwrap, stir gently and serve.

RICE PILAF WITH CHICKPEAS AND RAISINS
ALATLI PİLAV

Region:		Sivas, Central Anatolia
Preparation time:		15 minutes, plus 1 hour soaking
Cooking time:		55 minutes, plus 20 minutes resting
Serves:		4

400 g	medium-grain rice, washed	2 cups/ 14 oz
2½ tsp	salt	2½ tsp
100 g	ghee (see p.485)	scant ½ cup/ 3½ oz
400 g	lamb shoulder, (medium fat) diced into 1-cm (½-inch) cubes	14 oz
2 (240 g)	medium onions, finely sliced	2 (1⅝ cups/ 8½ oz)
80 g	split chickpeas (chana dal)	½ cup/3 oz
100 g	large raisins	¾ cup/3½ oz
1	cinnamon stick	1
10	black peppercorns	10
½ tsp	salt	½ tsp

p.309

This recipe is popular in Divriği. It is a dish for special occasions, which is made in large copper cauldrons.

If split chickpeas (chana dal) are unavailable, use the same amount of chickpeas (garbanzo beans), soaked overnight, then drained and peeled.

♦

Put the rice into a large bowl, add 2 teaspoons salt and pour over 1 litre (4¼ cups/34 fl oz) boiling water. Soak for 1 hour at room temperature. Drain and rinse the rice under cold running water, until the water runs clear. Drain the rice in a colander for 5 minutes.

Heat the ghee in a large saucepan over medium heat, then increase the heat to high, add the lamb and sauté for 10 minutes, stirring occasionally. Add the onions and sauté for another 10 minutes. Reduce the heat to medium, add the split chickpeas (chana dal), raisins, cinnamon stick, black peppercorns and remaining ½ teaspoon salt, along with 850 ml (3½ cups/28 fl oz) boiling water and cook, covered, for 15 minutes. Add the rice and bring to the boil over high heat, uncovered, for 5 minutes. Reduce the heat, cover again, and cook for a final 10 minutes.

Remove from the heat, tightly cover the pan with a dish towel, then seal tight with the pan lid. Wrap the entire pan in another dish towel and let rest for 20 minutes. Unwrap the pilaf, stir gently and serve.

♦

PLAIN RICE PILAF
ADİ PİLAV

Region:		İstanbul, all regions
Preparation time:		10 minutes, plus 1 hour soaking
Cooking time:		25 minutes, plus 20 minutes resting
Serves:		4

400 g	medium grain rice	2 cups/14 oz
2½ tsp	salt	2½ tsp
100 g	ghee (see p.485)	scant ½ cup/ 3½ oz

Some serve this pilaf with a sprinkling of black pepper, and some use chicken or meat stock instead of water. *Salma* is the name of this technique. Another technique involves frying the drained rice in hot oil for 10 minutes, mixing continuously. Hot water is added and the dish is finished off by simmering over low heat.

♦

Put the rice into a large bowl, add 2 teaspoons salt and pour over 1 litre (4¼ cups/34 fl oz) boiling water. Soak for 1 hour at room temperature. Drain and rinse the rice under cold running water, until the water runs clear. Drain the rice in a colander for 5 minutes.

In a large saucepan, combine 750 ml (3 cups/25 fl oz) hot water with the rice and remaining ½ teaspoon salt and cook over medium heat, covered, for 20 minutes.

Heat the ghee in a small saucepan over medium heat. Pour the hot ghee into the rice and cook for 2 minutes. Remove from the heat, tightly cover the pan with a dish towel, then seal tight with the pan lid. Wrap the entire pan in another dish towel and let rest for 20 minutes. Unwrap the pilaf, stir gently and serve.

SULTAN'S RICE
HÜNKAR PİLAVI

Region:		İstanbul, all regions
Preparation time:		10 minutes, plus 1 hour soaking, plus overnight soaking
Cooking time:		50 minutes, plus 20 minutes resting
Serves:		4

400 g	medium grain rice	2 cups/14 oz
3 tsp	salt	3 tsp
70 g	pistachios	¾ cup/2¾ oz
100 g	ghee (see p.485)	scant ½ cup/3½ oz
400 g	lamb meat, diced	14 oz
½ tsp	ground cloves	½ tsp
½ tsp	ground cardamom	½ tsp
1 tsp	ground cinnamon	1 tsp
¼ tsp	ground black pepper	¼ tsp
50 g	currants, soaked overnight in 200 ml (scant 1 cup/7 fl oz) water	scant ½ cup/2 oz

This dish is a specialty that was made in the Sultan's palace and mansions in İstanbul in bygone days.

♦

Put the rice into a large bowl, add 2 teaspoons salt and pour over 1 litre (4¼ cups/34 fl oz) boiling water. Soak for 1 hour at room temperature. Drain and rinse the rice under cold running water, until the water runs clear. Drain the rice in a colander for 5 minutes.

Soak the pistachios in 400 ml (1⅔ cups/14 fl oz) boiling water for 10 minutes. Drain and let rest for 30 minutes, then peel.

Heat the ghee in a large over medium heat, add the lamb and sauté for 10 minutes, stirring occasionally. Add the pistachios and sauté for 5 minutes. Add the cloves, cardamom, cinnamon, black pepper, the remaining 1 teaspoon salt and 750 ml (3 cups/25 fl oz) boiling water and cook, covered, for 20 minutes. Increase the heat to high, add the rice and bring to the boil, covered, for about 5 minutes. Reduce the heat and simmer for a further 7 minutes.

Remove from the heat, add the currants, tightly cover the pan with a dish towel, then seal tight with the pan lid. Wrap the entire pan in another dish towel and let rest for 20 minutes. Unwrap the pilaf, stir gently and serve.

♦

RICE PILAF WITH PINE NUTS AND RAISINS
İÇ PİLAV

Region:		İstanbul, all regions
Preparation time:		15 minutes, plus 1 hour soaking, plus overnight soaking
Cooking time:		30 minutes, plus 20 minutes resting
Serves:		4

400 g	medium grain rice	2 cups/14 oz
2½ tsp	salt	2½ tsp
100 ml	olive oil	scant ½ cup/3½ fl oz
1 (120 g)	medium onion, finely chopped	1 (¾ cup/4 oz)
400 g	lamb liver, finely diced	14 oz
1 tbsp	toasted pine nuts	1 tbsp
½ tsp	ground allspice	½ tsp
1 tsp	ground cinnamon	1 tsp
¼ tsp	black pepper	¼ tsp
50 g	raisins, soaked overnight in 200 ml (scant 1 cup/7 fl oz) water	⅓ cup/2 oz

This is a versatile special occasion dish. Delicious by itself, it is also used as a stuffing for lamb, goat and game birds. The spring version includes suckling-lamb's liver. Home cooks and restaurants serve this with tzatziki.

♦

Put the rice into a large bowl, add 2 teaspoons salt and pour over 1 litre (4¼ cups/34 fl oz) boiling water. Soak for 1 hour at room temperature. Drain and rinse the rice under cold running water, until the water runs clear. Drain the rice in a colander for 5 minutes.

Heat the olive oil in a large saucepan over medium heat, add the onions and sauté for 3 minutes. Add the liver and sauté for 5 minutes. Add the pine nuts, allspice, cinnamon, black pepper and remaining ½ teaspoon salt, along with 700 ml (2¾ cups/23 fl oz) water, and cook for 5 minutes. Increase the heat, add the rice, cover and cook for a further 5 minutes. Then reduce the heat to low and cook for a final 7 minutes.

Remove from the heat, add the raisins, tightly cover the pan with a dish towel, then seal tight with the pan lid. Wrap the entire pan in another dish towel and let rest for 20 minutes. Unwrap the pilaf, stir gently and serve.

LAMB AND ALMOND RICE PILAF
KUZU ETLİ BADEMLİ PİLAV

Region:		Antalya, all regions
Preparation time:		30 minutes, plus 1 hour soaking
Cooking time:		40 minutes, plus 20 minutes resting
Serves:		4

300 g	medium-grain rice	1½ cups/11 oz
2¾ tsp	salt	2¾ tsp
80 g	ghee (see p.485)	⅓ cup/3 oz
300 g	lamb meat, diced	11 oz
120 g	almonds, soaked in boiling water for 30 minutes, drained and peeled	1 cup/4 oz
¼ tsp	orange zest	¼ tsp
½ tsp	ground cardamom	½ tsp
pinch	saffron	pinch
60 g	dried apricots, diced	⅓ cup/ 2¼ oz

❧ ◐

For centuries this dish has been made on special occasions by affluent city dwellers.

◆

Put the rice into a large bowl, add 2 teaspoons salt and pour over 1 litre (4¼ cups/34 fl oz) boiling water. Soak for 1 hour at room temperature. Drain and rinse the rice under cold running water, until the water runs clear. Drain the rice in a colander for 5 minutes.

Heat the ghee in a large saucepan over medium heat, add the lamb and sauté for 10 minutes, then add the almonds and sauté for 5 minutes. Add the orange zest, cardamom, saffron, remaining ¾ teaspoon salt and 600 ml (2½ cups/20 fl oz) hot water and bring to a boil for 5 minutes. Increase the heat, add the rice and cook, covered, for 5 minutes. Reduce the heat, add the dried apricots and cook, covered, for 10 minutes.

Remove from the heat, tightly cover the pan with a dish towel, then seal tight with the pan lid. Wrap the entire pan in another dish towel and let rest for 20 minutes. Unwrap the pilaf, stir gently and serve.

MUSSEL RICE PILAF
MİDYE SALMASI

Region:		İstanbul, Marmara Region
Preparation time:		15 minutes, plus 1 hour soaking
Cooking time:		40 minutes
Serves:		4

400 g	medium grain rice	2 cups/14 oz
2½ tsp	salt	2½ tsp
400 g	tomatoes, finely diced	2 cups/14 oz
½ tsp	black pepper	½ tsp
1 tsp	dried mint	1 tsp
½ tsp	ground ginger	½ tsp
40	medium mussels in shell, cleaned and de-bearded	40

For the sauce:		
100 ml	olive oil	scant ½ cup/ 3½ fl oz
1 (120 g)	medium onion, finely chopped	1 (¾ cup/ 4 oz)
1	green chilli (chile), finely chopped	1

💧 ❧ ◐

Black mussels are used in this popular dish, made extensively during September.

◆

Put the rice into a large bowl, add 2 teaspoons salt and pour over 1 litre (4¼ cups/34 fl oz) hot water. Soak for 1 hour at room temperature. Drain and rinse the rice under cold running water, until the water runs clear. Drain the rice in a colander for 5 minutes.

In a large saucepan over medium heat, bring 600 ml (2½ cups/20 fl oz) owater, the tomatoes, the remaining ½ teaspoon salt, black pepper, dried mint and ginger to a boil for 5 minutes. Increase the heat, add the rice and cook for 5 minutes. Reduce the heat, add the mussels and cook, covered, for a further 10 minutes. Discard any mussels that have not opened at this point.

To make the sauce:
Heat the olive oil in a large saucepan over medium heat, add the onions and sauté for 3 minutes. Add the chilli (chile) and sauté for a further 3 minutes.

Stir the sauce into the pilaf, remove from the heat, tightly cover the pan with a dish towel, then seal tight with the pan lid. Wrap the entire pan in another dish towel and let rest for 15 minutes. Unwrap the pilaf, stir gently and serve.

AUBERGINE RICE PILAF
PATLICANLI PİLAV

Region:	İzmir, Aegean Region	
Preparation time:	20 minutes, plus 1 hour soaking	
Cooking time:	30 minutes, plus 15 minutes resting	
Serves:		4

300 g	medium-grain rice	1½ cups/11 oz
4½ tsp	salt	4½ tsp
600 g	aubergines (eggplants), peeled in stripes	2⅜ cups/ 1 lb 5 oz
4 tbsp	mastic (plant resin)	4 tbsp
1 tsp	sugar	1 tsp
100 ml	olive oil	scant ½ cup/ 3½ fl oz
60 g	onion, finely chopped	⅜ cup/2¼ oz
¼ tsp	black pepper	¼ tsp
pinch	saffron	pinch

This dish is best made in August during the aubergine season.

♦

Put the rice into a bowl, add 2 teaspoons salt and pour over 1 litre (4¼ cups/34 fl oz) hot water. Soak for 1 hour at room temperature. Drain and rinse under cold running water, until it runs clear. Drain in a colander for 5 minutes.

Meanwhile, soak the aubergines (eggplants) in 1.5 litres (6¼ cups/50 fl oz) water with 2 teaspoons salt for 15 minutes. Drain, rinse, squeeze out excess water and dry with paper towels. Dice into 1-cm (½-inch) pieces and set aside.

Pound the mastic with the sugar in a mortar and pestle and set aside.

Heat the olive oil in a saucepan over medium heat, add the onions and sauté for 3 minutes. Add the aubergines and sauté for 6 minutes. Add 500 ml (generous 2 cups/ 17 fl oz) boiling water, the mastic mixture, black pepper, saffron and the remaining ½ teaspoon of salt and cook for 3 minutes. Increase the heat, add the rice and cook for 5 minutes. Reduce the heat and cook for a final 10 minutes.

Remove from the heat, tightly cover the pan with a dish towel, then seal tight with the pan lid. Wrap the entire pan in another dish towel and let rest for 15 minutes. Unwrap the pilaf, stir gently and serve.

♦

FINE BULGUR PILAF
SİMİT AŞI (İNCE BULGUR PİLAVI)

Region:	Gaziantep, Southeastern Anatolia	
Preparation time:		10 minutes
Cooking time:		25 minutes
Serves:		4

100 g	ghee (see p.485)	scant ½ cup/ 3½ oz
1 (120 g)	medium onion, finely sliced	1 (¾ cup/4 oz)
2 tbsp	tomato paste (see p.492)	2 tbsp
2 tsp	red bell pepper paste (see p.492)	2 tsp
1 tsp	dried chilli (red pepper) flakes	1 tsp
200 g	kavurma (lamb confit, see p.497)	7 oz
½ tsp	salt	½ tsp
300 g	fine bulgur wheat	1⅓ cups/11 oz
¼ tsp	black pepper	¼ tsp

The preparation of this dish takes next to no time, so it is popular in Ramadan during *sahur*, the meal eaten just before the sun rises.

♦

Heat the ghee in a large saucepan over medium heat, add the onions and sauté for 2 minutes. Add the tomato paste, red bell pepper paste and dried chilli (red pepper) flakes and sauté for 3 minutes, then add the lamb confit and sauté for 5 minutes. Add the salt, pour in 1 litre (4¼ cups/34 fl oz) hot water, bring to the boil and cook for 5 minutes. Reduce the heat and add the bulgur wheat and black pepper. Cook, uncovered, for 7 minutes, until it becomes mushy. Serve immediately.

SWEET CARP RICE PILAF
ŞİRANİ PİLAV

Region:		Kars, Eastern Anatolia
Preparation time:		30 minutes, plus overnight soaking, plus 1 hour soaking
Cooking time:	1 hour 20 minutes, plus 10 minutes resting	
Serves:		4

60 g	chickpeas (garbanzo beans), soaked in water overnight, drained	⅓ cup/2¼ oz
300 g	medium-grain rice	1½ cups/11 oz
3½ tsp	salt	3½ tsp
400 g	carp fillet, diced into 2-cm (¾-inch) pieces	14 oz
60 ml	apple cider vinegar	¼ cup/2 fl oz
60 g	sultanas (golden raisins)	scant ½ cup/ 2¼ oz
100 ml	olive oil	scant ½ cup/ 3½ fl oz
1	cinnamon stick	1
½ tsp	ground turmeric	½ tsp
3	fennel seeds	3
2 tbsp	grape molasses	2 tbsp

◈ ❧

This sweet summer dish is traditionally eaten communally outdoors after the harvest. This dish is also popular when a suitor visits a young woman's family home to ask for her hand in marriage. It is known as *şirinleme* in some regions.

◆

Cook the drained chickpeas (garbanzo beans) in a saucepan of simmering water for 1 hour until soft. Drain and let cool a little, then peel the chickpeas. Set aside.

Meanwhile, put the rice into a large bowl, add 2 teaspoons of the salt and pour over 1 litre (4¼ cups/34 fl oz) hot water. Soak for 1 hour at room temperature. Drain and rinse the rice under cold running water, until the water runs clear. Drain the rice in a colander for 5 minutes.

Meanwhile, put the carp to soak in 3 litres (12 cups/100 fl oz) cold water with 1 teaspoon of salt and the apple cider vinegar. Soak for 1 hour, then drain and rinse. At the same time, put the sultanas (golden raisins) in a bowl with 200 ml (scant 1 cup/7 fl oz) water to soak for 1 hour.

Heat the olive oil in a large saucepan over medium heat. Add the carp and sauté for 2 minutes on each side, turning continuously. Drain the sultanas. Reduce the heat, add the sultanas, rice, chickpeas, cinnamon, turmeric, fennel seeds and remaining ½ teaspoon of salt, along with 550 ml (2½ cups/18 fl oz) hot water and cook, covered, for 10 minutes. Add the grape molasses and cook for another 3 minutes.

Remove from the heat, tightly cover the pan with a dish towel, then seal tight with the pan lid. Wrap the entire pan in another dish towel and let rest for 10 minutes. Unwrap the pilaf, stir gently and serve.

◆

BULGUR PILAF WITH CHESTNUTS
KESTANELİ BULGUR PİLAVI

Region:		Bursa, Marmara Region
Preparation time:		5 minutes
Cooking time:		25 minutes
Serves:		4

100 g	butter	½ cup/3½ oz
1 (120 g)	medium onion, finely sliced	1 (¾ cup/4 oz)
300 g	fine bulgur wheat	1⅓ cups/11 oz
500 g	chestnuts, peeled	1 lb 2 oz
½ tsp	salt	½ tsp

◗ V X ⬥

Ottoman archives state that this was the favourite dish of Mehmed the Conqueror, who conquered Constantinople (modern day İstanbul) in 1453. Made especially in the autumn, this dish is found in many special-occasion feasts.

◆

Heat the butter in a large saucepan over medium heat, add the onions and sauté for 3 minutes. Add the bulgur wheat, chestnuts and salt to the fried onions and sauté for a further 3 minutes. Reduce the heat, add 600 ml (2½ cups/20 fl oz) hot water and cook, covered, for 15 minutes. Let rest for 2 minutes, then gently stir and serve.

VEILED RICE PILAF
PERDE PİLAVI

Region:	Siirt, Southeastern Anatolia
Preparation time:	30 minutes, plus 1 hour soaking
Cooking time:	2 hours 55 minutes, plus 10 minutes resting
Serves:	4

300 g	medium-grain rice	1½ cups/11 oz
2½ tsp	salt	2½ tsp
2	partridges (not too lean)	2
2 (240 g)	medium onions, 1 quartered and 1 finely sliced	2 (1⅝ cups/ 4 oz)
120 g	butter	½ cup/4 oz
80 g	pine nuts, toasted	⅝ cup/3 oz
100 g	blanched almonds	¾ cup/3½ oz
½ tsp	black pepper	½ tsp
2 tsp	dried oregano	2 tsp
½ tsp	ground cardamom	½ tsp
100 g	currants, soaked in water for 1 hour, drained	¾ cup/3½ oz

For the pastry dough:

2	eggs	2
100 g	Greek yogurt	½ cup/3½ oz
¼ tsp	salt	¼ tsp
2 tbsp	olive oil	2 tbsp
150 g	plain (all-purpose) flour, plus extra for dusting	1 cup/5 oz
1 tsp	mahleb (cherry seed spice), crushed	1 tsp

p.315 📷

This dish is also known as 'wedding pilaf' and is offered to all guests. The almonds and pine nuts represent the husband and wife, the pastry the roof of the house, and the currants the children.

♦

Put the rice into a large bowl, add 2 teaspoons salt and pour over 1 litre (4¼ cups/34 fl oz) hot water. Soak for 1 hour at room temperature. Drain and rinse the rice under cold running water, until the water runs clear. Drain the rice in a colander for 5 minutes.

In a large saucepan, bring 2 litres (8½ cups/70 fl oz) water to the boil with the partridges and onion quarters and boil for 5 minutes. Reduce the heat and cook covered for 1 hour 45 minutes. Remove the cooked partridges from the pot, pull the meat off the bone and set aside in a bowl. Reserve the stock.

Heat 3 tablespoons of the butter in a large saucepan over medium heat, add the finely sliced onions and sauté for 3 minutes. Add the pine nuts and a third of the almonds and sauté for 3 minutes. Ladle 600 ml (2½ cups/20 fl oz) of the hot partridge stock into the pot and add the pulled partridge meat, black pepper, dried oregano, cardamom and remaining ½ teaspoon salt. Boil for 5 minutes. Increase the heat to high, add the rice and boil for 5 minutes, then reduce the heat and simmer for a further 10 minutes.

Remove from the heat and add the currants. Tightly cover the pan with a dish towel, then seal tight with the pan lid. Wrap the entire pan in another dish towel and let rest for 10 minutes.

To make the pastry dough:
Combine the eggs, yogurt, salt, olive oil, flour and mahleb in a large bowl and knead for 5 minutes. Divide the dough into quarters.

Preheat oven to 220°C/425°F/Gas Mark 7. Generously grease the bottom and sides of 4 souffle dishes or ramekins (about 9-cm/3½-inches in diameter) with the remaining butter. Use the remaining almonds to decorate the bottoms and sides of the dishes in diagonal lines.

On a lightly dusted work surface, roll out the pastry pieces to 33-cm (13-inch) diameter circles. Make sure the pastry is large enough to line the dishes with plenty left to hang over the edges. Line the dishes, aligning the middle of the circles with the middle of the dishes. Fill the dishes with the cooked rice and fold the pastry hanging down the sides back over the top of the pilaf. Cover with aluminium foil.

Bake in the hot oven for 30 minutes, then remove the foil and bake for another 5 minutes. Turn out onto plates making sure that the pastry remains intact.

BULGUR WITH LAMB'S LIVER
CİĞERLİ AŞ

Region:	Malatya, Eastern Anatolia	
Preparation time:	10 minutes	
Cooking time:	35 minutes	
Serves:	4	

80 g	butter	⅓ cup/3 oz
1 (120 g)	medium onion, finely sliced	1 (¾ cup/4 oz)
300 g	lamb liver, membrane removed, sinew trimmed, finely sliced	11 oz
225 g	coarse bulgur wheat	1 cup/ 8 oz
1 tsp	dried chilli (red pepper) flakes	1 tsp
¼ tsp	black pepper	¼ tsp
½ tsp	salt	½ tsp
½ bunch	flat-leaf parsley, finely sliced	½ bunch
4	fresh basil sprigs, finely sliced	4

Families who can afford it sacrifice sheep or lamb for *Eid-al-Adha* (the festival of the sacrifice). A portion of it is then cooked and distributed to neighbours and the poor. This is one of the popular dishes given away for charity. It can also be cooked into a kebab, but the pilaf is believed to bring abundance.

♦

Heat the butter in a large saucepan over medium heat, add the onions and sauté for 5 minutes, mixing continuously. Add the liver and sauté for 7 minutes, then add the bulgur wheat, dried chilli (red pepper) flakes, black pepper and salt and sauté for 5 minutes. Reduce the heat, add 500 ml (generous 2 cups/17 fl oz) hot water and cook, covered, for 15 minutes.

Sprinkle with parsley and fresh basil and serve immediately.

♦

SHEPHERD'S BULGUR
ÇOBAN AŞI

Region:	Ankara, Central Anatolia	
Preparation time:	10 minutes	
Cooking time:	35 minutes	
Serves:	4	

100 ml	olive oil	scant ½ cup/ 3½ fl oz
1 (120 g)	medium onion, finely chopped	1 (¾ cup/4 oz)
300 g	coarse bulgur wheat	1⅓ cups/11 oz
2	banana peppers (mild sweet peppers), finely diced	2
200 g	tomato, finely diced	1 cup/7 oz
100 g	potato, finely diced	½ cup/3½ oz
¼ tsp	black pepper	¼ tsp
½ tsp	salt	½ tsp
500 ml	milk (sheep's), hot	generous 2 cups/ 17 fl oz

This dish is made by the shepherd during his break with whatever he has at hand while he enjoys the green pastures. The ingredients show seasonal variations. *lor* (fresh curd cheese, see p.485), *kashk* (see p.485) and milk are popular and so is the plain bulgur pilaf. Originally a dish thrown-together by shepherds, it is now a culinary inspiration for home cooks.

♦

Heat the olive oil in a large saucepan over medium heat, add the onions and sauté for 5 minutes, mixing continuously. Add the bulgur wheat, banana peppers, tomato, potato, black pepper and salt and sauté for 5 minutes. Reduce the heat, add the hot milk and cook, partially covered, for 20 minutes. Transfer to plates and serve.

♦ V

BULGUR WRAPS
KARIN İÇİ (KARIN AŞI)

Region:		Hatay, Mediterranean Region
Preparation time:		10 minutes
Cooking time:		45 minutes
Serves:		4

4	crisp, thin white cabbage leaves, quartered	4
100 ml	olive oil	scant ½ cup/ 3½ fl oz
2 (240 g)	medium onions, finely chopped	2 (1⅝ cups/ 8½ oz)
4 tsp	red bell pepper paste (see p.492)	4 tsp
2 tbsp	tomato paste (see p.492)	2 tbsp
1 tsp	dried chilli (red pepper) flakes	1 tsp
½ tsp	ground cumin	½ tsp
½ tsp	salt	½ tsp
300 g	coarse bulgur wheat	1⅓ cups/11 oz

◗ ◗ V

This winter dish is eaten wrapped in cabbage leaves. Serve them on the side for everyone to use to scoop up the bulgur wheat.

◆

Bring 2 litres (8½ cups/70 fl oz) water to the boil in a saucepan, add the cabbage leaves and poach for 10 minutes, then drain and set aside.

Heat the olive oil in a large saucepan over medium heat, add the onions and sauté for 10 minutes, mixing continuously. Add the red bell pepper paste, tomato paste, dried chilli (red pepper) flakes, cumin and salt and sauté for 2 minutes, then add the bulgur and sauté for 5 minutes. Reduce the heat, add 500 ml (generous 2 cups/17 fl oz) hot water and cook, covered, for 15 minutes. Transfer to plates and serve with the cabbage leaves.

◆

POUNDED LAMB AND WHEAT
KEŞKEK

Region:		Muğla, all regions
Preparation time:		15 minutes, plus overnight soaking,
Cooking time:		2 hours 10 minutes
Serves:		4

150 g	cracked wheat, soaked overnight in water	1¼ cups/5 oz
50 g	chickpeas (garbanzo beans), soaked overnight in water	¼ cup/2 oz
500 g	lamb neck (on the bone)	1 lb 2 oz
60 g	onion, quartered	⅜ cup/2¼ oz
¼ tsp	black pepper	¼ tsp
½ tsp	salt	½ tsp
For the sauce:		
50 g	butter	¼ cup/2 oz
60 g	onion, finely chopped	⅜ cup/2¼ oz
60 g	walnuts, crushed	½ cup/2¼ oz
½ tsp	dried chilli (red pepper) flakes	½ tsp
½ tsp	ground sumac	½ tsp

This is a dish for weddings, funerals, celebrations of peace and other festive occasions and is made in the winter months. It is also known as *aşur, dövme, döğmeden, keşkah, harize* and *herseh*.

◆

Preheat oven to 160°C/325°F/Gas Mark 3.

In a large casserole dish (Dutch oven), combine the cracked wheat, chickpeas, lamb, onion quarters, black pepper and salt with 3 litres (12 cups/100 fl oz) water. Cover and cook in the hot oven for 2 hours. Pull the lamb meat away from the bone and discard the bone. Pound the lamb in the casserole dish with a pestle or the end of a wooden rolling pin for 15 minutes, until it is chewy.

To make the sauce:
Heat the butter in a sauté pan over medium heat, add the onions and walnuts and sauté for 3 minutes. Add the dried chilli (red pepper) flakes and sumac and sauté for another 2 minutes.

Transfer the dish to plates and serve topped with the sauce.

BULGUR WITH CUMIN AND CHILLI
KİMYONLU BİBERLİ AŞ

Region:		Hatay, Mediterranean Region
Preparation time:		10 minutes, plus overnight soaking
Cooking time:		1½ hours for the chickpeas, plus 35 minutes
Serves:		4

100 g	chickpeas (garbanzo beans), soaked overnight	½ cup/3½ oz
100 ml	olive oil	scant ½ cup/ 3½ fl oz
2 (240 g)	medium onions, finely chopped	2 (1⅝ cups/ 8½ oz)
2	hot red chillies (chiles), washed in hot water, seeded and crushed in a mortar and pestle	2
300 g	coarse bulgur wheat	1⅓ cups/11 oz
2½ tsp	ground cumin	2½ tsp
½ tsp	salt	½ tsp
1	Ayran (Salted Yogurt Drink, see p.452), to serve	1

This dish is a specialty of the Turkmen families in the region, who almost always have some chickpeas cooking away on the stove. This would be the go-to dish when an unexpected visitor appears out of the blue.

♦

Drain the soaked chickpeas (garbanzo beans), then cook in a saucepan of simmering water until soft, about 1½ hours. Drain, let cool, then shell. Set aside.

Heat the olive oil in a large saucepan over medium heat, add the onions and sauté for 10 minutes, mixing continuously. Add the crushed chillies (chiles) and sauté for 2 minutes, then add the bulgur wheat, cooked chickpeas, cumin and salt and sauté for 2 minutes. Reduce the heat, add 600 ml (2½ cups/20 fl oz) boiling water and cook, covered, for 15 minutes. Let rest, covered, for 5 minutes.

Serve with *Ayran*.

BULGUR WITH ORZO PASTA
ŞEHRİYELİ BULGUR PİLAVI

Region:		Mardin, all regions
Preparation time:		5 minutes
Cooking time:		25 minutes
Serves:		4

100 g	ghee (see p.485)	scant ½ cup/3½ oz
50 g	orzo pasta	½ cup/2 oz
300 g	coarse bulgur wheat	1⅓ cups/11 oz
¼ tsp	black pepper	¼ tsp
½ tsp	salt	½ tsp
875 ml	chicken stock (see p.489), hot	3½ cups/30 fl oz

This dish is made in Southeastern Anatolia especially in the spring. Popular with lamb dishes and yoghurt soup during *Nowruz* in March and April, this dish celebrates the arrival of spring.

♦

Heat the ghee in a large saucepan over medium heat, add the orzo pasta and sauté for 5 minutes, mixing continuously. Add the coarse bulgur wheat, black pepper and salt and sauté for a further 2 minutes. Reduce the heat, add the chicken stock and simmer, covered, for 10 minutes. Let rest, covered, for 5 minutes. Transfer to plates and serve.

HERB AND VEGETABLE BULGUR
KAPAMA AŞI

Region:	Gaziantep, Southeastern Anatolia	
Preparation time:		20 minutes
Cooking time:		35 minutes
Serves:		4

300 g	coarse bulgur wheat, washed	1⅓ cups/11 oz
200 g	mallow, finely chopped	7 oz
200 g	dock, finely chopped	7 oz
200 g	sorrel, finely chopped	7 oz
200 g	chicory, finely chopped	7 oz
300 g	fresh vine leaves, finely chopped	11 oz
1 tsp	dried chilli (red pepper) flakes	1 tsp
2 tsp	dried mint	2 tsp
200 ml	olive oil	1 cup/7 fl oz
1 (120 g)	medium onion, finely chopped	1 (¾ cup/4 oz)
6	garlic cloves, finely chopped	6
4 tsp	red bell pepper paste (see p.492)	4 tsp
2 tbsp	tomato paste (see p.492)	2 tbsp

⁝ ⬦ ⁚ V

This dish is made in Nizip and its surrounding areas in the spring. It works well with the first vine leaves of the season.

◆

Mix the bulgur wheat, mallow, dock, sorrel, chicory, vine leaves, dried chilli (red pepper) flakes and dried mint with ¼ teaspoon black pepper and ½ teaspoon salt in a large bowl for 5 minutes, until well combined. Set aside.

Heat half of the olive oil in a large saucepan over medium heat, add the onions and garlic and sauté for 5 minutes, mixing continuously. Add the red bell pepper paste and tomato paste and sauté for 2 minutes. Reduce the heat, add the bulgur mixture to the pan, drizzle with the remaining olive oil and cook, covered, for 20 minutes. Let rest, covered, for 5 minutes and serve.

◆

BULGUR PILAF WITH TOMATOES
DOMATESLİ AŞ

Region:	Hatay, Mediterranean Region, Southeastern Anatolia	
Preparation time:		10 minutes
Cooking time:		40 minutes
Serves:		4

100 ml	olive oil	½ cup/3½ fl oz
1 (120 g)	medium onion, finely chopped	1 (¾ cup/4 oz)
4	garlic cloves, quartered	4
2	green chillies (chiles), finely diced	2
2 tsp	red bell pepper paste (see p.492)	2 tsp
¼ tsp	black pepper	¼ tsp
1 tsp	dried chilli (red pepper) flakes	1 tsp
½ tsp	salt	½ tsp
1.2 kg	ripe tomatoes, finely diced	6 cups/2 lb 10 oz
300 g	fine bulgur wheat	1⅓ cups/11 oz

⁝ ⬦ ⁚ V

Sun-ripened tomatoes are at their best in August, and are the glorious stars of this dish. People in the region eagerly await the end of summer to taste this dish again.

◆

Heat the olive oil in a large saucepan over medium heat, add the onions and garlic and sauté for 5 minutes, mixing continuously. Add the green chillies (chiles) and sauté for 5 minutes. Add the red bell pepper paste, black pepper, dried chilli (red pepper) flakes and salt and sauté for 2 minutes. Add the tomatoes and cook for a further 10 minutes, mixing continuously. Reduce the heat, add the bulgur wheat and cook, covered, for a final 15 minutes.

BULGUR AND SPICED BEEF HOT POT
ÇÖMLEKTE PASTIRMALI PİLAV

Region:		Kastamonu, Black Sea Region
Preparation time:		10 minutes
Cooking time:		45 minutes
Serves:		4

100 ml	olive oil	scant ½ cup/ 3½ fl oz
400 g	potatoes, thinly sliced	14 oz
1 (120 g)	medium onion, finely sliced	1 (1¾ cups/4 oz)
700 ml	meat stock (see p.489)	2¾ cups/ 23 fl oz
½ tsp	salt	½ tsp
¼ tsp	black pepper	¼ tsp
200 g	*pastırma* (cured beef, see p.497), thinly sliced	7 oz
250 g	coarse bulgur wheat, washed	1⅛ cups/9 oz

This comforting winter is dish usually accompanied by *Ayran* (Salted Yogurt Drink, see p.452) and pickles.

♦

Preheat oven to 200°C/400°F/Gas Mark 6.

In a large saucepan, heat the olive oil over medium heat to 155°C/310°F. Place the potato slices into the hot oil and fry for 2 minutes on each side. Remove with a slotted spoon to a plate. Place the onion slices into the hot oil and fry for 5 minutes. Remove with a slotted spoon to a separate plate. Add the meat stock, salt and black pepper to the pan and cook for 5 minutes.

Layer the fried potato and *pastırma* slices in a casserole dish (Dutch oven). Make sure each slice half overlaps with the next. Sprinkle with the fried onions. Put the bulgur in the middle of the dish and top with the hot stock. Cover and bake in the hot oven for 20 minutes. Let rest for 5 minutes, then serve in the dish.

BULGUR PILAF
BULGUR PİLAVI

Region:		Sivas, all regions
Preparation time:		5 minutes
Cooking time:		20 minutes
Serves:		4

½ tsp	salt	½ tsp
300 g	coarse bulgur wheat	1⅓ cups/11 oz
100 g	butter	scant ½ cup/ 3½ oz

Some recipes add meat or chicken to bulgur pilaf. The water can be substituted with meat or chicken stock.

♦

In a large saucepan, bring 750 ml (3 cups/25 fl oz) water and the salt to a boil over medium heat. Reduce the heat, add the bulgur wheat and cook, covered, for 15 minutes.

Heat the butter in a separate pan until melted, then add to the cooked pilaf. Stir and serve.

♦ V X ⁘

BULGUR WITH MOREL MUSHROOMS
GÖBELEK AŞI

Region:	Çorum, Black Sea Region	
Preparation time:	10 minutes	
Cooking time:	30 minutes	
Serves:	4	

¾ tsp	salt	¾ tsp
300 g	coarse bulgur wheat	1⅓ cups/11 oz
100 g	butter	½ cup/3½ oz
1 (120 g)	medium onion, finely sliced	1 (1¾ cups/4 oz)
200 g	morel mushrooms, quartered	2⅔ cups/7 oz

V ⁘

Morel pickers cook these mushroom fresh for themselves and dry them on strings to sell. This spring delight is also enjoyed grilled and in soups.

♦

In a large saucepan, bring 600 ml (2½ cups/20 fl oz) water and the salt to a boil over medium heat. Reduce the heat, add the bulgur wheat and cook, covered, for 20 minutes.

Meanwhile, heat the butter in a large saucepan over medium heat, add the onion and sauté for 5 minutes. Add the mushrooms and sauté for 20 minutes, mixing continuously. Pour the sautéed mushrooms and any remaining butter into the cooked pilaf, stir to combine and serve.

♦

LENTIL BULGUR
HASPELİ (HASBELİ) AŞ

Region:	Şanlıurfa and Gaziantep, Southeastern Anatolia	
Preparation time:	5 minutes, plus 1 hour soaking	
Cooking time:	30 minutes	
Serves:	4	

100 g	unhulled red lentils, rinsed, soaked for 1 hour and drained	generous ½ cup/3½ oz
300 g	coarse bulgur wheat	1⅓ cups/11 oz
½ tsp	salt	½ tsp
100 ml	olive oil	scant ½ cup/3½ fl oz
2 (240 g)	medium onions, finely chopped	2 (1⅝ cups/8½ oz)
1 tbsp	tomato paste (see p.492)	1 tbsp
2 tsp	red bell pepper paste (see p.492)	2 tsp
¼ tsp	black pepper	¼ tsp

♦ ♦ V

At the beginning of autumn, village women go to the local river to wash their *kilims* (woven rugs). Once they are done, they trample upon dry leaves on the ground to get rid of their worries. They then make a fire out of the dried leaves and cook a pilaf. The ashes of the fire are tipped onto more leaves, a wish is made before the leaves float away on the river. This is an expression of gratitude for a summer well spent and a wish that the coming winter will be the same. Letting go of ashes signifies releasing negativity.

♦

In a large saucepan, bring 1.2 litres (5 cups/40 fl oz) water to the boil, add the lentils and simmer, covered, over medium heat for 20 minutes. When there is about 600 ml (2½ cups/20 fl oz) water left in the pan (if there is more water in the pan, discard the extra; if too little, add boiling water to make up the difference), add the bulgur wheat and salt and cook, covered, for a further 10 minutes, until all the water has been absorbed.

Meanwhile, heat the olive oil in a large saucepan over medium heat, add the onions and sauté for 5 minutes, mixing continuously. Add the tomato paste, red bell pepper paste and black pepper to the onions and sauté for 3 minutes. Gently mix this mixture into the pan with the lentils and bulgur wheat and cook, covered, for a further 10 minutes. Transfer to plates and serve.

POPPY SEED BULGUR
HAŞHAŞLI SARMA AŞI

Region:		Burdur, Mediterranean Region
Preparation time:		20 minutes
Cooking time:		25 minutes
Serves:		4

100 g	poppy seeds, roasted	¾ cup/3½ oz
1 (120 g)	medium onion, finely chopped	1 (¾ cup/4 oz)
70 g	walnuts, finely chopped	¾ cup/2¾ oz
300 g	coarse bulgur wheat, washed	1⅓ cups/11 oz
½ tsp	salt	½ tsp
100 g	goat's cheese, crumbled	½ cup/3½ oz
¼ tsp	dried mint	¼ tsp
½ bunch	flat-leaf parsley	½ bunch
20	fresh vine leaves, to serve	20

 V

This dish is made extensively in July and August after the poppy harvest.

◆

Put the roasted poppy seeds into a mortar and pestle and pound to extract their oils. Reserve both.

Heat the poppy seed oil in a large saucepan over medium heat, add the onion and sauté for 3 minutes, mixing continuously. Add the mashed poppy seeds and walnuts and sauté for 2 minutes. Reduce the heat, add the bulgur wheat and salt along with 600 ml (2½ cups/20 fl oz) boiling water and cook, covered, for 15 minutes Remove from the heat and let rest, covered, for 5 minutes.

Stir the goat's cheese, dried mint and parsley into the pilaf. Transfer to plates and serve with crisp, fresh vine leaves.

BULGUR WITH GOOSE MEAT
KAZ ETLİ BULGUR PİLAVI

Region:		Kars, Eastern Anatolia
Preparation time:		5 minutes
Cooking time:		1 hour 55 minutes
Serves:		4

2 (600 g)	goose drumsticks	2 (1 lb 5 oz)
1 (120 g)	medium onion, finely chopped	1 (¾ cup/4 oz)
4	garlic cloves, crushed	4
300 g	coarse bulgur wheat	1⅓ cups/11 oz
¼ tsp	black pepper	¼ tsp
½ tsp	ground turmeric	½ tsp
¾ tsp	salt	¾ tsp
60 g	goose fat	⅓ cup/2¼ oz

Goose is cut after the first snow of winter, salted and semi-dried before cooking. Goose is the trademark delicacy of the region enjoyed in many dishes. Goose farmers are usually female and are known as hard-headed women who rebel against the monotonous rural life in the region.

◆

In a large saucepan, bring 2 litres (8½ cups/70 fl oz) water to a boil over medium heat, add the goose drumsticks and onion and simmer, covered, for 1½ hours. Remove the drumsticks from the pan and measure the remaining water. If there is more than 600 ml (2½ cups/20 fl oz) water in the pan, discard the extra; if too little, add boiling water to make up the difference. Add the garlic, bulgur wheat, black pepper, turmeric and salt and cook, covered, for 10 minutes.

Meanwhile, pick the goose meat off the drumsticks.

Heat the goose fat in a saucepan over medium heat, add the goose meat and sauté for 5 minutes, mixing continuously.

Add the goose meat to the pan with the pilaf and cook, covered, for a further 5 minutes, without stirring. Let the pilaf rest for 5 minutes. Transfer to plates and serve.

BULGUR PILAF WITH LAMB
MEYHANE PİLAVI

Region:		Şanlıurfa, all regions
Preparation time:		15 minutes
Cooking time:		50 minutes
Serves:		4

120 g	ghee (see p.485)	½ cup/4 oz
1 (120 g)	medium onion, finely sliced	1 (¾ cup/4 oz)
200 g	carrot, finely diced	1½ cups/7 oz
4	garlic cloves, finely sliced	4
300 g	lamb, finely diced	11 oz
1½ tsp	tomato paste (see p.492)	1½ tsp
1 tsp	red bell pepper paste (see p.492)	1 tsp
1 tsp	dried chilli (red pepper) flakes	1 tsp
½ tsp	black pepper	½ tsp
½ tsp	salt	½ tsp
2 tbsp	lemon juice	2 tbsp
300 g	fine bulgur wheat	1⅓ cups/11 oz

This pilaf can also be made with rice in place of the bulgur wheat.

◆

Heat the ghee in a large saucepan over medium heat, add the onion, carrot and garlic and sauté for 5 minutes. Add the lamb and sauté for 10 minutes, then add the tomato paste, red bell pepper paste, dried chilli (red pepper) flakes, black pepper and salt and sauté for a further 2 minutes.

Pour in 750 ml (3 cups/25 fl oz) hot water and the lemon juice and bring to a boil. Boil for 10 minutes, then add the bulgur wheat and cook, covered, for 5 minutes, until it comes back to the boil. Reduce the heat and simmer, covered, for a further 10 minutes. Let the cooked pilaf rest for 5 minutes. Stir gently and serve.

BULGUR WITH EGGS
YUMURTALI AŞ

Region:	Gaziantep, Southeastern and Eastern Anatolia	
Preparation time:		5 minutes
Cooking time:		25 minutes
Serves:		4

2 tsp	salt	2 tsp
300 g	coarse bulgur wheat	1⅓ cups/11 oz
120 ml	olive oil	½ cup/4 fl oz
8	eggs	8

½ tsp	black pepper	½ tsp
8	spring onions (scallions)	8
1	*Ayran* (Salted Yogurt Drink, see p.452)	1

This dish is popular in rural areas. It is made in the spring, especially in Nizip and the surrounding areas. Chickens start laying eggs in the spring, increasing the popularity of egg dishes. People believe that eggs eaten in the spring will renew their cells. This dish is not made in warmer weather.

◆

In a large saucepan, bring 750 ml (3 cups/25 fl oz) water and ¾ teaspoon salt to a boil over medium heat. Reduce the heat, add the bulgur wheat and cook, covered, for 15 minutes. Let rest, covered, for 5 minutes.

Meanwhile, heat the olive oil in a sauté pan with a lid over medium heat. Crack the eggs into the hot oil, keeping the yolks intact and sprinkle with 1¼ teaspoons salt. Cover the pan and cook for 1 minute. Check to see whether the yolks have cooked, then cook for 1 further minute.

Stir the bulgur gently and transfer to serving plates. Top with the eggs, sprinkle with black pepper and serve with whole spring onions (scallions) and *ayran*.

MILK BULGUR
SÜTLÜ BULGUR AŞ

Region:		Tokat, Black Sea Region
Preparation time:		5 minutes
Cooking time:		25 minutes
Serves:		4

750 ml	milk	3 cups/25 fl oz
250 g	coarse bulgur wheat	1⅛ cups/9 oz
100 g	toasted almonds, crushed	¾ cup /3½ oz
¼ tsp	black pepper	¼ tsp
½ tsp	salt	½ tsp

Some recipes add butter or olive oil to this dish.

◆

In a large saucepan, heat the milk over medium heat. When hot, add the bulgur wheat, almonds, black pepper and salt and bring to a boil, stirring in the same direction all the while. Reduce the heat, add a metal spoon to the pan to prevent the milk boiling over and cook, partially covered, for 15 minutes. Let rest, covered, for 5 minutes. Transfer to plates and serve.

◆

RICE AND BULGUR MASH
LAPA

Region:		Ankara, all regions
Preparation time:		20 minutes
Cooking time:		55 minutes
Serves:		4

60 ml	olive oil	¼ cup/2 fl oz
1 (120 g)	medium onion, finely chopped	1 (¾ cup/4 oz)
2	garlic cloves, quartered	2
200 g	lamb shouider, finely chopped	7 oz
1	green bell pepper, finely chopped	1
1 kg	tomatoes, finely chopped	5 cups/2 lb 3 oz
2 tsp	red bell pepper paste (see p.492)	2 tsp
¼ tsp	black pepper	¼ tsp
1 tsp	dried chilli (red pepper) flakes	1 tsp
½ tsp	salt	½ tsp
100 g	medium grain rice, rinsed in cold water	½ cup/ 3½ oz
100 g	fine bulgur wheat	½ cup/3½ oz

4	dill sprigs, finely chopped	4
6	flat-leaf parsley sprigs, finely chopped	6

This mash is made in the autumn and winter. It is often made for the elderly, the unwell and the young. This dish needs to be eaten as soon as it is prepared. It is traditionally prepared right after prayers for rain.

◆

Heat the olive oil in a large saucepan over medium heat, add the onions and garlic and sauté for 3 minutes. Add the lamb and sauté for 10 minutes, then add the bell peppers, and sauté for 5 minutes. Add the tomatoes, red bell pepper paste, black pepper, dried chilli (red pepper) flakes and salt, along with 400 ml (1 ⅔ cups/14 fl oz) hot water, and cook uncovered for 5 minutes. Add the rice and cook for 10 minutes, then add the bulgur wheat and cook for 15 minutes, stirring occasionally, until the consistency reaches a mash.

Transfer to plates, sprinkle with dill and parsley and serve.

LENTIL MASH
MERCİMEK LAPASI

Region:	Gaziantep, Southeastern Anatolia	
Preparation time:	10 minutes	
Cooking time:	55 minutes	
Serves:	4	

200 g	red lentils, washed and drained	1 cup/7 oz
80 g	fine bulgur wheat	⅜ cup/3 oz
½ tsp	ground cumin	½ tsp
¼ tsp	black pepper	¼ tsp
½ tsp	salt	½ tsp
1 tbsp	dried basil	1 tbsp

For the sauce:		
100 ml	olive oil	scant ½ cup/ 3½ fl oz
2 (240 g)	medium onions, finely sliced	2 (1⅝ cups/ 8½ oz)
4	garlic cloves, crushed	4
1 tsp	dried chilli (red pepper) flakes	1 tsp

This dish is known as *mercimek lapası* in and around Nizip and as *malhutalı aş* in and around Hatay and Gaziantep. It is a winter dish that is enjoyed hot or cold, although the cold version is firmer in consistency.

♦

In a large saucepan, bring 2 litres (8½ cups/70 fl oz) water to a boil, reduce the heat to low, add the lentils and cook, covered, for 30 minutes. Combine well with a whisk, then add the bulgur wheat, cumin, black pepper and salt and cook for another 10 minutes, stirring occasionally, until the mixture turns into mash.

To make the sauce:
Heat the olive oil in a sauté pan over medium heat, add the onions and sauté for 10 minutes. Add the garlic and sauté for 1 minute, then add the dried chilli (red pepper) flakes and cook for another 10 seconds.

Stir the sauce into the lentil mash, sprinkle with dried basil and serve.

♦

POMEGRANATE MOLASSES, LAMB AND RICE PILAF
SİYAH DANE

Region:	İstanbul, all regions	
Preparation time:	10 minutes, plus 1 hour soaking	
Cooking time:	45 minutes, plus 10 minutes resting	
Serves:	4	

400 g	medium grain rice	2 cups/14 oz
2½ tsp	salt	2½ tsp
100 g	butter	½ cup/3½ oz
600 g	lamb shoulder, finely diced	1 lb 5 oz
60 g	onion, finely chopped	⅜ cup/2¼ oz
½ tsp	black pepper	½ tsp
2 tbsp	pomegranate molasses (see p.490)	2 tbsp

This dish is made in İstanbul, Southeastern Anatolia and the Eastern Mediterranean. Pomegranate molasses, fresh pomegranate seeds and dried pomegranate seeds all work well in this dish. It is known as 'sour pilaf' or 'pilaf with Hanar' in the region.

♦

Put the rice into a large bowl, add 2 teaspoons salt and pour over 1 litre (4¼ cups/34 fl oz) hot water. Soak for 1 hour at room temperature. Drain and rinse the rice under cold running water, until the water runs clear. Drain the rice in a colander for 5 minutes.

Heat the butter in a large saucepan over medium heat. Increase the heat, add the lamb and sauté for 15 minutes. Add the onion and sauté for 5 minutes. Add the black pepper and remaining ½ teaspoon salt along with 800 ml (3¼ cups/27 fl oz) boiling water and cook for 5 minutes. Add the rice and boil for 5 minutes, then cover with a lid, reduce the heat and simmer for 10 minutes.

Remove from the heat, tightly cover the pan with a dish towel, then seal tight with the pan lid. Wrap the entire pan in another dish towel and let rest for 10 minutes. Unwrap the pilaf, stir gently and serve.

FREEKEH PILAF
FİRİK BULGURU PİLAVI

Region:	Gaziantep, Mediterranean Region and Southeastern Anatolia	
Preparation time:	10 minutes, plus overnight soaking	
Cooking time:	1 hour 30 minutes	
Serves:	4	

1 (300 g)	turkey leg	1 (11 oz)
80 g	chickpeas (garbanzo beans), soaked overnight in water, drained and peeled	⅜ cup/3 oz
¾ tsp	salt	¾ tsp
150 g	freekeh	1 cup/5 oz
½ tsp	black pepper	½ tsp
70 g	ghee (see p.485)	⅓ cup/2¾ oz

 p.327

This is a dish for celebrations and special occasions such as weddings.

◆

In a large saucepan, bring 2 litres (8½ cups/70 fl oz) water to the boil, add the turkey leg, chickpeas (garbanzo beans) and ¼ teaspoon salt, reduce the heat to low and cook, covered, for 1 hour. Remove the turkey leg from the pan with a slotted spoon, pull the meat from the bone and shred.

Measure the remaining water in the pan. If there is more than 600 ml (2½ cups/20 fl oz) water in the pan, discard the extra; if too little, add boiling water to make up the difference. Add the freekeh and ¼ teaspoon black pepper and cook, covered, over low heat for 20 minutes. Let rest for 5 minutes.

Heat the ghee in a sauté pan over medium heat, add the pulled turkey meat and the remaining ½ teaspoon salt and sauté, mixing for 2 minutes. Serve the pilaf topped with the turkey and a sprinkling of the remaining ¼ teaspoon black pepper.

◆

LAMB AND CRACKED WHEAT
DÖVME AŞI

Region:	Şanlıurfa, Southeastern Anatolia	
Preparation time:	15 minutes, plus overnight soaking	
Cooking time:	1 hour 45 minutes	
Serves:	4	

200 g	cracked wheat	1⅔ cups/7 oz
80 g	chickpeas (garbanzo beans), soaked overnight	⅜ cup/3 oz
70 g	butter	⅓ cup/2¾ oz
2 (240 g)	medium onions, finely chopped	2 (1⅝ cups/8½ oz)
4	garlic cloves, finely chopped	4
300 g	lamb backstrap, finely chopped	11 oz
2 tsp	red bell pepper paste (see p.492)	2 tsp
1 tbsp	tomato paste (see p.492)	1 tbsp
1 tsp	dried chilli (red pepper) flakes	1 tsp
½ tsp	ground cumin	½ tsp
¼ tsp	black pepper	¼ tsp
½ tsp	salt	½ tsp

This winter dish is sometimes cooked with tomato paste. There is a plain as well as a spicy version. Start preparing the cracked wheat and chickpeas (garbanzo beans) the day before you plan to serve this dish.

◆

The day before, cook the cracked wheat in a saucepan of boiling water for 5 minutes. Remove the pan from the heat, cover and let rest overnight.

The next day, drain and cook the chickpeas (garbanzo beans) in a saucepan of simmering water for 1 hour until soft. Drain and let cool a little, then peel the chickpeas. Set aside.

Heat the butter in a large saucepan over medium heat, add the onions and garlic and sauté for 10 minutes, mixing continuously. Add the lamb and sauté for 10 minutes, then add the red bell pepper paste, tomato paste and dried chilli (red pepper) flakes and sauté for 3 minutes. Add the cracked wheat, chickpeas, cumin, black pepper and salt and sauté for 5 minutes, still mixing continuously. Reduce the heat, add 200 ml (scant 1 cup/7 fl oz) hot water and cook, covered, for 10 minutes. Transfer to plates and serve.

CRACKED WHEAT MASH
DÖVME ŞİLESİ

Region:		Van, Eastern Anatolia
Preparation time:		5 minutes
Cooking time:		20 minutes
Serves:		4

400 ml	tomato juice	1⅔ cups/14 fl oz
1 tbsp	ground basil	1 tbsp
½ tsp	salt	½ tsp
200 g	finely ground cracked wheat (or semolina)	1⅔ cups/7 oz

For the sauce:		
80 g	butter	⅓ cup/3 oz
100 g	walnuts, crushed	1 cup/3½ oz
2	garlic cloves, finely sliced	2
1 tsp	tomato paste (see p.492)	1 tsp
1 tsp	dried chilli (red pepper) flakes	1 tsp

This pilaf is usually eaten with salted or pickled fish and is made seasonally with vegetables, fruit, milk or rice.

◆

In a large saucepan, bring 400 ml (1⅔ cups/14 fl oz) water, the tomato juice, ground basil, salt and cracked wheat to a simmer and cook for 15 minutes, stirring continously in the same direction, until the mixture turns into mash.

To make the sauce:
Heat the butter in a sauté pan over medium heat, add the walnuts and sauté for 1 minute, then add the garlic and sauté for 10 seconds. Add the tomato paste and dried chilli (red pepper) flakes and cook for 1 minute, mixing continuously.

Transfer the mash to serving plates and make a hole in the middle of each. Pour the sauce into the holes and serve.

◆

WHITE BEAN AND WHEAT MASH
MIRDİK (KURU FASULYE) LAPASI

Region:		Erzincan, Eastern Anatolia
Preparation time:		15 minutes, plus overnight soaking
Cooking time:		20 minutes
Serves:		4

200 g	dried meat or *pastırma* (see p.497), pounded into strings	7 oz
250 g	dried cannellini beans, soaked overnight, peeled, mashed	1¼ cups/ 9 oz
50 g	fine cracked wheat	⅜ cup/2 oz
1	dried chilli (chile), crumbled	1
¼ tsp	black pepper	¼ tsp
½ tsp	salt	½ tsp
2 tsp	dried basil	2 tsp
2 tbsp	mulberry molasses	2 tbsp
100 g	butter	½ cup/3½ oz
60 g	walnuts, crushed	½ cup/2¼ oz

This dish is made in the winter months. Mırdik is the local name given to white beans in the region. It is known as a dish for the elderly especially because it is easy on the digestive system.

◆

In a large saucepan over medium heat, combine the dried meat, beans, cracked wheat, dried chilli (chile), black pepper and salt with 500 ml (generous 2 cups/17 fl oz) water, and mix together for 3 minutes. Reduce the heat and cook for 10 minutes, pounding the contents of the pot with a wooden pestle or the end of a rolling pin, and mixing continuously in the same direction. Add the dried basil and cook for another 2 minutes, until the mixture turns into mash.

Transfer to serving plates and flatten. Sprinkle over the mulberry molasses.

Heat the butter in a small saucepan over medium heat until hot. Drizzle the mash with the hot butter, sprinkle with crushed walnuts and serve immediately.

WHOLE WHEAT STEW
HEDİK

Region:		Gaziantep, all regions
Preparation time:		20 minutes, plus overnight soaking
Cooking time:		1½ hours
Serves:		4

150 g	whole wheat grain, soaked overnight in water, drained	1 cup/5 oz
80 g	chickpeas (garbanzo beans), soaked overnight in water, drained	⅜ cup/3 oz
100 g	shelled pistachios	1 cup/3½ oz
80 g	sour pomegranate seeds	1 cup/3 oz
80 g	blanched almonds	½ cup/3 oz
80 g	sultanas (golden raisins)	½ cup/3 oz
4	dried apricots, quartered	4
100 g	sugar-coated dried chickpeas	3½ oz
¼ tsp	ground fennel	¼ tsp
½ tsp	salt	½ tsp

♦ ♦ V

Hedik always appears at a celebration for the first tooth of a baby. Traditionally, the teething baby's family organizes an event where *hedik* is served and it is distributed to at least seven neighbours. Along with other rituals, a morsel of the *hedik* is placed on the baby's head. Some make *hedik* using 5 tablespoons of sugar instead of the sugared chickpeas (which are like sugared almonds) and some use no sugar at all.

♦

Cook the whole wheat grain in a saucepan with 1 litre (4¼ cups/34 fl oz) simmering water until soft, about 1½ hours. Drain.

Meanwhile, cook the drained chickpeas (garbanzo beans) in a separate saucepan of 1 litre (4¼ cups/34 fl oz) of simmering water for 1½ hours until soft. Drain and let cool a little, then peel the chickpeas.

In a large bowl, gently mix the wheat, chickpeas, pistachios, pomegranate seeds, almonds, sultanas (golden raisins), dried apricots, sugar-coated chickpeas, fennel and salt, until well combined. Transfer to plates and serve.

♦

YOGURT BULGUR WITH BUTTER SAUCE
GULUL

Region:		Hakkâri, Eastern Anatolia
Preparation time:		5 minutes
Cooking time:		40 minutes
Serves:		4

1 kg	Greek yogurt (sheep's milk)	5 cups/ 2 lb 3 oz
½ tsp	salt	½ tsp
200 g	fine bulgur wheat	⅞ cup/7 oz
60 ml	grape molasses	¼ cup/2 fl oz

For the sauce:		
140 g	butter	⅔ cup/4¾ oz
2 tbsp	plain (all-purpose) flour	2 tbsp

V

Gulul is served with the butter and molasses in the middle, either together or separately.

♦

In a large saucepan, whisk 400 ml (1⅔ cups/14 fl oz) water together with the yogurt and salt. Add the bulgur wheat and cook over low heat for 20 minutes, always stirring in the same direction, until it reaches the consistency of a thick mash.

To make the sauce:
Heat 3 tablespoons of the butter in a sauté pan over medium heat, add the flour and cook for 10 minutes, mixing continuously, making sure it doesn't burn. Transfer the roasted flour to a plate. In the same pan, heat the remaining butter for 1 minute.

Transfer the pilaf to serving plates and make a hole in the middle of each serving. Fill each with a little roasted flour, fried butter and molasses.

HOMEMADE NOODLES WITH KASHK
KEŞLİ ERİŞTE

Region:	Bolu, all regions
Preparation time:	5 minutes
Cooking time:	20 minutes
Serves:	4

250 g	homemade noodles (see p.493)	2¾ cups/ 9 oz
100 g	butter	½ cup/3½ oz
100 g	crushed walnuts	1 cup/3½ oz
100 g	*kashk* (see p.485), grated	3½ oz
4	flat-leaf parsley sprigs, finely sliced	4

V I ⁂   p.331 ◻

This rustic dish is made all over the country, all through the year, but it is especially popular around Bolu, Çankırı and Bartın.

♦

In a large saucepan, bring 3 litres (12 cups/100 fl oz) water to the boil over medium heat. Add the noodles and cook, covered, for 15 minutes.

Meanwhile, heat the butter in a frying pan (skillet) over medium heat, add the walnuts and sauté for 2 minutes. Add the dried curd and sauté for another 2 minutes.

Drain the cooked noodles and add to the pan with the sauce. Stir in the parsley and serve.

♦

HOMEMADE NOODLE PILAF WITH WOODCOCK
ERİŞTE PİLAVI (ÇULLUKLU)

Region:	Bingöl, all regions
Preparation time:	35 minutes
Cooking time:	1 hour
Serves:	4

250 g	homemade noodle dough (see p.493)	2¾ cups/ 9 oz
1 (1.5 kg)	woodcock (or turkey leg)	1 (3 lb 5 oz)
100 g	butter	½ cup/3½ oz
¼ tsp	black pepper	¼ tsp
½ tsp	salt	½ tsp

⁂

Throughout the autumn and winter, game birds, especially wild duck and woodcock, turn this pilaf into a great main course. This dish goes really well with lamb confit.

♦

Roll the homemade noodle dough out to a 40-cm (16-inch) square. Cut it into 2.5-cm (1-inch) strips and let dry for 30 minutes.

Meanwhile, put the woodcock or turkey into a pressure cooker with 1.5 litres (6¼ cups/50 fl oz) water and cook for 30 minutes. Remove and pick the meat from the bones. Reserve the stock.

Heat the butter in a large saucepan with a lid over medium heat, add the noodles and sauté gently for 15 minutes until they brown. Add the picked meat, the reserved stock, black pepper and salt and cook, covered, for 15 minutes. Transfer to plates and serve.

HOMEMADE COUSCOUS WITH CURED BEEF
KUSKUS PİLAVI (ERİŞTE KUSKUSU)

Region:		Niğde, Central Anatolia
Preparation time:		15 minutes
Cooking time:		20 minutes
Serves:		4

¾ tsp	salt	¾ tsp
300 g	couscous made from homemade noodles (see p.493)	4¼ cups/ 11 oz
80 g	butter	⅓ cup/3 oz
60 g	onion, finely chopped	⅜ cup/2¼ oz
4	garlic cloves, finely chopped	4
1	green chilli (chile), finely chopped	1
100 g	*pastırma* (cured beef, see p.497), finely chopped	3½ oz
300 g	tomatoes, finely chopped	1½ cups/11 oz
1 tsp	dried chilli (red pepper) flakes	1 tsp
4	flat-leaf parsley sprigs, finely chopped	4

This dish is known all over the country but particularly well loved in the Central Anatolia and Marmara regions.
◆
In a large saucepan, bring 2 litres (8½ cups/70 fl oz) water and ¼ teaspoon salt to a boil over medium heat. Once the water boils, add the noodle couscous and cook, covered, for 7 minutes.

Meanwhile, heat the butter in a large saucepan over medium heat. Add the onion, garlic and chilli (chile) and sauté for 3 minutes, mixing continuously. Add the *pastırma* and sauté for 2 minutes. Add the tomatoes, dried chilli (red pepper) flakes and remaining ½ teaspoon salt and cook for 10 minutes, mixing continuously.

Drain the couscous and serve with the sauce, garnished with the parsley.

p.333 ◻

◆

COUSCOUS WITH CHEESE
PEYNİRLİ KUSKUS PİLAVI

Region:		Çankırı, all regions
Preparation time:		10 minutes
Cooking time:		25 minutes
Serves:		4

¼ tsp	salt	¼ tsp
300 g	couscous (see p.495)	11 oz
100 g	butter	½ cup/3½ oz
80 g	walnuts, crushed	¾ cup/3 oz
150 g	fresh cheese (sheep's milk), crumbled	⅔ cup/ 5 oz
¼ tsp	black pepper	¼ tsp
6	flat-leaf parsley sprigs, finely chopped	6

V

This dish is traditionally shared from the middle of a communal table. Couscous pilaf is also made with *kashk* (see p.485), Greek yogurt, tomatoes, chillies (chiles) or spinach instead of cheese.
◆
In a large saucepan, bring 3 litres (12 cups/100 fl oz) water and the salt to a boil over medium heat. Once the water boils, add the couscous, reduce the heat and cook uncovered for 15 minutes. Drain and set aside in a bowl.

Heat the butter in a small saucepan over medium heat. Add the walnuts and sauté for 2 minutes, mixing continuously.

Add the walnut sauce to the drained couscous and stir gently. Add the cheese and black pepper, stir again and then add the parsley. Give a final stir, transfer to plates and serve.

♦

BREADS
&
PASTRIES

♦

TURKISH DOUGH CULTURE

Dough-based dishes are cherished and revered nationwide. Without them we would be incomplete – eating pilaf or homemade noodles with bread is endemic to our culture. Breads, pastries and pasta dishes that are baked in the oven, fried or poached are so numerous in the Turkish kitchen as to be almost endless. Every seasonal green creates a new recipe.

Açik Ekmek (Ridged Bread, see p.394), *Bazlama* (see p.394) and *Yufka Ekmeği* (Thin Flatbread, see p.378) are the first breads that spring to mind and accompany most meals. Filled flatbreads, such as *lahmacun* and *pide*, and filled pastries, such as *börek*, are substantial enough to be eaten on their own, accompanied by a drink on the side. Traditionally, local cooks prepare their own fillings for such dishes and take them to be baked at the bakery for a small fee. The depth of flavour that the bakery's wood-fired oven adds to a dish is something else.

DOUGH TECHNIQUES AND INGREDIENTS

I recommend using wholemeal (whole wheat) flour for these recipes. Unlike white flour, the nutritious bran and wheatgerm are not removed from wholemeal flour. You can of course use different types of flour for different recipes. Strong flour, for instance, will increase your success rate in recipes such as *Mantı* (Dumplings, see p.386) and *Erişte* (Homemade Noodles, see p.493).

I always use fresh yeast as a raising agent, but quantities for dried active yeast have also been given. If patience is your forte, try using the *Ekşi Maya* (Sourdough Starter, see p.483). If using the sourdough starter, then 30 g/1 oz starter and 2 hours proving time is needed for every 100 g/ ¾ cup/3½ oz of flour. The *Kül Mayasi* (Ash Starter, see p.482) will work very well in cookies instead of bicarbonate of soda (baking soda). Use 2 teaspoons of ash water for every 100 g/¾ cup/3½ oz of flour. You can use the *Nohut Mayasi* (Chickpea Starter, see p.482) for *Simit* (Sesame Bagels, see p.370). The ratio is 2 tablespoons of chickpea starter for every 100 g/¾ cup/3½ oz of flour. The recipes for the starters are in the Pantry chapter (see pp.482–483).

The most revered of our loaves of bread are sourdough varieties, baked in wood-fired ovens. The wood-fired oven also transforms *lahmacun*, flatbreads and *börek* from good to delicious. If you are lucky enough to have a wood-fired oven, always remember to preheat it before you bake bread. Oak or hornbeam are the best woods for baking. The baking times and temperatures in the recipes are all for standard ovens.

However, baking times vary, so always check on your bake every 10–15 minutes. Wood-fired ovens cook far more quickly than standard domestic ovens.

◆

DOUGH
RITUALS

Most of our pastries are full of cultural meaning, with rituals and stories attached to them. Weddings, funerals, religious festivals, celebrations are all adorned by these dishes.

One such ritual accompanies the *Hıdrellez* festivities, which celebrate the arrival of spring. Unleavened bread made with water and salt is covered with a dish towel and placed outside overnight. Bread is made from this dough the following day. If the bread is good, it is believed that *Hıdır* and *İlyas* have passed through and stopped at that house. A little bit of the dough is kept as starter for future loaves. This starter is believed to bring peace, health and good fortune and everyone wants some. Giving some away to the neighbours is at the owner's discretion. If the person asking for the starter is a good person, it is believed that the starter will thrive in their house. If the neighbour in question is an insidious, evil person, the starter will go off. And the owner of the starter must beware of the 'evil eye' issue. If someone badly wants a piece of the starter and is denied it, then this will bring bad luck to the owner. This widespread belief is still going strong, especially in the countryside of the Marmara Region.

The festivities of Easter, *Nowruz* and *Hıdrellez* are very close to one another in the calendar. As the Turks and Muslims celebrate *Hıdırellez*, the Armenian, Ottoman Greek and Assyrian Christians celebrate Easter, and Kurds and the Azeri celebrate *Nowruz*. This is when the *Paskalya Çöreği* (Easter Brioche, see p.360) and *İkliçe* (Mardin Cakes, see p.360) are made, with a coin hidden inside them. A wonderful, prosperous year awaits the finder of the coin. In Central Anatolia, they have the same ritual for *Kete* or *Sivas* (Kete Rolls, see p.367). And in Southeastern and Eastern Anatolia, *Kete* are made for *Nowruz* (New Year) in the hope that they will bring prosperity as nature and all living things reawaken. The fact that all of these different faiths are following similar rituals around food at the same time shows the richness and diversity of Turkish culture, which should be embraced and treasured.

BREAD AND CHICKPEA STEW
ÇÖREK AŞI

Region:	Hatay, Mediterranean Region
Preparation time:	20 minutes, plus overnight soaking
Cooking time:	1 hour 35 minutes
Serves:	4

100 g	chickpeas (garbanzo beans) soaked overnight	½ cup/ 3½ oz
100 ml	olive oil	scant ½ cup/3½ fl oz
1 (120 g)	medium onion	1 (¾ cup/4 oz)
3	banana peppers, finely diced	3
4	garlic cloves, quartered	4
2 tsp	red bell pepper paste (see p.492)	2 tsp
2 tsp	tomato paste (see p.492)	2 tsp
2 tsp	dried chilli (red pepper) flakes	2 tsp
600 g	tomatoes, finely diced	3 cup/1 lb 5 oz
1 tsp	ground cumin	1 tsp
250 g	dried stale bread	9 oz
4	flat-leaf parsley sprigs	4

💧 ◆ V p.341 📷

This is a go-to dish for when a lot of stale bread accumulates in the house. The stale bread is diced and dried at room temperature.

◆

Drain the chickpeas (garbanzo beans) and cook in a saucepan of simmering water for 1 hour until soft. Drain and let cool a little, then peel the chickpeas. Set aside.

Heat 5 tablespoons of the oil in a saucepan over medium heat. Finely dice the onion and sauté for 5 minutes, mixing continuously. Add the banana peppers and garlic. Sauté for 3 minutes, then add the chickpeas, red bell pepper paste, tomato paste and dried chilli (red pepper) flakes and sauté for another 3 minutes. Add the tomatoes and sauté for 5 minutes, mixing continuously. Reduce the heat, stir in the cumin, ¼ teaspoon black pepper and ½ teaspoon salt, cover and cook for 10 minutes.

Dice the dried stale bread into 1-cm (½-inch) cubes, add on top and cook, covered, for a further 5 minutes. Add the remaining 2 tablespoons of olive oil and cook, uncovered, for a final 2 minutes. Remove from the heat, transfer to plates and serve with a sprinkle of finely sliced parsley.

◆

BREAD 'MEATBALLS'
PİSİK KÖFTESİ

Region:	Şanlıurfa, Southeastern Anatolia
Preparation time:	20 minutes
Serves:	4

600 g	tomatoes	1 lb 5 oz
1 (120 g)	medium onion	1 (¾ cup/4 oz)
4	banana peppers (mild sweet peppers)	4
6	flat-leaf parsley sprigs	6
2	fresh basil sprigs	2
2	dried *Yufka Ekmeği* (Thin Flatbread, see p.378, or 300 g/11 oz stale bread), crumbled	2
100 g	fresh sheep's milk cheese (unsalted), crumbled	3½ oz
1½ tbsp	dried chilli (red pepper) flakes	1½ tbsp
2 tsp	dried mint	2 tsp
2 tsp	tomato paste (see p.492)	2 tsp
1 bunch	cress	1 bunch
8	lettuce hearts, halved	8

🌱 ◆ V ✗

This dish is made especially in the summer months to cool off. There is also a plain version, which is known as *Pisik Ovmacı* in Gaziantep and Adıyaman.

◆

Finely slice the tomatoes, onion, banana peppers, parsley and basil. Combine with the dried *yufka*, cheese, dried chilli (red pepper) flakes, dried mint, tomato paste, ¼ teaspoon black pepper and ½ teaspoon salt in a large bowl for 5 minutes, kneading gently. Divide the mixture into 12 equal parts and squeeze each piece into a ball shape with your fingers.

Serve on a bed of cress and lettuce hearts.

FRIED PASTIES
ÇİĞ BÖREK

Region:		Eskişehir, Central Anatolia
Preparation time:		30 minutes, plus 35 minutes resting
Cooking time:		20 minutes
Serves:		4

For the pastry:

250 g	plain (all-purpose) flour	2 cups/9 oz
1	egg	1
40 g	Greek yogurt	scant ¼ cup/1½ oz
2 tbsp	olive oil	2 tbsp
1 tbsp	grape vinegar	1 tbsp
1 litre	olive oil	4¼ cups/34 fl oz

For the filling:

320 g	veal brisket and shoulder, coarsely minced (ground)	11¼ oz
2 (240 g)	medium onions	2 (1⅝ cups/8½ oz)
2 tbsp	grape vinegar	2 tbsp
½ tsp	black pepper	½ tsp
100 ml	tomato juice	½ cup/3½ fl oz
4	flat-leaf parsley sprigs	4

This trademark dish of Crimean Tatars is known as *çi börek*.

♦

To make the pastry:
Combine the flour and ½ teaspoon salt in a bowl. Make a well and add the egg, yogurt, oil and vinegar with 2 tablespoons water. Gently mix until a dough forms. Cover with a damp dish towel and rest for 20 minutes.

Divide the dough into 8 equal parts. Dip your hand in olive oil, lightly coat the pieces of dough and let prove for another 15 minutes.

To make the filling:
Finely slice the onions and parsley. Combine all the filling ingredients in a large bowl with ½ teaspoon salt. Mix for 3 minutes, until well combined.

On an oiled work counter, use an oiled rolling pin to roll out each piece of dough to a 15-cm (6-inch) disc.

Divide the filling among the pastry discs: spread the filling on one half of the circle and fold over the other to enclose, then press on the edges with your fingertips to seal.

In a saucepan, heat the remaining olive oil over medium heat to 155°C/310°F. Working in batches of 2, fry the pastries in the hot oil for 3 minutes, turning occasionally. Remove with a slotted spoon and serve immediately.

FRIED FILO CHEESE ROLLS
SİGARA BÖREĞİ

Region:		Tekirdağ, all regions
Preparation time:		20 minutes
Cooking time:		20 minutes
Serves:		4

1 sheet	filo (phyllo) pastry (see p.496)	1 sheet
1	egg white	1
1 litre	olive oil	4¼ cups/34 fl oz

For the filling:

400 g	unsalted goat's cheese or *çökelek* (dry curd cottage cheese, see p.484)	4 cups/14 oz
3	spring onions (scallions)	3
1 bunch	flat-leaf parsley	1 bunch
½ bunch	dill	½ bunch
2 tsp	dried mint	2 tsp

This is a popular finger food for special occasions. Serve with a cup of *Çay* (Tea, see p.446).

♦

To make the filling:
Crumble the cheese or *çökelek* in a large bowl. Finely slice the spring onions (scallions), parsley and dill and add to the bowl with ¼ teaspoon black pepper and ½ teaspoon salt. Gently toss all the filling ingredients together. Divide the filling into 40 equal pieces.

Cut the filo (phyllo) pastry into 40 triangles. Put a triangular piece of filo pastry on the work counter. About 1 cm (½ inch) from the wider end, place a piece of the filling parallel to the edge. Roll the pastry towards the pointy end of the triangle, then fold in and seal the sides and the end with egg white. Repeat for all the pieces.

In a large saucepan, heat the olive oil over medium heat to 155°C/310°F. Working in batches, fry the pastries in the hot oil for 4 minutes. Remove with a slotted spoon and serve immediately.

♠ V

BREADS & PASTRIES

FRIED LAMB PASTIES
AĞZI AÇIK

Region:	Şanlıurfa, Southeastern Anatolia	
Preparation time:	30 minutes, plus 30 minutes resting	
Cooking time:		15 minutes
Serves:		4

For the pastry:

250 g	plain (all-purpose) flour	2 cups/9 oz
1	egg	1
50 g	Greek yogurt	¼ cup/2oz
3 tbsp	olive oil	3 tbsp
750 ml	olive oil	3 cups/25 fl oz

For the filling:

400 g	lean lamb, sinew removed, minced (ground)	14 oz
60 g	onion, finely sliced	⅜ cup/2¼ oz
2 tsp	isot (smoked dried chilli (red pepper) flakes)	2 tsp
1 tbsp	tomato paste (see p.492)	1 tbsp
2 tsp	red bell pepper paste (see p.492)	2 tsp
½ tsp	ground cloves	½ tsp
½ tsp	ground cinnamon	½ tsp
½ tsp	ground coriander	½ tsp
½ tsp	ground cumin	½ tsp
2 tbsp	pomegranate molasses	2 tbsp

These pasties are made on special occasions in the winter months. Another name for this dish is *ağzı yumuk*. Some prefer to fold the pastry in half like a crescent. This dish has several versions. In *ağzı yumuk*, the filling is completely enclosed in the pastry whereas in *ağzı açık* the filling is on top. There is a third version where the filling is enclosed but the pastry is crescent shaped.

◆

To make the pastry:
Combine the flour and ¼ teaspoon salt in a bowl. Make a well and add the egg, yogurt, 1 tablespoon olive oil and 3 tablespoons water. Knead for 5 minutes until a dough forms. Cover with a damp dish towel and rest for 20 minutes.

Divide the dough into 8 equal parts. Roll into balls and brush each with olive oil. Rest for a further 10 minutes.

To make the filling:
Combine all the filling ingredients in a large bowl with ½ teaspoon each of black pepper and salt. Mix for 3 minutes, until well combined. Divide the mixture into 8 equal parts.

On an oiled work counter, use an oiled rolling pin to roll out each piece of dough to a 8-cm (3-inch) disc.

Divide the filling among the pastry discs: leave a clear border of 1 cm (½ inch) all around. Fold the pastry edges inwards to enclose the edges of the filling.

In a saucepan, heat the remaining olive oil over medium heat to 155°C/310°F. Working in batches of 2, fry the pastries in the oil, filling side upwards, for 5 minutes, then place on paper towels to drain. Serve immediately.

◆

FRIED CHEESE AND SPICED BEEF ROLLS
PAÇANGA BÖREĞİ

Region:	İstanbul, Marmara Region	
Preparation time:		15 minutes
Cooking time:		10 minutes
Serves:		4

1	fresh *Yufka Ekmeği* (Thin Flatbread, see p.378)	1
1	egg white	1
200 ml	olive oil	scant 1 cup/7 oz

For the filling:

400 g	*pastırma* (cured beef, see p.497),	14 oz
400 g	*kaşer* (sheep's milk cheese)	14 oz

This is a traditional *meyhane* dish, served after the cold meze. Serve with a cup of *Çay* (Tea, see p.446).

◆

Cut the *yufka ekmeği* into 8 equal triangles and then cut the *pastırma* and *kaşer* cheese into 32 equal strips, each 3-mm (⅛-inch wide).

Put a triangular piece of *yufka ekmeği* on the work counter. About 2 cm (¾ inch) from the wider end, layer 2 strips of cheese, 4 strips of *pastırma*, then 2 more strips of *kaşer* cheese. Fold the *yufka* over itself towards the narrow end and seal the end with egg white. Repeat for all the pieces.

In a large saucepan, heat the olive oil over medium heat to 155°C/310°F. Reduce the heat and fry the rolls for 2 minutes, turning every 30 seconds. Remove with a slotted spoon and serve immediately.

WALNUT AND CREAM BOREK
İÇLİ BÖREK

Region:	Çankırı, Central Anatolia
Preparation time:	30 minutes, plus 20 minutes resting
Cooking time:	50 minutes
Serves:	4

3 tbsp	olive oil	3 tbsp
200 g	butter	scant 1 cup/7 oz
250 g	long homemade noodles (see p.493)	9 oz
200 g	*kaymak* (clotted cream, see p.486)	1 cup/7 oz
150 g	walnuts, crushed	1½ cups/5 oz
50 g	*kashk* (see p.485), grated	2 oz
1	egg	1

For the pastry:

100 g	plain (all-purpose) flour	¾ cup/3½ oz
¼ tsp	salt	¼ tsp
3 tbsp	milk	3 tbsp
1 tbsp	butter, melted	1 tbsp

◗ V

Locals are known to dig into this dish by hand.

◆

To make the pastry:
Combine the flour and salt in a large bowl. Make a well in the middle, add the milk and melted butter and mix until a dough forms. Divide the dough into 2 balls. Brush each one with 2 teaspoons of olive oil, cover with a damp dish towel and let rest for 20 minutes.

Meanwhile, heat 130 g (generous ½ cup/4½ oz) of the butter in a large saucepan over medium heat. Add the long noodles to the hot butter and sauté for 15 minutes, mixing occasionally.

Turn the rested balls of pastry out on to a work counter, brush with the remaining 4–5 teaspoons of olive oil and flatten with your hands. Roll the pastry out with a rolling pin to 20-cm (8-inch) circles.

Preheat oven to 180°C/350°F/Gas Mark 4. Butter a large baking sheet with 2 tablespoons of butter. Place 1 pastry circle on the baking sheet and brush with 1 tablespoon of butter. Layer the noodles on top, then add 150 g (¾ cup/ 5 oz) of the clotted cream, then add a layer of the walnuts and *kashk*. Cover with the other pastry circle and roll in the edges to seal.

In a separate bowl, mix the remaining 2 tablespoons of butter with the egg, and remaining 50 g (¼ cup/2 oz) of clotted cream. Pour the mixture on top of the pastry sheet and bake in the hot oven for 30 minutes, checking every now and then, until evenly browned.

Remove from the oven, cut into 4 pieces and serve.

PUMPKIN BOREK
KABAKLI BÖREK

Region:		Bolu, Black Sea Region
Preparation time:		25 minutes, plus 25 minutes resting
Cooking time:		1 hour, plus 20 minutes
Serves:		4

100 g	plain (all-purpose) flour, for dusting	¾ cup/ 3½ oz
80 g	butter	⅓ cup/3 oz

For the pastry:		
250 g	plain (all-purpose) flour	scant 2 cups/ 9 oz
¼ tsp	salt	¼ tsp
165 ml	milk	scant ¾ cup/ 5½ fl oz

For the filling:		
1 kg	pumpkin, peeled and diced	2 lb 3 oz
¼ tsp	black pepper	¼ tsp
½ bunch	flat-leaf parsley, finely sliced	½ bunch
½ tsp	salt	½ tsp
70 g	butter	⅓ cup/2¾ oz
1 (120 g)	medium onion, finely sliced	1 (¾ cup/4 oz)

This is one of those really quick snacks. All the women of a village would get together and roll out pastry sheets. They make this *börek* as a little pick-me-up during their breaks.
♦
Put the diced pumpkin on a baking sheet, cover with aluminium foil, and bake in a 180°C/350°F/Gas Mark 4 oven for 1 hour. Remove from the oven, then mash the pumpkin and set aside.

To make the filling:
Mix the mashed pumpkin, black pepper, parsley and salt in a bowl until well combined. Heat the butter in a large sauté pan over medium heat, add the onion and sauté for 10 minutes. Pour the cooked mixture into the bowl with the pumpkin and mix until well combined. Divide into 4 equal parts.

To make the pastry:
Combine the flour and salt in a large bowl, make a well in the middle and add the milk. Gently combine, then knead for 5 minutes until a dough forms. Cover the dough with a damp dish towel and let rest for 20 minutes.

Divide the dough into 4 equal parts and let rest for another 5 minutes. Sprinkle each piece of dough with flour, turn out on to a floured work counter and roll out to a 40-cm (16-inch) circle.

Spread the filling over half of each circle, fold the empty half over the top and seal the edges with wet fingers. Heat a large *sac*, griddle pan or iron skillet over high heat until very hot. Add 2 tablespoons of butter, then place the *börek* on the griddle and fry for 2 minutes. Turn the *börek*, add another 2 tablespoons of butter, and fry for 2 minutes. Turn and fry the *börek* for another 1 minute on each side, adding another 2 tablespoons of butter; 6 minutes in total. Transfer to plates and serve.

BREADS & PASTRIES

BOSNIAN BOREK
BOŞNAK BÖREĞİ

Region: Kocaeli, Marmara Region
Preparation time: 30 minutes, plus 20 minutes resting
Cooking time: 1 hours 20 minutes,
                              plus 20 minutes resting
Serves: 4

For the filling:

800 g	veal brisket and shoulder, coarsely minced (ground)	1 lb 12 oz
100 g	butter	½ cup/3½ oz
2 (240 g)	medium onions, finely sliced	2 (1⅝ cups/ 8½ oz)
1 kg	spinach, finely sliced	2 lb 3 oz
½ tsp	black pepper	½ tsp
½ tsp	salt	½ tsp

For the pastry:

250 g	plain (all-purpose) flour	scant 2 cups/ 9 oz
½ tsp	salt	½ tsp

60 ml	olive oil	¼ cup/2 fl oz
125 g	butter, melted	½ cup/4¼ oz
200 g	*kaymak* (clotted cream, see p.486)	1 cup/ 7 oz

p.347 ◻

Börek is the generic Turkish name for savoury pastries and pies, which have greatly influenced the Balkans. This recipe is called Bosnian Börek only in İstanbul, and not in the Balkans. The locals make this dish by stretching one piece of dough out to 2 metres (80 inches).

♦

To make the filling:
Heat a large sauté pan over medium heat until hot. Add the veal and sauté for 10 minutes, then add the butter and onions and sauté for 20 minutes. Add the spinach, black pepper and salt and sauté for another 10 minutes, mixing continuously. Remove from the heat, stir and let cool for 30 minutes.

To make the pastry:
Combine the flour and salt in a large bowl. Make a well in the middle and pour in 160 ml (generous ⅔ cup/ 5½ fl oz) water. Slowly work the flour and water together for 5 minutes, until a dough forms. Divide the pastry dough in half, cover with a damp dish towel and let rest for 20 minutes.

Oiling the work counter and your fingertips, turn the pastry out on to the counter and pull both pieces of dough out in all directions to large, very thin pieces. You are aiming for 60-cm (23-inch) circles, as thin as filo (phyllo) pastry, or even thinner.

Melt about 70 g (⅓ cup/2¾ oz) of the butter and 100 g (½ cup/3½ oz) of the clotted cream in a saucepan and spread on top of each piece of pastry.

Leaving a 2-cm (¾-inch) gap at the edge of the pastry, spoon a line of filling in a 2-cm (¾-inch) wide strip across the width of the pastry. Roll the pastry over the filling four times, then cut the rolled strip away from the circle and set aside. Repeat, until you have used up all the pastry and filling.

Preheat oven to 180°C/350°F/Gas Mark 4. Grease a large baking sheet with about 2 tablespoons of butter.

Coil one end of a piece of rolled pastry inwards, laying it on the prepared baking sheet in a spiral. Join the ends of the rolls by squeezing the dough together, starting in the middle of the sheet and working outwards, form one large spiral. Brush with the remaining butter and clotted cream and bake in the hot oven for 30 minutes, checking every now and then until golden brown.

Cut into quarters or eighths, transfer to plates and serve.

FRIED COFFEE-CUP DUMPLINGS
FİNCAN BÖREĞİ

Region:		İstanbul, all regions
Preparation time:		30 minutes, plus 20 minutes resting
Cooking time:		1 hour
Serves:		4

100 g	plain (all-purpose) flour, for dusting	¾ cup/ 3½ oz
1	egg white	1
1 litre	olive oil, for deep-frying	4¼ cups/ 34 fl oz

For the pastry:		
200 g	plain (all-purpose) flour	1½ cups/ 7 oz
3 tbsp	milk	3 tbsp
1	egg	1
1 tbsp	grape vinegar	1 tbsp
½ tsp	salt	½ tsp

For the filling:		
500 g	veal brisket and shoulder, sinew removed, coarsely minced (ground)	1 lb 2 oz
1 (120 g)	medium onion, finely sliced	1 (¾ cup/4 oz)
150 g	ghee (see p.485), melted	¾ cup/5 oz
70 g	pine nuts, toasted	½ cup/2¾ oz
60 g	currants	½ cup/2¼ oz
½ tsp	black pepper	½ tsp
1 tsp	ground cinnamon	1 tsp
½ tsp	salt	½ tsp
2	dill sprigs, finely sliced	2
4	flat-leaf parsley sprigs, finely sliced	4

Locals use coffee cups to cut this pastry, hence the name.

◆

To make the filling:
Heat a large sauté pan over medium heat until hot. Add the lamb and sauté for 10 minutes, then add the onions and 50 g (¼ cup/2 oz) of the ghee and sauté for 5 minutes. Add the pine nuts, currants, black pepper, ground cinnamon and salt and sauté for another 5 minutes. Let cool, then stir in the dill and parsley.

To make the pastry:
Combine the flour, milk, egg, grape vinegar and salt in a large bowl and knead for 5 minutes into a firm dough. Divide the dough into 4 equal parts, cover each with a damp dish towel and let rest for 20 minutes.

On a flour-dusted work counter, roll out each piece of dough to a 25-cm (10-inch) circle.

Cut 8 small discs out of each circle with a 7-cm (2¾-inch) wide coffee cup, ending up with 32 in total. Brush the edges of each disc with egg white. Divide the filling among 16 of the discs, then top with the other 16 discs and seal the edges with your fingertips.

In a large saucepan, heat the olive oil over medium heat to 155°C/310°F. Fry the pastries for 4–5 minutes on each side, turning frequently. Remove with a slotted spoon and serve immediately.

TURKISH BOREK
TÜRK BÖREĞİ

Region:		İstanbul, all regions
Preparation time:		40 minutes, plus 15 minutes resting
Cooking time:		55 minutes, plus 30 minutes cooling
Serves:		4

150 g	ghee (see p.485), melted	⅔ cup/5 oz
60 ml	olive oil	¼ cup/2 fl oz

For the pastry:		
200 g	plain (all-purpose) flour	1½ cups/7 oz
½ tsp	salt	½ tsp
1	egg	1

For the filling:		
50 g	butter	¼ cup/2 oz
1 (120 g)	medium onion, finely sliced	1 (¾ cup/4 oz)
600 g	mutton, finely chopped	1 lb 5 oz
100 g	toasted almonds	¾ cup/3½ oz
1 tsp	ground cinnamon	1 tsp
½ tsp	black pepper	½ tsp
2 tbsp	pine nuts	2 tbsp
½ tsp	salt	½ tsp
1 bunch	flat-leaf parsley, finely sliced	1 bunch
2 tbsp	grape vinegar	2 tbsp

This crisp, flaky pastry is also known as *katmer*.

♦

To make the filling:
Heat the butter in a large saucepan over medium heat, add the onion and sauté for 10 minutes, mixing continuously. Add the mutton and sauté for 10 minutes, then add the almonds, ground cinnamon, black pepper, pine nuts and salt and sauté for another 3 minutes. Let cool for 30 minutes.

To make the pastry:
Combine the flour and salt in a large bowl. Make a well in the middle and add the egg with 60 ml (¼ cup/2 fl oz) water, mix until well combined, then knead for 10 minutes. Divide the dough into 6 equal parts, flour lightly and roll into balls. Cover with a damp dish towel and let rest for 15 minutes.

Mix the melted ghee and olive oil together in a bowl. Oil the balls of rested dough with the ghee and olive oil mixture and flatten into discs, then use a rolling pin to roll them out to 20-cm (8-inch) circles. Oil the pastry circles with your fingers and fold in like an envelope. Roll them out again, one by one, into 20-cm (8-inch) circles. Fold into envelopes again and repeat this process 6 times, finally rolling them out to 20-cm (8-inch) circles.

Preheat oven to 180°C/350°F/Gas Mark 4 and oil a baking sheet.

Place 3 pastry sheets on top of one another on the baking sheet, brushing with oil between each layer. Spread the filling over the top, then layer the other 3 pastry sheets on top, oiling between each layer as before. Prick several times with a fork. Bake in the hot oven for 30 minutes.

Cut into 4, transfer to plates and serve.

WATER BOREK
SU BÖREĞİ

Region:		Bartın, all regions
Preparation time:		35 minutes, plus 25 minutes resting
Cooking time:		1 hour 20 minutes
Serves:		4

For the dough:

2	eggs	2
250 g	plain (all-purpose) flour	scant 2 cups/ 9 oz
1¾ tbsp	apple cider vinegar	1¾ tbsp
½ tsp	salt	½ tsp
100 g	plain (all-purpose) flour	¾ cup/ 3½ oz
2 tsp	salt	2 tsp
100 g	butter, melted	½ cup/3½ oz

For the filling:

400 g	unsalted Bulgarian or Greek feta cheese, crumbled	14 oz
½ bunch	flat-leaf parsley, finely sliced	½ bunch
2	fresh tarragon sprigs, finely sliced	2

For the egg glaze:

50 g	butter, melted	3½ tbsp/2 oz
60 ml	milk	¼ cup/2 fl oz
1	egg	1

V

This dish can also be cooked in the open air over hot barbecue ashes, for 20 minutes on each side, omitting brushing with the egg glaze.

♦

To make the dough:
Knead the eggs, flour, apple cider vinegar and salt in a large bowl for 10 minutes to a firm dough. Cover with a damp dish towel and let rest for 20 minutes.

Divide the dough into 8 equal pieces and let rest for another 5 minutes.

Sprinkle the pieces of dough with flour and, on a flour-dusted work counter, roll each one out to a 25-cm (10-inch) circle.

Bring a large saucepan with 3 litres (12 cups/100 fl oz) water to a boil over medium heat and add the salt.

Meanwhile, place a bowl of 3 litres (12 cups/100 fl oz) iced water nearby.

Working one at a time, place each sheet of dough into the boiling water, cook for 3 minutes then transfer to the bowl of iced water. Let chill for 3 minutes then remove and drain over an inverted colander.

Preheat oven to 180°C/350°F/Gas Mark 4.

To make the filling:
Mix the cheese, parsley and tarragon in a bowl.

Butter a deep, round baking pan with 2 tablespoons of the butter. Layer 4 sheets of the cooked dough at the bottom of the pan, brushing with 2 teaspoons of butter between each layer. Spread the filling evenly over the top. Top with the remaining 4 sheets of pastry, buttering between the layers as before.

To make the egg glaze:
In a bowl, whisk together the butter, milk and egg.

Brush the glaze generously over the top of the pastry. Bake in the hot oven for 30 minutes.

Remove from the oven, cut into 4 pieces and serve.

CRUMBED AND STUFFED PANCAKE ROLLS
AVCI BÖREĞİ

Region:		Balıkesir, all regions
Preparation time:		30 minutes, plus 30 minutes resting
Cooking time:		2 hour 20 minutes
Serves:		4

1 (700 g)	partridge	1 (1 lb 8½ oz)

For the batter:

1	egg	1
300 ml	milk	1¼ cups/10 fl oz
½ tsp	salt	½ tsp
120 g	plain (all-purpose) flour	scant 1 cup/ 4 oz

For the filling:

60 ml	olive oil	¼ cup/2 fl oz
150 g	coarsely minced (ground) veal	5 oz
1 (120 g)	medium onion, finely sliced	1 (¾ cup/4 oz)
100 g	chanterelle mushrooms, quartered vertically	3½ oz
150 g	pastırma (cured beef, see p.497), finely sliced	5 oz
½ tsp	black pepper	½ tsp
½ tsp	salt	½ tsp
50 g	walnuts	½ cup/2 oz
1	fresh fennel frond, finely sliced	1

90 g	butter	⅓ cup/3¼ oz
4	eggs	4
100 g	cornmeal (polenta)	⅔ cup/3½ oz

The pastries that hunters used to eat when out hunting were the inspiration for this recipe. The filling has become richer over the years.

♦

In a large covered saucepan, cook the partridge for 1 hour in 2 litres (8½ cups/70 fl oz) simmering water. Drain, then pick the partridge meat from the bone and set aside.

To make the batter:
Whisk the egg and milk together with the salt in a large bowl for 2 minutes. Gently fold in the flour, then whisk for another 5 minutes, until well combined.

Heat 1 tablespoon of the butter in a frying pan (skillet) over medium heat. Ladle ⅛ of the batter mixture into the pan and cook for 2 minutes on each side. Repeat until all the batter has been used up. Transfer the cooked pancakes to a plate, cover with a dish towel and let rest.

To make the filling:
Heat the olive oil in a large sauté pan over medium heat, add the veal and sauté for 10 minutes. Add the onion and sauté for 5 minutes, then add the chanterelle mushrooms and sauté for another 10 minutes. Add the *pastırma*, black pepper, salt, walnuts and picked partridge meat and sauté for 10 minutes. Remove from the heat, stir in the fresh fennel and let cool at room temperature for 30 minutes.

Divide the filling equally among the pancakes: spoon a line along one side, then fold the two sides of the pancake in and roll into a wrap.

Whisk the 4 eggs in a shallow bowl, then put the cornmeal (polenta) in a separate shallow bowl alongside. Heat the remaining butter (about 70 g/⅓ cup/2¾ oz) in a large sauté pan until hot. Coat the pancake rolls first in egg wash and then in cornmeal and place in the hot butter. Fry for 2 minutes on each side. Remove with a slotted spoon and serve immediately.

SWEET KURDISH BOREK
KÜRT BÖREĞİ

Region:		İstanbul, all regions
Preparation time:		30 minutes, plus 25 minutes resting
Cooking time:		30 minutes
Serves:		4

For the pastry:		
250 g	plain (all-purpose) flour	scant 2 cups/ 9 oz
½ tsp	salt	½ tsp

200 ml	sesame oil	scant 1 cup/ 7 fl oz
100 g	caster (superfine) sugar	½ cup/ 3½ oz

♦ ♦ V ❖   p.353 ◘

Most pastry chefs in İstanbul are from Bingöl and its environs. The dish is named after the many Kurdish cooks and vendors of this *börek*. This delicious pastry has a very short shelf life. It is made in the early hours of the day and is gone by mid-morning.

♦

To make the pastry:
Combine the flour and salt in a bowl, make a well in the middle and add 175 ml (¾ cup/6 fl oz) water. Gently combine, then knead for 10 minutes until a dough forms. Cover with a damp dish towel and let rest for 5 minutes.

Divide the dough into 4 equal parts and roll into discs. Dip your hand in sesame oil and coat the dough. Cover and let rest for another 20 minutes.

Preheat oven to 180°C/350°F/Gas Mark 4. Lightly grease a large baking sheet with sesame oil.

Oil a large, cold (ideally marble) work counter and a rolling pin with sesame oil and roll a piece of dough out to a 30-cm (12-inch) circle. Holding opposites side of the dough in each hand, between your thumb and fingers, slap the dough on the counter, then stretch it upwards. This has to happen fast, like shaking a towel. Repeat until the dough is 1-metre (40-inches) wide. Making sure the dough remains intact, oil 2 opposite sides with sesame oil and fold inwards. Repeat for the remaining 2 sides. After the folding, the dough should be 25-cm (10-inches) square. Repeat for each piece of dough.

Put the pastry sheets on the prepared baking sheet, making sure the folded sides are facing downwards and bake in the hot oven for 30 minutes, until both top and bottom are crisp.

Remove from the oven, cut into 4-cm (1¼-inch) squares, sprinkle with sugar and serve.

OLIVE BOREK
ZEYTİNLİ BÖREK (SEMSEK)

Region:	Gaziantep, Southeastern Anatolia	
Preparation time:	30 minutes, plus 45 resting	
Cooking time:	35 minutes, plus 1 hour cooling	
Serves:		4

For the filling:

200 ml	olive oil	scant 1 cup/7 fl oz
2 (240 g)	medium onions, finely diced	2 (1⅝ cups/ 8½ oz)
4	garlic cloves, finely sliced	4
2 tsp	red bell pepper paste (see p.492)	2 tsp
1 tbsp	tomato paste (see p.492)	1 tbsp
1 tsp	dried chilli (red pepper) flakes	1 tsp
100 g	walnuts, finely sliced	1 cup/3½ oz
300 g	unsalted green olives, soaked for 24 hours and then rinsed, pitted and finely sliced	1⅔ cups/ 11 oz
½ bunch	flat-leaf parsley, finely sliced	½ bunch
2	fresh tarragon sprigs, finely sliced	2
2 tbsp	pomegranate molasses (see p.490)	2 tbsp
¼ tsp	black pepper	¼ tsp
½ tsp	salt	½ tsp

For the pastry:

250 g	plain (all-purpose) flour	scant 2 cups/ 9 oz
½ tsp	salt	½ tsp
½ tsp	sugar	½ tsp
50 g	fresh yeast (or 3 sachets active dried yeast)	3 tbsp/2 oz
100 g	plain (all-purpose) flour	¾ cup/3½ oz

◖ ◉ ◗ V   p.355 ▣

This is a popular local snack made out of *halhalı*, the unsalted local green olives, resembling marbles. It is common to prepare the pastry at home and take it to the local bakery for cooking. Some versions of this recipe include meat, such as lamb mince, and some fold the pastry into a semi-circle.

◆

To make the filling:
Heat the olive oil in a saucepan over medium heat, add the onions and sauté for 15 minutes, mixing continuously. Add the garlic, red bell pepper paste, tomato paste and dried chilli (red pepper) flakes and sauté for 2 minutes, then add the walnuts and olives and sauté for 7 minutes. Remove from the heat and stir through the parsley, tarragon, pomegranate molasses, black pepper and salt. Let cool for 1 hour, then divide into 8 equal parts.

To make the pastry:
Combine the flour, salt and sugar in a large bowl. In a separate bowl, dissolve the fresh yeast in 175 ml (¾ cup/6 fl oz) water. Make a well in the middle of the flour mixture, add the dissolved yeast, mix until combined, then knead for 5 minutes. Cover the dough with a damp dish towel and let rest for 30 minutes at room temperature.

Divide the dough into 8 equal pieces, roll each into a ball and let rest for another 15 minutes.

Preheat oven to 240°C/475°F/Gas Mark 9.

Sprinkle flour over the rested dough balls and press with your hand to flatten. Flour the work counter and a rolling pin and roll the balls of dough into 15-cm (6-inch) circles. Spoon a line of filling in the middle of each pastry and fold each side of the pastry over itself to enclose. Press with your fingers to seal the edges. Arrange the pastries on a baking tray and bake in the hot oven for 9–10 minutes, until deep golden brown. Serve immediately.

GÖZLEME (FILLED FLATBREAD)
GÖZLEME

Region:		Muğla, all regions
Preparation time:	15 minutes, plus 20 minutes resting	
Cooking time:		10 minutes
Serves:		4

100 g	plain (all-purpose) flour, for dusting	¾ cup/3½ oz
200 g	butter	scant 1 cup/7 oz

For the pastry:		
200 g	plain (all-purpose) flour	1½ cups/7 oz

For the filling:		
300 g	çökelek (dry curd cottage cheese) see p.484)	1⅓ cups/11 oz
200 g	feta cheese (goat's milk)	1⅝ cups/7 oz
1 bunch	flat-leaf parsley	1 bunch
1 bunch	fresh mint	1 bunch
4	dill sprigs	4

◆ V

p.357

Milk, *Ayran* (Salted Yogurt Drink, see p.452) or *Çay* (Tea, see p.446) are all popular drinks to serve with *gözleme*.

◆

To make the filling:
Gently combine the *çökelek* and feta cheese in a large bowl. Finely slice the parsley, mint and dill and fold through the cheese. Season with ¼ teaspoon black pepper and ½ teaspoon salt. Set aside.

To make the pastry:
In a large bowl, combine the flour with ¼ teaspoon salt and 130 ml (generous ½ cup/4½ fl oz) water, then knead for 5 minutes into a firm dough. Divide the dough into 4 equal parts, cover each one with a damp dish towel and let rest for 20 minutes.

On a flour dusted work counter, use a rolling pin to roll each piece of dough to a 40-cm (16-inch) circle. Shake off the excess flour. Equally divide the filling among the pastry circles and add about 2 tablespoons of butter to each. Fold in the sides like an envelope.

Heat a large *sac*, griddle pan or iron skillet over high heat until very hot. Add 50 g (3½ tbsp/2 oz) butter, then place the *gözleme* on the griddle and fry for 2 minutes on each side. Add another 50 g (3½ tbsp/2 oz) butter to the pan, then turn and fry the *gözleme* for another 1 minute on each side; 6 minutes in total. Transfer to plates and serve.

◆

ANCHOVY BREAD
HAMSİ KOLİ (HAMSİLİ EKMEK)

Region:		Rize, Black Sea Region
Preparation time:		15 minutes
Cooking time:		30 minutes
Serves:		4

200 g	ground cornmeal (polenta)	1⅓ cups/ 7 oz
1 (120 g)	medium onion, finely chopped	1 (¾ cup/4 oz)
4	spring onions (scallions), finely chopped	4
1 bunch	chard, finely chopped	1 bunch
3	leeks, finely chopped	3
1 bunch	flat-leaf parsley, finely chopped	1 bunch
1 bunch	dill, finely chopped	1 bunch
100 ml	olive oil	½ cup (3½ fl oz)
300 g	anchovies in brine (or fresh), de-boned	11 oz

This fish bread is absolutely adored in the region. An autumn and winter dish, it can also be made using canned anchovies.

◆

Preheat oven to 180°C/350°F/Gas Mark 4.

Combine the cornmeal (polenta), onion, spring onions (scallions), chard, leeks, parsley, dill and olive oil in a large bowl. Season with ½ teaspoon black pepper and ½ teaspoon salt and knead for 10 minutes. Add the anchovies and knead for 5 minutes. Transfer to a deep baking pan. Bake in the hot oven for 30 minutes. Cut into quarters and serve.

◆ ❧ ◆

BOYOZ (TAHINI ROLLS)
BOYOZ

For the pastry:		
200 g	plain (all-purpose) flour	1½ cups/7 oz
½ tsp	salt	½ tsp
200 ml	sesame oil	scant 1 cup/7 fl oz
60 ml	tahini (sesame seed paste)	¼ cup/2 fl oz
8	eggs, hard-boiled for 12 minutes, peeled, quartered	8

Region:		İzmir, Aegean Region	
Preparation time:		45 minutes, plus 5 hours chilling, plus 1½ hours resting	
Cooking time:		30 minutes	
Serves:		4	

p.359

These pastries are bought at bakeries which specialize in *boyoz* with hard-boiled eggs. It is commonly enjoyed in the mornings with a cup of *Çay* (Tea, see p.446).

♦

To make the pastry:
Combine the flour and salt in a large bowl, make a well in the middle and pour in 120 ml (½ cup/4 fl oz) water. Mix, then knead for 10 minutes into a firm dough. Brush the dough with 2 tablespoons of sesame oil, cover with a damp dish towel and let chill in the refrigerator for 5 hours.

Oil a cold (ideally marble) work counter and a rolling pin with sesame oil. Roll the dough out to a 30-cm (12-inch) circle. Holding opposites side of the dough, between your thumb and fingers, working quickly, slap the dough on the counter, then stretch it upwards, like shaking a towel. Repeat until the dough is 1-metre (40-inches) wide. Fold the corners into an envelope shape. Smear the tahini all over the dough, then roll it up (like a Swiss roll) into a long roll. Cover with a damp dish towel and let rest for 1 hour.

Divide into 8 equal parts by hand and arrange the pastries on a baking sheet. Press down with your thumb in the middle of each piece and let rest for another 30 minutes.

Meanwhile, preheat oven to 180°C/350°F/Gas Mark 4. Bake in the hot oven for 30 minutes, transfer to plates and serve with the hard-boiled eggs.

♦

FLAKY PASTRY WITH TAHINI
TAHİNLİ KATMER

150 ml	sesame oil	⅔ cup/5 fl oz
100 ml	tahini (sesame seed paste)	½ cup/3 ½ fl oz
40 g	sesame seeds, toasted	⅓ cup/1½ oz
60 g	plain (all-purpose) flour, for dusting	scant ½ cup/ 2¼ oz

For the pastry:		
250 g	plain (all-purpose) flour	scant 2 cups/ 9 oz
½ tsp	salt	½ tsp
20 g	sugar	1½ tbsp/¾ oz

Region:		Kayseri, Central Anatolia
Preparation time:		35 minutes, plus 35 minutes resting
Cooking time:		20 minutes
Serves:		4

This breakfast staple takes its Turkish name from the way the pastry is folded.

♦

To make the pastry:
Combine the flour and salt in a bowl. Make a well and add the sugar and 165 ml (scant ¾ cup/5½ fl oz) warm water. Combine, then knead for 10 minutes into a dough. Cover with a damp dish towel and rest for 10 minutes.

Divide the dough into 4 equal parts. Form each piece into a disc, cover with a damp dish towel and rest for 10 minutes.

Meanwhile, in a small bowl, whisk together the sesame oil, tahini and the sesame seeds.

Dust the work counter with flour and use a rolling pin to roll out the pastry discs to 40-cm (16-inch) circles. Brush the tahini mixture over the pastry circles, and roll the circles into a rope, then coil the rope into a spiral and tuck one end under the outer edge of the coil. Cover with a damp dish towel and rest for 15 minutes.

Heat a *sac*, cast-iron pan or griddle over medium heat until hot. Cook the pastries for 2 minutes on each side, then serve.

EASTER BRIOCHE
PASKALYA ÇÖREĞİ

Region:		İstanbul, all regions
Preparation time:	25 minutes, 1 hour 20 minutes resting	
Cooking time:		35 minutes
Serves:		4

2 tbsp	butter, melted	2 tbsp
1	egg yolk	1
40 g	slivered almonds	¼ cup/1½ oz

For the pastry:

¼ tsp	mastic (plant resin)	¼ tsp
4 tsp	sugar	4 tsp
250 g	plain (all-purpose) flour	2 cups/9 oz
3 tbsp	milk	3 tbsp
30 g	fresh yeast	6 tsp/1 oz
1½ tsp	mahleb (cherry seed spice), crushed	1½ tsp
50 g	butter	¼ cup/2 oz
1	egg	1

Christians make this bread at Easter, adding a gold or nickel coin to the dough. The coin is believed to bring good fortune to its finder for the year.

♦

To make the pastry:
Pound the mastic with 1 teaspoon sugar in a pestle and mortar and set aside. Combine the flour and ½ teaspoon salt in a bowl. Make a well in the middle, add the milk, yeast, 3 teaspoons sugar, mahleb, butter, eggs and pounded mastic. Combine, then knead for 10 minutes into a dough. Cover with a damp dish towel and rest for 1 hour.

With oiled hands, divide the dough into 3 equal pieces, and form each into a 20-cm (8-inch) roll. Line them up, press the top ends together and plait them, pressing the ends together when you reach the end of the plait.

Preheat oven to 160°C/325°F/Gas Mark 3 and grease a baking sheet with butter. Put the pastry on to the prepared baking sheet, brush with egg yolk and sprinkle with slivered almonds. Let rest for 20 minutes.

Bake in the hot oven for 35 minutes. Cut into 4 pieces, transfer to plates and serve.

MARDIN CAKE
İKLİÇE (KİLİÇE)

Region:		Mardin, all regions
Preparation time:	25 minutes, 1 hour 25 minutes resting	
Cooking time:		30 minutes
Serves:		4

For the pastry:

250 g	plain (all-purpose) flour	2 cups/9 oz
100 ml	milk, warm	scant ½ cup/3½ fl oz
50 g	fresh yeast (or 3 sachets active dried yeast)	3 tbsp/2 oz
60 g	butter, melted	¼ cup/2¼ oz
1 tbsp	sugar	1 tbsp
1 tsp	ground fennel	1 tsp
½ tsp	ground cinnamon	½ tsp
½ tsp	ground allspice	½ tsp
1 tsp	mahleb (cherry seed spice)	1 tsp
1 tbsp	nigella seeds	1 tbsp

2 tbsp	olive oil	2 tbsp
2 tbsp	butter, melted	2 tbsp

Muslims make this pastry for their holy *Kandil* festivals and for *mevlits*; Christians make it for Easter with different patterns on top.

♦

To make the pastry:
Combine the flour and ½ teaspoon salt in a bowl. Make a well in the middle, add the milk, yeast, butter, sugar, fennel, cinnamon, allspice, mahleb and nigella seeds. Combine, then knead for 10 minutes into a soft dough. Cover with a damp dish towel and rest for 1 hour.

Divide the dough into 4 equal pieces, brush with olive oil, cover with a damp dish towel and rest for 10 minutes.

Preheat oven to 160°C/325°F/Gas Mark 3 and grease a baking sheet with 2 tablespoons of butter.

Brush the work counter with the remaining olive oil and roll the dough out to 15-cm (6-inch) circles. Make patterns on the sides with a fork.

Arrange the pastry on the prepared baking sheet and let rest for 15 minutes.

Bake in the hot oven for 30 minutes. Transfer to plates and serve.

BREADS & PASTRIES

WALNUT AND POPPYSEED TWISTS
HAŞHAŞLI BURMA ÇÖREĞİ

Region:		Amasya, Black Sea Region
Preparation time:		45 minutes, plus 55 minutes resting
Cooking time:		30 minutes
Serves:		4

For the filling:

100 g	poppy seeds, toasted, pounded	generous ¾ cup/ 3½ oz
100 g	walnuts, pounded	1 cup/3½ oz
1 generous tbsp	honey	1 generous tbsp
4 tsp	poppy seed oil	4 tsp

For the pastry:

250 g	plain (all-purpose) flour	scant 2 cups/ 9 oz
½ tsp	salt	½ tsp
1	egg	1
2 tbsp	poppy seed oil	2 tbsp
2 tbsp	butter, melted	2 tbsp
50 g	fresh yeast (or 3 sachets active dried yeast)	3 tbsp/2 oz

3 tbsp	poppy seed oil	3 tbsp

◗ V

These pastries are made both for holidays and for special occasions.
♦
To make the filling:
Mix the pounded poppy seeds, walnuts, honey and poppy seed oil until well combined and set aside.

To make the pastry:
Combine the flour and salt in a large bowl. Make a well in the middle and add the egg, poppy seed oil, butter and yeast, mix until well combined, then knead for 10 minutes into a dough. Cover the bowl with a damp dish towel and let rest for 30 minutes.

Divide the dough into 4 equal parts, brush with 2 teaspoons of poppy seed oil, cover with a damp dish towel again and let rest for another 10 minutes.

Preheat oven to 160°C/325°F/Gas Mark 3. Oil a 30-cm (12-inch) diameter circular baking pan with 4 teaspoons of poppy seed oil.

Transfer the rested dough to an oiled work counter. With oiled hands, form the pieces of dough into 20-cm (8-inch) circles. Top a circle of dough with a third of the filling mixture, then layer another circle of dough on top. Repeat, layering with the remaining filling and dough. Oiling your hands and a rolling pin, roll out the stack of filled dough to a 25-cm (10-inch) wide circle. Cut the pastry into 4-cm (1½-inch) wide strips. Oiling your hands again, twist and stretch the strips.

Arrange the twisted pieces of dough in the prepared baking pan, starting in the middle and working outwards, bending and twisting the strips in a spiral shape. Let rest for 15 minutes.

Bake in the hot oven for 30 minutes. Cut, transfer to plates and serve.

FORKED SAVOURY COOKIES
ÇATAL

	For the pastry:	
Region:		İstanbul, all regions
Preparation time:		25 minutes, plus 40 minutes resting
Cooking time:		30 minutes
Serves:		4

	For the pastry:	
200 g	plain (all-purpose) flour	1½ cups/7 oz
1 tbsp	sugar	1 tbsp
½ tsp	salt	½ tsp
2 tbsp	butter, melted	2 tbsp
50 g	Greek yogurt	¼ cup/2 oz
1 tsp	grape vinegar	1 tsp
¾ tsp	mahleb (cherry seed spice)	¾ tsp
1	egg	1

3 tbsp	olive oil	3 tbsp
1	egg yolk	1
2 tsp	nigella seeds	2 tsp

V

p.363

These savoury cookies get their name from their forked shape. Although found in pastry shops they fall squarely in the domain of street vendors. They are traditionally eaten with a cup of *Çay* (Tea, see p.446) or warm milk.

◆

To make the pastry:
Combine the flour, sugar and salt in a bowl. Make a well, add the butter, yogurt, grape vinegar, mahleb and egg, mix until well combined. Knead for 10 minutes into a firm dough. Cover with a damp dish towel and rest for 20 minutes.

Divide the dough into 4 equal parts and roll into balls. Brush with 2 teaspoons of olive oil and rest for 10 minutes.

Preheat oven to 180°C/350°F/Gas Mark 4. Oil a baking sheet.

Stretch the rested dough with oiled fingers into a 35-cm (14-inch) circle – you will need to use another 2 teaspoons of olive oil. Roll each circle into a sausage, then make a U shape and squeeze the edges together to join. Squeeze at the opposite end too, so that the shape resembles an eye. Arrange the pastries on the prepared baking sheet, brush the tops with egg yolk and sprinkle with nigella seeds. Cover with a damp dish towel and let rest for 10 minutes.

Bake in the oven for 30 minutes. Transfer to plates and serve.

◆

TAHINI CAKES
KÜLÇE

Region:		Hatay, Mediterranean Region
Preparation time:		25 minutes, plus 1 hour 25 minutes resting
Cooking time:		35 minutes
Serves:		4

3 tbsp	olive oil	3 tbsp
85 g	butter, melted	⅓ cup/3 oz
60 ml	tahini (sesame seed paste)	¼ cup/2 fl oz
2 tbsp	sesame seeds	2 tbsp
1 tsp	ground fennel	1 tsp
1 tbsp	nigella seeds	1 tbsp

	For the pastry:	
250 g	plain (all-purpose) flour	scant 2 cups/ 9 oz
50 g	fresh yeast (or 3 sachets active dried yeast), crumbled	3 tbsp/2 oz

V

Tahini cakes are part of the religious rituals of all 'people of the book'. Christians, Jews and Muslims make these cakes on special occasions, but using differing spices.

◆

To make the pastry:
Combine the flour and ½ teaspoon salt in a bowl. Make a well and add 165 ml (scant ¾ cup/5 ½ fl oz) water and the yeast. Combine, then knead for 10 minutes into a dough. Cover with a damp dish towel and rest for 1 hour.

Divide the dough into 4 equal parts and oil the top and bottom of each piece with olive oil. Cover with a damp dish towel and rest for a further 10 minutes.

Preheat oven to 160°C/325°F/Gas Mark 3 and grease a baking sheet with butter.

Oil the work counter. Apply a little butter to your hands. Stretch each piece of dough into a 25-cm (10-inch) disc. Brush with tahini and sprinkle with sesame, ground fennel and nigella seeds. Twist the pieces on both ends and coil. Arrange the pastries on the prepared baking sheet, cover with a damp dish towel and let rest for 15 minutes.

Bake in the oven for 35 minutes. Serve immediately.

TAHINI SWIRLS
TAHİNLİ ÇÖREK

Region:		Kütahya, all regions
Preparation time:		30 minutes, plus 1 hour resting
Cooking time:		20 minutes
Serves:		4

200 ml	tahini (sesame seed paste)	1 cup/7 fl oz
60 ml	grape molasses	¼ cup/2 fl oz
150 ml	sesame oil	⅔ cup/5 fl oz
1 tbsp	nigella seeds	1 tbsp
	For the pastry:	
250 g	plain (all-purpose) flour	2 cups/9 oz
½ tsp	salt	½ tsp
100 ml	milk	scant ½ cup/3½ fl oz
50 g	fresh yeast (or 3 sachets active dried yeast), crumbled	3 tbsp/2 oz

♠ V   p.365 〇

When women get together to make *Yufka Ekmeği* (Thin Flatbreads, see p.378) or noodles for the village, they make these swirls for their break. Also popular at celebrations, it is a dish made by new in-laws for each other. The two sides use these swirls to sweeten their relationship.

♦

Mix the tahini and molasses in a bowl and set aside.

To make the pastry:
Combine the flour and salt in a bowl. Make a well in the middle, add the milk, yeast and 75 ml (⅓ cup/2½ fl oz) water, mix to combine, then knead for 10 minutes into a dough. Divide the dough into 4 equal parts and roll into balls. Oil them lightly with 2 teaspoons of sesame oil, cover the bowl with a damp dish towel and let rest for 1 hour.

Preheat oven to 180°C/350°F/Gas Mark 4. Oil a baking sheet.

Oil each of the rested balls of dough with 2 teaspoons sesame oil. Use a rolling pin to roll them out to 40-cm (16-inch) circles. Brush each circle with another 4 teaspoons sesame oil, then brush with the tahini and molasses mixture, combining the oil, tahini and molasses well. With oiled hands, make a hole in the middle of the pastry with your index finger. Starting from the hole in the middle, roll the dough outwards to form a ring. Tear the ring apart in one place to end up with a roll. Shape this roll into a spiral, starting from the middle.

Arrange the pastries on the prepared baking sheet, press on the pastries gently and sprinkle with the nigella seeds.

Bake in the hot oven for 20 minutes. Transfer to plates and serve.

♦

EGG AND FLOUR MURTUGA
MURTUĞA

Region:		Van, Eastern Anatolia
Preparation time:		5 minutes
Cooking time:		20 minutes
Serves:		4

200 g	*yayik yaği* (yogurt butter, see p.487) or regular butter	scant 1 cup/7 oz
60 g	wholemeal (whole wheat) plain (all-purpose) flour	scant ½ cup/2¼ oz
¼ tsp	salt	¼ tsp
8	eggs	8

♠ V X ⬩⬩

This popular winter breakfast staple is also made for new mothers.

♦

Heat the *yayik yaği* or butter in a saucepan over medium heat until hot. Reduce the heat to low, add the flour and salt and cook for 15 minutes, mixing continuously.

Meanwhile, crack the eggs into a bowl, ensuring the yolks are intact. Gently muddle the yolks with a fork, but do not scramble.

Add the eggs to the flour and stir in gently. Reduce the heat to very low, cover the pan with a lid and cook for 1 minute. Making zigzag lines on the surface of the *murtuğa* with a fork, stir through for 1 minute. Serve on a single serving platter.

KETE ROLLS
KETE

Region:		Kayseri, Central Anatolia
Preparation time:		35 minutes,
		plus 1 hour 25 minutes resting
Cooking time:		30–40 minutes for boiling the fat,
		plus 45 minutes
Serves:		4

80 g	suet (kidney fat)	⅝ cup/3 oz
160 g	plain (all-purpose) flour	scant 1¼ cups/ 5 ½ oz
¼ tsp	salt	¼ tsp
50 g	butter, melted	¼ cup/2 oz
60 ml	tahini (sesame seed paste)	¼ cup/2 fl oz
1	egg yolk	1
1 tbsp	nigella seeds	1 tbsp
2 tbsp	sesame seeds	2 tbsp

For the pastry:		
250 g	plain (all-purpose) flour	scant 2 cups/ 9 oz
½ tsp	salt	½ tsp
100 ml	milk, warm	scant ½ cup/ 3½ fl oz
50 g	fresh yeast (or 3 sachets active dried yeast)	3 tbsp/2 oz

Muslims like making these rolls for the two main religious festivals, whereas the local Armenians distribute *kete* at Easter with red eggs. Mothers make these rolls for their children when they come home from abroad. It is customary to hide coins and beads inside the rolls. Whoever comes across one of these hidden treasures is supposed to have good fortune for life.

♦

Heat a large saucepan over medium heat, add the suet (kidney fat) and melt without letting it burn. Pour in 3 litres (12 cups/100 fl oz) water and boil until the fat rises to the surface of the water. Skim off the fat with a slotted spoon. Add fresh water to the pan and the skimmed fat back to the water. Repeat this boiling process three times until the smell of the fat disappears completely. Transfer the skimmed fat to a bowl and set aside.

Heat a sauté pan over medium heat until hot. Reduce the heat, add 60 g (scant ½ cup/2¼ oz) of the flour and the salt and cook for 10 minutes, mixing continuously. Set aside and let cool.

To make the pastry:
Combine the flour and salt in a large bowl, make a well in the flour and add the milk, yeast and 60 g (2¼ oz) of the suet (kidney fat). Mix until well combined, then knead for 10 minutes into a dough. Cover the bowl with a damp dish towel and let rest for 1 hour .

Divide the dough into 4 equal parts and brush each with the fat. Cover with a damp dish towel and rest for 10 minutes.

Preheat oven to 180°C/350°F/Gas Mark 4 and grease a baking sheet with the fat.

Grease a rolling pin, then roll the pieces of dough into 30-cm (12-inch) circles. Brush with melted butter and tahini, then roll each into a long sausage. Holding the rolled pastry at each end, twist the ends of the roll in opposite directions. Join the two ends of the twisted pastry to make a ring by pressing them firmly together to seal, making sure the ends overlap a little. Roll out with a rolling pin into 15-cm (6-inch) circles. Put some of the roasted flour into the middle of each pastry, then fold the pastry over like an envelope, making sure the folds overlap, to form parcels.

Arrange the pastries on the prepared baking sheet, make indentations on the pastry tops with a small fork, brush with egg yolk and sprinkle with nigella and sesame seeds. Cover with a damp dish towel and let rest for 15 minutes.

Bake in the hot oven for 35 minutes. Transfer to plates and serve immediately.

KETE ROLLS (SİVAS)
KETE (SİVAS)

Region:		Sivas, Central Anatolia
Preparation time:		35 minutes,
		plus 1 hour 35 minutes resting
Cooking time:		50 minutes
Serves:		4

250 g	butter, melted	scant 1¼ cups/ 9 oz
60 g	plain (all-purpose) flour	scant ½ cup/ 2¼ oz
100 g	walnuts, crushed	1 cup/3½ oz
¼ tsp	salt	¼ tsp
1	egg yolk	1

For the pastry:

250 g	plain (all-purpose) flour	scant 2 cups/ 9 oz
½ tsp	salt	½ tsp
75 ml	milk, warm	⅓ cup/2½ fl oz
50 g	butter	¼ cup/2 oz
50 g	fresh yeast (or 3 sachets active dried yeast)	3 tbsp/2 oz

V ♠

Folding *kete* is an art in itself with myriad variations. Everyone seems to have their own way. There are sweet and savoury versions. Kids in particular love *kete*.

♦

Heat 50 g (3½ tbsp/2 oz) of the butter in a large saucepan over medium heat. Add the flour, walnuts and salt and cook for 10 minutes, mixing continuously. Remove from the heat and set aside.

To make the pastry:
Combine the flour and salt in a large bowl. Make a well in the flour and add the milk, butter and yeast and 2 tablespoons warm water. Mix well and knead for 10 minutes. Cover the bowl with a damp dish towel and let rest for 1 hour.

Divide the rested dough into 4 equal parts and brush with butter. Cover with a damp dish towel and let rest for another 10 minutes.

Grease the work counter with butter and turn the rested dough out on to it. Use a greased rolling pin to roll the dough into 50-cm (20-inch) circles. Liberally brush 2 tablespoons butter over each circle. Cut the circles into 5-cm (2-inch) wide strips and stack them one on top of another – you will have 4 stacks. Use your index and ring fingers to roll each stack into a ring, then seal one end like a shallow cup. Fill with the roasted flour and walnut mixture. Stick the open ends together to seal, cover with a damp dish towel and let rest for 10 minutes.

Meanwhile, preheat oven to 180°C/350°F/Gas Mark 4 and grease a baking sheet with butter.

Press the rested pastries down and use a rolling pin to roll into 7-cm (2¾-inch) circles.

Arrange the pastries on the prepared baking sheet, brush with egg yolk and let rest for another 15 minutes.

Bake in the hot oven for 35 minutes. Transfer to plates and serve immediately.

MUSHROOMS, BREAD AND MILK
SÜTLÜ PAPARA

Region:	Çanakkale, Marmara Region	
Preparation time:	10 minutes	
Cooking time:	50 minutes	
Serves:	4	

100 g	butter	scant ½ cup/3½ oz
60 ml	olive oil	¼ cup/2 fl oz
2 (240 g)	medium onions, finely sliced	2 (1⅝ cups/ 8½ oz)
300 g	morel mushrooms, torn into strips	4 cups/11 oz
1.5 litres	hot milk	6¼ cups/50 fl oz
2	dried *Yufka Ekmeği* (Thin Flatbread, see p.378), crushed	2

This dish is usually eaten from the central of a communal dining table.

♦

Heat the butter and olive oil in a large sauté pan over medium heat, add the onions and sauté for 20 minutes, mixing every now and then. Add the morel mushrooms and sauté for 20 minutes. Add ¼ teaspoon black pepper and ¼ teaspoon salt, then mix well.

Reduce the heat to low, pour in the milk and add ¼ teaspoon each of black pepper and salt and, mixing continuously in one direction for 5 minutes. Reduce the heat to very low and keep simmering.

Meanwhile, spread the *yufka* over a deep heat-resistant tray and set it over medium heat. Pour over the hot milk and mushroom mixture and warm through for 3 minutes. Transfer to plates and serve.

BAKED LAMB PASTIES
HITAP

Region:	Adıyaman, Southeastern Anatolia	
Preparation time:	30 minutes, plus 45 minutes resting	
Cooking time:	10 minutes	
Serves:	4	

50 g	ghee (see p.485)	3½ tbsp/2 oz

For the pastry:		
250 g	plain (all-purpose) flour	scant 2 cups/ 9 oz
½ tsp	salt	½ tsp
50 g	fresh yeast (or 3 sachets active dried yeast)	3 tbsp/2 oz

For the filling:		
400 g	*kavurma* (lamb confit, see p.497), meat shredded	14 oz
6	spring onions (scallions), finely sliced	6
1	fresh garlic, finely sliced	1
½ bunch	flat-leaf parsley, finely sliced	½ bunch
2 tsp	dried chilli (red pepper) flakes	2 tsp
1½ tsp	tomato paste (see p.492)	1½ tsp
2	fresh basil sprigs, finely sliced	2
½ tsp	black pepper	½ tsp

Locals commonly prepare the filling for this wintertime dish and taking it to the local bakery who would bake it for a small fee. There is no salt in this recipe as the confit is already quite salty.

♦

To make the pastry:
Combine the flour and salt in a large bowl. In a separate bowl, dissolve the yeast in 175 ml (¾ cup/6 fl oz) water. Make a well in the flour and add the dissolved yeast, mix until combined, then knead the dough for 5 minutes. Cover with a damp dish towel and let rest for 30 minutes.

Divide the dough into 8 equal parts and roll into balls. Let rest for another 15 minutes.

To make the filling:
Mix all the filling ingredients in a large bowl, until well combined. Divide the mixture into 8 equal parts.

Preheat oven to 240°C/475°F/Gas Mark 9.

Sprinkle the rested balls of dough with flour and flatten them into discs. Dust the work counter and a rolling pin with flour and roll out each disc to a 15-cm (6-inch) circle. Cover half of each pastry circle with the filling, then fold the empty halves over and press with your fingers to seal. Arrange on a lined baking sheet and bake in the hot oven for 9–10 minutes, until golden brown.

Remove from the oven, brush with ghee and serve.

BREADS & PASTRIES

LAMB AND VEGETABLE PARCELS
TALAŞ BÖREĞİ

Region:	İstanbul, Marmara Region	
Preparation time:	30 minutes, plus 24 hours resting	
Cooking time:	1 hour 15 minutes	
Serves:	4	

For the pastry:

250 g	plain (all-purpose) flour	scant 2 cups/ 9 oz
½ tsp	salt	½ tsp
60 ml	olive oil	¼ cup/2 fl oz
2 tbsp	apple cider vinegar	2 tbsp
50 g	butter, cut into 10 pieces	3½ tbsp/ 2 oz

2 tbsp	olive oil	2 tbsp
1	egg yolk	1

For the filling:

80 g	butter	generous ⅓ cup/3 oz
500 g	lamb backstrap, finely diced	1 lb 2 oz
200 g	carrots, finely diced	7 oz
1 (150 g)	potato, finely diced	1 (5 oz)
100 g	fresh shelled peas	3½ oz
1	celery stalk, finely diced	1
1 tsp	dried oregano	1 tsp
3	spring onions (scallions), finely sliced	3
¼ tsp	black pepper	¼ tsp
½ tsp	salt	½ tsp
½ bunch	dill, finely chopped	½ bunch

The Turkish name for this classic restaurant favourite refers to the folding technique used to make the pastry.

♦

To make the pastry:
Combine the flour and salt in a bowl. Make a well and add the oil, vinegar and 5 tablespoons water, mix well and knead for 5 minutes. Roll the dough out to a 20-cm (8-inch) disc. Add the butter pieces, combine and roll out the dough to a 20-cm (8-inch) disc. Fold in half 3 times consecutively, then roll out again to a 20-cm (8-inch) disc. Transfer to a bowl, cover and rest in the refrigerator for 24 hours.

The next day, divide the rested dough into 4 equal parts and roll each into a 17-cm (6½-inch) disc. Set aside.

To make the filling:
Heat the butter in a saucepan over medium heat, add the lamb and sauté for 10 minutes. Add the carrots and sauté for 5 minutes, then add the potato, peas, celery, dried oregano, spring onions (scallions) black pepper and salt. Sauté for a further 5 minutes. Reduce the heat and cook, covered, for 20 minutes, until the vegetables soften. Drain, reserving the juices, and transfer to a bowl. Gently stir in the dill and divide the mixture into 4 parts.

Preheat oven to 180°C/350°F/Gas Mark 4 and oil a large baking sheet with 1 tablespoon of the olive oil.

Spoon the filling onto the middle of the pastry discs. Drizzle with cooking juices. Fold the pastry sides into the middle like an envelope and press to seal. Arrange the parcels, folded side down, on the baking sheet. With a sharp knife, score a small cross on top of each parcel. Whisk the egg yolk with the remaining 1 tablespoon olive oil and brush the parcels. Bake in the oven for 30 minutes until cooked on top and bottom. Serve immediately.

♦

CHEESE CORNMEAL (POLENTA)
MUHLAMA

Region:	Rize, Black Sea Region	
Preparation time:	5 minutes	
Cooking time:	15 minutes	
Serves:	4	

100 g	butter	½ cup/3½ oz
100 g	ground cornmeal (polenta)	¾ cup/3½ oz
500 ml	milk, hot	2 cups/17 fl oz
200 g	fresh sheep's milk cheese (low fat, reduced salt), grated	2 cups/ 7 oz

Some prefer to use water instead of milk to make this.

♦

Heat the butter in a saucepan over medium heat until hot. Reduce the heat, add the cornmeal (polenta) and cook, stirring, for 5 minutes. Add the milk and cook, stirring continuously, for 2 minutes. Add the cheese and cook, stirring continuously, for 3 minutes, then for another 2 minutes without stirring. Transfer to plates and serve.

🌿 ⬥ V Ⅹ ⁘

SESAME BAGELS
SİMİT

Region:		İstanbul, all regions
Preparation time:		30 minutes, plus 45 minutes resting
Cooking time:		20 minutes
Serves:		4

For the dough:

250 g	plain (all-purpose) flour	2 cups/9 oz
½ tsp	salt	½ tsp
50 g	fresh yeast (or 3 sachets active dried yeast), crumbled	3 tbsp/2 oz

1 tbsp	*kaymak* (clotted cream, see p.486)	1 tbsp
2 tbsp	milk	2 tbsp
100 g	sesame seeds	⅔ cup/3½ oz

♦ V   p.371

Baked in wood-fired ovens, different regions have their own versions of *simit* with names such as *gevrek* or *kahke*.

♦

To make the dough:
Combine the flour and salt in a bowl. Make a well and add the yeast and 175 ml (¾ cup/6 fl oz) water. Combine until a coarse dough forms. Knead the dough on a lightly floured surface for 10 minutes. Cover with a damp dish towel and rest for 15 minutes. Divide the dough into 4 equal pieces, cover with a damp cloth and rest for another 15 minutes.

Preheat oven to 200°C/400°F/Gas Mark 6 and line a baking sheet with baking (parchment) paper. Roll each piece of dough into a 70-cm (27½-inch) rope. Fold in two, stick the ends together, twist the dough and then form into rings.

Whisk the clotted cream and milk in a bowl for 3 minutes. Put the sesame seeds in a separate bowl nearby. Dip the dough rings into the cream mixture, then into the sesame seeds, turning to coat the rings thoroughly. Arrange on the lined baking sheet, cover with a damp dish towel and let rest for 15 minutes. Bake in the hot oven for 20 minutes.

♦

LAMB AND CHEESE PUFFS
PUF BÖREĞİ

Region:		İstanbul, all regions
Preparation time:		25 minutes, plus 2½ hours resting
Cooking time:		20 minutes
Serves:		4

For the pastry:

250 g	plain (all-purpose) flour	2 cups/9 oz
50 g	ghee (see p.485)	3½ tbsp/2 oz
90 ml	milk	6 tbsp/3 fl oz
2 tbsp	*Kül Mayasi* (Ash Starter, see p.482)	2 tbsp

1 litre	olive oil	4¼ cups/34 fl oz
2	egg whites	2

For the filling:

300 g	lean minced (ground) veal shoulder, pan-fried	11 oz
1 (120 g)	medium onion, finely sliced	1 (¾ cup/4 oz)
4	dill sprigs, finely sliced	4
6	flat-leaf parsley, finely sliced	6
200 g	feta cheese, crumbled	2 cups/7 oz

♦

Locals roll the pastry to a 1-metre (40-inch) wide disc by hand. They add the filling, cut the pastry, fold each piece into a crescent and fry. Some cooks make separate batches: half with minced (ground) meat and half with just cheese.

♦

To make the pastry:
Combine the flour and ghee in a bowl with ¼ teaspoon salt. Make a well, add the milk and ash starter, then knead for 5 minutes until a dough forms. Cover with a damp dish towel and let rest for 20 minutes. Divide the dough into 8 equal parts and let rest for a further 10 minutes.

Oil the rolling pin with olive oil and roll each piece of dough into a 20-cm (8-inch) disc. Layer on a baking sheet, brushing each disc with olive oil. Rest in the refrigerator for 2 hours. Roll the dough out to 60-cm (24-inch) discs.

To make the filling:
In a bowl, mix all the filling ingredients with ½ teaspoon each of black pepper and salt until combined, then divide into 16 equal parts. Dot the filling over one pastry disc at equal intervals. Lay another pastry disc on top and push down around the pieces of filling. Cut the 16 individual pastries out using a cookie cutter and press to seal the edges. Brush the pastries with egg white.

In a large saucepan, heat the remaining olive oil over medium heat to 155°C/310°F. Fry the pastries in the hot oil for 1–3 minutes, until both sides are golden brown. Remove with a slotted spoon and serve immediately.

BREADS & PASTRIES

MILLER'S BULGUR WHEAT BREAD
BULGUR EKMEĞİ (NAN-É SAVAR)

Region:	Diyarbakır, Southeastern Anatolia
Preparation time:	20 minutes, plus 1 hour 45 minutes resting
Cooking time:	25 minutes
Serves:	4

60 g	ghee (see p.485)	¼ cup/2¼ oz
1 (120 g)	medium onion, finely diced	1 (¾ cup/4 oz)
1 tsp	dried chilli (red pepper) flakes	1 tsp
1 tsp	ground coriander	1 tsp
100 g	fine bulgur wheat, soaked for 15 minutes	½ cup/3½ oz
150 g	wholemeal (whole wheat) plain (all-purpose) flour	generous 1 cup/ 5 oz
75 ml	ayran (salted yogurt drink, see p.452)	⅓ cup/ 2½ fl oz
50 g	plain (all-purpose) flour, for dusting	⅓ cup/2 oz

 ♦ V

This bread was prepared collectively by people waiting in line to grind their flour and was cooked on a *sac* griddle. These days, locals take their dough to the bakery to be cooked in their wood-fired oven. Some recipes add yeast.
♦

Heat the ghee in a sauté pan over medium heat, add the onion and sauté for 10 minutes. Add the dried chilli (red pepper) flakes, ground coriander and ½ teaspoon salt. Sauté for 1 minute. Remove from the heat and cool for 10 minutes.

Drain the bulgur wheat and combine with the wholemeal (whole wheat) flour and *ayran* in a bowl. Add the cooled onion mixture. Combine, then knead for 10 minutes into a dough. Cover with a damp dish towel and rest for 1 hour. Divide the dough into 4 equal pieces, cover with a damp dish towel and rest for another 20 minutes.

Preheat oven to 240°C/475°F/Gas Mark 9.

Lightly flour your hands and the work counter and roll the rested dough out to a 12-cm (4¾-inch) circle. Let rest for another 15 minutes. Put the dough on a baking sheet and bake in the hot oven for 15 minutes.

♦

MILLER'S BREAD
PAĞAÇ

Region:	Erzurum, Eastern Anatolia
Preparation time:	25 minutes, plus 1½ hours resting
Cooking time:	40 minutes
Serves:	4

For the pastry:		
100 g	ground cornmeal (polenta)	¾ cup/3½ oz
150 g	plain (all-purpose) flour	1 cup/5 oz
60 ml	warm milk	¼ cup/2 fl oz
2½ tbsp	butter	2½ tbsp
1	egg	1
50 g	fresh yeast (or 3 sachets active dried yeast), crumbled	3 tbsp/2 oz

2 tbsp	butter, melted	2 tbsp
100 g	plain (all-purpose) flour	¾ cup/3½ oz
1	egg yolk	1
1 tsp	nigella seeds	1 tsp
3 tsp	sesame seeds	3 tsp

♦ V

Pağaç is traditionally prepared by the people who mill their flour at the local mill. Made with the flour (*pağaç* in Turkish) that is stuck to the sides of the millstone, the pastry is prepared and eaten collectively outdoors by those waiting in line to grind their flour. Serve with a cup of *Çay* (Tea, see p.446).
♦

To make the pastry:
Combine the cornmeal and flour with ½ teaspoon salt in a large bowl. Make a well in the middle and add the milk, butter, egg and yeast, mix until well combined and knead for 10 minutes into a dough. Cover with a damp dish towel and let rest for 1 hour.

Grease a baking sheet with the melted butter. Knead the rested dough for another 10 minutes, dipping your fingertips in flour every now and then. Put the dough on the prepared baking sheet and stretch into a 20-cm (8-inch) circle with your fingers. Cover with a damp dish towel and let rest for 30 minutes.

Meanwhile, preheat oven to 160°C/325°F/Gas Mark 3.

Brush the dough with egg yolk and sprinkle with nigella seeds and sesame seeds. Bake in the hot oven for 40 minutes.

Divide into 4 equal parts, transfer to plates and serve.

RUSTIC SOURDOUGH LOAF WITH POTATO
KÖY EKMEĞİ

Region:		Kastamonu, all regions
Preparation time:		30 minutes, plus overnight resting,
		plus 4 hours resting
Cooking time:		1 hour, plus 30 minutes
Serves:		4

For the potato dough:

100 g	potato	½/3½ oz
¼ tsp	salt	¼ tsp
2 tsp	sugar	2 tsp
50 g	plain (all-purpose) flour	⅓ cup/2 oz
3 tbsp	*ayran* (salted yogurt drink, see p.452)	3 tbsp
100 g	*ekşi maya* (sourdough starter, see p.483)	3½ oz
½ tsp	*çemen* seeds	½ tsp
200 g	wholemeal (whole wheat) plain (all-purpose) flour	1½ cups/ 7 oz
½ tsp	salt	½ tsp
2	chard leaves	2

◓ V

Some recipes omit the potatoes. You could substitute the sourdough starter with 60 g (2¼ oz) of fresh yeast, reducing the proving time to 1 hour.

◆

To make the potato dough:
Cook the potato in 1 litre (4¼ cups/34 fl oz) boiling water for 1 hour, then drain reserving 100 ml (scant ½ cup/ 3½ fl oz) of the cooking water. Combine the potato and reserved cooking water in a bowl and mash, then add the salt, sugar and flour, knead into a dough, cover and let rest overnight.

The next day, combine the potato dough with 100 ml (scant ½ cup/3½ fl oz) water, the *ayran*, sourdough starter and *çemen* seeds and mix for 10 minutes. Add the wholemeal flour and salt, combine well and knead for 10 minutes. Cover with a damp dish towel and rest for 3 hours.

Knock back the rested dough, turn to eradicate any air bubbles and roll into a ball. Arrange the chard leaves in a casserole dish (Dutch oven) and place the dough on top. Wrap the dish in a damp dish towel and let rest for 1 hour at room temperature, until the dough proves.

Meanwhile, preheat oven to 180°C/350°F/Gas Mark 4. Transfer the dough to a baking sheet and bake in the hot oven for 30 minutes.

◆

CORN BREAD
MISIR EKMEĞİ

Region:		Rize, Black Sea Region
Preparation time:		10 minutes, plus 30 minutes resting
Cooking time:		35 minutes
Serves:		4

50 g	butter, melted	¼ cup/2 oz
250 g	ground cornmeal (polenta)	1⅔ cups/ 9 oz
½ tsp	salt	½ tsp
160 ml	milk, boiling	scant ¾ cup/ 5½ fl oz

❋ ◓ V ⁙

Also known as *cadi*, this bread is popular all around the Black Sea Region. There is a plain version made with boiling water and some recipes use water instead of milk.

◆

Preheat oven to 180°C/350°F/Gas Mark 4 and grease a heavy baking pan with 2 teaspoons of the butter.

Combine the cornmeal (polenta) and salt in a large bowl. Add the milk and the remaining butter and mix with a wooden spoon until well combined. Add the mixture to the prepared baking pan, cover with a damp dish towel and let rest for 30 minutes.

Make a cross on top of the dough with a knife, but don't go too deep. Bake in the hot oven for 35 minutes. Slice and serve.

LENTIL BREAD
MERCİMEK EKMEĞİ

Region:	Şanlıurfa, Southeastern Anatolia
Preparation time:	30 minutes, plus 15 minutes resting
Cooking time:	20 minutes
Serves:	4

100 g	wholemeal (whole wheat) flour, plus extra for dusting	¾ cup/3½ oz
150 g	red lentil flour	1 cup/5 oz
½ tsp	ground cumin	½ tsp
½ tsp	black pepper	½ tsp
1 tsp	dried chilli (red pepper) flakes	1 tsp
½ tsp	salt	½ tsp
200 g	tomato, grated	1 cup/7 oz
1	red bell pepper, finely sliced	1
1 (120 g)	medium onion, finely diced	1 (¾ cup/4 oz)
6	garlic cloves, crushed	6
2 tsp	red bell pepper paste (see p.492)	2 tsp
1 tbsp	tomato paste (see p.492)	1 tbsp

🌢 ◆ ◓ V   p.375 📷

This bread can be enjoyed warm or cold, dipped in olive oil or served with *Ayran* (Salted Yogurt Drink, see p.452).

Some recipes use only lentil flour only and fry the bread in oil. If you make the same recipe with ground cornmeal (polenta), you get cornbread.

◆

Combine the wholemeal (whole wheat) flour, lentil flour, cumin, black pepper, dried chilli (red pepper) flakes and salt in a large bowl. Make a well in the middle and pour in 60 ml (¼ cup/2 fl oz) lukewarm water, and add the tomato, bell pepper, onion, garlic, red bell pepper paste and tomato paste. Combine well and knead for 10 minutes into a dough. Transfer the dough to a floured work counter and knead for another 10 minutes. Divide the dough into 4 equal pieces, transfer to a bowl and cover with a damp dish towel. Let rest for 15 minutes.

Roll out the rested dough to 20-cm (8-inch) circles.

Heat a *sac*, cast-iron pan or griddle over medium heat until very hot, about 8 minutes. Cook the first side of the breads for 2 minutes and the second side for 1 minute. Serve immediately.

◆

MILLET LOAF
NAN-É GİLGİL (AKDARI) EKMEĞİ

Region:	Bitlis, Eastern Anatolia
Preparation time:	20 minutes, plus 2 hours resting
Cooking time:	35 minutes
Serves:	4

For the pastry:

200 g	millet flour	1⅓ cups/7 oz
½ tsp	salt	½ tsp
100 ml	*ayran* (salted yogurt drink, see p.452), warm	½ cup/3½ fl oz
50 g	*kashk* (see p.485), grated	2 oz
½ tsp	*poy* (see p.502)	½ tsp
1 tbsp	grape molasses	1 tbsp
50 g	fresh yeast (or 3 sachets active dried yeast), crumbled	3 tbsp/2 oz
70 g	butter, melted	⅓ cup/2¾ oz

2 tbsp	butter	2 tbsp

◓ V

Yet another way to celebrate the arrival of spring is to make this bread and offer some to the local birds and insects to ensure an abundance of crops. This act of generosity must also extend to at least seven neighbours. This bread is traditionally consumed with sheep's milk or goat's milk yogurt.

◆

Combine the millet flour and salt in a large bowl. Make a well in the middle and add the *ayran*, *kashk*, *poy*, grape molasses, yeast and 50 g (3½ tbsp/2 oz) of the butter. Mix until well combined, then knead for 10 minutes. Cover with a damp dish towel and let rest for 1 hour.

Brush a deep, 20-cm (8-inch) baking pan with 1 tablespoon of the butter. Transfer the dough to the pan, cover with a damp dish towel and let rest for another 1 hour.

Meanwhile, preheat oven to 180°C/350°F/Gas Mark 4.

Brush the dough with the remaining 1 tablespoon of butter and press down in the middle with your fist to make a hole without breaking the dough. Bake in the hot oven for 35 minutes.

PIDE RIDGED FLATBREADS
TIRNAKLI EKMEK

Region:	Gaziantep, all regions	
Preparation time:	15 minutes, plus 55 minutes resting	
Cooking time:		10 minutes
Serves:		4

For the dough:

250 g	wholemeal (whole wheat) flour, plus extra for dusting	scant 2 cups/ 9 oz
½ tsp	salt	½ tsp
1 tsp	sugar	1 tsp
50 g	fresh yeast (or 3 sachets active dried yeast), crumbled	3 tbsp/2 oz

For the flour paste:

2 tbsp	plain (all-purpose) flour	2 tbsp

⁞ ⬥ ⬦ V ⋰ p.377 ⬛

These flatbreads are consumed in Eastern and Southeastern Anatolia. The Turkish name *tırnaklı ekmek* (ridged flatbread) refers to the way the ridges of the bread are made by pressing with your fingertips. People go to bakeries and buy a fresh loaf for every meal in Southeastern Turkey. It is customary to sprinkle sesame seeds or caster (superfine) sugar on this bread. It is also prepared with olive oil, cartilage or lamb confit.

♦

To make the dough:
Combine the wholemeal (whole wheat) flour, salt and sugar in a large bowl. Make a well in the middle, add the yeast and 175 ml (¾ cup/6 fl oz) water, mix until well combined, then knead for 10 minutes into a dough. Cover the bowl with a damp dish towel and let rest for 30 minutes.

Divide the dough into 4 equal parts and roll into balls. Sprinkle with flour, flatten the balls of dough with your hands, cover with a damp dish towel and let rest for another 15 minutes.

Flour your hands and stretch out the dough to 15-cm (6-inch) circles. Cover with a damp dish towel and let rest for another 10 minutes.

Preheat oven to 240°C/475°F/Gas Mark 9. Put a heavy baking sheet in the oven to heat up.

To make the flour paste:
In a bowl, mix the flour with 75 ml (⅓ cup/2½ fl oz) water.

Brush the rested dough with the flour paste. Using the fingers of both hands spaced about 1 cm (½ inch) apart, make a line of indentations with your fingertips down the length of the dough, pressing firmly, starting 1 cm (½ inch) in from the edges. Make sure you do not break the dough. Turn the dough sideways and repeat to form a grid of ridges.

Put the breads on to the baking sheet and bake in the hot oven for 10 minutes.

THIN FLATBREAD
YUFKA EKMEĞİ

Region:		Adana, all regions
Preparation time:		15 minutes, plus 50 minutes resting
Cooking time:		18 minutes
Serves:		4

250 g	wholemeal (whole wheat) flour, plus extra for dusting	scant 2 cups/ 9 oz
½ tsp	salt	½ tsp

This bread is collectively made by rural women twice a year, in batches of 200 or 300. It is kept stocked at home for use all through the year. A sprinkle of water and a little rest in a dish towel is all it takes to get it ready to eat.

♦

Combine the flour and salt in a large bowl and make a well in the middle. Pour in 175 ml (¾ cup/6 fl oz) water and work into a dough, kneading for 10 minutes. Cover with a damp dish towel and let rest for 30 minutes.

Divide the dough into 4 equal parts, cover with a damp dish towel and let rest for another 20 minutes.

On a floured work counter, use a rolling pin to roll out each piece of dough to a 40-cm (16-inch) circle.

Heat a *sac*, cast iron pan or griddle over medium heat until very hot, about 10 minutes. Cook the flatbreads for 50 seconds on each side. Serve immediately.

♦

CIRIK CHEESE PASTA
KARNI CIRIK

Region:		Ardahan, Eastern Anatolia
Preparation time:		30 minutes, plus 15 minutes resting
Cooking time:		12 minutes
Serves:		4

100 g	plain (all-purpose) flour, for dusting	¾ cup/ 3½ oz
¾ tsp	salt	¾ tsp
200 g	blue cheese, crumbled	2 cups/7 oz
200 g	*kaşar* cheese (cow's milk) grated	2 cups/ 7 oz
80 g	butter, melted	⅓ cup/3 oz

For the dough:

250 g	plain (all-purpose) flour	scant 2 cups/ 9 oz
½ tsp	salt	½ tsp
1	egg, whisked	1

 V

This winter dish is popular around Kars, Ağrı and Artvin and is served in a tray in the middle of a communal table.

♦

To make the dough:
Combine the flour and salt in a large bowl. Make a well in the middle, add the egg and 95 ml (⅓ cup/3¼ fl oz) water and combine gently. Knead for 10 minutes into a firm dough. Divide into 2 equal parts. Cover with a damp dish towel and let rest for 15 minutes.

Sprinkle the rested dough with flour and use a rolling pin to roll each piece out to a 20-cm (8-inch) circle. Cut both circles into 1-cm (½-inch) squares. Pressing on one end of each square, roll it towards the other corner and stick together to make little rolls. Bring 2.25 litres (10 cups/ 80 fl oz) water with the salt to a boil over medium heat. Add the pasta to the boiling water and cook for 4 minutes, stirring gently to ensure they do not stick to one another. Drain the pasta, but reserve 60 ml (¼ cup/ 2 fl oz) of the cooking water.

Spread half of the blue cheese and *kaşar* cheese over a heat-resistant serving tray and layer with the pasta. Spread the remaining half of the two cheeses on top and spoon over the reserved cooking water. Top with the melted butter, and set the tray over a medium heat. Cook for 2 minutes, mixing to combine, then serve.

YOGURT PIE
ZIRFET

Region:		Elazığ, Doğu Anadolu
Preparation time:		25 minutes
Cooking time:		50 minutes
Serves:		4

For the pastry:

120 g	wholemeal (whole wheat) flour, plus extra for dusting	scant 1 cup/ 4 oz
1 tbsp	plain (all-purpose) flour	1 tbsp
120 g	cornmeal (polenta)	1¾ cups/ 4 oz
½ tsp	salt	½ tsp

For the yogurt sauce:

500 g	Greek yogurt (sheep's milk)	2½ cups/ 1 lb 2 oz
6	garlic cloves, crushed	6
¼ tsp	salt	¼ tsp

For the butter sauce:

400 g	freshly churned butter (see p.487) or regular butter	1¾ cups/ 14 oz

 V

Also known as *lere*, *zerfet*, *babuko*, *zarfet* and *kömbe*, this is a festive dish for special occasions, served with sultana compote. Traditionally, it is not eaten with cutlery but with the hands. In Karakoçan, everyone claims the piece of pastry in front of them and uses it as a spoon – this method is called '*sokum*'. Some recipes include meat or *kavurma* fillings.

♦

Preheat oven to 200°C/400°F/Gas Mark 6.

To make the pastry:
Combine the wholemeal (whole wheat) flour, plain flour, cornmeal (polenta) and salt in a large bowl. Make a well in the middle, pour in 175 ml (¾ cup/6 fl oz) water and knead for 10 minutes, working the mixture into a coarse dough.

Turn the dough out on to a floured work counter and knead for another 10 minutes, dipping your hand in flour every now and then, making the dough thicker. Roll the dough into a ball, then use a rolling pin to roll it out to a 25-cm (10-inch) circle. Using your finger, score a circle 2 cm (¾ inch) in from the edge.

Put the dough on to a large baking sheet and bake in the hot oven for 30 minutes. Remove from the oven and remove the inner circle of pastry. Break the circle of pastry into pieces and return to the baking sheet, arranging the pieces in a mound in the middle. Bake for another 20 minutes, checking regularly until golden brown.

To make the yogurt sauce:
Whisk the yogurt, garlic and salt in a large bowl for 1 minute, until well combined.

To make the butter sauce:
Heat the butter in a small saucepan until hot.

Pour the hot butter sauce over the pastry as soon you take it from the oven, then top with the yogurt sauce, making sure you stay within the circle. Serve immediately.

BREADS & PASTRIES

SPICED MEAT-TOPPED FLATBREAD
LAHMACUN (GAZİANTEP)

Region:	Gaziantep, Southeastern Anatolia	
Preparation time:	20 minutes, plus 35 minutes resting	
Cooking time:	1 hour, plus 5–20 minutes	
Serves:		4

100 g	plain (all-purpose) flour, for dusting	¾ cup/3½ oz

For the dough:

250 g	plain (all-purpose) flour	scant 2 cups/ 9 oz
½ tsp	salt	½ tsp
20 g	fresh yeast (or 1½ sachets of active dried yeast)	4 tsp/¾ oz

For the topping:

320 g	lamb (rack or shoulder), de-boned, trimmed of sinew, finely chopped	11¼ oz
200 g	tomato, finely sliced	1 cup/7 oz
1½ tsp	tomato paste (see p.492)	1½ tsp
4 tsp	red bell pepper paste (see p.492)	4 tsp
1	small red bell pepper, finely sliced	1
10	garlic cloves, finely sliced	10
1 bunch	flat-leaf parsley, finely sliced	1 bunch
4 tsp	dried chilli (red pepper) flakes	4 tsp
½ tsp	black pepper	½ tsp
½ tsp	salt	½ tsp

1 kg	aubergines (eggplants)	4 cups/ 2 lb 4 oz

p.381

Alternatively known as '*lahmacun* with vegetables', other flavours include fresh garlic, olive and truffle. *Ayran* (Salted Yogurt Drink, see p.452) makes a good accompaniment and it can also be served with radish, flat-leaf parsley and lemon.

♦

Bake the aubergines (eggplants) in a 200°C/400°F/Gas Mark 6 oven for 1 hour. Remove from the oven and let cool, then peel and set aside.

To make the dough:
Combine the flour and salt in a large bowl. In a separate bowl, dissolve the yeast in 175 ml (¾ cup/6 fl oz) water. Make a well in the middle of the flour and pour in the dissolved yeast mixture, combine well and knead for 5 minutes into a dough. Cover with a damp dish towel and let rest for 30 minutes.

Divide the rested dough into 8 equal pieces, roll into balls and let rest for another 5 minutes.

To make the topping:
In a large bowl, gently mix together all the topping ingredients with your hands, until well combined. Divide the topping into 8 equal pieces.

Preheat oven to 240°C/475°F/Gas Mark 9.

Sprinkle flour on the rested balls of dough, flatten them with your hands, then use a floured rolling pin to roll out to 15-cm (6-inch) circles. Arrange the topping on top of the circles, spreading it right to the edges, and stretch the dough out further to 20-cm (8-inch) circles. Arrange them on baking sheets (2 per sheet) and bake in the hot oven for 4–5 minutes.

Serve immediately with the baked aubergines.

LAHMACUN PIZZA WITH SPICED LAMB
LAHMACUN (ŞANLIURFA)

Region:	Şanlıurfa, Southeastern Anatolia	
Preparation time:	20 minutes, plus 35 minutes resting	
Cooking time:		5–20 minutes
Serves:		4

For the dough:

250 g	plain (all-purpose) flour	scant 2 cups/ 9 oz
½ tsp	salt	½ tsp
20 g	fresh yeast (or 1½ sachets of active dried yeast)	4 tsp/¾ oz

For the topping:

320 g	lamb rib and shoulder, de-boned, sinew trimmed, finely chopped	11¼ oz
3 (360 g)	medium onions, finely chopped	3 (2⅜ cups/12 oz)
1 bunch	flat-leaf parsley, finely chopped	1 bunch
250 ml	fresh tomato juice	1 cup/8 fl oz
4 tsp	red bell pepper paste (see p.492)	4 tsp
1 tbsp	tomato paste (see p.492)	1 tbsp
4 tsp	*isot* (smoky dried chilli (red pepper) flakes)	4 tsp
½ tsp	black pepper	½ tsp
¼ tsp	ground cinnamon	¼ tsp
½ tsp	salt	½ tsp

100 g	plain (all-purpose) flour, for dusting	¾ cup/3½ oz

200 g	red radish, thinly sliced	1¾ cups/7 oz
½ bunch	flat-leaf parsley, leaves picked	½ bunch
1	lemon, quartered	1

The topping for this dish is prepared at home, but can also be bought ready-made from the butcher. It is traditionally taken to the wood-fired oven of the local bakery where it is cooked. It is always enjoyed with a glass of *Ayran* (Salted Yogurt Drink, see p.452).

♦

To make the dough:
Combine the flour and salt in a large bowl. In a separate bowl, dissolve the yeast in 175 ml (¾ cup/6 fl oz) water. Make a well in the middle of the flour and pour in the dissolved yeast mixture, combine well and knead for 5 minutes into a dough. Cover with a damp dish towel and let rest for 30 minutes.

Divide the rested dough into 8 equal pieces, roll into balls and let rest for another 5 minutes.

To make the topping:
In a large bowl, gently mix together all the topping ingredients with your hands, until well combined. Divide the topping into 8 equal pieces and let rest for 5 minutes.

Preheat oven to 240°C/475°F/Gas Mark 9.

Sprinkle flour on the rested balls of dough, flatten them with your hands, then use a floured rolling pin to roll out to 15-cm (6-inch) circles. Gently spread the topping on top of the circles, spreading it right to the edges, then without breaking the dough, stretch the dough out further to 20-cm (8-inch) circles. Arrange them on baking sheets (2 per sheet) and bake in the hot oven for 4–5 minutes.

Serve immediately with sliced radishes, parsley and lemon quarters.

LAHMACUN PIZZA WITH LAMB AND ONIONS
SOĞANLI LAHMACUN

Region:	Gaziantep, Southeastern Anatolia	
Preparation time:	20 minutes, plus 35 minutes resting	
Cooking time:		5–20 minutes
Serves:		4

100 g	plain (all-purpose) flour, for dusting	¾ cup/3½ oz

For the dough:

250 g	plain (all-purpose) flour	scant 2 cups/ 9 oz
½ tsp	salt	½ tsp
20 g	fresh yeast (or 1½ sachets of active dried yeast)	4 tsp/¾ oz

For the topping:

320 g	lamb rib and shoulder, de-boned, sinew trimmed, finely chopped	11¼ oz
2 (240 g)	medium onions, finely chopped	2 (1⅝ cups/ 8½ oz)
100 g	walnuts, finely chopped	1 cup/3½ oz
2 tsp	red bell pepper paste (see p.492)	2 tsp
1 tbsp	tomato paste (see p.492)	1 tbsp
4 tsp	dried chilli (red pepper) flakes	4 tsp
½ tsp	black pepper	½ tsp
60 ml	pomegranate molasses (see p.490)	¼ cup/2 fl oz
½ tsp	salt	½ tsp

200 g	red radish, thinly sliced	1¾ cups/7 oz
½ bunch	flat-leaf parsley, leaves picked	½ bunch
4	fresh mint sprigs, leaves picked	4
1	lemon, quartered	1

This dish is made in the winter months, and always enjoyed with a glass of *Ayran* (Salted Yogurt Drink, see p.452). Some prefer to use pistachios and pine nuts instead of the walnuts.

◆

To make the dough:
Combine the flour and salt in a large bowl. In a separate bowl, dissolve the yeast in 175 ml (¾ cup/6 fl oz) water. Make a well in the middle of the flour and pour in the dissolved yeast mixture, combine well and knead for 5 minutes into a dough. Cover with a damp dish towel and let rest for 30 minutes.

Divide the rested dough into 8 equal pieces, roll into balls and let rest for another 5 minutes.

To make the topping:
In a large bowl, gently mix together all the topping ingredients with your hands, until well combined. Stir 100 ml (scant ½ cup/3½ fl oz) water into the mixture to loosen gently. Divide into 8 equal parts.

Preheat oven to 240°C/475°F/Gas Mark 9.

Sprinkle flour on the rested balls of dough, flatten them with your hands, then use a floured rolling pin to roll out to 15-cm (6-inch) circles. Gently spread the topping on top of the circles, spreading it right to the edges, then without breaking the dough, stretch the dough out further to 20-cm (8-inch) circles. Arrange them on baking sheets (2 per sheet) and bake in the hot oven for 4–5 minutes.

Serve immediately with sliced radishes, parsley, mint and lemon quarters.

YOGURT DUMPLINGS
BORANAŞI

Region:		Sinop, Black Sea Region
Preparation time:		30 minutes, plus 15 minutes resting
Cooking time:		10 minutes
Serves:		4

100 g	plain (all-purpose) flour, for dusting	¾ cup/3½ oz
¾ tsp	salt	¾ tsp

For the dough:		
250 g	plain (all-purpose) flour	scant 2 cups/ 9 oz
½ tsp	salt	½ tsp
1	egg, whisked	1

For the filling:		
400 g	strained Greek yogurt (cow's milk)	2 cups/14 oz
½ bunch	dill, finely chopped	½ bunch
4	garlic cloves, crushed	4
¼ tsp	salt	¼ tsp
¼ tsp	black pepper	¼ tsp

For the sauce:		
100 g	butter	scant ½ cup/ 3½ oz
4	dill sprigs, finely chopped	4
1 tsp	dried chilli (red pepper) flakes	1 tsp

V

A summer dish, these dumplings usually find their way into festivals and special occasion feasts.

♦

To make the dough:
Combine the flour and salt in a large bowl. Make a well in the middle, add the egg and 95 ml (⅓ cup/3¼ fl oz) water and combine gently. Knead for 10 minutes into a firm dough. Divide into 2 equal parts. Cover with a damp dish towel and let rest for 15 minutes.

Sprinkle the rested dough with flour and use a rolling pin to roll each piece out to a 40-cm (16-inch) circle. Cut both circles into 4-cm (1½-inch) squares.

To make the filling:
Mix all the filling ingredients in a large bowl until well combined.

Divide the filling mixture equally among the squares of dough, fold them into triangles and press to seal the sides.

In a large saucepan over medium heat, bring 2 litres (8½ cups/70 fl oz) water with ¾ teaspoon of salt to a boil. Add the dumplings to the boiling water and cook for 3–4 minutes, stirring gently to ensure they do not stick to one another. Use a slotted spoon to transfer to serving plates.

To make the sauce:
Heat the butter in a small saucepan over medium heat, add the dill and the dried chilli (red pepper) flakes and cook for 10 seconds.

Drizzle the sauce over the dumplings and serve.

TINY LAMB DUMPLINGS
BÖREK AŞI

Region:	Kayseri, Central Anatolia	
Preparation time:	30 minutes, plus overnight soaking, plus 15 minutes resting	
Cooking time:	1½ hours for the chickpeas (garbanzo beans), plus 15 minutes	
Serves:		4

For the dough:

250 g	plain (all-purpose) flour	scant 2 cups/ 9 oz
½ tsp	salt	½ tsp
1	egg, whisked	1

100 g	plain (all-purpose) flour, for dusting	¾ cup/3½ oz
100 g	butter	½ cup/3½ oz
6	garlic cloves, crushed	6
1½ tsp	tomato paste (see p.492)	1½ tsp
4 tsp	red bell pepper paste (see p.492)	4 tsp
1 tsp	dried chilli (red pepper) flakes	1 tsp
200 g	tomato, grated	1 cup/7 oz
100 g	chickpeas (garbanzo beans), soaked in water overnight, drained, pre-cooked for 1½ hours in 1.5 litres (6¼ cups/ 50 fl oz) water and peeled, or canned	½ cup/ 3½ oz
2 litres	meat stock (see p.489), hot	8½ cups/ 70 fl oz
½ tsp	salt	½ tsp
250 ml	sumac extract (see p.491)	1 cup/8 fl oz
2 tsp	dried mint	2 tsp

For the filling:

400 g	lamb, finely chopped with a cleaver or minced (ground)	14 oz
1 tsp	dried chilli (red pepper) flakes	1 tsp
½ tsp	salt	½ tsp
50 g	walnuts, finely chopped	½ cup/2 oz

Competent *manti* makers boast about fitting 40 of these tiny dumplings into a single tablespoon. If you find it impossible to make them as small as the instructions state, do try to get as close to that size as you can. Some enjoy this dish with a little plain yogurt drizzled over each dumpling just before serving.

♦

To make the dough:
Combine the flour and salt in a large bowl. Make a well in the middle, add the egg and 95 ml (⅓ cup/3¼ fl oz) water and combine gently. Knead for 10 minutes into a firm dough. Divide into 2 equal parts. Cover with a damp dish towel and let rest for 15 minutes.

Sprinkle the rested dough with flour and use a rolling pin to roll each piece out to a 40-cm (16-inch) circle. Cut both circles into 1-cm (½-inch) squares.

To make the filling:
In a bowl, knead the lamb, dried chilli (red pepper) flakes, salt and walnuts for 5 minutes, until well combined.

Divide the filling mixture equally among the squares of dough and gather the tops into little sacks, enclosing the filling.

Heat the butter in a small saucepan over medium heat, add the garlic and sauté for 10 seconds. Add the tomato paste, red bell pepper paste and dried chilli (red pepper) flakes and sauté for 2 more minutes. Add the tomatoes and chickpeas (garbanzo beans) and cook for 5 minutes, mixing occasionally.

In a large saucepan over medium heat, bring the meat stock and salt to a boil. Add the dumplings to the boiling stock and cook for 4 minutes, mixing occasionally to ensure they do not stick to one another.

Once cooked, remove the dumplings with a slotted spoon and transfer them to the tomato mixture in the other pan. Cook together for 1 minute, then stir in the sumac extract and dried mint and serve immediately.

DUMPLINGS
MANTI

Region:		Kayseri, Central Anatolia
Preparation time:		40 minutes, plus 15 minutes resting
Cooking time:		10 minutes
Serves:		4

For the dough:

250 g	plain (all-purpose) flour	scant 2 cups/ 9 oz
½ tsp	salt	½ tsp
1	egg, whisked	1
100 g	plain (all-purpose) flour, for dusting	¾ cup/3½ oz
¾ tsp	salt	¾ tsp

For the filling:

500 g	veal leg and brisket, finely chopped	1 lb 2 oz
60 g	medium onion finely sliced	⅜ cup/2¼ oz
½ tsp	salt	½ tsp
¼ tsp	black pepper	¼ tsp

For the yogurt sauce:

500 g	Greek yogurt (cow's milk)	2½ cups/ 1 lb 2 oz
¼ tsp	salt	¼ tsp
4	garlic cloves, crushed	4

For the butter sauce:

100 g	butter	scant ½ cup/ 3½ oz
1 tsp	dried chilli (red pepper) flakes	1 tsp

Sometimes these pasta dumplings are served with dried mint and sumac, and pickled peppers are also a popular side dish. These can also be made even smaller, with the pasta cut into 1-cm (½-inch) squares.

If you are not a big fan of yogurt, make a tomato sauce instead (with 1½ teaspoons tomato paste, 2 teaspoons red bell pepper paste, 4 garlic cloves, ¼ teaspoon ground sumac, and 250 ml/1 cup/8 fl oz fresh tomato juice).
♦

To make the dough:
Combine the flour and salt in a large bowl. Make a well in the middle, add the egg and 95 ml (⅓ cup/3¼ fl oz) water and combine gently. Knead for 10 minutes into a firm dough. Divide into 2 equal parts. Cover with a damp dish towel and let rest for 15 minutes.

Sprinkle the rested dough with flour and use a rolling pin to roll each piece out to a 30-cm (12-inch) circle. Cut both circles into 2-cm (¾-inch) squares.

To make the filling:
In a large bowl, knead the filling ingredients together until well combined.

Divide the filling mixture equally among the squares of dough and enclose to make little pockets, sealing them carefully.

In a large saucepan, bring 3 litres (12 cups/100 fl oz) water with ¾ teaspoon salt to a boil. Add the dumplings and cook for 5 minutes, stirring to ensure they do not stick to one another. Transfer the dumplings to a serving platter with a slotted spoon.

To make the yogurt sauce:
Whisk together the yogurt, salt and garlic for 3 minutes, until well combined.

To make the butter sauce:
Heat the butter in a saucepan over medium heat, add the dried chilli (red pepper) flakes and cook for 10 seconds.

Pour the yogurt sauce over the dumplings, followed by the hot butter sauce. Serve immediately.

GOAT CHEESE DUMPLINGS
PİRUHİ

Region:		Bilecik, all regions
Preparation time:		30 minutes, plus 30 minutes resting
Cooking time:		10 minutes
Serves:		4

For the dough:

250 g	plain (all-purpose) flour	scant 2 cups/ 9 oz
½ tsp	salt	½ tsp
1	egg, whisked	1

100 g	plain (all-purpose) flour, for dusting	¾ cup/3½ oz
¾ tsp	salt	¾ tsp

For the filling:

300 g	goat's cheese, crumbled	1⅓ cups/ 11 oz
2	spring onions (scallions), finely chopped	2
2	fresh mint sprigs, finely chopped	2
4	flat-leaf parsley sprigs, finely chopped	4
2	fresh basil sprigs, finely chopped	2
¼ tsp	salt	¼ tsp
¼ tsp	black pepper	¼ tsp

For the sauce:

100 g	butter	½ cup/3½ oz
1	spring onion (scallion), finely chopped	1
4	flat-leaf parsley, finely chopped	4
1	fresh basil sprig, finely chopped	1

V

Piruhi means cheese dumplings. *Lor*, *çökelek* and *kashk* are all popular fillings for these dumplings, there is a strained yogurt version too. They are all served with butter sauce.

◆

To make the dough:
Combine the flour and salt in a large bowl. Make a well in the flour, add the egg and 100 ml (scant ½ cup/3½ fl oz) water and combine gently. Knead for 10 minutes into a firm dough. Divide into 2 equal parts. Cover with a damp dish towel and let rest for 30 minutes.

Sprinkle the rested dough with flour and use a rolling pin to roll each piece out to a 40-cm (16-inch) circle. Cut both circles into 4-cm (1½-inch) squares.

To make the filling:
In a large bowl, knead the filling ingredients together for 5 minutes, until well combined.

Divide the filling mixture equally among the squares of dough, fold them into triangles and press to seal the sides.

In a large saucepan, bring 2 litres (8½ cups/70 fl oz) water with ¾ teaspoon salt to a boil. Add the dumplings and cook for 5 minutes, stirring to ensure they do not stick to one another. Transfer the dumplings to a serving platter with a slotted spoon.

To make the sauce:
Heat the butter in a saucepan over medium heat, add the chopped spring onion (scallion) and sauté for 1 minute. Add the parsley and basil and cook for another minute.

Drizzle the sauce over the dumplings and serve immediately.

TRAY DUMPLINGS
DİZME MANTI

Region:	Kayseri, Central Anatolia	
Preparation time:	30 minutes, plus 30 minutes resting	
Cooking time:		15 minutes
Serves:		4

100 g	plain (all-purpose) flour, for dusting	¾ cup/3½ oz
60 g	butter, melted	4 tbsp/2¼ oz
2	fresh basil sprigs, finely sliced	2
4	flat-leaf parsley sprigs, finely sliced	4
large pinch	ground sumac	large pinch
¼ tsp	black pepper	¼ tsp

For the dough:		
250 g	plain (all-purpose) flour	scant 2 cups/ 9 oz
½ tsp	salt	½ tsp
1	egg, whisked	1
75 ml	milk	⅓ cup/2½ fl oz
1 tbsp	olive oil	1 tbsp

For the filling:		
400 g	minced (ground) veal	14 oz
60 g	medium onion finely sliced	⅜ cup/2¼ oz
¼ tsp	salt	¼ tsp
½ tsp	dried chilli (red pepper) flakes	½ tsp
¼ tsp	black pepper	¼ tsp

For the sauce:		
150 g	butter, melted	⅔ cup/5 oz
4	garlic cloves	4
1 tsp	dried chilli (red pepper) flakes	1 tsp
1½ tsp	tomato paste (see p.492)	1½ tsp
200 g	tomato, finely sliced	1 cup/7 oz
½ tsp	salt	½ tsp
100 ml	veal stock (see p.489), hot	scant ½ cup/ 3½ fl oz

p.389 📷

Also known as 'oven dumplings', some like to serve this with an additional yogurt sauce (made with 500 g/2½ cups/1 lb 2 oz Greek yogurt, 3 crushed garlic cloves and a pinch of salt).

♦

To make the dough:
Combine the flour and salt in a large bowl. Make a well in the middle, add the egg, milk and olive oil and combine gently. Knead for 10 minutes into a coarse dough. Divide into 2 equal parts. Cover with a damp dish towel and let rest for 30 minutes.

Sprinkle the rested dough with flour and use a rolling pin to roll each piece out to a 30-cm (12-inch) circle. Cut both circles into 5-cm (2-inch) squares.

Preheat oven to 220°C/425°F/Gas Mark 7. Grease a 25-cm (10-inch) lipped baking sheet with 2 tablespoons of the butter.

To make the filling:
In a bowl, knead the veal, onion, salt, dried chilli (red pepper) flakes and black pepper for 5 minutes, until well combined.

Divide the filling mixture equally among the squares of dough, pair the corners and pinch them together leaving the middles open. Arrange the dumplings on the prepared baking sheet. Drizzle with the remaining 2 tablespoons of butter and bake in the hot oven for 8 minutes.

To make the sauce:
Meanwhile, heat the butter in a saucepan over medium heat, add the garlic cloves and sauté for 20 seconds. Add the dried chilli (red pepper) flakes and sauté for another 10 seconds. Add the tomato paste and sauté for 1 minute, then add the tomato and salt and cook for 5 minutes. Bring to a boil, then reduce the heat, add the hot stock and cook for another 3 minutes.

Pour the sauce over the cooked dumplings and sprinkle over the basil, parsley, ground sumac and black pepper. Return to the oven for 1 minute, then serve immediately.

CHEESE PASTRIES
PEYNİRLİ SEMSEK

Region:		Gaziantep, Southeastern Anatolia
Preparation time:		25 minutes, plus 45 minutes resting
Cooking time:		10 minutes
Serves:		4

100 g	plain (all-purpose) flour	¾ cup/3½ oz
60 ml	olive oil	¼ cup/2 fl oz

For the pastry:

250 g	plain (all-purpose) flour	2 cups/9 oz
50 g	fresh yeast (or 3 sachets active dried yeast)	3 tbsp/2 oz

For the filling:

400 g	unsalted sheep's milk cheese	14 oz
5	spring onions (scallions)	5
3	fresh garlic	3
½ bunch	flat-leaf parsley	½ bunch
2	fresh tarragon sprigs	2
1 tsp	dried mint	1 tsp
2 tsp	dried chilli (red pepper) flakes	2 tsp

◕ V

Called *peynirli semsek* in Nizip and its environs, and *peynirli börek* in and around Antep, these pastries are also known as cheese *börek*. Made in the spring with fresh sheep's or goat's milk cheese, preparing the dish at home and taking it to be cooked at the local bakery is common.

♦

To make the pastry:
Combine the flour and ½ teaspoon salt in a bowl. In a separate bowl, dissolve the fresh yeast in 175 ml (¾ cup/ 6 fl oz) water. Make a well in the flour, add the yeast, mix until combined, then knead for 5 minutes. Cover the dough with a damp dish towel and let rest for 30 minutes. Divide the dough into 8 equal parts, roll each into a ball and let rest for another 15 minutes.

To make the filling:
Crumble the cheese. Finely slice the spring onions (scallions), garlic, parsley and tarragon. In a bowl, gently mix all the filling ingredients together with ¼ teaspoon black pepper and ½ teaspoon salt. Divide into 8 equal parts.

Preheat oven to 220°C/425°F/Gas Mark 7. Sprinkle flour over the dough and flatten with your hands. Flour the work counter and roll out the dough to 15-cm (6-inch) discs. Place the filling in the pastry discs, fold in the edges by 1 cm (½ inch) and pinch the ends together to form an oval. Brush the edges with olive oil. Bake in the hot oven for 7–8 minutes, until golden brown Serve on plates.

♦

YOGURT NOODLES
ÖKSÜZ MANTI

Region:		Manisa, all regions
Preparation time:		5 minutes
Cooking time:		15 minutes
Serves:		4

250 g	homemade noodles (see p.493)	9 oz

For the butter sauce:

80 g	butter	⅓ cup/3 oz
2	garlic cloves, crushed	2
1 tsp	dried chilli (red pepper) flakes	1 tsp
1½ tsp	tomato paste (see p.492)	1½ tsp

For the yogurt sauce:

3	garlic cloves	3
500 g	Greek yogurt (sheep's milk)	2½ cups/ 1 lb 2 oz

V ✕

For some obscure reason the Turkish name of this dish, *Öksüz Mantı*, translates not to noodles but dumplings. The literal translation of the original title orphan dumplings refers to the fact that the noodles lack a filling. This dish is also known as 'poor man's dumplings'.

♦

In a saucepan, bring 3 litres (12 cups/100 fl oz) water and ¾ teaspoon salt to a boil over medium heat. Add the noodles and cook for 5 minutes. Remove from the heat and let rest for 2 minutes, while you finish the sauces.

To make the butter sauce:
Heat the butter in a saucepan over medium heat, add the garlic and dried chilli (red pepper) flakes and sauté for 10 seconds. Add the tomato paste and sauté for 2 minutes. Add 2 tablespoons of the noodle cooking water and cook for a further 2 minutes.

To make the yogurt sauce:
Pound the garlic to a paste. Whisk together with the yogurt and ¼ teaspoon salt for 3 minutes, until well combined.

Drain the noodles and transfer to plates. Spoon over the yogurt sauce and then the butter sauce and serve.

STACKED NOODLES
SİRON

Region:		Tunceli, all regions
Preparation time:		30 minutes, plus 30 minutes resting
Cooking time:		30 minutes
Serves:		4

100 g	wholemeal (whole wheat) plain (all-purpose) flour, for dusting	scant ½ cup/ 3½ oz

For the dough:

250 g	wholemeal (whole wheat) plain (all-purpose) flour	scant 2 cups/ 9 oz
½ tsp	salt	½ tsp

For the yogurt sauce:

500 g	yogurt (sheep's milk)	2½ cups/ 1 lb 2 oz
4	garlic cloves, pounded to a paste	4
1 tsp	dried chilli (red pepper) flakes	1 tsp
¼ tsp	salt	¼ tsp

For the butter sauce:

100 g	butter	½ cup/3½ oz
1 tsp	dried chilli (red pepper) flakes	1 tsp

2	fresh basil sprigs, finely chopped	2
4	flat-leaf parsley sprigs, finely chopped	4

V

This dish is also known locally as *ziron*, *silor*, *sırın* and *sırım*. It is made on special occasions and served stacked in a tray at a communal table. There are also versions of the recipe made with meat and chicken.

◆

To make the dough:
Combine the flour and salt in a large bowl. Make a well in the middle, add 165 ml (scant ¾ cup/5½ fl oz) water and combine. Knead for 10 minutes into a firm dough. Divide into 2 equal parts and roll into balls. Cover with a damp dish towel and let rest for 30 minutes.

Sprinkle the rested dough with flour and use a rolling pin to roll each piece out to a 40-cm (16-inch) circle.

Preheat oven to 200°C/400°F/Gas Mark 6.

Heat a sac, cast iron pan or griddle over medium heat until very hot, about 10 minutes. Cook each side of the sheets of dough for 50 seconds, then roll them up as tightly as possible. Cut the rolls into 2-cm (¾-inch) strips. Arrange them on a baking sheet, spirals facing up, and bake in the hot oven for 15 minutes.

To make the yogurt sauce:
Whisk together the yogurt, garlic, dried chilli (red pepper) flakes and salt for 3 minutes, until well combined.

To make the butter sauce:
Heat the butter in a saucepan over medium heat, add the dried chilli (red pepper) flakes and cook for 10 seconds.

Stack the cooked noodle spirals on a serving plate in a tower of three layers. Pour the yogurt and butter sauces over the top, sprinkle with fresh basil and parsley, then place in the middle of the table for everyone to serve themselves.

HANGEL NOODLES
HANGEL

Region:		Kars, Eastern Anatolia
Preparation time:		20 minutes, plus 15 minutes resting
Cooking time:		15 minutes
Serves:		4

100 g	plain (all-purpose) flour, for dusting	¾ cup/3½ oz
¾ tsp	salt	¾ tsp

For the dough:		
250 g	plain (all-purpose) flour	scant 2 cups/ 9 oz
½ tsp	salt	½ tsp
1	egg, whisked	1

For the sauce:		
100 g	butter	scant ½ cup/3½ oz
2 (240 g)	medium onions, sliced	2 (1⅝ cups/ 8½ oz)
¼ tsp	salt	¼ tsp

V

Hangel noodles are usually eaten after the main meal all through the year, but especially in winter.

♦

To make the dough:
Combine the flour and salt in a large bowl. Make a well in the middle, add the egg and 95 ml (⅓ cup/3¼ fl oz) water and combine gently. Knead for 10 minutes into a firm dough. Divide into 2 equal parts. Cover with a damp dish towel and let rest for 15 minutes.

Sprinkle the rested dough with flour and use a rolling pin to roll each piece out to a 30-cm (12-inch) circle. Cut both circles into 2-cm (¾-inch) squares.

To make the sauce:
Heat the butter in a saucepan over medium heat, add the onions and sauté for 10 minutes. Stir through the salt and cook for 1 more minute.

Meanwhile, bring 2.25 litres (10 cups/80 fl oz) water with ¾ teaspoon of salt to a boil. Add the noodles to the boiling water and cook for 3–4 minutes, stirring gently to ensure they do not stick to one another. Use a slotted spoon to transfer to serving plates.

Spoon 2 tablespoons of the cooking water over the noodles, then drizzle with the sauce and serve.

♦

DUCK NOODLES
ÖRDEKLİ MANTI

Region:		Çanakkale, Marmara Region
Preparation time:		15 minutes
Cooking time:		1 hour 50 minutes
Serves:		4

1 (1.5 kg)	wild (or farmed) duck	1 (3 lb 5 oz)
6	garlic cloves, crushed	6
5	black peppercorns	5
¾ tsp	salt	¾ tsp
400 g	*uzun erişte* (long homemade noodles) (see p.493)	14 oz

If a husband came home after hunting with a duck, then his wife would prepare this dish for the family. Duck noodles are frequently eaten in the winter.

♦

Put the duck into a saucepan with 3 litres (12 cups/ 100 fl oz) water and bring to a boil over medium heat. Skim off the foam on the surface with a slotted spoon. Reduce the heat, add the garlic, black peppercorns and salt and simmer for 1½ hours. Remove the duck from the water and pick the meat off the bones. Set the meat aside. Reduce the heat further and keep simmering the cooking stock.

Preheat oven to 220°C/425°F/Gas Mark 7.

Cut the long noodles in half. Add half the quantity to a roasting pan and layer half of the duck meat on top. Top with the remaining noodles and layer the remaining duck meat on top. Pour over the simmering stock.

Bake in the hot oven for 20 minutes.

Transfer to plates and serve.

NOODLE STEW
ŞİŞ BÖREK

Region:	Gaziantep, Southeastern Anatolia and Mediterranean Region	
Preparation time:	40 minutes, plus overnight soaking plus 10 minutes resting	
Cooking time:		1½ hours
Serves:		4

600 g	lamb shoulder, diced into 2-cm (¾-inch) pieces	1 lb 5 oz
100 g	chickpeas (garbanzo beans), soaked overnight in water, drained	½ cup/3½ oz
¾ tsp	salt	¾ tsp
100 g	plain (all-purpose) flour, for dusting	¾ cup/3½ oz
¼ tsp	black pepper	¼ tsp

For the dough:		
250 g	plain (all-purpose) flour	scant 2 cups/ 9 oz
½ tsp	salt	½ tsp

For the filling:		
400 g	mutton leg, finely chopped	14 oz
60 g	onion, finely chopped	⅜ cup/2¼ oz
½ tsp	salt	½ tsp
¼ tsp	black pepper	¼ tsp

For the yogurt sauce:		
300 g	strained yogurt (sheep's milk)	1½ cups/11 oz

For the butter sauce:		
60 g	butter	¼ cup/2¼ oz
2 tsp	dried mint	2 tsp

This dish is made on special occasions. There is a version of the recipe made with tomato paste, one made with garlic and a sour version with pomegranate molasses. Some also add walnuts to the filling mixture.

♦

Put the lamb shoulder and chickpeas (garbanzo beans) into a large saucepan with 3 litres (12 cups/100 fl oz) water and ½ teaspoon of the salt and bring to the boil over medium heat. Skim off the foam on the surface with a slotted spoon. Reduce the heat, cover and cook for 1 hour 20 minutes.

To make the dough:
Combine the flour and salt in a large bowl. Make a well in the middle, add 165 ml (scant ¾ cup/5½ fl oz) water and combine. Knead for 10 minutes into a firm dough. Divide into 2 equal parts and roll into balls. Cover with a damp dish towel and let rest for 10 minutes.

Sprinkle the rested dough with flour and use a rolling pin to roll each piece out to a 30-cm (12-inch) circle. Cut both circles into 2-cm (¾-inch) squares.

To make the filling:
In a large bowl, knead the filling ingredients for 5 minutes until well combined.

Divide the filling mixture equally among the squares of dough and gather the tops into little sacks, enclosing the filling.

To make the yogurt sauce:
In a small saucepan over medium heat, whisk the strained yogurt with 250 ml (1 cup/8 fl oz) water for 3 minutes. Reduce the heat and stir in the same direction until the yogurt boils. Cook for 2 minutes, then remove from the heat.

Add the filled noodle dumplings to the pan with the lamb and cook, uncovered, for 5 minutes. Add the yogurt sauce and black pepper and cook for a further 2 minutes.

To make the butter sauce:
Heat the butter in a saucepan over medium heat, add the dried mint and cook for 10 seconds.

Transfer the cooked stew to plates, pour over the butter sauce and serve.

RIDGED BREAD
AÇIK EKMEK

Region:	Gaziantep, Southeastern Anatolia and Mediterranean Region
Preparation time:	10 minutes, plus 25 minutes resting
Cooking time:	20 minutes
Serves:	4

For the dough:

250 g	wholemeal (whole wheat) flour	scant 2 cups/ 9 oz
½ tsp	salt	½ tsp
50 g	fresh yeast (or 3 sachets active dried yeast)	3 tbsp/2 oz

For the flour paste:

2 tbsp	plain (all-purpose) flour	2 tbsp
60 g	plain (all-purpose) flour	scant ½ cup/ 2¼ oz

◊ ◊ ◖ V ⁘

There is another version of this bread without the flour paste; cooked over a *tandir*, it is called a *lavash*. Instead of using a rolling pin, cooks use their hands dipped in flour.
◆

To make the dough:
Combine the flour and salt in a bowl, make a well and add the fresh yeast and 175 ml (¾ cup/6 fl oz) water. Slowly combine and knead for 10 minutes into a dough. Cover with a damp dish towel and rest for 15 minutes.

Divide the dough into 4 equal pieces. Roll into balls, cover with a damp dish towel and rest for another 10 minutes.

Preheat oven to 240°C/475°F/Gas Mark 9. Put a pizza stone or a heavy baking sheet in the oven to heat up.

To make the flour paste:
In a bowl, mix the flour with 75 ml (⅓ cup/2½ fl oz) water.

Take the rested dough, sprinkle each piece with flour and flatten with your palm. Roll each piece out to a 30 × 20-cm (12 × 8-inch) rectangle with a rolling pin. Apply the flour paste to the tops making ridges with the backs of your fingers. Make ridges in the paste with your fingertips.

Bake the breads, one at a time, on the pizza stone or baking sheet in the hot oven for 4 minutes.

BAZLAMA FLATBREAD
BAZLAMA

Region:	Bolu, Black Sea Region, Marmara Region and Central Anatolia
Preparation time:	20 minutes, plus 1 hour resting
Cooking time:	20 minutes
Serves:	4

250 g	wholemeal (whole wheat) flour	scant 2 cups/9 oz
½ tsp	salt	½ tsp
75 ml	milk, warm	⅓ cup/2½ fl oz
50 g	fresh yeast (or 3 sachets active dried yeast)	3 tbsp/2 oz
2 tsp	sugar	2 tsp

◖ V ⁘

This flatbread is usually made on a *sac* (concave iron plate), slate or ceramic plate. It is widely consumed in the Marmara, Western Black Sea and Central Anatolia regions.
◆

Combine the wholemeal (whole wheat) flour and salt in a large bowl. In a separate bowl, mix the milk, yeast and sugar with 100 ml (scant ½ cup/3½ fl oz) warm water. Make a well in the middle of the flour, pour in the liquids, mix well and knead for 10 minutes. Press into the dough with your hands to get rid of any air bubbles and roll into a ball. Divide into 2 pieces, cover with a damp dish towel and let rest for 30 minutes.

Stretch out the rested dough to a 15-cm (6-inch) circle, cover with a damp dish towel and let rest for another 30 minutes.

Heat a *sac*, cast iron pan or griddle over medium heat until very hot, about 10 minutes. Cook the breads for 10 minutes, turning every 2 minutes.

FRIED BREAD
PİŞİ

Region:		İstanbul, all regions
Preparation time:		15 minutes, plus 40 minutes resting
Cooking time:		35 minutes
Serves:		4

250 g	plain (all-purpose) flour	scant 2 cups/ 9 oz
1 tsp	salt	1 tsp
20 g	fresh yeast (or 1½ sachets active dried yeast)	4 tsp/ ¾ oz
500 ml	olive oil	generous 2 cups/ 17 fl oz

Traditionally, this fried bread is made and distributed when you have a dream about someone you have wronged. Generic *pişi* dough is thicker than the Şanlıurfa version. *Pişi* is associated with that olive harvest in Bursa and its environs where it is eaten with *helva* root foam.

◆

Combine the flour and salt in a large bowl. In a separate bowl, dissolve the yeast in 200 ml (scant 1 cup/7 fl oz) lukewarm water. Make a well in the flour and add the yeast. Mix gently and knead for 5 minutes into a dough. Cover with a damp dish towel and rest at room temperature for 30 minutes.

Divide the dough equally into 8 parts. Stretch the pieces of dough out to 15-cm (6-inch) discs and poke a hole in the middle of each disc with your finger. Cover with a damp dish towel and let rest for another 10 minutes.

In a large saucepan, heat the olive oil over medium heat to 155°C/310°F. Fry each bread in the hot oil for 4 minutes, turning continuously. Serve immediately.

ŞANLIURFA-STYLE FRIED FLATBREAD
PİŞİ (ŞANLIURFA)

Region:		Şanlıurfa, Southeastern Anatolia
Preparation time:		15 minutes, plus 40 minutes resting
Cooking time:		30 minutes
Serves:		4

250 g	plain (all-purpose) flour	scant 2 cups/ 9 oz
½ tsp	salt	½ tsp
1 tsp	sugar	1 tsp
1 tsp	nigella seeds	1 tsp
40 g	fresh yeast (or 2½ sachets active dried yeast), crumbled	2½ tbsp/ 1½ oz
500 ml	olive oil	generous 2 cups/ 17 fl oz

Here the dough is rolled out really thin, like *lahmacun*, and fried into a crispy flatbread in olive oil. It is sprinkled with sugar and cinnamon, then distributed for charity.

◆

Combine the flour, salt, sugar and nigella seeds in a bowl. In a separate bowl, dissolve the yeast in 150 ml (⅔ cup/ 5 fl oz) water. Make a well in the flour and add the yeast. Mix gently and knead for 5 minutes into a dough. Cover the bowl with a damp dish towel and rest for 30 minutes.

Divide the dough into 8 equal parts. Shape into balls, cover with a damp dish towel and rest for another 10 minutes.

Use a rolling pin to roll the rested balls of dough out to 20-cm (8-inch) circles.

In a large saucepan, heat the olive oil over medium heat to 155°C/310°F. Fry each bread in the hot oil for 1 minute on each side, then turn and cook for another 30 seconds on each side; 3 minutes in total. Serve immediately.

LAMB FLATBREAD
ETLİ EKMEK (MARDİN)

Region:		Mardin, Southeastern Anatolia
Preparation time:		25 minutes, plus 45 minutes resting
Cooking time:		10 minutes
Serves:		4

For the dough:

250 g	plain (all-purpose) flour	2 cups/9 oz
50 g	fresh yeast (or 3 sachets active dried yeast)	3 tbsp/2 oz
400 g	lamb brisket and backstrap	14 oz
1½ tsp	tomato paste (see p.492)	1½ tsp
½ tsp	mahleb (cherry seed spice)	½ tsp
2 tsp	dried oregano	2 tsp
½ tsp	ground cloves	½ tsp
¼ tsp	ground fennel	¼ tsp

50 g	plain (all-purpose) flour	⅓ cup/2 oz
60 ml	olive oil	¼ cup/2 fl oz

A popular flatbread all through the year, *etli ekmek* goes well with slices of watermelon in the summer. Locals take this to the nearest bakery to be cooked in their wood-fired oven. There is a hot version with chillies (chiles) too.

◆

To make the dough:
Combine the flour and ½ teaspoon salt in a bowl. Dissolve the yeast in 175 ml (¾ cup/6 fl oz) water. Make a well in the flour and mix in the yeast. De-bone, trim and finely chop or mince (grind) the lamb. Add the lamb, tomato paste, mahleb, dried oregano, ground cloves and ground fennel with ¼ teaspoon black pepper. Knead for 10 minutes into a dough, cover with a damp dish towel and rest for 30 minutes. Divide the dough into 4 equal parts, roll into balls and rest, covered with a damp dish towel, for a further 10 minutes.

Preheat oven to 240°C/475°F/Gas Mark 9. Sprinkle the tops and bottoms of the balls of dough with flour and flatten into discs. Oil your hands and stretch each disc into to a 15-cm (6-inch) circle. Arrange on a baking sheet, cover with a damp dish towel and rest for 5 minutes. Bake in the hot oven for 9–10 minutes. Remove from the oven, brush with olive oil and serve immediately.

◆

LAMB FLATBREAD PIZZA
ETLİ EKMEK

Region:		Konya, Central Anatolia
Preparation time:		25 minutes, plus 45 minutes resting
Cooking time:		10 minutes
Serves:		4

For the dough:

250 g	plain (all-purpose) flour	2 cups/9 oz
50 g	fresh yeast (or 3 sachets active dried yeast)	3 tbsp/2 oz

For the topping:

400 g	lamb brisket and shoulder	14 oz
1 (120 g)	medium onion	1 (¾ cup/4 oz)
2	banana peppers (mild sweet peppers)	2
200 g	tomato	1 cup/7 oz
4	flat-leaf parsley sprigs	4
2 tsp	red bell pepper paste (see p.492)	2 tsp
1 tsp	dried chilli (red pepper) flakes	1 tsp

100 g	plain (all-purpose) flour, ¾ cup/3½ oz	

The topping for this dish is prepared at home and then the pizza is baked in the wood-fired oven of the local bakery for a small fee. Bakeries specialize in this dish in the region, preparing one long 60 cm x 1 metre (23½ x 39 inch) pizza.

◆

To make the dough:
Combine the flour and ½ teaspoon salt in a bowl. Dissolve the yeast in 175 ml (¾ cup/6 fl oz) water. Make a well in the flour and mix in the yeast. Knead for 5 minutes into a dough, cover with a damp dish towel and rest for 30 minutes. Divide the into 4 equal parts, roll into balls and rest, covered, for a further 15 minutes.

To make the topping:
De-bone, trim and finely chop or mince (grind) the lamb. Finely slice the onion, banana peppers, tomato and parsley. Gently combine all the topping ingredients in a bowl. Season with ¼ teaspoon black pepper and ½ teaspoon salt. Divide into 4 equal parts.

Preheat oven to 240°C/475°F/Gas Mark 9. Sprinkle the dough with flour and flatten into discs. Flour your hands and stretch each disc into a 8 × 30-cm (3 × 12-inch) rectangle. Spread the filling evenly over each. Arrange on a baking sheet and bake in the oven for 6–7 minutes.

Remove from the oven, cut the pizzas into 4-cm (1½-inch) strips and serve.

BREADS & PASTRIES

CHEESE FLATBREAD PIZZA
KATIKLI EKMEK

For the dough:		
250 g	plain (all-purpose) flour	2 cups/9 oz
50 g	fresh yeast (or 3 sachets active dried yeast)	3 tbsp/2 oz

Region: Hatay, Mediterranean Region
Preparation time: 25 minutes, plus 35 minutes resting
Cooking time: 10 minutes
Serves: 4

For the topping:		
1 quantity	*sürk* (see p.484),	1 quantity
1 (120 g)	onion, finely chopped	1 (4 oz)
2 tsp	red bell pepper paste (see p.492)	2 tsp
2 tsp	dried chilli (red pepper) flakes	2 tsp
½ tsp	ground cumin	½ tsp
2 tsp	dried oregano	2 tsp
½ tsp	sesame seeds	½ tsp
3 tbsp	dried basil	3 tbsp
200 ml	olive oil	scant 1 cup/7 fl oz

100 g	plain (all-purpose) flour	¾ cup/3½ oz

V

This pizza is most often baked in tandoor ovens in the villages and home ovens in the cities. Locals like taking this dish to the nearest bakery to be cooked in their wood-fired oven. You can substitute the *sürk* (see p.484) with 200 g/7 oz *lor* (fresh curd cheese, see p.485) and 100 g/3½ oz feta cheese (goat's milk), if wished.

◆

To make the dough:
Combine the flour and ½ teaspoon salt in a bowl. Dissolve the yeast in 175 ml (¾ cup/6 fl oz) water. Make a well in the flour and mix in the yeast. Knead for 5 minutes into a dough, cover with a damp dish towel and rest for 30 minutes. Divide the dough into 4 equal parts, roll into balls and rest, covered, for a further 15 minutes.

To make the topping:
Crumble the *sürk* into a bowl. Add the other topping ingredients with ¼ teaspoon black pepper and ½ teaspoon salt, then combine by hand. Divide into 4 equal parts.

Preheat oven to 240°C/475°F/Gas Mark 9.

Sprinkle the dough with flour and flatten into discs. Flour your hands and stretch each disc into a 20-cm (8-inch) circle. Spread the filling evenly over each circle. Arrange on a baking sheet and bake the hot oven for 6–7 minutes.

Transfer to plates and serve.

PIDE FLATBREAD WITH VEAL
KAVURMALI PİDE

Region: Giresun, Black Sea Region
Preparation time: 25 minutes, plus 40 minutes resting
Cooking time: 10 minutes
Serves: 4

For the dough:		
250 g	plain (all-purpose) flour	2 cups/9 oz
1 tsp	sugar	1 tsp
50 g	fresh yeast (or 3 sachets active dried yeast)	3 tbsp/2 oz

100 g	plain (all-purpose) flour	¾ cup/3½ oz
500 g	veal confit	1 lb 2 oz
50 g	butter, melted	¼ cup/2 oz

1	*Çoban Salatası* (Shepherd's Salad, see p.54)	1

Made in local bakeries at the break of dawn, this *pide* is a favourite of weekend breakfasts, served with a glass of *Ayran* (Salted Yogurt Drink, see p.452).

◆

To make the dough:
Combine the flour and sugar with ½ teaspoon salt in a bowl. Dissolve the yeast in 175 ml (¾ cup/6 fl oz) water. Make a well in the flour and mix in the yeast. Knead for 5 minutes into a dough, cover with a damp dish towel and rest for 30 minutes. Divide the dough into 4 equal parts, roll into balls and rest, covered, for a further 15 minutes.

Preheat oven to 240°C/475°F/Gas Mark 9. Flour your hands and flatten the dough. Stretch each disc into a 20-cm (8-inch) circle. Spread the veal confit on one half of each circle and fold the other half over, pressing to seal the edges. Stretch and gently lengthen the sides.

Put the filled breads on a baking sheet. Bake in the oven for 9–10 minutes, making sure they are cooked all around. Remove from the oven and brush with melted butter. Slice into 4-cm (1½-inch) strips and serve with *Çoban Salatası*.

BREADS & PASTRIES

PIDE FLATBREAD WITH SPICED BEEF
PASTIRMALI PİDE

Region:		Kayseri, Central Anatolia
Preparation time:		25 minutes, plus 45 minutes resting
Cooking time:		10 minutes
Serves:		4

For the dough:

250 g	plain (all-purpose) flour	2 cups/9 oz
1 tsp	sugar	1 tsp
50 g	fresh yeast (or 3 sachets active dried yeast)	3 tbsp/2 oz

100 g	plain (all-purpose) flour, for dusting	¾ cup/3½ oz
400 g	*pastırma* (cured beef, see p.497), thinly sliced	14 oz
8	eggs	8
50 g	butter, melted	¼ cup/2 oz

p.399

A *Ramadan* favourite, *pide* is crescent shaped and cooked on a *sac* griddle. Substitute the *Pastırma* with *Sucuk* (Spiced Salami, see p.496) to make *Sucuklu Pide*.

◆

To make the dough:
Combine the flour and sugar with ½ teaspoon salt in a bowl. Dissolve the yeast in 175 ml (¾ cup/6 fl oz) water. Make a well in the flour and mix in the yeast. Knead for 5 minutes into a dough, cover with a damp dish towel and rest for 30 minutes. Divide the dough into 4 equal parts, roll into balls and rest, covered, for a further 15 minutes.

Preheat oven to 240°C/475°F/Gas Mark 9. Flour your hands and flatten the dough. Stretch each disc into a 12 × 25-cm (4¾ x 10-inch) rectangle. Divide the *pastırma* among the rectangles, placing it parallel to the long edges. Fold 3 cm (1¼ inch) of dough in all around and join the corners.

Put the flatbreads on a baking sheet. Bake in the oven for 7 minutes. Remove from the oven, crack 2 eggs on each flatbread, keeping the yolks intact, and brush the sides with butter. Return to the oven for 3 minutes. Remove from the oven, cut into 4-cm (1½-inch) strips and serve.

◆

PIDE FLATBREAD WITH CHEESE
PEYNİRLİ PİDE

Region:		İstanbul, all regions
Preparation time:		25 minutes, plus 45 minutes resting
Cooking time:		10 minutes
Serves:		4

For the dough:

250 g	plain (all-purpose) flour	2 cups/9 oz
1 tsp	sugar	1 tsp
50 g	fresh yeast (or 3 sachets active dried yeast)	3 tbsp/2 oz

For the filling:

4	spring onions (scallions)	4
1 bunch	flat-leaf parsley	1 bunch
5	dill sprigs	5
300 g	unsalted sheep's milk cheese, crumbled	11 oz
2	eggs	2
½ tsp	dried chilli (red pepper) flakes	½ tsp

100 g	plain (all-purpose) flour	¾ cup/3½ oz
50 g	butter, melted	¼ cup/2 oz

◆ V

This is a popular summer snack. Other cheeses also work well in this recipe and there is an egg version, where the egg is either mixed with the cheese or cracked on top of the flatbread, as in *Pastırmalı Pide* (Pide Flatbread with Spiced Beef, see above).

◆

To make the dough:
Make the dough following the instructions given above.

To make the filling:
Crumble the cheese into a bowl. Finely chop the spring onions (scallions), parsley and dill and add to the bowl with all the other filling ingredients. Season with ¼ teaspoon black pepper and ½ teaspoon salt and gently combine by hand. Divide the filling into 4 equal parts.

Preheat oven to 240°C/475°F/Gas Mark 9. Flour your hands and flatten the dough. Stretch each disc into a 10 x 25-cm (4 × 10-inch) rectangle. Spread the filling equally among the rectangles. Fold 2 cm (¾ inch) of dough in all around and join the corners of the short sides together.

Put the flatbreads on a baking sheet. Bake in the oven for 9–10 minutes, making sure they are evenly baked. Remove from the oven, brush with melted butter, cut into 4-cm (1½-inch) strips and serve.

BREADS & PASTRIES

SWEET CRESCENT ROLLS
AY ÇÖREĞİ

Region:		İstanbul, all regions
Preparation time:		40 minutes, plus 55 minutes resting
Cooking time:		30 minutes
Serves:		4

For the filling:

80 g	raisins	generous ½ cup/ 3 oz
100 g	walnuts, crushed	1 cup/3½ oz
1 tbsp	sugar	1 tbsp
3 tsp	ground cinnamon	3 tsp
1	sour apple, grated	1
1 tsp	ground cloves	1 tsp

For the pastry:

200 g	plain (all-purpose) flour	1½ cups/7 oz
2 tbsp	sugar	2 tbsp
½ tsp	salt	½ tsp
1¾ tbsp	milk	1¾ tbsp
50 g	butter, melted	¼ cup/2 oz
¾ tsp	mahleb (cherry seed spice)	¾ tsp
1	egg white	1
50 g	fresh yeast (or 3 sachets active dried yeast), crumbled	3 tbsp/2 oz

100 ml	olive oil	scant ½ cup/ 3½ fl oz
1	egg yolk	1
50 g	slivered almonds	⅓ cup/2 oz

V

p.401 📷

Legend has it that in pagan times people made these sweet crescents in gratitude to the Gods for granting their wishes. Butter pastries are made to celebrate Easter, *Nowruz*, *Hıdrellez*, *Ramadan* and *Eid-al-Adha*. These pastries are also distributed to celebrate accomplishments. Traditionally the women of the village hand them out.

◆

To make the filling:
In a mortar and pestle, pound the raisins, walnuts, sugar, ground cinnamon, apple and cloves into a fine paste. Divide into 4 equal parts.

To make the pastry:
Combine the flour, sugar and salt in a large bowl and mix well. Make a well in the middle and pour in the milk, butter, mahleb, egg white and yeast. Mix well and knead for 10 minutes into a firm dough. Cover with a damp dish towel and let rest for 10 minutes.

Divide the dough into 4 equal parts, brush lightly with 2 teaspoons of olive oil and let rest for another 10 minutes.

Roll out each piece of dough to a 30-cm (12-inch) circle. Brush the middle of each circle with 1 teaspoon of olive oil and fold into an envelope shape. Let rest for another 10 minutes.

Using an oiled rolling pin and oiling each piece as you go, roll out the pastry envelopes to 6 × 15-cm (2½ × 6-inch) ovals. Cover with a damp dish towel and let rest for 10 minutes.

Preheat oven to 180°C/350°F/Gas Mark 4 and oil a large baking sheet.

Spoon the filling along the long length of the oval and roll up, brushing again with olive oil.

Shape the rolled pastries into crescents and arrange on the prepared baking sheet. Brush the pastries with egg yolk, cover the tray with a damp dish towel, making sure it does not touch the pastries and let rest for 15 minutes.

Sprinkle the pastries with the slivered almonds and bake in the oven for 30 minutes. Transfer to plates and serve.

◆

DESSERTS

◆

DESSERTS IN
TURKISH CULTURE

Baklava, *kadayif*, *helva*, fruit desserts, milk puddings, pancakes, sweet sausages, pastries, jellies and desserts with cheese, molasses and honey make up our rich dessert culture. These desserts are all closely intertwined with tradition. Pastries of filo (phyllo) and *kadayif* (see p.436) are the queens of the Turkish dessert kitchen, closely followed by milk puddings.

There is an ideal time for every dessert. Milk puddings are popular all year round but especially in the summer months, served cold. Compotes are also enjoyed cold. The abundance of fruit in the warmer months yields a great variety of fresh fruit desserts. And obviously ice creams and desserts made with snow and ice are preferred in the summer.

Winter is time for dried fruit desserts, sweet pastries and sweets made from winter fruits. Warm desserts with sherbet are eaten throughout the winter months. Then there are jams, which are eaten for breakfast. Sweet sausages, fruit leathers and dried fruit are all tastes of the winter months, as well as egg-based desserts.

Baklava, *kadayif* and sweet pastries make holidays, weddings, engagement parties and other special occasions more spectacular. Another dessert for holidays and celebrations is rice pudding, which is popular all year round.

DESSERT TECHNIQUES

The usual size of the filo (phyllo) pastry for *baklava* is 40–50 cm (16–20 inches) wide, as *baklava* are traditionally made in 4–5 kg (9–11 lb) trays. This filo is rolled out with a special rolling pin called an *oklava* and wheat starch flour. In order to modify the recipes to suit the home kitchen and serve an average of four people, I have reduced the filo size to 25-cm (10-inch) sheets. Homemade *Baklava Yufkası* (Filo (Phyllo) Pastry, see p.496) will carry your *baklava* to new heights, but store-bought filo will work just fine too.

Baklava and all other tray bakes are even more delicious when baked in a wood-fired oven and using a copper tray makes them taste even better. Obviously, if this is not possible you will have to make do with standard ovens and equipment, which are detailed in the recipes.

The crucial tip for milk puddings, especially *Muhallebi* (Rice Custard, p.414) and *Tavuk Göğsü* (Chicken Breast Pudding, p.432), is to go the extra mile and make your own slaked rice emulsion. The result is far superior.

DESSERT RITUALS

There are numerous cultural dessert rituals – some desserts are made for wakes, such as the Ottoman Greek *Koliva*, or for distributing for charity, such as *Lokma*. Traditional wedding banquets will always feature a compote, especially in villages. Another widespread tradition is the making of *Aşure* (Noah's Pudding, p.418), which is made and distributed in the month of *Muharrem* after the fast. The Armenians, on the other hand, make *Anuşabur* (Sweet Porridge with Dried Fruit, see p.438), which is similar to *Aşure*, on New Year's Eve.

Then there is the important role of *baklava* in matrimony. Once a union has been agreed to, a betrothal ceremony is organised. This traditionally takes place at the bride's home, where the groom and his family visit bearing a kilim rug or a carpet and a tray of *baklava*. Where I come from, this visit is called the *şirinleme* (the sweeting). If things go sour soon after the ceremony, the bride's family returns all the gifts saying 'sweet has turned sour', which opens the way for both sides to exchange unpleasantries. This however is the worst case scenario, usually most problems are resolved over a tray of sweets.

In my hometown of Nizip, Gaziantep, a *bayram* (holiday) would only be a proper *bayram* if there was a dish of *Sütlaç* (Rice Pudding, see p.426). My mother always made this exclusively for *bayrams*, never at other times.

Helvas are winter staples and bear many functions and meanings. The first thing to do when someone dies is to roast a *helva* for their soul. The first choice here would be *Un Helvası* (Flour Halva, see p.410). This tradition is followed by families all over the country. *Helvas* are made and distributed to family and neighbours on the seventh and fortieth day after a death. Not sampling any would be considered bad manners – even a tiny morsel is believed to bring good fortune.

As a final note, there is an amusing saying for pregnant women who long for a boy: *ye tatlı'yı çıkar Hakkı'yı* (eat your dessert, push out Bert!). It is slightly ridiculous, but indicates just how seriously the role of desserts is taken in our culture.

TAHINI HALVA
TAHİNLİ HELVA

Region:		Kastamonu, all regions
Preparation time:		15 minutes
Cooking time:		30 minutes, plus 1 hour setting
Serves:		4

This rich dessert is mostly made in the winter months. The summer version is less sweet. It is customary to share this dish with seven neighbours each time it is made, so its aroma permeates the neighborhood.

♦

150 g	unsalted butter	⅔ cup/5 oz
100 g	plain (all-purpose) flour	¾ cup/3½ oz
¼ tsp	salt	¼ tsp
150 g	icing (confectioner's) sugar	1½ cups/5 oz
120 ml	tahini (sesame seed paste), diluted with 5 tbsp water	½ cup/ 4 fl oz
80 g	walnuts, crushed and toasted	¾ cup/3 oz
2 tbsp	sesame seeds, toasted	2 tbsp

Heat the butter in a large saucepan over medium heat until hot. Reduce the heat to low, slowly add the flour and cook for 15 minutes, mixing continuously with a wooden spoon. Reduce the heat to very low, add the salt, icing (confectioner's) sugar and 100 ml (scant ½ cup/ 3½ fl oz) of the tahini and mix well for 5 minutes. Add the remaining tahini and mix for another 5 minutes. Add the walnuts and sesame seeds and stir.

Transfer the mixture to a bowl and let set for 1 hour at room temperature. Serve on plates.

◐ ♦ V

p.409 📷

♦

CRUMBLY SEMOLINA HALVA
İRMİK HELVASI

Region:		Antalya, all regions
Preparation time:		10 minutes
Cooking time:		30 minutes
Serves:		4

This winter dish is traditionally made at wakes and on the seventh day after a death, when it is given away for charity. It is also said that seeing a recently deceased loved one in a dream is a good excuse to make and distribute this dish.

♦

150 g	sugar	¾ cup/5 oz
¼ tsp	orange zest	¼ tsp
200 ml	orange juice	scant 1 cup/ 7 fl oz
½ tsp	lemon zest	½ tsp
2 tbsp	lemon juice	2 tbsp
1	cinnamon stick	1
120 g	unsalted butter	½ cup/4 oz
3 tbsp	pine nuts	3 tbsp
120 g	semolina	⅔ cup/4 oz
¼ tsp	salt	¼ tsp

Combine the sugar, orange zest and juice, lemon zest and juice and cinnamon stick with 500 ml (generous 2 cups/ 17 fl oz) water in a large saucepan and bring to a boil over medium heat. Reduce the heat and keep simmering for 15 minutes.

Meanwhile, heat the butter in a separate small saucepan over medium heat until hot. Reduce the heat, add the pine nuts, semolina and salt and sauté for 20 minutes, stirring to ensure that it does not burn. Remove from the heat.

Pour the boiling syrup over the semolina mixture and stir together for 2 minutes. Cover the pan with a dish towel and let rest for 5 minutes.

Stir the semolina halva, transfer to plates and serve.

V

FLOUR HALVA
UN HELVASI

Region:		Çorum, all regions
Preparation time:		5 minutes
Cooking time:		25 minutes
Serves:		4

1 litre	milk	4¼ cups/34 fl oz
150 g	sugar	¾ cup/5 oz
150 g	unsalted butter	⅔ cup/5 oz
100 g	plain (all-purpose) flour	¾ cup/3½ oz

V X ⁙

p.411

Flour halva is associated with death rites. It is made and distributed by the family of the recently departed. The ritual is repeated on the seventh, fortieth and fifty-second day of the death. It is also popular at *mevlits* and *kandils* (Holy days for Muslims commemorating milestones in Mohammed's life). It is believed that the aromas released as the flour is roasted will give peace to the soul of the dead.

♦

Bring the milk and sugar to the boil in small saucepan over medium heat, then reduce the heat and keep simmering for 15 minutes.

Meanwhile, heat the butter in a separate small saucepan over medium heat until hot. Reduce the heat to low, add the flour and cook for 15 minutes, mixing continuously with a wooden spoon, until it starts to brown. Make sure it does not burn. Reduce the heat to very low and gradually pour the boiling milk mixture into the pan. Cook, stirring, for 5 minutes. Remove from the heat and let rest, covered, for 2 minutes. Transfer to plates and serve.

♦

WALNUT SLICE
NEVZİNE

Region:		Kayseri, Central Anatolia
Preparation time:		20 minutes
Cooking time:	1 hour, plus 1 hour 30 minutes resting	
Serves:		4

For the syrup:

200 g	sugar	1 cup/7 oz
1 tbsp	lemon juice	1 tbsp
2 tbsp	grape molasses	2 tbsp

2 tbsp	butter, for greasing	2 tbsp

For the pastry dough:

200 g	plain (all-purpose) flour, plus extra for dusting	1½ cups/7 oz
¾ tsp	baking powder	¾ tsp
2 tbsp	sesame seeds	2 tbsp
40 ml	tahini (sesame seed paste)	3 tbsp/1¼ fl oz
35 g	unsalted butter, melted	2 tbsp/1¼ oz
2 tbsp	olive oil	2 tbsp
40 ml	milk	3 tbsp/1¼ fl oz
100 g	walnuts, finely chopped	1 cup/3½ oz

V

This is a popular slice made extensively in the region for weddings, when a prospective groom asks for a woman's hand in marriage and also for new mothers.

♦

To make the syrup:
Combine the sugar, lemon juice, grape molasses and 300 ml (1¼ cups/10 fl oz) water in a small saucepan over medium heat. Heat until the temperature reaches 95°C (203°F) on a cooking thermometer, about 20 minutes, stirring until the sugar has dissolved. Remove from the heat and let cool for 1 hour.

Preheat oven to 180°C/350°F/Gas Mark 4. Brush a deep 20-cm (8-inch) square pan with 2 tablespoons of butter.

To make the pastry dough:
In a large bowl, combine the flour, baking powder and sesame seeds with ¼ teaspoon salt, make a well in the middle and add the tahini, butter, olive oil and milk. With flour-dusted hands, knead for 5 minutes. Transfer to a work counter and knead for another 5 minutes, until you have an elastic dough. Add the walnuts and knead in for another 5 minutes.

Put the dough into the prepared baking pan, pressing down and stretching to cover the entire pan. Flatten the top and use a sharp knife to cut into 3-cm (1¼-inch) squares. Bake in the hot oven for 40 minutes.

Remove from the oven, pour the syrup evenly over and let rest for 30 minutes. Transfer to plates and serve.

MA'AMOUL-FILLED COOKIES
KEREBİÇ (GEREBİÇ)

Region:	Kilis and Hatay, Mediterranean Region and Southeastern Anatolia
Preparation time:	25 minutes
Cooking time:	40 minutes, plus cooling
Serves:	4

For the pastry:

200 g	plain (all-purpose) flour	1½ cups/7 oz
120 ml	olive oil	½ cup/4 fl oz

For the filling:

150 g	walnuts, finely chopped	1½ cups/5 oz
3 tsp	ground cinnamon	3 tsp
60 g	sugar	⅓ cup/2¼ oz
1½ tsp	ground cinnamon	1½ tsp
2 tbsp	icing (confectioner's) sugar	2 tbsp

💧 ◗ ◆ **V**   p.413 📷

Some recipes prefer to use butter to make these cookies, but only olive oil is used around Kilis and the surrounding areas. If you do not have the special ma'amoul mould, you can shape them by hand.
◆
Preheat oven to 160°C/325°F/Gas Mark 3. Line a baking sheet with baking (parchment) paper.

To make the pastry:
Knead the flour and oil together in a bowl for 5 minutes. Transfer to a work counter and knead for another 10 minutes, until a stretchy dough. Divide into 8 equal parts.

To make the filling:
Combine the walnuts, cinnamon and sugar in a bowl and mix until well combined. Divide into 8 equal parts.

Put each piece of pastry dough in the ma'amoul mould, add a piece of the filling, close, then remove from the mould. Alternatively, use your hands to mould each piece of pastry dough into a flat oval shape. Make a cavity in the middle, add a spoonful of the filling and close.

Arrange the cookies on the lined baking sheet and bake in the hot oven for 30–40 minutes. Let the cookies cool for a few minutes before transferring to a wire cooking rack to cool to room temperature.

Once cooled, sprinkle with sifted icing (confectioner's) sugar and cinnamon and serve.

◆

KURABIYE COOKIES
UN KURABİYESİ

Region:	Antalya, all regions
Preparation time:	20 minutes
Cooking time:	1 hour 30 minutes
Serves:	4

100 g	ghee (see p.485), melted	scant ½ cup/3½ oz
100 g	sugar	½ cup/3½ oz
5 drops	vanilla extract	5 drops
1 tsp	baking powder	1 tsp
200 g	plain (all-purpose) flour	1½ cups/7 oz
50 g	icing (confectioner's) sugar	⅓ cup/2 oz

◗ **V**

These tea-time favourites are made for special occasions. The shape has many local variations. It is customary to distribute these when wishes come true. for charity and at funerals. If the deceased was young, a savoury version is made; if they were old, a sweet version is prepared.
◆
Preheat oven to 110°C/225°F/Gas Mark ¼. Line a baking sheet with baking (parchment) paper.

Put the melted ghee and sugar into a large bowl, mix well, then knead for 5 minutes. Add the vanilla extract, baking powder and flour and knead into a stretchy dough. Divide into 2 equal parts and roll into balls.

Roll each ball out on a work counter, stretching them into 15-cm (6-inch) rolls. Cut the rolls diagonally into 4-cm (1½-inch) thick slices, place on the baking sheet and bake in the oven for 1½ hours, until the cookies are fully cooked.

Dust with icing (confectioner's) sugar and serve.

BAKLAVA
BAKLAVA

Region:		Gümüşhane, all regions
Preparation time:		20 minutes
Cooking time:		40 minutes, plus 15 minutes resting
Serves:		4

175 g	ghee (see p.485), melted	¾ cup/6 oz
30 (25-cm) sheets	filo (phyllo) pastry (see p.496)	30 (10-inch) sheets
250 g	walnuts, finely chopped	2½ cups/9 oz
250 g	sugar	1¼ cups/9 oz
1 tbsp	lemon juice	1 tbsp

◆ V ⁂   p.415 ▢

Celebrations are never complete without *baklava*. Make it with pistachios or hazelnuts, depending on local preference.
◆
Preheat oven to 180°C/350°F/Gas Mark 4. Generously brush a deep 20-cm (8-inch) square baking pan with 2 tablespoons ghee. Layer 15 sheets of filo (phyllo) pastry into the pan, brushing each sheet with ghee before adding the next. Spread the walnuts over the sheets, then cover with the remaining 15 pastry sheets, brushing each with ghee as before. Push the pastry at the edges down into the pan. Cut through the pastry layers in diagonal strips about 3-cm (1¼-inches) wide, then cut in the opposite direction to obtain diamond-shaped portions. Pour over the remaining ghee and bake in the oven for 30–40 minutes.

Meanwhile, heat the sugar, lemon juice and 350 ml (1½ cups/12 fl oz) water in a saucepan over medium heat until the temperature reaches 100°C (212°F), about 20 minutes.

Remove the pan from the oven and drain away excess ghee, if there is any. Evenly pour the syrup over the pastry and let rest for 15 minutes. Transfer to plates and serve.

◆

MUHALLEBI RICE CUSTARD
MUHALLEBİ

Region:		Bursa, all regions
Preparation time:		15 minutes
Cooking time:		30 minutes, plus 6 hours resting
Serves:		4

1 litre	milk	4¼ cups/34 fl oz
¼ tsp	mastic (plant resin) pounded with 1 tsp sugar	¼ tsp
4 drops	vanilla extract	4 drops
120 g	sugar	½ cup/4 oz
1 tsp	ground cinnamon, to serve	1 tsp

For the slaked rice:		
100 g	medium-grain rice (or 100 g/¾ cup/ 3½ oz rice flour)	½ cup/3½ oz

💧 ◆ V

A Persian cook once presented this historic milk pudding to an Arab general, al Muhallab bin Abi Sufra, who loved it so much that he named it after himself. *Muhallebicis* (pudding shops) are a venerable culinary institution, which spread to other major cities from İstanbul. Getting cosy with your beloved at a *muhallebici* is İstanbul tradition. What makes a good *muhallebi* is the use of fresh buffalo milk and the preparation of the rice slurry through a stone mill. The home version uses rice flour, wheat starch or corn starch as a thickening agent.
◆
To make the slaked rice:
Soak the rice in 400 ml (1⅔ cups/14 fl oz) water for 4 hours. Transfer the mixture to a food processor and process until smooth.

Whisk the milk, slaked rice, mastic, vanilla extract and sugar in a large saucepan for 2 minutes, until well combined. Set over medium heat and bring to the boil, whisking continuously, for 5 minutes. Cook on a low heat for a further 20–30 minutes, until the custard coats the back of a spoon.

Transfer to serving glass bowls. Let rest at room temperature for 1 hour, then chill in the refrigerator for 5 hours. Sprinkle with ground cinnamon and serve.

♦

CUSTARD SLICE
PAPONİ (LAZ BÖREĞİ)

Region:		Rize, Black Sea Region
Preparation time:		15 minutes
Cooking time:		1 hour 15 minutes, plus 1 hour cooling, plus 15 minutes resting
Serves:		4

For the syrup:

250 g	sugar	1¼ cups/9 oz
1 tbsp	lemon juice	1 tbsp

For the custard:

70 g	wheat starch	½ cup/2¾ oz
400 ml	milk	1⅔ cups/14 fl oz
10	black peppercorns	10
2 tsp	sugar	2 tsp
¼ tsp	salt	¼ tsp

30 (20-cm) sheets	filo (phyllo) pastry (see p.496)	30 (8-inch) sheets
175 g	unsalted butter, melted	¾ cup/6 oz

V   p.417

Any excuse is a good excuse to prepare this dish. Originally cut into four, one slice was for maker, one for her parents, one for her children, and the last slice for neighbours.

♦

To make the syrup:
Combine the sugar, lemon juice and 350 ml (1½ cups/ 12 fl oz) water in a saucepan over medium heat. Heat until the temperature reaches 95°C (203°F) on a cooking thermometer. Remove from the heat and cool for 1 hour.

To make the custard:
In a saucepan, mix the wheat starch and milk until well combined then bring to a boil over medium heat. Cook for 20 minutes, reduce the heat, add the black pepper, sugar and salt and cook, stirring, for another 10 minutes, until the custard coats the back of a spoon. Let cool for 1 hour.

Preheat oven to 180°C/350°F/Gas Mark 4. Brush a 20-cm (8-inch) square pan with 2 teaspoons butter. Layer 15 sheets of pastry into the pan, brushing each with butter. Spread the custard over, then cover with the remaining pastry sheets, brushing each with butter. Using a sharp knife, cut the pastry into quarters through the layers. Pour over the remaining butter and bake in the oven for 30–40 minutes.

Remove from the oven, pour over the syrup and let soak for 15 minutes. Transfer to plates and serve.

♦

CREAM BAKLAVA
ŞÖBİYET

Region:		Gaziantep, Southeastern Anatolia
Preparation time:		30 minutes
Cooking time:		45 minutes, plus 1 hour cooling, plus 15 minutes resting
Serves:		4

320 g	ghee (see p.485)	1½ cups/11¾ oz
16 (20-cm) sheets	filo (phyllo) pastry (see p.496)	16 (8-inch) sheets
160 g	shelled pistachios	1½ cups/5½ oz

For the clotted cream:

400 ml	sheep's milk	1⅔ cups/14 fl oz
80 g	semolina	½ cup/3 oz

For the syrup:

300 g	sugar	1½ cups/11 oz
1 tbsp	lemon juice	1 tbsp

◆ V

This is also known as *muska baklavası* by some locals.

♦

To make the clotted cream:
In a saucepan, bring the milk and semolina to a boil over medium heat. Cook for 10 minutes, until thickened. Remove from the heat and cool. Divide into 16 portions.

Preheat oven to 180°C/350°F/Gas Mark 4. Brush a 25-cm (10-inch) square pan with 2 tablespoons ghee. Spread a pastry sheet on a work counter and cut into 3 strips. Brush each with 1 teaspoon ghee and layer on top of one another. Finely chop the pistachios and spoon 1 teaspoon towards one end of the strip, top with clotted cream, then another 1 teaspoon pistachios. Fold one corner of pastry over to enclose the filling in a triangle. Continue folding to make a triangular parcel, until the end of the pastry is reached. Repeat for all 16 sheets. Arrange in the prepared pan, with the corners of the triangles touching. Pour the remaining ghee over and bake in the oven for 30 minutes.

To make the syrup:
Follow the instructions given above. Remove the pan from the oven and drain any excess ghee. Pour the syrup over the pastry and rest for 15 minutes. Transfer to plates and serve.

BREAD PUDDING WITH SOUR CHERRIES
VİŞNELİ EKMEK KADAYIFI

Region:		Afyon, all regions
Preparation time:		10 minutes
Cooking time:	1 hour 30 minutes, plus 4 hours resting	
Serves:		4

1 (15-cm)	round loaf of wholemeal bread, crust only	1 (6-inch)

For the syrup:		
300 g	sugar	1½ cups/11 oz
350 ml	sour cherry juice	1½ cups/12 fl oz
1	cinnamon stick	1
3	cloves	3

100 g	walnuts, crushed	1 cup/3½ oz
200 g	clotted cream (or *lor*, fresh curd cheese, see p.485)	1 cup/7 oz

♦ V   p.419

This is made in the summer months when fresh sour cherries are abundant. The winter version uses molasses or sugar syrup.
♦
Preheat oven to 120°C/250°F/Gas Mark ½.

Put the bread crust on a baking sheet and dry in the oven for 1 hour.

To make the syrup:
In a small saucepan, bring the sugar, sour cherry juice and cinnamon to a boil over medium heat, until the temperature of the mixture reaches 87°C (188°F) on a cooking thermometer.

Add the cloves. Reduce the heat, add the bread and cook for 10 minutes on each side.

Remove from the heat and let cool at room temperature for 1 hour. Transfer to the refrigerator and chill for 3 hours.

Cut into 4 pieces, sprinkle with walnuts and serve with clotted cream.

♦

NOAH'S PUDDING
AŞURE

Region:		Tunceli, all regions
Preparation time:	10 minutes, plus overnight soaking	
Cooking time:	1 hour 35 minutes, plus 6 hours cooling	
Serves:		4

100 g	pearl barley, soaked overnight	½ cup/3½ oz
70 g	chickpeas (garbanzo beans) soaked overnight	⅜ cup/ 2¾ oz
70 g	haricot (navy) beans, soaked overnight	⅓ cup/ 2¾ oz
100 g	dried apricots	½ cup/3½ oz
100 g	sultanas	¾ cup/3½ oz
100 g	walnuts, crushed	1 cup/3½ oz
60 g	hazelnuts	½ cup/2¼ oz
150 g	sugar	¾ cup/5 oz
50 g	sesame seeds, toasted	⅓ cup/2 oz
2 tbsp	pine nuts	2 tbsp
½ tsp	orange zest	½ tsp
50 g	dried figs	⅓ cup/2 oz
50 g	dried mulberries	½ cup/2 oz
100 g	pomegranate seeds	1¼ cups/3½ oz

💧 🌿 ♦ V

Alevi Moslems fast during the month of *Muharrem*, the first month of the lunar year. *Aşure* is the name of the tenth day of *Muharrem*, the day Hüseyin was killed at Kerbela. This mourning dish is traditionally distributed to seven neighbours at the end of the fast. Sunni Moslems make this dish too since they deem the month of *Muharrem* sacred. Legend goes that Noah made this dish with the leftovers in his ship to celebrate his survival. There is always some sort of competition among home cooks for the most delicious *aşure*.
♦
Cook the chickpeas (garbanzo beans) and haricot (navy) beans, then drain. Bring 2.25 litres (10 cups/80 fl oz) water to a boil in a saucepan over medium heat. Add the pearl barley, reduce the heat and simmer for 5 minutes. Skim the surface with a slotted spoon. Cover and cook for 55 minutes. Add the cooked chickpeas and haricot beans and cook for 10 minutes. Quarter the dried apricots and then add with the sultanas, two-thirds of the walnuts, hazelnuts, sugar, sesame seeds, pine nuts and orange zest and cook for 15 minutes. Add the dried figs and dried mulberries and cook for another 5 minutes.

Remove from the heat. Divide among 4 serving bowls and rest at room temperature for 1 hour. Decorate with the remaining walnuts and the pomegranate seeds, then chill in the refrigerator for 5 hours before serving.

DESSERTS

HAZELNUT COOKIES IN SYRUP
ŞEKERPARE

For the syrup:		
300 g	sugar	1½ cups/11 oz
1 tbsp	lemon juice	1 tbsp

	butter, for greasing	
1	egg, separated	1
80 g	icing (confectioner's) sugar	½ cup/3 oz
50 g	semolina	¼ cup/2 oz
100 ml	olive oil	½ cup/3½ fl oz
300 g	plain (all-purpose) flour	2¼ cups/11 oz
1 tsp	baking powder	1 tsp
4 drops	vanilla extract	4 drops
100 g	ghee (see p.485)	½ cup/3½ oz
16	hazelnuts, peeled	16

Region: Bursa, all regions
Preparation time: 25 minutes
Cooking time: 40 minutes, plus 20 minutes resting
Serves: 4

V   p.421 📷

This dish is traditionally made for holidays.

♦

To make the syrup:
Combine the sugar, lemon juice and 350 ml (1½ cups/ 12 fl oz) water in a saucepan over medium heat. Heat until the temperature of the mixture reaches 95°C (203°F) on a cooking thermometer, about 20 minutes. Remove from the heat and let cool.

Preheat oven to 180°C/350°F/Gas Mark 4. Lightly butter a large lipped baking sheet.

Meanwhile, put the egg white into a large bowl and whisk with the icing (confectioner's) sugar and semolina for 5 minutes. Add the oil and whisk for another 1 minute. Add the flour, baking powder, vanilla extract and ghee with ¼ teaspoon salt. Knead for 5 minutes into an elastic dough. Divide the dough into 16 equal parts and flatten into discs. Arrange on the prepared baking sheet, brush each disc with the egg yolk and decorate each with a hazelnut. Bake in the hot oven for 20 minutes.

Remove from the oven and pour the cooled syrup over the cookies. Let rest for 20 minutes until the syrup has entirely soaked in. Serve cold.

♦

WALNUT COOKIES IN SYRUP
KALBURABASTI

For the syrup:		
300 g	sugar	1½ cups/11 oz
1 tbsp	lemon juice	1 tbsp

50 g	unsalted butter, melted	¼ cup/2 oz
70 g	plain yogurt	scant ½ cup/2¾ oz
40 ml	olive oil	3 tbsp/1¼ fl oz
1	egg	1
350 g	plain (all-purpose) flour	2⅔ cups/12 oz
¼ tsp	salt	¼ tsp
1¼ tsp	baking powder	1¼ tsp
10	walnuts, quartered	10

Region: Sivas, all regions
Preparation time: 25 minutes
Cooking time: 30 minutes, plus 20 minutes resting
Serves: 4

♦ V

The Turkish name *kalburabastı* roughly translates to 'pressed with a sieve'. The cookies are made on special occasions and during the holy month of Ramadan.

♦

To make the syrup:
Combine the sugar, lemon juice and 350 ml (1½ cups/ 12 fl oz) water in a small saucepan over medium heat. Heat until the temperature of the mixture reaches 102°C (215°F) on a cooking thermometer, about 20 minutes. Remove from the heat and let cool.

Preheat oven to 160°C/325°F/Gas Mark 3. In a bowl, combine the butter, yogurt, oil, egg, flour, salt and baking powder and knead for 5 minutes. Transfer to a work counter and knead for a further 5 minutes, stretching and kneading into an elastic dough. Divide into 16 parts and roll into balls. Press an indentation into each ball, add 2 walnuts pieces and close the dough around them. Roll on the counter into flat, oval discs, then press the dough on to the fine side of a grater or sieve to give texture. Line a baking sheet with parchment paper, arrange the cookies on the sheet and bake in the oven for 20–30 minutes.

Remove from the oven and pour over the syrup. Let the cookies soak for 20 minutes. Transfer to plates and serve.

DESSERTS

◆

CANDIED PUMPKIN CRUNCH
KABAK (BOYNUZ) TATLISI AYVA TATLISI

Region:		Hatay, all regions
Preparation time:		15 minutes, plus 1 day and
		5 hours pickling
Cooking time:		1 hour 20 minutes,
		plus 3 hours cooling
Serves:		4

For the pickling lime water:

250 g	food-grade pickling lime (see p.502)	½ cup/9 oz
800 g	pumpkin, peeled, seeded, cleaned and cut into 4 slices	1 lb 2 oz

For the sugar syrup:

350 g	sugar	1 ¾ cups/12¼ oz
1 tbsp	lemon juice	1 tbsp
¼	vanilla pod	¼
80 g	walnuts, pounded	¾ cup/3 oz
60 ml	tahini (sesame seed paste)	¼ cup/2 fl oz

◦ ✿ ◦ V   p.423 ▢

This popular dessert has many local names, including *reçel*, *murabba* and *macun*. Quinces, tomatoes, aubergines (eggplants), bell peppers, beans, melons, watermelons and olives are all candied using the same technique, which makes a crunchy dessert. The sugar can be substituted by 200 ml (scant 1 cup/7 fl oz) grape molasses, and the pickling lime water can be recycled up to ten times. Some like adding honey or grape molasses to this winter delight.
◆
To make the pickling lime water:
Combine 3 litres (12 cups/100 fl oz) water and the pickling lime in a glass or stainless steel bowl. Stir until dissolved. Rest for 5 hours, until the lime sinks to the bottom.

Put the pumpkin slices into a separate glass or stainless steel bowl and add 2.25 litres (10 cups/80 fl oz) of the lime water. Rest for 24 hours. Take the pumpkin slices out of the lime water (reserving it for later use) and thoroughly rinse 5 times with plenty of cold water, to eradicate the lime.

Bring 2 litres (8½ cups/70 fl oz) water to a boil in a large saucepan. Add the pumpkin slices, boil for 5 minutes and drain. Rinse the pumpkin again with plenty of cold water.

To make the sugar syrup:
Boil the sugar, lemon juice, vanilla and 600 ml (2½ cups/20 fl oz) water in a saucepan for 5 minutes. Reduce to medium, add the pumpkin, cover and simmer for 1 hour.

Remove the pan from the heat and rest at room temperature for 1 hour, then chill in the refrigerator for another 2 hours. Serve with a sprinkle of walnuts and drizzle of tahini.

◆

CANDIED PUMPKIN
FIRINDA BALKABAĞI TATLISI

Region:		Sakarya, all regions
Preparation time:		5 minutes, plus 1 day resting
Cooking time:		1 hour, plus 1 hour resting
		and 3 hours chilling
Serves:		4

4 (3 × 6-cm) slices	pumpkin	4 (1¼ × 2½-inch) slices
1	cinnamon stick	1
160 g	sugar	¾ cup/5½ oz
100 g	*kaymak* (clotted cream, see p.486)	½ cup/3½ oz
80 g	walnuts, crushed	¾ cup/3 oz

✿ ◆ V ⸭

This pumpkin dish can be made in a saucepan, however a wood-fired oven improves the taste greatly. Some like to add tahini as well as crushed walnuts just before serving.
◆
Arrange the pumpkin slices and cinnamon stick in a small roasting pan and sprinkle with the sugar. Cover and let rest in the refrigerator for 24 hours.

The next day, preheat oven to 180°C/350°F/Gas Mark 4.

Pour 250 ml (1 cup/8 fl oz) water over the pumpkin, cover with aluminium foil and cook in the hot oven for 40 minutes. Reduce the heat to 160°C/325°F/Gas Mark 3, remove the foil and cook for another 20 minutes. Remove from the oven and let rest at room temperature for 1 hour.

Transfer to the refrigerator and chill for 3 hours. When chilled, transfer to serving plates, drizzle with the syrup from the pan and serve with clotted cream and walnuts.

CANDIED FRESH WALNUTS
TAZE CEVİZ TATLISI

Region:		Hatay, all regions
Preparation time:		10 minutes, plus 1 week soaking,
		plus 1 day and 5 hours pickling
Cooking time:	2 hours 35 minutes, plus 4 hours cooling
Serves:		4

16	fresh green walnuts, outer skin peeled	16
5	cloves	5
250 g	sugar	1¼ cups/9 oz

For the pickling lime water:

250 g	food-grade pickling lime (see p.502)	½ cup/9 oz

100 g	*lor* (fresh curd cheese, see p.485)	3½ oz

❧ ◆ **V**

This time-consuming recipe is the definition of a 'labour of love'. A true delicacy, this is for the most esteemed guests. Made with soft, fresh walnuts picked in May and June, country folk place the nuts in hessian sacs in riverbeds for a week. The ever-changing water, smaller and fresher walnuts all add to the taste. Served with a glass of cold water, the candied walnuts can be dipped in the water. Green walnuts, when cut open, leak a colourless liquid that will badly stain your fingers – do use gloves and a potato peeler to peel them. They will require soaking for a week. The pickling lime water can be recycled up to ten times.

◆

Soak the peeled walnuts in 2 litres (8½ cups/70 fl oz) water for 1 week, changing the soaking water and rinsing the walnuts every 24 hours. Make sure you wear gloves to protect your hands.

To make the pickling lime water:
Combine 2 litres (8½ cups/70 fl oz) water and the pickling lime in a glass or stainless steel bowl. Stir until dissolved. Rest for 5 hours, until the lime sinks to the bottom.

Put the walnuts into a separate glass or stainless steel bowl and add 1.5 litres (6¼ cups/50 fl oz) of the lime water. Rest for 24 hours. Take the walnuts out of the lime water (reserving the water for another use) and thoroughly rinse 5 times with plenty of cold water, to eradicate all the lime.

Bring 2 litres (8½ cups/70 fl oz) water to a boil in a large saucepan, add the walnuts, boil for 5 minutes, then drain over a bowl, reserving 300 ml (1¼ cups/10 fl oz) of the cooking water. In a separate pan, immediately combine the reserved hot water, walnuts, cloves and sugar, tightly cover and cook over very low heat for 15 minutes. Remove from the heat and let rest for 15 minutes.

Return the pan to a very low heat, cook for 5 minutes, then remove from the heat and let rest for 15 minutes. Repeat this 4 times. Then cook for 15 minutes one final time. Let cool at room temperature for 1 hour, then chill in the refrigerator for 3 hours.

Serve with fresh *lor*.

WALNUT AND CINNAMON PANCAKES
ŞİLKİ (ŞILLIK) TATLISI

Region:	Adıyaman, Southeastern Anatolia	
Preparation time:		20 minutes
Cooking time:		40 minutes
Serves:		4

For the batter:

200 ml	milk	scant 1 cup/ 7 fl oz
½ tsp	salt	½ tsp
200 g	plain (all-purpose) flour	1½ cups/7 oz

3 tbsp	unsalted butter	3 tbsp

For the filling:

200 g	walnuts, crushed	2 cups/7 oz
1½ tsp	ground cinnamon	1½ tsp

For the syrup:

120 ml	grape molasses	½ cup/4 fl oz

100 g	ghee (see p.485)	scant ½ cup/3½ oz

◆ V

This dish is the reward for the hard work of local women when they collectively make huge amounts of *Yufka Ekmeği* (Thin Flatbread, see p.378) as it is made from the leftover dough.

◆

To make the batter:
In a large bowl, whisk the milk and salt together with 200 ml (scant 1 cup/7 fl oz) of water for 2 minutes, until well combined. Gradually add the flour and whisk for another 5 minutes, until smooth.

Heat a non-stick *sac* griddle (or cast iron frying pan/ skillet) until very hot. Brush the pan with about 1 teaspoon of the butter. Pour a ladleful of the batter into the pan and spread out to a thin pancake. Cook for 2 minutes on each side. Repeat until the batter is finished, adding more butter between cooking each pancake – you should have enough batter for 8 pancakes.

To make the filling:
Mix the walnuts and cinnamon in a bowl and divide into 7 equal portions.

In a large deep tray, lay out 1 pancake and spread 1 portion of filling on top. Add another pancake layer, then another portion of filling. Repeat until you have used up all the pancakes and filling. Cut the filled pastry into 8 equal parts (about 4-cm/1½-inch squares).

To make the syrup:
In a small saucepan, bring 60 ml (¼ cup/2 fl oz) of water and the grape molasses to a boil.

In a separate pan, heat the ghee until very hot.

Pour the boiling syrup over the pastries, then pour over the hot ghee. Transfer to plates and serve.

ROSE PETAL JAM
GÜL REÇELİ

Region:		Isparta, all regions
Preparation time:		5 minutes, plus overnight resting
Cooking time:		15 minutes, plus 3 days resting
Serves:		4

200 g	pink rose petals, white bits trimmed, washed, still moist	7 oz
1 tbsp	lemon juice	1 tbsp
200 g	sugar	1 cup/7 oz

♦ ❧ ◐ ♦ V ⁙   p.427

A breakfast staple, rose petal jam is made in big batches and preserved for later use. City folk preserve their jam in sealed containers, whereas rural folk keep jam uncovered. Some recipes have no added water and skip the boiling phase, but instead leave in the sun for 3 days. This technique can be used to make strawberry, sour cherry, cherry and quince jam.

♦

Mix the pink rose petals, lemon juice and sugar in a large non-reactive saucepan. Add 200 ml (scant 1 cup/7 fl oz) hot water and let rest, covered, for 24 hours.

The next day, give the mixture a gentle stir, bring to a boil and boil for 10 minutes. Skim off the foam on the surface with a slotted spoon or paper towel. Transfer the mixture to a glass bowl, place in a sunny spot and let rest for 3 days, taking it indoors when the sun sets. Cover overnight and transfer to the same sunny spot once the sun rises.

♦

RICE PUDDING
SÜTLAÇ

Region:		Trabzon, all regions
Preparation time:		10 minutes
Cooking time:		40 minutes, plus 6 hours cooling
Serves:		4

100 g	aromatic short-grain rice, washed, drained	generous ½ cup/ 3½ oz
1.5 litres	milk	6¼ cups/50 fl oz
2 tbsp	rice flour	2 tbsp
150 g	sugar	¾ cup/5 oz
4 drops	vanilla extract	4 drops
1	egg yolk	1

100 g	hazelnuts, toasted, finely sliced	¾ cup/ 3½ oz

❧ V

Also known as *sütlü aş* (milky meal), there are numerous variations on this recipe. Some recipes omit eggs, some substitute the rice with bulgur and some omit the vanilla extract. Some cooks also like to bake the pudding in clay pots in a 220°C/425°F/Gas Mark 7 oven for 5 minutes, which browns the top. Rice pudding is loved all around the country. Where I grew up, *sütlaç* was the preferred dessert of all festivals. It was made just with the starch of the rice. Local women believe doom and gloom will come to an end once they make this pudding.

♦

Bring the rice and 250 ml (1 cup/8 fl oz) water to a boil in a large saucepan and boil for 5 minutes. Reduce the heat to low, add 1.3 litres (5½ cups/43 fl oz) of the milk and cook for 30 minutes. Put a metal spoon in the pan to stop the milk from boiling over.

Meanwhile, dissolve the rice flour in the remaining 200 ml (scant 1 cup/7 fl oz) milk. Add to the pan and cook for 10 minutes, then add the sugar and the vanilla extract and cook for another 10 minutes. Remove from the heat.

Put the egg yolk into a small bowl, remove 60 ml (¼ cup/ 2 fl oz) hot milk from the pan and whisk into the egg yolk. Slowly add the mixture back into the pan, stirring continuously.

Divide the rice pudding among 4 serving bowls. Let cool at room temperature for 1 hour, then chill in the refrigerator for 5 hours. Sprinkle with hazelnuts and serve.

BURNED MILK PUDDING
KAZANDİBİ

Region:		İstanbul, Marmara Region
Preparation time:		5 minutes
Cooking time:		55 minutes, plus 7 hours resting
Serves:		4

80 g	unsalted butter	⅓ cup/3 oz
100 g	rice flour	⅔ cup/3½ oz
25 g	plain (all-purpose) flour	scant ¼ cup/1 oz
1.5 litres	milk	6¼ cups/50 fl oz
¼ tsp	mastic (plant resin) pounded with 1 tsp sugar	¼ tsp
200 g	sugar	1 cup/7 oz
4 drops	vanilla extract	4 drops
1 tsp	ground cinnamon	1 tsp

V

p.429

Legend has it that one day the pudding was burnt by mistake. When the makers realised it was delicious, they burnt it deliberately. The burnt version of *Tavukgöğsü* (Chicken Breast Pudding, see p.432) is also popular. Milk puddings spread throughout the country from İstanbul.

♦

Heat the butter in a saucepan over medium heat until hot. Reduce the heat, add the flours and cook for 3 minutes, mixing continuously. Add the milk and mastic and whisk for 3 minutes. Increase the heat to medium and bring to the boil for 5 minutes. Reduce the heat and cook for another 20–30 minutes, until the mixture thickens. Add 150 g (¾ cup/5 oz) of the sugar and the vanilla extract, cook for another 5 minutes, then remove from the heat.

Put the remaining sugar and 20 ml (4 tsp/¾ fl oz) water into a 20 × 25-cm (8 × 10-inch) flame-proof aluminium or cast-iron baking pan and spread evenly with a rubber spatula. Heat the sugar over high heat until it melts, making sure it doesn't burn. Pour the milk mixture over and mix thoroughly. As you do this, keep a close eye on the sugar at the base. The moment it burns, remove from the heat and let rest for 2 minutes. Let rest for 2 hours at room temperature, then chill in the refrigerator for 5 hours.

Cut the pudding into squares with a rubber spatula. Serve each slice burned bottom up, sprinkled with cinnamon.

♦

ALMOND RICE PUDDING
KEŞKÜL

Region:		İstanbul, all regions
Preparation time:		10 minutes, plus 4 hours soaking
Cooking time:		35 minutes, plus 6 hours resting
Serves:		4

For the rice slurry:		
100 g	medium-grain rice (or 100 g/⅔ cups/ 3½ oz rice flour)	½ cup/3½ oz

1 litre	milk	4¼ cups/34 fl oz
1	egg yolk	1
4 drops	vanilla extract	4 drops
150 g	sugar	¾ cup/5 oz
60 g	almond meal	½ cup/2¼ oz
50 g	pistachios, pounded into pistachio meal	½ cup/2 oz

🌱 ◆ V

This pudding has been nurturing the infatuation of many generations. It is more like a snack than an after-meal dessert. These days, *keşkül* is mostly eaten at special eateries called *muhallebici*.

♦

To make the rice slurry:
Soak the rice or rice flour in 400 ml (1 ⅔ cups/14 fl oz) water for 4 hours. Transfer the mixture to a food processor and process until smooth.

In a large saucepan, whisk the milk, egg yolk, vanilla extract and rice slurry for 2 minutes, until well combined. Set over medium heat and cook, whisking continuously, for 20 minutes. Add the sugar and cook for another 5 minutes. Add the almond meal and pistachio meal and cook for 5 minutes, whisking continuously.

Transfer the pudding to glass serving bowls. Let rest at room temperature for 1 hour, then chill in the refrigerator for 5 hours before serving.

SEED AND NUT MEMORIAL PUDDING
KOLİVA

Region:		İstanbul, Marmara Region
Preparation time:		overnight plus 1 hour soaking, plus 20 minutes
Cooking time:		15 minutes
Serves:		4

100 g	cracked wheat	½ cup/3½ oz
1 tbsp	plain (all-purpose flour), roasted for 5 minutes	1 tbsp
100 g	almond meal	¾ cup/3½ oz
100 g	hazelnuts	¾ cup/3½ oz
100 g	walnuts, crushed	1 cup/3½ oz
10 g	sugar-coated coriander seeds	⅓ oz
50 g	sour pomegranate seeds	½ cup/2 oz
40 g	currants, soaked for 1 hour in 250 ml (1 cup/8 fl oz) water	⅓ cup/1½ oz
½ tsp	ground cinnamon	½ tsp
¼ tsp	ground cumin	¼ tsp
2 tbsp	sugar	2 tbsp

30 g	icing (confectioner's) sugar	3½ tbsp/1 oz
50 g	sour pomegranate seeds	½ cup/2 oz
10 g	sugar-coated coriander seeds	⅓ oz
10 g	sugar-coated almonds	¼ oz
1 tsp	ground cinnamon	1 tsp

Eaten at festivals symbolizing renewal and rebirth, such as Christmas, New Year and Easter, wheat berry dishes have ancient roots. There is a fourteenth-century Byzantine manuscript with a *Koliva* recipe at the British Library. This popular funeral cake is believed to have pagan roots, its ingredients referring to Greek gods. It is traditionally distributed at Eastern Orthodox funerals with a portion left on the grave of the dearly departed. The ritual is repeated on subsequent anniversaries and on All Souls Day. This dessert is popular in the Black Sea, Aegean and Central Anatolia.

◆

In a large saucepan, bring 1 litre (4¼ cups/34 fl oz) of water to a boil. Add the cracked wheat and bring back to a boil, skimming off the foam on the surface with a slotted spoon. Cover and cook for 5 minutes. Remove from the heat and let rest overnight.

The next day, combine the following ingredients in a deep serving tray or pan in this order: the cracked wheat, flour, almond meal, hazelnuts, walnuts, sugar-coated coriander seeds, sour pomegranate seeds, currants, ground cinnamon, ground cumin and sugar. Mix gently.

Sprinkle with the icing (confectioners') sugar. Decorate around the edge with the sour pomegranate seeds and sugar-coated coriander seeds, alternating the pomegranate seeds and sweet coriander seeds. Add the sugar-coated almonds on one side and dust the top with the ground cinnamon in the shape of a cross. Serve immediately.

◆

HONEY CUSTARD
HİLİNDOR (XİLİNDOR)

Region:		Erzincan, Eastern Anatolia
Preparation time:		5 minutes
Cooking time:		20 minutes, plus 1 hour cooling
Serves:		4

1 litre	milk	4¼ cups/34 fl oz
6	eggs, whisked	6
80 g	honey (oregano flower)	3 oz

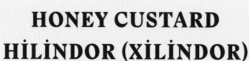

Honey custard is traditionally made with the first milk from a cow after calving. Some versions omit the honey.

◆

Whisk the eggs and the milk together for 3 minutes in a large saucepan. Cook, covered, over low heat for 20 minutes. Let cool at room temperature for 1 hour.

Divide among 4 serving bowls, drizzle with the honey and serve.

SAFFRON PUDDING
ZERDE

Region:	İstanbul, all regions
Preparation time:	overnight soaking, plus 1 hour soaking, plus 10 minutes
Cooking time:	40 minutes, plus 6 hours cooling
Serves:	4

80 g	rice, soaked in 500 ml (generous 2 cups/17 fl oz) water for 1 hour, drained and thoroughly rinsed	½ cup/3 oz
30 g	cornflour (cornstarch), slaked for 5 minutes in 60 ml (¼ cup/2 fl oz) cold water until smooth	¼ cup/1 oz
60 ml	rosewater	¼ cup/2 fl oz
pinch	saffron, soaked in 2 tbsp hot water for 1 hour	pinch
3 tbsp	pine nuts	3 tbsp
200 g	sugar	1 cup/7 oz
1 tbsp	lemon juice	1 tbsp
⅛ tsp	lemon zest	⅛ tsp
80 g	currants, soaked overnight in 500 ml (2 cups/17 fl oz) water	generous ½ cup/3 oz
40 g	sour pomegranate seeds	½ cup/1½ oz

Some like to eat this pudding warm, poured over rice.

◆

Bring 2 litres (8½ cups/70 fl oz) water to a boil in a saucepan over high heat, add the rice and cook for 5 minutes. Skim the surface with a slotted spoon. Reduce the heat to low and cook for another 15 minutes. Add the slaked cornflour (cornstarch) and cook for 5 minutes, whisking continuously. Add the rosewater, saffron, pine nuts, sugar, lemon juice, lemon zest and currants and cook for another 10 minutes, stirring vigorously.

Divide among 4 serving bowls and let cool at room temperature for 1 hour, then chill in the refrigerator for 5 hours. Garnish with pomegranate seeds and serve.

◆

FIGS IN GOAT'S MILK
TELEME

Region:	Adıyaman, all regions
Preparation time:	35 minutes
Cooking time:	5 minutes, plus overnight resting
Serves:	4

1 litre	goat's milk	4¼ cups/34 fl oz
250 g	dried figs, finely chopped	9 oz
100 g	walnuts, toasted and crushed	1 cup/3½ oz

Also known as shepherd's dessert, *teleme* is freshly made cheese, un-drained. At the end of a day in the mountains with his flock, the shepherd makes this dish when he feels like a pick-me-up. After milking the goat, the shepherd adds figs or fig leaves to curdle the milk, then a little sugar or honey... and that's it! This dish has many local names like *incir donması*, *incir uyutması*, *incir kestirmesi*.

◆

Bring the milk to a boil in a small saucepan, then let cool to 50°C (122°F) on a cooking thermometer.

In a large bowl, combine the dried figs with 500 ml (generous 2 cups/17 fl oz) of the milk and mash with the back of a wooden spoon, until the milk is fully absorbed. Add the remaining milk and keep mashing until the milk is absorbed, about 30 minutes. (You could also use a stick blender, adding the milk very slowly.)

Stir through the walnuts and transfer to serving bowls. Cover and let rest at room temperature for 1 hour, then chill in the refrigerator for 24 hours before serving.

CHICKEN BREAST PUDDING
TAVUKGÖĞSÜ

Region:		İstanbul, all regions
Preparation time:		15 minutes, plus overnight soaking
Cooking time:		1 hour and 50 minutes, plus 6 hours cooling
Serves:		4

1 (100 g)	fresh chicken breast	1 (3½ oz)
1.5 litres	milk	6¼ cups/50 fl oz
4 drops	vanilla extract	4 drops
200 g	sugar	1 cup/7 oz
1 tsp	ground cinnamon	1 tsp

For the slaked rice:

250 g	medium-grain rice, soaked overnight in 500 ml (generous 2 cups/ 17 fl oz) water (or 250 g/ 1⅔ cups/3½ oz rice flour)	1½ cups/9 oz

🌿 p.433

Milk puddings with chicken have been a part of Turkish culinary culture for centuries. Early sources refer to this dish as 'Byzantine Slurry'. Traditionally made at home, these days *muhallebicis* are where people get their *tavuk göğsü*. It is essential to use fresh chicken, but once it goes into the refrigerator, you can forget about it. If you are unable to make rice slurry, rice flour is an acceptable shortcut. The caramelizing method for making *Kazandibi* (Burned Milk Pudding, see p.428) is also used for this pudding. It is traditionally made with water buffalo milk.

◆

In a saucepan, bring 2 litres (8½ cups/70 fl oz) water to a boil, add the chicken and poach over low heat, covered, for 30 minutes. Remove the chicken from the pan and shred into thin strips. Thoroughly rinse 3 times in cold water, until it no longer smells. Wrap the chicken in a muslin (cheesecloth) and pound with your fist to work the chicken into thin strings. Rinse again in cold water.

To make the slaked rice:
Put the soaked rice or rice flour into a food processor and blend into a smooth liquid.

Mix the milk and slaked rice in large saucepan over medium heat and bring to a boil for 5 minutes. Reduce the heat and continue cooking for 30 minutes. Add the chicken breast and vanilla extract and cook for another 30 minutes, whisking vigorously, making sure that the chicken strings entirely dissolve. Whisk in the sugar and cook for another 15 minutes. Remove from the heat.

Moisten a 20 × 25-cm (8 × 10-inch) deep tray and pour the pudding mixture into it. Let cool at room temperature for 1 hour, then chill in the refrigerator for 5 hours. Divide into equal pieces and shape into rolls. Serve inverted, with the bottom bit on top and sprinkled with cinnamon.

◆

MILK SQUASH PUDDING
SÜTLÜ KABAK

Region:		Rize, Black Sea Region
Preparation time:		10 minutes
Cooking time:		55 minutes, plus 5 hours resting
Serves:		4

500 g	kabocha squash (Japanese pumpkin), peeled, seeded, finely diced	1 lb 2 oz
1 litre	milk, boiling	4¼ cups/34 fl oz
100 g	sugar	½ cup/3½ oz
100 g	hazelnuts, toasted	¾ cup/3½ oz

Made in the autumn and winter months when Japanese pumpkin is abundant, this local dessert is absolutely adored by the locals.

◆

In a large saucepan, bring 250 ml (1 cup/8 fl oz) water to the boil, add the squash and simmer, covered, for 30 minutes. Mash the cooked squash with a wooden spoon. Add the boiling milk, simmer for 15 minutes, then add the sugar and cook for another 5 minutes.

Transfer to glass serving bowls, let rest at room temperature for 1 hour, then chill in the refrigerator for 4 hours. Sprinkle with the hazelnuts and serve.

🌿 ◗ V ⬧

DESSERTS

CARROT SLICE
HAVUÇ DİLİMİ

Region:		Gaziantep, Southeastern Anatolia
Preparation time:		15 minutes
Cooking time:		40 minutes, plus 15 minutes resting
Serves:		4

175 g	ghee (see p.485), melted	¾ cup/6 oz
30 (25-cm) sheets	filo (phyllo) pastry (see p.496)	30 (10-inch) sheets
200 g	pistachios, slivered	2 cups/7 oz

For the syrup:		
250 g	sugar	1¼ cups/9 oz
1 tbsp	lemon juice	1 tbsp

V ⁙

p.435 📷

This sweet is served in triangular, square or diamond shapes of various sizes. The technique is called *baklava*.
♦
Preheat oven to 180°C/350°F/Gas Mark 4. Generously brush a deep 20-cm (8-inch) square baking pan with 2 tablespoons ghee. Layer 15 sheets of filo (phyllo) pastry into the pan, brushing each with ghee before adding the next. Spread the pistachios over, then cover with the remaining 15 pastry sheets, brushing with ghee as before. Push the pastry spilling over the edges down into the pan. Using a sharp knife, cut a 5-cm (2-inch) circle in the middle of the pastry, then make 8 cuts in the shape of carrots, at regular intervals between the circle and the side of the pan. Pour the remaining ghee over the pastry and bake in the hot oven for 30–40 minutes.

To make the syrup:
Combine the sugar, lemon juice and 350 ml (1½ cups/ 12 fl oz) water in a saucepan over medium heat. Heat, stirring continuously, until the temperature reaches 100°C (212°F), about 20 minutes. Remove from the heat.

Remove the pan from the oven. Drain away excess ghee, if there is any. Re-cut the incisions made earlier, going all the way through. Evenly pour the syrup over the pastry and let rest for 15 minutes. Transfer to plates and serve.

♦

SEMOLINA CAKE
REVANİ

Region:		İstanbul, all regions
Preparation time:		25 minutes
Cooking time:		20 minutes, plus 30 minutes, plus 4 hours cooling
Serves:		4

2	eggs	2
2 tbsp	sugar	2 tbsp
80 g	Greek yogurt	scant ½ cup/3 oz
75 ml	olive oil	⅓ cup/2½ fl oz
2 drops	vanilla extract	2 drops
⅛ tsp	lemon zest	⅛ tsp
45 g	plain (all-purpose) flour	⅓ cup/1½ oz
85 g	semolina	½ cup/3 oz
1¼ tsp	baking powder	1¼ tsp
2 tsp	unsalted butter	2 tsp

For the syrup:		
275 g	sugar	scant 1½ cups/9¾ oz

V

This recipe has been made at home for centuries. It is often associated with İstanbul and the Ottoman Palace. Some call it 'yogurt cake', others 'egg cake'. There used to be eateries specialising in *revani*, *tulumba* and *lokma* in İstanbul. Nowadays, home cooks carry on the tradition.
♦
To make the syrup:
Combine the sugar and 400 ml (1⅔ cups/14 fl oz) water in a saucepan over medium heat. Heat, stirring continuously, until it reaches 87°C (188°F) on a cooking thermometer, about 15 minutes. Remove from the heat and rest for 1 hour.

Meanwhile, preheat oven to 160°C/325°F/Gas Mark 3. Whisk the eggs in a large bowl for 5 minutes. Add the sugar and whisk for another 5 minutes. Add the yogurt, olive oil, vanilla extract and lemon zest and whisk for 5 minutes. Add the flour, semolina and baking powder and whisk for another 5 minutes, until well combined.

Grease a deep 20-cm (8-inch) square baking pan with the butter. Pour in the batter. Bake in the oven for 30 minutes. Remove from the oven and pour over the syrup. Cover the pan with a dish towel, making sure it does not touch the cake. Let rest at room temperature for 1 hour, then chill in the refrigerator for 3 hours. Divide into 4 pieces and serve.

SHREDDED KADAIFI WITH WALNUTS
CEVİZLİ TEL KADAYIF

Region:		Şanlıurfa, all regions
Preparation time:		10 minutes
Cooking time:	1 hour 10 minutes, plus 15 minutes resting	
Serves:		4

400 g	kadaifi pastry	14 oz
150 g	ghee (see p.485), melted	⅔ cup/5 oz
200 g	walnuts, finely sliced	2 cups/7 oz

For the syrup:

300 g	sugar	1½ cups/11 oz
1 tbsp	lemon juice	1 tbsp

◐ V ⁘   p.437 ◘

Kadaifi is the fine (1-mm/¹⁄₃₂-inch) pastry strands made with flour and water. It can also be made from the same quantity of thin, long homemade noodles (see p.493), cut very finely. The walnuts can be substituted with pistachios, clotted cream, fresh cheese, cheese, rice or bulgur wheat.
◆

Preheat oven to 180°C/350°F/Gas Mark 4. Put the kadaifi pastry into a bowl or tray and pour over a third of the ghee. Shred the noodles with your fingers until they are all about 5-mm (¼-inch) in size. Generously brush a deep 20-cm (8-inch) square baking pan with another third of the ghee, add the pastry and shake the pan to ensure even distribution. Remove half of the pastry from the pan and press down the remaining pastry. Sprinkle over the walnuts. Arrange the pastry back on top of the walnuts and press down. Cover the pan with aluminium foil and bake in the oven for 30 minutes. Pour the remaining ghee over the *kadaifi* in the tray, return to the oven and bake uncovered for 15–20 minutes, until it gets some colour. Remove from the oven. Invert onto a large serving plate.

To make the syrup:
Combine the sugar, lemon juice and 350 ml (1½ cups/ 12 fl oz) water in a saucepan over medium heat. Heat, stirring continuously, until the temperature reaches 102°C (215°F) on a cooking thermometer, about 20 minutes. Remove from the heat. Pour the syrup evenly over the top of the walnut *kadaifi* and let rest for 15 minutes before serving.

◆

RICE WAFERS WITH NUTS AND POMEGRANATES
GÜLLAÇ

Region:		İstanbul, Marmara Region
Preparation time:		10 minutes, plus 2 hours chilling
Cooking time:		5 minutes, plus 30 minutes cooling
Serves:		4

1 litre	milk	4¼ cups/34 fl oz
150 g	sugar	¾ cup/5 oz
60 ml	rosewater	¼ cup/2 fl oz
4 (25-cm square)	rice paper sheet wafers	4 (10-inch square)
150 g	slivered almonds, blanched	1¾ cups/5 oz
150 g	walnuts, crushed	1½ cups/5 oz
100 g	pistachios, peeled	1 cup/3½ oz
150 g	sour pomegranate seeds	1¾ cups/5 oz

 V

Made during *Ramadan*, this recipe is garnished with seasonal fruit such as berries, cherries, or pomegranates. Versions with pistachios or walnuts are popular too. It can be made with store-bought rice paper wafers.
◆

Bring the milk, sugar and rosewater to a boil in a saucepan over medium heat. Pour the mixture into a tray or pan, large enough to fit the wafers, and let cool for 30 minutes.

When cooled, soak the rice paper sheet wafers in the mixture until thoroughly wet. Cut the first rice paper sheet (if necessary) to snugly fit into another deep tray, placing it in the bottom of the tray. Arrange any rice paper offcuts evenly on top of the first rice paper layer. Repeat with the second rice paper sheet. Evenly sprinkle over half of the slivered almonds, walnuts, pistachios and pomegranate seeds. Layer the two remaining rice paper sheets over the top as before. Sprinkle over another layer of the nuts and pomegranate seeds, reserving a few pomegranate seeds for decoration. Transfer to the refrigerator and chill for 2 hours.

Remove from the refrigerator, cut into 4 squares and serve sprinkled with the pomegranate seeds.

SEVILLE ORANGE MARMALADE
TURUNÇ REÇELİ

Region:	Antalya, Mediterranean Region
Preparation time:	10 minutes
Cooking time:	2 days resting plus 30 minutes
Makes:	1 small jar

5	Seville oranges	5
300 g	sugar	1½ cups/11 oz
2 tbsp	Seville orange juice	2 tbsp

This marmalade is popular in Adana, Hatay and Mersin. The recipe also works well with bergamot, orange and mandarin. You will need a 30-cm (12-inch) piece of cotton string and a heavy-duty needle.

◆

Peel the rind from the oranges in one piece, with no bitter pith attached. Cut each piece into quarters. Put the orange rind into a saucepan with 2 litres (8½ cups/70 fl oz) water and bring to the boil. Boil for 3 minutes, then drain and add another 2 litres (8½ cups/70 fl oz) water. Repeat this process 3 times a day, for 2 days. After the rind is drained for the last time, squeeze out any water, bring the ends of each rind together and run the needle and string through them all. Tie the ends of the string together.

Put the sugar and orange juice, along with 500 ml (generous 2 cups/17 fl oz) water, into a saucepan and bring to the boil over medium heat. Boil for 5 minutes, mixing continuously. Reduce the heat, add the rind string and cook until a cooking thermometer reaches 108°C (226°F), about 5 minutes. Remove from the heat.

Transfer to a sterilised jar while warm.

◆

SWEET PORRIDGE WITH DRIED FRUIT
ANUŞABUR

Region:	İstanbul, all regions
Preparation time:	10 minutes, plus overnight soaking, plus 1 hour soaking, plus 5 minutes
Cooking time:	35 minutes, plus 1 hour resting
Serves:	4

150 g	cracked wheat, washed	1 cup/5 oz
60 ml	rosewater	¼ cup/2 fl oz
¼ tsp	orange zest	¼ tsp
100 g	dried apricots, finely diced, soaked in 500 ml (generous 2 cups/17 fl oz) water for 1 hour	1 cup/3½ oz
100 g	sultanas (golden raisins), soaked in 500 ml (generous 2 cups/17 fl oz) water for 1 hour	generous ½ cup/3½ oz
100 g	sugar	½ cup/3½ oz

Anoush in Armenian means sweet, *anoush'ella* means bon appetite and *anoushabour* means sweet soup. This is a sacred Armenian dessert made for the New Year and at Lent. Pomegranates and walnuts are popular serving suggestions. Some serve this dessert warm.

◆

In a large saucepan, bring 1.5 litres (6¼ cups/50 fl oz) water to a boil. Add the cracked wheat and bring back to a boil, skimming off the foam on the surface with a slotted spoon. Cover and cook for 10 minutes. Remove from the heat, wrapped the pan in a dish towel and let soak overnight.

The next day, bring the cracked wheat and 500 ml (generous 2 cups/17 fl oz) water to the boil in a large saucepan over medium heat. Boil for 5 minutes, then add the rosewater and orange zest and cook, covered, for 10 minutes. Add the dried apricots and sultanas (golden raisins) and cook for another 15 minutes. Add the sugar and cook for another 5 minutes, mixing continuously.

Remove from the heat and let cool at room temperature for 1 hour. Transfer to bowls and serve.

SWEET LAYERED KATMER PASTRY
TATLI KATMER

Region:	Gaziantep, Southeastern Anatolia	
Preparation time:	15 minutes, plus 24 hours resting, plus 30 minutes	
Cooking time:		30 minutes
Serves:		4

For the pastry:

150 g	strong (bread) flour	1 cup/5 oz
¼ tsp	salt	¼ tsp
60 ml	olive oil	¼ cup/2 fl oz

For the filling:

200 g	pistachios, finely chopped	1½ cups/7 oz
120 g	ghee (see p.485)	½ cup/4 oz
300 g	lor (fresh curd cheese, see p.485)	11 oz
160 g	sugar	generous ¾ cup/ 5½ oz
2 tbsp	pistachios, crushed	2 tbsp
1½ tsp	ground cinnamon	1½ tsp

◨ V

This dish is a breakfast staple. Local masters stretch the dough by hand, without a rolling pin. The making of it – a labour of love – is a communal affair, after which the makers almost always reward themselves with a *katmer*. The family of a prospective groom takes a tray of *baklava* to the home of the bride-to-be when certain that the marriage will go ahead. This is the initial sweetening or *şirinleme*. After the wedding, the groom's family sends a tray of sweet layered katmer pastry to the bride's parents to express their happiness with the new addition to their family.

◆

To make the pastry:
Put the flour and salt into a bowl. Make a well and pour in 100 ml (½ cup/3½ fl oz) of water. Mix until combined, then knead for 5 minutes. Transfer to a work counter and knead for a further 5 minutes into an elastic dough. Roll into a ball and divide into 4 parts. Brush with 1 tablespoon oil, making sure each piece is well oiled. Cover with a damp dish towel and rest in the refrigerator for 24 hours.

Preheat oven to 160°C/325°F/Gas Mark 3.

Transfer the chilled dough to a work counter. Put a bowl with 3 tablespoons oil nearby. Dip your fingers into the oil, stretch the dough pieces out to 10-cm (4-inch) diameter circles, then use a rolling pin to roll out to 40-cm (16-inch) diameter circles. Divide the pistachios, ghee, *lor* and sugar into 4 equal parts. Fold two dough edges in, like an envelope, until the edges touch and layer with the pistachio kernels, ghee and *lor* in this order. Sprinkle with sugar and fold in the remaining two edges into a square. Fold the corners into an envelope. Repeat for all the pastry sheets.

Transfer to a 40-cm (16-inch) baking sheet and bake in the hot oven for 30 minutes. Transfer to plates, sprinkle with crushed pistachios and cinnamon, and serve.

◆

FRUIT LEATHER PANCAKES
PESTİL ÇULLAMASI

Region:	Erzurum, Eastern Anatolia	
Preparation time:		5 minutes
Cooking time:		5 minutes
Serves:		4

4	eggs	4
200 g	grape leather (straps), thinly sliced	7 oz
100 g	unsalted butter	½ cup/ 3½ oz
50 g	walnuts, toasted, finely chopped	½ cup/2 oz

 ◨ V X ✢

This dish is made in the winter months.
◆
Mix the eggs and grape leather slices in a bowl.

Heat the butter in a frying pan (skillet) over medium heat. Pour the egg mixture into the pan and cook, covered, for 30 seconds. Uncover, stir gently and cook for another 3 minutes. Sprinkle with walnuts, transfer to plates and serve.

◆

BEVERAGES

◆

DRINKS IN
TURKISH CULTURE

Beverages vary according to taste. Coffee, tea, *Ayran* (Salted Yogurt Drink, see p.452), *sherbet* (cordial), *Tükenmez* (Bottomless Mulled Fruit, see p.450), *Salep* (Orchid Tuber Milk, see p.450), *Şalgam Suyu* (Turnip Juice, see p.454) and many others make up our vast array of popular drinks. Then there are *rakı*, wine and liqueurs. There are warming drinks, and drinks with and without alcohol. Although many recipes require fermentation, I have also included numerous recipes that need little or none.

Coffee and tea are consumed on a daily basis. *Ayran* and *şalgam suyu* accompany kebabs, *lahmacun* and filled flatbreads, with regional variations. *Rakı* and wine are preferred both with kebabs and *lahmacun*. When it comes to alcoholic beverages, *rakı* is by far the most popular.

Beverages, like our food, are also seasonal. *Boza* (Fermented Grain Smoothie, see p.454) and *salep* are drinks for the winter months in İstanbul and its surrounding areas. *Salep* warms us up in the mornings and *boza* is for the evenings. And it is the fruit sherbets that give summer its unique taste.

TEA AND
COFFEE

Our days start with a cup of *Çay* (Tea, see p.446) with breakfast. An average tea aficionado would probably go through 20 to 30 cups a day. Every morning starts with between three and five cups of tea, accompanied by olives, cheese, honey, clotted cream, butter, jam, eggs, *simit*, bread, *börek* and pastries. I can comfortably claim that there would not be a single household without a cup of tea in the morning. Tea steals the show in homes and coffeehouses.

Our coffee culture is even older than that of tea. Coffee consumption started in the sixteenth century and increased in popularity. Although tea replaced coffee as the favoured drink in the mid-twentieth century, coffee is treated with a different level of deference. The Turkish word for breakfast is *kahvaltı*, which is a composite word of *kahve* (coffee) and *altı* (under). The idea is to have a few bites before the morning coffee. And the social space where tea is drunk is, in fact, called a coffeehouse. The average coffee aficionado has between three and five cups a day.

Turkish coffee has to be freshly ground and foamy on top. Once the coffee is finished, the cup is inverted and left to cool for the 'coffee-cup reader'. Your fortune, destiny, troubles and current gossip are all revealed by the grounds. A cheeky ritual takes place when the prospective groom visits the house of his intended with his parents to ask for her hand in marriage. The prospective bride adds salt to the groom's coffee, so he gets an idea of who will wear the pants if the marriage goes ahead.

SHERBERT

Other hugely popular drinks are the cordials that we call sherbets. The culture of sherbet making is preserved in the Mediterranean, Southeastern and Eastern Anatolia regions. Sherbet makers sell liquorice sherbet in markets in the summer months.

The custom of *sebil* (distributing drinks to the poor) is still popular, particularly in commemoration of the dead. A patron arranges for the sherbet maker to make the preferred sherbet of the recently deceased and distribute it for the benefit of the deceased's soul. The sherbet maker chants the name of the deceased person as he distributes his sweet wares. People line up with their cups to drink. This part of our beverage culture is so popular that it is still widely practiced.

THE STORY OF KAYNAR

Kaynar (Spiced Herbal Tea, see p.446) is a spiced sweet herbal tea, traditionally served around the time of a birth. A pregnant woman will be taken to the Turkish baths for a birth preparation ceremony, 15 days before her due date. Her friends and family massage her belly with a paste made of spices, honey and molasses before washing her with 41 bowls of water – a tradition for easy delivery of a healthy baby. Any paste not used is preserved, diluted with hot water and kept boiling on the stove. It is offered to guests wishing the new mother and baby well and the first cup is sprinkled with ground walnuts and offered to the new mother in order to stimulate milk production.

If the new mother is not Muslim, the paste is boiled with wine. Alternatively, it is placed at the front door, so that everyone has a fingerful of sweet herbal tea. This an important tradition surviving to this day.

TEA
ÇAY

Region:		Rize, all regions
Preparation time:		5 minutes
Cooking time:		25 minutes
Serves:		4

10 g	black loose tea leaves	5 tsp/¼ oz

 ♨ ◉ ♦ V X ❖   p.447 ▣

Tea has been grown in Turkey since the 1930s and has overtaken coffee to become the national drink. It is the primary tool for social interaction. Anytime is a good time for a cup of tea – the average daily tea intake is between five and twenty cups. One is essential at breakfast with olives, cheese, eggs, jam, honey and clotted cream.
A Turkish tea set is made up of two kettles. The larger one at the bottom is for hot water to dilute the tea brewed in the smaller kettle above to the required strength. Boiling water can be used for brewing, in which case the brewing time would be only 10 minutes. Some drink it with sugar.

♦

Put the tea into the smaller pot of a Turkish tea kettle, along with 300 ml (1¼ cups/10 fl oz) water. Pour 700 ml (2¾ cups/23 fl oz) water into the larger, bottom pot. Plug the spout of the smaller pot with a mushroom or piece of cloth. Bring to a boil over low heat for 20 minutes.

To serve, pour about 60 ml (¼ cup/2 fl oz) through a tea strainer into a cup from the top pot. Top up with about 75 ml (⅓ cup/2½ fl oz) hot water from the bottom pot.

♦

SPICED HERBAL TEA
KAYNAR

Region:	Adana and Mersin, Mediterranean Region	
Preparation time:		10 minutes
Cooking time:		25 minutes
Serves:		4

10	allspice berries	10
3	pieces of dried ginger root	3
10	cloves	10
1	cinnamon stick	1
¼ tsp	ground cloves	¼ tsp
120 g	honey (oregano)	scant ½ cup/4 oz
40 g	walnut flour (meal)	⅜ cup/1½ oz
60 g	walnuts, crushed	½ cup/2¼ oz
¼ tsp	ground cinnamon	¼ tsp

♨ ❧ ◉ V

In the community, women take their pregnant friend to the Turkish bath house and massage her belly with this spiced herbal tea mixture. It is believed to help with a speedy and less painful delivery. After the birth, the mixture is then diluted into a cordial. The new mother takes the first sip and the rest is offered to well-wishers. Kaynar is only made at these occasions.

♦

Put all the spices into a saucepan or tea kettle along with 750 ml (3 cups/25 fl oz) water. Cover and bring to the boil. Boil for 15 minutes, then add the honey and boil for a further 5 minutes. Strain and pour into cups. Garnish with walnut flour (meal), then with crushed walnuts and finally sprinkle with the cinnamon in the middle. Serve immediately.

TURKISH COFFEE
KAHVE

Region:		İstanbul, all regions
Preparation time:		5 minutes
Cooking time:		10 minutes
Serves:		4

30 g	freshly roasted coffee, finely ground	6 tbsp/1 oz
4	pieces of Turkish Delight	4

💧 🌿 ◗ ✕ ✛   p.449

Coffee is made with varying amounts of sugar: little (about ¼ tsp), medium (about ½ tsp), lots (1 tsp), or none. The coffee grounds sink to the bottom of the cup in the classic brew. However, in Southeastern Anatolia, a cardamom pod is added to the pot and the grounds are incorporated with longer brewing. This version is known as *mırra*. If you don't have a *cezve*, a Turkish copper coffee pot, you can use a porcelain or chrome-plated coffee pot. Nuts and sugar-coated almonds can also be served with coffee instead of Turkish Delight.

◆

Put the coffee and 250 ml (1 cup/8 fl oz) cold water into a *cezve* (copper coffee pot) and mix for 30 seconds. Slowly bring to a boil over very low heat, without stirring. Watch over it, making sure it does not spill over. A thick froth will start forming on top. As soon as the froth starts boiling over, remove the pot from the heat.

A good cup of coffee is a frothy cup, so divide the froth among the cups first. Top off with the rest of the coffee, pouring gently to protect the froth. Serve with Turkish Delight on the side.

◆

TURKISH COFFEE WITH ALMOND SPRINKLES
CİLVELİ KAHVE

Region:		Manisa, Aegean Region
Preparation time:		5 minutes
Cooking time:		10 minutes
Serves:		4

30 g	freshly roasted coffee, finely ground	6 tbsp/1 oz
½ tsp	sugar	½ tsp
40 g	ground almonds, double-roasted	¼ cup/1½ oz

💧 🌿 ◗ ◆ V ✕ ✛

When a man likes a woman, tradition demands he send his family to the woman's home to ask for her hand in marriage. If consent is given, this is the coffee she makes. It is made in a *cezve*, a Turkish copper coffee pot and served in Turkish coffee cups, which are similar in size to espresso cups.

◆

Put the coffee, sugar and 250 ml (1 cup/8 fl oz) water into a *cezve* and stir to combine. Slowly bring to a boil over very low heat, without stirring. Watch over it, making sure it does not spill over. A thick froth will start forming on top. As soon as the froth starts boiling over, remove the pot from the heat.

A good cup of coffee is a frothy cup, so divide the froth among the cups first. Top off with the rest of the coffee, pouring gently to protect the froth. Sprinkle with the ground roasted almonds and serve.

TEREBINTH COFFEE
MELENGİÇ KAHVESİ

Region:		Gaziantep, Southeastern Anatolia
Preparation time:		5 minutes
Cooking time:		20 minutes, plus cooling
Serves:		4

100 g	terebinth berries	3½ oz
250 ml	milk	1 cup/8 fl oz
60 g	sugar	⅓ cup/2¼ oz

✿ V X ❖

Terebinth coffee is in fact not coffee at all. Terebinth berries are roasted and pounded to prepare this drink; although it is often made using a widely available paste.
◆
Heat a dry griddle or cast-iron pan until hot. Add the berries and roast for 10 minutes. Transfer to a plate and let cool. Pound the berries into a paste with a mortar and pestle.

Mix the berries, milk and sugar with 250 ml (1 cup/8 fl oz) water in a coffee pot or saucepan. Bring to the boil over low heat, mixing continuously. Remove from the heat once the froth is boiling over. Fill the coffee cups half way up first, then fill them all the way and serve.

ORCHID TUBER MILK
SALEP

Region:		İstanbul, all regions
Preparation time:		5 minutes
Cooking time:		40 minutes
Serves:		4

20 g	salep (orchid tuber) flour	¾ oz
120 g	sugar	scant ⅔ cup/4 oz
2 litres	milk	8½ cups/70 fl oz

✿ ◗ V ❖

Salep is made from the tubers of several species of orchid. It is a soul-warming winter drink, believed to be a cure-all. Traditionally it was prepared by vendors who were out in the streets at dawn. It was a popular drink in Britain in the seventeenth and eighteenth centuries until coffee came to dominate the market in the second half of the nineteenth century.
◆
Add the ground salep and sugar to a saucepan and mix well. Pour over the milk and whisk until well combined. Cook for 40 minutes over low heat, mixing continuously, until the mixture thickens. Pour into cups and serve.

BOTTOMLESS MULLED FRUIT
TÜKENMEZ

Region:		İstanbul and Bursa, Marmara Region
Preparation time:		15 minutes, plus 5 days fermentation
Serves:		4

100 g	muscovado sugar	½ cup/3½ oz
1	each of quince, pear and apple	1
300 g	medlars, quartered	11 oz
1½ tsp	black mustard seeds	1½ tsp
2 tbsp	sultanas (golden raisins)	2 tbsp

◗ ✿ ◗ ◗ V

Made in a traditional wooden barrel, a glass is filled with this fruit drink under the tap at the base of the barrel. The barrel is then topped up with the same volume of water, which is why the drink is called 'bottomless'. To minimise the alcohol content, keep the fermentation time short.
◆
Put the sugar in a 20-cm (8-inch) wooden barrel or sterilized glass fermenting jar, just in front of the tap at the bottom. Cut the quince, pear and apple into 8 pieces, then add to the jar with the medlars, crushed mustard seeds, sultanas (golden raisins) and 2 litres (8½ cups/70 fl oz) water. Seal and let rest in a cool, dark spot for 5 days.

After 5 days, transfer to the refrigerator and chill for 4 hours. Serve in glasses.

GRAPES FERMENTED WITH MUSTARD SEEDS
HARDALİYE

Region:		Kırklareli, Marmara Region
Preparation time:	10 minutes, plus 30 days fermentation, plus chilling	
Serves:		4

2 kg	black grapes, each quartered	4 lb 6 oz
100 g	sour cherry leaves	3½ oz
20 g	black mustard seeds, crushed	¾ oz
1 litre	dark grape juice	4¼ cups/34 fl oz

This drink is made with the dark grapes left on the vines in September and preserved in barrels for winter consumption. Sour cherries with the stones left in can be used instead of the leaves, and a glass fermenting jar can be substituted for a wooden barrel.

◆

Divide the black grapes and the sour cherry leaves in half. In a 20-cm (8-inch) wooden barrel or sterilized fermenting jar with a tap at the bottom, arrange a layer of black grapes, then a layer of sour cherry leaves, another layer of black grapes, then the black mustard seeds and a final layer of sour cherry leaves. Pour the dark grape juice over and seal the barrel or jar. Store in a cool, dark place for 30 days.

Every 5 days, empty the juice into a bowl using the tap at the bottom of the barrel or jar, pour it back over the leaves and seal again.

After 30 days, strain the liquid, chill and serve in glasses.

◆

PICKLING BRINE
TURŞU SUYU

Region:		Ankara, all regions
Preparation time:	30 minutes, plus 30 minutes chilling and 4 days resting	
Cooking time:		10 minutes
Serves:		4

100 g	white cabbage	3½ oz
100 g	Savoy cabbage	3½ oz
1	carrot	1
1	turnip	1
200 g	red tomatoes	1 cup/7 oz
200 g	green tomatoes	1 cup/7 oz
250 ml	grape vinegar	1 cup/8 fl oz
60 ml	lemon juice	¼ cup/2 fl oz
2 tsp	salt	2 tsp
6	garlic cloves, quartered	6
1	sweet chilli (chile), quartered	1
1	hot chilli (chile), quartered	1
1	celery stalk	1
4	black peppercorns	4
2 tsp	dried chilli (red pepper) flakes	2 tsp
5	chickpeas (garbanzo beans)	5
60 g	honey	scant ¼ cup/2¼ oz
2	dill sprigs	2
2	flat-leaf parsley sprigs	2
2	fresh mint sprigs	2

Pickling brine is made in the winter months. A large wooden barrel is the preferred container for fermenting, but this recipe works well in a glass fermenting jar too. The actual fermentation time varies according to taste. Families with young children tend to keep it short, since the alcohol percentage increases over time. Whenever a glass is tapped from the bottom of the barrel, the same amount of water is added back into the top, which gives rise to the drink's other name – *tükenmez*, which means 'endless' in Turkish – due to its constantly renewing itself. Adding vegetables to the brine is optional.

◆

Slice the cabbages, carrot, turnip and tomatoes into 2-cm (¾-inch) pieces.

Put the grape vinegar, lemon juice, salt, garlic, chillies (chiles), celery stalk, cabbages, carrot, turnip, tomatoes, black peppercorns and dried chilli (red pepper) flakes into a large saucepan with 1.5 litres (6¼ cups/50 fl oz) water and bring to the boil. Boil for 5 minutes, then remove from the heat. Add the chickpeas (garbanzo beans) and honey and chill in the refrigerator for 30 minutes.

Pour the mixture into a large glass sterilized fermenting jar with a tap at the bottom and add the dill, parsley and fresh mint. Press everything down and seal. Let rest for 3 days at room temperature, then transfer to the refrigerator for a further 1 day.

Serve in glasses.

SALTED YOGURT DRINK
AYRAN

Region:		Diyarbakır, all regions
Preparation time:		10 minutes
Serves:		4

| 500 g | Greek yogurt | 2½ cups/1 lb 2 oz |
| ¾ tsp | salt | ¾ tsp |

♨ ◈ V ⟡ ⁘   p.453 ▣

This is a summer beverage. It can be enjoyed on its own or served with ice, or as a refreshing accompaniment to kebabs, pilafs and pitas.

◆

Whisk the yogurt together with the salt and 1 litre (4¼ cups/34 fl oz) cold water in a large bowl for 5 minutes. Pour the mixture into another large bowl from a height of 50 cm (20 inches) to produce more froth. Return to the first bowl, pouring from the same height. Repeat 5 times to maximize the froth. Pour into glasses and serve chilled.

VERJUICE WITH ONIONS
SOĞANLI GORUK SUYU (KORUK SUYU)

Region:		Isparta, Mediterranean Region
Preparation time:		10 minutes, plus 2 hours chilling
Serves:		4

500 g	unripe grapes, washed	1 lb 2 oz
2 (240 g)	medium onions, sliced	2 (1⅝ cup/ 8½ oz)
¾ tsp	salt	¾ tsp

◉ ♨ ◈ V ⁘

Made in the months of July and August when unripe grapes are in abundance, this is a type of onion pickle in verjuice that resembles pickling brine. It goes really well with tandoor style kebabs and pilafs.

Put the grapes through a juicer. Transfer the juice to a bowl, add 1 litre (4¼ cups/34 fl oz) water. Mix for 1 minute.

Squeeze the onions to release the juices, then put into a colander and rinse thoroughly under running water. Combine the onions and salt in a bowl. Strain the grape juice and pour over. Chill in the refrigerator for 2 hours.

Serve in bowls.

ALMOND MILK
SOMATA

Region:		Manisa, Aegean Region
Preparation time:		10 minutes
Cooking time:		1 hour 10 minutes
Serves:		4

20	blanched bitter almonds	20
40	blanched almonds	40
100 g	sugar	½ cup/3½ oz
1 tsp	ground cinnamon	1 tsp

◉ ♨ ◈ ◈ V ⁘

Almond milk is prepared in large quantities and chilled. It is boiled with hot water before serving. The hot version, called kınalı in İstanbul, is served with cinnamon.

◆

Pound the almonds in a mortar and pestle into almond meal. Add the sugar and mix until combined. Put the mixture into a saucepan with 1 litre (4¼ cups/34 fl oz) water and cook over a low heat for 1 hour, mixing continuously. Strain off the pulp and return the liquid to the pan. Pour in 500 ml (generous 2 cups/17 fl oz) boiling water and boil for a further 3 minutes.

Pour into cups, sprinkle with cinnamon and serve.

TURNIP JUICE
ŞALGAM SUYU

Region:		Adana, Mediterranean Region
Preparation time:		15 minutes, plus 28 days fermentation
Serves:		4

For the starter culture:

60 g	fine bulgur wheat	generous ¼ cup/ 2¼ oz
1 tbsp	whole wheat flour	1 tbsp

400 g	purple carrots, peeled, quartered lengthwise then halved	3 cups/14 oz
1 kg	turnips, peeled and sliced	6⅔ cups/ 2 lb 4 oz

💧 🌿 ◆ V   p.455 📷

Originally a winter beverage, these days turnip juice is consumed throughout the year and is popular around Hatay, Mersin and their surrounding areas. There are even special vendors, who sell only turnip juice. Often consumed first thing in the morning, it is also a great accompaniment to bulgur wheat dishes and other pilafs and kebabs. Sometimes a dried hot chilli (chile) is added.

◆

To make the starter:
Mix the bulgur wheat and flour in a bowl with ¼ teaspoon salt and 2 tablespoons water. Put the mixture into a muslin (cheesecloth) and tie the top. Transfer to a sterilized glass jar, seal and set aside for 3 days.

After 3 days, dissolve 2 teaspoons salt in 3 litres (12 cups/ 100 fl oz) water in a bowl. Add the carrots, turnip and the muslin starter bag to a wooden barrel or sterilized fermenting jar, seal and store in a dark spot for 25 days.

After 25 days, remove the muslin starter bag. Chill before serving the juice with the pickled vegetables.

◆

FERMENTED GRAIN SMOOTHIE
BOZA

Region:		İstanbul, Marmara Region
Preparation time:		5 minutes, plus 3 days resting and 5 hours chilling
Cooking time:		1 hour 10 minutes
Serves:		4

150 g	millet, crushed	¾ cup/5 oz
50 g	cracked rice	⅓ cup/2 oz
1 tbsp	grape vinegar	1 tbsp
100 g	white grape molasses (or 200 g/1 cup/7 oz sugar)	⅓ cup/3½ oz
1 tsp	ground cinnamon	1 tsp

💧 🌿 ◗ ◆ V

Millet is the main ingredient of *boza*, a fermented grain drink. The degree of fermentation varies from 5 hours to 5 days, depending on personal taste. Believed to be an aphrodisiac, *boza* is drunk well into the long, dark winter nights. *Boza* sellers have almost disappeared from İstanbul. According to Mevlut, a *boza* seller who is the main character of Orhan Pamuk's novel *A Strangeness in My Mind*, what really sells the *boza* is the passion in the vendor's voice. *Boza* and *leblebi* are a marriage made in heaven. *Leblebi* is made by soaking and roasting chickpeas. The traditional method of embedding soaked chickpeas under hot sand and ashes is still practised in smaller villages. At home a pan will also give good results. *Leblebi* is sold in the ever-present Turkish nut shops. White, yellow, candied and spicy varieties are all popular.

◆

Put the millet and cracked rice into a large saucepan with 3 litres (12 cups/100 fl oz) water, cover with a dish towel and leave to rest overnight.

The next day, bring to the boil and cook for 4–5 minutes over medium heat. Skim the surface with a slotted spoon. Reduce the heat and cook for 1 hour, mixing occasionally, until the mixture resembles pancake batter. Strain and discard the pulp. Add the vinegar and white grape molasses or sugar and let rest for 2 days at room temperature. After 2 days, transfer to the refrigerator and chill for 5 hours. Serve in glasses with a sprinkle of ground cinnamon.

GRAPE CORDIAL
ŞIRA

Region:	Bursa, all regions
Preparation time:	5 minutes, plus 4 days fermentation and 5 hours chilling
Serves:	4

1.5 litres	dark grape juice	6¼ cups/50 fl oz
2	cloves	2
1 tbsp	barley, tied into a muslin (cheesecloth) bag	1 tbsp

p.457 📷

Şıra is made from crushed raisins in the winter months, while fresh grapes are used during the summer. Popular drunk on its own, it is also delicious served with kebabs, pilafs and *böreks*.
◆
Put the grape juice, cloves and barley into a sterilized glass fermenting jar and let rest in the refrigerator for 4 days.

After 4 days, stir and strain the mixture. Return to the refrigerator for a further 5 hours.

Serve chilled in glasses.

TAMARIND CORDIAL
DEMİRHİNDİ ŞERBETİ

Region:	İstanbul, Marmara Region
Preparation time:	10 minutes, plus 1 day resting and 5 hours chilling
Serves:	4

| 150 g | tamarind, peeled | 5 oz |
| 200 g | honey (flower) | 7 oz |

Traditionally, special sherbet makers are paid to make this popular summer drink and then distribute it to the poor for charity – this is called *sebil*.
◆
Mix the tamarind, honey and 1 litre (4¼ cups/34 fl oz) freshly boiled water in a bowl. Cover and let rest for 1 day.

The next day, mix and knead the mixture well, until the tamarind pips are all out. Strain and transfer the liquid to a jug (pitcher). Transfer the tamarind pulp to a bowl and cover with another 500 ml (generous 2 cups/17 fl oz) freshly boiled water. Mix for 1 minute, then strain again and pour the liquid into the jug. Cover the jug and chill in the refrigerator for 5 hours. Serve chilled.

MELON SEED CORDIAL
SÜBYE

Region:	İzmir, Aegean Region
Preparation time:	15 minutes, plus 4 hours chilling
Serves:	4

| 150 g | melon seeds | 5 oz |
| 130 g | sugar | ⅔ cup/4½ oz |

This is a summer drink, known as *şemmame-e sübi* in Eastern Anatolia and made by special sherbet makers in the region.
◆
Pound the melon seeds and sugar in a mortar and pestle into a thick paste. Transfer to a jug (pitcher), pour over 1.2 litres (5 cups/40 fl oz) water and let dissolve until it turns milky. Strain through a piece of muslin (cheesecloth), then transfer to the refrigerator and chill for 4 hours. Serve chilled, in glasses.

RHUBARB CORDIAL
IŞKIN ŞERBETİ

Region:		Hakkâri, Eastern Anatolia
Preparation time:		25 minutes, plus 4 hours chilling
Serves:		4

300 g	rhubarb, peeled	3 cups/11 oz
2 tbsp	sugar	2 tbsp
100 g	honey (oregano)	⅓ cup/3½ oz

˙ ✣ ◓ V ✣   p.461 ▣

Rhubarb is picked when it first appears in the spring. It is peeled and eaten raw, used in cooked dishes and turned into this sherbet.

◆

Pound the rhubarb and the sugar to a paste in a mortar and pestle for 10 minutes. Put into a large bowl with the honey and 1.2 litres (5 cups/40 fl oz) cold water and mix every 5 minutes for 15 minutes. Strain into a jug (pitcher), then cover and chill for 4 hours.

◆

OAK HONEYDEW CORDIAL
GEZO (KUDRET) ŞERBETİ

Region:		Bitlis, Southeastern Anatolia
Preparation time:		5 minutes, plus 5 hours chilling
Cooking time:		1 hour 10 minutes
Serves:		4

500 g	oak tree leaves with honey dew	1 lb 2 oz

˙ ✣ ◓ ˙ V ✣

Every 15 or 20 years, at the end of summer, a honey-like substance appears on the leaves of oak trees. This signals to locals that it is *gezo* time. The collected leaves are dipped into cauldrons of boiling water to collect the honey, which is turned into molasses. Any molasses left in the cauldron is diluted with snow from the mountains to make cordial.

◆

Bring 1.5 litres (6¼ cups/50 fl oz) water to a boil in a pan over medium heat, add the leaves and boil for 5 minutes. Remove the leaves with tongs, shaking to make sure the honey stays in the water. Transfer the leaves to a bowl. Pour over 500 ml (2 cups/17 fl oz) freshly boiled water to collect any remaining honey, remove the leaves and transfer the water to the pan. Reduce the heat and boil for 1 hour. Strain the cordial, transfer to a glass jar or jug (pitcher) and let cool for 1 hour. Once cooled, cover and chill in the refrigerator for 4 hours. Serve chilled.

◆

VERJUICE CORDIAL
KORUK ŞERBETİ

Region:		Aydın, all regions
Preparation time:		35 minutes, plus 4 hours chilling
Serves:		4

500 g	unripe grapes, washed	1 lb 2 oz
150 g	sugar	¾ cup/5 oz

˙ ✣ ◓ ˙ V ✣

Verjuice cordial is made of unripe grapes in July. Syrup (a more concentrated cordial) is made at the same time. It is made by local street vendors and in homes where it is offered to important guests.

◆

Put the unripe grapes and sugar into a large bowl and press and mix thoroughly for 10 minutes to extract the juice. Cover and let rest at room temperature for 20 minutes. Pour in 1.2 litres (5 cups/40 fl oz) water and mix for a further 2 minutes. Strain, discard the pulp and add the juice back to the mixture. Chill for 4 hours and serve.

SOUR CHERRY LIQUEUR
VİŞNE LİKÖRÜ

Region:	İstanbul, all regions
Preparation time:	10 minutes, plus 97 days
Serves:	4

1 kg	sour cherries	2 lb 3 oz
300 g	sugar	1½ cups/11 oz
400 ml	pure alcohol (vodka)	1⅔ cups/14 fl oz
30 g	cloves	6 tbsp/1 oz
30 g	fresh ginger	1 oz
3	cinnamon sticks	3
1	nutmeg	1

p.461 p.461

Local Christians serve this liqueur to guests, but especially at wakes, either by itself or with coffee. It is made out of other fruits too, but the sour cherry is the most popular.

Put the sour cherries with their leaves and stems, sugar and alcohol along with 1 litre (4¼ cups/34 fl oz) water into a large (4-litre/1-gallon) sterilized glass preserving jar.

Put the whole spices into a calico bag and pound until smooth. Tie the bag and add to the jar. Seal the jar and leave in a sunny spot for 1 week, turning it upside down every day. After 1 week, transfer the jar to a dark place and let rest for 3 months.

After 3 months, chill and serve the liqueur with or without the sour cherries.

PISTACHIO CORDIAL
FISTIK ŞERBETİ

Region:	Gaziantep, Southeastern Anatolia
Preparation time:	20 minutes, plus 5 hours chilling
Cooking time:	10 minutes
Serves:	4

150 g	shelled pistachios	1½ cups/5 oz
150 g	sugar	¾ cup/5 oz

This cordial is made from fresh pistachios in September and dried in the other months. Traditionally it is made for a prospective groom when visiting a bride's home. Offered after the salty coffee, it represents the change from salty to sweet and ends the visit on a good note.

Crush the pistachios and sugar to a powder in a mortar and pestle for 15 minutes. Bring a saucepan with 1.2 litres (5 cups/40 fl oz) water to the boil, add the powder and whisk vigorously for 5 minutes. Strain and discard the pulp. Let rest for 1 hour at room temperature, then chill in the refrigerator for 4 hours before serving.

GRAPE VINEGAR CORDIAL
SİKENCEBİN

Region:	İstanbul, all regions
Preparation time:	15 minutes, plus 1 day resting
Serves:	4

60 ml	grape vinegar	¼ cup/2 fl oz
2 tbsp	lemon juice	2 tbsp
110 g	honey (flower)	generous ⅓ cup/3¾ oz

Traditionally offered with pilafs, this drink is distributed to the poor as an act of charity in the summer months. The original name of this cordial as mentioned in old sources is *sikencebin* or *sirkencebin*.

Pour 1 litre (4¼ cups/34 fl oz) boiling water, the grape vinegar and lemon juice into a jug (pitcher). Cover and rest for 10 minutes, then stir in the honey. Re-cover and rest for 1 day. Chill in the refrigerator for 4 hours, before serving in glasses.

SUMAC CORDIAL
SUMAK ŞERBETİ

Region:		Siirt, Southeastern Anatolia
Preparation time:		10 minutes, plus overnight resting
Serves:		4

200 g	sumac berries	1¼ cups/7 oz
150 g	sugar	¾ cup/5 oz

✦ ❦ ◈ ✦ V ✤   p.463 ◻

Ground sumac, often found in salads, can be used to make this cordial if you cannot find sumac berries. Offered with earthy meat dishes, this cordial is popular all year round.

♦

Put the sumac berries into a large bowl and pour over 1.2 litres (5 cups/40 fl oz) boiling water. Cover and let rest at room temperature overnight.

The next day, thoroughly squeeze the sumac berries with your hands. Strain and discard the pulp. Add the sugar to the strained juice and mix for 3 minutes. Cover and chill in the refrigerator for 4 hours. Serve chilled, in glasses.

MULBERRY SYRUP
DUT ŞURUBU

Region:		Hatay, all regions
Preparation time:		10 minutes, plus 1 hour resting
Cooking time:		25 minutes
Serves:		4

200 g	sour black mulberries	7 oz
1 tbsp	lemon juice	1 tbsp
50 g	sugar	¼ cup/2 oz

✦ ❦ ◈ ✦ V ✤

Traditionally mulberry syrup is made in June and July. The concentrated syrup, similar to jam, is a popular breakfast spread. Otherwise, it is diluted before use.

♦

Put the sour mulberries, lemon juice and sugar into a saucepan and crush together for 5 minutes. Cover and let rest for 1 hour.

Pour over 500 ml (generous 2 cups/17 fl oz) water and bring to the boil. Boil for 20 minutes. Strain and discard the pulp. Dilute the syrup with 500 ml (generous 2 cups/17 fl oz) cold water, then refrigerate. Serve chilled.

SAFFRON CORDIAL
SAFRAN ŞERBETİ

Region:		Karabük, all regions
Preparation time:		15 minutes, plus 4 hours chilling
Cooking time:		15 minutes
Serves:		4

pinch	saffron	pinch
2 tsp	sugar	2 tsp
½ tsp	ground ginger	½ tsp
1	lemon, thinly sliced	1
110 g	honey	⅓ cup/3¾ oz

✦ ❦ ◈ V ✤

This cordial is a welcome relief on long, hot summer days. It is believed to be a staunch protector against the 'evil eye'. If someone trips on a flat path, out of the blue, it is blamed on the evil eye and so a drop of saffron cordial is poured on the spot where the accident took place for protection.

♦

Pound the saffron and sugar in a mortar and pestle to a fine powder. In a saucepan, bring 1 litre (4¼ cups/34 fl oz) water, with the ground ginger and lemon slices, to a boil. Boil for 2 minutes, then remove from the heat. Stir in the saffron and sugar powder and let rest for 10 minutes. Stir in the honey, then cover and chill in the refrigerator for 4 hours.

Serve chilled (no need to remove the lemon slices).

ROSE SYRUP
GÜL ŞURUBU

Region:		Isparta, all regions
Preparation time:	10 minutes, plus 2 hours, overnight rest	
Cooking time:		30 minutes
Serves:		4

250 g	fresh pink aromatic rose petals	9 oz
2 tbsp	lemon juice	2 tbsp
100 g	sugar	½ cup/3½ oz

♦ ☙ ◗ ♦ V ⸭

p.465 📷

Mountain snow is kept frozen to enjoy in the summer with rose syrup. If no snow is available, ice shavings will suffice. This is a favourite taste of my childhood.

♦

Put the petals, lemon juice and sugar into a bowl and knead for 5 minutes. Cover and rest for 2 hours. Pour over 500 ml (2 cups/17 fl oz) boiling water, cover and rest overnight.

The next day, strain the mixture, squeezing all the juice from the pulp. Put the juice into a saucepan and bring to the boil over medium heat. Boil for 5 minutes, then reduce the heat and cook for 20 minutes. Dilute with 500 ml (generous 2 cups/17 fl oz) cold water. Chill before serving.

♦

NOWROZ (NEW YEAR) CORDIAL
NEVRUZ ŞERBETİ

Region:		Ağrı, Eastern Anatolia
Preparation time:	35 minutes, 30 minutes rest	
Serves:		4

100 g	watercress, finely sliced	½ cup/3½ oz
100 g	sorrel, finely sliced	½ cup/3½ oz
2	dill sprigs, finely sliced	2
2	mallow leaves, finely sliced	2
1	fresh basil sprig, finely sliced	1
50 g	chickweed, finely sliced	2 oz
1	green apple, grated	1
100 g	wheat sprouts, finely sliced	3½ oz
2 tbsp	lemon juice	2 tbsp
150 g	honey (oregano flower)	½ cup/5 oz

♦ ◗ V

Nowruz, the festivities that mark the arrival of spring, are a big deal in Eastern Anatolia. This cordial is offered with a special dessert made of pounded wheat sprouts in March and April. Locals believe that these rituals will align them with Mother Nature, ward off evil and herald a fresh start to the year, not unlike the English tradition of wassailing.

♦

In a mortar and pestle, pound the watercress, sorrel, dill, mallow leaves, basil, chickweed, green apple, wheat sprouts, lemon juice and honey to a pulp. Transfer to a bowl and slowly mix in 1.2 litres (5 cups/40 fl oz) cold water. Mix for 5 minutes, until thoroughly combined, then let rest for 30 minutes. Mix for another 10 minutes, then strain and transfer to a jar or jug (pitcher). Seal or cover with clingfilm (plastic wrap) and refrigerate for 4 hours. Serve chilled, in glasses.

♦

GUEST CHEFS

♦

SABIT İSKENDEROĞLU

KEBAPÇI İSKENDER, BURSA

Kebapçı İskender was founded by İskender Dede
(son of Mehmet) at the Kayhan Mall in Bursa. It is now
run by fourth-generation family members.

DÖNER KEBAB
DÖNER KEBABI

Preparation time: 30 minutes, plus overnight chilling
Cooking time: 50 minutes
Serves: 4

1 kg	leg of lamb, sinew removed, minced (ground)	2 lb 3 oz
1 (120 g)	medium onion, grated	1 (¾ cup/ 4 oz)

For the tomato sauce:

250 ml	juice of charred tomatoes	1 cup/8 fl oz
250 ml	meat stock (see p.489)	1 cup/8 fl oz
1	garlic clove, crushed	1

100 g	butter (goat's milk)	scant ½ cup/ 3½ oz
300 g	sourdough ridged flatbread, dried, sprinkled with water, cubed	11 oz
300 g	Greek yogurt	1½ cups/11 oz
400 g	*shish köfte* (lamb rib meat, minced (ground), grilled on skewers), cut into 8 pieces	14 oz
4 (400 g)	*külbastı* (grilled beef fillets), each cut into 3 pieces	4 (14 oz)
480 g	tomatoes, quartered, charred	2½ cups/ 1 lb 1 oz
8	banana peppers (mild sweet peppers), charred	8

This recipe requires a döner kebab (rotisserie) grill.

In a large bowl, knead the minced (ground) lamb and grated onion with 1 teaspoon salt. Chill in the refrigerator overnight. Divide into 4 equal parts.

The next day, heat a rotisserie döner kebab grill (using oak embers if wood-fired). Mould the meat on to the skewer, making sure it is tightly attached. Secure the skewer to the grill and cook for 6 minutes. Shave a thin slice off the sides of the meat with a döner (serrated) knife. Knead the meat cut off for 5 minutes, then mould it back on to the skewer. Cook for a further 30 minutes, until cooked through. Thinly shave off the cooked meat with the döner knife, with a movement as if you were playing the violin. Repeat the cooking and shaving until the döner is finished.

To make the tomato sauce:
In a large saucepan, combine the tomato juice, meat stock and garlic with ¼ teaspoon black pepper and ½ teaspoon salt, bring to a boil for 10–15 minutes, then set aside.

Heat the butter in a small saucepan and keep warm.

Warm 4 plates, put the sourdough ridged bread pieces on the plates, then top with 200 ml (scant 1 cup/7 fl oz) tomato sauce. Whip the yogurt and serve a portion on one side of the plate. Layer with the shaved döner meat and add the pieces of *shish köfte* (lamb kebabs) and *külbastı* (grilled beef). Add the charred tomatoes and peppers. Top with the remaining tomato sauce and hot butter. Serve immediately.

ALI ELHAKAN

MARDIN KEBAP EVI, YENIŞEHIR, DIYARBAKII

Ali Elhakan's Mardin Kebap Evi has been
in business since 1965.

HOT AND SPICY KEBABS
ACILI KEBAP

Preparation time:	20 minutes, plus overnight chilling	
Cooking time:		15 minutes
Serves:		4

1 kg	sheep (male) leg and brisket, sinew trimmed	2 lb 3 oz
250 g	sheep (male) tail fat	9 oz
¾ tsp	salt	¾ tsp
60 g	onion	⅜ cup/2¼ oz
10	flat-leaf parsley sprigs	10
50 g	hot red bell pepper paste (see p.492)	¼ cup/2 oz

1	*Piyaz Salatsı* (Onion Salad, see p.67)	1

◦ ✿

Chop the meat and the tail fat finely together with a *zırh* (a curved cleaver) or a regular meat cleaver, until well minced (ground). Put into a bowl, mix with the salt, cover and chill in the refrigerator overnight.

The next day, remove the meat from the refrigerator. Finely slice the onion and parsley, then add to the meat with the red bell pepper paste, kneading until well combined. Divide into 4 equal pieces, then run a skewer through each piece and squeeze flat between your palms at regular intervals, making sure that the two ends are tightly secured. You should end up with four 15-cm (6-inch) semi-flat rolls.

Prepare a barbecue for cooking. Set the skewers 8 cm (3 inches) above the hot barbecue embers and grill for 3 minutes on each side, turning every 30 seconds.

Transfer the kebabs to plates and serve with *Piyaz Salatsı*.

MURAT KARGILI

KANAAT LOKANTASI, ÜSKÜDAR, İSTANBUL

Kanaat Lokantası has been around since 1933. The same
family from Thrace has been running it for a long time.

SUCKLING LAMB CASSEROLE
ELBASAN TAVA

Preparation time:		30 minutes
Cooking time:		2 hours 20 minutes
Serves:		4

1	leg of suckling lamb, quartered, soaked in 2 litres (8½ cups/70 fl oz) water for 30 minutes, then drained	1
¾ tsp	salt	¾ tsp
2	eggs	2
150 g	yogurt (sheep's milk)	¾ cup/ 5 oz
100 g	butter	scant ½ cup/ 3½ oz
130 g	plain (all-purpose) flour	scant 1 cup/ 4 ½ oz
50 g	tomato paste (see p.492)	¼ cup/ 2 oz
250 ml	meat stock (see p.489)	1 cup/ 8 fl oz

Put the lamb pieces and the salt into a saucepan with
3 litres (12 cups/100 fl oz) water, cover and cook over
medium heat for 2 hours. Remove the lamb from the
pan and reserve the stock. Take the meat off the bone
and set aside.

Whisk the eggs and yogurt together in a bowl for
3 minutes and set aside.

Heat the butter in a saucepan over medium heat, add
the flour and cook for 3 minutes, mixing continuously.
Add the yogurt and egg mixture, along with 750 ml
(3 cups/25 fl oz) of the reserved stock. Mix thoroughly
for 1 minute.

Preheat oven to 220°C/425°F/Gas Mark 7.

Arrange the lamb in a large roasting pan and pour over
the gravy mixture. Dilute the tomato paste with the
meat stock then add that to the pan. Cook in the hot oven
for 15 minutes, until the meat starts to brown.

Transfer to plates and serve.

SEFA BOYACIOĞLU

BOĞAZIÇI LOKANTASI, ULUS, ANKARA

Founded by Mehmet Recai Boyacıoğlu, Boğaziçi Lokantası
has been in business since 1956.

ANKARA HOTPOT
ANKARA TAVA

Preparation time:		20 minutes
Cooking time:	2 hours 5 minutes, plus 15 minutes resting	
Serves:		4

200 g	unsalted butter	1 cup/7 oz
4 × 250-g	lamb brisket pieces, on the bone, washed	4 × 9-oz
1 (120 g)	medium onion	1 (¾ cup/4 oz)
2	bay leaves	2
5	black peppercorns	5
2 tsp	salt	2 tsp
480 g	medium-grain rice, soaked in 2 litres (8½ cups/70 fl oz) water for 20 minutes, drained	2½ cups/ 1 lb 1 oz
360 g	tomatoes, quartered	1¾ cups/12½ oz
4	sweet green chillies (chiles), quartered	4
100 g	butter, salted	½ cup/3½ oz

❧

Melt the unsalted butter in a large casserole dish (Dutch oven). Add the lamb to the casserole dish and sauté over medium heat. Add the onion, bay leaves, black peppercorns and salt. Pour in 3 litres (12 cups/100 fl oz) water, or just enough to cover the meat, cover and cook for 1½ hours.

Preheat oven to 220°C/425°F/Gas Mark 7.

Strain the cooked lamb, reserving the cooking juices, but discarding the onions, bay leaves and peppercorns. Return the lamb and its cooking juices to the casserole dish, add the rice and cook, covered, until the rice has absorbed all the juices, about 20 minutes. Add the tomatoes and chillies (chiles). Cook, uncovered, in the hot oven for 10 minutes, until the tomatoes and chillies have some colour and the rice has absorbed all the juices. Remove from the oven.

Meanwhile, heat the salted butter in a small saucepan over medium heat. Pour the melted butter into the casserole dish. Cover and let rest for 15 minutes. Transfer to plates and serve.

FERIDUN ÜGÜMÜ

HÜNKÂR LOKANTASI, NIŞANTAŞI, İSTANBUL

The brothers Galip, Feridun and Faruk Ügümü have been
running Hünkâr Lokantası since 1998. If the cooked dish
has an excess of cooking liquid, ladle out the juice, simmer
in a separate pan until reduced, then return it to the dish.

LAMB AND QUINCE STEW
AYVALI YAHNİ

Preparation time:		15 minutes
Cooking time: 2 hours 15 minutes, plus 15 minutes resting		
Serves:		4

60 ml	sunflower oil	¼ cup/2 fl oz
600 g	lamb shoulder, diced into 2-cm (¾-inch) pieces	1 lb 5 oz
100 g	butter	½ cup/ 3½ oz
2 (240 g)	medium onions, sliced	2 (1⅝ cup/ 8½ oz)
1 (250 g)	quince, cut into 16 pieces	1 (9 oz)
1 tsp	salt	1 tsp
1 tsp	ground cinnamon	1 tsp
2 tbsp	grape molasses (or mulberry molasses)	2 tbsp

Heat the sunflower oil in a large saucepan over medium heat, add the lamb shoulder, turn the heat to high and sauté for 15 minutes. Reduce the heat to low, cover and cook without stirring for about 10 minutes, until the lamb has reabsorbed its own juices. Continue to cook over medium heat, stirring occasionally, until the lamb is caramelized, about 15 minutes. Add 400 ml (1⅔ cups/ 14 fl oz) hot water, reduce the heat to low once again, cover and simmer for 1 hour.

Meanwhile, heat half of the butter in a separate saucepan over medium heat, add the onions and cook until caramelized, about 20–30 minutes. Remove the onions and set aside. Add the remaining butter and the quince and cook until caramelized, about 15 minutes. Add the onions back to the pan, along with 100 ml (scant ½ cup/3½ fl oz) hot water, bring to a boil and cook for 5 minutes.

Pour the onion and quince mixture into the pan with the lamb, then stir in the salt, cinnamon and molasses. Cook for 30 minutes over low heat. Remove from the heat and let rest for 15 minutes. Serve warm.

ŞENOL ÖZTÜRK

DENIZ RESTAURANT, ALSANCAK, İZMIR

Deniz Restaurant was founded in 1981 by Yılmaz Ramazan
Çelikkaya and nowadays is managed by his sons.

SEA BASS IN BECHAMEL SAUCE
SÜTLÜ BALIK

Preparation time:		15 minutes
Cooking time:		1 hour 10 minutes
Serves:		4

1.5 kg	sea bass, cleaned, filleted	3 lb 5 oz
50 g	butter	¼ cup/2 oz
50 g	plain (all-purpose) flour	⅓ cup/2 oz
500 ml	milk	generous 2 cups/17 fl oz
1	egg	1
50 g	*kaşar* cheese, grated	2 oz
1	sweet red bell pepper, diced	1
5	mushrooms, sliced	5

Put the sea bass fillets into a saucepan with 1.5 litres (6¼ cups/50 fl oz) water, bring to the boil, then reduce the heat and simmer for 30 minutes. Drain, cool, then de-bone.

Preheat oven to 200°C/400°F/Gas Mark 6. Heat half of the butter in a saucepan over medium heat, add the flour and cook for 10 minutes, stirring, until it browns. Gradually pour in the milk, mixing continuously. Crack the egg into the pan, mix well and cook for a further 10 minutes, stirring occasionally. When thickened, remove from the heat.

Pour half of the sauce into a roasting pan. Add the fish and remaining sauce, mix until combined. Stir in the *kaşar* cheese, red bell pepper, mushrooms and remaining butter with ½ teaspoon salt. Bake for 20 minutes, until browned. Transfer to plates.

◆

LEVON BALIKÇIOĞLU

LEVON PATISSERIE, İÇERENKÖY, İSTANBUL

Levon Patisserie was founded in 2000 by chef Levon Balıkçıoğlu,
to provide delicious, healthy foods for people who live and work
locally. It caters for special occasions and business functions for its
clientele all over İstanbul.

BAKED CUSTARD
HAVİDZ

Preparation time: 5 minutes
Cooking time: 1 hour 5 minutes, plus 4 hours chilling
Serves: 4

120 g	butter	½ cup/4 oz
70 g	plain (all-purpose) flour	½ cup/2¾ oz
1 litre	milk	4¼ cups/34 fl oz
200 g	sugar	1 cup/7 oz
50 g	breadcrumbs	½ cup/2 oz
1 tsp	ground cinnamon	1 tsp

V

Heat 100 g (scant ½ cup/3½ oz) of the butter in a large
saucepan over low heat, add the flour and cook for
20 minutes, mixing continuously, until golden brown.
Increase heat to medium and gradually add the milk,
mixing continuously. When the milk starts to boil,
add the sugar. Reduce the heat and cook for a further
15 minutes, stirring occasionally.

Preheat oven to 180°C/350°F/Gas Mark 4.

Brush a 20-cm (8-inch) baking dish (preferably glass) with
the remaining butter and sprinkle with the breadcrumbs.
Pour the custard over and bake in the hot oven for
25 minutes, until the breadcrumbs are nicely browned.

Chill in the refrigerator for 4 hours. Dust with the ground
cinnamon before serving.

ABDULLAH KORU

HACI ABDULLAH LOKANTASI, BEYOĞLU, İSTANBUL

Hacı Abdullah is one of the oldest restaurants in İstanbul,
embracing traditional Turkish culinary culture.

FRUIT STEW
KARIŞIK HOŞAF

Preparation time:		10 minutes
Cooking time:		15 minutes, plus 5 hours chilling
Serves:		4

---

400 g	sugar	2 cups/14 oz
4	cloves	4
1	quince, peeled, quartered	1
1	apple, peeled, quartered	1
1	pear, peeled, quartered	1
1	peach, peeled, quartered	1
4	apricots	4
8	sour cherries	8
4	black plums	4

---

100 g	sour pomegranate seeds	1¼ cups/3½ oz
20	black mulberries	20
1	banana, cut into 16 thin slices	1

Put the sugar and cloves into a large saucepan with
1 litre (4¼ cups/34 fl oz) water and bring to a boil over
medium heat.

Reduce the heat, add the quince, apple, pear, peach,
apricots, sour cherries and black plums and simmer for
a further 10 minutes.

Remove from the heat and let cool at room temperature
for 1 hour. Transfer to the refrigerator and chill for
4 hours.

Serve in bowls, topped with the pomegranate seeds,
black mulberries and banana slices.

♦ ❧ ◗ ♦ V

♦

PANTRY

♦

LINDEN BLOSSOM STARTER
ÇİÇEK MAYASI

Region:		İstanbul, all regions
Preparation time:		15 minutes
Cooking time:	5 minutes, plus overnight resting	
Makes:		1

30 g	linden blossoms with leaves	1 oz
20 g	honey	2 tbsp/ ¾ oz
100 g	whole wheat flour	¾ cup/3½ oz
¼ tsp	salt	¼ tsp

This starter produces aromatic bread. The ratio for use is 2 tablespoons of starter to every 100 g (¾ cup/3½ oz) flour. The fermentation time is between five hours and one day. Add 50 g (⅓ cup/2 oz) flour every day to feed the starter. It can also be made from roses, geraniums and hops.

◆

Pound the blossoms and leaves in a pestle and mortar with the honey. Transfer to a saucepan, add 3 tablespoons of unchlorinated water, cover and bring to a boil over medium heat. Remove from the heat, wrap the pan in a dish towel and let rest overnight.

The next day, knead the mixture, then strain and discard the pulp, reserving the extracted liquid. Mix the flour and salt in a small bowl, add the linden blossom liquid, combine well, then knead for 5 minutes.

◆

ASH STARTER
KÜL MAYASI

Region:		Sivas, all regions
Preparation time:	5 minutes, plus overnight resting	
Makes:		1

100 g	powdered oak ashes, sifted	3½ oz

Bicarbonate of soda replaced the ash starter in cookies, cakes, *kalburabastı* and *şekerpare*, but traditional cooks still swear by it. It can also be used as a starter for bread by adding flour. The ratio for use is 20 ml (4 tsp/¾ fl oz) starter to every 100 g (¾ cup/3½ oz) flour. It can be prepared a day ahead, but it doesn't keep and you cannot feed it.

◆

Combine the oak ashes with 500 ml (generous 2 cups/ 17 fl oz) of water in a bowl and mix for 1 minute, until well combined. Cover and let rest overnight in a warm place. Take out the required amount and strain before use.

◆

CHICKPEA STARTER
NOHUT MAYASI

Region:		Yozgat, all regions
Preparation time:	5 minutes, plus overnight resting	
Makes:		1

50 g	canned chickpeas (garbanzo beans), crushed in a mortar and pestle	⅓ cup/2 oz

A chickpea starter makes oily pastries like *çörek*, *külçe* and *kete* crisper and sweeter. Also known as the 'sweet starter', this is used both in bread making and baking *Simit* or *Kahke* (Sesame Bagels, see p.370) and *çörek*. The ratio for use is 40 g (2½ tbsp/1¼ oz) starter to every 100 g (¾ cup/3½ oz) of flour. You can place it in a very low oven for 2 hours to encourage froth formation.

◆

Add the crushed chickpeas (garbanzo beans) to a glass jar. Pour over 500 ml (generous 2 cups/17 fl oz) lukewarm water and let rest overnight in a warm place. The starter is alive and working if there is froth on top.

SOURDOUGH STARTER
EKŞİ MAYA

Region:		Tekirdağ, all regions
Fermentation time:		minimum 5 hours
Preparation time:		15 minutes, plus 2 days resting
Makes:		1

3.1 kg	whole wheat flour	23 cups/6 lb 13 oz
¼ tsp	salt	¼ tsp
20 g	grape molasses	4 tsp/¾ oz
2 tbsp	grape vinegar	2 tbsp
10	fresh vine leaves	10

Sourdough starter is used to make bread and *pide*. Locals keep this starter buried in flour to use for breads and other recipes and it will last forever if fed regularly with fresh dough. The longer you let the dough rest, the more sour it will become – this is a matter of personal taste. The sourdough starter is half the amount of the flour needed for the loaf. If you want your dough to be more sour, you can use equal amounts of flour and starter. The starter should be diluted with water before use. Once a new loaf is proved, take a little of the dough and add it back to the mother starter to use for the next loaf. Each feeding improves the quality of the starter. The ratio for use is 40 g (2½ tbsp/1½ oz) starter to every 100 g (¾ cup/3½ oz) flour. Sourdough starter can also be made with fermented fruit.

♦

Mix 100 g (¾ cup/3½ oz) flour, salt, 60 ml (¼ cup/2 fl oz) water, the grape molasses and grape vinegar in a large bowl, then knead for 5 minutes until well combined. Transfer the dough on to a flour-dusted work counter and knead for 10 minutes, to a smooth and elastic dough.

Put the remaining 3 kg (22¼ cups/6 lb 9½ oz) flour into a large bowl. Wrap the dough in fresh vine leaves, bury deep in the flour and let rest for 2 days before using. The starter can be kept in flour for a few weeks: the taste of the bread depends on the maturity of the starter.

♦

CHEESE
PEYNİR

Region:		Gaziantep, all regions
Preparation time:		5 minutes
Cooking time:		20 minutes, plus 3 hours resting,
		plus 1 hour straining
Makes:		1 kg (2 lb 3 oz)

5 litres	milk (fresh sheep's, if possible)	20 cups/ 160 fl oz
50 g	sheep omasum (or 1 tbsp rennet)	2 oz

There are many local varieties and methods, but the majority of cheese production uses fresh, springtime milk. Locals do not boil the milk – they start with sheep omasum and add freshly milked sheep's milk. Sheep's, goat's, water buffalo's, camel's and cow's milk can be used, depending on availability and preference. The cheese is preserved in brine for 6 months before consumption. The whey strained off during the process is curdled with lemon juice to make *lor* (fresh curd cheese, see p.485).

♦

Heat the milk in a large saucepan to 40°C (104°F) on a cooking thermometer. Add the omasum or rennet and keep cooking until it reaches 45°C (113°F), then remove from the heat. Cover the pan with a dish towel and let rest at room temperature for 3 hours.

Remove the omasum. Transfer the milk curds to a bowl lined with a muslin (cheesecloth). Place a 500 g (1 lb 2 oz) weight on top of the curds to facilitate straining and let strain for 1 hour. Remove the cheese from the cloth and enjoy. Reserve the whey for making *lor* (see p.485).

DRY CURD COTTAGE CHEESE
ÇÖKELEK

Region:	Çankırı, all regions
Preparation time:	5 minutes
Cooking time:	20 minutes, plus 27 hours resting
Makes:	600 g (1 lb 5 oz)

2 tbsp	lemon juice	2 tbsp
3 kg	Greek yogurt	15 cups/6 lb 9½ oz

❧ ◈ V ⁙

Ekşimik and *minci* are other local names for this cheese, which is made from the milk of sheep, goats, water buffalo, camels and cows, depending on availability and preference. In some regions, the whey from making the *çökelek* is kept in large jars and consumed as a sour drink or boiled into a thick molasses and enjoyed as a tart side dish. The yogurt can also be substituted with *Ayran* (Salted Yogurt Drink, see p.452).

◆

Combine the lemon juice and yogurt with 1 litre (4¼ cups/ 34 fl oz) of water in a large saucepan. Bring to a boil over low heat and cook without stirring for 15 minutes, until it begins to curdle. Putting a metal ladle into the pan is the best way to prevent it boiling over.

Remove from the heat and let rest for 3 hours.

Put the yogurt into a large piece of muslin (cheesecloth), tie its corners together and hang over a large bowl in the refrigerator. The *çökelek* will be ready in 24 hours, once all the liquid has strained into the bowl. Remove the muslin and enjoy. Keep refrigerated and consume within 3 days. Storing in a jar of olive oil can extend the shelf life.

SPICY HATAY CHEESE
SÜRK

Region:	Hatay, Mediterranean Region
Preparation time:	15 minutes
Cooking time:	5 hours drying, plus 15 days resting
Makes:	600 g (1 lb 5 oz)

400 g	*lor* (see opposite)	3⅓ cups/14 oz
400 g	*çökelek* (see above)	3⅓ cups/14 oz
100 g	Bulgarian or Greek feta cheese, crumbled	¾ cup/3½ oz
30 g	dried chilli (red pepper) flakes	⅓ cup/1 oz
1 tsp	ground za'atar	1 tsp
¾ tsp	ground cumin	¾ tsp
1 tsp	ground coriander	1 tsp
¼ tsp	ground fennel	¼ tsp
120 ml	olive oil	½ cup/4 fl oz
½ tsp	salt	½ tsp

❧ ◈ V

The traditional method has the *sürk* dried in a cool place for a day, wrapped in moist paper and kept cool in glass jars until it becomes moldy. It is also made by fermenting in earthenware jugs. Locals crumble *sürk* and cover it with generous amounts of olive oil for breakfast. It is popular as a side to salads, with pastries at breakfast and as an accompaniment to *rakı*. When added to *çoban salatası* with pomegranate molasses and olive oil, this version is called *sürk salatası*.

◆

Preheat oven to its lowest possible temperature (75°C/165°F or as near as possible) and line a baking sheet with baking (parchment) paper.

Knead the *lor*, çökelek, feta cheese, dried chilli (red pepper) flakes, za'atar, cumin, coriander, fennel, olive oil and salt in a large bowl for 10 minutes, until well combined. Divide the mixture into small balls. Roll each ball in your hand and form one end into a point. Place each cheese on the prepared baking sheet.

Dry in the oven for 5 hours, then let cool at room temperature. Once cooled, cover with a moist dish towel and rest in the refrigerator for at least 15 days. Keep refrigerated.

FRESH CURD CHEESE
LOR

Region:	Muş, all regions
Preparation time:	5 minutes
Cooking time:	15 minutes plus 27 hours resting
Makes:	400 g (14 oz)

| 3 litres | strained whey (from making cheese, see p.481) (or 2 litres/8½ cups/70 fl oz milk, 2 tbsp lemon juice and 2 litres/8½ cups/70 fl oz cow's milk) | 12 cups/ 100 fl oz |

❧ ◆ V ⁂

Lor, or milk curd cheese, is produced by acidulating milk with lemon juice or vinegar. The leftover whey is commonly used in baking. The milk of goats, water buffalo, camels and sheep can be used, depending on availability and preference.

◆

Combine the strained whey or milk, lemon juice and cow's milk in a large saucepan and boil for 15 minutes, until the milk forms curds. A metal ladle in the pan is the best way to prevent it boiling over. Remove from the heat and let rest uncovered for 3 hours.

Transfer the contents into a muslin (cheesecloth), tie the ends and hang over a bowl in the refrigerator. Let rest for 24 hours, until all the whey has drained into the bowl below. Remove the *lor* from the cloth and enjoy.

◆

KASHK
KEŞ

Region:	Van, all regions
Preparation time:	15 minutes, plus 7 days resting
Makes:	200 g (7 oz)

200 g	strained Greek yogurt	1 cup/7 oz
200 g	*lor* (see above) or *çökelek* (see opposite)	7 oz
50 g	butter	¼ cup/2 oz

❧ ◆ V ⁂

Also known as *keşk*, *cortan*, *paskan*, *torak* and *kurut*, *kashk* is a vital ingredient for homemade noodles, *keledoş* and various soups. It can be made with any milk, depending on availability and preference, and can also be made with plain strained yogurt, unstrained yogurt and *çökelek* (see opposite). It keeps well in the refrigerator.

◆

Mix the yogurt, *lor* or *çökelek* and butter with 2 teaspoons salt for 2 minutes in a bowl. Knead well, getting rid of all the air bubbles. Shape into 5-cm (2-inch) wide domes and arrange on a piece of muslin (cheesecloth). Let dry for a week in a cool, dark place, turning them over after 3 days. Store at room temperature, hanging in a muslin bag.

◆

GHEE
SADEYAĞ

Region:	Şanlıurfa, all regions
Preparation time:	5 minutes
Cooking time:	10 minutes, plus 1 hour cooling time
Makes:	160 g (5½ oz)

| 200 g | raw butter (sheep's milk) | 1 cup/7 oz |

❧ ◆ V ⁂

Ghee can be made from any kind of milk, according to preference. It lasts for up to a year when kept refrigerated.

◆

Put the butter in a saucepan and melt over low heat, making sure the temperature does not exceed 130°C (266°F) on a cooking thermometer. Skim the surface with a slotted spoon until the butter is clear. Line a sieve (strainer) with cotton wool and filter the melted butter through it into a bowl. Pour the filtered butter into a sterilized glass jar. Let cool at room temperature for 1 hour, then cover and keep refrigerated.

CLOTTED CREAM
KAYMAK

Region:		İstanbul, all regions
Preparation time:		5 minutes
Cooking time:		2 hours, plus 26 hours resting
Makes:		300 g (11 oz)

3 litres	fresh water buffalo milk	12 cups/100 fl oz

The milk of sheep, goats, camels and cows can all be used to make clotted cream, depending on availability and preference. It is usually served with dessert or at breakfast with honey. The leftover milk can be used as a starter for making yogurt (see below), cheese (see p.481) or *lor* (fresh curd cheese, see p.485), or can be curdled with lemon for making milk curd.

Bring the milk to the boil in a heavy saucepan over low heat. Remove from the heat as soon as it boils and let rest at room temperature for 30 minutes. Return the pan to low heat and bring it to the boil again, without stirring. Remove from the heat as soon the milk boils. Repeat this process 3 times.

Let rest at room temperature for 2 hours, then refrigerate for 24 hours. Use a cotton thread to collect the clotted cream formed on the surface of the milk. Serve fresh.

YOGURT
YOĞURT

Region:		Ankara, all regions
Preparation time:		5 minutes, plus overnight resting
Cooking time:		20 minutes plus 5 hours, plus overnight resting
Makes:		2 kg (4 lb 6 oz)

2 litres	fresh milk	8½ cups/70 fl oz
5	canned chickpeas (garbanzo beans), crushed	5

Sheep's, goat's, water buffalo's, camel's and cow's milk can be used, depending on availability and preference. Locals like to reserve 4 teaspoons of the starter and the yogurt for future batches.

♦

To make the yogurt starter, heat 2 tablespoons of the milk in a small saucepan to 45°C (113°F) on a cooking thermometer. Pour the milk into a small bowl. Add the crushed chickpeas (garbanzo beans), cover with a dish towel and a lid. Wrap the bowl in another dish towel and let rest overnight.

The next day, bring the remaining milk to a boil in a large saucepan, cooking for about 10 minutes. Froth and cool the milk by pouring back and forth from a height of 50 cm (20 inches) between two large bowls. Bring the temperature to 45°C (113°F).

Uncover the yogurt starter, then strain and remove the chickpeas. Gently stir the starter into the milk in the bowl. Cover with a lid and wrap in a dish towel. Let rest at room temperature for 5 hours, then chill overnight in the refrigerator. Keep refrigerated.

◆

STRAINED YOGURT
SÜZME YOGURT

Region:	Edirne, all regions
Preparation time:	5 minutes, plus 24 hours resting
Makes:	1.25 kg (2 lb 12 oz)

The yogurt of sheep, goats, water buffalo, camels and cows can be used, depending on availability and preference. The leftover liquid is a popular substitute for water in baking.

◆

| 2 kg | Greek yogurt (sheep's milk) | 10 cups/4 lb 6 oz |

Pour the yogurt into a muslin (cheesecloth), tie the corners and hang over a bowl in the refrigerator. Let rest for 24 hours, until the yogurt is fully strained.

❧ ◗ V ⁝

◆

YOGURT BUTTER
YAYIK YAĞI (YOĞURT TEREYAĞI)

Region:	Giresun, all regions
Preparation time:	2 hours 10 minutes
Makes:	400 g (14 oz)

The yogurt from sheep, goat, water buffalo, camels and cows can be used, depending on availability and preference.

◆

| 3 kg | Greek yogurt | 15 cups/6 lb 9½ oz |
| 4 | ice cubes | 4 |

Put the yogurt and 2 litres (8½ cups/70 fl oz) cold water into a butter churn. Churn for 2 hours, adding 1 ice cube every 30 minutes. Keep the lid and the central hole of the churn sealed to prevent air flow. Scrape off the butter formed on the lid and sides of the churn with your hands. Roll the butter into a ball, rinse, squeeze and place on a plate. Keep refrigerated.

❧ ◗ V ⁝

◆

BUTTER
TEREYAĞI

Region:	Erzincan, all regions
Preparation time:	2 hours and 10 minutes
Makes:	500 g (1 lb 2 oz)

Depending on availability and preference, any milk can be used. The same method applies if you are using a wooden butter churn or a machine. Any buttermilk can be turned into curds by adding 2 tablespoons of vinegar or lemon. Cook it for 15 minutes, strain in a muslin (cheesecloth) bag and you get *lor* (fresh curd cheese, see p.485).

3 litres	fresh milk	12 cups/100 fl oz
500 g	fresh clotted cream (see opposite)	2½ cups/ 1 lb 2 oz
4	ice cubes	4

◆

Put the milk and clotted cream into a butter churn. Churn for 2 hours, adding 1 ice cube every 30 minutes. Keep the lid and the central hole of the churn sealed to prevent air flow. Scrape off the butter formed on the lid and sides of the churn with your hands. Roll the butter into a ball, rinse, squeeze and place on a plate. Keep refrigerated.

❧ ◗ V ⁝

VEGETABLE STOCK
SEBZE SUYU

Region:	Aydın, all regions
Preparation time:	15 minutes
Cooking time:	45 minutes
Makes:	2.25 litres (10 cups/80 fl oz)

6	flat-leaf parsley sprigs, chopped	6
2	fresh mint sprigs, chopped	2
1	fennel frond, chopped	1
1	fresh basil sprig, chopped	1
2	shallots, peeled, diced	2
120 g	potato, diced	generous ½ cup/ 4 oz
70 g	carrot, diced	½ cup/ 2¾ oz
100 g	celeriac (celery root), diced	⅔ cup/ 3½ oz
5	black peppercorns	5
¾ tsp	salt	¾ tsp
60 ml	olive oil	¼ cup/2 fl oz

This stock can be strained or added to soups as is with the diced vegetables. It is believed to have healing properties and will be added to soups for convalescents who cannot handle solids. It has numerous variations: some like adding barley, orzo pasta or wheat; some make it with tomatoes and oregano; some with only carrots, or substituting the potato with courgettes (zucchini). Another recipe uses wild herbs such as mallow, hyssop, sorrel, lamb's ear and pigweed. Some recipes do not roast the vegetables, instead boiling them in the water from cold. Dried or fresh fruit is poached using the same method and the juice added to soups and other dishes.

◆

Preheat oven to 200°C/400°F/Gas Mark 6.

Put all the ingredients, along with 500 ml (generous 2 cups/17 fl oz) water, into a large roasting pan and mix until well combined. Roast in the hot oven for 20 minutes.

Put the roasted mixture into a large saucepan over medium heat, pour over 2.25 litres (10 cups/80 fl oz) boiling water and simmer for 20 minutes. Skim off the foam on the surface with a slotted spoon as needed. Strain or use as is. Keep refrigerated and use within 3 days. Alternatively, freeze in ice cube trays or freezer bags and use within 2 months.

◆

FISH STOCK
BALIK SUYU

Region:	İstanbul, Marmara and Aegean Regions
Preparation time:	10 minutes
Cooking time:	2 hours and 15 minutes
Makes:	3 litres (12 cups/100 fl oz)

60 ml	olive oil	¼ cup/2 fl oz
4 (1 kg)	gurnard heads	4 (2 lb 3 oz)
1	celery stalk	1
1	fennel frond	1
½ bunch	flat-leaf parsley	½ bunch
70 g	carrot, quartered	½ cup/2¾ oz
1 (120 g)	medium onion, quartered	1 (¾ cup/ 4 oz)
6	garlic cloves	6
10	black peppercorns	10
120 g	potato, quartered	generous ½ cup/ 4 oz
4	bay leaves	4
¾ tsp	salt	¾ tsp
1	lemon, halved	1

This can be made with the leftover heads and bones of any fish. After straining, pick the flesh off the fish heads and simply add to the stock with some vegetables for a delicious soup. The pulled fish also makes a great salad drizzled with olive oil.

◆

Heat the olive oil in a large casserole dish (Dutch oven) or stock pan over medium heat. Add the fish heads, celery, fennel, parsley, carrot, onion, garlic, peppercorns, potato, bay leaves and salt and cook for 10 minutes, stirring continuously. Pour over 3 litres (12 cups/100 fl oz) water. Juice the lemon halves, add the juice and the halves to the pan and cook for another 5 minutes. Skim off the foam on the surface with a slotted spoon. Cover with the lid and cook for 2 hours over low heat.

Strain the stock before using. Keep refrigerated and use within 2 days. Alternatively, freeze in ice cube trays or freezer bags and use within 2 months.

MEAT STOCK
ET SUYU

Region:		İzmir, Aegean Region
Preparation time:		10 minutes
Cooking time:		3 hours 10 minutes
Makes:		2 litres (8½ cups/70 fl oz)

500 g	lamb shanks, on the bone	1 lb 2 oz
500 g	lamb neck	1 lb 2 oz
2	lamb bones, with marrow	2
1 (120 g)	medium onion, quartered	1 (¾ cup/ 4 oz)
70 g	carrot, quartered	½ cup/2¾ oz
4	garlic cloves	4
4	black peppercorns	4
1 tbsp	lemon juice	1 tbsp
4	bay leaves	4
¾ tsp	salt	¾ tsp

Meat stock can also be made with goat, mutton or beef shanks. Dilute with hot water before use – a ratio of 1 litre (4¼ cups/34 fl oz) water to 500 ml (generous 2 cups/ 17 fl oz) meat stock is good. The meat can be enjoyed cold once the stock is strained off; it is widely used in omelettes, pilafs and soups, such as *Beyran Çorbası* (Lamb and Rice Soup, see p.42) and *Demirci Kebabı* (The Ironmonger's Kebab, see p.200). It can also be enjoyed as is, without straining. This recipe takes 1 hour in a pressure cooker with 2 litres (8½ cups/70 fl oz) water.

◆

Put all the ingredients into a large casserole dish (Dutch oven) or stock pan, along with 4 litres (16 cups/130 fl oz) water. Bring to a boil and cook over medium heat for 5 minutes. Skim off the foam on the surface with a slotted spoon. Simmer for 3 hours over low heat.

Strain the stock before using. Keep refrigerated and use within 3 days. Alternatively, freeze in ice cube trays or freezer bags and use within 2 months.

CHICKEN STOCK
TAVUK SUYU

Region:		Manisa, all regions
Preparation time:		10 minutes
Cooking time:		2 hours 10 minutes
Makes:		4 litres (16 cups/130 fl oz)

1 (2.5 kg)	chicken	1 (5 lb 8 oz)
200 g	celeriac (celery root), diced	1¼ cups/ 7 oz
120 g	potato, diced	generous ½ cup/ 4 oz
70 g	carrot, quartered	½ cup/2¾ oz
200 g	shelled peas	1⅓ cups/7 oz
½ bunch	flat-leaf parsley	½ bunch
2½ tsp	cumin seeds	2½ tsp
10	fennel seeds	10
10	black peppercorns	10
¾ tsp	salt	¾ tsp
½	lemon	½

This stock is a great addition to many dishes, especially pilafs. The strained chicken can be pulled and the vegetables finely sliced and used in dishes such as *Arabaşı* (Spicy Dumpling Soup, see p.224), *Perde Pilavı* (Veiled Rice Pilaf, see p.314) and *Tavuk Çullama* (Fried Poached Chicken, see p.230). It can be made out of other fowl or game using the same method, either roasted or fresh. Another method puts the chicken on the upper level of a steamer, with the other ingredients in the bottom pan, letting the chicken cook in the aromatic steam. Dilute with hot water before use – a ratio of 1 litre (4¼ cups/34 fl oz) water to 500 ml (generous 2 cups/17 fl oz) chicken stock is good. This recipe takes 1 hour in a pressure cooker with 2 litres (8½ cups/70 fl oz) water.

◆

Put all the ingredients into a large casserole dish (Dutch oven) or stock pan, along with 4 litres (16 cups/130 fl oz) of water, squeezing the lemon half over and adding the lemon half to the pan too. Bring to a boil and cook over medium heat for 5 minutes. Skim off the foam on the surface with a slotted spoon. Reduce the heat, cover and simmer for 2 hours, skimming off the foam on the surface as needed.

Strain the stock before using. Keep refrigerated and use within 2 days. Alternatively, freeze in ice cube trays or freezer bags and use within 2 months.

BONE BROTH
KEMİK SUYU

Region:	Ankara, all regions
Preparation time:	5 minutes
Cooking time:	3 hour 5 minutes
Makes:	4 litres (16 cups/130 fl oz)

4	lamb bones with marrow, not too meaty, halved	4
2	lamb tail bones, halved	2
1 (120 g)	medium onion, quartered	1 (¾ cup/4 oz)
70 g	carrot, quartered	½ cup/2¾ oz
4	garlic cloves	4
¾ tsp	salt	¾ tsp
1 tbsp	lemon juice	1 tbsp

Goat and sheep bones are more popular than beef for this broth, then the bones are enjoyed separately after straining. Dilute with hot water before use – a ratio of 1 litre (4¼ cups/34 fl oz) water to 500 ml (generous 2 cups/17 fl oz) meat stock is good. This recipe takes 1 hour in a pressure cooker. Locally, bones are dried, salted and kept in earthenware vessels, ready to be used to make bone broth when needed.

♦

Put all the ingredients into a large casserole dish (Dutch oven) or stock pan, along with 4 litres (16 cups/130 fl oz) water. Bring to a boil and cook over medium heat for 5 minutes. Skim off the foam on the surface with a slotted spoon. Cover, reduce the heat and simmer for 3 hours, until the broth becomes clear.

Strain the stock before using. Keep refrigerated and use within 2 days. Alternatively, freeze in ice cube trays or freezer bags and use within 2 months.

POMEGRANATE MOLASSES
NAR EKŞİSİ

Region:	Hatay, Mediterranean Region and Southeast Anatolia
Preparation time:	5 minutes
Cooking time:	20 minutes
Makes:	1 litre (34 fl oz)

5 litres	pomegranate juice, freshly squeezed and strained	20 cups/160 fl oz

Locally, pomegranates are boiled for 2 hours in the open air, under the sun. The juice is transferred to a deep basin and left in direct sunlight for 15 days, stirring occasionally. In another version of this recipe, pomegranate seeds are harvested in bulk (50–100 kg/110–220 lb) in a hessian sack and pressed tightly. The sack is placed on a tripod over a basin on the roof of a house and left in the sun for 15 days.

Simmer the pomegranate juice in a large saucepan, until it reaches 108°C (226°F) on a cooking thermometer, making sure it doesn't burn. Skim off the foam on the surface with a slotted spoon.

Let cool, then pour into a sterilized bottle and seal tightly. It will keep for up to a year when stored in a cool place.

CRANBERRY EXTRACT
KIZILCIK EKŞİSİ

Region:		Artvin, all regions
Preparation time:		15 minutes
Cooking time:		1 hour, plus 1 hour resting
Makes:		1.5 litres (6¼ cups/50 fl oz)

1 kg	fresh cranberries	10 cups/2 lb 4 oz
1 tbsp	olive oil	1 tbsp

Cranberry products, such as molasses, sherbet and fruit leather straps are widely popular. This extract is made at the end of summer and in the autumn.

♦

Put the cranberries and 1.2 litres (5 cups/40 fl oz) water into a saucepan and simmer over low heat for 1 hour. Remove from the heat and rest for 1 hour at room temperature.

Crush the cranberries by hand and remove their seeds. Run through a sieve (strainer) and collect the extracted juice in a bowl. Pour the juice into a sterilized bottle. Pour the olive oil on top, seal the bottle and keep refrigerated. It will keep for up to a year when stored in a cool place.

♦

SOUR PLUM EXTRACT
ERİK (KORUĞU) EKŞİSİ

Region:		Ordu, all regions
Preparation time:		15 minutes
Cooking time:		1 hour, plus 1 hour resting
Makes:		1 litre (34 fl oz)

1 kg	unripe greengages or sour plums	6 cups/ 2 lb 4 oz
¾ tsp	salt	¾ tsp
1 tbsp	olive oil	1 tbsp

This is added to dishes such as *dolmas* and other stuffed dishes. It can also be preserved without straining.

♦

Put the plums, salt and 1 litre (4¼ cups/34 fl oz) of water into a large saucepan and simmer, covered, over low heat for 1 hour.

Remove from the heat and let rest for 1 hour at room temperature.

Crush the plums by hand and remove their pits. Run the plums through a sieve (strainer) and collect the extracted juice in a bowl. Pour the juice into a sterilized bottle. Pour the olive oil on top, seal the bottle and keep refrigerated. It will keep for up to a year when stored in a cool place.

♦

SUMAC EXTRACT
SUMAK EKŞİSİ

Region:		Diyarbakır, Southeastern Anatolia
Preparation time:		10 minutes
Cooking time:		1 hour resting
Makes:		1 litre (34 fl oz)

200 g	sumac	1¼ cups/7 oz
¾ tbsp	salt	¾ tbsp

Sumac extract is prepared and used fresh to add a sour note to *dolmas* (stuffed dishes) and sherbets. Another technique prepares the same recipe with cold water, one day ahead.

♦

Put the sumac and salt into a large bowl. Pour over 1 litre (4¼ cups/34 fl oz) boiling water, stir and let rest for 1 hour. Knead the mixture and strain. Use immediately.

RED BELL PEPPER PASTE
BİBER PEKMEZİ (SALÇASI)

Region:	Gaziantep, all regions
Preparation time:	20 minutes
Cooking time:	1 hour, plus 3 days resting
Makes:	1 kg (2 lb 3 oz)

1.5 kg	sweet red bell peppers, halved, stems removed, de-seeded	3 lb 5 oz
500 g	hot red bell peppers, halved, stems removed, de-seeded	1 lb 2 oz
2 tsp	salt	2 tsp

A local version of this recipe omits the cooking process, simply running the bell peppers through a mincer (grinder) and sun-drying them in deep trays. The peppers are left in the hot sun for a week, and mixed twice daily.

◆

Simmer the bell peppers in a large saucepan with 4 litres (16 cups/130 fl oz) water for 20 minutes. Skim off the foam on the surface with a slotted spoon. Drain the bell peppers well and let rest for 10 minutes.

Run the bell peppers through a mincer (grinder), or process to a coarse texture in a food processor.

Put the pepper mixture into a large saucepan and cook over low heat for 30 minutes. Add the salt and mix for 1 minute. Spread the mixture over a large baking sheet and leave in direct sunlight for 3 days covered with a muslin cloth. Alternatively it can be dried in a low 50°C/120°F oven. Give the mixture a good stir, twice daily. Store in a cool, dry place in well-sealed sterilized glass jars. It will keep for up to a year when stored in a cool place.

◆

TOMATO PASTE
DOMATES PEKMEZİ (SALÇASI)

Region:	Gaziantep, all regions
Preparation time:	5 minutes
Cooking time:	2 hours, plus 3 days resting
Makes:	400 g (14 oz)

2 litres	tomato juice, freshly squeezed from ripe tomatoes	8¼ cups/70 fl oz
2 tsp	salt	2 tsp

Locals boil the tomato juice for 30 minutes, then spread over deep trays and let rest in direct hot sunlight, mixing twice daily.

◆

Simmer the tomato juice in a large saucepan for 2 hours, regularly skimming off the foam from the surface with a slotted spoon. Stir in the salt, then transfer the juice to a deep tray. Let rest in a sunny spot for 3 days covered with a muslin cloth, mixing twice daily. Alternatively it can be dried in a low 50°C/120°F oven. Keep in a cool place in sealed, sterilized glass jars. It will keep for up to a year when stored in a cool place.

LONG HOMEMADE NOODLES
UZUN ERİŞTE

Region:	Ağrı, all regions
Preparation time:	30 minutes, plus 1 hour 20 minutes resting
Makes:	150 g (5 oz)

200 g	strong (bread) flour	scant 1½ cups/ 7 oz
¼ tsp	salt	¼ tsp
2	eggs	2
60 g	plain (all-purpose) flour	scant ½ cup/ 2¼ oz

◒ ◕ V ⋮

The thickness of these noodles varies among regions.

◆

Put the strong (bread) flour and salt into a large bowl and make a well in the middle. Slowly add the eggs and knead for 10 minutes, into an elastic dough. Divide in half, cover with a moist dish towel and let rest for 20 minutes.

Roll the balls out using a rolling pin to about 8-mm (⅓-inch) thick. Wrap the dough around the rolling pin, slide the rolling pin out and cut the dough into 3-mm (⅛-inch) strips. The dough should be 1 mm thick at this point. Sprinkle over some plain (all-purpose) flour and cut into 1-mm (¹⁄₁₆-inch) strips. Sprinkle over more flour and toss the strips of dough until well covered. Let rest for 1 hour, then shake off the excess flour.

◆

HOMEMADE NOODLES
ERİŞTE

Region:	Kars, all regions
Preparation time:	30 minutes, plus 35 minutes resting
Makes:	150 g (5 oz)

200 g	strong (bread) flour	scant 1½ cups/ 7 oz
¼ tsp	salt	¼ tsp
2	eggs	2
60 g	plain (all-purpose) flour	scant ½ cup/ 2¼ oz

◒ ◕ V ⋮

The recipe for *tutmaç* (noodles cut into 1-cm squares) is based on the same dough, cut into 1-cm (½-inch) squares after resting. This can also be made into 'noodle couscous' by cutting into 2-mm (⅛-inch) squares.

◆

Put the strong (bread) flour and salt into a large bowl, add the eggs, mix and knead for 5 minutes. Transfer the dough to a smooth, flat surface and knead for another 10 minutes. Cover with a moist dish towel and let rest for 10 minutes.

Divide the dough into quarters. Cover with a moist dish towel and rest for another 10 minutes. Roll out with a rolling pin on a lightly floured surface to 1-mm (¹⁄₁₆-inch) thick, then cut into 2-cm × 3-mm (¾ × ⅛-inch) strips. Sprinkle with the plain (all-purpose) flour and rest for 15 minutes. It will keep for 1 year when dried and stored in a muslin bag.

POWDERED TARHANA
TOZ TARHANASI (UN TARHANASI)

Region:		Bolu, all regions
Preparation time:		35 minutes
Cooking time:		20 minutes, plus 15 minutes cooling, plus up to 13 days resting
Makes:		500 g (1 lb 2 oz)

100 g	tomato, quartered	½ cup/3½ oz
2	chillies (chiles), crushed	2
2	fresh mint sprigs	2
1 (100 g)	onion, cut into 8 pieces	1 (⅔ cup/ 3½ oz)
3	garlic cloves	3
50 g	tomato paste (see p.492)	¼ cup/2 oz
1 tsp	paprika	1 tsp
¾ tsp	salt	¾ tsp
300 g	Greek yogurt (sour), strained	1½ cups/11 oz
200 g	whole wheat flour	1½ cups/7 oz

◓ V

Powdered tarhana is great for thickening winter soups. The grain used in this recipe varies according to local taste and preference. The flour can be replaced by semolina, barley, ground cornmeal or millet flour. Other flavourings include fruit and vegetables (cranberries, asparagus, wild pear), dried meat, or milk.

◆

Put the tomatoes, chillies (chiles), mint, onion, garlic, tomato paste, paprika and salt into a large saucepan and cook, covered, for 20 minutes over medium heat. Crush the mixture with a wooden spoon, strain over a bowl and discard the pulp. Let the strained juice cool for 15 minutes.

Add the Greek yogurt to the strained juice and mix for 2 minutes. Add the flour and mix for another 5 minutes. Cover with a moist dish towel and let rest at room temperature for 1 week, kneading the dough and changing the moist towel daily, until the dough stops proving.

Lay a 50-cm (20-inch) square piece of muslin (cheesecloth) on a flat surface. Tear 5-cm (2-inch) pieces from the dough and arrange on the muslin. Let dry indoors, uncovered, for 5–6 days.

When dried, use your hands or a food processor to crumble the *tarhana* mixture and run through a fine sieve (strainer). Further crumble the pieces that did not go through and sieve again. Repeat for the entire batch.

It will keep for up to a year when sealed in a jar and stored in a cool place.

◆

VERJUICE
KORUK EKŞİSİ

Region:		Kilis, all regions
Preparation time:		10 minutes
Cooking time:		1 hour, plus 5 hours resting
Makes:		1.25 litres (42 fl oz)

1 kg	unripe grapes, washed and crushed	2 lb 4 oz
2 tsp	salt	2 tsp
1 tbsp	olive oil	1 tbsp

Verjuice cordial is made of unripe grapes in July. A syrup (a more concentrated cordial) is made at the same time. It is made by local street vendors and in homes where it is offered to important guests.

◆

Put the crushed grapes, pulp and all, into a saucepan. Add 1 litre (4¼ cups/34 fl oz) water and the salt and simmer for 1 hour.

Remove from the heat and let rest for 1 hour at room temperature.

Crush and mix the grapes further by hand, then strain over a bowl. Pour the juice into a sterilized bottle. Pour the olive oil on top, seal the bottle and refrigerate for 4 hours. It will keep for up to a year when stored in a cool place.

HULLED TARHANA
DÖVME TARHANA (DİŞ TARHANA)

Region:	Şanlıurfa, all regions
Preparation time:	35 minutes
Cooking time:	10 minutes, plus overnight resting, plus 2 hours, plus 4 days/10 hours drying
Makes:	350 g (12½ oz)

150 g	threshed wheat	1 cup/5 oz
2 tsp	salt	2 tsp
600 g	sour, strained Greek yogurt (sheep's milk)	3 cups/1 lb 5 oz

◒ V ⁘

The shape of *tarhana* varies among regions: some like circles, triangles or flat discs; some poke a hole in the middle; the technique in the Kahramanmaraş province dries it on reeds as a single thin, flat piece. Flavours vary from fruit (blackthorn), vegetables (cabbage), legumes and dried goat's meat. It is consumed as is, and added to soups. It is used for soups, salads, pilafs and tirit. It is a popular snack enjoyed usually with nuts.

◆

Bring 1.5 litres (6¼ cups/50 fl oz) water to the boil in a large saucepan. Add the wheat just before the water reaches boiling point and cook for 5 minutes. Skim off the foam on the surface with a slotted spoon. Remove the pan from the heat and let rest overnight, covered.

The next day, add another 1.5 litres (6¼ cups/50 fl oz) water to the pan. Cook, covered, over low heat for 1½ hours, until all the liquid is absorbed. Add the salt, mix in thoroughly and remove from the heat. Let rest for 30 minutes with the lid ajar.

Add the yogurt and mash it in with a wooden spoon for 30 minutes, making sure it is well combined. Divide the mixture into 8 equal pieces, squeezing the pieces between your fingers. Leave to dry in direct sunlight for 4 days, making sure the tarhana is well aerated from the top and bottom. Alternatively, dry it out in a very low oven (about 75°C/165°F or as near as possible) for 10 hours.

◆

COUSCOUS
KUSKUS

Region:	Çanakkale, Marmara Region and Central Anatolia
Preparation time:	25 minutes, plus 3 days resting
Makes:	200 g (7 oz)

200 g	coarse bulgur wheat, washed and dried	1 cup/7 oz
1	egg, whisked	1
¼ tsp	salt	¼ tsp
150 g	plain (all-purpose) flour	1 cup/5 oz

💧 ◒ V ⁘

Couscous can be enjoyed in a pilaf, salad or stew with tomato/bell pepper paste. Cheese, Greek yogurt, *kashk* (see p.483) and walnuts are also popular flavourings. Some recipes use semolina and fine bulgur wheat instead of the coarse bulgur wheat, and the egg can be substituted with 250 ml (1 cup/8 fl oz) of both milk and water.

◆

Put the bulgur wheat, egg and salt into a large bowl and mix with your fingertips for 1 minute. Add the flour and keep mixing and rubbing with your fingertips for 20 minutes, until the mixture combines into tiny balls or grains. Spread the couscous grains over a large tray and let dry in a cool place for 3 days, stirring occasionally. Keep in a well-sealed glass jar. It will keep for up to a year when dried and stored in a muslin (cheesecloth) bag.

FILO (PHYLLO) PASTRY
BAKLAVA YUFKASI

Region:		Gaziantep, all regions
Preparation time:		35 minutes, plus 30 minutes resting
Makes:		800 g (1 lb 12 oz/40 sheets)

350 g	strong white flour, plus extra for dusting (about 200 g/1½ cups/7 oz)	2½ cups/12 oz
¼ tsp	salt	¼ tsp
1	egg, whisked	1
1 tsp	lemon juice	1 tsp
1 tbsp	grape vinegar	1 tbsp

◦ ◆ V ⁖

Professional bakers roll out filo pastry to 40 cm (16 inches) with starch whereas home cooks prefer flour. There should be no flour or starch left on the pastry sheets. The fresher the filo pastry, the crispier the baklava will be. Some recipes use wheat starch instead of extra flour for rolling.
◆
Put the flour and salt into a bowl, add the egg, lemon juice, vinegar and 175 ml (¾ cup/6 fl oz) water, mix thoroughly and knead for 5 minutes. Transfer the dough to a flat surface and knead for a further 10 minutes until elastic. Cover with a moist dish towel and let rest for 20 minutes.

Cut the dough into 40 balls. Cover with a moist dish towel and let rest for another 10 minutes. Flatten the discs, first by hand, then with a rolling pin on a flour-dusted work counter, into 10-cm (4-inch) circles.

Working swiftly, divide the dough into 4 batches of 10 discs. Take a batch of 10 discs and place them on top of one another, sprinkling flour between each layer. Wrap around an *oklava,* or a thin, long wooden rolling pin, shake off the excess flour and roll out all the discs together to 25-cm (10-inch) circles. Repeat for the remaining 3 batches.

Arrange the pastry sheets on a baking sheet in layers. Make sure to grease between each layer. Use immediately unless making *cendere baklavası,* a kind of baklava that is made of dried filo sheets.

◆

SPICED SALAMI
SUCUK

Region:		Kayseri, all regions
Preparation time:		1 hour 5 minutes, plus 8 days plus 1 hour resting
Makes:		1.5 kg (3 lb 5 oz)

2 kg	minced (ground) goat, medium fat	4 lb 6 oz
100 g	garlic, crushed	3½ oz
50 g	ground paprika	½ cup/2 oz
3 tbsp	dried chilli (red pepper) flakes	3 tbsp
1¾ tbsp	ground cumin	1¾ tbsp
1 tbsp	*poy* (see p.502)	1 tbsp
1 tbsp	black pepper	1 tbsp
1 tbsp	salt	1 tbsp
1	sheep's gut sausage casing	1
250 ml	grape vinegar	1 cup/8 fl oz

◦ ☙ ◆

Beef, sheep and even camel can also be used to make *sucuk.*
◆
Combine the goat, garlic, paprika, dried chilli (red pepper) flakes, cumin, *poy,* black pepper and salt in a large bowl and knead for 20 minutes. Cover and chill in the refrigerator for 24 hours.

The next day, cover the sausage casing with 1 litre (4¼ cups/34 fl oz) water and the vinegar in a bowl. Cover and rest for 1 hour. Meanwhile, remove the sausage filling from the refrigerator and knead for 20 minutes.

Drain the casing and rinse well. Attach a funnel to one end of the casing and start filling it with the filling mixture. Squeeze with your hand to move the filling along towards the end of the casing. Tie a tight knot at each end of the casing, making sure you get rid of all the air trapped inside. Hang the salami to dry in a well-aerated, cool place for 1 week. Store in the refrigerator. It will keep for 6 months when stored in a cool place or the refrigerator. Once cut, the whole lot should be eaten within 2 weeks.

CURED BEEF
PASTIRMA

Region:		İstanbul, all regions
Preparation time:		15 minutes, plus 23 days resting,
		plus 10 minutes
Makes:		1.7 kg (3 lb 11 oz)

2.5 kg	veal entrecote (rib-eye steak), surface sinew trimmed	5 lb 8 oz
3 kg	rock salt	6 lb 9½ oz

For the spice rub paste:

8 tbsp	*poy* (see p.502)	8 tbsp
100 g	ground paprika	1 cup/3½ oz
1½ tbsp	dried chilli (red pepper) flakes	1½ tbsp
3 tbsp	ground cumin	3 tbsp
20	garlic cloves, crushed	20
1¼ tsp	black pepper	1¼ tsp
¾ tsp	salt	¾ tsp

Pastırma are dried at the end of summer and the beginning of autumn. The warm and sunny days during this period, our Indian summer, is called the *pastırma* summer. Some local versions make the *pastırma* out of minced (ground) meat. Some recipes use fillets placed in hessian sacks, tripe or omasum, and cured underground. Some recipes omit the spice rub, and some make it with bone-in meat. It is eaten shaved into extremely thin slices.

◆

Put the veal entrecote (rib-eye steak) into a deep tray. Add the rock salt and make sure it covers the meat entirely. Put a 4 kg (9 lb) weight on top. Let rest for 7 days, cleaning away the liquid that oozes out.

Day 8: rinse the meat in plenty of water. Put the meat in a bowl of cold water to soak. Replace the water in the bowl every 2 hours. Repeat 5 times, then leave it in the water overnight.

Day 9: remove and dry the meat. Tie it up with kitchen string and hang it outdoors, somewhere sunny but cool. Let rest for 4 days, protecting the meat from flies by storing in a meat safe.

Day 13: make the spice rub paste by combining the *poy*, paprika, dried chilli (red pepper) flakes, cumin, garlic, black pepper and salt with 250 ml (1 cup/8 fl oz) water in a large bowl and mix for 5 minutes into a paste.

Cover the entire piece of meat with the spice rub paste. Hang it in a well-aerated place and let dry for 10 days. Wrap in muslin (cheesecloth) and keep in the refrigerator.

◆

LAMB CONFIT
KAVURMA (TOPAÇ)

Region:		Gaziantep, all regions
Preparation time:		10 minutes
Cooking time:	1 hour 10 minutes, plus 1 hour resting
Makes:		1.3 kg (2 lb 13 oz)

2 kg	leg of lamb, shoulder and brisket (fatty), diced into 2-cm (¾-inch) pieces	4 lb 6 oz
2½ tsp	salt	2½ tsp

Kavurma is made with beef in the Black Sea and Eastern Anatolia regions whereas the rest of the country uses mostly lamb and goat. Ox, veal and mutton are also preserved this way. The roasted meat is preserved in large, wide earthenware vessels for years. Known as *topaç kavurması* from its shape.

◆

Put the lamb meat into a heavy saucepan and cook over medium heat for 1 hour, stirring occasionally. Sprinkle over the salt and keep cooking for another 10 minutes.

Remove from the heat and let rest at room temperature for 1 hour.

Stir the meat for a minute, then roll into 8-cm (3-inch) balls and place them on plates. Let rest until the fat solidifies. It will keep for up to 6 months when stored in a cool place, in a very well-sealed, airtight container.

◆

GLOSSARY

◆

BÖREK
The generic name for savoury pastries and pies.

CEMALCİ
This post-harvest festival starts with gunshots fired into the air in Biga, Çanakkale. The shots are to prepare people for door-knockers. Young men who have not done their military service gather around the graveyard, rub their torso black, pray for the dead and visit the houses in the village. The leader is dressed as a male goat and rings a bell. Everyone else follows him. Doors are knocked one by one and donated ingredients are collected. A communal feast is prepared with a small portion of the ingredients and the rest is distributed to the village youth who will be getting married soon.

CEZVE
A copper coffee pot.

ÇİNÇAR
The local name for nettles in North Eastern Anatolia. Nettles grown in shade are believed to have stronger healing properties.

ÇİROZ
Mackerel migrate to the Black Sea. Caught on their way back by fishermen of the Marmara Sea, exhausted and skinny, these mackerel are hung with strings and dried for 10–15 days. When dried, the mackerel – or *çiroz* – can be lightly grilled, then pounded in a mortar and pestle to remove the skin and bones.

DİBLE
The local name given to a cooking technique native to Ordu and Giresun in which grain and a minimal amount of water is added to a well in beans. No stirring is necessary. Many fruit and vegetables are prepared this way.

GÂH OR HÂH
Dried meat or fruit, especially dried apples and quinces. *Gâh* is a popular snack in the winter.

GELBERİ
An L-shaped utensil used to manage fire in the kebab oven.

GEZO
Every 15 to 20 years, at the end of summer, a sticky honey-like substance appears on the leaves of oak trees. This signals to locals that it is *gezo* time. They rush to the trees with pots and collect the honeyed leaves. A fire is lit to boil water in cauldrons. The leaves are dipped in this water and taken out to collect the honey, which is turned into molasses.

GOGOL
Little balls of dough.

GOŞTEBERG
Goşteberg means lamb meat in Kurdish, but it is also the name of a local herb. The lamb meat is chopped into pieces, mixed with *goşteberg* and placed in tripe, which is then sealed in sheepskin. Locals dig a hole in the ground, and a fire is lit within the hole. Once the hole is hot enough, the fire is removed, stones are placed insdie, on top of which the sheepskin goes. Another fire is lit on the sheepskin and the dish is cooked for 4–5 hours. Jumping over fire is a *Nowrouz* (New Year) tradition. People dance, play music and celebrate spring.

HAMURSUZ (PESACH)
Jews of the Iberian peninsula took refuge in the Ottoman Empire after the Inquisition in 1492. *Pesach* (*Hamursuz* in Turkish and Passover in English) falls around Easter and starts with a spring clean at home. Pastry shops in some İstanbul neighborhoods fill their windows with delicious unleavened products. *Haggadahs* (the text setting out the order of rituals for the seder meal) used in Turkey has many stories to tell in a disappearing language, Ladino, a mix of Castilian Spanish and Turkish.

HELİSE
Helise is usually made with lamb, but game, poultry, sheep and goat are popular variations. Also known as *harisa, herise, herse, aşir, aşür, dövme, keşkek* and *keşka*, this dish symbolizes peace and is popular at weddings and special occasions. Some recipes omit honey altogether, others use molasses instead. This dish is made in the winter months.

HIDRELLEZ
The Romani and Alevis in the Marmara, Central Anatolia regions and in Antalya start *Hıdrellez* with a thorough cleaning of homes in the first week of May. Jewellery is collected in water jars, then placed at the roots of a rose tree in the evening. The items are pulled out of the jar one by one, accompanied by a few verses. The prophets Hıdır (Al-Khidr) and İlyas (Elijah) are believed to pass through as the verses are recited. Unleavened bread is made. If the bread turns out well, it is a sign that Hıdır and Ilyas have actually passed through. The bread is leavened later and used as a starter until *Hıdrellez* the following year. Hızır and Ilyas are believed to be the creators of spring and the word *Hıdrellez* is a combination of their names. *Hıdrellez* is also known as the Festival of Shepherds. All milk on the day is made into *hoşmerim* (a sweet set fresh cheese) and distributed as charity. Goats and sheep (males only) are kept until *Hıdrellez* for slaughter, and their meat is distributed to pasture owners, in thanks for the food the animals have enjoyed. The purpose of the ritual is to guarantee the arrival of Hızır and Ilyas (Elijah), who hopefully grant everyone's wishes.

HODAN
In Turkey, wild borage heralds the spring as the snow starts to melt. It tastes like mushrooms and is loved in the Marmara and western Black Sea regions. Locally, it's known as *zılbıt, zıbıdık, ıspıt, tomara* and *galdirik*. Often pickled, the flowers used

in *kaygana*, *maya* and mash. Other local variations include a fried version, as well as recipes using *kavurma* (lamb confit, see p.497), eggs and *pastırma* (cured beef, see p.497).

KADAYIF
Kadayif, or kadaifi, consists of fine (1-mm/¹⁄₃₂-inch) pastry strands made with flour and water. Often made on a *sac* (concave iron plate), *kadayif* was traditionally made on stone. A thick, square, flat stone with legs is placed on a wood fire and warmed thoroughly. Runny leavened batter is ladled on the stone and cooked on both sides.

KALBUR
A 2-mm (¹⁄₁₆-inch) wide fine strainer made from either linen or cotton threads. It is also used to shape *kalburabastı* (see p.420), a well-known traditional dessert. This is done with a grater.

KAPAMA
A cooking method in which some embers are set aside and a tray containing meat, *börek* or vegetables are placed on top. It is covered with a *sac* lid and some branches are placed on top to provide heat from the top as well. Lamb *kapama* and *kapama böreği* is made this way. The trick with this dish is not to stir at all during cooking and to make sure that the pot is completely airtight. The name *kapama* (sealed) refers to this technique.

KASHK
Kashk is a very popular snack with pregnant women. It leaves a tangy taste in the mouth. *Kashk* is added to soups, ayran and many other dishes. It is believed to have healing and energy enhancing properties. It is consumed cold in the summer months and warm with added butter in the winter.

KETE
Muslims make these rolls for the two main religious festivals whereas the local Armenians distribute *kete* at Easter with red eggs. Mothers make these rolls for their children when they come home from abroad. It is customary to hide coins and beads inside the rolls. Whoever comes across one of these is supposed to have good fortune for life.

KÜLEK
A spruce *külek* has a very pleasant aroma and keeps its contents cool. Different varieties are used for making yogurt or butter. This is different to the *ibrik*, which is usually mistaken for a water jug although is traditionally only used for ablutions.

KURBAN BAYRAMI
Kurban bayramı, or *Eid-al-Adha*, the Festival of the Sacrifice, is one of the two main Muslim festivals that commemorate Abraham's willingness to sacrifice his son, whereupon a lamb replaced his son as the object of sacrifice. The traditional way to celebrate is to sacrifice a lamb, goat or another animal and share the meat with friends,

neighbours and among the poor. The well-off sacrifice a lamb and keep only one-third for themselves, and the rest is distributed among the poor. People who have debts are not supposed to sacrifice lambs. In the Black Sea region, families tend to get together and sacrifice a cow. It is always the ram or male goat that is slaughtered. People used to have meat only at these times.

LOQUAT
The loquat is also known as a Maltese plum in Turkey. The thin-skinned version is better for cooking, however if not available thick-skinned loquats can be used. The best results will be achieved with just-ripe fruit.

LUNAR ECLIPSE
Children beating tin drums collect ingredients from the village houses for a communal meal in Nizip. Adults fire shotguns to ward off the lunar eclipse.

LÜFER
Bluefish is the signature fish of İstanbul. It is so integral to the city's culinary culture that the locals have a different name for each size of this fish. *Yaprak*, *çinekop*, *sarıkanat*, *lüfer* and *kofana* all refer to bluefish at different stages of growth. Mostly *lüfer* (28–35 cm/11–14 inches long) are caught these days in order to protect the species, and always with a handline. The varying sizes of bluefish do taste slightly different: *lüfer* is by far the most delicious. Bluefish is traditionally eaten by hand. If you cannot source bluefish, seabass, turbot, mackerel or bonito can be used instead.

MAHLEPI
An aromatic spice made by grinding the seeds of a type of wild cherry.

MARUL BAYRAMI
The Lettuce Festival. Lettuce is a symbol of rebirth. Young girls are cleansed in Turkish baths before they go into the lettuce field where they celebrate the end of spring, make wishes and look for a good husband. Fresh lettuce sprinkled with lemon, sugar or molasses is well loved in Southeastern Anatolia. No one makes salad when lettuce is in season. The ideal temperature to grow lettuce is 22°C to 24°C. It goes to seed over 30°C. Eggs, lettuce and molasses eaten together is believed to increase fertility for married couples. *Yazidis* (a religious minority from Northern Mesopotamia) do not eat anything with large leaves, since it signifies the sacred peacock. During the month of April, women in Southeastern Anatolia, and especially in the towns of Adıyaman and Malatya, go to the local baths in large groups. This cleansing ritual continues in the lettuce fields, which are believed to spread calm and serenity. They pick the lettuce, eat some in the fields and take the rest home. Lettuce is good to eat for seven to ten days after it is picked: after this time it acquires a bitter taste. Kids stealing lettuce from the fields is the worst nightmare of lettuce growers.

MEVLID (MEVLİT)

Mevlid is the name of death rites, as well as the hymns chanted during those rites. They commemorate the milestones in Mohammed's life. Meat and pilaf are traditional offerings as well as *halva*, with flavours believed to soothe the soul of the recently departed. All food prepared for a *mevlid* is distributed to a minimum of seven neighbours and then to guests.

MEYHANE

A *meyhane* is a local tavern serving a multi-course 'tapas'-style meal, always served with *rakı*, a local aniseed-based liquor.

MÜLHİYE

A popular herb, *molokhia* (or *mulukhiyah*) is used in a variety of dishes. Legend goes that the slaves escaping the Pharaoh in Ancient Egypt had this herb with them. It is also known as 'the Pharaoh herb' and is believed to give good health and long life. Use fresh *molokhia* when in season; dry some in the spring for use in winter.

NEVRUZ

Legend goes that Assyrian King Dehak the Tyrant had terrible headaches. Doctors came from near and far to find a cure but to no avail. One doctor suggested he ate young human brains. His subjects would indulge him begrudgingly, until one day Kawa the ironmonger chopped off his head. Dehak's Arabic kingdom collapsed. *Nevruz* ('New Day' in Farsi) is celebrated on March 21st by many locals, though not Arabs. Fires are lit and fun is had with many youngsters jumping over them.

OBRUKÇU

Fresh new season's cheese prepared in an earthenware pot, sheepskin or goatskin, is handed over to a *obrukçu* (pothole owner) in the spring. The cheese is buried in a pothole in the mountains for maturation. The *obrukçu* checks if the cheese is ready in January, but depending on the owner's taste, the cheese may spend up to three years in the pothole. Once returned to its owner, traditionally the first seven portions are distributed to neighbours with flatbread to protect the produce from the evil eye.

OKLAVA

The domestic version of this rolling pin is 2 cm (¾ inch) wide and 60–70 cm (24–28 inches) long. Every kitchen has five to ten such pins. The most popular woods are pear, hornbeam and oak – all dry woods with their own distinct aromas. The *oklava* is used to make flatbreads, *börek*, *manti* and *baklava*. The rolling pin is a relatively recent addition to traditional homes in Turkey.

PAPARA

Yet another dish to use up stale bread, there is a plain meatless version as well as one with chicken. Papara and tirit are the two names of the same dish prepared by cooking stale bread in meat stock. The toppings depend on what the family can afford. Meat stock, chicken stock, minced meat, lamb confit are all popular. This dish is presented in a tray and is shared by the whole family. Most families make *tirit* or *papara* at least 15 to 20 times a year. Many a story is shared around this humble dish. Some like it with *topa. kavurması* and with lemon, garlic and chili. These dishes are mentioned in ancient culinary records.

PASKALYA (EASTER)

Turkish Armenians observe Lent, which comes with special restrictions. Often olive oil dishes are consumed at these times. The end of Lent is celebrated with a feast where fish and meat are eaten. *Topik* (see p.85) is a favourite Lent food of Armenians. The Rum (Ottoman Greeks) and Armenians of İstanbul make the traditional plaited *Paskalya Çöreği* (Easter brioche, see p.360). *Kete* (see p.366) or *çörek*, with simpler shapes, are more widely made. Eggs are dyed with red onion skins and distributed with the brioche to neighbours and friends. Easter brioche is available in pastry shops in İstanbul throughout the year

PESTİL

Grape juice is mixed with wheat starch and dried on calico to make *pestil*, a fruit leather.

PICKLING LIME

Food grade calcium hydroxide, more commonly knows as pickling lime or slaked lime, is made by mixing calcium oxide (called lime or quicklime) with water. Use a long, steel spoon to mix the calcium hydroxide with water, wear eye protection and use a stainless steel pot.

PILEKI

The *pileki* are plate-shaped stones used for making pickles, bread and sometimes for baking fish. They are preheated for an hour by lighting a fire inside. Once ready, the bread is placed on the cleaned stone and baked covered. There is also an earthenware version.

POY (ÇEMENOTU)

Fenugreek is the main ingredient of this paste rubbed onto *pastırma* (cured beef, see p.497).

PÜRPÜRÜM

The wild variety of purslane, which grows everywhere in the summer, is most flavoursome. Purslane salad with yogurt is loved all over the country as well purslane soups, and wraps. People believe purslane strengthens the bones. When the wild version is in abundance, storks are expected to deliver babies for those yearning couples. The Turkish idiom 'seeing the stork in the air' means you will be travelling a lot. All you need to do to enjoy all these side effects is to eat some purslane! This dish is a local favourite in Southeastern Anatolia and the Mediterranean. It is enjoyed hot or cold at home. The oil-free version is very popular in the heat.

RAKI

Rakı is distilled grape juice, a version of ouzo and arak (called *arakı* in Southeastern Anatolia.) There is a homemade version called *boğma*. In Thrace and Bulgaria it is often made from plums.

RAMAZAN BAYRAMI

Ramazan bayramı or *Şeker Bayramı* means Sugar Festival. One of the two Muslim festivals, *Eid-el-Fıtr* is celebrated at the end of *Ramadan*, the ninth month of Hijri, the Muslim lunar calendar. Hijrah, an Arabic word meaning migration, marks the migration of Prophet Muhammed from Mecca to Medina in 622 AD. The lunar year is eleven days shorter than the 365 days of the Western calendar, so significant dates in the Muslim calendar come earlier every year. Muslims eat before sunrise and fast until sunset when a communal feast is shared. The end of *Ramadan*, the holiest month of the Muslim calendar, is celebrated by enjoying elaborate feasts. Children kiss the hands of their elders and are given sweets and pocket money. Those who do not get along make peace at these times.

SAC

A concave iron plate, 2-mm (¹⁄₁₆-inch) thick and 1-m (40-inches) wide used to cook flatbreads, *bazlama* and other pastries, but also meat and vegetables. Traditionally placed on a crescent-shaped oven over a layer of firewood, it can be inverted and used like a wok to make lamb confit. A stone sac is a 2-cm (¾-inch) and 60-cm (24-cm) wide, thick stone used to cook flatbreads.

SAHAN

A shallow pan with two handles.

SALEP

Salep is made from the tubers of several species of orchid. It is believed to be a cure-all as well as a soul-warming winter drink. It was prepared by Turkish vendors in the streets at dawn and went on to become a popular drink in Britain during the seventeenth and eighteenth centuries until coffee dominated in the nineteenth century.

SOLAR ECLIPSE

Oil, salt, flour, clotted cream and firewood are collected by the Hemşin in the eastern Black Sea region. Adults start a fire and from copper cauldrons one ladle of oil is thrown into the air in this ritual that hopes to get sunshine in return.

SUMAC

Widely used in the Eastern Mediterranean, Eastern and Southeastern Anatolia, sumac berries are dried and powdered to add a sour note to dishes. Make sure ground sumac is not pre-salted.

TANDIR

A tandoor oven, which has many varieties. The shallow ovens are used to bake flatbreads. *Kuyu tandırı* (tandoor) is 2.5m (8 feet) deep with a wood fire at the base. Lamb and goat are baked on the warm ashes. Vegetables and salted water are placed in a pot on the pre-heated *tandır* oven at the bottom of a pit. The lamb or goat carcass is lowered and the pit is sealed. The fat in the meat renders down into the salty water and the meat is steamed. This method is called *büryan*. It is also called *kuyu kebab* or *büryan kebab* in some regions.

TAPPUŞ

A local term to Antakya and its environs, *tappuş* describes how patties are made into flattened balls.

TARHANA

There are legends associated with the origins of this popular cure for colds. A local tent-dwelling couple have a fight. The husband goes to town, the wife starts a soup with yogurt and crushed wheat. When she sees him returning home, she pours the soup onto the reeds in anger. She realises later on that the soup has dried and became more delicious. Another legend goes that Sultan Selim asked for this soup when he visited Maraş. He then set off for his Tehran campaign. The locals poured the soup over the reeds to dry as a memento from the Sultan. The soup has since then been known as 'tarhana'.

TARATOR

A sauce commonly served with roasted and fried vegetables. The main ingredient is stale bread. It is especially popular in the Marmara, Aegean and Mediterranean regions. In winter, tarator is served with leeks and fish, but it is also drizzled on pastries and meat dishes. Pine nuts, walnuts or hazelnuts may be used instead of almonds.

TAVLAMA

The roasting of onions and other vegetables in a little bit of oil in a pan or pot.

TİRİT

A cooking method in which squares of bread are topped with meat, chicken stock or yogurt. It is also known as *papara*, *banduma* or *siron* in other regions. *İskender*, a popular kebab, uses the same technique.

TİRŞİK (YILAN PANCARI)

Curly dock, a wild herb is also known as snake beet. Locals have myriad names for this spring herb and as many ways to cook it.

TULUG

This is a vessel made of goat skin, prepared the same way as the *tulum*. Water is added, the skin is tied at the ends and buried in the ground horizontally. It keeps drinks nice and cool. It is also used as a churn for making *ayran* and butter. It has wooden and earthenware versions.

TULUM

A method of cooking using the salted, dried skin of a goat. Cheese is prepared, placed in the prepared skin and buried in the ground or hung to mature in caves.

INDEX

INDEX

ABOUT THE AUTHOR

Musa Dağdeviren was born in Nizip, Gaziantep in 1960. He started working at his uncle's bakery when he was five years old. While growing up, Musa held various jobs until he opened a restaurant with two friends in Gaziantep. In 1977 he moved to İstanbul and worked with his uncle at a wood-fire oven. Musa learned about kebabs, *pide* and meze. In 1981 he became Chef Tomato Memed's apprentice. The two had long discussions about food and Musa learnt the art of soup-making.

While doing his military service, Musa served as a cook and sergeant, responsible for the kitchen of the Officer's Club near Çanakkale between 1983 and 1984. After his return to İstanbul, he worked in restaurants making kebabs and meze. Later, Musa returned to İstanbul and worked as the master chef of kebab and appetizers in a few restaurants and also worked in a bakery. Then in 1987, Musa opened Çiya/Kebap-Lahmacun with three friends, later becoming the sole owner. Çiya means spark in Laz, brazier in Ottoman Greek and mountain in Kurdish. It is the name of a Georgian childrens' game and a popular song. This boutique hole-in-the-wall is still remembered with affection by aficionados. Musa would take orders for special dishes and cook them for the patrons who would enjoy them accompanied by classical music.

In 1990, Zeynep Calışkan, who would later become his wife, joined the Çiya family. Musa's research substantially enriched the kebab menu with about 100 items. He made the first vegetarian lahmacun and kebab. In 1998 he opened Çiya Sofrası. He created a unique menu with local food, desserts and drinks canvassing a large part of the country. In 2001 he started another kebab restaurant, Çiya Kebap II.

Musa currently carries out fieldwork all over Turkey to revive disappearing cooking techniques, vessels and ingredients. He has a collection of written sources, ephemera, local diaries and cookbooks, home and restaurant menus. He passionately mentors local producers. He started *Yemek ve Kültür* (*Food and Culture*), a quarterly magazine, in 2005 to contribute to culinary history, folklore, literature, art, etymology and culture. His publishing house, Çiya Yayınları reprinted the first Ottoman-Turkish cookbook as well as many others on Anatolian food, dishes of the early republic and other important works by international authors. He has many local and international awards in recognition of his contributions to Turkish cuisine. He has presented at conferences and led workshops around the world, and has collaborated extensively with NGOs and academia on many aspects of culinary culture.

AUTHOR ACKNOWLEDGEMENTS

My better half, Zeynep, deserves the biggest thanks for always being one step ahead. The creative process for this book was nurtured by her and our daughter Elifsu's abundant support and patience. Members of the Çiya family and the team at *Yemek ve Kültür* shared my enthusiasm all the way and contributed extensively to this project.

Nazlı Pişkin's work during the conceptual stages of the project with the format and initial communication with the publisher was invaluable. Yusufcan Hamarat, Aysu Erensoy and Hasan Hüseyin Çinay spent many days putting recipes onto paper. Assistant Professor Özge Samancı reviewed the chapter introductions and provided valuable feedback. Abdullah Koçak, Cenk Sinör and Büşra Macit worked meticulously rendering recipes with format and precision.

Şengül Yüksel Toraman helped in so many ways through the process.

Nevin Göltaşı, who would not be able to follow a recipe to save her life, nurtured us at home with her traditional recipes from the heart.

Burçak Gürün Muraben became my voice in English. She was enthusiastic and efficient all through the process and an absolute pleasure to work with. Many thanks to Yusuf Muraben who proofread the translations and made them flow.

I would like to mention Necdet Kaygın with affection. He always wanted to be a part of this book, but did not live to see it.

Phaidon's commissioning editor Emily Takoudes nurtured this book from the very early stages and made sure it was smooth sailing throughout. Eve O'Sullivan started the project editor process. Lisa Pendreigh has been a hard-working and meticulous editor. The copy editor Emily Preece-Morrison has been the definition of dilligent. The book design is a very thoughtful visual translation of my culinary world with Toby Glanville's 'less is more' photography. I am indebted to Julia Hasting for personally embarking on the task and the sublime output.

RECIPE NOTES:

Milk is always whole.

Cream is always heavy (whipping).

Butter is always unsalted, unless specified otherwise.

Eggs are always large (US)/medium (UK).

Herbs, unless indicated otherwise, are always fresh,
and parsley is always flat-leaf.

Sugar is always granulated white, unless specified
otherwise.

Kosher salt is Diamond Crystal.
(UK, please use coarse salt in its place.)

Medium-grain rice is baldo rice or a risotto rice,
such as arborio.

Chickpeas and cannellini beans are dried, unless specified
otherwise, but canned can be substituted.

Cooking and preparation times are for guidance only,
as individual ovens vary. If using a fan (convection) oven,
follow the manufacturer's instructions concerning
oven temperatures.

To test whether your deep-frying oil is hot enough,
add a cube of stale bread. If it browns in 30 seconds,
the temperature is 180–190°C/350–375°F, about right
for most frying. Exercise a high level of caution when
following recipes involving any potentially hazardous
activity, including the use of high temperature and
open flames. In particular, when deep-frying, add the
food carefully to avoid splashing, wear long sleeves,
and never leave the pan unattended.

Some recipes include raw or very lightly cooked eggs.
These should be avoided by the elderly, infants, pregnant
women, convalescents, and anyone with an impaired
immune system.

Both metric and imperial measures are used in this book.
Follow one set of measurements throughout, not a mixture,
as they are not interchangeable.

All spoon measurements are level, unless specified
otherwise.

When no quantity is specified, for example of oils,
salts, and herbs used for finishing dishes, quantities are
discretionary and flexible.

Exercise caution when making fermented products,
ensuring all equipment is spotlessly clean, and seek expert
advice if in any doubt.

All herbs, shoots, flowers, and leaves should be picked
fresh from a clean source. Exercise caution when
foraging for ingredients; any foraged ingredients should
only be eaten if an expert has deemed them safe to eat.
Mushrooms should be wiped clean.

Phaidon Press Limited
Regent's Wharf
All Saints Street
London N1 9PA

Phaidon Press Inc.
65 Bleecker Street
New York, NY 10012

phaidon.com

First published 2019
© 2019 Phaidon Press Limited

ISBN 978 0 7148 7815 7

A CIP catalogue record for this book is available from
the British Library and the Library of Congress.

Commissioning Editor: Emily Takoudes
Project Editors: Eve O'Sullivan, Lisa Pendreigh
Production Controller: Sarah Kramer
Translator: Burçak Gürün Muraben
Artworker: Michael Wallace
Photography: Toby Glanville

Designed by Julia Hasting

Printed in China.

The publisher would like to thank Burçak Gürün
Muraben, Nazlı Pişkin, Emily Preece-Morrison,
Kelsey Kins, Jo Ireson, Vanessa Bird, Lesley Malkin
and Jane Ellis for their contributions to the book.